Educational Measurement and Evaluation

EDUCATION FOR LIVING SERIES

under the editorship of

H. H. REMMERS

Educational
Measurement and
Evaluation

REVISED EDITION

H. H. REMMERS

Professor of Education and Psychology
Director, Division of Educational Reference, Purdue University

and

N. L. GAGE

Associate Professor of Education
Bureau of Educational Research, College of Education
University of Illinois

HARPER & BROTHERS   PUBLISHERS   NEW YORK

EDUCATIONAL MEASUREMENT AND EVALUATION, REVISED EDITION

Copyright, 1943, 1955, by H. H. Remmers and N. L. Gage

Library of Congress catalog card number: 55-5899

CONTENTS

PART ONE: ACHIEVEMENT

PART TWO: ABILITIES

PART THREE: ADJUSTMENT

PART FOUR: ATTITUDES:
OPINIONS, INTERESTS, APPRECIATIONS, ETC.

PART SIX: PHYSICAL ASPECTS OF PUPILS

PART SEVEN: ADMINISTERING AND INTERPRETING THE EVALUATION PROGRAM

FOREWORD TO THE FIRST EDITION

The reasons for writing books are many and varied—as varied as the individual writers. Apart from ego-inflationary reasons which are generally not socially acceptable, the following constitute a framework of principles which have motivated and guided the writing of this book.

1. The modern psychological concept of the whole individual—not just the academic to-be-taught-subject-matter individual—in his various socially significant dimensions needs to be guided and stimulated to grow in terms of these dimensions.

2. The constant interaction between the individual and his environment in all relevant dimensions, the needs of the individual and the needs of the society in which he lives—these constitute the frame of reference for the scope of this book. Hence in addition to the traditional topics of "achievement" and "intelligence" testing there are included such chapters as those dealing with the physical aspects of pupils, their emotional and social adjustment, their attitudes and their environment and background, together with a chapter on the evaluation of the teacher as a high important part of that environment.

3. This entails psychological understanding and insight on the part of teachers and counselors. Hence the first part of the book is concerned not a little with psychological theory. Education will have juice, bounce, and vitality to the extent that teachers are themselves well educated and oriented to the world in which they live, including especially the youngsters whom they teach as part of that world.

4. Theory without practice is futile and practice without theory becomes dangerous immediate time-serving. In one sense, to be sure, we are all time-servers. It is only in the time perspective that we differ—in the units of time that we serve. Human finiteness forbids the presumption of attempting to build for eternity, but

human needs require greater than day-to-day foresight. Hence the second part of the book presents practice in harmony with the theory of the first part, designed to implement not only the day-to-day purposes of educational endeavor but also the long-time view with which education worthy of the name must concern itself.

5. There is at present little uniformity in the prerequisite requirement of elementary statistical concepts for courses in evaluation and measurement. Reasonable mastery of such statistical concepts is, however, a necessity for any safe use of measurement and evaluation devices and techniques. This dilemma has been resolved by placing at the end of the book a chapter covering the minimum essentials of statistics which teachers in training are likely to master. The instructor can if he chooses teach this chapter first, last, or in parallel with the other chapters requiring statistical insight.

6. The book makes no pretense of being a handbook for guidance. It is rather concerned with providing the methods and techniques for obtaining the facts and evaluative data necessary for valid guidance.

The authors' intellectual debts are many and varied. Grateful acknowledgment is due Doctor Frank Peyton, who read and criticized the manuscript of Chapter III particularly with a view to its orientation to the medical profession. Doctor Arthur E. Traxler, Associate Director of the Educational Records Bureau, made valuable constructive suggestions on Chapters I to XV. Professor Harry C. Steinmetz, Head of the Department of Psychology of San Diego State College, gave generously of his experience and insight for the major part of the manuscript. Students too numerous to mention who as teachers in service took the course for which this book was prepared made many suggestions that found their way into the manuscript. Any errors of either omission or commission are not, however, chargeable to these friends and colleagues. For these the authors must be held responsible. In the typing of the manuscript Miss N. Elizabeth Brant gave highly competent service.

FOREWORD TO THE REVISED EDITION

Our purposes in making this revision can best be stated by describing how this edition differs from the first. In form, we have tried to make the book more teachable and readable by changing the sequence of the chapters and by thoroughly revamping most chapters, many sections and paragraphs, and innumerable sentences. In content, we have attempted to make the book reflect the most desirable and significant developments in the more than a decade since the first edition went to press. The changes in content consist of both deletions and additions. What experience and research have shown to be obsolescent, obsolete, or no longer relevant we have deleted.

Not a single chapter has remained unchanged. Several chapters have been entirely or almost entirely rewritten. Much new knowledge has been developed in the behavioral sciences, and our criterion for inclusion of material from them has been its relevance to the tasks of teacher and guidance worker. The general areas ordinarily subsumed under the headings of personality development, mental hygiene, and social-emotional adjustment have continued to receive much emphasis. Measurement techniques related to these areas and extensively developed in the last decade and a half—such as uni-dimensional scaling, sociometry, disguising attitude measurement, projective techniques—have been included.

Another of our objectives has been to clarify and sharpen various important concepts in the light of scientific thinking of the last one or two decades. Examples of such concepts are general intelligence and special ability, validity as including relevance and reliability, instructional objective, and adjustment. The reader will find in the present edition much new and more extensive illustrative material designed to make the book more readable and teachable.

The chapters have been rearranged into six parts. Each part

deals with a major aspect of learners. The "what" and "how" for each aspect are now together in a single part. This arrangement, we think, will coincide more happily with predilections of instructors and students.

In basic outlook this book remains the same; we still hold to a holistic philosophy. Again we have gone beyond what a narrower tradition considers relevant for teachers or school personnel. Using many concepts from other disciplines, we have tried to make the book as many-sided as modern education requires, on the premise that the horizons of education cannot be too broad. All natural and social phenomena impinge on the education of a child. Some things matter more than others, of course, and we have tried to make our emphases reflect valid principles from the behavioral sciences. For example, we discuss the concepts of status and role—not ordinarily treated in textbooks of this sort—because of a conviction that these are powerful tools for understanding social behavior, in school and out. The same justification would apply to our inclusion of many other ideas.

In short, we have not devoted chapter on chapter to the measurement of achievement in reading, writing, arithmetic, Latin, geometry, chemistry, history, and so on. Rather, we have attempted to lay out the principles for all these subject matter areas in relatively few chapters. Then we have gone ahead to what we consider equally important matters: ability, adjustment, attitude, environmental background, and physical aspects.

We are, obviously, indebted to many colleagues and publishers both for ideas and for permission to quote. Like every textbook, this one draws upon the thought and research of leaders in the field. We hope our references to their work will be viewed not only as acknowledgments but as thanks. Not the least of the sources of ideas for which we are grateful are the students who have taken our courses.

Finally, we gladly record our debt to our wives for moral support well beyond the call of duty. Along with our children, they willingly if not gladly forewent vacations so that we could go ahead with what at times appeared to be a Sisyphean task.

December, 1954   H. H. REMMERS
                                                    N. L. GAGE

Educational Measurement and Evaluation

CHAPTER I

Why Evaluate?

ABSTRACT

Determining the rightness of pupils and educations for one another requires evaluation. This is because of the heterogeneity of pupils in all aspects affecting their adjustment to themselves and society and the heterogeneity of educational and economic activities available for students in a democracy. The necessary evaluation of pupils must be both continuous and comprehensive if it is to serve optimally in its major role of enabling the guidance of pupils. Data from evaluation should fit into the guidance process in various ways. Such data belong in the school guidance program regardless of its basic orientation—"directive," "nondirective," or other. The standards-maintenance function of evaluation, when properly conceived, becomes more of a standards-revelation function. The selection function is similarly yielding to the guidance function. The motivation function must pay heed to the quality as well as the quantity of the learning effort. The diagnostic function of revealing pupil strengths and weaknesses requires special techniques other than general single-score tests. The appraisal function can be realized only in the form of controlled, statistically analyzed experimentation. The instructional function can be realized only when evaluations are allowed to be self-imposed self-criticisms. Such "self-evaluation" must be valid and can be taken seriously only in educational programs where there is no strong competition for the social rewards of education. Evaluation includes measurement along with values, or purposes; but the logical distinction between measurement and evaluation has been lessened by recent usage.

.~.~.~.

"To enable the right pupils to receive the right education from the right teachers" may be considered the aim of the good educational system. Although at first glance this definition seems merely a truism, it does provide an approach to the question of why pupils should be evaluated. For the present discussion, let us assume that the right teacher has been discovered and is operating, and even becoming "righter" as he reads this book. But the right teacher must be concerned whether he has the right pupils and is giving them the right education. And to satisfy these concerns he must evaluate his students and discover whether the learning process in which he is leading them is bearing desirable fruit for them individually and for the society they should serve. The right pupil is the pupil whose personal attributes and opportunities enable him to profit fully from the education offered him. The right education is the education best suited to the needs of both society and the pupil. Obviously, the task of determining this "rightness" of pupils and educations is a task for the process of evaluation. Pupils' attributes and opportunities must be ascertained. Pupil behavior must be evaluated at all stages of the interaction between pupil and education to determine the fitness of one for the other.

Contemporary education is divided, at all age levels, into numerous subject-matter fields, such as mathematics, social studies, and the like. Whether the teaching process itself is thus segregated, or whether it encompasses all subjects in one activity program, the conceptualization of the modern educational curriculum into "subjects" is inevitable, for man's interests, activities, and problems are themselves thus divisible. And in each of these subject-matter areas it is possible for many varied mental processes, such as rote memory or logical inference, to take place. Each of these mental processes has some value, great or small, in each of the subject-matter areas. The differences between subject-matter areas in the degrees to which they involve various mental processes, in the societal needs they satisfy, in the vocations to which they are most relevant, in the personal values or types to which they appeal, all operate to render the modern school curriculum a heterogeneous, variegated thing.

In the same way, the economic and social activities in which pupils may now or in the future engage differ among themselves very widely. Some jobs require great muscular strength and little mental ability, while others require the opposite combination. Some social activities and roles require a knack for leadership or dominance, while others can be undertaken successfully only by adaptable followers. For all the thousands of different occupations, recreations, and civic activities engaged in by our millions of citizens there are needed different combinations of strengths and weaknesses in all the various "mental" and "physical" aspects of persons.

Similarly, pupils differ, both within themselves and among themselves, in all aspects of their personalities and especially in all those dimensions which determine their fitness for success in the various subject-matter areas and social roles afforded by contemporary society. Pupils differ, like all living things, in the behavior and responses of which they are capable, in intelligence, interests, and opportunities. These individual differences result in differences in the types of activities, educational and vocational, from which pupils may best profit and in doing which they may best serve society. To illustrate, let us examine an extreme case of physical differences. Society does not fit the weak or the feminine into activities requiring great physical stamina. Invalids do not work as lumberjacks. In the same way, society must prevent the intellectually weak from filling positions requiring intellectual strength. And the centers which society provides for cultivating the mental strengths it needs to keep itself going—that is, the schools—are the places where this process of fitting pupils to curricula, and citizens to social roles, is carried out with the best results for individual adjustment and social welfare.

In the schools this fitting process is *guidance,* i.e., the guidance of pupils differing in all ways within and among themselves into activities, curricula, and vocations which differ within and among themselves in the capacities they require, so as to make the best fit between pupil and education.

THE ROLE OF EVALUATION IN GUIDANCE

[Guidance requires the evaluation of pupils so that their specific capacities, both strengths and weaknesses, may be determined. As pupils proceed up the educational ladder in elementary school, with its general curriculum providing the common core of skills (reading, writing, arithmetic, etc.) that everyone in our civilization must acquire, the process of evaluation must operate upon them so as to reveal differences in their aptitudes, abilities, achievements, interests, environmental backgrounds, and all other relevant attributes.] It is during this elementary schooling that pupils set off on diverging paths, some toward one set of interests and goals and some toward another. By the time they reach secondary schools the pupils on the various paths are already far apart from one another in their educational needs and capacities. At this point the knowledge of the pupil which the teacher has gained during the elementary schooling should crucially affect the decision of the pupil (and his parents) as to the type of secondary education to be selected. This knowledge must be the result of *continuous* evaluation throughout the six or eight years of the elementary educative process. And the evaluation must have been *comprehensive* throughout those six or eight years, involving as many important aspects of the pupil's personality as it is possible for a teacher to perceive. Similarly, guidance and evaluation should operate during and at the end of the secondary schooling.

The *continuity* of the evaluation process implies that it should go on during all the time that the teacher can observe the pupil, not only on the special occasions when tests are given or report-card grades are determined. Every recitation, every assignment, every conversation, every behavioral detail that the teacher can observe may be material for the evaluation process and the basis for a record whereby he may accumulate knowledge of the pupil and pass this accumulated record of evaluations and evidence on to the pupil's next teacher. The specific content and techniques of continuous evaluation in the actual school situation are the substance of later chapters of this book. At present our thesis is that guidance requires of the teacher a continuously evaluating point of view.

The *comprehensiveness* of the evaluation process refers to its extent over the whole personality of the pupil, rather than merely his intellectual achievement. Evaluation of a pupil's knowledge is, of course, extremely important in guiding him. But also important for his happiness and for fitting him into the world of work is evidence concerning his aptitudes and interests, his temperament, his attitudes, his social adaptability, his habits of work and play, his physical characteristics. Each of these aspects of the pupil's personality, and many more, must be evaluated both with respect to its position in relation to other aspects or dimensions of the pupil and with respect to its position in relation to similar aspects of the population at large.

With such broadly continuous and comprehensive evaluative evidence concerning its pupils, a school can properly undertake its important function of guidance. Such guidance is not to be considered as operating only at the students' entrance into or exit from a particular level of schooling or vocation, although this is its most striking occurrence. Rather guidance should operate within the schooling period. For example, evaluations should assist in the solution of such guidance problems as choice of elective subjects. Should a pupil take a twelfth-year English course or instead a course in typewriting? Which laboratory science should a pupil elect, physics, biology, or chemistry? Why is a certain pupil becoming a disciplinary problem? Answers to such questions, of which those here presented are only a small illustrative sample, all come under the broad heading of guidance. And the answers should not be given without a basis of valid evaluative data on the pupil.

How are the data gathered by the evaluation and measurement techniques used in guidance? In many instances the process goes something as follows. A need for guidance arises routinely as a normal part of a pupil's school career. Or it has a more urgent basis, as when a pupil shows signs of serious emotional distress, or comes to his teacher asking for help with a personal, educational, or vocational problem. Generally the pupil and the teacher will discuss the problem in one or more interviews, exploring it, getting it clearly understood. In the process of seeking a fuller understanding of the problem, and possible solutions, various kinds of data become necessary. These may be facts about the pupil collected by any of the methods described in this book, or information about the world at large, such as the educational requirements of certain occupations. Either the pupil or the teacher may suggest the need for such data and ways of gathering the necessary information.

After the facts have been marshaled, their implications for the alternative solutions to the problem are discussed jointly by teacher and pupil. The teacher's own interpretations of the data may be offered and the pupil's reactions to these interpretations brought into the picture. By means of interviewing, counseling, and guidance procedures, a synthesis of the pupil's and teacher's attitudes, in interaction with the data concerning the pupil and the outside world, is achieved. Finally there results at least a tentative program of action.

This general procedure which this volume assumes may seem to be brought into question in the writings of the "nondirective" group of counselors and psychotherapists. Rogers (7, 8),[1] for example, has indicated that psychometric tests have little if any place in the procedures of nondirective counselors. The permissive, client-centered, nonevaluative relationships they seek to foster with their clients are endangered and broken down when the counselor tests his client. The administration of tests, says Rogers, suggests to the client that the teacher or counselor knows what to do about the problem, can find out all about the pupil, and can tell him what to do. Giving tests, according to Rogers, shifts the responsibility for the exploration and solution of the problem to the counselor, whereas every effort of the nondirective counselor must be aimed at inducing the pupil to take the responsibility for understanding himself, examining himself, and developing a new and more realistic concept of himself. Rogers will admit tests into the counseling situation when they are requested as a real desire of the client after an extensive preliminary exploration of his own problem. But if the pupil does not know that tests are available, he cannot ask for them. If this is so, then tests will simply not be used.

Carrying this point of view to its logical limits would make it unnecessary for schools to engage in the kind of evaluation for guidance purposes that this volume considers. Schools might continue to collect evaluative data for other purposes, but seldom would these data be used in guidance. The question ultimately is

---

[1] Numbers in parentheses refer to the References at the end of the chapter.

whether diagnosis (the collection and interpretation of measurement and evaluation data concerning pupils) has a role in the guidance process. Our position is that diagnosis of some kind must be regarded as inevitable and indispensable. The actual issue is whether diagnosis should be carried out solely by the client in the course of a series of nondirective interviews (as Rogers' position implies) or by the client operating together with his counselor in the examination of all the pertinent evidence that can be brought to bear.

The apparently nondiagnostic mode of operation advocated by Rogers and his students will seldom serve alone with maximum effectiveness in handling the kind of guidance problems that make up the vast majority of those arising in schools. We cannot assume that most of the task of guidance in schools arises from the kind of neuroses with which most nondirective psychotherapists have been concerned. It is true that many problems of pupils that seem to the pupils, and at first glance even to their teachers, to be straightforward educational or vocational problems prove, on deeper examination, to be essentially emotional problems. But this may not always, or even most often, be the case. Not all pupils in our schools who have guidance problems need psychotherapy; indeed it seems likely that the vast bulk of the guidance function of contemporary schools stems from the need of normal, mentally healthy pupils for assistance in resolving personal, educational, and vocational problems on a logical and intellectual basis *as well as* through procedures oriented to their emotions.

The following discussion by Bordin (1) illustrates our position on the compatibility between tests and counseling:

Somehow I find it neither credible nor fruitful to conceive of individuals as having vocational problems which are not at the same time personal problems or vice versa. I find it hard to reconcile such distinctions with our growing awareness of the dynamic organization of human attitudes and motives. I find it hard to reconcile these distinctions with specific instances such as I encountered recently in talking to a student veteran about his vocational plans. For two interviews we went through a process familiar to those who think of their job as vocational counseling. The student took tests; we discussed test results and their significance for various vocational alternatives; we discussed general information about the jobs involved. At the end of two interviews we had reviewed all the surface aspects of the decision facing him and were beginning to dig a little deeper into the attitudes that might be the final determinants of his vocational choice. No sooner had we started on this process than our discussion took an entirely new turn. In talking about some of his vocational motivations he was directly led to expressions of some of his attitudes toward his life goal, and this in turn led him to discuss factors that had influenced these attitudes.

The central factor, the one which was apparently placing the largest obstacle in the way of his clarity of vision, was the problem of his parents' adjustment to each other and his adjustment to them. His pent-up feelings came out in a flood. He poured out his hatred toward his mother and his desire to get away from her. Yet he also identified with his father and felt the need to stand by him.

We went on for four more hour-interviews, exploring the ramifications of these feelings. He analyzed and re-analyzed his parents' relationship to each other and what position he could take on the matter. This problem had been puzzling him for a number of years. The direction he took in solving this difficulty would have an important influence on the direction he took with other problems. It involved such things as where he wanted to work, whether he wanted to get married, and whether he could ever have a feeling of security about himself. Eventually he came to a resolution of this central problem and turned once more to the question of vocational choice, this time dispatching it with decisiveness and reality.

I do not imply by this illustration that this man solved his vocational problem simply by solving his personal problem. In fact I wish to convey the opposite. I wish to point out that these two problems were aspects of one adjustment situation, and that self-knowledge obtained through tests and discussions about job characteristics and self-knowledge obtained through clarification and exploration of his attitudes toward his parents and their relationship to his life goal were both necessary for the resolution of his problem.

This obviously does not mean that guidance should be undertaken in the manner of the physician who diagnoses and then prescribes, with the patient "asking no questions" and taking essentially a passive role. The pupil's attitudes need always to be taken into account when tests or other procedures are introduced, while they are being administered, and especially when they are being interpreted and an understanding of their meaning is being acquired by the pupil.

In this matter all the strictures of nondirective counselors about the misuse of tests have often been well justified. Too often, guidance workers have taken their function in communicating the results of measurements and evaluations to pupils as the task of simply telling the pupil what must be done—or at best of selling, convincing, and persuading him as to the validity of the teacher's or counselor's own interpretation of the results. Pupils have been given too little opportunity to react to the results, to express a feeling about their significance, and to have these feelings accepted and reflected by the counselor. Too little attention has been given to the need for an emotional assimilation of the information resulting from the measurements and evaluations undertaken in the guidance process. Too much emphasis has been placed on the intellectualized communication of results through informal "lectures," percentages, coefficients, tables, and charts. The nondirective point of view at this stage of the guidance process calls for allowing full opportunity for the pupil to evaluate the data as they apply to himself, while the teacher, remaining neutral toward both the data and the pupil's feelings, attempts to facilitate the pupil's self-evaluation.

Measurement and evaluation often become central to the guidance process by virtue of the ethical need for teachers and counselors to provide information of vital significance to the pupil and society. When the pupil makes plans that might be radically modified if he were aware of certain facts about his tested abilities or interests, is it not the teacher's responsibility to provide that information? If a pupil and his parents are strongly embarked on a program of education leading toward a medical degree, for example, whereas test data of the most valid kind indicate that his abilities and interests are distinctly unsuited for such an occupation, is it not the school's responsibility to bring this evidence to bear in the process of vocational guidance? Conversely, a pupil's abilities and interests might indicate exceedingly high promise for success in pursuits for which society has an urgent need, such as significant research in social science. But the pupil and his parents may be proceeding as if unaware of the rare talent and its prime importance to society. ~~Must not~~ the school in its guidance function *should* use the most valid evidence, including measurements and evaluations of the kind described in this book, so that appropriate changes in the pupil's educational and vocational plans can be made for the benefit of both the pupil and the society of which he is a part? This volume assumes affirmative answers to these questions.

OTHER PURPOSES OF EVALUATION

In the course of satisfying the need for data on which to base the guidance of pupils, the teacher will acquire evidence enabling the school to serve many other purposes. These purposes include the many "uses of tests and measurements" put forth since educational measurement began. These uses are usually ascribed to educational evaluation conceived more narrowly as the ranking of pupils with respect to individual differences in their *achievement in a particular course of study*. Given the instruments with which to make such rankings, the teacher or administrator may then use them for the following purposes:

1. To maintain standards
2. To select students
3. To motivate learning
4. To guide teaching
5. To appraise teachers, teaching methods, books, curricular content, etc.
6. To furnish educational experience

Each of these uses of tests, or reasons for evaluating pupils, can take several forms of varying validity and desirability. Let us now examine them critically, to clarify and furnish an understanding of their benefits and dangers, of how they can best be realized.

1. MAINTAINING STANDARDS

(Standards are necessary to society in carrying on its social and economic life.) In the production of economic goods and the performance of vital social services, standards define the minimum degrees of excellence which society can accept. Airplane mechanics, doctors of medicine, pharmacists, practitioners of law, teachers, dentists, engineers, plumbers, carpenters, professionals in all the learned fields—all must meet certain standards, as set forth, for example, in professional licensing examinations, before society will permit them to practice in their fields. Standards may exist at all the earlier stages of the educational ladder, in promotion from one class to another, in admission to secondary and higher education, in the granting of honors, in graduation, in transfer from one institution to another. At all these junctures, standards furnish the means of social control, and evaluations become the means whereby society determines whether the standards are satisfied and the candidate may "pass." Such social control, and the implied maintenance of standards and evaluations necessary to enforce minimum degrees of attainment, where society can get along with nothing less, are a legitimate and valid use of educational evaluation.

But when standards and evaluations are employed to enforce uniform curricula or courses of study, in violation of the fact of individual differences and of the truth that men can serve themselves and society in many different ways, they become a hindrance to individual adjustment and the proper use of human resources. Illustrations of such misuse of standards and evaluations are numerous in the history of American education. Schools and colleges with large proportions of failures and dismissals may be considered to be perverting rather than maintaining their standards, through a failure to provide for individual differences. Schools which provide only one curriculum for students of varying abilities and interests are similarly abusing their standards. Thus the charge can still be justifiably leveled at many secondary schools that they are maintaining high but false academic standards by providing academic, or pre-college, training for students who will never, and perhaps should never, go to college. Where standards thus become a matter of prescribing the bookish attainments suited to the selected pupils of forty years ago for the relatively unselected millions who go to school today, these standards and the evaluations and examinations which implement them will cause untold damage and misery to vast numbers of pupils at all levels of education and waste precious resources of human society. Such attempts to force the widely varying kinds and degrees of human capacities and

interests into one uniform academic mold have thwarted and
warped many pupils into social misfits.

This misuse and potential danger of educational evaluation,
when it is used to maintain standards in violation of individual
differences and other than as indispensable social controls, is perhaps more a misunderstanding of curriculum construction than of
the functions of evaluation. The argument against the use of
evaluations to uphold invalid standards should, however, prevent
their misuse by teachers in this respect. The teacher will thus
recognize the need for more and more standards, highly differentiated and adaptable to as many kinds and degrees of interests and
abilities as the evaluation of students may reveal. And the major
function of teacher evaluations will no longer be standards maintenance but rather standards revelation. Each pupil will be evaluated to discover the educational directions and distances he is best
fitted to travel. This point of view in turn shifts much of the
"standards" function of evaluation back into the realm of guidance.)

2. SELECTING PUPILS

The selection of pupils as a function of educational evaluation
is a form of guidance in reverse. Fig. 1 shows how selection and
guidance differ. Selection picks among many persons for admission
to one job, one college, one officer training program. Guidance
picks among many possible careers for pursuit by one person.
Selection is usually made with the advantages of the institution,
say college, as the primary consideration, with the advantages to
students in being rejected as probable misfits only an incidental
by-product of the selection. Such educational selection is becoming
increasingly rare in American educational institutions, being at
present confined to a small minority of the institutions of higher
learning and to the relatively small number of private schools at
the primary and secondary levels. At the college level perhaps the
foremost agency of educational measurement for selection purposes is the College Entrance Examination Board, which annually
measures the scholastic achievement and aptitudes of thousands of
applicants for admission to its member colleges.

The use of educational measurements for selection purposes is

4. GUIDING TEACHING

Evaluations can guide teaching when they furnish diagnoses of specific strengths and weaknesses in the pupil's achievements or capacities. The teacher may then seek either to eliminate the weaknesses by using special teaching methods and emphases, or to circumvent them by directing learning toward areas where the pupil's efforts will be more fruitful. The causes of weakness in a specific subject can be traced by tests to any one of the various possible pupil inadequacies underlying it. Weakness in a history or geography course may be found to be due to lack of either comprehension power or speed in reading, as revealed by a test of reading ability. Or it may be due to lack of general intelligence, or to lack of the presupposed background material, a lack which could be revealed by tests designed to measure achievement at a lower level of the subject. Similarly, a pupil's difficulties in arithmetic may be traced by means of tests to a specific inadequacy, such as inability to deal with certain combinations of digits, or lack of a correct technique for carrying, or the use of a cumbersome method of short division. Diagnostic testing may thus reveal the precise sources of a pupil's shortcomings and guide the teacher to the optimum way of overcoming them. Inadequately equipped pupils may thus be studied and given special attention aimed at the basic roots of the "failure." They may be shown in what parts of a subject or what outcomes of the course they are weak. Teachers may discover what parts of a topic or unit need to be retaught, or taught differently. The pupils who are capable of doing exceptional work may be discovered by evaluation procedures and they may be guided toward special tasks and references.

Certain modifications in the construction procedure for an achievement test may be desirable, to build into the test, by means of the classification of item content, the means whereby it can be used diagnostically. That is, if the test builder is careful to analyze his objectives and to apportion a sufficient number of specific items to each objective, the total test score may later be broken down into part scores which furnish measures of the specific outcomes. Gross disparities in a pupil's achievement of the various objectives can be thus revealed and laid open to remedial treatment.

5. Appraising Educational Instrumentalities

The use of evaluations in the appraisal of educational instrumentalities such as teachers, teaching methods, and textbooks is easily understood but not easily practiced. The principle underlying all such uses of evaluations is that whatever yields the greatest realization of the educational objectives is the best teacher, teaching method, textbook, or other instrumentality of the educative process. And since most educational objectives may be stated in terms of desired changes in pupils, educational evaluations of those pupils will provide a measure of the degree to which the objectives are attained and of the effectiveness of the instrumentality concerned. The difficulty in using educational evaluations for these purposes is that no worth-while, reliable results can be obtained unless the appraisal becomes a controlled investigation, with significant variables held constant and with statistical tests of significance applied to the results. The complexity and refinement of the procedures and precautions that are necessary may be appreciated from reading textbooks (3, 4) in statistics and educational research.

Factors pointed to as having to be held constant to justify ascribing an effect to any "treatment," such as teaching method, are, for example, intelligence of pupils, previous educational background of pupils, study habits of pupils, home environment of pupils, teacher skill, school conditions, and the like. The subtleties of experimental design that are involved in the valid use of educational evaluations for appraisal research should prevent evaluation from being used in this way by any but qualified research workers. Principals, superintendents, and others who make appraisals must therefore either acquire a mastery of these scientific methods for themselves, or turn the problems over to experts, or cease to use evaluations for the appraisal of educational instrumentalities.

6. Furnishing Educational Experience (Self-Evaluation)

In recent years, increasing attention has centered on the notion of "self-evaluation," the carrying out of all steps in evaluation by the pupils themselves (2, 6, 9, 10, 11). Usually this concept is linked to a pattern of education that goes as follows. Pupils determine to a large extent, with the guidance of their teachers, what they will undertake to learn. They identify the problems with which they wish to be concerned. These problems may take the form of traditional subjects and be recognizable as problems in arithmetic, physics, or geography. Or more likely, problems may cut across traditional subject-matter lines, as when pupils attack the problem of preventing the sewers in their neighborhood from overflowing after heavy rain and find themselves concerned with the physics of fluids, with sewerage engineering, politics, public opinion, taxation, and health.

Whatever form the problem may take, many educators (10) insist that more of the responsibility for identifying and selecting the problems that pupils should work on should be given to the pupils themselves. Pupils will need help, of course, in identifying and solving their problems. They will get this help from their teachers. They will need to learn how to use reading and community resources effectively in identifying and solving their problems. They will learn to keep personal educational records to facilitate their learning. They will learn to work together in groups in identifying and solving their problems. And they will develop improved reading skills of a kind necessary for problem solving which may differ in significant respects from the kinds of reading that they have hitherto done for school purposes. Above and beyond these is the necessity for developing skills in self-evaluation.

Why has such an educational program, including self-evaluation, been proposed? (1) It accords with the idea of making learning more significant by giving greater responsibility to the learner. Motivation will be stronger and more genuine when pupils work on problems that they themselves have identified and selected as of real significance to themselves. Their "ego involvement" in the learning process and the transfer of what they learn in school to the activities and problems of out-of-school life will be greater when they have acquired skill in identifying and solving their own problems. The ability to continue learning and to teach oneself should exist to a higher degree in adults who have had to develop the necessary skills during their school days. And if the entire process is to be truly significant it must be accompanied by self-evaluation, whereby the pupils themselves largely determine what is to be evaluated and how the evaluation is to be carried out.

(2) The idea of self-evaluation stems from the concern of educators with the democratic process. If schools are to develop adults who live democratically, their own organization should exemplify the tenets of democracy. Many educators conclude that schools in which the pupils have no voice in determining what they are to study or how they are to study it, in determining on what grounds they are to be evaluated or how the evaluation is to be made, are not furthering the democratic ideals that teachers profess.

But, the reply goes, there must be realistic and severe limits to how far self-determination can be allowed to go. Democracy does not mean that everybody is qualified to do anything, that everyone can have responsibility and authority for every phase of the educative process. The patient on the operating table, to use an extreme analogy, does not have and does not want the right to discuss with the surgeon whether he should have an appendectomy or how it should be done. By the same logic, the six-year-old child is not qualified to have a voice in deciding what he should study or how. Indeed, at all levels of education, it is the teachers and other mature citizens who should primarily determine the curriculum. For them to give away any important share of this responsibility to the "consumers" of education would amount to their failing to put their superior training and competence to full use. For pupils to have any large share in evaluating themselves as to their achievement of the objectives of going to school would amount to the blind leading the blind. To introduce value-laden terms like democracy into a discussion of these issues, it is charged, is to becloud the issue. What we need are the educational methods, under any label, that lead to the greatest achievement of the most valid educational objectives by the greatest number of pupils. Teachers are the agents of society, selected and trained to be highly qualified in determining what pupils need to learn and how they can learn it, and in evaluating pupils to determine how well they have learned.

It is exactly at this point, however, that many teachers in recent years have taken the position that (a) democratic ways of living must be learned in schools as well as elsewhere; (b) the best and perhaps the only way to learn democratic ways of living is by experiencing a democratic way of life including a democratically organized system of education; (c) the boredom, inertia, and ineffective learning that characterize many pupils in present-day schools result inevitably from teaching that is not attuned to actual needs and concerns as pupils experience them; (d) the remedy for the inadequacies of our schools both as trainers in democratic living and as centers where children can learn what they need is to be found by destroying the teachers' monopoly in curriculum building and the evaluation of learning.

This is not the place for any full discussion of alternative approaches to curriculum building, classroom management, and the general organization of the learning process in modern schools. But insofar as these approaches imply the need for self-evaluation, we must consider them here. Is self-evaluation desirable? Our answer must be affirmative, but qualified as follows.

(1) Self-evaluations by pupils must be "taken seriously" by teachers if they are to have optimum effect on learning. Evaluations of the achievement of pupils have always been used as bases for the distribution of rewards (high marks, honors, admissions, prizes, and the like) and deprivations. If self-evaluations are taken seriously, this means that they should be similarly used as bases for distributing rewards. Whatever these rewards and deprivations may be in more democratically oriented, pupil-centered, problem-process systems of education, some analogue of them, perhaps more intrinsic than grades and marks, must exist. If not "taken seriously" as bases of rewards, self-evaluations will lose whatever good effect they can have on the learning process.

(2) Self-evaluations should have as much validity as possible. This means that teachers will need to guide and train their pupils in carrying out their self-evaluations to maximize their validity. We cannot rely solely on pupils' feelings of satisfaction or dissatisfaction with their performance and achievement. The mere fact that a pupil feels he has achieved an objective of education is no evidence of the desirability of the learning process he has completed. People tend to feel satisfied with the results of their visits to fortunetellers, or quacks of other kinds. Similarly we must reject

as insufficient evidence the unsupported statements of students that they have achieved new insights or new understanding in a given learning activity.

That pupils' untrained self-evaluations may sometimes even have negative validity is indicated by Mitchell's study (5) in which a negative relationship (−.50) was found between pupils' predictions of their own achievement in high school and their actual grades at the end of the first six weeks of their high-school careers. Merely having pupils evaluate themselves by whatever techniques occur to them might prove worse than no evaluation at all. If evaluation is to be done by the pupils, the teacher may need to provide, at a level appropriate to the pupils, whatever training in evaluation becomes necessary to insure adequate validity. By validity we mean, of course, the extent of agreement between evaluation and some a priori accepted measure, the criterion, of what is evaluated. In one sense, self-evaluations must always be valid by definition, if the criterion is the student's own judgment. But such individualistic criteria must often be supplanted by socially accepted criteria, the judgments of experts, authorities, and agents of society, such as teachers. The task thus becomes inculcating in pupils the socially accepted criteria of their achievement and then helping them develop measures and evaluations that are valid in those terms.

(3) It may be that the degree to which the learning process can be pupil-oriented depends on how much the educational achievement serves as a "gateway" to highly desired social roles. When achievement in a curriculum constitutes the path to higher, more rewarded positions in society, self-determination and self-evaluation of learning seem to become less admissible as factors to be "taken seriously" by schools as bases for rewards and deprivations. We can see this in professional education. The kinds of preparation that are necessary for entrance into, say, medical or legal practice can be determined by the student to a much lesser degree than can the content and method of learning in general education at, say, the fifth grade. In the former case, society must set standards to govern the competition for admission and for its own protection must enforce these standards through systems of evaluation that are anything but "self-evaluation." In the fifth grade, on the other

hand, what a pupil learns and how he goes about learning it may much more realistically be left in his own hands, and his own evaluation of his learning can go on without the regulation of social mobility which educational measurement and evaluation could provide. What seems to us to make the difference in the feasibility of self-evaluation is the extent to which high achievement of instructional objectives is a vehicle to social rewards *for which there is real competition.* There can be more widespread distribution of the rewards to which high achievement in the fifth grade leads than of those to which adequate achievement in, say, medical courses leads. Realistic understanding of self-evaluation and its possibilities in American society must, it seems to us, take this factor into account.

DISTINCTION BETWEEN MEASUREMENT AND EVALUATION

The dictionary defines the verb *evaluate* as meaning "to ascertain the value or amount of; appraise carefully." The verb *measure* means the "act or process of ascertaining the extent, dimensions, quantity, etc., of something, esp. by comparison with a standard." From this it is clear that *evaluation* is the more inclusive concept. It includes the concept of *measurement* as this is used in psychology and education. Measurement, however, does not necessarily imply evaluation. Evaluation assumes a purpose, or an idea of what is "good" or "desirable" from the standpoint of the individual or society, or both.

Evaluation is the more recent technical term; it gained currency particularly with the revolt represented by the progressive education movement against the traditional curriculum. It was given technical status and currency especially by Tyler (12). The textbooks designed to orient the student to the application of the scientific method in education that appeared before the 1930's carried such titles as "Measurement in Education," "Educational Measurement," "Experimentation in Education," and the like. More recently—because educators have come to realize that education is designed to help in achieving human *values,* to change students in desirable ways—the notions of evaluation and measurement have been joined, perhaps a bit redundantly.

The two terms are rather closely analogous in meaning to two other technical concepts—*validity* and *reliability*—of which more later. *Evaluation is to validity as measurement is to reliability* states the analogy formally.

While evaluation and validity always imply purpose, and measurement and reliability do not, the sharp logical separation of the two pairs of concepts that we have just made is not generally maintained in educational writing, for usually some purpose is being served by any measurement. When the measurements are interpreted in relation to their purpose—as when we decide whether a pupil is tall enough or understands scientific method well enough for certain purposes—we are evaluating as well as measuring.

HOW THIS BOOK IS ORGANIZED

In the preceding pages we have dealt with the question, *Why* should pupils be evaluated? Having given some justification for concern with the evaluation of students, we must now approach the questions, *What* aspects of pupils should be evaluated? *How* can the evaluations be made?

Our answer to the first question must, of course, be determined in its major outlines by the answers we have given to why pupils should be evaluated; that is, what we should evaluate depends on why we are evaluating. Since the major purpose of evaluation is to furnish data for guidance, in serving which we also serve the other purposes of evaluation, the content of our evaluations should be whatever is needed as a basis for guidance. Since guidance seeks "the fullest realization by each pupil of his potentialities for desirable participation in the social order," the data it needs are in turn determined by the needs of society on the one hand, and of the individual on the other. For example, society requires that its members be able to communicate with one another through spoken and written language; similarly, individuals living in society must possess such language abilities. Innumerable other abilities, skills, habits, attitudes, informations, and so on are needed by both society and the individual. It is these mutual needs of both society and individuals that determine the aspects of pupils, or kinds of data, with which the evaluation of pupils must be concerned.

This book is built around the following breakdown of the aspects of pupils important to both society and the individual, and consequently essential to guidance:

1. Achievement of instructional objectives
2. Mental abilities, general and special
3. Emotional and social adjustment
4. Attitudes
5. Environment and background
6. Physical aspects

Discussions of each of these aspects will be given in the subsequent parts of this book. The first chapter in each part deals with the *meaning and importance* of the given aspect of pupils, and with theories as to its organization and determiners, all in terms of how schools need to be concerned with these matters. The remaining chapters of each part deal with the *techniques* that schools can use in evaluating that aspect of pupils.

SUGGESTED READINGS

Mathewson, R. H., *Guidance Policy and Practice,* New York: Harper & Brothers, 1949. Introduction, "Review of the Current Scene," pp. 3–17.

Russell, D. H., "What does research say about self-evaluation?" *Journal of Educational Research,* 46:561–574 (1953).

Super, D. E., *Appraising Vocational Fitness,* New York: Harper & Brothers, 1949. "To Diagnose or Not to Diagnose," pp. 2–6; "Non-Directive Test Interpretation," pp. 550–555.

Traxler, A. E., *Techniques of Guidance,* New York: Harper & Brothers, 1945. Chapter 1, "Background and Orientation," pp. 1–13.

Tyler, R. W., "Evaluation: a challenge to progressive education," *Progressive Education,* 12:552–556 (1935).

REFERENCES

1. Bordin, E. S., "Counseling points of view, non-directive and others," in Williamson, E. G. (ed.), *Trends in Student Personnel Work,* Minneapolis: University of Minnesota Press, 1949, pp. 120–121.

2. Giles, H. H., *Teacher-Pupil Planning,* New York: Harper & Brothers, 1941.

3. Good, C. V., Barr, A. S., and Scates, D. E., *The Methodology of Educational Research,* New York: Appleton-Century-Crofts, 1936.

4. Lindquist, E. F., *Design and Analysis of Experiments in Education and Psychology,* Boston: Houghton Mifflin Company, 1953.

5. Mitchell, C., "How valid are pupils' self-evaluations?" *Clearing House,* 19:486–488 (1945).

6. Orata, P. T., "Evaluating evaluation," *Journal of Educational Research,* 33:641–661 (1940).

7. Rogers, C. R., *Counseling and Psychotherapy,* Boston: Houghton Mifflin Company, 1942.

8. Rogers, C. R., "Psychometric tests and client-centered counseling," *Educational and Psychological Measurement,* 6:139–144 (1946).

9. Russell, D. H., "What does research say about self-evaluation?" *Journal of Educational Research,* 46:561–574 (1953).

10. Simpson, R. H., *Improving Teaching-Learning Processes,* New York: Longmans, Green & Co., Inc., 1953.

11. Troyer, M. E., "Self-evaluation in teacher education," *Journal of Educational Research,* 35:528–542 (1942).

12. Tyler, R. W., "Evaluation: a challenge to progressive education," *Progressive Education,* 12:552–556 (1935).

PART ONE

Achievement

CHAPTER II

The Nature of Achievement

ABSTRACT

Achievement in school consists of moving toward instructional objectives. Such objectives must guide both teaching and evaluation. The evidence concerning the specificity of achievement is conflicting but nonetheless implies that evaluation must directly concern itself with all important objectives. Teachers, pupils, and other citizens need to formulate objectives because of the inadequacy of most statements of objectives furnished them. The distinction between general and specific objectives should be made to facilitate the comprehension of objectives. Explicit statements of objectives are even more essential to evaluation than to instruction. Objectives should be stated in the form of observable pupil changes, understandably and singly, and should be grouped. Statements of objectives should contain only actual guiding purposes, should deal with mental processes, and should be determined by individual and social needs. Illustrations are given of statements of objectives for instruction in general, for reading and arithmetic at the elementary level, for English and mathematics at the secondary level. The "taxonomy of educational objectives" provides the most careful definitions yet made.

·~·~·~·

Achievement of instructional objectives is the degree to which the pupil has moved toward the objectives of the school. These objectives are the goals in the direction of which the curriculum seeks to change pupils. Here the curriculum is defined as *all the experiences used* by the school to attain the aims of education. "Objective" is, of course, a normative concept, carrying value

27

implications of the good, the desirable, and reflecting the purpose-fulness of the educational process.

What are the objectives of schools, of specific courses, curricula, teachers? In what ways are these social instrumentalities trying to change pupils? This question, although it constitutes mainly a curriculum problem, is also basic in evaluating educational achievement. For not only the content and methods of instruction but also the evaluating instruments must be determined by the objectives set up. The importance of objectives in designing evaluating instruments has been effectively stressed in the writings of Peters (19 : 148–159) and Tyler (26 : 5–6). This point of view —that the first and last steps in educational evaluation should be, respectively, the formulation of objectives and the validation of the evaluating instrument against the objectives—is so appealing to common sense as to seem platitudinous. However, it is only since this point of view has been adopted by evaluation workers that evaluation has begun to escape from stultifying emphasis on one type of objective, memorization of information, that char-acterized it in the past. Looking to the objectives of instruction for the determiners of evaluation methods has exposed the failure of many evaluation programs to deal with the many objectives long eulogized by curriculum builders.

THE SPECIFICITY OF INSTRUCTIONAL OBJECTIVES

Emphasis on objectives as the springboard for the evaluation of educational achievement has come from evidence concerning the low correlations between achievements of various objectives. The earlier standpoint of Wood (32 : 163), that high relationships were to be found between measures of information and of ability to think in a field, has been thrown into doubt. Different results have been found by various investigators.

The following discussion shows the differences between those investigations which have found high and low correlations between achievements of various objectives of courses. Thus Johnson (12) concluded on the basis of correlational studies that the ability to acquire information on the part of students in human biology, physics and chemistry, and basic health courses was accompanied to a substantial extent by the ability to apply this information.

Similarly Eurich (7) found that the thirteen subtests of a comprehensive examination designed to measure achievement of thirteen objectives of an English course were so intercorrelated as to "indicate practically no relationship between achievement in terms of some objectives *while between others it is relatively high.*" (Italics ours.) Fotos and Remmers (8), working with objectives and examinations in French courses, obtained high intercorrelations between vocabulary, English to French translation, French to English translation, and knowledge of verb forms; they conclude that "the language pattern tends to develop as a whole."

McConnell (17 : 3–8) used a more elaborate approach to the problem of differential achievement. In three subject-matter divisions he analyzed tests intended to measure achievement of three kinds of objectives: knowledge of vocabulary, knowledge of facts and principles, ability to apply facts and principles. His analysis was made not only by the usual method of intercorrelating the three tests, which yielded an average correlation of .66, but also by the method of item discrimination. That is, did test items for one objective discriminate among students of high and low achievement better when the criterion of achievement was the total score in its own objective, or did these items discriminate better when the criterion was total score on a test devised to test some other objective? He found that differences in item-discriminating power were greater between subject-matter sections than between the sections for the three different objectives. This means that the three objectives differed less among themselves than the three subjects differed among themselves.

A different group of researches has, however, emphasized the specificity of, or low correlation between, achievements of various objectives. Tyler's studies (30) in numerous courses at Ohio State University showed correlations of only about .40 between the scores on *recall of information* tests, on tests that demanded the *application of principles,* and on tests of *ability to draw inferences* from new data. He concluded that students did not develop corresponding degrees of achievement in mere recall and in achievement in such higher mental processes as applying principles and drawing inferences. Similarly Brown (3 : 59–60) found that "in a college foods class the correlations between a *knowledge of the scientific principles* underlying cookery and the *quality of the food cooked,* or the *ability of people to manage their work* in the laboratory, was less than .50." Other studies, such as those by Amidon, Botto, Jones, Segner, and Brown, are also cited by Brown as having furnished evidence indicating low correlation between achievements of various objectives of home economics courses.

Furst (9) reported low median correlations among 29 measures of achievement of different objectives of general education for high-school and college students over a two-year period of instruction; these were as follows:

	College Group		High-School Group	
	Initial Tests	Final Tests	Initial Tests	Final Tests
Median *r*'s:	.312	.347	.229	.311

Wittenborn and Larsen (31) reported intercorrelations of from .60 to .75 among achievement scores in German reading, vocabulary, and grammar; and correlations of from .50 to .59 between semester grades and these achievement scores. Comrey (5) found that the generality of achievement in courses at West Point varied considerably from one subject to another.

The intercorrelations in these and similar studies, even if they could be made comparable by correcting for the unreliability of the measures and the differences in range of talent measured, fall in general much below that required to establish the case for generality of achievement. The correlations tend to be positive but relatively low.

These differences in conclusions concerning the specificity of objectives may be due to various factors. (1) Differences in instructional emphasis may lead to either a high or a low relationship between achievement of various objectives. If teachers consistently strive to relate facts and principles to their applications, and to relate practice to theory, their pupils may perhaps exhibit higher relationships between these objectives. (2) Also, as McConnell (17) pointed out, "Research on the transfer of training suggests that the relationship between information and application would change with the difficulty of the application problems, and also with the degree of similarity between the original learning situations and those to which the facts and principles were to be applied in the examination. One might expect, also, to find a lower correlation between a knowledge of facts and principles tested verbally and applications tested in performance, than between knowledge and application when both were measured in purely verbal situations." (3) The degree of correlation may be a function of the age or maturity of the learner. For example, the correlation between knowledge of facts and ability to apply them might be, say, .30 for the third-grade pupils and .60 or .70 for college students. (4) Unreliability of the measuring instruments will also produce low correlations.

The practical consequence of this research for the educator is probably that *each objective must be clearly defined in terms of the measures of its attainment. The attainment of a particular objective cannot be inferred from the measured attainment of another objective.*

WHO FORMULATES OBJECTIVES?

Leary (15) reported in 1938 that teachers participated in making 63 percent of the 1660 curricula she analyzed. Supervisors, principals, and superintendents also serve on many curriculum committees, and professors in institutions of higher education act as consultants or provide, through graduate courses, inspiration or immediate opportunity for practical curriculum work.

In the interests of living democratically and making education more functional, curriculum planning and construction in recent years have also increasingly involved pupils and the public, the "consumers" of education (14, 21).

GENERAL AND SPECIFIC OBJECTIVES

Educational objectives may, of course, be classified in many ways. One distinction is that between *general* and *specific* objectives. This distinction is not a sharp one but rather a continuum from extreme generality to extreme specificity. General objectives are those which control the general learning situation, such as "a happy and useful life in society" or acquisition of "the ability to reason scientifically." Specific objectives, on the other hand, are the narrower, day-to-day goals, such as acquisition of "the ability to use the possessive singular correctly," or "the ability to make subjects agree with verbs in number," or "the ability to use the tabular key in indenting for paragraphs," or the "use of the proper form in introducing one person to another." Both types are, of course, necessary in any clear formulation of objectives, since the achievement of general objectives depends upon the contribution made by each specific factor in relation to every other. Fig. 2 gives

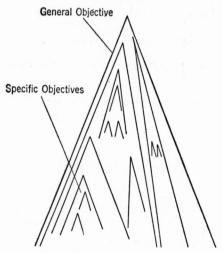

FIG. 2. Graphic Illustration of Relationship Between General and Specific Objectives.

a graphic illustration of this interdependence of general and specific objectives.

That statements of objectives may therefore often be inadequate is evident from the findings of Leary (15): "General objectives are included in 76 percent of all the courses analyzed. They represent the only kind of objective mentioned in 46 percent of the courses. . . . Specific objectives are stated in 42 percent of the total number of courses, and represent the only kind mentioned in approximately 10 percent. . . . Both general and specific objectives occur in 31 percent of all the courses analyzed. . . ."

It may be argued that excellent teaching practices can exist without the conscious and explicit formulation of objectives. The work of the interschool committees for evaluating the Eight-Year Study of the Progressive Education Association indicated that "vagueness of statement does not necessarily mean vagueness of purpose" (27). But the clarification of objectives is necessary to the *evaluation* of teaching practices and pupil achievement, even when it is not essential to instruction. And such clarification will usually assist in teaching toward the objectives because of the directive influence which objectives exert upon the selection of content, activities, and experiences (2).

HOW TO FORMULATE OBJECTIVES

To assist in formulating objectives we present a brief discussion of the desirable *form* and *content* for statements of objectives, and *illustrations* of objectives both for education in general and for special subjects.

FORM FOR STATING OBJECTIVES

1. Objectives should be worded in terms of changes expected in the pupil rather than as duties of the teacher, since attainment of objectives must in any case be evaluated in terms of pupil changes. The difference between the two ways of stating objectives may be seen from the following illustration.

Teacher's objective: To teach the knowledges, skills, habits, and attitudes involving the multiplication table in arithmetic.
Pupil objectives:
Knowledge—To know the multiplication table.
Skill—To be able to apply the multiplication table to problem solving.
Habit—To use smaller numbers as multipliers.
Attitude—To respect the power and value of the multiplication table.

2. An objective should be put in terms of observable changes in the pupil between the beginning and end of his experiences in a defined segment of the educative process. Unless we can tell whether pupils are changed, we shall have difficulty in justifying an objective, however worthy it may appear on philosophical grounds.

3. The terminology of the objective should be understandable;

it should have its meaning defined in terms that pupils, parents, and other teachers can appreciate. This requirement, it is readily understood, can often be met only after much thought, discussion, questioning, wording, and rewording.

4. Each statement should be unitary and contain one objective only, to prevent confusion and facilitate ready identification of the objective. To illustrate, such an objective as "To be able to translate French into English and English into French, with correct use of idioms" is less clear than the statement of these objectives in the form of three separate objectives.

5. Objectives should be grouped for purposes of economy and clarity, and for use in guiding pupil activities, in the organization of units of work, and in the construction of evaluation devices. That is, specific objectives should be grouped under the objective that is general to them.

CONTENT OF STATEMENTS OF OBJECTIVES

1. Statements should contain only "real" objectives, and not those to which lip service only is given. Schools may be tempted to formulate a glib statement rather than to think through their own serious purposes. They should ask themselves whether they intend actually to do something about each objective and about each phrase in the statement of the objective.

2. The list of objectives should contain references not only to the subject matter of a course but also to the mental processes to be applied to the subject matter. By mental processes are meant such types of behavior as remembering, reasoning, appreciating, being interested, and so on. And, especially for the higher mental processes, statements of objectives should be comprehensive. The higher mental processes are those to which the individual makes a large contribution through his own conscious effort. Such mental processes as sensation or mere memory are considered to be lower in the intellectual hierarchy because the individual makes less contribution; he is more "active" when he compares, infers, and abstracts. The value of the higher mental processes is largely a social one. Deductive and inductive reasoning are more powerful in solving most human problems than is mere recall of facts or the mechanical application of rules to familiar types of problems. As

Judd (13 : 4) says, "If by any means the educational system can discover how to promote even in the slightest measure the development of the higher mental processes, great advantage will be gained for civilization."

Differences of opinion exist among evaluation workers concerning the relative merits of various "mental process" objectives. Tyler (28 : 15) and his co-workers include and emphasize in their lists of objectives such types as "reasoning, or scientific method, which includes induction, testing hypotheses, and deduction." These types have been derived from the demands of teachers for tests which measure the attainment of the major outcomes they seek to achieve in their students. Wood and Beers (33) on the other hand, disparage the hope of teachers to "create thinkers," and uphold instead the social value of the knowledge of facts. Evidence adduced by Tyler (29) indicated (a) the relatively low retention of ability to recall information and the high retention of such outcomes as ability to recall principles, to apply principles, and to draw inferences from new data, and (b) the low correlations (13 : 6–17) (r equals about .40) between these types of achievement. This evidence is interpreted in different ways by these two schools of thought. On the one hand these findings are interpreted as showing that these tests of "higher mental processes" really measure activities which are independent of the educative process; thus "the relatively slight loss indicated by 'problem' tests given at intervals after completion of a course reflects the relative powerlessness of the teacher to alter the thinking ability of students" (33 : 494). On the other hand these findings are interpreted as showing that these "higher outcomes" are more permanent results of teaching and consequently more worth striving for and evaluating.

The classroom teacher will profit from the consideration and formulation of various mental process objectives as well as of the various subject-matter objectives. Such consideration, even if it does not *improve* thinking ability, will lead to more vital, interesting teaching and presentation of subject matter, in more varied forms and in forms more recognizable by pupils as related to their needs. It will also lead to more effective construction of evaluation devices.

3. The content of statements of objectives should be determined

by community and individual needs. Such needs can be discovered by investigations, studies, and reports of the activities and interests of the pupils and of the social milieu in which they will have to function. Detailed description of these methods of curriculum making would be out of place here. Many thoughtful works (14, 23) have been devoted to this problem and references to them may here serve the purposes of our discussion.

ILLUSTRATIONS OF OBJECTIVES

Before considering objectives for specific subjects it will be valuable to examine explicit attempts which have been made to formulate lists of *general* objectives for the work of the schools. Such formulations are, of course, the proper task of educational philosophers, scholars, scientists, administrators, curriculum builders, and other thoughtful citizens. The views of such thinkers reflecting the social forces of their environment have largely determined the nature of the teaching that goes on in the schools. But formulations of educational objectives have also been made by those concerned chiefly with the *evaluation* of pupil achievement. One such formulation, derived from work in constructing achievement tests for several departments of Ohio State University, has been presented by Tyler (26):

Type A. Information, which includes terminology, specific facts, and general principles.

Type B. Reasoning, or scientific method, which includes induction, testing hypotheses, and deduction.

Type C. Location of relevant data, which involves a knowledge of sources of usable data and skill in getting information from appropriate sources.

Type D. Skills characteristic of particular subjects, which include laboratory skills in the sciences, language skills, and the like.

Type E. Standards of technical performance, which include the knowledge of appropriate standards, ability to evaluate the relative importance of several standards which apply, and skill or habits in applying these standards.

Type F. Reports, which include the necessary skill in reporting projects in engineering or reporting experiments in science and the like.

Type G. Consistency in application of point of view, which is most apparent in philosophy.

Type X. Character, which is perhaps the most inclusive, involving many specific factors.

Another list of objectives resulted from a classification of the wide variety of objectives submitted by the thirty secondary schools participating in the Eight-Year Experimental Study of the Progressive Education Association. To observe the effects of a different type of instruction, these thirty schools were freed of the influence of college entrance requirements upon their work by the colleges' agreeing to accept all recommended candidates. Raths (20) was able to classify all the objectives submitted by these schools under the following eight headings:

1. Functional information
2. Aspects of thinking
3. Attitudes
4. Interests, aims, purposes
5. Study skills and work habits
6. Social adjustment and social sensitivity
7. Creativeness
8. A functional social philosophy

These attempts of evaluation workers to formulate lists of objectives have, of course, both determined and reflected the actual content of courses of study now operating in schools. Leary's analysis (15) of the objectives of 1660 courses of study shows the percentages of occurrence of various objectives as follows:

Objectives	Total Percentage in State, City, and County Courses
1. Attainment of knowledge and acquisition of skills in particular fields...........................	68
2. Development of desirable attitudes, appreciations, and understandings.........................	66
3. Development of specific habits and abilities.......	45
4. Promotion of enriched living and social well-being .	27
5. Development of personality....................	21

SPECIFIC OBJECTIVES

From the consideration of *general* objectives we may now proceed to formulations of objectives within *specific subject matters*.

On the one hand is the subject matter as determined by textbook content, courses of study, definitions of requirements. On the other hand are the mental processes that can operate upon that subject matter, the behaviors a given teacher will seek to bring about in his pupils in that particular subject-matter field. It is possible to present here only a few formulations of objectives to serve as illustrations of the results of this step in the construction of evaluation devices.

ELEMENTARY-SCHOOL OBJECTIVES

At the elementary school level, the subject matter may be classified into four divisions:
1. Language arts—Handwriting, spelling, composition (written and oral), grammar, reading
2. Arithmetic—Computation, problem solving
3. Social studies—Geography, history, civics
4. Others—Art, music, science, hygiene, home economics, industrial arts, etc.

To illustrate the formulation of objectives at the elementary level, we shall present representative attempts in two of these subjects—reading and arithmetic—in specific school grades.

OBJECTIVES OF INSTRUCTION IN READING

Grade I

Reading readiness, which involves (10 : 48–64) acquisition of the intelligence, visual and auditory perception, language development, background of experience, and social behavior necessary before a child can learn to read. Some of these objectives cannot be aimed at explicitly by the teacher, because their attainment is largely a function of certain processes of maturation which we have not yet learned how to affect with specific variations in environment, or of factors like home background, which cannot be readily changed for instructional purposes.

Grade III

Know the sounds of all the letters of the alphabet and of most of the common phonograms.

Be able to work out the pronunciation of unfamiliar words without help.

Read silently with greater speed than is attained in reading orally.

Read silently without pointing or lip movements.

Like to read, and read widely in varied sources.

Be able to read fourth-grade material with satisfactory understanding.

Grade VI

Read widely so as to extend and enrich experience.

Continue improvement of basic skills in word recognition and comprehension.

Read silently with *much* greater speed than is attained in reading orally.

Acquire training in the use of books and in the location of information in dictionaries and other reference works.

Acquire skills involved in the reading of factual material.

Achieve seventh-grade level in reading ability.

OBJECTIVES OF INSTRUCTION IN ARITHMETIC

Arithmetic objectives may be put in two classes: *computation,* as represented by the sixteen combinations possible between the four kinds of operations (addition, subtraction, multiplication, division) and the four kinds of numbers (whole numbers, mixed numbers, common fractions, decimal fractions); and *problem solving,* which may be analyzed into five somewhat distinct abilities: (1) comprehension, (2) ability to determine what is given, (3) ability to determine what is called for, (4) ability to conceive the probable answer, and (5) ability to produce the correct solution.

In selecting the teaching materials in arithmetic instruction the trend has been away from basing the selection on disciplinary value for the mind to basing it on the social usefulness of the materials. Also, demonstrations of the absence of correlation between arithmetic abilities with apparently similar materials, such as ability to add columns of two numbers and ability to add columns of three numbers, have caused curriculum makers to analyze arithmetic objectives in great detail. For example, Merton (18) listed eighteen distinct objectives in teaching the addition of whole numbers.

SECONDARY-SCHOOL OBJECTIVES

At the secondary school level the subject matter may traditionally be classified into eight divisions:

1. English—Composition and literature
2. Mathematics—Algebra, geometry, trigonometry
3. Foreign languages—Latin, French, German, Spanish, Italian
4. Social studies—Civics, American and world history, economics, sociology, social psychology
5. Natural sciences—General science, biology, chemistry, physics
6. Commercial subjects—Bookkeeping, shorthand, typewriting, business practice
7. Home economics—Clothing, foods, housing, family relationships
8. Industrial arts—Mechanical drawing, shop work (metal, wood, etc.), related mathematics, related science, blueprinting, etc.

To illustrate objectives at the secondary level we shall present representative attempts in two of the subjects.

OBJECTIVES OF INSTRUCTION IN ENGLISH (11 : 381)

Literature or assimilative objectives

Attainment of ability to read literary materials with facility and understanding

Development of critical judgment and appreciation of literature

Enlarged acquaintance with literature and with literary history

Broadening of experience vicariously through reading

Formation of desirable attitudes toward reading, namely, increased appetite and taste for what is good in literature

Attainment of some competence in the use of the resources of libraries

Language or reproductive objectives

Attainment of ability to speak and write intelligibly, agreeably, and effectively

  Skill in correct language usage
  Power of expression
Development of desirable attitudes toward the translation of experience into spoken and written words.

Objectives of Instruction in Mathematics (25)

Utilitarian aims
Skill in the fundamental processes of arithmetic
Command of the language of algebra
Such knowledge of the fundamental laws of algebra as will equip one to understand and use elementary algebraic methods
Skill in interpreting graphic representation
Familiarity with the geometric forms common in nature, industry, and life. This involves acquaintance with the more fundamental properties and relationships of these forms.
Disciplinary aims
The acquisition, in precise form, of those ideas and concepts in terms of which the quantitative thinking of the world is done, and the development of the ability to think clearly in terms of such ideas and concepts
The acquisition of mental habits and attitudes which will make the above training effective in the life of the individual: a seeking for relations, an attitude of inquiry, a love of precision, a desire for orderly and logical organization, etc.
Training in thinking in terms of the idea of relationship of dependence
Cultural aims
Appreciation of beauty in the geometric forms of nature, art, and industry
Ideals of perfection as to logical structure, precision of statement and of thought, logical reasoning, etc.
Appreciation of the power of mathematics
  These objectives of mathematics instruction differ among themselves of course in their "immediacy," those labeled "utilitarian" being far more directly associated with the actual subject-matter content of courses of study than those called "disciplinary" and "cultural." Greater immediacy and ease of realization need not,

however, decrease the teacher's efforts to realize the other objectives.

THE TAXONOMY OF EDUCATIONAL OBJECTIVES

As the reader has looked over the foregoing lists of general and specific objectives, he may have been impressed with the variety and ambiguity of the terms used. For example, what is meant by "information" and "knowledge"? Are these the same or should some distinction be made in them? Similarly, what is meant by "critical judgment" as against "appreciation"? When two curricula or statements of objectives use a given term, do they assign the same meaning to it? When teachers make up a statement of objectives, can they have any feeling of satisfaction that they have considered and thought through any of the important possibilities? Or may they wonder whether they have not overlooked, through accident or personal blind spots, some of the objectives with which they should be concerned?

About 1949 a group of college and university examiners became concerned with just these kinds of questions. Under the informal chairmanship of Benjamin S. Bloom of the University of Chicago, they organized a "Taxonomy Group." Over several years this group worked toward a comprehensive classification of educational objectives to be used for several purposes: to facilitate communication among teachers, examiners, and other educational workers; to set up a comprehensive, systematic list of the types of behavior at which educational procedures may aim; to provide a source of hypotheses and questions for methods of developing curricula, teaching methods, and testing techniques; to arrange educational behaviors, or objectives, from simple to complex; and, in general, to lay bare many of the hitherto concealed assumptions underlying the statements of objectives that educators have developed in the past.

Although the taxonomy is still tentative, and will probably remain so for some time to come, it has been developed to the point where it can serve some of these purposes effectively. The following brief description of the taxonomy is intended merely to introduce the student to this highly significant development.

THREE DOMAINS

In the first place, the Taxonomy Group has differentiated objectives into three major "domains"—the Cognitive, the Affective, and the Psychomotor. The Cognitive domain has thus far been most fully mapped, and our examples will be drawn from it. The Affective domain will include attitudes, appreciations, emotional and social adjustments, and the like. The Psychomotor domain will presumably contain types of small and large muscle skills and coördinations such as those involved in, say, surgery, physical training, and vocational education for various mechanical and clerical trades.

Within the Cognitive domain,[1] the taxonomy thus provides for two major classes—knowledge, and intellectual abilities and skills.

KNOWLEDGE

The first of these major classes—1.00: Knowledge—has in turn been defined as follows:

Knowledge as defined here includes those behaviors and test situations which emphasize the remembering, either by recognition or recall, of ideas, material, or phenomena. The behavior expected of the student in a recall situation is very similar to the behavior he was expected to have during the original learning situation. In the learning situation the student is expected to store in his mind certain information and the behavior expected later is the remembering of this information. Although some alterations may be expected in the material to be remembered, this is a relatively minor part of the knowledge behavior or test. The process of relating and judging is also involved to the extent that the student is expected to answer questions and problems which are posed in a different form in the test situation than in the original learning situation.

In the classification of the knowledge objectives, the arrangement is from the specific and relatively concrete types of be-

[1] Benjamin S. Bloom, Max Engelhardt, Edward Furst, Walker Hill and David R. Krathwohl, *A Taxonomy of Educational Objectives—The Cognitive Domain*, New York: Longmans, Green, & Co., Inc., Preliminary Edition, 1954.

haviors to the more complex and abstract ones. Thus, the knowledge of specifics refers to types of information or knowledge which can be isolated or remembered separately, while the knowledge of universals and abstractions emphasizes the interrelations and patterns in which information can be organized and structured.

While it is recognized that knowledge is involved in the more complex major categories of the taxonomy (2.00 to 6.00), the knowledge category differs from the others in that remembering is the major psychological process involved here, while in the other categories the remembering is only one part of a much more complex process of relating, judging, and reorganizing.

Following this definition, Knowledge is broken down into the following types:

1.10: Knowledge of Specifics—the recall of specific and isolable bits of information

1.11: Knowledge of Terminology—of referents for specific verbal and nonverbal symbols

1.12: Knowledge of Specific Facts—of dates, events, persons, places, sources of information, etc.

1.20: Knowledge of Ways and Means of Dealing with Specifics—of the ways of organizing, studying, judging, and criticizing ideas and phenomena

1.21: Knowledge of Conventions—of characteristic ways of treating and presenting ideas and phenomena

1.22: Knowledge of Trends and Sequences—of the processes, directions, and movements of phenomena with respect to time

1.23: Knowledge of Classifications and Categories—of the classes, sets, divisions, and arrangements which are regarded as fundamental or useful for a given subject field, purpose, argument, or problem

1.24: Knowledge of Criteria—of the criteria by which facts, principles, opinions, and conduct are tested and judged

1.25: Knowledge of Methodology—of the methods of inquiry, techniques, and procedures employed in a particular subject field as well as those employed in investigating particular problems and phenomena

1.30: Knowledge of the Universals and Abstractions in a Field—of the major schemes and patterns by which phenomena and ideas are organized

1.31: Knowledge of Principles and Generalizations—of particular abstractions which summarize observations of phenomena

1.32: Knowledge of Theories and Structures—of the body of principles and generalizations, together with their interrelations, which present a clear, rounded, and systematic view of a complex phenomenon, problem, or field.

The Taxonomy Group has also developed illustrative objectives and test items for each of the categories of knowledge. For example, under 1.11: Knowledge of Terminology would be included such objectives as "Ability to define technical terms by giving their attributes, properties, or relations" and "Knowledge of the vocabulary of the fine arts sufficient to be able to read and converse intelligently." An illustrative test item in this field is the following:

A synapse can best be described as
  1 a mass or layer of protoplasm having many nuclei but lacking distinct cell boundaries.
  2 a lapse of memory caused by inadequate circulation of blood to the brain.
  3 the pairing of maternal with paternal chromosomes during maturation of the germ cells.
  4 the long cylindrical portion of an axon.
  5 the point at which the nerve impulse passes from one neuron to another.

For 1.31: Knowledge of Principles and Generalizations, illustrative educational objectives are "The recall of major generalizations about particular cultures" and "Knowledge of biological laws of reproduction and heredity." An illustration of an item for testing knowledge of principles and generalizations is the following:

If the volume of a given mass of gas is kept constant, the pressure may be diminished by
  1 reducing the temperature.
  2 raising the temperature.
  3 adding heat.
  4 decreasing the density.
  5 increasing the density.

Intellectual Abilities and Skills

Under this second major heading of the Cognitive Domain are the following categories of objectives, each of which, with its sub-categories, is carefully defined. Each is also illustrated with objectives and test items from actual subject-matter fields.

2.00 Comprehension
    2.10 Translation
    2.20 Interpretation
    2.30 Extrapolation
3.00 Application
4.00 Analysis
5.00 Synthesis
6.00 Evaluation

REFERENCES

1. *American College Dictionary,* text edition, New York: Harper & Brothers, 1950.
2. Bristow, W. H., and Frederick, O. I., "Curriculum development," in Monroe, W. S. (ed.), *Encyclopedia of Educational Research,* New York: The Macmillan Company, rev. ed., 1950.
3. Brown, Clara M., *Evaluation and Investigation in Home Economics,* New York: Appleton-Century-Crofts, 1941.
4. Caswell, H. L., and Campbell, D. S., *Curriculum Development,* New York: American Book Company, 1935.
5. Comrey, A. L., "A factorial study of achievement in West Point courses," *Educational and Psychological Measurement,* 9:193–210 (1949).
6. Draper, E. M., *Principles and Techniques of Curriculum Making,* New York: Appleton-Century-Crofts, 1936.
7. Eurich, A. C., "Measuring the achievement of objectives in freshman English," *Studies in College Examinations,* Minneapolis: University of Minnesota, Committee on Educational Research, 1934, pp. 50–66.
8. Fotos, J. T., and Remmers, H. H., "The functional interrelationships of certain aspects of modern language learning," *Modern Language Journal,* 18:481–493 (1934).
9. Furst, E. J., "Effect of the organization of learning experiences

upon the organization of learning outcomes. I. Study of the problem by means of correlation analysis," *Journal of Experimental Education*, 18:215–228 (1950); II. Study of the problem by means of factor analysis, *ibid.*, 18:343–352 (1950).

10. Harris, A. J., *How to Increase Reading Ability*, New York: Longmans, Green & Co., Inc., 1940.

11. Hawkes, H. E., Lindquist, E. F., and Mann, C. R., *Construction and Use of Achievement Examinations*, Boston: Houghton Mifflin Company, 1936.

12. Johnson, P. O., "Differential functions of examinations," *Studies in College Examinations*, Minneapolis: University of Minnesota, Committee on Educational Research, 1934, pp. 43–50.

13. Judd, C. H., *Education as Cultivation of the Higher Mental Processes*, New York: The Macmillan Company, 1936.

14. Krug, E. A., *Curriculum Planning*, New York: Harper & Brothers, 1950.

15. Leary, B. E., *A Survey of Courses of Study and Other Curriculum Materials Published Since 1934*, U.S. Office of Education, Bulletin 1937, No. 31, Washington: Government Printing Office, 1938.

16. Mathews, C. O., "Issues in the construction and use of educational measurements," *Journal of Educational Research*, 33:452–456 (1940).

17. McConnell, T. R., "A study of the extent of measurement of differential objectives of instruction," in *An Appraisal of Techniques of Evaluation, Symposium*, Washington: American Educational Research Association, National Education Association, February 26, 1940.

18. Merton, C. L., "Remedial work in arithmetic," *Second Year Book of Department of Elementary School Principals*, 1933.

19. Peters, C. C., "The relation of standardized tests to educational objectives," *Second Yearbook of the National Society for the Study of Educational Sociology*, New York: Teachers College, Columbia University, 1929.

20. Raths, L. E., "Evaluating the program of a school," *Educational Research Bulletin*, 17:57–84 (1938).

21. Remmers, H. H., and Shimberg, B., *Manual, SRA Youth Inventory*, Chicago: Science Research Associates, 1949.

22. Smith, B. O., *Logical Aspects of Educational Measurement*, New York: Columbia University Press, 1938.

23. Smith, B. O., Stanley, W. O., and Shores, H., *Fundamentals of Curriculum Development*, Yonkers: World Book Company, 1950.

24. *Summary Report, College and University Examiners' Taxonomy Conference,* (mimeographed), Champaign: University of Illinois, Bureau of Research and Service, College of Education, November, 1949, pp. 16–17.

25. *The Reorganization of Mathematics in Secondary Education,* Mathematical Association of America, Inc., 1923.

26. Tyler, R. W., *Constructing Achievement Tests,* Columbus: Ohio State University, 1934. (Reprints from *Educational Research Bulletin.*)

27. Tyler, R. W., "Defining and measuring objectives of progressive education," *Educational Record,* Supplement No. 9, pp. 78–85, 1936.

28. Tyler, R. W., "Evaluation: A challenge to progressive education," *Progressive Education,* 12:553–556 (1935).

29. Tyler, R. W., "Permanence of learning," *Journal of Higher Education,* 4:203–204 (1933).

30. Tyler, R. W., "The relation between recall and higher mental processes," in Judd, C. H., *Education as Cultivation of the Higher Mental Processes,* New York: The Macmillan Company, 1936, pp. 6–17.

31. Wittenborn, J. R., and Larsen, R. P., "A factorial study of achievement in college German," *Journal of Educational Psychology,* 35:39–48 (1944).

32. Wood, B. D., *Measurement in Higher Education,* Yonkers: World Book Company, 1923.

33. Wood, B. D., and Beers, F. S., "Knowledge versus thinking," *Teachers College Record,* 37:487–499 (1936).

CHAPTER III

Achievement Testing

ABSTRACT

After weighing the relative merits of essay tests and short-answer tests in the light of twelve considerations, we conclude that the essay test may readily have the advantage as a motivational device, as an instructional device for increasing ability to write good English, and as a device for evaluating that ability. On other counts the short-answer test has been found either equal or superior to the essay test. The practical implications of these conclusions for the classroom teacher are that in most circumstances it will be advantageous to use: (1) short-answer tests, in all the varied forms described in Chapter IV, to evaluate types of achievement other than the ability to write essays; (2) the essay test as one way to evaluate ability to write essays and all that such writing implies; (3) the essay test to motivate pupils to learn certain materials (selected carefully for their worth-whileness) in such a way that they will be able to recall the materials in an organized fashion and to know facts when cues are not given. For this purpose the essay test should be used in the improved forms described in Chapter VII.

The chief advantages of standardized tests are their possession of norms and their greater technical refinement. Teacher-made tests can fit instructional objectives better, yield greater benefits to the teacher, and be adapted to continuous evaluation during a semester. The more extensive interpretations possible with some standardized tests can be achieved only through careful selection of the tests according to the meaningfulness of their norms; they are most useful in the tool subjects, where the objectives may vary least from classroom to classroom and where achievement is to be considered, for guidance purposes, as an aptitude for prediction of future achievement. Where intrapupil

49

differences in achievement from subject to subject and from year to year are to be studied, standard tests have a major advantage. For comparison of one pupil with another and of one classroom with another, teacher-made tests can easily be supplied with the necessary norms.

What are the techniques with which we can evaluate the aspects of pupils discussed in Chapter II? We shall present a full treatment of all the steps in the evaluation of the pupil's achievement of instructional objectives. Especially in the field of achievement evaluation there has been accumulated a large fund of practical technique. For this reason it is well that our presentation of evaluation techniques begins with achievement of instructional objectives. When we have completed our treatment of achievement testing we shall have taken up many of the practical and theoretical ideas needed in the evaluation of any aspect of pupils.

FIVE MAJOR STEPS IN EVALUATION

It is helpful to think of the evaluation process as consisting of five major steps.

1. Statement of the Purpose and Content of Evaluation

This step in evaluation procedure has, of course, been treated in the preceding two chapters. It is mentioned here merely to serve as a liaison with those chapters. In Chapter II we presented sample definitions, descriptions, and discussions of the kinds of achievement which should be evaluated. These were in turn determined by the purposes of evaluation considered in Chapter I, which centered around the function of providing data for guidance. Hence the preceding chapters have been designed to help teachers carry out this first step in the evaluation process.

2. Construction or Selection of an Evaluating Device

This step should proceed in close touch with Step 1, of course, since only the devices that have been aimed at specific materials and purposes can be expected to provide worth-while data on those materials and for those purposes. The microscope, for example, can furnish data concerning only very small objects because it was designed for the visual examination of objects of certain sizes. This obvious point has frequently been forgotten in the construction of evaluation devices for the aspects of pupils with which we are concerned. Instruments have been designed to evaluate achievement without close and critical regard for what was meant by achievement. Consequently, many devices intended to evaluate achievement of instructional objectives have reflected a narrow conception of this task. Failure to make sure that construction or selection of evaluation devices was attuned to purposes and objectives has frequently resulted in damage to learning, instruction, and guidance.

3. Administration of the Evaluating Device

This step is easily understood in terms of illustrations from everyday life. If our purpose is to measure the length of a room and we have selected or constructed a device for this purpose in the form of a foot rule, we administer this device by placing it as many times as possible end-for-end along the lengthwise dimension of the room. We administer the device for evaluating a pupil's temperature by placing a fever thermometer underneath his tongue. For each of the evaluating devices to be discussed, the method of administration—how it should be given—will have to be specified either explicitly or by inference from the classification to which the device belongs.

4. Interpretation of the Data Yielded by the Evaluating Device

Any set of data acquire meaning only after they have been interpreted and related to the purpose and content of evaluation. The number of times the foot rule is placed along the side of the room is interpreted as the length of the room. The position of the column of mercury in the fever thermometer must be interpreted in terms of the pupil's temperature and health. The scores and other data derived from the evaluating devices to be described here must be interpreted for what they show about pupil achievement.

5. Evaluation of the Evaluating Device

After the device has been administered and the resulting data interpreted, the device itself may be evaluated in terms of the success with which it serves its purpose and the degree to which it can be improved. The criteria by which evaluating devices should be judged—that is, the concepts of validity and practicality—will be our major concern under this heading.

A SEQUENCE OF QUESTIONS

Let us assume that the objectives of instruction have already been stated in accordance with the rules presented in Chapter II. At this point, then, the teacher is equipped with a set of objectives stated in the form of grouped, unitary, understandable, and observable changes in pupils, toward which instructional effort is actually directed, which involve both subject matter and mental processes, and which have been determined by community and individual needs.

From this point onward, the construction or selection of the evaluating device requires that answers be given to the following questions:

1. At what objective or group of objectives is the evaluation device aimed?
2. Which of the following types of devices is best suited to evaluate the achievement of these objectives?
   a. Devices involving symbols (verbal, mathematical, musical, spatial, etc.)
   b. Devices involving " real things" rather than symbols
   c. Devices involving the direct observation of behavior or performance
3. If a device involving language (verbal or other symbols) is chosen, should it be an essay test or a short-answer test?[1]
4. If a short-answer test is chosen, should it be an externally made, standardized, purchasable test or a teacher-made test?
5. If a teacher-made short-answer test is chosen, what types of questions should be used and how should they be apportioned and composed?
6. If an externally made, standardized, short-answer test is to be used, how should it be chosen from among the many available?

---

[1] "Short-answer test" as used in this book refers to the whole class of objectively scored test items rather than only to the type in which the pupil's response is a single word, phrase, or sentence. It seems to be a better term than "objective" or "objectively scorable" test because it is more directly opposite in meaning to "essay test."

7. If a nonlanguage product or behavior device is to be used, how should it be constructed?

8. If an essay test is to be used, how should it be constructed?

In this chapter we shall consider Questions 1 to 4. Note that in these questions we have selected the answers for Questions 1 to 5 so as to narrow our problem to an immediate and practical concern of most classroom teachers. That is, many teachers use devices involving symbols in the form of short-answer tests which they make themselves, as was indicated in a study by Lee and Segel (14 : 6–12) of the testing practices of about 1500 high school teachers.

OBJECTIVES AND EVALUATION DEVICES

1. *At what objective or group of objectives is the evaluation device aimed?* Different objectives require different evaluation devices. Frequently, not all the objectives of a class of instruction can be approached by even the same type of device. Consequently, the first step in constructing an evaluation device after the objectives have been formulated is to single out the objective, or objectives, at which each device is to be aimed. This procedure of singling out an objective so that evaluation devices may be constructed to fit its peculiar requirements has been well illustrated by Tyler (24 : 8):

Each of the eight objectives set up for elementary courses in zoology was defined in terms of the behavior expected of students. In defining the first objective, a fund of information about animal activities and structures, the specific facts and general principles which the student should be able to recall without reference to textbooks, or other sources of information, were indicated. The second objective, an understanding of technical terminology, was defined by listing the terms which the student himself should be able to use in his own reports, and another list of terms which he would not be expected to use, but should be able to understand when he finds them in zoological publications. The third objective, an ability to draw inferences from facts, that is, to propose hypotheses, was defined by describing the types of experiments which an elementary student should be able to interpret. The fourth objective, ability to propose ways of testing hypotheses, was defined by listing the types of hypotheses which an elementary student should be able to validate by experiment, or to propose ways of validation. The fifth objective, an ability to apply principles to concrete situations, was defined by listing the principles which elementary students should be able to apply, and types of concrete situations in which the student might apply these principles. The sixth objective, accuracy of observation, was defined by listing the types of experiments in which the elementary student should be able to make accurate observations. The seventh objective, skill in the use of the microscope and other essential tools, was defined by describing the types of microscopic mounts and types of dissections which elementary students should learn to make. The eighth objective, an ability to express effectively ideas related to zoology, was defined by indicating the nature of the reports, both written and oral, which zoology students are expected to make and the qualities demanded for these reports to be effective.

TYPE OF EVALUATING DEVICE

2. *Which of the following three general types of devices is best suited to evaluate the achievement of these objectives?*
   a. *Devices involving language, either verbal or mathematical*
   b. *Devices involving "real things" rather than symbols*
   c. *Devices involving direct observation of performance*

These types may be illustrated by reference to the objectives listed in the quotation from Tyler. Devices involving language (by language we mean any system of communication using symbols) would apply to the first, second, third, fourth, fifth, and eighth objectives. Devices involving real things would be applicable to the seventh objective, skill in use of the microscope and other essential tools, since this skill would be reflected in the quality of the microscopic mounts and types of dissection made by the students. Devices involving direct observation of behavior would similarly be applicable to the sixth and seventh objectives, since the evaluator directly observes the student's behavior, the movements of his body and eyes, the position and vantage points adopted, the skill in manipulating instruments. The first type of device, that involving language, is represented by the "paper and pencil" test, which is by far the most frequently used type of evaluation device. The preponderance of written language or paper and pencil devices in the evaluation of achievement merely reflects how important language is in the school curriculum and in our civilization.

Devices involving nonsymbolic materials are usually in the form of a check list or rating scale upon which may be indicated the presence or absence, or degree of quality, of the salient features of the product. Typical products are those which pupils turn out in art courses, chemical laboratories, home economics laboratories, woodwork and metalwork shops, and in many other kinds of school work. Thus under the heading of nonlanguage products may be listed such objects as drawings, precipitates, pies, dresses, chairs, book ends, and wrenches. Devices involving behavior are those which enable an observer using his eyes and ears to evaluate on a rating scale or check list a pupil's achievement of desirable ways of moving or speaking. Typical observations under this heading would be clarity of speech, posture, habits of recitation in class, physical education achievement, and speed and efficiency in handling scientific apparatus or laboratory equipment.

Obviously, in the majority of cases, teachers will find devices involving language most suited to their instructional objectives.

ESSAY VS. SHORT-ANSWER TESTING

3. *If a device involving language is chosen, should it be an essay test or a short-answer test?* Let us compare the merits and limitations of essay tests and short-answer tests as to each of the following:

    a. Reliability[2] of grading or scoring
    b. Extensiveness of the sampling of achievement
    c. Possibility of the pupil's guessing or bluffing
    d. Pretest, or motivational, effects on pupil achievement
    e. Posttest, or instructional, effects on pupil achievement
    f. Labor required in construction
    g. Labor required in scoring or grading
    h. Cost of administering
    i. Attitudes of pupils toward each type of test
    j. Intellectual pleasure and growth derived by teacher from constructing and scoring

[2] Reliability may be roughly defined for the present as the consistency with which a device yields the same results. If the device does not yield consistent measurements, it is unreliable. A quick glance, for example, would probably be an unreliable technique for measuring the circumference of a cylinder, because different judges would give different guesses from one to another.

   k. Distorting effects on achievement of the medium of expression

   l. Fitness for evaluation of complex achievement

The purpose of this discussion will be primarily to review the kinds of arguments that have been introduced during decades of controversy. The considerations are not necessarily taken up in order of their importance. The references cited are representative rather than exhaustive.

RELIABILITY OF GRADING OR SCORING

In general, the short-answer test can be graded more reliably, or consistently, than the essay test. This means that a given short-answer test paper will be given the same score no matter who grades it or on how many different occasions it is graded by the same person, if we disregard clerical errors. On the other hand, essay tests will not be graded in the same way either by different people or by the same person at different times. The unreliability of rating essay tests has been demonstrated repeatedly by many experiments beginning with those of Starch and Elliott (22) in 1912. Hartog (10) in 1935 reported similar results from studies in

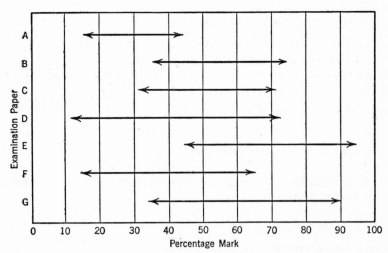

FIG. 3. Range of Percentage Marks Assigned by 12 Home Economics Teachers to 7 Essay-Type Examination Papers of 9th-Grade Students. (After 2 : 17.)

British schools. All these investigators found that scores on essay tests *graded according to the usual methods* by different graders vary widely. Brown (**3** : 33) reports on "an experiment, conducted with home economics seniors who had completed their supervised teaching and graduate students who were experienced teachers, [which] showed that essay-type tests in home economics were as difficult to score accurately as were tests in other subjects. The range of scores assigned by these judges to seven ninth-grade papers is shown in Figure 2." (Our Fig. 3.)

As Freeman (**8**) has pointed out, however, "It is obvious that a large part of this variation may be due, not to the unreliability of scoring, but to a difference in the standard required for passing. This variation in standards also affects the scores on objective tests when these scores are transformed into marks."

Among other factors which may be responsible for unreliability in grading essay tests are:

1. Psychological factors, such as fatigue, affecting ability to distinguish between closely allied degrees of merit. As a test grader proceeds through a large pile of papers there are systematic changes, resulting from factors which, while varying for different graders, grossly affect the test scores.

2. The influence of handwriting; for example, James (**11**) and Sheppard (**20**) both found a positive relationship between the quality of handwriting and the grade accorded to test papers identical in content.

In Chapter VI we shall see that certain techniques can materially reduce the unreliability of scoring essay tests. But our present conclusion must be that short-answer tests are superior in reliability of scoring.

EXTENSIVENESS OF THE SAMPLING OF ACHIEVEMENT

The usual short-answer test containing, say, fifty items or questions draws upon a far wider range of pupil achievement than does the usual essay test containing less than fifteen questions. Consequently, short-answer tests run less danger of permitting chance variations in student preparation and achievement to have a great effect on test scores. Such effects occur when pupils do or do not happen to guess correctly which one or more of a small number of essay questions would be asked. Furthermore, the extensive coverage of subject matter and mental processes made possible by short-answer tests may produce less variation among teachers in the content selected for tests.

Possibility of the Pupil's Guessing or Bluffing

The charge is often made that the restricted number of alternatives which multiple-choice tests present lets a pupil achieve a higher score than is warranted by his true achievement. That is, in a test of one hundred items each presenting two choices, pupils could on the average make fifty correct responses by following the advice of a tossed coin. Various statistical formulas have been offered to correct for this chance factor. The problem of guessing cannot be entirely eliminated by such mechanically applied statistical corrections, since they are based on either theorems of probability or on statistical studies of average effects, neither of which can correct for the *individual* pupil's spurious achievement through guessing.

Nonetheless, as the logic of estimating test reliability shows (see Chapter V), when a test has adequate reliability we know that the factor of chance success is negligible.

The essay test, however, may be similarly thwarted if it is not well constructed and graded. A pupil who knows scarcely anything about a subject may often take advantage of the positive effect on grades of such factors as speed of writing, literary style, and ability to "free-associate" around a question. Here, however, the effect of bluffing and guessing can be counteracted in the case of *individual* students by the use of valid, constant scoring standards.

Pretest, or Motivational, Effects on Pupil Achievement

Does expectation of a short-answer test have a different effect on pupil preparation and achievement than expectation of an essay test? Students certainly think so when they insist on knowing whether they will have an essay or a short-answer test. Several experiments have attempted to answer this question. Terry (23) found that two classes in educational psychology prepared for an objective test by emphasizing details, whereas expectation of an essay test led them to emphasize larger units of subject matter. Similarly, Douglass and Tallmadge (6) found that the short-answer test directs attention to detail and exact wording, while the essay test encourages study methods involving organization, perception of relationships and trends, and personal reactions.

Meyer (16) studied the effect of essay and short-answer test expectation on both preparation and achievement. Dividing 124 students of Civil War history into four groups he directed one group to study for a true-false test, the second group for a multiple-choice test, the third group for a completion test, and the fourth group for an essay test. At the end of the study period all groups were given all four types of tests. He found that all four types of tests were equally good for motivating the learning of facts, but that the groups which had studied for completion and essay tests achieved higher scores when the students were tested again five weeks later. Consequently he concluded that achievement was more permanent when the student anticipated an essay type of test. Also the methods of study were superior, involving more worth-while units of subject matter and less attention to rote learning, when the students studied for essay tests. Vallance (25) more recently used high-school seniors studying a pamphlet on the life of migratory farm laborers in comparing the effects of (1) preparing for and (2) taking short-answer and essay tests. He found no significant differences between the two types as estimated by testing subsequent retention of the subject matter.

The conclusion on this issue probably cannot be general. It depends on what kinds of essay and short-answer tests students have experienced in the past, what expectations they have developed concerning such tests, and the mental processes required by the content of the test questions.

Posttest, or Instructional, Effects on Pupil Achievement

This consideration may be broken down into (1) the suggestive effect of the untrue material included in short-answer tests and (2) the potentialities of the two kinds of tests for use in increasing various kinds of achievement. Negative suggestion refers to the possibility that the false statements in true-false tests and the incorrect alternatives in multiple-choice tests may implant misinformation in the minds of pupils. That is, students may retain the false elements of tests and later on believe them to be correct. However, research (**19** : 358–365) has shown that in addition to the weakness of the psychological basis for such a possibility in disregarding mental set, the small amount of negative suggestion is fully offset by an even greater positive suggestion, leaving a positive net effect. So, on the whole, pupils learn more than they lose by taking true-false tests.

The value of the two types of tests for instructional purposes can take two forms. One such value for the essay test is urged forcefully by Krey (**13**):

There is one skill which may, indeed has been, seriously impaired by the excessive use of the new-type tests. This is skill in expression, the ability to set forth some topic in social science clearly, convincingly, and agreeably. Teachers in college have begun to remark that students who come to them from school systems in which the new-type test has been used almost exclusively for a number of years are unable to express themselves cogently either orally or in writing. In school systems in which the new-type test has been used extremely, it has been possible for students to avoid writing a single complete sentence except in courses in English composition. Inasmuch as coherent and cogent composition is still one of the most widely used, as it is one of the most valuable, skills in social science, it would seem essential to continue to use the essay-type examination, if for no other reason than to afford practice in this skill.

Although Krey applies his argument only in the social sciences, his point of view has been argued in many other fields of subject matter. Granted the importance of the skills he mentioned, the essay test becomes essential as a motivator and instructional device for the development of those skills. It should be pointed out, however, that ability to write "coherent and cogent composition" is a very important instructional objective that should by no means be left to incidental learning while taking an examination. On the contrary, it should be carefully provided for in the instructional program and separately evaluated.

Short-answer tests may also be of instructional value, as shown by a study by Curtis and Woods (**5**), who compared the teaching values of four common practices in correcting examination papers. The following four methods were compared:

1. Pupils corrected own papers while the teachers read the correct answers. Free discussion followed.
2. Teacher checked incorrect items but made no corrections. Papers were later returned and discussed item by item.
3. Teacher carefully wrote in all corrections. Papers were later returned and discussed item by item.
4. Teacher carefully wrote in all corrections. Papers were later returned but only the questions pupils asked about were discussed.

On the next day and also after six weeks, the test containing one hundred items in various short-answer forms was repeated without warning. The first method, in which the teacher is least active and the pupils most active, resulted in the greatest improvement in scores.

The *SRA Self-Scorer*[3] is a device intended to promote learning by showing immediately whether short-answer test questions have been answered correctly. The student punches a hole in the space appropriate to the answer he selects. If his choice is correct, he sees a red dot through the hole; if it is incorrect, no red dot appears. He continues punching holes for each test item until he sees the red dot. The manual for this device cites research indicating its effectiveness in improving learning.

We may conclude that short-answer tests can have instructional value when they are used in such a way as to provide the practice necessary for increasing achievement. So both the essay test and the short-answer test can have distinct positive effects on achievement, each in its special way. The instructional value of the essay test is for the highly important ability to marshal and organize ideas with a minimum of outside help; the instructional value of the short-answer test can be aimed at the wide variety of other objectives that can be tested in this form.

LABOR REQUIRED IN CONSTRUCTION

To make the essay test in its usual form requires far less effort than does the short-answer test. This follows from the differences

[3] Published by Science Research Associates.

between the two types of tests in the number and precision of the questions put to the pupil. As will be seen in the following chapter, good short-answer test items can be composed only by dint of thoughtful, detailed, and intensive adherence to instructional objectives, and the application of much general intelligence. Essay test questions are fewer in number, usually less specific in content, and generally not as carefully composed with regard to subtle psychological values. Furthermore, it is possible to accumulate short-answer test questions from year to year; they merely require editing to keep them up to date. Such accumulation increases (1) the sampling of the subject matter, (2) the flexibility available for constructing tests for special purposes, (3) the possibility of constructing "equivalent" forms of tests for determining reliability. Finally, the accumulation of questions eventually reduces to a small amount the effort required for constructing short-answer tests.

LABOR REQUIRED IN SCORING OR GRADING

Here the short-answer test is superior because of the speed and little skill with which it may be scored. While an essay test may be constructed in, say, less than one hour, it may require perhaps ten hours for grading, whereas a short-answer test may require ten hours for construction and perhaps one hour for scoring. The essay test requires expert knowledge for both construction and grading, whereas a short-answer test requires an expert only for its construction. Although the illustrative time estimates just given would probably never fit a real case, it is clear that there is little difference between the two types in the total quantity and quality of the work involved, unless the number of pupils tested becomes far greater than is usual in the average classroom. In this case, the short-answer test acquires great advantage from its greater scorability.

COST OF ADMINISTERING

Short-answer tests usually are reproduced by mimeograph or some other method, so that each pupil may have a copy. Essay tests, on the other hand, can escape the cost of reproduction by being written on the blackboard or dictated orally to the pupils. The importance of these factors depends on the availability of reproducing devices to the classroom teacher. Since most present-day schools have a mimeograph, hectograph, or other means of reproducing test material, this consideration should probably not be allowed to have any considerable effect on the teacher's choice between these two types of tests.

ATTITUDES OF PUPILS TOWARD THE TWO TYPES OF TESTS

The evidence on this question has differed. Some investigators report that pupils prefer essay tests and others report preferences for the short-answer test. Odell (17 : 193) claims that pupils, realizing that marks on essay tests are relatively unreliable, consider them unjust and prefer short-answer tests for the objectivity and reliability of scoring which they insure. However, Jones (12) found that the statement, "I think one's ability is far better shown through discussion questions than through short objective questions," was agreed to by 68 percent of the students in colleges which gave senior comprehensives, and 55 percent of the superior students in other colleges. Alumni taking both types of examinations offered even more favorable comments on the essay test, because they felt that it was more important to be able to discuss an issue than merely to check it. Similarly, Hanford (9) concluded from a survey of the examination system of Harvard College that undergraduates favor the "reasoning," speculative type of examination.

Ruch (19 : 132–137) concluded from his summary of the studies on this question that essay tests and short-answer tests were both regarded as unpleasant tasks by both teachers and pupils, with about equal proportions of students favoring either type.

More recently, Bender and Davis (1) concluded from a survey of opinion that students in Colorado secondary schools preferred fairly difficult essay tests, on applications, at weekly intervals, with advance notice.

Since attitudes are learned, students' feelings on this issue will depend on their experience with the two kinds of tests. Teachers can probably shift these attitudes in either direction according to the skill and wisdom they apply to using the two kinds in their classrooms.

Intellectual Pleasure and Professional Growth Derived by the Teacher

Since most of the work in short-answer testing goes into the construction of the test while most of the work in essay testing goes into grading the test, how do the two types compare in the pleasure of the work involved? Vernon's preference (26 : 247) is one with which most teachers will agree: ". . . The setting of a new-type test is a fascinating occupation, which can be done in odd moments throughout the year; and the marking is simply a routine matter which involves no mental strain. By contrast, the marking of large numbers of essay-type scripts in psychology is the most trying work that he has ever had to do." (It has, indeed, become possible to have a machine do the scoring of short-answer tests.)

Constructing short-answer tests probably results in greater professional growth for the teacher than does constructing essay tests. The need for thinking through instructional objectives, for intensive attention to subject matter, for sophistication in the logical theory of measurement, for insight into pupil difficulties and errors is greater in short-answer testing. In satisfying these needs the teacher should acquire desirable skills that will carry over into all phases of teaching.

Distorting Effect on Manifested Achievement

Here we are concerned with whether essay tests and short-answer tests introduce factors between evaluator (that is, the teacher) and achievement which distort the expression of the latter, in the same way that colored glasses change things. Do essay tests involve behavior on the part of the pupil that colors his achievement? Similarly, do short-answer tests elicit behavior that reflects not only achievement but also intelligence and test sophistication operating to provide him with correct answers even when he could not really claim to have the achievement at which the test is aimed? Essay tests measure ability in expression, breadth of vocabulary, speed of writing, and other aspects of pupils which may be considered irrelevant to the evaluation of a particular kind of achievement. The "halo" effect of the teacher's general impression of a pupil also comes between the pupil's achievement and the teacher's evaluation of it.

Short-answer tests, however, are not necessarily free from this distortion. A pupil must be able to follow the instructions given in a test and then manipulate his knowledge and intellectual resources in such a way as to fit them to the requirements of the question. Ebel (15 : 221–223) has presented an excellent summary of the "irrelevant cues" which may twist the achievement of a pupil below or above its true value. Short-answer testing requires skill in anticipating the mental devices which, although not a part of instructional objectives, enable a pupil to obtain a higher score on a test than his achievement of instructional objectives warrants. The tricks of test question phrasing that will reduce this distortion to a minimum will be discussed in Chapter IV. Here we wish only to note that short-answer tests as well as essay tests can exert an influence on what they are testing so as to distort it.

FITNESS FOR EVALUATION OF COMPLEX ACHIEVEMENT

It is frequently charged that short-answer tests measure only small elements of achievement in the form of details of information and collections of facts, and that essay tests are necessary to the evaluation of general understanding, interpretation, capacity for organizing and formulating knowledge, and other complex mental operations. This belief is reflected in the findings concerning differences in the way pupils prepare for the two kinds of tests.

Short-answer tests *can,* however, be designed to get at these complexly organized types of achievement. The Evaluation Staff in the Eight-Year Study of the Progressive Education Association (21), recognizing the importance of such objectives of instruction and the necessity for evaluating achievement of them, has constructed short-answer tests with such titles as Interpretation of Data, Application of Principles of Thinking (several subject fields), Problems Relating to Proof in Mathematics, Critical-mindedness in the Reading of Fiction, and others. These are described in Chapter IV. The claim to measure complex achievements which these titles reflect indicates that at least the essay test has not been unchallenged for this purpose.

We can say here, without subjecting these new types of short-answer test questions to critical discussion, that they do succeed in measuring some types of mental processes that are far more complex than mere rote memory, factual knowledge, unrelated bits of information, and other so-called "elementaristic" types of achievement. When such tests have been correlated with essay examinations aimed at the same achievement, the correlations have ranged from about .75 to .85 (21, 27); that is, the short-answer tests tapped much the same achievement as the essay examinations.

Similarly, the yearbook, "The Measurement of Understanding" (4), has described in detail the techniques that can be used to evaluate higher mental processes in various school subjects. Many of these techniques involve short-answer testing. The success of the yearbook's authors in devising and describing such techniques indicates that essay tests have no monopoly on the possibilities of evaluating complex achievement.

In conclusion, the following statement by Freeman (8) merits quotation: "I would not cast out the objective tests on which so much ingenuity has been expended. They have their uses. I would, however, protest vigorously against the casting out of what is con-temptuously called the essay examination. . . . I suggest that we recover our balance, confining objective tests to those uses to which they are fitted, and restoring the free expression of thought to the position which it deserves."

TEACHER-MADE VS. STANDARDIZED TESTS

4. *If a short-answer test is chosen, should it be an externally made, standardized, purchasable test or a teacher-made test?* Illustrative of standardized tests are the New Stanford Achievement Tests in the elementary-school subjects and the tests of the many coöperative state high-school testing services. These, of course, are probably not typical because they are among the best of the available standardized tests.

Let us now compare standardized tests and teacher-made tests in the light of the following considerations:
1. Closeness of fit to instructional objectives
2. Refinement of construction
3. Interpretations possible
4. Expenditures and gains of the teacher

CLOSENESS OF FIT TO INSTRUCTIONAL OBJECTIVES

Whether instructional objectives refer only to subject matter or to both subject matter and mental processes, the teacher-made short-answer test can usually, if not always, achieve a closer fit to the instructional objectives of a particular classroom, school, or school system than can a standard test. The standardized test must strive for content which is common to a great many schools, whereas the content of the teacher-made test can fit not only objectives which a particular teacher has in common with other teachers but also those which are peculiar to his and his pupils' unique conception of objectives as they reflect the abilities and needs of pupils and community. As a result, standardized tests may evaluate the pupils' achievement of objectives with which they have not been concerned, while neglecting other objectives that have guided a major part of school work.

This shortcoming of standard tests will vary in different subjects, of course, in proportion to the degree of variability among classrooms, schools, and systems in objectives. In tool subjects, such as reading, writing, and arithmetic, the differences between classrooms, teachers, and school systems may not be so great as those in the social studies and the natural sciences. In any case, the teacher who uses standard tests should be prepared to face the charge of "testing what hasn't been taught." The teacher-made test can almost always fit more closely the learning in a particular classroom.

REFINEMENT OF CONSTRUCTION

Under this heading we may consider the selection and expression of test content, the procedure for administering the test, and the means furnished for interpreting the scores. The content of standard tests usually is selected by groups of subject-matter experts in close contact with the most respected textbooks and courses of study, statements of objectives, teaching methods, and expressions of the "philosophy" of a subject. Each item of the content usually has been subjected to the criticism of many other experts and tried out on pupils; from these preliminary tryouts have been computed statistical measures of the difficulty and validity[4] of the item.

On the basis of these statistical measures poor items are weeded out. The remaining items are usually arranged in order of difficulty and divided into two or more groups to give equivalent forms of the same test. Standardization of administrative procedure means that definite directions have been worked out, with provisions for practice exercises, time limits, oral directions to pupils, all designed to result in the best possible testing conditions held uniform from one classroom to the next. Standardization of interpretation means that scoring directions, question weightings, and corrections for guessing have been definitely worked out as an inseparable part of the test itself.

It is possible for classroom teachers to standardize their own tests in all these respects by acquiring and applying the intensive and technical statistical techniques required. But it is extremely improbable that most teachers will have the resources necessary for extensive preliminary tryouts of tests and for statistical treatment of the results. The technical and time-consuming nature of the standardization process will prevent most teachers from producing evaluation devices as refined as the better standard tests.

INTERPRETATIONS POSSIBLE WITH EACH TYPE OF TEST

Standard tests are supplied with norms which enable comparisons with other groups of pupils. Thus a teacher may compare the achievement of his class with that of pupils throughout the nation; the standardization group of pupils may be divided according to age, sex, or grade and made representative either of the nation at large or of urban groups, rural groups, etc. The meaningfulness of comparisons of classroom achievement or of individual pupil achievement depends almost entirely on the degree to which the sample used in the standardization process succeeds in representing the specific group it claims to represent. That is, if a set of norms for twelve-year-old arithmetic achievement is

---

[4] Item validity may be roughly defined here as the success with which an item discriminates between good pupils and poor pupils, in terms of their achievement of instructional objectives.

based on a small group of pupils, or on a group which is not representative with respect to certain factors affecting arithmetic achievement such as intelligence, socioeconomic status, or sex, the comparisons will be misleading and the teacher will be unjustified in interpreting a given pupil's achievement as above or below that of the average twelve-year-old.

Furthermore, the group used in standardizing an arithmetic test, for example, may be different from that used in standardizing a geography test, so that even though both tests may have sets of norms for twelve-year-olds, there is an unknown degree of uncertainty in comparing a pupil's relative achievement in the two subjects; one could not say that a pupil who had the same standing on the norms in these two tests really had the same relative standing in the two subjects. Only tests of the same quality and form, with norms established at the same time and under the same conditions for the same groups of pupils and schools, will make possible such comparisons between subject and subject and from year to year. Only then can teachers interpret test scores as indicators of differences *within* individual pupils from subject to subject and from year to year.

Comparisons between pupils and between groups, moreover, are valuable only insofar as the nature of the "normative" group is known and appreciated. Since it is improbable that tests constructed independently by different classroom teachers will meet these requirements for comparability, standardized tests are clearly superior for the types of interpretations they allow. Not all standardized tests, however, can meet these requirements; tests that are independently constructed and standardized on different groups under different conditions are *not* comparable. The Stanford Achievement Test is typical of those which have been so standardized as to meet requirements for comparability.

The desirability of "intersubject" comparability and the shortcomings of independently standardized tests in this respect have been well expressed by Flanagan (7 : 30):

Norms which are defined in terms of the groups who happen to be taking the various subjects in a particular year are bound to fluctuate from year to year, no matter how adequate the sample. For instance, norms established only a few years ago were not proved satisfactory as a representation of our present secondary school population because of the great increase in the enrollment of certain types of students in the secondary schools. Also, in particular subjects, various factors such as the temporary dominance of some educational doctrine or the alteration of college entrance requirements may change very greatly the type of individual enrolled in a subject. *From the point of view of individual guidance this lack of comparability in the norms from subject to subject is a greater deficiency than the failure to be representative of current groups.* [Italics ours.] It is very difficult to get a clear picture of an individual's relative achievement in various subjects if the scores are not directly comparable.

EXPENDITURES AND GAINS OF THE TEACHER

Under this heading we may first be concerned with the relative amounts of intellectual pleasure and professional growth provided by standardized and teacher-made tests. Teacher-made tests involve much more activity on the part of the teacher in all steps of the evaluation procedure. On the other hand, standardized tests allow the teacher to devote more effort to instruction and other activities. But, as was noted above, the work of constructing an objective test yields real benefits to him in professional growth. Perhaps similar benefits would follow from the careful study and selection of standardized tests, their construction, administration, and interpretation, but the difference in any case will usually be in favor of teacher-made tests.

The monetary cost of standard tests, which may become considerable when many pupils or frequent testings are involved, must enter into the choice of many teachers and school systems between the two types. Also the availability of standardized tests for only whole subjects or large units of subject matter makes them at best suitable for only occasional use. That is, they can seldom be adapted for evaluation of achievement other than at the beginning or end of the semester. This is reflected in the finding of Lee and Segel (14 : 4) that only 15 percent of the 1242 responding teachers gave three or more standardized achievement tests during one semester, whereas teacher-made tests were used about eight times during one semester by the average teacher (14 : 2).

REFERENCES

1. Bender, W., and Davis, R. A., "What high-school students think about teacher-made examinations," *Journal of Educational Research,* 43:58–65 (1949).
2. Boucher, C. S., *The Chicago College Plan,* Chicago: University of Chicago Press, 1935.
3. Brown, Clara M., *Evaluation and Investigation in Home Economics,* New York: Appleton-Century-Crofts, 1941.
4. Brownell, W. A. (chairman), "The measurement of understanding," *Forty-Fifth Yearbook of the National Society for the Study of Education,* Chicago: University of Chicago Press, 1946, Part I.
5. Curtis, F. D., and Woods, G. G., "A study of the relative teaching values of four common practices in correcting examination papers," *School Review,* 37:615–623 (1929).
6. Douglass, H. R., and Tallmadge, M., "How university students prepare for new types of examinations," *School and Society,* 39:318–320 (1934).
7. Flanagan, J. C., "The interpretation of the Cooperative Achievement Test Scores," *The Cooperative Achievement Tests: A Handbook Describing Their Purpose, Content, and Interpretation,* New York: The Cooperative Test Service, October, 1936.
8. Freeman, F. N., "The monopoly of objective tests," *Educational Forum,* 10:389–395 (1946).
9. Hanford, A. C., "Tests and examinations at Harvard College," *Proceedings, 1936,* Institute for Administrative Officers of Higher Institutions, Chicago: University of Chicago Press, 1936, pp. 5–26.
10. Hartog, P., and Rhodes, E. C., *An Examination of Examinations,* International Institute Examinations Inquiry, London: Macmillan & Company, Ltd., 1935.
11. James, A. W., "The effect of handwriting on grading," *English Journal,* 16:180–205 (1927).
12. Jones, E. S., "The relationship of examinations and instructions," *Proceedings, 1936,* Institute for Administrative Officers of Higher Institutions, Chicago: University of Chicago Press, 1936.
13. Kelley, T. L., and Krey, A. C., *Tests and Measurements in the Social Sciences,* New York: Charles Scribner's Sons, 1934.
14. Lee, J. M., and Segel, D., *Testing Practices of High School Teachers,* U.S. Office of Education, Bulletin No. 9, Washington: Government Printing Office, 1936.

15. Lindquist, E. F., *et al.*, *Educational Measurement*, Washington: American Council on Education, 1951.
16. Meyer, G., "An experimental study of the old and new types of examination," *Journal of Educational Psychology*, 25:641–661 (1934), and 26:30–40 (1935).
17. Odell, C. W., *Traditional Examinations and New Type Tests*, New York: Appleton-Century-Crofts, 1928.
18. Progressive Education Association, *Evaluation Materials Developed for Various Aspects of Thinking*, Chicago: Evaluation in the Eight Year Study, Progressive Education Association, 1939.
19. Ruch, G. M., *The Objective or New-Type Examination*, Chicago: Scott, Foresman & Company, 1929.
20. Sheppard, E. M., "The effect of the quality of penmanship on grades," *Journal of Educational Research*, 19:102–105 (1929).
21. Smith, E. R., Tyler, R. W., *et al.*, *Appraising and Recording Student Progress*, New York: Harper & Brothers, 1942.
22. Starch, D., and Elliott, E. C., "Reliability of the grading of high school work in English," *School Review*, 20:442–457 (1912).
23. Terry, P. W., "How students review for objective and essay tests," *Elementary School Journal*, 33:592–603 (1933).
24. Tyler, R. W., *Constructing Achievement Tests*, Columbus: Ohio State University, 1934.
25. Vallance, T. R., "A comparison of essay and objective examinations as learning experiences," *Journal of Educational Research*, 41:279–288 (1947).
26. Vernon, P. E., *The Measurement of Ability*, London: University of London Press, 1940.
27. Wrightstone, J. W., "Measuring some major objectives of the social studies," *School Review*, 43:771–779 (1935).

CHAPTER IV

Constructing Short-Answer Tests

Our consideration of the first four questions has led to the conclusion that in many situations the teacher should use a short-answer test constructed by himself for the purpose of evaluating the pupil's achievement of instructional objectives. We are therefore confronted with the following question:

5. *If a teacher-made short-answer test is chosen, what types of questions should be used, and how should they be apportioned and composed?*

The answer to this question has already been implied by Chapter II and by our description of the first major step of evaluation, i.e., the formulation of instructional objectives. Here we shall apply the principles and reasoning of these statements to the specific problem of constructing a short-answer achievement test.

The first step in constructing such a test is to draw up an outline or table of specifications, indicating in terms of subject matter and mental processes the instructional objectives whose achievement is to be evaluated. The second step is to compose the individual items or questions so as to correspond with specific items in the plan of specifications. The third step is to arrange these items in the order and form that yield best results, prepare the directions to pupils taking the test, prepare the scoring key, and arrange other mechanical features of the test. Let us now describe each of these steps in turn.

TABLE OF SPECIFICATIONS

The table of specifications draws its material from the statements of instructional objectives whose nature, form, and content were described in Chapter II. It differs from the statement of objectives in that it is designed specifically to aid in test construction, rather than to serve as a guide for teaching. Furthermore, the table of specifications for an achievement test will contain only that part of the statement of objectives which can be evaluated by its means and will omit those parts whose achievement cannot be evaluated by means of a device involving symbols in the form of a teacher-made short-answer test.

The table of specifications should contain some indication of the relative importance of each of the subdivisions of the instructional objectives, in terms of the time allotted to each subdivision or of its significance in relation to other important objectives. The subdivisions of the table of specifications should, of course, be made on more than one basis so that no important points of view will be omitted or unduly emphasized. For a history course, subdivisions would usually be made in terms of chronological periods, types of subject matter (social, political, economic), types of mental processes (interpreting data, applying generalizations, recognizing cause-and-result relationships), and any other bases considered important according to the statement of instructional objectives. For an algebra course, a table of specifications might be subdivided into vocabulary, types of computations, types of problems, familiarity with formulas, and so forth. That is, the construction of the test should aim at proper emphasis on each of the subdivisions arrived at by each of these types of classification.

Table 1 shows a table of specifications that might be drawn up for an examination in a first course in educational measurement and evaluation. The teacher and students in the course could probably express their ideas as to the proper emphasis on various objectives by means of such a table. The actual percentages of items would probably change as construction of the test went on. The teacher would get new ideas about matters that should be understood or known. He would also probably find his efforts to make up meaningful questions unsuccessful in some areas; for these areas the percentages might be reduced. In short, the table of specifications *interacts* with the process of writing the questions. Each influences the other. The table of specifications serves to keep the teacher aware of what emphases he is building into his test.

By tallying each item as it is prepared in the appropriate sub-division in the table of specifications it will be possible to maintain the distribution of the items in accordance with the emphasis determined by the statement of objectives.

TABLE 1. Hypothetical Table of Specifications for a Short-Answer Test of Achievement in a First Course in Educational Measurement and Evaluation

Subject-Matter Area	Type of Behavior (Mental Process)		
	Understanding of Basic Concepts and Considerations (35%)	Ability to Recall and Apply Principles and Rules to Practical Problems (45%)	Knowledge of Facts About Existing Tests, Programs, etc. (20%)
Achievement of instructional objectives (25%)..........	10%	10%	5%
Abilities, general and special (12%)................	5%	5%	2%
Attitudes: interests, opinions, appreciations (8%)........	3%	3%	2%
Adjustment, emotional and social (20%)............	5%	10%	5%
Environment and background (5%)...................	2%	2%	1%
Administering testing programs (15%)................	5%	7%	3%
Interpreting and using measurement data (15%)........	5%	8%	2%
	35%	45%	20%

Does the number of items dealing with a given objective indicate how much those items determine the total score? For example, if 15 percent of the items of a history test deal with "knowledge of facts about the Civil War," does this mean that 15 percent of the differences among students in total score are contributed by these items? The answer depends on the difficulty and intercorrelations of the items in the test. Vaughn (**18** : 168–169) has described the statistical reasoning that leads to the conclusion that, roughly speaking, the number of items is proportional to the desired contribution of the part to the total score. Since this is only a rough approximation, however, it means that test authors need not follow the percentages exactly in their tables of specifications.

The actual weighting of a given part in the total test score can only approximately be determined by the number of items allotted to that part.

COMPOSING TEST ITEMS

The next step is to compose the individual items. Short-answer test items can take a large number of forms, such as true-false, multiple-choice, completion, matching, and many others. Which form should be used for testing the particular item of content or objective is a matter of psychological insight into the mental operations required. But the fitness of any form of test item for testing a particular objective or mental operation is a function not only of the form of the item but also of the way in which it is applied. True-false or multiple-choice items may test merely memory but they can also be designed to test interpretation, organization, ability to infer, or any other mental process.

Before we discuss the form of short-answer test items, it will be profitable to consider some of the principles which apply to all of them. Some of these principles are merely admonitions to use common sense, but they are justified by the frequency with which teacher-made tests violate them. Others reflect research and experience accumulated by test experts and would not be apparent to newcomers in the field.

Avoid obvious, trivial, meaningless, and ambiguous items.

Observe the rules of rhetoric, grammar, and punctuation.

Avoid items that have no answer upon which all experts will agree.

Avoid "trick" or "catch" items, that is, items so phrased that the correct answer depends on a single obscure key word, to which even good students are unlikely to give sufficient attention.

Avoid items which contain "irrelevant cues." These are items whose phrasing is such that the correct answer may be determined merely by the exercise of intelligence without real possession of the achievement at which the item is aimed. The kinds of irrelevant cues which may occur vary with different types of test items and will be discussed specifically in connection with each type. Illustrative of an irrelevant cue which can occur in all types is the following item: "Man is an (1) plant, (2) reptile, (3) animal, (4) bird." The irrelevant cue here is the article "an," which indicates that the correct answer must begin with a vowel. (This is perhaps not the only flaw in this item.)

Avoid items which furnish the answers to other items, because one of the items will be rendered useless for evaluation purposes by this mistake.

Require all pupils to take the same test, and permit no choice among items. Pupils cannot be compared with one another unless they all take the same test.

TYPES OF TEST ITEMS

Two major types of short-answer test items have been distinguished by Ebel (4 : 193) as *supply type* and *selection type*. These have in the past been called "recall" and "recognition" types respectively. But the latter terms imply that all items measure merely memory of either of these two kinds. Since this is untrue, it is better to use the terms supply and selection, which tell whether the pupil must supply the words, numbers, or other symbols for his answer or whether he must select his answer from the alternatives provided.

What is tested by a specific type of test item depends not only on what it gives to the pupil and what sort of response it requires of him but also on the way in which a particular material has been taught. Questions which may require interpretative thinking on the part of the pupils in one classroom may require only rote memory on the part of the pupils in a classroom in which the desired response has been taught explicitly.

In constructing test items the teacher must therefore ask himself such questions as "What type of test item—true-false, completion, multiple-choice, etc.—is best suited to evaluate the French vocabulary of my pupils in the light of the way in which vocabulary has been learned by them?" "What type of test item is best suited to the evaluation of my pupils' ability to reason arithmetically?" "What type of test item is best suited to evaluate my pupils' understanding of the relative importance of the various causes of the American Revolution?" In answering these questions he will employ as much psychological insight into the teaching situation, the pupils' learning, and the relationship of both to instructional objectives, as he can.

The *supply type* includes the following kinds of short-answer test items:

1. Simple question
2. Completion

The *selection type* includes the following kinds of short-answer test items:

3. Constant alternatives, items requiring choice between constant alternatives, such as
   a. True-false, yes-no, right-wrong, synonym-antonym, agree-disagree (two alternatives)
   b. True-false-doubtful, true-false-converse (three constant alternatives)
   c. True or false with corrections
   d. True or false for a series of statements based on a given topic or body of material
   e. True or false with inferences
   f. True or false with qualifications
   g. True or false with diagrams
   h. Check list or no-check for a given characteristic (check list)
   i. Master list of characteristics or explanations or evaluations
4. Changing alternatives, i.e., items that require choice between changing alternatives on the basis of which one is the
   a. Correct or best answer
   b. Incorrect or worst answer
   c. Common principle or most inclusive
   d. Most dissimilar
   e. Result from among causes
   f. Cause from among results
5. Matching
   a. Simple matching
   b. Compound matching
6. Analogies

7. Rearrangement
   a. Chronological order
   b. Logical order
   c. Ranking
   d. Pied outlines

We shall take up each of these kinds in turn, with definitions, illustrations, discussion of advantages and limitations, and suggestions for using it in the best way.

SUPPLY-TYPE ITEMS

SIMPLE-QUESTION ITEMS

Simple-question items are usually in the form of a direct question, a specific direction or stimulus to which the pupil responds with a word, number, phrase, or sentence. Illustrations:

What are the two main gases found in air? ....
Who was the first President of the United States? ....
Explain in one sentence or phrase what connection each of the following people had with Abraham Lincoln.

  Stephen A. Douglas ....
  Chester A. Arthur ....
  Ulysses S. Grant ....
  Dred Scott ....

The *advantages* of this type are: It eliminates almost entirely the possibility of guessing. It constitutes a "natural" form of questioning, requiring little adaptation by the pupil. It is easily prepared. As we saw in the discussion of the relative values of essay and short-answer tests, recall tests serve as motivators of better learning and the development of the ability to recall. This type of item is particularly useful in problem situations in mathematics and the physical sciences, where the result of a complex reasoning and computational process can be expressed in a few symbols.

Among the *disadvantages* of the simple-question type of test item are: Its scoring is not as completely objective as is that of selection types of test items. Almost inevitably certain pupils will make responses that only expert judgment can distinguish from the correct response included in the scoring key. In subjects other than mathematics and the physical sciences the simple-question item tends to become too much a matter of identifying, naming, and associating facts; interpretative, inferential handling of complicated concepts may be slighted. As will be noted below, the simple-question type is relatively unfit for testing understanding of definitions or other achievement that cannot be expressed in a single, unique word, phrase or number.

Suggestions for the Improvement of Simple-Question Items.
1. *Short, definite, clean-cut answers should be required.* Only in the degree to which this suggestion is followed will objectivity of scoring be possible. Example:

Faulty: What kind of process is evaporation? . . . .
Improved: To what does a liquid change when it evaporates? . . . .

2. *If several correct answers (e.g., synonyms) are possible, each should be considered correct.* Example:

What method is used to preserve meats which are transported over long distances? . . . .

Here the correct answer may be "refrigeration," "cooling," "icing," "canning," "cold-packing," "salting," "pickling," or "smoking." Provision should be made in scoring this item for counting each of these responses as correct, or the item should be changed so as to restrict the correct answer to only one of these.

3. *Spelling should be either disregarded or given special attention in the form of a separate score for spelling correctness.* Accuracy in spelling should usually be distinguished from knowledge of the correct response as a separate instructional objective and therefore separately evaluated.

4. *Minimize the use of textbook expressions or stereotyped language in phrasing the questions.* Such phrasing rewards and motivates rote memorization of textbook materials, which is not always associated with a real understanding independent of terminology.

5. *Specify the terms in which the response is to be given.* Failure to observe this rule will result in responses all of which may be correct while evading the issue at which the item is aimed. Example:

Faulty: Where is the world's tallest building located? . . . .
Improved: In what city is the world's tallest building located? . . . .

In the first case the correct answer could be anything from "North America" to "the Atlantic seaboard." The second example forces the pupil to face the issue squarely.

With computational problems it should be indicated to the pupil how precise (e.g., to how many decimal places) his answer should be and whether or not "units" are to be given with it. Example:

What is the density of a piece of metal having a volume of 100 cc. and weighing 180 grams?

Ways of requiring the answer

....

.... grams per cc.

Answer .... Units ....

The second and third ways of providing for the pupil's answer are obviously preferable to the first. In the case of the third line explicit provision should be made for scoring or disregarding the "unit" part of the answer.

6. *In testing for a knowledge and understanding of definitions it is often better to provide the term and require a definition than to provide a definition and require the term,* because a higher level of achievement is thereby required. Since definitions cannot usually be phrased in the form of a "short answer," it is obvious that the simple-question type of test item is largely unfit for testing understanding of definitions. Example:

Faulty: What is the general term for vertebrates which suckle their young? ....

Improved: Define "mammal." ....

Other types of test items, such as the multiple-choice, are probably better adapted to testing this kind of achievement.

7. *Direct questions are probably preferable to incomplete declarative sentences,* especially for younger, less "test-sophisticated" pupils, because the former are more similar to the forms in which ordinary discourse is carried on. Example:

Faulty: America was discovered in the year ....

Improved: In what year was America discovered? ....

8. *Hints concerning the correct answer, in the form of the first letter of a word, or a number indicating the number of letters in a word, should generally not be employed.* Such hints may tend to confuse pupils when the answer upon which they have decided, although it is a correct synonym, does not coincide with the given hint. Guessing and responses to superficial cues may also result from this practice.

9. *The position of the space for the response should usually be at the right of the question,* for it has been found that most pupils prefer this position. This preference is probably due to the fact that the right-handed pupil will not have to cover the question while writing his answer.

10. *The amount of space allowed for the response should be sufficient to provide for legible writing.* In arranging this space, account should be taken of the usually larger handwriting of younger pupils.

11. *Arranging response spaces in a column at the right-hand margin of the page makes the scoring process more convenient.*

Completion Items

Completion items require the pupil to "write in" a word which has been omitted from either an isolated statement or connected discourse. Examples:

The joule is a unit of ....

Most automobile engines are .... cycle engines.

The mother called to her child, "Please go to the store and .... me some apples."

The greatest nation of the western hemisphere is ....
the head of which is the ...., who exercises the chief
.... power of the government but whose power is checked
and .... by the legislature, called ...., and
by the chief judiciary body, called ...., all of which carry
on their functions in the city of ....

The *advantages* and *limitations* of completion items are similar to those of the simple-question type. Good completion items usually cannot be made merely by leaving out one or more words from a sentence or passage taken from the textbook. This is so because such words or passages often make sense only as a result of their context. When the context is removed, the sentence or passage can yield only an ambiguous completion item. This means that teachers should generally write completion items in their own words, make them self-contained, and make sure that they limit possible correct responses to exactly the kind of achievement intended.

SELECTION-TYPE ITEMS

CONSTANT-ALTERNATIVE ITEMS

a. Constant-alternative items require the pupil to choose his answer from two or more alternatives *that remain the same for a whole series of items.* They may be in the form of statements concerning whose truth or falsity the pupil is required to make a judgment. Examples:

Directions: For each of the following statements encircle T if the statement is true and F if the statement is false.

The Crusades were successful in converting many Mohammedans to the Christian faith. .... T F

The head of a newborn baby is about one-fourth of the total body length. .... T F

b. The number of alternatives furnished may be increased to three by permitting such answers as doubtful, can't say, or can't tell, in addition to true or false. In another three-alternative type the pupil is required to say whether two variables are positively related, negatively related, or unrelated. Example:

Directions: Below is given a list of variables influencing test reliability. After each variable write:

+, if reliability is positively related to it.
—, if reliability is negatively related to it.
o, if reliability is not related to it.

Number of items ....

Range of item difficulty ....

Interdependence of items ....

Time allowed with fixed number of items ....

Reliability of criterion ....

The two-alternative form may be further varied to require the pupil to indicate not only whether the item is true or false but also whether the converse is true or false. Example:

Directions: Below are statements for which you are to encircle the two correct answers from among the following:

> T: The statement is true.
> F: The statement is false.
> CT: The converse is true.
> CF: The converse is false.

A cube is always a rectangular parallelepiped.	T	F	CT	CF
Two dihedral angles are equal if their plane angles are equal.	T	F	CT	CF
All vertebrates are mammals.	T	F	CT	CF

c. Another variation of the constant-choice item requires the pupil to make the proper changes in a single word so as to make false statements correct. Example:

Directions: For each of the following statements if the statement is true, underline the word True. If the statement is false, underline the word False, and write the substitute for the underlined word necessary to make it true.

Nitrogen supports combustion.	True	False	Oxygen
Water is a chemical element.	True	False	Compound
NaCl is the symbol for common salt.	True	False	

d. True-false statements may be based upon a given topic, paragraph, or body of material. Example:

The Constitution of the United States sets forth:

The exact number of justices necessary for the Supreme Court.	T	F
The exact number of Cabinet officers for the President's Cabinet.	T	F
The age at which one may exercise the right of suffrage.	T	F
The President as commander-in-chief of the Army and Navy.	T	F
An exact minimum age for Senators and Representatives.	T	F

e. The pupil may be required to indicate whether a statement is true or false and then to judge the truth or falsity of inferences drawn from the statement which he marked true. Example:

The President of the United States is commander-in-chief of
the Army and Navy. .... T F

The President of the United States can declare war whenever he sees fit. .... T F

The President would be the commander-in-chief of a separate air force. .... T F

f. True-false items with qualifications require the pupil to indicate whether the item is true or false or whether it can be made
true only by adding certain qualifications to be given or selected
by him. Examples:

Statements

The President has the power to appoint justices of the
Supreme Court. .... T F 1

The President can propose taxation measures. .... T F 2

The President may appoint ambassadors to other coun-
tries. .... T F 3

The President may appoint Senators-at-large. .... T F ___

Qualifications

1. With the consent of the Senate
2. With the consent of the House of Representatives
3. No qualification

g. True-false items with diagrams present to the pupil a series of
diagrams concerning which he is to make one of a small number
of possible judgments (see Fig. 4). Diagrams of the Wheatstone

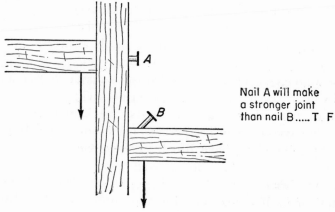

Nail A will make
a stronger joint
than nail B ..... T F

FIG. 4. True-False Item with Diagram.

bridge for measuring electrical resistance have been used in this manner in physics courses, the pupil marking each diagram with a plus sign if it was balanced and with a minus sign if it was unbalanced or if the wiring diagram was incorrect. Diagrams of tools, geometrical figures, housing plans, and similar materials can all be treated in this way.

Advantages. The merits of the constant-choice type of item in its most used form, the true-false test, can easily be outweighed by its limitations unless far more care than usual is exercised in constructing it. (1) One type of achievement to which it is well adapted is the ability to distinguish popular misconceptions and superstitions from scientifically validated truths. For this kind of material the true-false test provides a mode of presentation that is similar to an actual life situation in which the pupil must make a judgment concerning the truth or falsity of statements occurring in the layman's literature on any subject. (2) Another type of material for which the true-false item is peculiarly well suited is that in which the material does not lend itself to the construction of more than two or three plausible alternatives. An example of this is the following item: "Emergency exits from office buildings should open outwardly." Here there are only two possible choices, inwardly or outwardly, so that the construction of a multiple-choice item would lead to absurdities. Phrasing this question as a completion item, "Emergency exits from office buildings should open: ....," would leave too indefinite the terms in which the answer was expected. (3) Perhaps the major advantage of true-false items is that they enable the teacher to evaluate achievement of objectives related to a comparatively large sample of subject matter in a short period of time, because pupils can generally answer more of this type of item per unit of time than of other types.

Disadvantages. This fact has led to its major shortcomings as used by many teachers. (1) Its use as a time-saving device has often been accompanied by hurried, careless, mechanical construction so that this type of item has perhaps been more abused than any other type. Teachers have lifted sentences out of textbooks to provide true statements and inserted "nots" to provide the required number of false statements. (2) Apart from this, the true-false test of itself tends toward greater ambiguity than do other types. Only statements that are *absolutely* true or false should be used. In subject matter like mathematics or science, such statements may be made readily. In other subjects, however, many important materials are matters of judgment and are not absolutely true or false; these may be inferences, interpretations, explanations, or generalizations which may be probably true or require qualifications of one sort or another. Such material, often important in education, cannot readily be put into true-false form. Teachers who attempt to do so often produce bewildered, confused, cynical, or antagonized students. (3) The most serious disadvantage of true-false tests and all other constant-alternative forms arises from their tendency to be influenced by response sets (3). Response sets are tendencies to respond to all the questions on a test in a constant way unrelated to the purpose of the test. For example, students tend to answer "true" to true-false items whose answer they are ignorant or unsure of. Or they may tend to say "agree" to opinion questionnaire items, or "like" to interest inventory items.

Response sets have been found to occur almost always in constant-alternative tests. By definition, they are consistent within a given test for a given individual. What makes response sets undesirable? *Individuals differ* significantly from one another in the degree to which they exhibit these tendencies to say "true," "agree," "like," and so forth, in answer to difficult questions or questions whose answer they are unsure of. And since these differences between individuals are seldom the characteristics at which the test is aimed, they becloud the differences in achievement, attitude, and the like, that the test *is* intended to reveal. If a true-false test of achievement in history yields scores that reflect both differences in achievement and differences in tendency to say "true," the scores have a mixed significance. The validity of the scores, a concept dealt with in Chapter V, has been impaired.

Response sets appear primarily in constant-alternative tests, but hardly at all in changing-alternative types. They constitute a strong reason for avoiding the constant-alternative types of test when possible and increasing the use of changing-alternative types, such as multiple-choice items.

Suggestions for Composing True-False Items. 1. *The number* *of true statements should be approximately equal to the number of false statements.* Otherwise the pupils may begin to see whether the preponderance of statements are true or false and begin to guess accordingly. This would be an irrelevant cue.

2. *Avoid "tricking" the pupil by distracting his attention from the crucial part of the item.* Do not put the false part of the statement in a qualifying phrase, for pupils usually assume these phrases to be correct and are misled into concentrating upon the major statement. Example:

Faulty: The President of the United States, a naturalized citizen, holds office for four years in a single term. . . . .   T   F
Improved: The President of the United States is a naturalized citizen. . . . .   T   F

In general, such misdirection of attention can be avoided by having the crucial element of the true-false statement come toward the end of it. If there are several sentences in the statement, the student should be told in the directions that the introductory sentences may be considered correct, the last sentence determining the truth or falsity of the item.

In statements concerning the "why" or the "reason" for something, the false elements if any should be contained in the "reason" part of the statement. In this way the pupil's attention will be directed toward that part of the statement which should contain the crucial elements if the statement is really a test of what it appears to test, namely, understanding of a reason or cause. Example:

Faulty: There was very little dissension among the American colonists, since all were united in hatred of England. . . . . . .   T   F
Improved: There was much dissension among the colonists, because (either correct or incorrect reasons). . . . .   T   F

In the "faulty" illustration, the statement appears to test knowledge of a reason while merely testing facts; in the "improved" illustration the statement does not pretend to test something other than what it really tests.

3. *Avoid "specific determiners," that is, words or modes of expression that are usually associated with a true statement or a false statement.* Analyses of large numbers of teacher-made true-false

tests have shown that the vast majority of statements containing "only," "alone," "all," "no," "none," "nothing," "always," "never," "cause," or "reason," were false. On the other hand, statements containing "should," "may," "most," "some," "often," or "generally" were usually true. Furthermore, statements containing enumerations, or more than twenty words, were also usually true. Such words and characteristics as these cease to be specific determiners when they are approximately evenly balanced among true and false statements; that is, if the teacher makes a conscious effort to counteract the tendency to convert true statements into false ones by using "not," "only," "all," etc., these words will cease to be specific determiners. Specific determiners are undesirable, of course, because they provide clues which enable pupils to respond correctly without real knowledge or understanding.

4. *Ambiguity can be reduced by the use of quantitative rather than qualitative language wherever possible.* Direct comparisons, for the same reason, should be used wherever a quantitative description is impossible. This means that the use of such terms as "few," "great," "many," "more," and "important" should be minimized. Example:

Faulty: Stevenson received a large number of votes in the election of 1952. .... T F

Improved: Stevenson received more than 40 percent of the votes in the election of 1952. .... T F

But this should not be allowed to result in the testing of unimportant precision of factual knowledge.

5. *Avoid involved, complex sentence structures with many dependent clauses, double negatives, or unfamiliar language. Similarly, unless the intention is to test technical vocabulary, word questions in simple, nontechnical language.* Examples:

Faulty: Only after having analyzed his problem and set up an hypothesis should the experimenter, who should be familiar with the literature in his field, decide upon an experimental technique. .... T F

Improved: An experimenter should know what others have done in his field before deciding upon a technique to test his hypothesis. .... T F

Faulty: There was marked efflorescence of inventive activity
   in the nineteenth century. ....   T   F
Improved: There was a marked increase in inventive activity
   during the nineteenth century. ....   T   F

6. Instructions against guessing on true-false or other two-alternative tests have been used by some test technicians and avoided
by others. Such directions may be considered desirable on the
ground that they decrease the element of chance success which
enters into responses on selection-type tests. Consequently it is
reasoned that such directions should result in a more valid measurement of actual achievement. On the other hand it is argued
that they can never achieve their purpose because pupils do not
know when they have complete knowledge of the correct response,
no knowledge, or partial knowledge. Many guesses are not "pure"
in the sense of being based on no knowledge whatsoever. Rather,
students may frequently respond correctly on the basis of partial
knowledge or "hunches."

Essentially, such directions usually introduce a "personality,"
or nonintellectual, factor into the measurement of achievement.
This is the pupil's tendency to gamble, or his willingness to respond on the basis of partial knowledge rather than only when
completely certain of the correct response. Since pupils differ in
this personality trait, instructions against guessing will make the
test scores depend on both intellectual and "personality" factors
in unknown proportions. (See the discussion of response sets
above.)

It has been argued that instructions to answer all items may lead
pupils to lose respect for tests and to regard them as guessing
games. Whatever effect of this kind such instructions may have can
probably be counteracted quite readily if teachers will explain the
purpose of these instructions in simple terms.

In summary, *we urge that no instructions against guessing be
used with selection-type tests. Rather, pupils should be instructed
to answer every item without omissions.*

7. A further issue in the use of selection-type tests, especially
those presenting only two alternatives per item, is the desirability
of a scoring formula intended to correct for chance successes, or

guessing. The general and two-choice forms of the scoring formula used for this purpose are as follows:

<table>
<tr><td></td><td align="center">General Form</td><td align="center">Two-choice Form</td></tr>
<tr><td>(1)</td><td>$S = T - \dfrac{n}{n-1}W - O$</td><td>$S = T - 2W - O$</td></tr>
<tr><td>(2)</td><td>$S = R - \dfrac{W}{n-1}$</td><td>$S = R - W$</td></tr>
<tr><td>(3)</td><td>$S = R + \dfrac{O}{n}$</td><td>$S = R + \dfrac{O}{2}$</td></tr>
</table>

where S = score

T = number of items in the test

R = number of right responses

W = number of wrong responses

O = number of omitted responses

n = number of response alternatives presented in each item

These three formulas, while differing in the kinds of counting required, yield scores that correlate perfectly with one another. The third formula, which requires that R's and O's be counted, is more acceptable to pupils because it gives full credit for right responses and an additional fractional credit for items omitted rather than wrong.

All these formulas are based on the assumption that guessed responses in two-choice tests will be right as often as wrong. This assumption is at best justifiable only on the average rather than for any individual pupil. Insofar as it is not justified, the formulas over- or under-penalize wrong responses.

When every pupil answers every item, the formulas need not be used because in such a case there is a perfect correlation between simple (number right) scores and corrected scores.

h. Before proceeding to the next class of test items we should deal with the constant-alternative types known as the "check list" and the "master list." The *check list* requires the student to go through a list of phrases or statements and mark each one that fulfills certain requirements set up in the directions. Example:

Directions: Place a check in front of each of the following that is part of an airplane:

✓	aileron			windbeacon
✓	rudder	✓	strut
	gear shift	✓	propeller
	mast			periscope
✓	stabilizer	✓	stick
	accelerator			helium bag
✓	throttle			ripcord

It is evident that the check list is almost indistinguishable from the true-false item with respect to scoring, advantages, and disadvantages.

i. The *master list* requires the pupil to select from a constant group of alternatives, usually more than two, the one that best applies to a group of items. Example:

Directions: From the list at the top select the kind of vote required by the phrases below and place its number on the line at the right.

1. Majority
2. Two-thirds majority
3. Three-fourths majority
4. Unanimous

Number of jury votes necessary to convict a criminal ....

Number of votes necessary to expel a member of either House of the United States Congress ....

Number of members necessary for a quorum of each House ....

Number of votes needed to pass a bill over the President's veto ....

Number of votes necessary to propose amendments to the United States Constitution ....

Number of state legislatures that must ratify an amendment before it becomes valid ....

As will be seen later, the master list differs from the matching form in that the numbers of items contained in the two groups of the master list are much more disproportionate, so that items from one of the lists must be used more than once. The master list differs from the multiple-choice form in that the alternatives remain the same instead of changing for each question.

CHANGING-ALTERNATIVE ITEMS

a. Changing-alternative items require the pupil to select the best one of a group of several alternatives which change with each item. The most usual form of this kind is the multiple-choice item. Example:

A fuse is placed in an electric circuit to (1) measure the current, (2) affect the current, (3) prevent excessive flow of current, (4) lower the resistance. ....

Although the variety of bases on which the pupil can be instructed to select the correct answer is almost infinite, only a few of them are used with any frequency. Among them are the best answer, the correct answer, the worst answer, the least satisfactory answer, the most inclusive term, the most dissimilar term, the result from among causes, the cause from among results, etc. Examples:

b. *Worst Answer:*

Directions: Of the four alternatives presented as completions to each statement, choose the worst and write its number in the space at the right.

An isosceles triangle is one in which (1) two sides are equal, (2) two angles are equal, (3) one of the altitudes is perpendicular to its side, (4) the base equals the altitude. ....

c. *Most Inclusive Answer:*

Directions: Following are sets of four words or terms, one of which includes the other three. You are to select the inclusive term from each set and write its number in the space to the right of the set.

(1) smallpox, (2) tuberculosis, (3) scurvy, (4) disease ....
(1) tapeworm, (2) typhoid bacillus, (3) parasite, (4) dodder ....

d. *Most Dissimilar Answer:*

Directions: Following are sets of four words or terms, one of which does not belong with the other three. Select the word or term which does not belong and write its number in the space to the right of the set.

(1) Abraham Lincoln, (2) Ulysses S. Grant, (3) Stephen A. Douglas, (4) Chester A. Arthur ....
(1) shark, (2) ape, (3) giraffe, (4) kangaroo ....

e. *Result from Among Causes:*

Directions: In each group of four events given below there is one
result together with three causes which contributed to bringing about
this result. Select the result and write its number on the line at the
right of the item.
(1) Sinking of the *Lusitania,* (2) unrestricted submarine warfare,
     (3) declaration of war in 1917, (4) invasion of Belgium . . . .

f. *Cause from Among Results:*

Directions: From the following groups of four historical events or
conditions, select the one that may best be considered to be a cause of
the other three.
(1) English religious intolerance, (2) settlement of Jamestown,
     (3) American freedom of religion, (4) sailing of the *Mayflower*   ....

The number of alternatives presented can vary from two to any
larger number, but the most frequently used numbers are four and
five.

Advantages and Limitations.   (1) The changing-alternative type
of test item or the multiple-choice item can be adapted to testing
the higher mental processes, such as inferential reasoning and fine
discrimination, as well as the rote memorization of isolated facts.
It is the most flexible kind of test item available for varying types
of mental process according to specific kind of subject matter. (2)
The multiple-choice item is frequently preferable to the simple
question when the correct response is lengthy or involved or can
be written in several correct forms. (3) In proportion as the number of alternatives is greater than two, the possibility of guessing
the correct answer is less than in the true-false test; the greater the
number and plausibility of these alternatives the less chance there
is for a guessed answer to be correct. (4) Finally, multiple-choice
tests tend to be free of response sets which, as previously said, may
seriously dilute with irrelevant factors what is measured by constant-alternative tests.

Disadvantages of the multiple-choice test item are: (1) It is much
more difficult to construct well than are other forms of test items.
The necessity for devising plausible incorrect alternatives places
a heavy burden on the ingenuity and psychological insight of the
teacher. Constructing a single multiple-choice item with four alter-

natives often requires as much work as constructing four true-false or simple-recall items. (2) Multiple-choice items require more time per item than do some other types. In the practical classroom situation this factor serves to bring the multiple-choice item closer to the true-false item in net total merit. That is, the true-false item may be as efficient for the available time as the more reliable multiple-choice item. The greater reliability of the latter arising from its large number of alternatives may thus be counteracted by the larger number of true-false items it is possible to present to pupils during a given period of time. *But the same economy of time, without the appearance of response sets, can be obtained with multiple-choice items that have only two choices per item.*

Suggestions for Constructing Multiple-Choice Items. Multiple-choice items consist of an introductory part, or stem, and several alternatives which may be divided into the answer and the false alternatives, or distractors.

1. *The stem may be in the form either of a direct question or of an incomplete statement.*

2. *If the incomplete statement form of stem is used it should be meaningful in itself and imply a direct question rather than merely lead into a collection of unrelated true-false statements.* Example:

Faulty: The United States of America (1) has more than 150,-000,000 people, (2) grows large amounts of rubber, (3) has few good harbors, (4) produces most of the world's automobiles. ....
Improved: The population of the United States is characterized by (1) a stable birth rate, (2) varied nationality backgrounds, (3) its even distribution over the area of the United States, (4) an increasing proportion of young people. ....

3. *The distractors should be plausible, so that the pupils who do not possess the achievement being evaluated will tend to select them rather than the correct answer.* Plausibility may be attained by making the distractors as familiar as the correct answer, related to the same concept as the correct answer, and as reasonable and natural as the correct answer. One method of securing plausible distractors is to use the introductory statement as a completion test and then tabulate the incorrect responses of pupils. Stalnaker

and Stalnaker (16) found that distractors selected in this way for a five-choice best-answer vocabulary test were marked more often by uninformed pupils than were distractors selected at random; since there was no interference by these selected distractors with the discriminatory power of the item, their use was recommended. On the other hand Kelley (8) concluded that the test maker's judgment was about as valid as tabulating the responses from recall tests as a method of securing the incorrect responses for vocabulary tests. Whatever method is chosen the goal must be the same: plausible distractors that will attract uninformed pupils away from the correct answer.

4. *The length or precision of statement of the alternatives should not vary systematically with their correctness.* Otherwise pupils may come to learn that the long distractors are usually the correct ones, or vice versa.

5. *The arrangement of alternatives should be uniform throughout the test.* If possible, the alternatives should come at the end of the statement if the incomplete-statement form of introduction is used. If space permits, they should be listed one under the other rather than placed in a paragraph, because listed alternatives are easier to read and consider separately. Example:

Faulty: The cheapness of land and scarcity of labor in the West created (1) an aristocratic class of landowners, (2) a large class of wage-earning men, (3) a system of servitude, (4) a large class of small freeholders. ....

Improved: The cheapness of land and scarcity of labor in the West created

    1. an aristocratic class of landowners. ....
    2. a large class of small freeholders. ....
    3. a system of servitude. ....
    4. a large class of wage-earning men. ....

6. *Grammatical consistency should be maintained throughout the item.* It should be possible to form a correct sentence by attaching any of the alternatives to the introductory incomplete statement. Example:

Faulty: The best way to employ leisure time is (1) read good books and magazines, (2) movies are usually enjoyable and educational,

(3) minding your own business, (4) in playing cards and working out puzzles.

Improved: The best way to employ leisure time is to (1) use it reading good books and magazines, (2) go to the movies, (3) mind your own business, (4) use it playing cards and working out puzzles.

7. *The number of alternatives should be four or five if possible.* It should be less if it is impossible to construct others without involving absurdities or obviously false distractors. It is unnecessary to have the same number of alternatives for every item unless a formula to correct for chance guessing is applied to the score.

8. *Corrections for guessing need not be applied in the usual classroom testing situation.* In standardized multiple-choice tests where statistical evidence for the equal plausibility of the distractors has been obtained, the application of the correction for guessing formula may yield worth-while results.

9. *When the simple-question type is more suitable, the multiple-choice form should not be used.* Such situations may occur when the answer required by the simple-question item requires little more writing than does the multiple-choice item, in computational questions where the response is in numerical form.

10. *The level of mental process required by an item is dependent in large part upon the homogeneity of the alternatives presented by it.* Examples:

Less homogeneous: Which city is nearest to Chicago? (1) Los Angeles, (2) New York, (3) St. Louis, (4) Miami. . . . .

More homogeneous: Which city is nearest to Chicago? (1) Minneapolis, (2) St. Louis, (3) Cleveland, (4) Milwaukee. . . . .

Less homogeneous: Archimedes' Law deals with (1) falling bodies, (2) liquid-displacing bodies, (3) heated bodies, (4) light-giving bodies. . . . .

More homogeneous: Archimedes' Law states that a floating body (1) will seek its own level, (2) will displace a volume of liquid whose weight equals the body's weight, (3) will receive pressure from the liquid which is equal in all directions, (4) cannot float midway between the surface of the liquid and the bottom of the vessel. . . . .

11. *Understanding of definitions is better tested by furnishing the name or word and requiring choice between alternative defini-*

tions than by presenting the definition and requiring choice between alternative names or words. Example:

Faulty: Water enters the air by a process called (1) osmosis, (2) filtration, (3) condensation, (4) evaporation. . . . .
Improved: Evaporation is a process by which (1) vapors turn into liquids, (2) liquids pass between two porous surfaces, (3) solids dissolve in liquids, (4) liquids turn into vapors. . . . .

12. *Distractors can often be made attractive and plausible by expressing them in textbook phraseology,* the correct response being expressed in original terms.

MATCHING

Matching exercises consist of two sets of items which are to be associated on some basis furnished by the directions. The variety of bases upon which the two lists of items can be matched is almost infinite. Examples of bases are: events and dates, events and places, events and results, inventions and inventors, books and authors, processes and products, usages and rules, names and definitions, causes and effects. Similarly, the lists may be presented in many varying forms; diagrams, maps, pictures, chronologically or logically arranged items with numbered gaps between them may all be used if they are appropriately labeled and proper directions are given. Example:

Directions: After each animal write the number of its gestation and incubation period.

Gestation and Incubation Period	*Animals*	
1. 280–283 days	1. Swine	. . . .
2. 330–340 days	2. Poultry	. . . .
3. 143–150 days	3. Mares	. . . .
4. 112–114 days	4. Sheep	. . . .
5. 67–70 days	5. Cattle	. . . .
6. 20–21 days		

A variation of the matching form is *compound matching,* which requires matching three or more lists with one another on indicated bases. Example:

Directions: After each city write first the number of its state and then the letter of its major industry.

States	Major Industries	Cities
1. Illinois	a. Autos	1. Detroit ....
2. Indiana	b. Airplanes	2. Akron ....
3. Michigan	c. Flour milling	3. St. Paul ....
4. Minnesota	d. Meat packing	4. Chicago ....
5. New Jersey	e. Electrical equipment	5. Schenectady .. ..
6. New York	f. Publishing	6. Pittsburgh ... .
7. Ohio	g. Rubber	
8. Pennsylvania	h. Steel	
9. Texas	i. Telephones	

The matching form is frequently modified in various ways. It is sometimes arranged so that each item in the list of alternatives may be used more than once as a response; this makes it impossible to answer correctly by a process of elimination. It may be arranged so as to require the use of more than one alternative for some test items; this enables the testing of ability to recognize terms which share meanings in common with other terms. The alternatives may be arranged so as to make it easy to find the number of the alternative if its meaning has already been decided upon; such arrangements may be alphabetical, chronological, or logical, or have other meaningful bases.

Advantages and Limitations. The compactness of the matching form, resulting from its use of the same response alternatives for a whole group of questions, makes it highly efficient in terms of space required and testing time per item. It is peculiarly well suited for making a rapid survey of a specific aspect of a field of subject matter, such as its leading personalities, the time orientation of a group of events, or definitions of basic terms.

Perhaps the chief disadvantage of the matching form is that it requires even greater care than other forms if it is not to be rendered invalid by irrelevant clues, implausible alternatives, and awkward arrangement.

Suggestions for Constructing Matching Items. 1. *Homogeneity of response alternatives, and consequently homogeneity of the items with which these alternatives are to be matched, are impor-*

tant factors in the effectiveness of a matching set. For example, if the set is aimed at definitions and distinctions between terms involved in the human respiratory system, only such terms should be included, not terms referring to such physiological groupings as the digestive, skeletal, or nervous systems. Example:

Faulty:

1. Auricle	1. Main respiratory organ . . . .
2. Lung	2. Major subdivision of windpipe . . . .
3. Trachea	3. Windpipe . . . .
4. Vagus	4. Breastbone . . . .
5. Bronchus	5. Cranial nerve for lung . . . .
6. Esophagus	6. Chamber of heart . . . .
7. Sternum	

Improved:

1. Lung	1. Windpipe . . . .
2. Trachea	2. Subdivision of windpipe . . . .
3. Vagus	3. Respiratory nerve . . . .
4. Bronchus	
5. Bronchiole	

One test for homogeneity is whether it is possible to label each column of the matching set with one term which accurately delimits its content. Perhaps the only way to determine whether the matching exercise really elicits the type of achievement desired is to take each question and examine the way in which the correct response alternative will have to be selected. Can it be selected directly on the basis of real knowledge? Or, if the selection has to proceed by elimination of incorrect responses, will such elimination be based upon the gross unfitness for matching, either logically, grammatically, or generically, of all but the correct alternative? If so, the matching exercise is not calling for the desired achievement.

2. *The chances of guessing the correct response may be reduced by* increasing the number of response alternatives beyond the number of items, permitting some of the response alternatives to be used more than once in the same matching set, requiring more than one response alternative to be matched with some of the test items.

3. The basis upon which the matching is to be done should always be clearly indicated if it is not obvious. This should be done both in the directions and in the headings of the columns of items to be matched. Example:

Faulty:

1. Brazil	1. rice ....
2. Iowa	2. corn ....
3. China	3. rubber ....
4. Germany	4. silk ....
5. India	
6. Japan	

Instructing the pupil merely to match these groups of items without giving him some basis for doing so will give the teacher no justification for considering some responses correct and others incorrect.

Improved:

Test to Identify Fibers	*Fibers*
a. Tears easily with a shrill sound and ends of yarn are even and curled.	1. silk ....
b. Tears with difficulty, with dull sound; leaves irregular edge.	2. wool ....
c. Tears with difficulty, with dull sound; leaves ends of yarn straight.	3. rayon ....
d. Tears easily with shrill sound, leaving threads of uneven length.	
e. Tears with shrill sound, with threads long and uneven in length.	

In this illustration the basis for matching is clearly indicated, the pupil knows what is expected, and a definite criterion for determining correct responses has been set up.

4. Single words, short phrases, numbers, and other quickly examined types of material should constitute one of the lists of items to be matched. Also it is preferable that this list of short terms be the list of response alternatives. This, of course, is what makes the matching form less suitable for testing understanding of terms and definitions than the multiple-choice forms, which can require the pupil to select from among definitions rather than from among terms.

5. *The list of response alternatives should be arranged in some order that will enable the pupil to find his response quickly once he has decided what he is looking for.* Dates should be arranged chronologically and names should be arranged alphabetically.

6. *The number of response alternatives should seldom be greater than ten or twelve.* Longer lists will require the pupil to spend too much of his time finding the correct response. *For machine-scored (IBM) answer sheets,* matching sets generally are made to consist of three items to be matched against five response alternatives. Example:

Test Booklet		Answer Sheet

Author	Test		1 2 3 4 5
56. Thorndike	1. TAT	56.	∷ ▊ ∷ ∷ ∷
57. Thurstone	2. CAVD	57.	∷ ∷ ∷ ▊ ∷
58. Terman	3. Army Alpha	58.	∷ ∷ ∷ ∷ ▊
	4. Primary Mental Abilities		
	5. Stanford-Binet		

7. *A single page should contain all the matching set* so that the pupil will not be required to look for a response on a different page from the one that contains the question.

ANALOGIES

Analogies are not a distinct form of test item, but a way of putting questions to which any of the other forms may be adapted. The pupil is presented with two terms whose relationship he must infer. A third term is then given for which he must either supply or select a fourth term whose relationship to the third is the same as that between the first two. Examples:

Animals : oxygen :: plants : (carbon dioxide).
Two points are to a straight line as (two lines) to a plane.
Verb is to adverb as noun is to (adjective).

Any of the other forms of short-answer test item may be used with analogies. The pupil may be required to furnish the missing terms as in completion items. The missing term may be selected from a group of changing alternatives for each analogy, as in multiple-choice items. A list of analogies may be presented with a list of response alternatives, as in matching items. Complete analogies may also be furnished, the pupil being required to judge them true or false.

Advantages and Disadvantages. Intelligence and mental ability tests have made more use of analogies than have achievement tests, perhaps because the artificiality of the analogies form requires more general mental ability for a correct adaptation or response than specific achievement of instructional objectives. Analogies do, however, provide a compact way in which to put a question. If pupils can be made thoroughly familiar with this form so that it loses its artificiality for them, it can become an efficient testing device. The advantages in brevity of the analogies form may be seen in the following examples:

Oxygen : O :: chlorine : Cl
instead of
What is the chemical symbol for chlorine?

Animals : oxygen :: plants : carbon dioxide
instead of
What gas is indispensable in the respiration of plants?

Suggestions for Constructing Analogies Items. The necessary precautions are the same as those required in constructing the type of item to which the analogies form is applied. That is, if the analogies are to be supply-type items, the suggestions for constructing the latter items should be considered. Perhaps the only rule unique to analogies is that the directions, especially for younger, less "test-wise" pupils, should be especially clear. Practice exercises and close observation by the teacher are usually necessary to insure that all the pupils understand what the analogies form requires of them.

REARRANGEMENT

Rearrangement items require the pupil to put into some specified order a series of randomly presented material. The specified order may be of any kind, such as chronology, difficulty, importance, length, weight, logical order, etc. Examples:

a. *Chronological Order:*

Directions: Given below are groups of three events or men whose numbers are to be written in chronological order in the space at the right of the items.

1. were Presidents of the United States . . . (1) Wilson, (2) Lincoln, (3) Washington. ....

2. were religious groups who settled in America . . . (1) Catholics, (2) Quakers, (3) Puritans. ....

b. *Logical Order:*

Directions: A greenhouse catches and holds much of the heat radiation from the sun. Place a cross (x) before the statements below which help to explain this phenomenon. (Some of the statements are false; some of them are true but do not apply.)[1]

.... 1. The glass transmits the longer heat waves more readily than the shorter heat waves.

.... 2. Objects inside the greenhouse, once warmed, radiate very long heat waves.

.... 3. The heated glass radiates the shorter waves to objects within the greenhouse.

.... 4. The glass roof reflects the longer heat waves.

.... 5. The shorter heat waves from the sun are transmitted readily through the glass.

.... 6. The glass roof absorbs long heat waves.

Now rearrange the pertinent statements above in the proper order to give a thoroughly complete explanation. *Use the numbers.*   ....
Answer

The pupil may also be required to rearrange items and statements in outline form with the proper headings, classifications, and subordinations.

Advantages and Limitations. More than in most other types, the mental processes involved in rearrangement items depend

---

[1] This example, and examples of the pied outline form, are included in M. W. Richardson, *et al., Manual of Examination Methods,* Chicago: University of Chicago Book Store, preliminary ed., June, 1933.

upon how the subject matter has been presented in the classroom. If the proper order has been explicitly presented in class, the test may measure only rote memory. Higher levels of understanding are elicited only if the pupil is required to make the rearrangement originally.

Suggestions for Scoring Rearrangement Tests. Apart from its scoring, the considerations in designing rearrangement tests are similar to those for other forms.

When the number of parts to be arranged is small, say four or less, it is often sufficient to consider the response correct only if the rearrangement is correct for all parts, and to give one point for the correct answer. When more than four parts are to be arranged, a practical scoring scheme is to add the squares of the differences between the student's order and the correct order.

Correct order:	1	2	3	4	5
Worst possible answer:	5	4	3	2	1
Differences:	4	2	0	2	4
Squares of differences:	16	4	0	4	16

The sum of the squared differences between the correct and the worst possible arrangement is 40. If a pupil's arrangement is 3 1 2 4 5, the sum of the squared differences from the correct arrangement is 6. The more correct the pupil's response the lower the value; by subtracting this score from the worst possible one, the higher the result the better the answer.

When each item consists of three elements to be ranked, the pupil needs to indicate only the "most" and "least." If a separate answer sheet is used, it may look as follows for each item:

Directions: Cross out the *m* opposite the activity that would probably have the most attraction for an "extrovert," and *l* opposite the activity that would have the least.
21. listening to classical records ....21. m ✗
22. going to a prize fight ....22. ✗ l
23. going fishing ....23. m l

The scoring key should be punched with holes over the two correct responses; the number of cross-out marks showing through (2, 1, or 0) is the score on the item. For added discrimination, another key punched with the opposite of the correct answer (e.g., 21 with m and 22 with l) can be used; all items showing two cross-out marks through this key should be scored minus one (-1).

EVALUATION TECHNIQUES EXPLICITLY AIMED AT HIGHER MENTAL PROCESSES

THE EIGHT-YEAR STUDY

In the course of the Eight-Year Study of the Progressive Education Association (1) an evaluation staff under the direction of Ralph W. Tyler constructed a series of evaluation devices aimed at instructional objectives not explicitly approached by most of the earlier achievement tests. Among the tests constructed for the Eight-Year Study are the following:[2]

Test 1.3. Application of Principles—Aspects of Thinking

Test 1.3b. Application of Principles in Science

Test 1.31. Application of Principles in Chemistry

Test 1.32. Application of Principles in Physics

Test 2.5. Interpretation of Data

Test 5.1. Problems Relating to Proof in Mathematics

Test 5.11. Application of Certain Principles of Logical Reasoning

Test 5.21. Nature of Proof

One distinguishing feature of these tests is their presentation of original problem material differing from that presented in classrooms and textbooks. A second feature is their orientation to a single, somewhat specific instructional objective expressed primarily in terms of a mental process, such as "ability to apply principles," rather than in terms of knowledge of subject matter, such as history or chemistry. A third characteristic is their use of everyday problems.

The steps involved in constructing a representative evaluation device of this type, a test of ability to apply principles, have been described by Raths (12). The first step is to decide upon the facts, principles, and definitions which have been taught and ability to apply which is to be tested. The second is to set up a group of problems involving each of the facts, principles, and definitions. The

---

[2] Evaluation instruments of the Eight-Year Study are available from the Educational Testing Service, Princeton, New Jersey.

specific terms in which the problem is put should be new rather than familiar to the pupils; these terms, or settings, should be interesting and should represent important aspects of the life experiences of pupils. The third step is to present two or more plausible alternative solutions to each problem, from which the pupil will select the one he considers most reasonable in the light of his knowledge or most consistent with the facts given. The fourth step is to formulate a series of reasons or statements from which the pupil will choose those supporting his solution of the problem. This series should include plausible statements supporting each of the alternative solutions or conclusions.

Illustrative of the end product of this procedure is the following problem from Test 1.3b, Application of Principles in Science.

Problem II

Two new electric irons (each 110 volts, 500 watts) have been used for an equal length of time. *The heating efficiency of both irons has decreased by approximately the same amount.*

Directions: A. If you are *uncertain* about the truth or falsity of the italicized statement, place a mark in the box on the answer sheet under *A*.

B. If you think that the italicized statement is quite likely to be *true,* place a mark in the box on the answer sheet under *B*.

C. If you *disagree* with the italicized statement, place a mark in the box on the answer sheet under *C*.

Directions for Reasons: If you placed a mark under *A,* select from the *first ten reasons* given below *all* those which help you to explain thoroughly why you were *uncertain* and place a mark in Column *A* opposite each of the reasons you decide to use.

If you placed a mark under *B,* select from reasons *11 through 24 all* those which help you to explain thoroughly why you *agreed* with the italicized statement and place a mark in Column *B* opposite each of the reasons you decide to use.

If you placed a mark under *C,* select from reasons *11 through 24 all* those which help you to explain thoroughly why you *disagreed* with the italicized statement and place a mark in Column *C* opposite each of the reasons you decide to use.

Reasons to be used if you are UNCERTAIN:

1. I have never used electric irons enough to know whether they consistently give more or less heat after they have been used for a time.
2. The heating efficiency of an iron may be affected by the voltage and constancy of the electric current maintained in the power line.
3. The frequent removal of the plug from an iron while it is being used may result in more rapid destruction of the contacts.

.   .   .   .   .

7. The phrase "approximately the same amount" needs to be made more definite.

.   .   .   .   .

9. I do not know what factors may affect the heating efficiency of an iron.

.   .   .   .   .

Reasons to be used if you AGREE or DISAGREE:

11. It is commonly observed that electrical appliances lose their efficiency at a constant rate.
12. It is silly to think that the use of two irons for the same length of time would not result in about equal amounts of deterioration.
13. A reduction in the flow of current through an iron is accompanied by a reduction in the heat developed by the iron.
14. Irons that have been used for equal lengths of time will deteriorate about equally.
15. The gradual oxidation of the wires in the heating element of irons introduces additional resistance in the form of an insulating layer.
16. An electrical current flowing in an iron must spend some of its energy in overcoming the additional resistance that nature gradually develops to prevent its flow.

.   .   .   .   .

19. Just as the wires in an electric light bulb will in time become burned and less efficient, so will the heating element in an electric iron become worn with use.
20. Manufacturers of electric irons say that irons kept in good repair will maintain their heating efficiency.

.   .   .   .   .

22. Burned wires decrease the heat developed in electric irons just as decreasing the friction in automobile brakes develops less heat.

.   .   .   .   .

The pupil's achievement on the test presenting eight such problems is analyzed for the extent to which he reaches valid conclusions and also for the kinds of reasons he selects to explain his decisions about the stated conclusions. The reasons from among which the pupils choose are classified into various types. The classifications of the reasons quoted from the above problem are as follows:

Reason　1 is based on Lack of Experience.

Reason　2 is based on Control.

Reason　3 is based on Control.

Reason　7 is based on Definition of Term.

Reason　9 is based on Lack of Knowledge.

Reason 11 is based on Poor Practice.

Reason 12 is based on Ridicule.

Reason 13 is based on Right Principle.

Reason 14 is based on Assuming the Conclusion.

Reason 15 is based on Wrong Principle.

Reason 16 is based on Teleology.

Reason 19 is based on Analogy.

Reason 20 is based on Authority.

Reason 22 is based on Poor Analogy.

These various types of reasons are considered representative of those given by pupils in essay tests presenting similar problems. The concrete meaning of each type of reason is probably best set forth by the illustrative item given for it above. The pupil's choice of a conclusion and his supporting reasons can be analyzed into the types of reasoning responsible for the correctness or incorrectness of the choice. For each pupil's test paper a set of scores is obtained showing the percentages of desirable and undesirable choices from among the total number of opportunities for choosing each type of reasoning.

Ability to interpret data has been evaluated by tests constructed according to the following procedure. Several sets of data, such as statistics in a table, or graphs, maps, cartoons, and pictures are selected for interpretation by the pupils. For each set of data a series of conclusions are drawn, some of which are fully supported (true), partially supported (probably true), not supported (uncertain), partially contradicted (probably false), and completely contradicted (false) by the set of data. The pupil is required to indicate for each conclusion the one of these five classes into which it falls.

His responses are then scored for general accuracy, accuracy with probably true and probably false statements, accuracy with uncertain statements, general tendency to go beyond the data, tendency to ascribe more truth to statements than is warranted, tendency to ascribe greater falsity than is warranted, and tendency to make such crude errors in judgment as confusing probably true with probably false or true with false statements. The following problem is used by Raths (12 : 101–102) to illustrate a test of ability to interpret data.

Percentage Distribution of Gainfully Occupied Persons in the United States Sixteen Years of Age and Over, 1870–1930

Occupation Group	1870	1880	1890	1900	1910	1920	1930
(1)	(2)	(3)	(4)	(5)	(6)	(7)	(8)
Agriculture.............	52.8	48.1	41.2	35.9	30.3	25.8	21.3
Mining........	1.5	1.6	1.8	2.1	2.6	2.7	2.0
Manufacturing...........	22.0	24.8	26.3	27.5	28.6	30.5	28.6
Trade and transportation...	9.1	10.7	13.6	16.3	17.4	18.0	20.7
Clerical service...........	1.7	2.0	2.5	2.8	4.6	7.2	8.2
Domestic and personal service...............	9.6	8.8	9.7	10.0	10.6	8.8	11.3
Public service...........	.6	.7	.9	1.0	1.1	1.6	1.4
Professional service.......	2.7	3.3	4.0	4.4	4.8	5.4	6.5
Total..............	100.0	100.0	100.0	100.0	100.0	100.0	100.0

Directions: Assuming that the data in the above table are true, you are to evaluate each of the following statements, by writing after each statement the number

> 1—if the statement is true
> 2—if the statement is probably true
> 3—if the evidence is not sufficient to indicate that there is any degree of truth or falsity in the statement
> 4—if the statement is probably false
> 5—if the statement is false

Statements:

1. There has been a persistent decline in the percentage of gainfully occupied persons in the United States, sixteen years of age and over, in the field of agriculture from 1870 to 1930.
2. The number of ministers has increased from 1870 to 1930.

3. In 1910, the largest percentage of occupied persons was to be found in manufacturing.
4. In Great Britain shifts in occupations of people gainfully employed have taken place which are similar to those in the United States.
5. In 1930 the percentage of gainfully occupied persons was greater than in 1850 for all occupations excepting agriculture.
[and so on for 11 more statements]

A further variation of these tests aimed at types of "thinking" is the technique used to evaluate the pupil's understanding of the nature of proof. A problem and conclusion are presented, followed by a randomly arranged series of statements expressing facts, implicit assumptions, restatements of the conclusion, irrelevant statements, and inconsistent or contradictory statements. The pupil is required to indicate the class in which each statement belongs, to select three crucial assumptions of the argument, and to demonstrate in other ways his ability to deal with various forms of argument. His responses may be analyzed diagnostically into various total and subscores in a fashion similar to that described for the test of ability to interpret data. The following is a typical problem from Test 5.21, Nature of Proof.

The following advertisement appeared in a teachers' association magazine:

"The gentle, rhythmic chewing of gum helps increase the blood flow to your head. This tends to make you feel more wide awake and hence keener-minded. And, at the same time, sweet, pleasant-tasting chewing gum supplies a quick pick-up of energy. That is why chewing gum helps keep you alert at your work. There's a time and place for Chewing Gum." Mary, after reading this advertisement, decided that *she would be more alert in school if she chewed gum.*

Statements:

1. Chewing gum contains some ingredient which is a source of energy.
2. The chewing of gum helps keep the teeth in better condition.
3. It is quite possible for a person to be wide awake and yet not have a keen mind.
4. The chewing of gum increases the flow of blood to the brain.
5. Chewing gum is socially acceptable.

6. An increase in the flow of blood to the brain results in one's being more wide awake.
7. Many people enjoy chewing gum.
8. The source of energy in chewing gum can be quickly utilized.
9. People who are wide awake usually have keen minds.
10. The chewing of gum may actually decrease the amount of food and oxygen reaching the brain.
11. Many good magazines advertise chewing gum.
12. Even if the chewing of gum did increase the flow of blood to the brain, the increase would probably be too small to have any real effect.
13. Many school children chew gum.
14. People who are wide awake and keen-minded are usually alert.

The relevance and reliability of the various tests of this type have been reported in the volume summarizing the work of the Evaluation Staff of the Eight-Year Study (15). In general, the reliability in terms of the Kuder-Richardson formula (see below) was found to cluster around .90 for individual grades in various private and public schools. The argument for the relevance of the tests was based on (1) the procedures used in selecting test material, and (2) correlations between the test scores and essay tests of pupils' ability to write original interpretations of data and applications of logical reasoning. It is evident from the illustrations that the types of test items employed represent no radical departure from the constant-alternative and changing-alternative types described earlier in this chapter. The constant-alternative items used here are, like all such items, open to contamination by response sets. Rather it is the nature of the problems presented, their subject matter, and their more thorough orientation to defined objectives (other than factual knowledge) that constitute the major change from more traditional achievement tests.

Are the abilities approached by tests of this type amenable to improvement through teaching and instructional procedures? Or, on the other hand, are they determined mainly by factors affecting a pupil's mental growth independent of classroom instruction? In short, are they "achievement" or "intelligence" tests? As we noted in Chapter II, the evidence that the achievements evaluated by these tests are relatively more permanent than those evaluated by more traditional tests may mean that (1) these tests evaluate achievements not of *instructional* objectives but rather of the goals of general mental development or (2) they evaluate achievements of instructional objectives which represent the more fundamental and functional goals of educational endeavor.

There is evidence, summarized by Glaser (6), that reasoning tests are not the same as intelligence tests. The correlations are consistently positive but far from perfect, even when allowances are made for the imperfect reliability of the tests. Furst (5) has made a logical analysis of the two kinds of test. He concludes that ". . . considerable learning underlies the cultivation of critical thinking in any subject field. This is necessarily so. In most subject fields the development of critical thinking is dependent on the acquisition of specialized knowledge . . . [but also on] instruction which encourages the learner to perceive relations among ideas, apply facts previously learned, recognize implicit assumptions, identify elements crucial to the solution of problems, and so on."

In short, it seems likely that tests of higher mental processes, like those developed by the Eight-Year Study, Glaser, Furst, and others, are not mere tests of intelligence. They do get at something that can be taught in schools and "achieved" by pupils.

THE MEASUREMENT OF UNDERSTANDING

In 1946, the National Society for the Study of Education sponsored a yearbook (2) on methods of evaluating achievement of types of instructional objectives that could be denoted by the term "understanding." In addition to chapters on the importance of teaching for understanding and on the nature of understanding, the yearbook had a general chapter on methods of obtaining evidence of understanding. Among the major principles set forth are the following:

1. Novel, but not too novel, evaluation situations are necessary to bring forth evidence of understanding. The task or situation should not require only insights or reasons that have been taught and learned as facts. Too much novelty, however, will merely confuse. In arithmetic, for example, either content or process, but not both, should be novel in the same problem.

2. Since understanding can exist at different levels of com-

plexity and subtlety, the evaluation must be aimed at a level appropriate to the maturity of the pupil. Intellectual and social distance of the evaluation situation from what was originally learned can be manipulated to make the level appropriate.

3. Primary reality must be appreciated by pupils before they can show any valid understanding. The terms used in solving problems requiring understanding must be more than mere verbalisms. Using pictures, requiring examples, and referring to real situations can help in this.

4. The ability to recognize the relevance and sufficiency of data should be evaluated in many attempts to tap understanding.

5. Originality of performance can give evidence of understanding. Creative effort in writing, building, drawing, and the like, are involved here. The teacher must avoid imposing repressive and restrictive evaluative standards but must try to represent to the pupil the viewpoints of various social groups.

Illustrative procedures for evaluating understanding are given in the second section of this yearbook. Separate chapters deal with objectives and evaluative procedures in social studies, science, mathematics, language arts, fine arts, health and physical education, home economics, agriculture, technical education, and industrial arts.

ARRANGING THE SHORT-ANSWER TEST

After the test items have been constructed, they must be arranged to maximize efficiency of administration and interpretation. This involves attention to the following:

1. Assembling items into parts
2. Editing the items
3. Determining the order of difficulty within parts
4. Arranging items for efficient scoring
5. Preparing the scoring key
6. Providing directions for the pupil
7. Providing directions for the test administrator

ASSEMBLING ITEMS INTO PARTS

After constructing the test items, the teacher will have a collection of them in varying forms. The number of items will be whatever is sufficient to cover adequately the instructional objectives at which the test is aimed. Enough items must be used to make the test sufficiently reliable; as is brought out in the next chapter, test reliability depends on the number of items.

EDITING THE ITEMS AND ARRANGING THEM IN ORDER OF DIFFICULTY WITHIN PARTS

These two steps are discussed together because they can be conveniently carried out at the same time. In editing the items a final check should be made to see that all the suggestions for constructing that form of item have been observed. If possible, the opinions of other teachers should be obtained by having them read each item carefully and attempt to answer it. During or after the editing, an attempt should be made to arrange the items of each type in order of difficulty. Since it has been found experimentally that subjective estimates of the difficulty of an item are seldom more than rough approximations of the difficulty as measured by the percentage of pupils failing an item, no attempt should be made to obtain more than a rough order of difficulty. Rather than being ranked, the items should be classified into a few categories, such as "very difficult," "fairly difficult," "average," "fairly easy," "very easy."

If the purpose is to make the test maximally efficient in measuring individual differences in achievement, the items should range in difficulty from very easy to very difficult, with equal numbers of items at any point along this range. No item should be so easy that 100 percent of the pupils succeed with it, nor should any be so difficult that no one succeeds. Because they do not discriminate between good and poor pupils, such items can serve no purpose in evaluation except, perhaps, to emphasize and motivate achievement of certain objectives to be evaluated in future tests. If the difficulty of the items has been properly adjusted, the average score will be about half the possible score and the range of scores for the group tested will tend to approximate the whole possible range, from almost zero to almost perfect. Perfect scores are undesirable because they indicate that the good pupil has been denied an opportunity to show the full extent of his achievement; similarly, zero scores fail to indicate what little achievement the poor pupil possesses.

The statements in the preceding paragraph apply only when test items tap achievement of objectives that are important to the individual and his society. Suppose true achievement in a certain course of instruction exists at a uniformly high level in all the pupils tested; then the valid items to evaluate it will be passed by high percentages, say 80 or 90 percent, of the pupils. To make the items center around the 50 percent level of difficulty in this situation might be possible only by asking "trivial," less valid questions. In short, the validity of test items should take precedence over their difficulty in achievement test construction. It is only when achievement is not at such a uniformly high level that test authors can meet both the validity and the difficulty requirements for optimum functioning of the test.

This point may be illustrated by the experience of psychologists in constructing tests of skill in radar navigation. One of the tasks of these navigators during World War II was to "compute winds," i.e., to use data on ground speed, true heading, air speed, and the like, for determining wind direction and velocity. For practical purposes, it was necessary that such computations be accurate only to within, say, 5 miles per hour in velocity and about 10 degrees in direction. About 80 to 90 percent of the student navigators on training flights were able to perform this task with this desired degree of accuracy; the same was true of them for most of the other important tasks of this air crew job. Achievement tests that were valid could thus not have the "50 percent level" of difficulty that would have been desirable on purely measurement grounds. Attempts to make the tests have this level of difficulty—as by giving credit only if the direction was accurate to within 5 degrees—almost invariably resulted in items that were unrealistic, unimportant, and irrelevant to the navigator's task. In cases like this, it is better to accept the situation than to insist on "efficient measurement" at the expense of validity.

This situation can occur in any area—handwriting, typing, shorthand, computational speed, woodworking—in which there are objective and external limits on the desirable degree of skill or level of achievement. In a shorthand test consequently, a speed of more than so many words per minute is an adequate and valid standard regardless of whether it is achieved by 50 or by 100 percent of the students in a given group. To raise the standard for the sake of bringing the level of difficulty closer to 50 percent is to sacrifice validity for discriminating power.

Within each type of test item, the order of presentation should be from "easy" through "moderately difficult" to "most difficult." An order of increasing difficulty may lead to better distribution of working time and to better morale while taking the test. Pupils, especially those of mediocre or low achievement, may become discouraged and confused if they are confronted with more difficult items at the beginning of the test. Time will be lost which could more profitably be employed on the easier items. Furthermore, only the better pupils are discriminated or "spread out" from one another by the more difficult items. Weaker pupils coming upon difficult items at the end of the test will already have had an opportunity to indicate their full achievement; they will consequently not be adversely affected by discouragement and loss of working time. As in a high-jump competition in a track and field contest, competitors begin at low heights and work up to progressively higher hurdles, the less able dropping out along the way.

Arranging Items for Easy Scoring

The spaces for the pupil's responses should usually be arranged in a column running from top to bottom of the page. This arrangement can be followed for all types of test items. In simple-question and completion items, when the omitted words or phrases are scattered in the middle of sentences or connected discourse, the scattering of these blanks may be circumvented by inserting a number in them which refers to a specific space for the response at the right side of the page. Example:

Items should be arranged in 1 order of difficulty   1. Increasing
   mainly in order to affect pupil 2 in a desirable way.   2. Morale

True-false items, multiple-choice items, matching items, and all the others can be similarly arranged so that the spaces for pupil responses will be in a vertical column at one side of the page.

When tests are to be scored electrically by means of the International Test Scoring Machine the teacher can secure help in arranging the test from a special manual (7).

PREPARING THE SCORING KEY

If one copy of a mimeographed test is filled out with the correct responses it may be used as a scoring key, the test scorer placing it next to the pupil's responses and checking them according to their correctness or incorrectness. Needless to say, the scoring key should be checked and rechecked by the teacher and other subject-matter experts before it is used in scoring test papers.

DIRECTIONS TO THE PUPIL

General directions to the pupil for the entire test may appear on the front page with regard to (1) writing his name and other identifying data in the proper spaces, (2) when to begin to work, (3) amount of time to be allowed, (4) observing and following directions for each part of the test, (5) distributing his time on easy and hard items, (6) whether going back to preceding parts is permitted, (7) stopping work when told, (8) asking questions, (9) guessing and the penalties or rewards for guessing. The teacher's judgment is a fairly safe guide in deciding the extent of these general directions. It is better, of course, to err in the direction of excessively detailed directions than to run the risk of omitting anything important.

Directions to the pupil for specific parts of the test should tell him what each type of item gives him and what it requires of him. The form of the directions is determined mainly by the pupils' age and their familiarity with the type of test item being used. Brevity, simplicity, and completeness should be attained as far as possible. Wherever necessary, sample items already answered should be provided to show the pupil how to proceed. Similarly, practice exercises may be provided. If the test is a time-limit test such exercises should be given outside the time limit of the test itself. The pupil should gain from the directions a clear idea of what he is to do and of where and how he is to record what he has done.

DIRECTIONS TO THE TEST ADMINISTRATOR

Whether the teacher gives a test of his own or one that was made elsewhere, directions for administering it should give him a clear idea of what to do and what *not* to do. He should make whatever special provisions are necessary for (1) furnishing pupils with pencils and other equipment such as answer sheets, (2) passing out test booklets, (3) reading directions with the pupils and answering questions concerning them, (4) giving starting and stopping signals, (5) observing total and part-time limits, and (6) collecting test papers and other equipment.

REFERENCES

1. Aikin, W. I., *The Story of the Eight-Year Study,* New York: Harper & Brothers, 1942.
2. Brownell, W. A. (chairman), "The measurement of understanding," *Forty-Ninth Yearbook of the National Society for the Study of Education,* Chicago: University of Chicago Press, Part I, 1946.
3. Cronbach, L. J., "Further Evidence on Response Sets and Test Design," *Educational and Psychological Measurement,* 10:3–31 (1950).
4. Ebel, R. L., "Writing the test item," in Lindquist, E. F., *et al., Educational Measurement,* Washington: American Council on Education, 1951, Chapter 7.
5. Furst, E. J., "Relationship between tests of intelligence and tests of critical thinking and knowledge," *Journal of Educational Research,* 43:614–625 (1950).
6. Glaser, E. M., *An Experiment in the Development of Critical Thinking,* New York: Teachers College, Columbia University, 1941.
7. International Business Machines Corporation, Department of Education, *Methods of Adapting Tests for Scoring by the IBM Electric Test Scoring Machine,* New York: The Corporation, 1947.
8. Kelley, V. H., "An experience with multiple-choice vocabulary tests constructed by two different procedures," *Journal of Experimental Education,* 5:249–250 (1937).
9. Lee, J. M., and Segel, D., *Testing Practices of High School Teachers,* Washington: U.S. Office of Education, Bulletin No. 9, Washington: Government Printing Office, 1936.
10. Lindquist, E. F., in Hawkes, H. E., *et al., The Construction and Use of Achievement Examinations,* Boston: Houghton Mifflin Company, 1936.
11. Odell, C. W., *Traditional Examinations and New Type Tests,* New York: Appleton-Century-Crofts, 1928.

12. Raths, L. E., "Techniques for test construction," *Educational Research Bulletin,* 17:83–114 (1938).
13. Richardson, M. W., *et al., Manual of Examination Methods,* Chicago: University of Chicago Book Store, preliminary ed., 1933.
14. Sims, V. M., "Note on scoring the rearrangement test," *Journal of Educational Psychology,* 28:302–304 (1937).
15. Smith, E. R., Tyler, R. W., *et al., Appraising and Recording Student Progress,* New York: Harper & Brothers, 1942, vol. 3.
16. Stalnaker, J. M. and Ruth C., "Chance vs. selected distractors in a vocabulary test," *Journal of Educational Psychology,* 26:161–168 (1935).
17. Tyler, R. W., *Constructing Achievement Tests,* Columbus: Ohio State University, 1934.
18. Vaughn, K. W., "Planning the objective test," in Lindquist, E. F., *et al., Educational Measurement,* Washington: American Council on Education, 1951, pp. 159–184.

CHAPTER V

Choosing Standardized Tests

ABSTRACT

This chapter reviews the considerations in evaluating standardized and teacher-made tests. If the former are to be used, they should be chosen on the basis of their validity, administrability, and interpretability. These concepts also apply to all other types of educational and psychological test. Validity consists of relevance and reliability. Relevance is the correspondence between the test and a criterion, or accepted standard, of what the test is intended to measure. The major types of criteria, and of relevance, are logical and empirical. Reliability, or accuracy of measurement, takes several forms: internal consistency, equivalence, and stability. Methods of estimating, factors affecting, and standards for interpreting reliability are described. Administrability refers to ease, cost, and training required in giving the test. Interpretability refers to the ease of obtaining scores and of using meaningful norms.

．～．～．～．

In this chapter we shall be concerned with the sixth question listed at the beginning of Chapter III:

6. *If an externally made, standardized short-answer test is to be used, how should it be chosen from among the many available?*

Certain considerations in selecting a standardized test apply to all evaluation devices, including teacher-made short-answer tests, essay tests, product and behavior rating devices, and evaluation devices for all other aspects of pupils. Consequently, the present discussion will lay the general foundation for understanding how all evaluation devices should be judged. In later chapters we shall consider the methods of applying these criteria to specific other kinds of evaluation devices.

It will be recalled, from the discussion of the relative merits of standardized vs. teacher-made tests in Chapter III, that the chief advantages of standardized tests are their norms and their technical refinement. On the other hand, teacher-made tests usually coincide more closely with the instructional objectives of particular classes, yield greater benefits to the teacher, and are more adaptable to continuous evaluation throughout a semester. For certain kinds of evaluations, for certain instructional objectives, and for certain kinds of interpretations the standardized test is superior. The problem of maximizing the usefulness of standardized tests resolves itself into two parts: Under what circumstances should the standardized test be used? How can the best standardized test for a particular situation be selected from among the many available?

In general, standardized tests should be used when the instructional objectives whose achievement is to be evaluated are objectives for which such tests have been designed. The objectives will usually be those that are common to a great many classrooms, teachers, and school systems. The objectives of instruction in arithmetic, reading, writing, and other tool subjects do not often vary so much from one classroom to another and from one school system to another that standardized tests designed for widespread use will be found grossly unfit for a particular situation. In other subjects, such as American history and general science, there is still enough in common between the objectives of different teachers and school systems so that valuable standardized achievement tests can be made. Granted the communality of instructional objectives in various classrooms, the problem becomes one of selecting the proper standardized test.

The basic characteristics of evaluation devices are (1) validity, which consists of (a) relevance and (b) reliability, (2) administrability, and (3) interpretability.

VALIDITY

The validity of an evaluation device is the degree to which it measures what it is intended to measure. This definition can be broken down into two parts: (1) "the degree to which it measures," and (2) "what it is intended to measure." The degree to which a test measures anything, and measures it accurately, is the *reliability* of the test. "What it is intended to measure" is the criterion for the *relevance*[1] of the test.

The relationships between these concepts are shown in Fig. 5.

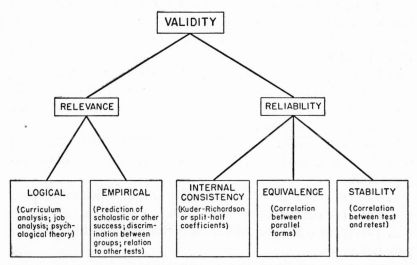

FIG. 5. The Components of Validity and Methods of Estimating Them.

This diagram also shows the operations usually carried out to estimate or establish the various kinds of relevance and reliability.

RELEVANCE

Relevance must always refer to a specific purpose or objective and a specific group of pupils. Within a given set of instructional objectives, an evaluation device may be relevant to achievement of one objective but not of others. Thus a history test may be relevant for evaluating ability to recall facts and definitions but irrelevant for evaluating ability to interpret data. The concept of relevance has meaning only in relation to specific purposes, subject matters, and instructional objectives.

[1] We are here following Cureton's original and useful clarification of the validity, relevance, and reliability concepts (8). Most writers prior to Cureton used the term validity as synonymous with relevance on some occasions, and as inclusive of both relevance and reliability on others. We shall attempt to make clear, in citing earlier writers, in which sense they seem to be using the term.

The quantitative nature of the concept of relevance may be inferred from the method by which relevance is frequently estimated. The purpose of a test or other evaluating device is realized to the degree in which the results of the test *correlate* with data obtained by some method or criterion whose validity is already known or assumed. The relevance of a foot rule may be defined as the degree to which results obtained with that foot rule agree with the results obtained with some standard yardstick, for example, in the U.S. Bureau of Standards. The relevance of a history test will vary in the degree to which scores obtained on it agree with other accepted evidence, such as the teacher's ratings, of achievement in history. The standard used as a basis of comparison in determining relevance is the *criterion*.   •

What kinds of criteria are used in estimating the relevance of tests? Relevance and the methods used to estimate it are of two related kinds:

1. Logical relevance, which uses criteria with which to compare test *content* or the *behaviors* called forth by tests.

2. Empirical relevance, which uses criteria with which to compare test *scores*.

ESTIMATING LOGICAL RELEVANCE

Criteria against which the logical relevance of a test may be determined may take the following forms: analyses of courses of study and jobs, statements of instructional objectives, analyses of textbooks, analyses of teachers' final examination questions, pooled judgments of competent persons, concepts of social utility, and, especially, logical or psychological analyses of mental processes, motor performances, or other behaviors.

Mosier (18) identified four different meanings of the concept of *face validity* (he used the term face validity to denote an aspect of what we are calling logical relevance. (1) Validity *by assumption:* A given test *looks as if* it ought to measure a particular characteristic or the achievement of a stated objective; hence the assumption is made that it does so. This is in general *not* permissible and may be very wide of the truth. (2) Validity *by definition:* If it is desired, for example, to measure student attitudes toward specified characteristics of teachers, a rating scale designed for that purpose may be said to be valid by definition. The validity of the ratings will then be the same as their reliability (see below). The validity of many educational measurements falls under this heading. (3) Validity *by appearance:* In addition to curricular or statistical validity it is generally desirable to have tests accepted by the persons taking them as valid measures of whatever is being tested. The tests should appear to be "fair." (4) Validity *by hypothesis:* There may be some slight evidence of validity and further validation would be highly desirable, but action that depends on the measurements must be taken now. The person making the measurement is fully aware of the lack of established validity and does not naïvely assume it. But in the circumstances the measurement obtained is the best basis available for immediate action and he therefore goes ahead in the belief that further research will bear out his as yet inadequate findings.

Obviously, relevance must eventually be thought of as relevance to the interacting needs of individuals and society. Fig. 6 illustrates

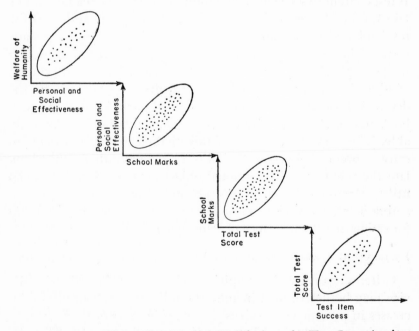

FIG. 6. Diagram Illustrating Implicit Validation of a Test Item Against a Series of Criteria Increasingly Remote from the Test Item.

the chain of criteria from test item to "welfare of humanity" that may be implicitly involved in validating a single test item. Each criterion may be validated against a "more ultimate" criterion.

On this ground, many school evaluation programs can immediately be declared at least partly irrelevant because of their lack of comprehensiveness, since they relate to only a few relatively minor educational objectives. It is of course the aim of the present book to increase the comprehensiveness of evaluation by outlining techniques for the evaluation not only of information and verbal and numerical skills, but of ways of thinking, attitudes, work habits, study skills, general and specific mental abilities, physical aspects, and social environment. Evaluation will become more relevant insofar as it becomes more comprehensive in terms of these aspects of pupils.

Estimating the relevance of achievement test content to the content of textbooks is useful because it insures to a high degree that pupils will be evaluated on the basis of what they have read. If test content so selected is then found wanting, the blame must be laid not on the test constructors but rather on the author of the textbook and those who have made use of it. Of course, the statement of instructional objectives which is embodied and implicit in any textbook has a specific and definite form, whereas statements of objectives embodied in the usual course of study are far less detailed. Especially for subjects new to the curriculum, the textbook may embody the most useful statement of objectives available. The danger in the use of this method is that it is likely to cause a premature crystallization of objectives rather than stimulate the progress of instructional objectives toward greater social utility. Analyses of courses of study and of teacher-made final examinations have similar advantages and disadvantages as criteria for estimating the relevance of achievement tests.

ESTIMATING EMPIRICAL RELEVANCE

Criteria against which empirical relevance of an evaluating device may be determined include the following: school marks, increases in percentage of success in successive ages or grades, differences in scores obtained by any two or more groups known to be widely separated in whatever is being measured, ratings by competent raters, and scores on other tests.

Estimating empirical relevance requires the application of statistical techniques. The test must first be administered to the group of pupils for whom the relevance of a given test is being estimated. For each pupil given a score on the test, a criterion score is obtained. The criterion score may be a teacher's mark or rating, a score on another test whose validity is known or assumed, a measure of the pupil's success or standing in whatever the test is being used to measure. The relationship between test scores and criterion scores is then examined by the appropriate statistical techniques. The principle of these techniques is to determine whether the average score on the test rises as the average score on the criterion becomes higher. For example, the average score on an arithmetic test of fifth-grade pupils should be higher than that of fourth-grade pupils, because the latter have had less instruction in arithmetic. If the expected difference in the average test scores is not obtained, either the test is irrelevant or the arithmetic instruction has not been effective. The better the agreement between criterion scores and test scores, the more relevant the test.

Of these two types of relevance, logical and empirical, the one more frequently applied to standardized achievement tests is logical relevance, involving test content rather than test scores, for it is very difficult to secure established valid criterion scores in quantitative form for school learning. Teachers' marks are often unsatisfactory as a criterion because they may be influenced by many other factors than those which should determine scores on achievement tests. Such marks are influenced partly by achievement but also by attendance, classroom behavior, recitations, work habits, general mental ability, socioeconomic status, sex, and other aspects of pupils which may or may not be related to achievement test scores.

How can a teacher discover what degree of relevance a standardized test possesses? This information can usually be obtained from the manual for the test. Such manuals should contain information concerning how the test items were chosen, the characteristics and composition of the sample of students upon whom the test was standardized, the criteria used in validating the test, and the degree of relevance the test had against these criteria. The absence of such information should incline one to judge that the test is of doubtful relevance. Of the thousands of standardized tests that have been published, only a small minority have been accompanied by manuals giving sufficient information to make possible an accurate judgment of relevance. To supplement the information in these manuals, or as a substitute if there is no manual, one may consult various educational journals which report experimental studies of the test.

Extremely valuable in this connection are the *Mental Measurements Yearbooks* edited by Buros (4). These volumes present critical evaluations, by competent experts, of standardized achievement tests in most of the subject-matter fields, and also tests of other aspects of pupils. The reviews cover not only newly published tests but older, widely used ones. Competent reviewers representing a variety of points of view among curriculum specialists and test technicians are selected to criticize each test. A reading of these yearbooks before selecting any standardized test will give those responsible for the selection of tests much data on which an intelligent judgment can be based.

Time may not permit one to obtain specimen copies of tests from the test publishers or to subject a fairly large number of tests in a given field to the necessary critical appraisal. Such an appraisal may nevertheless be made after the test has been used and may considerably modify the interpretation of the results obtained with it. If on inspection a test has been found to have important shortcomings with respect to relevance, reliability, etc., or to neglect or overemphasize certain instructional objectives, the interpretation of scores should be appropriately modified. There is no substitute for familiarity with whatever evaluation devices are used. And, of course, one of the best ways to acquire this familiarity is to take the test before giving it.

SOME SOURCES OF IRRELEVANCE OF TESTS

Factors that tend to make tests irrelevant to their purposes should be recognized. Among them are (1) cultural influences, particularly in so-called intelligence and aptitude tests; (2) response sets; (3) increase in reliability at the expense of relevance; and (4) difficulty or lack of clarity in directions to pupils.

Cultural influences. Recent work (**9, 13, 19**) has shown the effect of *culture*—socioeconomic status, social class structure, differential sex roles, etc.—on general mental ability as measured by tests. Among Hopi Indians, for example, the average boys' intelligence quotient on the Goodenough Draw-a-Man test was 123; the average girls', 102. Navaho boys and girls, on the other hand, did not differ significantly—107 and 110 respectively. Cultural anthropologists explain these differences in terms of the opportunities for learning to draw as determined by the different ways of bringing up boys and girls in the different tribes. Navaho boys and girls have similar experiences and opportunities to learn art. But Hopi Indian girls are restricted to routine household tasks, whereas the boys are stimulated to observe and work with their world.

A group of workers at the University of Chicago (**9**) have shown that eight different standardized group tests of intelligence vary enormously in their social class loading, i.e., the proportion of test items that discriminate between groups of children of upper and lower socioeconomic status. The smallest proportion of such test items, 46 percent, was found in the Otis Alpha (nonverbal) test; the largest proportion, 100 percent, in the Terman-McNemar Test of Mental Ability and the Thurstone Reasoning Test. Except for the Otis Alpha, considerably more than half the items favored the high socioeconomic group. Obviously these tests of "mental ability" measure different things to a significant degree. As a concrete illustration of a loaded item we show results for two items which required knowledge of the terms "sonata" and "cutting tool":

	Percentage of Each Socioeconomic Group Knowing Meaning of Word	
	High	Low
"Sonata"	74	28
"Cutting tool"	76	79

Such cultural effects have often been underestimated or not recognized at all. In a brief vocabulary test a national sample of high-school students, divided on the basis of religious preference, showed widely different degrees of understanding. Of the Catholic students, 32 percent defined the word "absolve" correctly, as contrasted with 14 percent of Protestant and 18 percent of Jewish students. Of the Jewish students, on the other hand, 56 percent knew the meaning of "incite" as against 41 percent of the Protestants and 44 percent of Catholics (19). "Subcultures" in our total culture thus complicate the problems of relevance enormously. There is much evidence, as Anastasi (2) points out, that "cultural differentials" are present not only in the more complex forms of behavior, but even in motor and discriminative, or perceptual, responses.

Response Sets.   Response sets, discussed in Chapter IV, are test-taking habits which affect persons' scores, usually in ways irrelevant to the purpose of the test. Cronbach (**6, 7**) has summarized the phenomenon as follows:

. . . Response sets have been identified in tests of ability, personality, attitude and interest, and in rating scales. Among the most widely found sets are acquiescence (tendency to say "True," "Yes," "Agree," etc.), evasiveness (tendency to say "?," "Indifferent," "Uncertain," etc.), and similar biases in favor of a particular response when certain fixed alternatives are offered. Other sets include the tendency to work for speed rather than accuracy, the tendency to guess when uncertain, the tendency to check many items in a checklist, etc. Response sets become most influential as items become difficult or ambiguous. Individual differences in response sets are consistent throughout a given test. . . . Response sets dilute a test with factors not intended to form part of the test content and so reduce its logical validity. These sets may also reduce the test's empirical validity. Response sets tend to reduce the range of individual differences in score (**6** : 3–4).

Increase in Reliability at the Expense of Relevance.   Suppose a teacher of mathematics finds that a test he constructed to measure ability to solve verbal problems is not adequately reliable. He knows (as is explained below) that increasing the number of test items will generally increase the reliability of a test. The test must also be administered during a class period. Hence he decides to add a considerable number of items calling for the less complex skills required in solving verbal problems—such skills as removing parentheses in algebra, factoring, and the like. It is quite possible that a student who has learned many of these skills in a rote memory fashion will receive a higher score than the student who has greater ability to solve verbal problems but has "memorized" fewer of the less complex skills. The test now yields a higher reliability coefficient, but its relevance may have been actually reduced.

Difficulty or Lack of Clarity of Directions to Pupils. Poor directions may for some pupils render the test a measure of something much different than the test author intended. For example, if the directions for a sixth-grade geography test include vocabulary of tenth-grade difficulty, the test becomes to a great extent one of ability to understand directions rather than a test of ability in geography.

RELIABILITY

Reliability is the accuracy with which a test measures whatever it does measure. What a test measures may not be what it is used to measure; i.e., a test may be irrelevant. But if it measures something accurately, it is reliable. If height is used as a measure of

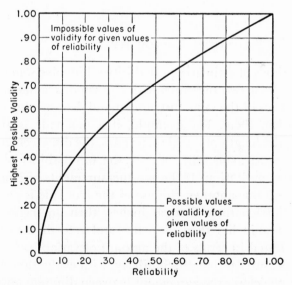

FIG. 7. Curve Showing Relationship Between Given Values of Reliability and Highest Possible Validity Coefficients. Validity$_{(max)}$ = $\sqrt{\text{Reliability}}$.

intelligence it will give reliable, consistent results but will have no relevance, and hence no validity, for that purpose; although less reliable, ratings of intelligence by teachers would be far more valid, because more relevant, for this purpose. An unreliable measuring instrument if relevant may be more valid than a reliable instrument applied to purposes for which it is irrelevant. Reliability is thus seen to be included in the concept of validity; it is one aspect of validity, necessary but not sufficient to it. Reliability puts an upper limit to the validity of a test. Fig. 7 shows the maximum validities possible for various reliability coefficients when relevance is perfect.

KINDS OF RELIABILITY

Reliability pertains to a *class* of test characteristics. The specific characteristics of this class are stability, equivalence, and internal conistency. Different techniques are used to estimate each of these kinds of reliability. These techniques, and the different meanings of the three kinds of coefficients obtained with them, are described below.

METHODS OF ESTIMATING RELIABILITY

The methods of estimating reliability all involve some means of securing at least two measures with the same instrument or with different forms of the same instrument and determining the agreement between them. For example, if a foot rule is applied to measuring the length of a table ten times, the disagreement among the ten measurements will indicate the unreliability of the foot rule and its application. If the ten measurements of length agree perfectly with one another, the use of the foot rule is perfectly reliable; if the length is first 50 inches, then 49 inches, then 51 inches, then 50 inches, then 48 inches, and so forth, the unreliability can be stated in terms of the amount of variability among the different measures of length. Similarly, with evaluation devices in education, the closer the agreement between different applications of the device, the greater its reliability.

1. The *test-retest method* requires that the same evaluation device be applied more than once to the same group of pupils. The

agreement between the scores from two or more applications of the same test is determined by means of a correlation coefficient which, for this method, is sometimes called a *coefficient of stability*. This method, however, has the following disadvantages: Repeating the test at too short an interval introduces the memory factor and tends to make the self-correlations of the test too high, unless, of course, the memory factor is what one wants to measure. On the other hand, repeating the test after a longer time interval permits such factors as growth, intervening learning, and unlearning to come into play so as to make the self-correlation lower than it should be.

2. The *equivalent-forms method* of estimating reliability makes it possible to avoid the disadvantages of too short or too long a time interval between successive administrations of the evaluating device. Two equivalent forms of the device must be constructed that will be as similar as possible in content, mental processes required, length, difficulty, and all other respects. One form of the test is given to the pupils and then, as soon as possible, the other form is given. The agreement between the two is again determined by means of a correlation coefficient which for this method is sometimes called a *coefficient of equivalence*. If the agreement is high, we can say that each form does an accurate job of measurement.

The question may occur to the reader how two forms can be equivalent while differing in specific content or test items. The notion of equivalent forms may become clearer when it is compared with the process of sampling from any large population. When a medical technician examines a droplet of blood for the number of red corpuscles it contains, he may determine the reliability of his count by examining another droplet from the same person. The two droplets are equivalent and yet distinct, in that no corpuscle of one is contained in the other. Similarly, a test may be considered to be a sampling of test items from a large "population" of possible test items. Each sample of test items or form of test can be equivalent to the others, although not a single test item is common to both forms. If the two forms or samples are administered to a group of pupils, the scores on the two forms will correlate or agree in proportion to the equivalence of the two samples of test items.

3. The *split-test method* of estimating reliability yields what is sometimes referred to as a *coefficient of internal consistency*. In this method the items of a single test are divided into halves, usually by pooling odd-numbered items for one score and even-numbered items for another score. The odd-even method of splitting usually makes the two scores obtained from a single testing reasonably equivalent in such respects as practice, fatigue, distractions, boredom, mental set, item difficulty and content. After the test has been given, two scores are obtained for each pupil, one in the odd-numbered and the other on the even-numbered items. The agreement between these two scores on the same test as determined by a correlation coefficient measures the reliability of the test. Since this reliability holds only for one-half the whole test, the reliability of the whole test must still be obtained. This is so because the reliability of tests varies with the number of functioning items they contain; hence the reliability of a half test is lower than that of the whole. But we have a technique for estimating the reliability of a whole test from that of its halves. This technique, the Spearman-Brown prophecy formula, requires merely the substitution of the calculated reliability of the half test in the following equation in order to estimate the reliability of the whole test:

$$\text{Reliability of lengthened test} = \frac{nr}{1 + (n - 1)r}$$

where n = number of times test is lengthened

r = original reliability coefficient

When the r is between scores on two half tests, this formula becomes:

$$\text{Reliability of whole test} = \frac{2\,(\text{reliability of half test})}{1 + (\text{reliability of half test})}$$

The applicability of the Spearman-Brown formula depends on the degree to which certain assumptions are met. The two halves of the test must be as equivalent as possible in average score, variability of scores, content, and type of items. The formula has been found experimentally to give results in agreement with the actual reliabilities of whole tests; that is, predicted and obtained whole-test reliabilities have been found to be approximately the same.

Two other split-test methods of estimating reliability which "involve no assumptions contradictory to the data" (5) do not require computing the correlation coefficient or correcting by the Spearman-Brown formula. As shown in the following formula, the first of these (12) requires only the standard deviations of each half test and of the total test:

$$r = 2\left(1 - \frac{s_o{}^2 + s_e{}^2}{s_t{}^2}\right)$$

where s_o = standard deviation of odd half
  s_e = standard deviation of even half
  s_t = standard deviation of total test
(Methods of computing standard deviations and coefficients of correlation are described in Chapter XXI.)

The second formula which will yield the same results requires only the standard deviation of the differences, s_d, between half-test scores and the standard deviation of the total test (21).

$$r = 1 - \frac{s^2{}_d}{s^2{}_t}$$

Kuder and Richardson (16) have presented methods for estimating reliability coefficients which do not require splitting a test into halves and rescoring and calculating a correlation coefficient. The only data required for this simpler method are the number of items in the test, the standard deviation of the test, and the arithmetic mean of the total scores on the test. Assuming that all the items in the test measure essentially a single ability, that the correlations between the items are all equal, and that all items are of the same difficulty, they arrive at the following formula:

$$r = \frac{n}{n - 1} \cdot \frac{s^2_t - n\bar{p}\bar{q}}{s^2_t}$$

where n = number of items in the test
  s_t = the standard deviation of the total test scores
  $\bar{p} = \dfrac{\text{arithmetic mean of test scores}}{n} = \dfrac{M_t}{n}$
  $\bar{q} = 1 - \bar{p}$

This formula underestimates the reliability of the test if there is variation in difficulty among the items; in any case, its estimate is usually lower than that obtained by the split-test methods. If the test items do not vary greatly in difficulty, it is probable that the quick estimate made possible by this formula is good enough for all practical purposes.

Another Kuder-Richardson formula for estimating internal consistency has been shown by Cronbach (5) to yield a coefficient equal to the mean of all the possible split-half coefficients of the test. This formula, called Kuder-Richardson's "20" (or, by Cronbach, "alpha") is:

$$r = \frac{n}{n-1} \cdot \frac{s_t^2 - \Sigma pq}{s_t^2}$$

where n = number of items in the test

s_t = standard deviation of the total test scores

p = proportion of persons passing each item

$q = 1 - p$

This formula requires counting the number of persons passing on each item, dividing this by the number of persons taking the test, subtracting the resulting proportion p from 1 to obtain q, getting pq from a table, and adding the pq's for all items to get Σpq. Since p is often valuable as part of the item analysis of a test in computing the difficulty of each item, the labor required in determining p for each item can serve more than one purpose.

FACTORS AFFECTING RELIABILITY

1. The *length of the test* has already been mentioned in connection with the Spearman-Brown formula as a factor influencing its reliability. Certain other factors should also be discussed here in connection with interpreting a reliability coefficient.

2. The *range of talent,* achievement, or ability of the pupils on whom the reliability is based has a direct effect on the reliability coefficient. The greater the variability in the group of pupils, the higher the reliability coefficient. Consequently, the reliability coefficient of a test given to several grades is higher than that of the same test given to a single grade because the range of achievement is larger in the first case. Figs. 8 and 9 show this fact graphically. The reliability coefficient should therefore always be determined on a group of pupils whose range of achievement is similar to that of the group who are to be discriminated from one another

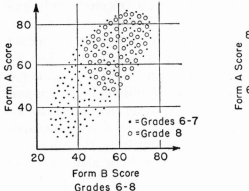

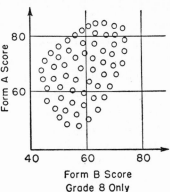

FIG. 8. Scatter Diagrams Showing How Restriction of Range of "Talent" Results in Lower Reliability Coefficients.

by the test. The reliability of a test designed to reveal differences in achievement in a single classroom should be determined on a group of pupils within a similarly restricted range of achievement. Reliability determined on pupils in several classrooms or different geographic areas or differing in certain other factors that affect achievement will give a false picture of the reliability of the test when used in a single classroom.

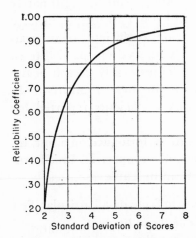

FIG. 9. Increase in the Reliability Coefficient as the Test Is Applied to an Increasingly Heterogeneous Group.

3. The *conditions of test administration* and scoring may raise or lower the reliability of a given test. The mental set of the pupils for accuracy, speed of work, motivation or incentive, and emotional stability affects the reliability of their scores. Distractions and accidents, like breaking a pencil or finding a defective test blank, lower reliability. Cheating by pupils and inaccuracy in scoring due to clerical errors affect reliability adversely.

4. The *construction of the test,* the form of test items, their dif-

ficulty, the objectivity of scoring, and such factors as interdependent items and item wording also affect reliability.

Test reliability increases as the number of response alternatives presented by each item increases, up to certain limits. Other factors being equal, a multiple-choice test containing five alternatives per item will be more reliable than a multiple-choice test containing three alternatives per item. Remmers and others (20, 10) have shown that this increase in reliability resulting from more alternatives can be predicted quite accurately by the Spearman-Brown formula. That is, a 5-choice test will be about as much more reliable than a 2-choice test as if the length, or number of items on the 2-choice test, had been multiplied by 2.5 (i.e., $5 \div 2$). These considerations, however, belong more properly under the heading of test construction than test evaluation, and have already been partly discussed in Chapter IV.

5. A consideration often overlooked in standardizing tests is that not all methods of estimating reliability can be legitimately applied to speeded tests, i.e., tests in which not all the pupils have time to attempt all the items. The various coefficients of internal consistency cited here may not properly be used on speeded tests. The *equivalent-forms* method may be so used only if each of the forms is given and timed independently. Because of failure to observe this consideration, the reliability coefficients reported for standardized tests may be spuriously high.

The possible sources of differences in performance on a test, including sources of unreliability, are well summarized by Thorndike (23) and are shown in adapted form in Table 2.

TABLE 2.   Possible Sources of Differences in Score on a Particular Test

I. *Lasting and general characteristics of the individual*
    A. Level of ability on one or more general traits which operate in a number of tests
    B. General skills and techniques of taking tests
    C. General ability to comprehend instructions

II. *Lasting but specific characteristics of the individual*
    A. Specific to the test as a whole (and to parallel forms of it)
        1. Individual level of ability on traits required in this test but not in others
        2. Knowledges and skills specific to particular form of test items

B. Specific to particular test items
1. The "chance" element determining whether the individual does or does not know a particular fact. (Sampling variance in a finite number of items, not the probability of his guessing the answer.)
III. *Temporary but general characteristics of the individual* (Factors affecting performance on many or all tests at a particular time)
A. Health
B. Fatigue
C. Motivation
D. Emotional strain
E. General test-wiseness (partly lasting)
F. Understanding of mechanics of testing
G. External conditions of heat, light, ventilation, etc.
IV. *Temporary and specific characteristics of the individual*
A. Specific to a test as a whole
1. Comprehension of the specific test task (insofar as this is distinct from IB)
2. Specific tricks or techniques of dealing with the particular test materials (insofar as distinct from IIA2)
3. Level of practice on the specific skills involved (especially in psychomotor tests)
4. Momentary "set" for a particular test
B. Specific to particular test items
1. Fluctuations and idiosyncrasies of human memory
2. Unpredictable fluctuations in attention or accuracy superimposed upon the general level of performance characteristic of the individual
V. *Systematic or chance factors affecting the administration of the test or the appraisal of test performance*
A. Conditions of testing—adherence to time limits, freedom from distractions, clarity of instructions, etc.
B. Unreliability or bias in subjective rating of traits or performances
VI. *Variance not otherwise accounted for (chance)*
A. "Luck" in selection of answers by "guessing"

How High Should Reliability Be?

Correlation coefficients may range from minus 1.00 through .00 to plus 1.00. If the correlation is perfect and positive, so that the pupils have exactly the same relative standing on one form of a test as on another form of it, the correlation coefficient will be plus 1.00. If pupils' scores on the two forms are completely unrelated, so that it is impossible to tell what one score will be on the basis of the other, the correlation coefficient will be .00. A perfect negative correlation, minus 1.00, means that the higher the score on one test, the lower the score on the other and in the same degree. Intermediate values of correlation, such as plus .65, mean that the agreement between the scores on the two forms is neither perfect nor completely absent, that there is a distinct tendency for higher scores on one form to be associated with higher scores on the other.

How high should the reliability coefficient be? It is obvious that evaluation devices are never perfectly reliable. How unreliable may a test be and still be useful for evaluation purposes? This depends mainly on the fineness of the discrimination for which the test scores will be used. A basis for decisions about individual pupil scores has been provided by Bloom (3) in the form of Table 3, which gives the limits within which true percentile scores may be expected to fall 95 times out of 100. A "normal" distribution of the scores is assumed. (See Chapter XXI for the meaning of percentile score and normal distribution.)

The important characteristic of the statistics in Table 3 is that they show that we can be more precise—more certain—about extreme scores than about those in the middle range of the distribution. The table is read as follows.

If the reliability of a test is .80 and a pupil's percentile score is 90, the true percentile score for this pupil will fall (95 times in 100) within the limits 66 and 99. Another way of saying this is that the betting odds are 19 to 1 that this pupil's true percentile score is between 66 and 99. The ratio 19 : 1 is, of course, the ratio 95 : 5. The reader will note that as reliability coefficients and percentile ranks increase, the range of probable true scores decrease, and conversely. As the percentile ranks become more and more extreme, we can with the same degree of confidence assign the pupil's true rank to a narrower and narrower range of possible true ranks.

In general, most standardized tests published for use in schools have reliability coefficients, of one kind or another, of at least .80

in the populations for which they are designed. For research purposes, psychologists may find tests useful if their reliability coefficients are as low as .50.

TABLE 3. Given a Specified Reliability Coefficient and Specified Percentile Score Based on a Normal Distribution, the Fiducial Limits Which May Be Expected 95 Out of 100 Times (After Bloom, 3)

Percentile Score[a]	Reliability Coefficients							
	.40	.50	.60	.70	.80	.85	.90	.95
99	999+ 791	999+ 827	999+ 861	999+ 895	999 926	999 942	998 956	997 971
98	999+ 704	999+ 748	999+ 792	999 837	998 881	998 902	996 924	994 947
97	999+ 642	999 690	999 739	998 790	997 842	996 867	994 869	990 896
96	999+ 592	999 642	999 695	998 751	996 809	994 839	991 871	986 905
95	999 550	999 602	998 657	997 716	994 779	992 812	988 847	981 886
90	997 407	996 460	994 517	991 582	985 657	979 699	971 746	957 801
85	995 315	992 363	989 420	983 485	972 564	964 609	951 662	930 725
80	991 249	987 293	981 345	972 408	957 486	945 533	928 588	900 657
70	980 160	972 195	961 237	945 291	919 362	900 407	874 462	832 534
60	962 103	949 129	932 162	908 206	871 267	844 307	809 357	755 427
50	936 065	917 083	892 108	859 142	810 190	776 224	732 268	669 331

[a] The complements of the above figures may be used for percentile scores below 50.

It is sufficient, perhaps, to say that the teacher should seek a standardized test whose reliability is as high as possible. But this reliability coefficient must be interpreted in the light of the groups of pupils on which it is based, of the variability of this group, and of the method used in estimating reliability. Coefficients of stability tell how similar the scores may be expected to be over a specified time interval. Coefficients of equivalence tell how similar the scores on one form of a test will be to the scores on another form. Coefficients of internal consistency tell how much all the items, combined to yield a single score, may be considered to measure the same homogeneous characteristic of the persons tested.

One method of expressing the reliability of scores on a test which has the advantage of being independent of the range of talent used in determining reliability is *the standard error of a true score*. It is computed as follows:

$$\text{S.E.}_{(\text{Meas})} = s_t \sqrt{1 - r_{tt}}$$

where s_t = standard deviation of the scores on the test
$\quad r_{tt}$ = reliability coefficient of the test
This statistic is the one on which Table 3 is based. It tells the range within which scores on the same test would be expected to fall two-thirds of the time if a very large number of the tests, equivalent in all respects, were given to the pupil.

ADMINISTRABILITY

The administrability of evaluation devices refers to the ease and accuracy with which the directions to pupils and evaluator can be carried out. Requirements of good directions have already been listed in Chapter IV. Here we wish to point out the need for concern with administrability. An example of a highly valuable and reliable test that is difficult to administer is the Stanford-Binet Intelligence Test. This test can be given to only one individual at a time and requires approximately an hour for the individual and about an hour and a half for the examiner. The directions for the examiner are very detailed and complex; indeed, a university course of one semester is usually required for the training necessary for the proper administration of this test.

In many tests the administration time is divided among several subtests with specific time limits; in such cases the examiner must be provided with an accurate timepiece with a second hand so that serious errors in administration will not be committed. In speed tests especially, slight errors in timing can make the norms and interpretations worthless.

Other tests require little supervision by the examiner; such "self-administering" tests require merely passing out test papers, giving the starting and stopping signals, and collecting the papers. These tests are obviously very desirable when they are to be administered in widely separated classrooms by examiners who differ greatly in testing ability. A further aid is to separate the directions to the pupils from the directions to the examiner so that the pupils will not be confused or distracted by material they do not need. For maximum administrability in schools, the time required for giving a test should preferably fit into the normal classroom period of about forty minutes; tests requiring more time than this can be made more reliable and valid by this additional length, but only at the sacrifice of administrability. Many test publishers have had to shorten their tests to meet this need. Obviously, such shortened tests must be more highly refined in content so as to reduce the sacrifice of validity and reliability to a minimum. The mechanical features of the test, such as the paper on which it is printed, the typography, and the spaces for pupil's responses, are further considerations.

The monetary cost of standardized tests also affects their administrability. Other things being equal, the best test is the cheapest test. But cost should always be figured in relation to test validity.

Administrability may be increased by using separate answer sheets for pupils' responses. These answer sheets are easier to handle during the scoring process and they make it possible to use the same test booklet more than once. An analysis of the scoring process in terms of the time required to score a single test, the complexity of the operation, the provision of schemes for checking the scoring and summation of responses, may all throw valuable light on the test's administrability. Evaluation devices whose cost of scoring is high may be severely limited in usefulness for many schools.

INTERPRETABILITY

The interpretability of an evaluation device refers to the ease and meaningfulness with which scores may be derived and understood. The first step in interpreting a test is obviously applying the scoring key to obtain "raw" scores. Some of the considerations in maximizing scorability have already been discussed in Chapter IV with respect to teacher-made tests. Obviously scoring is easiest when it requires merely the counting of simple marks or numbers. It becomes more effort-consuming when weights and correction formulas must be applied. For a large-scale testing program the problem of scoring may assume considerable proportions. Numerous mechanical scoring devices have been invented to lessen this labor.

After the "raw" score has been obtained, it must be given meaning in relation to other pupils. Tables of norms are usually provided for this purpose. The nature of these norms and the groups on whom they are based must be considered in relation to the kinds of interpretation required. Some norms enable comparisons of pupils of the same and different ages, or grades, or other types of groupings. Norms may be provided for each part of a test so that separate scores may be interpreted. Here again we are concerned only with the need for considering interpretability in selecting evaluation devices. A fuller discussion of the interpretation of evaluation devices is presented in Chapter XXII.

A TEST EVALUATION FORM

Following is a form that may prove useful in describing and evaluating any standardized test. The major headings follow those in this chapter. The reader will understand the ideas in this chapter better if he fills out this form for one or two tests. For some tests the information under various headings may be lacking or scanty; this form will at least make the test user aware of what he does not know about a test.[2]

[2] *Technical Recommendations for Psychological Tests and Diagnostic Techniques* have been developed by the Committees on Test Standards of the American Psychological Association, the American Educational Research Association, and the National Council on Measurements Used in Education. These *Recommendations* cover the ground of this chapter in more detail and with many technical refinements. Advanced readers of this book who have had at least one course in statistics and in tests and measurements will find these *Recommendations* invaluable. Test publishers and authors should be guided by these *Recommendations* in preparing tests and, especially, test manuals for widespread distribution. See *Psychological Bulletin,* 51, 1954, No. 2, Part 2.

A FORM FOR DESCRIBING AND EVALUATING TESTS
A. *Identifying Data*

1. Title: 2. Authors:

3. General purpose: 4. Group to which applicable:

5. Year of publication: 6. Cost, booklet:

                                                answer sheet:

7. Time required: 8. Forms available:

9. Publisher's name and address:

B. *Validity*

1. Relevance, logical: Names of scores as given by authors, mental or behavioral function represented by each score as seen by present analyst of the test (response sets, speed?), basis for selecting items, basis for scoring items (correction formulas, empirical weighting, etc.)

2. Relevance, empirical: Criteria, size and nature of samples, correlation coefficients obtained, etc.; correlations with other tests, specifying subjects used.

3. Reliability in the sense of internal consistency: Method of estimating, size and nature of sample, coefficients obtained.

4. Reliability in the sense of equivalence: Method of estimating, size and nature of sample, coefficients obtained.

5. Reliability in the sense of stability: Method of estimating, time interval used, size and nature of sample, coefficients obtained.

C. *Administrability*

1. Rapport, special problems or methods in establishing:

2. Directions to test taker: Adequacy, clarity, etc.

3. Special problems: Timing, effect of practice or previous experience with test, mental sets to be sought, etc.

D. *Interpretability*

1. Provisions for scoring: Hand scoring keys, machine scorability, self-scorability, scoring costs, etc.

2. Norms: Type of derived score, size and nature of sample on which based.

3. Special interpretations: Cutting scores, meaning of various patterns of scores, need for local norms, etc.

E. *Summary Evaluation*

1. Comments of reviewers in Buros' *Yearbooks, Review of Educational Research,* research journals, etc.

2. Advantages and disadvantages in local situation:

F. *References*

SOURCES OF INFORMATION CONCERNING TESTS

This book mentions only a small number of the tests published in the various fields. Only the general nature and content of any particular area of educational and psychological measurement and various important practical considerations are presented. The reasons for limiting the discussion in this fashion are twofold. (1) Limitations of space prohibit any attempt to provide detailed specific information, evaluations, and recommendations concerning the large numbers of tests available in each of the fields discussed. (2) The availability of publications which can satisfy far more thoroughly than is possible here the need for an exhaustive listing and evaluation of available tests makes such an attempt superfluous for a general textbook manual in educational measurement and evaluation. We refer here specifically to Hildreth's *Bibliog-*

raphy of Mental Tests and Rating Scales (14) and to Buros' *Mental Measurements Yearbooks* (4). Not only are they specifically designed for the functions which this book avoids, but they also have the advantage of being *recurrent*. At the present writing, several editions of both of these works have already been published (Hildreth's *Bibliography* in 1933, 1939, and 1945; Buros' *Yearbooks* in 1938, 1940, 1949, and 1952) and further editions will probably appear.

A further source of information concerning the ongoing development of evaluation devices is the *Review of Educational Research* (1). The issues entitled "Psychological Tests and Their Uses," "Educational Tests and Their Uses," "Methods of Research and Appraisal in Education," and "Counseling and Guidance" are especially rich in references to new tests and to research findings with old tests. These appear in three-year cycles and critically evaluate the literature of the preceding three years in a given field.

The Encyclopedia of Educational Research (17) provides information useful in judging and selecting tests. It will be valuable in the professional library of any school.

The catalogues of test publishers are a further source of information as to available tests. Schools can readily keep an up-to-date collection of such catalogues. These catalogues tell how to obtain specimen sets of tests (consisting generally of test booklet, manual, answer sheet, scoring key, norms, etc.). Publishers' test catalogues and manuals obviously present their tests as favorably as possible. But the intelligent test user can make wise decisions by inspecting the specimen set, applying the concepts and principles set forth in this chapter and elsewhere in this volume, and consulting the critical and research literature on the test.

Every classroom teacher and school administrator should have access to these sources when selecting evaluation devices. When this is impossible, teachers and administrators can write to the educational research bureaus of universities for specific information concerning available tests in a particular field. Such inquiries are answered most helpfully by such bureaus when they state specifically the purposes, time limits, financial resources, and other factors affecting the proposed testing program.

REFERENCES

1. American Educational Research Association, *Review of Educational Research,* Washington: American Educational Research Association.
2. Anastasi, Anne, "Some implications of cultural factors in test construction," *Proceedings, 1949 Invitational Conference on Testing Problems,* Princeton: Educational Testing Service, 1950.
3. Bloom, B. S., "Test reliability for what?" *Journal of Educational Psychology,* 33:517–526 (1942).
4. Buros, O. K. (ed.), *Mental Measurements Yearbooks,* Highland Park, New Jersey: The Mental Measurements Yearbook, 1938, 1940, 1949, 1953.
5. Cronbach, L. J., "Coefficient alpha and the internal structure of tests," *Psychometrika,* 16:297–334 (1951).
6. Cronbach, L. J., "Further evidence on response sets and test design," *Educational and Psychological Measurement,* 10:3–31 (1950).
7. Cronbach, L. J., "Response sets and test validity," *Educational and Psychological Measurement,* 6:475–494 (1946).
8. Cureton, E. E., "Validity," in Lindquist, E. F. (ed.), *Educational Measurement,* Washington: American Council on Education, 1951, Chapter 16.
9. Eells, K., Davis, A., Havighurst, R. J., Herrick, V. E., and Tyler, R., *Intelligence and Cultural Differences; a Study of Cultural Learning and Problem-Solving,* Chicago: University of Chicago Press, 1951.
10. Gage, N. L., and Damrin, Dora, "Reliability, homogeneity and number of choices," *Journal of Educational Psychology,* 41:385–404 (1950).
11. Guilford, J. P., "New standards for test evaluation," *Educational and Psychological Measurement,* 4:427–438 (1946).
12. Guttman, L., "A basis for analyzing test-retest reliability," *Psychometrika,* 10:255–282 (1945).
13. Havighurst, R. J., Gunther, M. K., and Pratt, I. E., "Environment and the Draw-a-Man Test: the performance of Indian children," *Journal of Abnormal and Social Psychology,* 41:50–63 (1946).
14. Hildreth, G. H., *A Bibliography of Mental Tests and Rating Scales,* New York: The Psychological Corporation, 1939.
15. Jackson, R. W. B., and Ferguson, G. A., *Studies in the Reliability of Tests,* Toronto: Department of Educational Research, University of Toronto, Bulletin No. 12, 1941.

16. Kuder, G. F., and Richardson, M. W., "The theory of the estimation of test reliability," *Psychometrika,* 2:151–160 (1937).
17. Monroe, W. S. (ed.), *The Encyclopedia of Educational Research,* Rev. ed., New York: The Macmillan Company, 1950.
18. Mosier, C. I., "A critical examination of the concept of face validity," *Educational and Psychological Measurement,* 7:191–206 (1947).
19. Remmers, H. H., and Drucker, A. J., "High school youth re-ponder some national problems and issues," *Purdue Opinion Panel,* vol. 9, No. 3, 1950.
20. Remmers, H. H., and Sageser, H. W., "The reliability of multiple-choice measuring instruments as a function of the Spearman-Brown Prophecy Formula, V," *Journal of Educational Psychology,* 32:445–451 (1941).
21. Rulon, P. J., "A simplified procedure for determining the reliability of a test by split-halves," *Harvard Educational Review,* 9:99–103 (1939).
22. Symonds, P. M., "Factors influencing test reliability," *Journal of Educational Psychology,* 9:73–87 (1928).
23. Thorndike, R. L., "Reliability," in Lindquist, E. F. (ed.), *Educational Measurement,* Washington: American Council on Education, 1951, Chapter 15.

CHAPTER VI

Product and Procedure Evaluation

ABSTRACT

This chapter begins with a review of the purposes of product and procedure evaluation in terms of fields of study involving this evaluation. The construction of product evaluation devices requires (1) an analysis of the product or procedure into various features and (2) a method for scoring each feature. The analysis into features involves considering the instructional objectives which the product should reflect and the amenability of each feature to evaluation. Grouping and weighting the features may improve validity. Providing a scoring method for each feature calls for decisions concerning the number of levels at which each feature is to be evaluated, and arrangements, such as graphic scales, for presenting the various levels. The psychophysical methods may have value in defining the various levels of excellence of each feature. Finally we discuss representative evaluation devices in different fields.

·~·~·~·

As we noted in Chapter III, not all achievement of instructional objectives can be expressed in symbols—verbal, mathematical, or other kinds. Whether the curriculum is organized in subject-matter fields or in activities and projects, we often find that short-answer tests of the type thus far discussed are inadequate. The inadequacy of tests for such objectives as "coherent and cogent composition" and "organized expression," already discussed, was found to point toward the need for essay tests. But there remains a large sphere of educational activity still untouched by either of these kinds of evaluation devices. This is the area in which a pupil's achievement is expressed by means of a *product* or a *procedure,* something that is a direct indication of his application of information, skill, and understanding.

The purpose of this chapter is to make clear the nature and logic of the methods of product and procedure evaluation. A product is well illustrated in industrial arts and home economics —a piece of woodwork or metalwork, a mechanical drawing, chairs, tables, lamps, funnels, dustpans, sets of bookends. Products such as these and often the procedures used in producing them must be evaluated.

Similarly, in home economics the understanding of food preparation and clothing construction must be evaluated in terms of pupil products and procedures, as well as by tests involving linguistic expression of ideas. The quality of the foods and clothing produced and of the selection and arrangement of home furnishings is at least as important an indication of achievement in these fields as scores on a verbal test.

In other subjects products may similarly constitute an important aspect of achievement. In English—notebooks, compositions, and term papers; in the social studies, such as history, civics, economics, and geography—maps, tables, notebooks, and term papers; in art—drawings and models; in the natural sciences, such as biology, chemistry, and physics—laboratory setups, specimen preparations, models, notebooks, precipitates, and general procedures. In the elementary grades, handwriting is a kind of achievement that must be evaluated as a product.

We are therefore ready to take up the seventh of the questions listed at the beginning of Chapter III:

7. *If a nonlanguage product or behavior device is to be used, how should it be constructed?*

CONSTRUCTION OF PRODUCT AND PROCEDURE EVALUATION DEVICES

Products may be evaluated in terms of their component features, or of their overall "general merit" in which features are not considered separately. Devices of the first type are called score cards or check lists. Devices of the second type, which may also be applied to the specific features involved in the first type, are either rating scales or quality scales. When rating scales or quality scales are applied to the specific features of products, the evaluation device becomes a collection of scales, each feature requiring a separate scale. Let us consider the procedure in constructing each of these.

In general, product evaluation devices are a way to systematize and organize judgments concerning the product. Perhaps this point is best clarified by an analogy to short-answer tests. In a short-answer test the pupil's "product" is his set of responses to the test items and this "product" is evaluated by means of the scoring key. The products here considered are, however, far more complex and detailed than responses to short-answer test items. Consequently the evaluation device analogous to the scoring key must be analytical, so as to reduce the single complex product to a series of more simple features analogous to test items. In other words, just as the short-answer test forces the analysis of a complex achievement into a number of simpler, more unitary test item responses, so the product evaluation device must furnish an analysis of complex, multi-featured products into a number of more unitary features. Each feature can then be separately considered and evaluated. The total evaluation of the product is usually the sum of the evaluations of the separate features. The separate features may sometimes be differently weighted.

Furthermore, just as each item in the short-answer test must be scored, usually either right or wrong, so each feature of the product must be given a score, usually, as we shall see, along a multi-valued continuum. So constructing a product evaluation device adds up to (1) analyzing the product into specific features, and (2) providing various levels of quality for scoring each feature.

ANALYSIS OF THE PRODUCT INTO SPECIFIC FEATURES

The features into which a product is analyzed should first possess relevance to the *instructional objectives* at which the training in making the product is aimed. Here again, evaluation must proceed in close touch with instructional objectives. Products should not be evaluated in terms of features that are irrelevant to the skills and abilities which the product has been designed to require of pupils. For example, a product should not be evaluated on the basis of the feature "neatness" unless neatness has been an objective of instruction.

A second consideration determining the features into which a product should be analyzed is *amenability to reliable evaluation*. Only such features should be considered as are sufficiently explicit, definite, and unambiguous that competent judges will tend to agree in their evaluations of them. This point is illustrated by the results of attempts to construct rating scales for personality traits. Judges agree well on such traits as quickness, efficiency, perseverance, scholarship, and leadership, but they agree poorly on such traits as tactfulness, unselfishness, courage, and integrity. Obviously, for products whose features can be evaluated by physical measurements, as with rulers or thermometers, there will be greater amenability to evaluation in the sense of greater agreement among judges than there will be for subjective features like "decorative value," grace, or general merit. But before we regard a feature of a product as too intangible for evaluation, we should realize that many such features can be made scorable by means of techniques such as the quality scale, to be discussed below. Furthermore, the analysis into features must not concentrate on easily scorable properties at the expense of more intangible properties that may provide a more important approach to the objectives of instruction. Relevance must not be sacrificed to reliability.

The features into which the product is analyzed should be *grouped* on some basis that will increase the efficiency and meaningfulness of the judgment. The features may be arranged in the order in which the product is examined, or the arrangement may be in terms of general and specific features. Newkirk and Greene (12 : 151–152) recommend that the features be grouped according to the method of judgment to be used. Their examples of analyses of industrial arts products grouped according to method of judgment are as follows:

Woodwork	*Drawing*
Inspection	Inspection
Utility	Neatness
Design	Placement
Proportion	Arrowheads
Finish	

Woodwork (cont'd.)	*Drawing (cont'd.)*
Physical Measurement	Physical Measurement
Squareness	Circle
Dimensions	Accuracy
	Dimensions
Rating Scale or Inspection	Rating Scale or Inspection
Nailing	Lettering
Screw joints	Lines
Glue joints	Numbering
Wood filing	
Sawed edges	
Plane edges	
Sanding	

Another method of arranging the features, especially valuable when the product evaluation device is used also for instructional purposes, is in the order in which they emerge during the development of the product itself. Some features are best judged before the product is completed because they may be obscured or altered by subsequent operations or parts of the product.

The analysis of a product into features should also, if possible, provide a *weighting* of each of the features according to its importance as a determiner of the total merit of the product. The total of the weightings may equal some such figure as 100, with each of the component features contributing a proportion or percentage of this total in accordance with its importance.

But before proceeding, we should note how the analyzing process is parallel to our discussion of instructional objectives in Chapter II, and the table of test specifications in Chapter IV. Evaluation must depend on the purposes or objectives of the endeavor being evaluated.

Provision for Scoring Specific Features of a Product

The problem of scoring specific features breaks down into two related problems: (1) the number of points or values it is possible for the feature to have, and (2) the description and definition of the various points along the scale on which the feature is scored. The simplest solution for both of these problems is twofold scoring, such as "present or absent," "good or bad." This converts the product evaluation device into a simple check list, each of the features being checked according to whether it is present or absent in the product. The total score for the product is the total number of desirable features it possesses, as represented by the number of check marks. Although this method has the advantage of simplicity, most features are not completely present or absent but rather are present in degrees varying between these two extremes. Twofold scoring may lead to considerable loss of refinement, accuracy, and reliability in the evaluation.

Hence we often present several levels of quality of the feature under consideration. The number of levels or steps or scale units or alternatives presented for each feature depends on the fineness of discrimination possible and desirable for that feature. Features that can be objectively measured, such as accuracy of dimensions, may be evaluated on a large number of levels of quality, whereas more subjective features, such as neatness or legibility, will necessarily be evaluated on fewer levels. In general, the more levels or the finer the discrimination possible, the more reliable will be the resulting evaluation or measurement. Consequently the number of levels presented should be as large as practical discrimination permits, so as to maximize reliability. With human personality traits it has been suggested (13 : 79) that the reliability of rating reaches its maximum when about seven levels of discrimination are presented for each trait; more than seven yield no increase in reliability and less than seven lead to an appreciable sacrifice of reliability. If the various levels are defined by means of scaling techniques which assign scores to various products chosen to illustrate different levels of quality, more levels may be used. The Thorndike Handwriting Scale presents fifteen samples of handwriting, each sample defining some point along the range from poorest to best in "general merit."

How should the various levels for each feature be presented? In twofold scoring, this question is answered by simply defining the two levels as "present or absent" or "good or bad." For three or more levels an intermediate term may be inserted: "excellent, average, poor." Each of these terms may be given a numerical value such as 3, 2, 1.

A modification is to furnish a *graphic scale* in the form of a

straight line whose ends and intermediate points are properly labeled, as follows:

Very poor	Average	Very good
1	2	3

In making his rating the judge places a check mark on this line
at the point which, to his mind, represents the merit of the feature.
This mark is then given a score proportional to the distance from
the "poor" end of the line, say the number of "half-inches" from
that end.

Instead of *general* descriptive adjectives like "good" and "poor,"
the points along the graphic scale or the levels of quality may be
defined in *specific* terms. The Minnesota Score Card for Meat
Roast presents the levels for different features in this way.

FOOD SCORE CARDS
(Adapted from Clara M. Brown and others)
Meat Roast

		1	2	3	Score
APPEARANCE	1.	Shriveled		Plump and slightly moist	1. ....
COLOR	2.	Pale or burned		Well browned	2. ....
MOISTURE CONTENT	3.	Dry		Juicy	3. ....
TENDERNESS	4.	Tough		Easily cut or pierced with fork	4. ....
TASTE AND FLAVOR	5.	Flat or too highly seasoned		Well seasoned	5. ....
	6.	Raw, tasteless, or burned		Flavor developed	6. ....

APPLYING THE PSYCHOPHYSICAL METHODS

Some products must be frequently evaluated and will be produced in many different classes over a period of years. Such products occur in teaching handwriting, woodworking, qualitative
analysis, and art. For these it may be worth while to apply one of

the psychophysical methods: *paired comparisons, rank order,* or *equal-appearing intervals.* Each of these provides a means of defining the levels of quality for specific features of a product in such a way that rather accurate psychological values for quality, or merit, may be assigned.

Each of these methods has most frequently been applied in scaling the general merit of various products taken *as a whole,* or in scaling *single* features of various stimuli. They require so much work that applying them to more than one feature of a product, or to the scaling of all the features into which a product has been analyzed, is usually impracticable. Although we discuss these methods here at a logical point in our treatment of the methods by which the various levels of different features may be defined, these methods will probably be more useful in constructing general quality or merit scales, or scales of affective (emotionally toned) values, in which a product or stimulus is considered from one general point of view.

1. *The method of paired comparisons* requires that each product be judged in turn as better or worse, with respect to the feature under consideration, than every other product in the group. The number of comparisons to be made increases rapidly as the number of products, n, increases, because it is equal to $\frac{n(n-1)}{2}$. For example, if there are 30 pupil products, the number of comparisons by this method is $\frac{30 \times 29}{2}$, or 435. The large number of comparisons required makes it wearying for the judges who do the comparing. For this reason it is desirable to reduce to a minimum the number of pairs of products which must be compared. This can be done in two ways. (a) Select from all the products in the class a limited number to become the standard for the scale. These should be chosen at what seem to be equal intervals along the scale and the quality of their features should be as unambiguous as possible. The method of paired comparisons may then be applied to these standard values which are fewer in number than if all the products of a given class were used. (b) Establish the approximate rank order of all the products (either by the method of equal-appearing intervals or any other method) and

then obtain paired comparisons only between neighboring pairs or with a limited number of neighbors on either side of each product.

Several methods of treating the proportion of preferences for each product so as to obtain scale values have been proposed. We shall refer here to only the simplest one, proposed by Guilford (6 : 236–238). For details on the procedure of deriving scale values by this method we refer the reader to Guilford's volume.

The use of these scale values is straightforward. Any product being evaluated is compared or matched with the products whose scale values have been determined. The product being evaluated is given the scale value of the product it most resembles.

How many judges should be used in determining scale values? This depends on the accuracy of the judges, the amenability to accurate judgment of whatever is being evaluated, and the degree of accuracy needed. Generally, the more judges the more reliable the scale values. For most educational scaling jobs, somewhere between 20 and 100 judges should be enough. They should be teachers and pupils who can understand what the judging task requires of them.

2. *The method of rank order* requires that the products be ranked in serial order according to the evaluator's judgment of their merit. The mean rank for each product is computed for all the judges. (The mean is the sum of the ranks given by all the judges divided by the number of judges.) These mean rankings give merely the final rank order representing the pooled judgments of a number of evaluators; they cannot be considered scale values unless the products are about evenly scattered over the continuum of quality for the specific feature, with no piling up or grouping at any place. When the products are not so distributed but rather tend to pile up around the middle of the range of values so that more are average in merit and fewer are at the extreme good or the extreme bad end of the continuum, the average rank cannot stand for units on a scale. Guilford (6 : 250–251) has presented a relatively simple method of deriving scale values from pooled judgments of rank order.

With the scale values thus derived, a number of products may be chosen to represent equal steps along the continuum of quality.

This scale is also used by matching the product to be evaluated with the various products whose scale values have been derived.

3. *The method of equal-appearing intervals* requires the group of judges to sort the products into a set of categories, usually nine or eleven in number, defined so that the difference in apparent quality of the product with respect to the given feature is the same from one to the next. Then the number of times each product occurs in each category for all judges is determined and the median score for that product is obtained. (The median is the point below which lie half the cases.) At the same time there is obtained a measure of the spread of the categories into which each product was placed; usually in terms of the quartile deviation. (The quartile deviation is half the difference between the product score below which 75 percent of the judgments fell and the product score below which 25 percent of the judgments fell.) The scale value for each product is the median category into which it was placed by the judges. But if a high quartile deviation is found for a product, it is rejected as a definer of a scale value because this means that the judges were not able to agree well with one another on what scale value that product deserved.

This method requires that a large number of products and many raters be used in the first sorting of products, since some products will be rejected as having too wide a dispersion over the scale, and a large number of judges is necessary to make the results reliable. Also the preliminary samples used should cover the entire range of quality from very poor to very good. A large number of sample products of widely varying quality used in the preliminary sorting afford much greater room for the selection of the most unambiguously scaled products at evenly spaced intervals. Thurstone (17) has used this method in the construction of attitude scales so that the distance between one statement of an attitude and the others may be readily determined and a person's attitude defined as the average of the scale values of the statements he endorses. Similarly, Hollingworth (7) classified jokes into ten categories as to degree of humor by this method and found the procedure quicker, less monotonous, and less fatiguing than the ranking method.

Comparison of the Three Methods. This discussion has provided only an introduction to these methods; for a more extended discussion the reader is referred to Guilford (6). They require so much work that they can be profitably applied only to products and procedures that need to be evaluated again and again.

The ranking method is probably easiest to apply but is not suitable when many products must be scaled. The paired comparisons technique is perhaps most accurate but also most laborious. The rating, or equal-appearing intervals, technique may incorporate the best combination of applicability, validity, and practicability. While not so accurate or valid under many circumstances, it sometimes provides the only practicable technique.

SPECIFIC PRODUCT EVALUATION DEVICES

The reader will understand the preceding discussion better if he becomes familiar with some of the rating scales, score cards, check lists, and quality scales developed in various fields. Let us begin with handwriting scales, since these come first both historically and on the educational ladder. Then we shall discuss, in order, the evaluation of drawings; food products and food preparation procedures; clothing; industrial arts; laboratory, shop, and agricultural products and procedures. The ideas and principles used in these illustrations can be applied to whatever kinds of products or procedures especially interest the reader.

HANDWRITING

Thorndike's handwriting scale, developed in 1910, provided the first scientifically derived "means of measuring the quality of a sample of handwriting." The condition he tried to improve is described as follows (15 : 1):

At present we can do no better than estimate a handwriting as very bad, bad, good, very good, or extremely good, knowing only vaguely what we mean thereby, running the risk of shifting our standards with time, and only by chance meaning the same by a word as some other student means by it. We are in the condition in which students of temperature were before the discovery of the thermometer or any other scale for measuring temperature beyond the very hot, hot, warm, lukewarm, and the like of subjective opinion.

Thorndike used two methods in constructing his Scale for Quality of Handwritings of Children in Grades 5 to 8: the method of equal-appearing intervals, checked by the method of paired comparisons. The two methods did not give results that agreed exactly. He assigned to his samples of handwriting the values 7, 8, 9, 10, 11, 12, 13, 14, 15, 16, and 17; the sample value 14 is as much better than 13 as 13 is than 12 as 12 is than 11, etc. Several samples were furnished for some levels of quality, the samples being of equal merit but in different styles. The scale is used by putting the specimen of handwriting to be evaluated alongside the scale and determining what point in the scale it is closest to. Thorndike was confident concerning the increase in reliability made possible by the scale: "Observers will disagree in their measurements made with the scale but not nearly so much as in measurements made without it" (15 : 44).

The Ayres Handwriting Scale (4 : 46–57) substituted "legibility" for Thorndike's "general merit" as the criterion of quality, on the grounds that legibility is both more functional and more objectively scorable, as the time required for reading, than general merit. He secured 1578 preliminary samples of handwriting by asking pupils to write a list of words thrown out of context so as to require every word to be read. These samples were then read by ten competent paid assistants who recorded, by means of a stop watch, the exact time it took to read each sample. The average time required by the ten readers for each sample was computed, and the rate in words per minute by dividing the average time by the number of words in the sample. To counteract increases in reading speed due to practice the first 75 papers were reread at the end of the 1578 samples, and new times were recorded. The samples were then classified into five types of style: vertical, medium slant, extreme slant, backhand, and mixed.

The scale values of the samples were obtained by arranging them in order of legibility, or speed with which read, and picking out those which fell at tenths of the whole series. That is, the sample below which 20 percent of the samples fell was given the scale value 20, that below which 30 percent fell was scaled at 30, and so on. The rates of reading of the eight samples thus chosen were 131.2, 149.4, 163.5, 175.7, 186.1, 195.8, 202.9, and 209.6 words per

MEASURING SCALE

20	50
Four score and seven years ago our fathers brought forth upon this continenta new nation, conceived in liberty, and dedicat-	*Four scores and seven years ago our fathers brought forth upon this continent a new nation, conceived in liberty, and dedicated to the*

"This scale for measuring the quality of handwriting is a revised edition of a scale first published in 1912 and subsequently reprinted 12 times with several minor revisions and with a total of 62,000 copies. The purpose of the changes introduced in the present edition is to increase the reliability of measurements of handwriting through standardizing methods of securing and scoring samples, and through making numerous improvements in the scale itself designed to reduce variability in the results secured through its use. The present scale may be referred to as the 'Gettysburg Edition' in order to distinguish it from other editions. The original or 'Three Slant Edition' and the scale for adult handwriting are not superseded by the present scale.

minute, respectively. It is apparent that the differences in time rate become progressively smaller in proceeding from the worst to the best sample, as would be expected from realizing that the gain in legibility grows smaller and smaller as handwriting improves. The scale, illustrated on this and the preceding page, is used in the same way as the Thorndike Scale.

Freeman (5) developed a Chart for Diagnosing Faults in Handwriting which enabled the scoring of a specimen of handwriting on five features: uniformity of slant, uniformity of alignment, quality of line, letter formation, and spacing. For each of these features a three-step product scale is provided.

FREEHAND DRAWING

To Thorndike (16) also belongs credit for the first product scale for drawing. He constructed it by securing rankings of fifteen children's drawings, already selected for suitability, from 376 raters: 60 artists listed in *Who's Who in America*, 80 supervisors of art

FOR HANDWRITING

60	90
Four score and seven years ago our fathers brought for theupon this continent a new nation, conceived in liberty, and dedicated to the proposition that all	*Fourscore and seven years ago our fathers brought forth upon this continent a new nation; conceived in liberty*

"*To secure samples of handwriting* the teacher should write on the board the first three sentences of Lincoln's Gettysburg Address and have the pupils read and copy until familiar with it. They should then copy it, beginning at a given signal and writing for precisely two minutes. They should write in ink on ruled paper. . . .

"*To score samples* slide each specimen along the scale until a writing of the same quality is found. The number at the top of the scale above this shows the value of the writing being measured. Disregard differences in style, but try to find on the scale the *quality* corresponding with that of the sample being scored. . . ."

(These portions of the Ayres Scale are reproduced by permission of the Russell Sage Foundation, the publisher of the scale.)

teaching, and 236 students of education and psychology. The difference in merit between any two drawings was taken as the percentage of judges who judged each drawing superior to the other. If 94.85 percent judged B superior to A, and 84.5 percent judged C superior to B, the B — A difference is greater than the C — B difference. While the exact relationship between "units of difference" and percentages of preferences is not known, Thorndike decided to call the difference judged similarly by 75 percent of the judges (and otherwise by 25 percent) equal to 1.00. A difference one-tenth as great, or 0.10, would be judged similarly by 52.69 percent, two-tenths as great by 55.36 percent, etc. Likewise, given percentages of similar judgments or preferences, the units of difference may be obtained. The necessary figures are given in Table 4.

After the unit differences between successive pairs of products, i.e., $a - b$, $b - c$, $c - d$, etc., are obtained, the differences are successively added to the lowest product, which is considered as zero.

The successive sums are the scale values of the respective products. It should be apparent that Thorndike here used a technique for combining order-of-merit judgments.

This method yielded Thorndike's Scale for the Merit of Drawings by Pupils 8 to 15 Years Old. It contained thirteen drawings

TABLE 4.   The Amounts of Difference $(x - y)$ Corresponding to Given Percentages of Judgments That $x > y$. $\%r$ = the Percentage of Judgments That $x > y$. $\triangle/P.E. = x - y$, in Multiples of the Difference Such That $\%r$ Is 75

$\%r$	$\triangle/P.E.$	$\%r$	$\triangle/P.E.$	$\%r$	$\triangle/P.E.$	$\%r$	$\triangle/P.E.$	$\%r$	$\triangle/P.E.$
50	.000	60	.376	70	.778	80	1.246	90	1.900
51	.037	61	.414	71	.821	81	1.300	91	1.987
52	.074	62	.453	72	.865	82	1.355	92	2.083
53	.112	63	.492	73	.909	83	1.412	93	2.188
54	.149	64	.532	74	.954	84	1.472	94	2.305
55	.186	65	.571	75	1.000	85	1.536	95	2.439
56	.224	66	.612	76	1.046	86	1.601	96	2.596
57	.262	67	.653	77	1.094	87	1.670	97	2.790
58	.299	68	.694	78	1.143	88	1.742	98	3.045
59	.337	69	.736	79	1.194	89	1.818	99	3.450
								99.5	3.818
								99.75	4.166

whose scale values were, in order, 2.4, 3.9, 5.7, 6.5, 7.8, 8.6, 10.5, 11.8, 12.6, 13.5, 14.4, 16.0, and 17.0. It should be remembered that the unit of these scale values is the difference between products whose direction 75 percent of the judges agreed in perceiving.

Another drawing scale is that by Kline and Carey (10). This scale differs from Thorndike's in presenting four scaled series of drawings, each on a separate subject: house, rabbit, tree, and boy running. In this way the authors tried to overcome the disadvantage of Thorndike's scale, which, in dealing with a variety of subjects, makes it difficult to determine the exact value of any drawing by comparing it with a standard on its own subject. Also the range of applicability of the Kline-Carey scale is greater, extending from the primary kindergarten group to the high-school senior level.

To secure finer discrimination for the primary kindergarten group and to have the advantage of several subjects for the drawings at each level of quality, McCarty (11) constructed another drawing scale. Three subjects were selected in accordance with evidence of children's major drawing interests: persons, house, and trees. The pictures were to be judged not for their artistic feeling or aesthetic merit, but rather for their accuracy, clarity, and vividness in *representation*.

The 1070 or more drawings on each of the three subjects were sorted and sifted three times, and each time the drawings found too variable in rating or unnecessary for representation of their scale value were eliminated. The first sorting was done by the method of equal-appearing intervals; the second and third sortings were made by Thorndike's process with the rank-order method. By the third sorting the number of drawings on each subject had been reduced to thirty-four. After the third rating by many judges, the three scales for drawings of human beings, houses, and trees contained 16, 16, and 12 drawings, respectively.

Tiebout (18), requiring a drawing scale emphasizing aesthetic qualities rather than representation, constructed another device. Finer discrimination than that possible with the Kline-Carey scale was also desired, so that separate scales were constructed for each of the grades from one through seven. Also colors were used in the paintings, unlike other scales. As the result of a preliminary sorting of 2227 paintings by five experts, thirty were chosen for each grade so as to represent, in the judges' opinions, five degrees of artistic quality. Small groups—fourteen to seventeen—of highly qualified judges rated these thirty paintings by arranging them in each grade in five ranks of artistic merit, giving due consideration to the attainment of rhythm, balance, unity, and other aesthetically significant qualities. The method of equal-appearing intervals was then applied and nine-step scales for each grade were derived. The reliability of the judgments of the paintings was found, in several ways, to be above .90.

Some evidence concerning the advantages of drawing scales has been obtained by Brooks (2). He found that the use of either the Thorndike or the Kline-Carey scale decreased the inaccuracy of ratings to approximately one-half of what it was when no scale was used. Furthermore, the Thorndike scale yielded more stable results than the Kline-Carey.

FOOD PRODUCTS AND PROCEDURES

In this field the score card, check list, and rating scale have been used more than quality scales.

In the Check List for Student Performance in Dining-Room Waitress Service shown below, each feature is described verbally, but the levels for all features of performance are presented in one general form.

CHECK LIST FOR STUDENT PERFORMANCE IN DINING-ROOM WAITRESS SERVICE

*(Adaptation of form developed at Rochester Athenaeum and Mechanics Institute, Rochester, New York)

Directions for rating: In the blank in front of each item write the number which represents the level you think describes the person's performance.

Key

1—Usually below minimum standard acceptable in institution dining room

2—Occasionally falls below minimum standard

3—Meets minimum standard, acceptable to patrons lacking in discrimination

4—Meets maximum standard, acceptable to patrons desiring high-grade service

Personal Appearance and Neatness

.... 1. Uniforms clean and well pressed
.... 2. Hair clean, tidy, held in place with net or band
.... 3. Shoes—low heels; clean; heels straight
.... 4. Hose—no holes or runs; seams straight
.... 5. Body—no odor
.... 6. Cosmetics becomingly applied and used in moderation
.... 7. Posture erect but not tense
.... 8. Hands and fingernails clean and well manicured
.... 9. Hands washed after using handkerchief, arranging hair, or visiting lavatory

Preparation Before Guests Arrive

.... 10. Temperature, ventilation, and light in room satisfactory
.... 11. Tables correctly and suitably set

Table Service

.... 12. Loading of trays in kitchen done quickly and without inconveniencing others
.... 13. Food service correct and rapid

.... 14. Needs of guests recognized and cared for

.... 15. Loading of trays with soiled dishes done quickly and quietly

Dismantling Table After Guests Leave

.... 16. Returned food properly cared for

.... 17. Soiled and wet linen properly cared for

.... 18. Dining and serving tables cleared and in order

Salesmanship

.... 19. Helpfulness

.... 20. Courtesy

.... 21. Diplomacy in meeting complaints and unusual situations

CLOTHING

For clothing evaluation both quality scales and check lists have been developed. Murdoch in 1919 developed the first product evaluation device in any field of home economics. Her Sewing Scale is described by Brown (**3** : 443–444).

Other clothing evaluation devices are the Murdoch Analytic Sewing Scale for Measuring Separate Stitches, the Stiebling-Worcester Chart for Diagnosing Defects in Buttonholes, the Winn Analytic Sewing Scale, the Hickey Checklist for Fitted Facings on Garments, and the Score Card for Judging Garments of 4-H Clothing Project I. All of these are discussed by Brown (**3**).

INDUSTRIAL ARTS

Newkirk and Greene (**12**) have presented a Rating Scale for Mechanical Drawings which contains an analysis into 45 features, each of which is verbally defined at one level and is scorable at ten levels. A suggestion concerning the use of quality scales for judging such features as lettering figures and lines is included in the Directions for Use. These authors also discuss in detail the construction of quality scales by the order-of-merit method.

For an extensive and thoughtful treatment of techniques for evaluation in industrial arts, the reader should consult the book by Micheels and Karnes (see Suggested Readings).

LABORATORY PRODUCTS AND PROCEDURES

The check list technique was applied to products and procedures in the laboratory sciences by Tyler (**19** : 37–41) in determining the nature of students' difficulties in using a microscope. Students having difficulty are selected from among others in a large class by first administering a group test to the entire class seated at microscope tables in the laboratory. The students are required to find an object under the microscope within three minutes; by quickly passing from microscope to microscope, the instructor can note those who are unable to pass this preliminary test. The class is retested several days later. Students who fail both tests are given the following individual test.

One student at a time is called into a special room by the instructor. Here a microscope is placed on a table, together with yeast culture, slide covers, cloth, and lens paper. The student is asked to find a yeast cell under the microscope. A record of the time is kept

but instead of writing down his actions [the observer uses] the check list [which] contains all of the actions both desirable and undesirable which have been observed thus far. The observer records the sequence of actions by placing the figure *1* after the description of the student's first action, a figure *2* after his second, and so on. . . . By reading the actions in the order they are numbered one gets a detailed description of the student's procedure in finding an object under the microscope.

An examination of the sample will serve to indicate the usefulness of the test. It is clear that this student is very deficient in microscope skill. He used eleven minutes without finding the cell, whereas the better students find an object in approximately two minutes. He does not adjust mirror or diaphragm, he closes one eye and turns down the coarse adjustment while his eye is at eyepiece—all habits which must be remedied before he can use a microscope skillfully. As would be expected, he has poor light on the object, has a smeared objective, and is unable to find the object. He needs training in each of the specific phases of microscope skill. Hence, this test record gives the instructor an analysis of the student's behavior which permits the selection of the individual students who need training and a determination of the specific phases of training which each student needs.

This illustrates the wide applicability of the check list technique to the evaluation of products and procedures. Any scientific laboratory apparatus and any procedures, such as those used in caring for infants, in baking and preparing meals, can be evaluated with check lists similar in principle to Tyler's. The sequential feature, where steps are numbered in the order in which they are per-

TABLE 5. Check List of Student Reactions in Finding an Object Under the Microscope

STUDENT'S ACTIONS	Sequence of Actions	STUDENT'S ACTIONS (Continued)	Sequence of Actions
a. Takes slide	....1....	ah. Turns up fine adjustment screw a great distance	....
b. Wipes slide with lens paper	....2....	ai. Turns fine adjustment screw a few turns	....
c. Wipes slide with cloth	....	aj. Removes slide from stage	...16...
d. Wipes slide with finger	....	ak. Wipes objective with lens paper	....
e. Moves bottle of culture along the table	....	al. Wipes objective with cloth	....
f. Places drop or two of culture on slide	....3....	am. Wipes objective with finger	...17...
g. Adds more culture	....	an. Wipes eyepiece with lens paper	....
h. Adds few drops of water	....	ao. Wipes eyepiece with cloth	....
i. Hunts for cover glasses	....4....	ap. Wipes eyepiece with finger	...18...
j. Wipes cover glass with lens paper	....5....	aq. Makes another mount	....
k. Wipes cover with cloth	....	ar. Takes another microscope	....
l. Wipes cover with finger	....	as. Finds object	....
m. Adjusts cover with finger	....	at. Pauses for an interval	....
n. Wipes off surplus fluid	....	au. Asks, "What do you want me to do?"	....
o. Places slide on stage	....6....	av. Asks whether to use high power	....
p. Looks through eyepiece with right eye	....	aw. Says, "I'm satisfied"	....
q. Looks through eyepiece with left eye	....7....	ax. Says that the mount is all right for his eye	....
r. Turns to objective of lowest power	....9....	ay. Says he cannot do it	..19, 24..
s. Turns to low-power objective	...21...	az. Told to start new mount	....
t. Turns to high-power objective	....	aaa. Directed to find object under low power	...20...
u. Holds one eye closed	....8....	aab. Directed to find object under high power	....
v. Looks for light	....		
w. Adjusts concave mirror	....		
x. Adjusts plane mirror	....		
y. Adjusts diaphragm	....		
z. Does not touch diaphragm	...10...		
aa. With eye at eyepiece turns down coarse adjustment	...11...		
ab. Breaks cover glass	...12...		
ac. Breaks slide	....		
ad. With eye away from eyepiece turns down coarse adjustment	....		
ae. Turns up coarse adjustment a great distance	..13, 22..		
af. With eye at eyepiece turns down fine adjustment a great distance	..14, 23..		
ag. With eye away from eyepiece turns down fine adjustment a great distance	...15...		

NOTICEABLE CHARACTERISTICS OF STUDENT'S BEHAVIOR

a. Awkward in movements	....
b. Obviously dexterous in movements	....
c. Slow and deliberate	...√...
d. Very rapid	....
e. Fingers tremble	....
f. Obviously perturbed	....
g. Obviously angry	....
h. Does not take work seriously	....
i. Unable to work without specific directions	...√...
j. Obviously satisfied with his unsuccessful efforts	...√...

SKILLS IN WHICH STUDENT NEEDS FURTHER TRAINING	Sequence of Actions	CHARACTERIZATION OF THE STUDENT'S MOUNT	Sequence of Actions
a. In cleaning objective	...√...	a. Poor light	...√...
b. In cleaning eyepiece	...√...	b. Poor focus	....
c. In focusing low power	...√...	c. Excellent mount	....
d. In focusing high power	...√...	d. Good mount	....
e. In adjusting mirror	...√...	e. Fair mount	....
f. In using diaphragm	...√...	f. Poor mount	....
g. In keeping both eyes open	...√...	g. Very poor mount	....
h. In protecting slide and objective from breaking by careless focusing	...√...	h. Nothing in view but a thread in his eyepiece	....
		i. Something on objective	....
		j. Smeared lens	...√...
		k. Unable to find object	...√...

formed, is especially useful in observing procedures. The technique can be further refined by using rating scales for the quality of each feature of a product or step in a procedure. When numbering for sequence, the number could be placed at a point along a scale of quality or excellence.

Shop

A highly flexible technique for evaluating shop procedures and products is illustrated in the following.[1]

Each student observes several shop situations or "setups" in succession, reads one or more questions related to each situation, and records the number of his choice of answer on a form like that shown below.

MACHINE SHOP TEST

Name ....   Class period ....

Instructions

You will be assigned a position to start this test at a place in the shop where there is a question typed on a 5 x 8 card, and also several possible answers. Pick out the answer that you think is correct, and note the *number* in front of that answer. Write *this number* in the answer space below, *after* the correct question number. Be sure that the first answer you write is after the correct number. Then the others will follow in order.

You will be given two minutes to answer each question. At the sound of the bell, change to the question with the next higher number, with the exception that from question number "20" you will go to question number "1." Do not go ahead. Do not talk. You may figure on the back of this sheet, but do not write on the question card.

If a question pertains to a setup on a machine, DO NOT CHANGE ANYTHING ON THE SETUP UNLESS THE QUESTION CARD TELLS YOU TO DO SO. Otherwise you may make it impossible for the next student to answer that question.

1.	7.	14. ....
2.	8.	15. ....
3.	9.	16. ....
4.	10.	17. ....
5.	11.	18. ....
6.	12.	19. ....
	13.	

[1] For this illustration we are indebted to Emil W. Ross.

20. Write your answer below. You may continue writing on the other side if necessary, but be very brief.

[*Sample questions:* The following questions illustrate either different methods of phrasing questions, or different types of situations appropriate to this particular form of test. For actual use, each of these questions and its alternative answers are typed on a separate card. Note that any one of the starred responses could be made the desired response. Comments on each question are included after the question.]

1. Which one of the following is a correct statement?
   *(1) The hacksaw blade is in the frame backwards.
   *(2) A finer toothed blade should be used on this job.
   *(3) The piece protrudes too far from the vise.
   (4) One should saw on the other side of the vise.

[The required setup consists of a hacksaw, a vise holding a piece of work, and a saw cut started.]

2. Which one of the following statements tells what is wrong with this shaper setup? You may engage the clutch.
   *(1) The stroke is too long.
   *(2) The stroke position is wrong.
   (3) Paper should not have been left under the work.
   *(4) The vise is turned wrong.

["What is wrong" can apply to a great many shop situations.]

.   .   .   .

4. Which one of the following measurements is nearest the diameter of this piece? Use the micrometers provided.
   *(1) 1.091"
   *(2) 1.116"
   *(3) 1.191"
   *(4) 1.216"

[These are easily confused micrometer readings. The question form is equally well adapted to other methods of measurement.]

5. Which one of the following statements explains why this lathe tool bit cut rough?
   (1) The feed is too high.
   (2) The speed is too fast.
   (3) The work is too loose between centers.
   *(4) The cutting edge is too high.

[The cause of faulty work requires careful observation. The setup should show the actual operation partly finished.]

6. Which one of these drills is made of "high-speed steel," as determined by a grinding wheel spark test? You are to touch the

drill points to the grinding wheel, but do not grind away drill material unnecessarily.

(1)
(2)
(3)   }Observe the number on the tag tied to the selected drill
(4)

[This is a simple performance check that can be adapted to many other situations.]

7. [A piece being turned in a lathe is smaller at the tailstock end than in the middle.] To correct this situation before the next cut the operator should:

*(1) Move the tailstock toward the rear.
(2) Move the tailstock toward the front.
(3) Clamp the tailstock tighter.
(4) Back the cross slide out as the cut progresses.

[Several shop situations require such reasoning. The situation is probably presented in more valid form in this way than in words or pictures.]

20. Rules are necessary either to prolong the life of equipment or to improve the appearance of a shop. Name five things wrong on this lathe, according to the rules of this particular shop.

[Such a question requires more space and so is last on the answer form.]

It is obvious that the situational items can be devised either as products or as features of a process in making a more complex product. Such items can be adapted realistically to any laboratory work in which various phases of an ongoing process can be identified and scored.

AGRICULTURE

A final example is a procedure for evaluating ability in setting out trees and shrubs (1).

Provide the following material at the approximate location at which the tree is to be planted: one hardwood tree about 10 feet high, one pick, one spade, one shovel, one "tamper," 300 lbs. of well-rotted barnyard manure, 3 guy wires, 3 stakes, 2 yards of burlap, one pair of hand pruning shears.

Direct the student to set out the tree with the use of one or more members of the class as assistants where help is needed. Check and record the time from the start until all operations are completed.

Using the accompanying form for recording observations of procedure, observe his actions and check the quality of each action as, for example, good, fair, poor, in Column A. In Column B, write the time when the action was completed. In Column C, trace his actions by placing a figure 1 after his first action, a figure 2 after his second action, and so on, in the order of performance of the different operations.

Skills

Student's Actions	A Quality	B Time	C Sequence
1. Locates according to plan..........			
2. Lays out diameter of hole to fit root system of tree....................			
3. Loosens soil with pick (if necessary)...			
11. Places tree so roots lie normally......			
12. Holds tree erect.................			
13. Places top soil in hole with shovel.....			
20. Removes broken and diseased limbs...			
21. Makes smooth, clean cuts..........			
22. Prunes to balance the tree..........			

After the tree has been planted, ask questions that will give the student an opportunity to explain why he performed certain actions as he did and why the operations performed followed the particular sequence. For example, "I noticed you tamped the top soil and manure mixture in the bottom of the hole. Why?" From an examination of your notations, make a list of actions and other aspects of the student's behavior that you think he could improve and record these items and suggested remedies in the space provided for "Comments." Also record any improvising which seemed to reflect understanding on the part of the student.

It should be noted that such instruments as paper forms, and outlines of procedures such as check lists, rating scales, and the like are no guarantee of relevant and reliable measurement and evaluation. In a very real sense the judge or rater is the instrument and the paper form merely a convenient and systematically organized aid. Hence the important task is to train the judge or observer.

SUGGESTED READINGS

Adkins, Dorothy, *et al., Construction and Analysis of Achievement Tests.* Chapter 5, "Special Problems in the Development of Performance Tests," pp. 211–265.

    Although concerned primarily with Civil Service examinations, this treatment provides many excellent illustrations and ideas that could be applied to the evaluation of products and procedures in schools.

Brownell, W. A. (chairman), "The Measurement of Understanding," *Forty-fifth Yearbook of the National Society for the Study of Education,* Chicago: University of Chicago Press, 1946, Part I. Chapters 10 (Fine Arts), 11 (Health Education), 12 (Physical Education), 13 (Home Economics), 14 (Agriculture), 15 (Technical Education), and 16 (Industrial Arts).

    Each of these chapters includes illustrations of product and procedure evaluation devices.

Micheels, W. J., and Karnes, M. R., *Measuring Educational Achievement,* New York: McGraw-Hill Book Company, Inc., 1950. Chapters 11 (Object Tests), 12 (Manipulative-Performance Tests), 13 (Observation and Evaluation), and 14 (Evaluating Major Projects).

    Draws illustrations primarily from wood- and metal-working, but the detailed presentation and discussion of these may provide many suggestions for other fields.

Ryans, D. G., and Frederiksen, N. "Performance tests of educational achievement," in Lindquist, E. F. (ed.), *Educational Measurement,* Washington: American Council on Education, 1951, Chapter 12.

    In addition to many ingenious and stimulating illustrations, this chapter contains a discussion of the problems of selecting the particular tasks, features, or procedures to be included in simulated and work-sample tests.

REFERENCES

1. Aderhold, A. C., and Ekstrom, G. F., "A suggested technique for constructing tests in vocational agriculture," *Agricultural Education Magazine,* 10:136–137 (1938).
2. Brooks, F. D., "The relative accuracy of ratings assigned with and without the use of drawing scales," *School and Society,* 27:518–520 (1928).
3. Brown, Clara M., *Evaluation and Investigation in Home Economics,* New York: Appleton-Century-Crofts, 1941.

4. Chapman, J. C., and Rush, Grace P., *The Scientific Measurement of Classroom Products,* New York: Silver, Burdett & Company, 1917.
5. Freeman, F. N., *The Teaching of Handwriting,* Boston: Houghton Mifflin Company, 1914.
6. Guilford, J. P., *Psychometric Methods,* New York: McGraw-Hill Book Company, Inc., 1936.
7. Hollingworth, H. L., "Judgment of the comic," *Psychological Review,* 18:132–156 (1911).
8. Hudelson, E., "English composition: its aims, methods, and measurement," *Twenty-second Yearbook of the National Society for the Study of Education,* Bloomington: Public School Publishing Company, 1923, Part I.
9. Hudelson, E., "The effect of objective standards upon composition teachers' judgments," *Journal of Educational Research,* 12:329–340 (1925).
10. Kline, L. W., and Carey, G. L., "A measuring scale for free-hand drawing," *Johns Hopkins Studies in Education,* No. 5, Part I, 1922; Part II, 1933.
11. McCarty, Stella A., *Children's Drawings,* Baltimore: The Williams & Wilkins Company, 1924.
12. Newkirk, L. V., and Greene, H. A., *Tests and Measurements in Industrial Education,* New York: John Wiley & Sons, Inc., 1935.
13. Symonds, P. M., *Diagnosing Personality and Conduct,* New York: Appleton-Century-Crofts, 1931.
14. Theisen, W. W., "Improving teachers' estimates of composition specimens with the aid of the Trabue Nassau County Scale," *School and Society,* 7:143–150 (1918).
15. Thorndike, E. L., "Handwriting," *Teachers College Record,* 11:1–93 (1910).
16. Thorndike, E. L., "The measurement of achievement in drawing," *Teachers College Record,* 14:1–38 (1913).
17. Thurstone, L. L., "Attitudes can be measured," *American Journal of Sociology,* 33:529–554 (1928).
18. Tiebout, Carolyn, "The measurement of quality in children's painting by the scale method," *Psychological Monographs,* 48:85–94 (1936).
19. Tyler, R. W., "A test of skill in using a microscope," *Constructing Achievement Tests,* Columbus: Ohio State University, 1934.
20. Van Wagenen, M. J., "The Minnesota English Composition Scales; their derivation and validity," *Educational Administration and Supervision,* 7:481–499 (1921).

CHAPTER VII

Essay Testing

ABSTRACT

Essay tests are best used to evaluate such kinds of achievement as writing ability and ability to assimilate, organize, and evaluate subject matter. Constructing valid essay tests may be helped by awareness of the variety of forms into which essay questions can be put. Lists of types of essay questions provide illustrations. Methods of grading essay tests include the percentage-passing, the quality scale, the sorting or rating, the check-list point-score, and the "projective interpretation" methods. The check-list point-score method makes possible highly reliable grading. It depends for its best results on rigorous training of the test graders. Further aids to grading essay tests are grading anonymously, considering single questions at a time, double grading, and considering the mechanical aspects of a pupil's answers separately.

•~•~•~•

In the preceding chapter we discussed the pupil product as an evaluation device. In the construction and scoring of essay tests the same general principles apply that were presented for product evaluation devices. The essay test is given separate treatment, however, because of its distinctive position in the thinking and practice of evaluation workers.

The discussion of the relative merits of essay and short-answer tests in Chapter III came to the conclusion that for certain purposes essay tests are to be preferred. Let us briefly review these purposes and situations. In the first place, such courses as English composition and journalism have as one of their main objectives the ability to write essays which essay tests can elicit directly.

Knowledge of sentence structure, punctuation, and spelling is an essential tool in essay writing and can be evaluated by short-answer tests, but only the essay test can provide sufficient indication of the ability to express oneself in an organized fashion (9 : 514–516). The essay test must always be used for this purpose.

Similarly, the ability to assimilate, organize, and evaluate complex bodies of subject matter is usually an important objective. This is, of course, especially true in the social studies. Whatever short-answer devices may be used to get at objectives similar to these, they must always fail to elicit certain mental processes involved in writing answers to essay or "thought" questions. It is true that many essay questions have been such that short-answer testing would have been more suitable for the purpose. But at its best, the essay or "thought" question calls out behaviors that are difficult or impossible to get at by other means and yet may be extremely important objectives. Furthermore, as we have seen, the essay test may be superior for motivating pupils to recall material in an organized fashion, to know facts when cues are not given, and to learn to write organized prose.

Sims (5) has pointed out certain unique values of essay testing in getting at the "structure, dynamics and functioning of the student's mental life as it has been modified by a particular set of learning experiences." The student projects his personality into his answers on certain essay tests; he has freedom of choice and makes a complex response which the tester can interpret in terms of its pattern as well as its separate features. The hidden as well as the manifest content of the answer is useful in understanding the pupil's learning processes and achievement. Especially for diagnosing individuals, as against grading or ranking them, do projective essay tests have value. And not only maximum performance or abilities, but also typical behaviors or habits, including attitudes and values, can be revealed by the essay examination.

Stalnaker has indicated (9 : 496) that such "projective" values of essay tests may be difficult to achieve. Students may not respond sincerely, and interpretations of responses as "projections" may not be dependable and valid for estimating achievement of many kinds of educational objectives.

At any rate, the first step in improving the essay test is to appreciate when it should and should not be used. It should not be used when the short-answer test will require similar mental processes and yet be far superior in objectivity of scoring. Recall of information, interpretation of data, and application of principles can usually be better evaluated with short-answer tests.

CONSTRUCTION OF ESSAY TESTS

At this point we can take up the last of the questions listed at the beginning of Chapter III:

8. *If an essay test is to be used, how should it be constructed?*

Once we have decided to restrict the use of the essay test to the type of evalution for which it is best suited, we are faced with the task of defining achievement in terms of mental processes—ways in which subject matter may be handled. The operation of a mental process assumes the presence of some material or subject matter to be processed or handled by the pupil. To find out whether he has the knowledge or "raw material" it is usually sufficient to use the short-answer type of test. This does not mean that short-answer or "objective" tests must be restricted to the testing of factual information but rather that they are better suited for this purpose than the essay test. The essay test has long been used in a confused way for the simultaneous testing of both factual information and the ability to handle or process this information in various ways. This failure to restrict essay testing to the purposes for which it is best suited has resulted in lost efficiency, time, and effort, and also in lower validity of evaluation.

One reason for failure to use the essay test only where it is suitable is the unfamiliarity of teachers with the short-answer forms of test items. Another is that teachers have not been sufficiently aware of the variety of types of essay question and of the need for framing questions so as to require the mental processes which constitute instructional objectives. The latter reason may be largely eliminated if teachers become familiar with types of question like those presented by Monroe and Carter (2) in 1923. These authors listed twenty types of "thought" questions. Although this list cannot claim to be exhaustive or composed of mutually exclusive items or based on experimental research, it should prove suggestive to teachers who wish to realize the full potentialities of the essay question. We must remember that the question does not alone determine the mental processes required or elicited; the way in which the subject matter has been taught and the methods of study used by the student also make a difference. The same question may require "thought" from one student, memory from a second, and other mental processes from a third. The thought question for a given student today may be a memory question for the same student tomorrow.

Following is the list of types of thought questions made by Monroe and Carter, together with illustrations of each type drawn whenever possible from these authors:

1. Selective recall—basis given.
   Name the Presidents of the United States who had been in military life before their election.
   What do New Zealand and Australia sell in Europe that may interfere with our market?
2. Evaluating recall—basis given.
   Which do you consider the three most important American inventions in the nineteenth century from the standpoint of expansion and growth of transportation?
   Name the three statesmen who have had the greatest influence on economic legislation in the United States.
3. Comparison of two things—on a single designated basis.
   Compare Eliot and Thackeray in ability in character delineation.
   Compare the armies of the North and South in the Civil War as to leadership.
4. Comparison of two things—in general.
   Compare the early settlers of the Massachusetts colony with those of the Virginia colony.
   Contrast the life of Silas Marner in Raveloe with his life in Lantern Yard.
5. Decision—for or against.
   Whom do you admire more, Washington or Lincoln?
   In which in your opinion can you do better, oral or written examinations?
6. Causes or effects.
   Why has the Senate become a much more powerful body than the House of Representatives?

What caused Silas Marner to change from what he was in Lantern Yard to what he was in Raveloe?

7. Explanation of the use or exact meaning of some phrase or statement in a passage.

Tell how a siphon works.

What did Hamlet mean by "be" when he said "To be or not to be, that is the question"?

8. Summary of some unit of the text or of some article read.

State the plot of *The House of Seven Gables* in about one hundred words.

Tell briefly the contents of the Declaration of Independence.

9. Analysis. (The word itself is seldom involved in the question.)

What characteristic of Silas Marner makes you understand why Raveloe people were suspicious of him?

Mention several qualities of leadership.

10. Statement of relationship.

Why is a knowledge of botany helpful in studying agriculture?

Tell the relation of exercise to good health.

11. Illustration or examples (your own) of principles in science, construction in language, etc.

Give two examples of the use of pure carbon in industrial work.

Illustrate the *in*correct use of a relative pronoun with a parenthetical phrase.

12. Classification. (Usually the converse of number 11.)

Group the following words according to their part of speech and name each group: red, boy, run, house, in, with, small, slowly, ball, etc.

What do four of the five men named below have in common? How do they differ historically?

Aristotle, Pericles, Homer, Cicero, Phidias.

13. Application of rules or principles in these situations.

Would you weigh more or less on the moon? On the sun? Why?

If you sat halfway between the middle and one end of a seesaw, would a person sitting on the other end have to be heavier or lighter than you in order to make the seesaw balance in the middle? Why?

14. Discussion.

Discuss the Monroe Doctrine.

Discuss early American literature.

15. Statement of aim—author's purpose in his selection or organization of material.

What was the purpose of introducing this incident?

Why did he discuss this before that?

16. Criticism—as to the adequacy, correctness, or relevancy of a printed statement or a classmate's answer to a question on the lesson.

Why were the Articles of Confederation doomed to failure?

What is wrong with the following menu? (Menu given below.)

17. Outline.

Outline the foreign policy of the federal government during the Civil War.

Outline the steps required in computing the square root of a five-figure number.

18. Reorganization of facts. (A good type of review question to give training in organization.)

The student is asked for reports where facts from different organizations are arranged on an entirely new basis.

19. Formulation of new questions—problems and questions raised.

What question came to your mind?

What else must be known in order to understand the matter under consideration?

20. New methods of procedure.

Suggest a plan for proving the truth or falsity of some hypothesis.

How would you change the plot in order to produce a certain different effect?

It should be clear that some of these types, such as numbers 1, 2, 11, 12, and 19, can be formulated in short-answer form, such as completion or simple-recall items.

Weidemann (10) has attempted to refine still further the analysis of written essay questions into a series of definable types. He suggested eleven new essay-type questions proceeding from simple to complex, and for examination purposes only, as follows:

1. what	2. list	7. explain
who	3. outline	8. discuss
when	4. describe	9. develop
which	5. contrast	10. summarize
where	6. compare	11. evaluate

For each of these a standard definition was proposed according to which teachers were to ask pupils to pattern their responses and by which the answers were to be graded. For example, a pupil's response to a "contrast" question should consist of a list of items of fact identifying dissimilarities between two concepts. In response to a "compare" question the response should consist of two lists of items of fact concerning two concepts, one of the lists identifying similarities, and the other dissimilarities. In response to an "explain" question the response should be a list of items of fact, with each fact supported by a reason. In response to a "discuss" question the response should consist of a multiple type of the "explain" essay in the form of three lists: (1) a list of affirmative arguments with reasons supporting them; (2) a list of negative arguments with reasons supporting each argument; and (3) a list of arguments refuting each negative argument and giving reasons supporting each argument.

If pupils are instructed to pattern their responses along these lines, we may get consistency in each pupil's understanding of what he is required to do by a certain question and in the way the teacher can grade pupils' responses to that question. The first two types listed by Weidemann are, of course, similar to recall tests that may be arranged in short-answer form so as to increase objectivity of scoring.

The care that can be taken in the preparation of essay tests is well illustrated by the work of the College Entrance Examination Board, particularly with its English examination (3). The examination is aimed at the student's power to think through and to organize the materials contained in the books he has read, to read poetry and prose intelligently at sight, and to express his ideas in an effective way. A conscious effort is made to define as accurately as possible the instructional objectives at which each question is aimed. All the candidates are asked "to run the same race" by having them write on a single essay topic rather than select one that supposedly provides the most "inspiration." Each question is pretested before it is used by giving it to a group of students similar to those who will eventually take the English examination. This allows the examiners to find out how their questions are most likely to be misunderstood, assists in the selection of material, such as passages of prose or poetry, that will produce the best results, and enables an estimate of the time that should be allotted to each question.

A further control for essay questions that will serve to define more closely what is required of the pupils is to limit the amount of writing to a maximum number of words. This gives the pupil some indication of how expansive his response should be, how general or specific.

Sims (5), in using the essay test as a projective technique, would abandon all these devices that tell the student what to do in answering a question. It is exactly these limits on behavior, says Sims, that must be removed if we are to realize the possibilities of essay testing in getting to understand the student's abilities, difficulties, and ways of thinking as a basis for guiding his learning. Hence essay questions should allow a free and extended response. Instead of "Discuss the Articles of Confederation with respect to their origin, their working out in practice, and their relationship to the present federal constitution," Sims' question would read simply: "Discuss the Articles of Confederation." He argues further that essay questions should set up novel problems, at some reasonable intellectual distance from the original learning situation (see our discussion of the measurement of understanding in Chapter IV). The student should be encouraged to choose and defend his own interpretation of the question, his way of answering—in short, his frame of reference. Finally, reliability should be obtained not through many simple responses but through a few, but representative, deep and complex responses.

We may now summarize the suggestions for improving the construction of essay questions.

1. Use essay questions to evaluate achievement of only those instructional objectives not as well or better tested by the short-answer forms.

2. Phrase the questions so as to require as precisely as possible the specific mental processes operating on specific subject matter that are embodied in the instructional objective at which the questions are aimed.

3. Unless the essay test is to be used as a projective technique, as Sims has elaborated it, phrase the questions so as to give as many hints concerning the organization of the pupil's answers as are not inconsistent with the instructional objective at which the questions are aimed. Pupils should not be asked merely to discuss a specific

topic but should also be given the basis of discussion. Hints concerning organization of answers should not be given, of course, if part of the objective at which the question is aimed is the pupil's ability to distinguish the relevant bases for his discussion. Such assistance to the pupil really operates to increase the number of questions or subquestions in an essay examination and to reduce the length of the answer to each. As such, the more specific the essay question becomes, the more similar it becomes to short-answer test items. Carried to an extreme, this technique would rob the essay question of its unique value in testing the pupil's ability to organize and express his answers. Each teacher must therefore maintain some balance between generality and specificity in essay questions. We can attempt to elicit as much organizational effort from the pupils as possible while giving them a common set of reference points so that their answers will be comparable.

4. Permit no choice among questions. Only by requiring all pupils to answer all questions can their achievement be compared. It is almost impossible to equate optional questions for difficulty without an elaborate pretesting program. The teacher who permits pupils to choose among optional questions can never know whether all of them have taken a test of equal difficulty (7). Nor can pupils be relied upon to choose essay questions from a series of options that will enable them to exhibit their achievement in the best possible light. Some pupils may think that by choosing more difficult questions they will receive greater leniency and more credit from the teacher, but others in the same classroom will not reason in this way. Meyer (1) found that pupils' rankings of the quality of their responses to essay questions agreed poorly with the rankings given by the teachers grading these responses. If pupils had been allowed to choose only the questions they thought they could answer best, they would not always have chosen the ones which subsequent grading showed they could answer best.

5. Balance the questions in difficulty so that the pupil can actually write adequate answers to all of them within the allotted time if he possesses the required achievement. Furthermore, the questions should be arranged in order of difficulty for the same reasons as were mentioned in connection with the short-answer test form.

GRADING THE ESSAY TEST

In general, five different methods have been used or suggested for grading essay questions: (1) the percentage-passing method, (2) the quality scale, (3) the sorting or rating method, (4) the check-list point-score method, and (5) projective interpretation.

PERCENTAGE PASSING

The percentage-passing method involves giving each question a definite value and marking every answer to that question on the scale of 100. Some arbitrary percentage, such as 60 or 70, is commonly chosen as the "barely passing" grade. "Barely passing" is usually vaguely defined in such terms as "showing minimum ability to do work at this grade level." This system of grading is still in vogue in many school systems for report-card grades. Its major disadvantage is that the standard of "passing" varies widely from teacher to teacher. Also, it permits such a wide range of scores—from zero to 100—that it gives a spurious notion of the fineness of discrimination between qualities of answers that it is possible for teachers to make. Furthermore, it is usually unaccompanied by any system of analysis of answers into specific features so that a definite and unambiguous criterion of excellence of response is usually unavailable. The shortcomings of this method have been shown by the many studies of the reliability of grading essay questions, for this is the method usually used in these studies. The wide fluctuation in grades given a single paper by different teachers, which these studies have shown, may be expected in most of the cases where the method is used.

QUALITY SCALES

The method of quality scales has been studied by Odell (4). To nine of the twenty types of thought questions listed by Monroe and Carter, Odell secured over 23,000 pupils' answers in essay tests in physics, general science, American history, and English literature. On the basis of a preliminary rating of the answers, one question in each of the nine types in each of the four subjects was chosen. Eleven answers to each of these thirty-six questions were selected, which, according to the average judgment of several raters, most nearly deserved ratings of 0, 1, 2, and so on up to 10. Criticisms of these answers were prepared. For each question the set of eleven answers and the accompanying criticisms formed a quality scale. Both with and without these scales, over 23,000 pupil answers to questions similar to but not identical with those in the scale, and also over 5000 answers to some of the questions in the scale, were then rated. Reliability coefficients were computed for two ratings without the scale and two ratings with the scale. On the whole, the reliability of ratings given with the scale was not found to be significantly higher than of those given without the scale. So this elaborate attempt to increase the reliability of grading essay questions by using quality scales was largely a failure. But these results should not be considered conclusive because the raters had not made the rather careful study of the scales, in addition to acquiring practice in employing them, which Hudelson found necessary in improving the rating of English compositions with quality scales. Similarly, greater success has been obtained with English composition scales because the values of the specimens included in them have been derived more precisely than was true of those in Odell's scale.

SORTING OR RATING

The sorting or rating method has been used by Sims (6). His procedure involved the following steps:

a. On the basis of a quick reading, sort the papers into five groups labeled very superior, superior, average, inferior, very inferior. (The proportion of papers in each group if the papers were "normally distributed" would be 10 percent, 20 percent, 40 percent, 20 percent, 10 percent, but no attempt should be made to conform rigidly to these proportions.)

b. Reread the papers in each group and shift any that this second reading indicates have been misplaced.

c. Give no numerical grades or separate evaluations of individual questions; group each paper according to general total merit.

d. Assign the same letter grades to the papers in each group, A for very superior, B for superior, etc.

This procedure is, of course, preceded by the rater's working out, with the use of the textbook and other materials on which the examination is based, a set of acceptable answers to the essay questions. It may be objected that this method sacrifices refinement of grading in cases where more than five levels of general merit can be distinguished in pupil's answers. Considerable diagnostic value may also be sacrificed by disregarding separate questions and considering merely the general merit of the examination paper as a whole. Teachers may have difficulty in placing papers that have one distinctly superior answer along with a distinctly inferior one. In such a case, the "general merit" of the paper would be highly ambiguous, telling little of the pupil's specific achievement. Of course, the rating method may be used with separate questions, the pile of papers being sorted for one question and resorted for the next. Here again, however, rating according to general merit can easily become a vague procedure, subjective and without any helpful quantitative basis.

CHECK-LIST POINT-SCORE

The check-list point-score method involves analyzing the ideal response to the essay question into a series of features or points, each specifically defined. The pupil's answer is then judged with respect to each feature and a point is awarded if the feature is present in the response. This method is well illustrated by the procedure of the readers of the English examination of the College Entrance Examination Board (3). Each of the readers is rigorously trained and retrained during the week of examination grading in the following procedure:

Each question is graded on a series of points suggested by the terms and the purpose of the question itself, and determined by a careful analysis of the answers written by the students. Each reader will deal, at most, with only a third of any answer book, and he will grade it according to standards which he himself has helped to define and establish. He is trained to analyze each answer to discover the presence or absence of certain qualities, or elements. The new analytical method of grading has proved especially valuable in dealing with the essay question. As all English teachers know, marking themes is a ticklish business. Many elements have to be considered: the student's organization of his material; technical points of composition such as spelling and punctuation; sentence and paragraph structure; the right or wrong use of words, and so forth. Our present system, by giving definite and predetermined values to each of these elements, makes it possible for all the readers to use approximately the same yardstick, and hence has contributed immensely to the increase in reliability of reading. Last year, for example, the maximum grade for the essay question was eleven points. Four were awarded for accuracy in writing, or technique of composition. Three were given for organization in paragraph structure, and four for varying knowledge and skill in the use of books required by the topic.

An illustration of this method is the way in which the Board graded the following item on the interpretation of sight passages:

A metaphor is a transfer of meaning, one thing or act being named or implied when another is meant. It is the commonest and most serviceable figure in language. . . . There is at least one metaphor in each of the following passages. Indicate the metaphors in each passage and translate them in such a way as to show your understanding of the author's use of them. Allow about twenty-five minutes for this question. The model below is intended to suggest the kind of an answer expected. [Model omitted.]
  1. "Poverty is the banana skin on the doorstep of romance." *P. G. Wodehouse.*

The pupil's answers to questions in this series were to be marked on a maximum of five points:
    Adequate comprehension of the passage as a whole, 1 point
    Explicit indication of the principal metaphors (banana skin and doorstep), 1 point
    Adequate translation of these terms, 1 point
    More than a merely adequate understanding of the passage, i.e., recognition of Wodehouse's humorous purpose, 1 point
    Composition—To all answers not incoherent or marred by serious grammatical errors, 1 point
For example, the following response would receive credit for only the fifth point: "In this sentence Wodehouse means the banana skin to be an aid rather than a hindrance to romance. By this Wodehouse shows that a person does not stop to think about falling in love merely because of poverty." The pupil failed to comprehend the meaning of the passage, indicated only one of the meta-

phors, mistranslated that one, and loses the fourth point for not having more than a merely adequate comprehension. He receives the fifth point because his answer is reasonably grammatical and has no misspellings, and the sentences are properly punctuated.

The following answer receives credit for all points except the second: "Wodehouse is humorously saying that poverty is the danger that romance faces at its beginning." The student gained the first point because he clearly understood the passage, lost the second for failure to indicate the metaphors explicitly, and won the third for translating both metaphors, the fourth for recognizing the humorous purpose, and the fifth for composition.

The reliability of grades obtained with this method of scoring has been shown by Stalnaker (8) to be very high, ranging above .90 for all College Entrance Board examinations except English, for which the reliability of reading was .84. It must be emphasized that such excellent results can be obtained only when the persons who grade the essay test papers have undergone a careful training or self-training program.

In grading according to this system the teacher must work out a rigorous analysis of the things desired in the pupil's response to a question in the definite and explicit forms indicated in the above example. This means that he should write out an answer to the questions that will contain all the ideas desired from pupils. Perhaps another list of ideas which are not to be regarded as acceptable for credit should also be made.

PROJECTIVE INTERPRETATION

In considering essay tests as projective techniques, Sims (5) would handle them as follows:
a. Use an inductive method; only after inspecting the answers should you work out a point of view for interpreting them. (If the right answer can be predetermined, short-answer rather than essay questions should be used.)
b. Distinguish between manifest and hidden content, between the results of the curriculum and the manifestations of general personality, between the answers and the inferences from them. Style, omissions, rationalizations, or attitudes can be as revealing as what is consciously written in a paper.

c. Identify clearly and exactly what is to be looked for and develop an organized and systematic method for observing and inferring from the data. (Presumably this implies techniques like those described for the check-list point-score method.)

d. Read the papers for what they reveal about the learning of individual students rather than for simple counts of objective facts. Clues and suggestions for further work with individual students should usually be obtained.

e. If it is necessary to determine grades, identify the most frequent pattern of response and classify the deviates into categories on one or more continua. If possible, develop check sheets, rating scales, or sets of objective questions for the reader to use in evaluating answers. (Here Sims again seems to have in mind the check-list point-score method.)

f. Avoid overly broad generalizations. Since essay tests are limited samples of behavior, conclusions about personality based on them should be tentative.

Projective techniques for appraising personality (see Chapter XII) require years of scientific effort before they become established as trustworthy. Some of these techniques, such as the Rorschach inkblots, are still arousing heated debate as to their validity after several decades of research. Essay tests can be used as projective techniques in only a figurative sense until they have been similarly systematized and validated. Sims has nonetheless pointed out a basic aspect of essay testing that explains the appeal of such tests to many teachers. Essay tests can give insights into personality and achievement that are available through no other means.

FURTHER AIDS IN GRADING ESSAY TESTS

The following procedures and devices have also been suggested as ways to improve the reliability, or objectivity, of grading essay examination papers:

1. Grade papers anonymously so that the grader does not know whose paper is being graded. Personal factors such as teacher-student relationships can thus be largely eliminated and the paper graded solely on its merit. A teacher's general opinion of a pupil,

his prejudice for or against the pupil, cannot then affect the grade assigned to the paper. Anonymity may be secured by having the pupils write their names either on the back or at the end of the examination paper, or by assigning randomly selected numbers to the pupils in such a way that they are unknown to the teacher, and later having the pupils put their names opposite the list of numbers.

2. Grade only one question at a time. In this way one pupil's answer to a given question is more easily compared with all the other answers to the same question. This procedure requires the teacher to keep only one list of points in mind at a time; he does not have to waste time in continually refreshing his memory concerning the points required in successive questions.

3. Use multiple grading wherever possible, especially with important examinations that determine promotion, graduation, and so on. Multiple grading means simply having more than one person grade a paper. The graders should, of course, have the same standards and consider the same points in grading. Such agreement between graders, and equal competency of graders, are difficult to secure without additional time and effort. Whenever two graders disagree sharply with each other, the papers should preferably be read by a third grader rather than arbitrated by the two original graders; in the latter situation the grade may be determined by the opinion of the grader with the more aggressive and dominant personality.

4. Make special provision for considering sentence structure, paragraphing, writing ability, spelling, and so forth. Should these factors be permitted to affect the student's score on an essay question which is primarily concerned with other instructional objectives? It will, of course, require a conscious effort on the part of the teacher to prevent himself from being influenced adversely by poor spelling and grammar, or, on the other hand, favorably prejudiced by neat handwriting, extensive vocabulary, and fine prose. While all these factors in pupils' answers to essay questions, with the probable exception of quality of handwriting, may in the long run be found to be correlated with pupils' achievement of other objectives, they are, strictly speaking, often irrelevant to the

specific kinds of achievement at which the essay test is aimed. In any case, the teacher should consciously make a decision on this question.

REFERENCES

1. Meyer, G., "The choice of questions in essay examinations," *Journal of Educational Psychology*, 30:161–171 (1939).
2. Monroe, W. S., and Carter, R. E., *The Use of Different Types of Thought Questions in Secondary Schools and Their Relative Difficulty for Students*, Bureau of Educational Research, Bulletin No. 14, College of Education, University of Illinois, 1923.
3. Noyes, E. S., "Recent trends of the comprehensive examination in English," *Educational Record, Supplement No. 13*, 21:107–119 (1940).
4. Odell, C. W., *The Use of Scales for Rating Pupils' Answers to Thought Questions*, Bureau of Educational Research, Bulletin No. 46, University of Illinois, 1929.
5. Sims, V. M., "The essay examination is a projective technique," *Educational and Psychological Measurement*, 8:15–31 (1948).
6. Sims, V. M., "The objectivity, reliability, and validity of an essay examination graded by rating," *Journal of Educational Research*, 24:216–223 (1931).
7. Stalnaker, J. M., "A study of optional questions on examinations," *School and Society*, 49:829–832 (1936).
8. Stalnaker, J. M., "Essay examinations reliably read," *School and Society*, 46:671–672 (1937).
9. Stalnaker, J. M., "The essay type of examination," in Lindquist, E. F. (ed.), *Educational Measurement*, Washington: American Council on Education, 1951, Chapter 13.
10. Weidemann, C. C., "Review of essay examination studies," *Journal of Higher Education*, 12:41–44 (1941).

PART TWO

Abilities

The Nature of Mental Abilities

A B S T R A C T

Conceptions of intelligence, although not yet agreed upon, center around higher mental processes rather than sensory discriminations. Binet, Spearman, Thorndike, Stoddard, and others have given verbal formulations, but tests are the operational definitions of the concept. Theories of the organization of intelligence differ as to the degree of specificity or generality of intelligence; current theory and research (especially factor analysis) reject thoroughgoing specificity and agree that there are general and group factors. The nature-nurture controversy is still unsettled, but the practical implication remains that intelligence tests should be interpreted in the light of the individual's background, environment, and training. Educational-vocational differences in intelligence have implications for guidance and for practical understanding of the concept of intelligence. Special abilities may be considered from the standpoint of both primary factors and educational or vocational "aptitudes." Vocational information belongs in any realistic analysis of special abilities.

·~·~·~·

What do we mean by "the mental abilities of pupils"? Scientific psychology has not been able to find any real agreement within itself on the answer to this question. That is, the nature of mental ability, although a very practical matter, is still largely unclear. This statement, however, is not as pessimistic as it may sound. A similar statement can be made concerning basic physical concepts such as electricity and magnetism, despite our obvious mastery of these concepts for practical purposes. The practical importance of intelligence is so great that, in the fields of measurement and of educational policy based on pupil intelligence, practice has left theory far behind. Psychologists and teachers have been measuring intelligence for practical purposes for more than a generation despite the controversy that still goes on as to the question of the nature and the determiners of mental ability.

Acquaintance with the terms in which the discussion concerning intelligence has been carried on will be helpful in understanding what is meant by the mental abilities of pupils. Let us consider the concept of intelligence under the following interrelated headings:

1. General definitions of intelligence
2. The organization of intelligence
3. The relative influence of "environment" and "heredity" on intelligence
4. Educational-vocational differences in mental ability
5. Special mental abilities of pupils

GENERAL DEFINITIONS

Definitions of intelligence have been offered throughout the history of philosophy. But we are concerned only with the meaning of the term in the field of psychology and education during the past half century. During the period from 1880 to around 1900 the definition of intelligence was reflected in the attempts to approach it through human sensorimotor processes. It was assumed that sensory discrimination provided the key to the determination of intelligence. The attempts proceeded on the following assumption, as stated by Francis Galton (8 : 27): "The only information that reaches us concerning outward events appears to pass through the avenues of our senses; and the more perceptive the senses are of the differences, the larger is the field upon which our judgment and intelligence can act." However, attempts to measure intelligence based on this assumption proved unsuccessful.

Toward the end of this period another point of view, of which Alfred Binet was the leader, focused attention on a concept of intelligence that emphasized the more complex mental activities, such as memory, association, judgment, and attention. In 1905 Binet wrote: "To judge well, to comprehend well, to reason well, these are the essential activities of intelligence" (4). Binet's approach has sometimes been referred to as a "global" approach. The ultimate purpose of intelligence according to Binet was the continuous adjustment of the individual to his environment, accomplished as the result of an organization in which several mental functions (comprehension, invention, direction, and criticism) are involved.

Charles Spearman (14) gave his definition in a statement of a series of "qualitative" and "quantitative" principles (referred to by him as the noegenetic laws). The expression of intelligence according to him consists of three "laws" and all their possible combinations:

1. The apprehension of one's own experience, or the degree of a person's possession of the power to observe what goes on in his own mind. A person cannot only feel, he must also know what he feels; he cannot only strive, he must also know that he strives; he cannot only know, he must also know that he knows. This is illustrated when a person says, "I like this" or "I am thinking of the past."

2. The eduction of relations, or the degree of a person's power to bring to mind any relations that essentially hold between two or more ideas in his mind. This law is illustrated whenever a person make such statements as "Seven is more than five" or "Sugar is sweeter than salt."

3. The eduction of correlates, or the degree of a person's power to bring into mind the correlative idea (when he has in mind any idea together with a relation). For example, when an individual has in mind the number five and the relationship "two times as great as," he may be able to educe the correlative idea of the number ten.

In 1921 the editors of the *Journal of Educational Psychology* published a symposium (10) on intelligence and its measurement, which produced the following definitions:

Thorndike, "We may define intellect, in general, as the power of good responses from the point of view of truth or fact."

Terman, "Intelligence is the ability to think in terms of abstract ideas."

Pintner, "Intelligence [is] the ability of the individual to adapt himself adequately to relatively new relations in life" implying "ease in breaking old habits and in forming new ones."

Henmon, "Intelligence is capacity for knowledge and knowledge possessed."

Thurstone, "(a) inhibited capacity; (b) analytical capacity; and (c) perseverance."

Woodrow, "Intelligence is the capacity to acquire capacity."

Dearborn, "Intelligence is the capacity to learn or profit by experience."

Haggerty, "Intelligence is a practical concept . . . connoting a group of complex mental processes traditionally defined in systematic psychology as sensation, perception, association, memory, imagination, discrimination, judgment, and reasoning . . . while emotions, instincts, will activities, and so-called character traits are for the most part excluded."

In 1927 Thorndike conceived of intelligence as including "operations such as we may call attention, retention, recall, recognition, selective and rational thinking, abstraction, generalization, organization, inductive and deductive reasoning, together with knowledge and learning in general" (20 : 22). He also distinguished between four different *aspects* of intelligence: (1) altitude or level, which is apparently native and determines the limits of response with respect to difficulty; (2) range, the number of tasks at any given degree of difficulty that we can perform; (3) area, or totality of response, contributed to by both altitude and range; and (4) speed of response.

The most comprehensive attempt to define intelligence has been made by Stoddard (16): "Intelligence is the ability to undertake activities that are characterized by (1) difficulty, (2) complexity, (3) abstractness, (4) economy, (5) adaptiveness to a goal, (6) social value, and (7) the emergence of originals, and to maintain such activities under conditions that demand a concentration of energy and a resistance to emotional forces." Stoddard discusses each of these attributes of intelligent activity at length. His main point is that all these attributes must be present simultaneously; we must not achieve difficulty merely through the rarity of a task, for example. "Difficulty" is measured by percentage passing; "complexity," by number of kinds of tasks; "abstractness," by distance from the physical, explicit, and complete; "economy," by speed of accomplishing mental tasks; "adaptiveness to a goal" and "social value," by the activity's utility for satisfying the individual's and society's needs; the "emergence of originals," by the newness and uniqueness of intellectual products. The more a given activity has *all* of these attributes, the more intelligence it demands. None of the ingredients can be lacking.

This listing of definitions of intelligence may make the reader question the satisfactoriness of abstract definitions. It is this inadequacy of words to define anything so basic and complex as intelligence that has caused many psychologists to resort to the statement that intelligence is whatever the intelligence tests measure. Obviously, however, this is merely begging the question. But the full meaning of any concept of intelligence for practical purposes emerges only when we do something about it, as when we perform *operations* to measure intelligence. As is usual in science, it is here a case of interaction between the conceptual end and the practical means. A fuller understanding will come when we take up the question, how to measure intelligence, in Chapter IX.

THE ORGANIZATION OF INTELLIGENCE

The main theories concerning the organization of intelligence may be described in terms of degrees of specificity. Thorndike has humorously designated the three major theories as the "sand" theory, the "gravel" theory, and the "cobblestone" theory. In accordance with this classification, Thorndike's hypothesis concerning the organization of intellect is a "sand" theory (20). Defining intellect as the ability to succeed with certain tests and measuring it by taking a fair sampling of the tests that require intellectual power, he notes the customary sharp distinction between two levels of intellect: one involving mere connection-forming, the association of ideas, the acquisition of information, and specialized habits of thinking; and the other, the second or higher level, characterized by abstraction, generalization, the perception and use of relations, the selection and control of habits in inference or reasoning, and ability to manage novel or original tasks. Only surface intelligence can be divided into these two levels, however. The deeper nature of intellect requires a different formulation. Thorndike's hypothe-

sis holds that quality of intellect depends on quantity of connections. Connections are the physiological mechanisms whereby a
nerve stimulus is conducted to and excites action in specific nerve
cells, muscles, and glands. Differences in the number of connections or bonds of the associative type are sufficient to account for
both quantitative and qualitative differences in degree of intellect.
No special qualitative differences in mental organization are required.

The "gravel" theory of intelligence posits a relatively small number of distinct mental abilities, thought of as being relatively independent of each other, rather than the large number of un-
grouped connections conceived by Thorndike. These distinct
mental abilities, few in number, were called "faculties" earlier in
the history of psychology. As this theory has developed out of the
statistical work of such men as T. L. Kelley and L. L. Thurstone,
they are called primary abilities, or functional unities. Using the
method of factorial analysis of the intercorrelations among many
tests, Thurstone (22) has arrived at the following list of primary
mental abilities: number facilities; word fluencies; visualizing;
memory of words, names, and numbers; perceptual speed; induction; and verbal reasoning. That is, Thorndike's large number of
mental abilities or "atoms" or connections are grouped by these
theories into a much smaller number of primary abilities.

The third or "cobblestone" theory of the organization of mental
ability holds that all abilities may be classified into one of two
types. This two-factor theory, first formulated by Spearman, is also
based on the statistical examination of correlations between various tests. The first factor has been called the "general" factor,
denoted by the letter "g." It is so named because, although varying in amount from individual to individual, it remains the same
for any one individual for all the correlated abilities. It more or
less pervades all the tests in a given set. The second kind of mental
ability is called the "specific" factor, denoted by the letter "s"; it
varies not only from individual to individual, but even for any one
individual from one ability to another. When these specific factors
overlap they are called group factors. But in general, according to
the two-factor theory, any mental task involves a certain amount
of general ability, g, which is common to all other mental tasks,

and a certain amount of specific ability, s, which is involved in no other mental tasks.

The different kinds of factors that can be found by different methods and approaches to factor analysis are shown in Fig. 10.

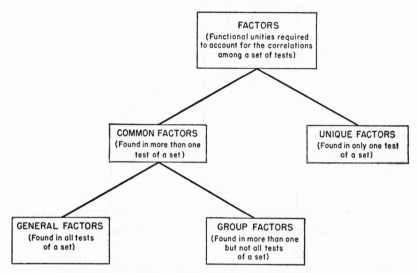

FIG. 10. Diagram Showing Relationships Between Different Types of Factors Found in Factor Analyses of Mental Tests.

Spearman's two-factor theory would call for the existence of only general and unique factors. Later, Spearman revised his position and admitted group factors. Thurstone has used methods which find only group and unique factors; but *since the group factors are themselves often correlated, the general factor again crops up.*

Perhaps the best way to illustrate the problem of factor analysis is by citing the methods and results of one study (23) of this kind. Twenty-one selected mental ability tests of various kinds were given to 437 eighth-grade children. One item from each of these tests is given here to show, better than the name does, what each test measured:

IDENTICAL NUMBERS (1)

The number at the top of each of the columns is repeated one or more times in that column. Find those numbers as quickly as possible and put a mark under each of them. Go right ahead.

634	876	795	423	279	374
693	643	583	837	363	282
850	328	795	115	643	663
634	932	189	423	279	539
513	879	342	528	375	314
398	375	795	969	470	475
696	470	896	274	887	576
634	697	247	423	699	374
574	876	319	627	291	850
628	294	468	423	983	677
634	982	543	962	585	846

The test contained thirty columns of numbers.

FACES (2)

Here is a row of faces. One face is different from the others. The face that is different is marked.

Here are more pictures for you to practice on. In each row mark the face which is different from the others.

The test contains sixty rows of faces.

Mirror Reading (3)

The first word in each column below is printed forward. Below it are four words printed backward. One of the four words printed backward is the same as the word at the top of the column. The word which is the same as the first word is marked.

flag town

The test contains fifty columns of four words.

First Names (4)

In each row below is written a name. You are to learn the names so well that when the last name is given you can write the first name. On the next page the last names are listed in a different order. You will be asked to write the first names.

If writing helps you to remember, you may copy the first and last names on the blanks below. Study silently until you are told to stop. Begin studying now. Do not wait for any signal.

First Name	Last Name	First Name	Last Name
Mary	Brown		
John	Davis		
Ruth	Preston		
Fred	Smith		

In the first row the correct first name has been written. Write the correct first names in the other blanks.

First Name	Last Name
Ruth	Preston
———	Brown
———	Smith
———	Davis

The test consisted in memorizing twenty first names which were to be associated with given surnames.

Figure Recognition (5)

Study the figures below so that you can recognize them when you see them again.

In the list below put a check mark (√) after each of the figures that were listed above.

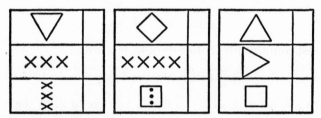

In a similar manner study the list below so that you can check these figures when you see them again on the next page.

In the test proper twenty figures were shown, and these were to be checked in a longer list of sixty figures presented on a separate sheet.

Word-Number Recall (6)

Each object in the list below has a number. The number of *box* is 66, the number of *chair* is 21, and so on. You are to remember the number of each object. On next page, the names of the objects are listed in a different order. You will be asked to write the number of each object.

If writing helps you to remember, you may copy the pairs of words and numbers on the blanks below. Study silently until you are told to stop. Begin studying now. Do not wait for any signal.

Object Number	Object Number	Object Number
box 66	_____	_____
chair 21	_____	_____
fan 92	_____	_____
lamp 77	_____	_____

Do not turn back this page.

In the first row the correct number has been written.
Write the number of each of the other objects. Go right ahead.

Object	Number
chair	*21*
lamp	_____
box	_____
fan	_____

The test proper contains fifteen word-number combinations.

SENTENCES (7)

This test was taken from the Chicago Reading Tests and is a
sentence-completion test.

VOCABULARY (8)

This test was taken from the Chicago Reading Tests and is a
synonyms test.

COMPLETION (9)

The following sentence has a word missing at the place indicated
by the parentheses. You are to think of the word that best completes
the meaning of the sentence. The number in parentheses is the number of letters in the missing word.

A (4) is a contest of speed..........
B═   F═   M═   P═   R━

The test contained sixty definitions.

FIRST LETTERS (10)

Look at the words below. Each word begins with *D*.

doll   dinner   daisy   doughnut

On the blanks below, write several words which begin with *P*. One
word you might write is *pretty*. Go ahead and write more words which
begin with *P*.

The instructions for the test were as follows:

Write as many words as you can which begin with *S*.

Four-Letter Words (11)

Each of the words in the list below has four letters and begins with *B*.

bear   bone   bald   bent

On the blanks below write several four-letter words which begin with *M*.

The instructions for the test were as follows:

Write as many words as you can which have four letters and begin with *C*.

Suffixes (12)

Look at the words in the following list. Each of them ends with *able*.

capable   valuable   comfortable   hospitable

Write in the blanks below several words ending with *ent*. Go ahead.

The instructions for the test were as follows:

Write as many words as you can which end with *tion*.

Flags (13)

Here are two pictures of a flag. These two pictures of the flag are the same. You can slide one picture around to fit exactly on the other picture.

S is marked to show that the pictures are the *same*.

The next two pictures of the flag are different. You cannot slide the pictures around to make them fit exactly.

D is marked to show that the pictures are *different*.

The test contained forty-eight items.

Figures (14)

Some of the figures in the row are like the first figure. Some are made backward. The figures like the first figure are marked.

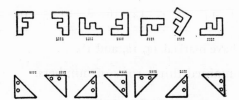

The test proper contained sixty rows of seven figures.

Cards (15)

Below is another row of cards. Mark all the cards which are like the first card in the row, when you slide them around on the page.

The test contained twenty rows of seven figures.

Addition (16)

Below are two columns of numbers which have been added. Add the numbers for yourself to see if the sums are correct.

16	42
38	61
45	83
99	176
R —	R =
W =	W —

The first sum is right, so the R below it is marked. The second sum is wrong, so the W is marked.

The test contained fifty-six colums of six two-place numbers.

Multiplication (17)

Below are two multiplication problems which have been worked out. Multiply the numbers for yourself to see if the products are correct.

$$\begin{array}{r} 64 \\ 7 \\ \hline 448 \end{array} \qquad \begin{array}{r} 39 \\ 4 \\ \hline 166 \end{array}$$

R ▬   R ═
W ═   W ▬

The first answer is right, so the R below it is marked. The second answer is wrong, so the W is marked.

The test contained seventy problems.

THREE-HIGHER (18)

Here is another row of numbers. Mark every number that is exactly 3 more than the number just before it.

4   11   14   10   9   12   16   8   10   3   15   18   9
═   ═   ═   ═   ═   ═   ═   ═   ═   ═   ═   ═   ═

You should have marked 14, 12, and 18.

The test contained thirty rows of numbers.

LETTER SERIES (19)

Read the row of letters below.

a b a b a b a b _____

The next letter in this series would be a. Write the letter *a* in the blank at the right.

Now read the next row of letters and decide what the next letter should be. Write that letter in the blank.

c a d a e a f a _____

You should have written the letter g.

The test contained twenty-five series.

PEDIGREES (20)

Look at this chart.

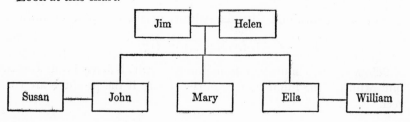

This chart tells you that Jim and Helen were married and had three children, John, Mary, and Ella. John married a girl named Susan, and Ella married a man named William.

Now answer these questions by consulting the chart.

Mary's brother is _____.
How many children did Helen have? _____.
How many brothers-in-law does Harry have? _____.
How many brothers-in-law does Ella have? _____.
Jim's daughter-in-law is _____.
William's mother-in-law is _____.
How many daughters has Jim? _____.
Helen's husband is _____.
Susan married _____.
Ella's sister-in-law is _____.

The test consisted of a more elaborate chart, followed by 22 questions.

LETTER GROUPING (21)

Here is another problem. Three of the groups are alike in some way. Can you find three groups which are alike? Mark the one that is different.

XVRM   ABCD   MNOP   EFGH

The test contained twenty lines.

After the tests were scored, each test was correlated with each of the others. This resulted in the 210 correlation coefficients in Table 6. Each coefficient shows the degree to which pupils tended to have the same relative standing on the two tests correlated. The higher the coefficient, the closer the relationship between the two sets of scores and, consequently, the more the two tests measure the same ability. For only a few tests, say four or five, it might be possible by inspection of the coefficients to determine whether the tests could be clustered meaningfully into groups that had high intercorrelations among themselves and low correlations with tests outside the group. Whatever such a group of tests seemed to have in common could then be the basis for naming the group and denoting it as a special type of mental ability or a group factor, a set of mental functions that operated more or less as a unit.

Table 6. Product-Moment Correlation Coefficients for the Selected Test Battery[a] (23 : 90)

	1	2	3	4	5	6	7	8	9	10	11	12	13	14	15	16	17	18	19	20	21
1		461	430	129	156	129	261	247	204	297	239	231	181	143	221	434	497	369	292	259	348
2			505	209	338	175	297	264	400	256	221	183	416	402	424	339	334	433	378	398	401
3				263	224	209	343	349	332	447	372	350	279	291	298	317	354	347	418	385	460
4					280	478	295	364	282	286	299	311	103	046	061	196	268	261	320	381	285
5						292	151	242	234	243	184	122	227	183	252	121	040	155	290	254	217
6							234	260	251	240	217	236	100	078	166	216	203	140	249	254	192
7								829	768	419	356	407	108	033	108	298	309	351	492	555	425
8									775	472	415	482	115	061	125	323	347	369	468	525	381
9										428	354	433	272	205	238	296	271	385	446	523	396
10											654	557	176	092	127	293	348	319	391	355	398
11												514	192	165	144	261	308	334	367	323	381
12													100	009	066	233	254	293	305	319	303
13														636	626	249	183	369	271	185	279
14															709	138	091	254	180	147	191
15																190	103	291	225	179	245
16																	654	527	399	262	356
17																		541	407	296	394
18																			471	437	429
19																				613	610
20																					496
21																					

[a] Decimals are omitted.

But with 210 coefficients, such an inspectional technique is too confusing and inefficient. The various techniques of factor analysis are therefore used. These techniques are more objective and quantitative than inspection could be. The battery of 21 tests was factor analyzed by Thurstone's centroid method; it resulted in the "rotated factor matrix" shown in Table 7.

TABLE 7.   Rotated Factor Matrix (23 : 91)

Test	P	N	W	V	S	M	R	Residual
1.............	.42	.40	.05	−.02	−.07	−.06	−.06	.08
2.............	.45	.17	−.06	.04	.20	.05	.02	−.12
3.............	.36	.09	.19	−.02	.05	−.01	.09	.12
4.............	−.02	.09	.02	.00	−.05	.53	.10	.02
5.............	.20	−.10	.02	−.02	.10	.31	.07	−.17
6.............	.02	.13	−.03	.00	.01	.58	−.04	.04
7.............	.00	.01	−.03	.66	−.08	−.05	.13	.07
8.............	−.01	.02	.05	.66	−.04	.02	.02	.05
9.............	−.01	.00	−.01	.67	.15	.00	−.01	−.11
10.............	.12	−.03	.63	.03	−.02	.00	−.00	−.08
11.............	−.02	−.05	.61	−.01	.08	−.01	.04	−.05
12.............	.04	.03	.45	.18	−.03	.03	−.08	.10
13.............	−.04	.05	.03	−.01	.68	.00	.01	−.07
14.............	.02	−.06	.01	−.02	.76	−.02	−.02	.07
15.............	.07	−.03	−.03	.03	.72	.02	−.03	.13
16.............	.01	.64	−.02	.01	.05	.01	−.02	−.03
17.............	.01	.67	.01	−.03	−.05	.02	.02	.01
18.............	−.05	.38	−.01	.06	.20	−.05	.16	−.12
19.............	−.03	.03	.03	.02	.00	.02	.53	.02
20.............	.02	−.05	−.03	.22	−.03	.05	.44	−.02
21.............	.06	.06	.13	−.04	.01	−.06	.42	.06

P: perceptual speed   S: space
N: number   M: associative memory
W: word fluency   R (or I): general reason-
V: verbal comprehension   ing (or induction)

This table is read as follows. The entries along the top are the names of the factors. The tests are listed along the left-hand side. Each entry in the body of the table shows the loading of the test with a factor. The higher the loading, the more the scores on the test are weighted with the kind of ability specified by the factor.

Note that each test has high loadings (.40 or higher) on only one or two factors. Also, each factor has high loadings on only a few tests; this is why they are called group factors. The meaning of each factor is best understood from the nature of the tests on which it has the highest loadings. For example, the perceptual speed factor (P) is largely the abilities needed on Tests 1 (Identical Numbers) and 2 (Faces). The reasoning factor (R) is largely the abilities needed on Tests 19 (Letter Series), 20 (Pedigrees), and 21 (Letter Grouping).

This work by the Thurstones shows the purpose and results of factor analysis. It is a way of bringing order out of the chaos of mental testing. It is conceivable that an infinite number of different mental ability tests could be invented. Can this infinite variety be "boiled down" into a manageable, meaningful number of functional unities? Factor analysis is an attempt to do this kind of job.

ORGANIZATION OF ABILITY AS A FUNCTION OF AGE

If there is a *general* factor in mental ability, is it equally important at different ages? If it decreases in importance, this means, as Garrett (9) has stated, that with increasing age (from 8 to 18) there appears to be a gradual breakdown of an amorphous general ability into a group of fairly distinct aptitudes. It would then be even more desirable to measure the intelligence of older pupils through several scores rather than a single index of general intelligence. The evidence on this matter is, however, not yet conclusive; Doppelt (6), for example, found that the general factor tends to maintain rather than lose its importance as age increases from 13 to 17.

THE RELATIVE INFLUENCE OF "ENVIRONMENT" AND "HEREDITY" ON INTELLIGENCE

We may ask why people differ in intelligence. The student will have noticed that in this chapter we have persistently put quotation marks around the words "environment" and "heredity." This was done to indicate that these two concepts are abstractions that in human beings have not been found separable. They are more usefully thought of as representing the extremes of a continuum on which the factors influencing human development may be placed. At one extreme are such traits as eye color and height; at the other such characteristics as the language one speaks and one's taste in clothes. The fact of the matter is that to ask which is more important, environment or heredity, in one sense poses a question impossible to answer. The two are always necessary to produce all the characteristics of a given individual.

In another sense, however, the question of the relative importance of two indispensable kinds of determinants like heredity and environment can be meaningful. This is so if we ask which is more important in producing differences among people. Height is a dimension on which differences among people are due more to differences in heredity than in environment. Attitude toward polygamy is a dimension on which differences are due more to differences in environment (culture) than in heredity. What about intelligence— are differences in it among people due more to differences in their heredity or in their environment? The reader can probably think of many reasons why this question has practical significance.

In Chapter V we provided evidence on various factors that affect test scores. Among these factors, the cultural influences on the individual are especially in point here (7).

The first successful intelligence tester, Alfred Binet, believed that intelligence was something that could be substantially raised or lowered with training (3 : 118): "With practice, ambition, and especially method one can succeed in increasing his attention, memory, and judgment, and in literally becoming more intelligent than before."

On the other hand Terman, the foremost exponent of the Binet method in the English language, placed the emphasis on heredity as the determiner of intelligence: "It would, of course, be going too far to deny all possibility of environmental conditions affecting the result of an intelligence test. Certainly no one would expect that a child reared in a cage and denied all intercourse with other human beings could by any system of mental measurement test up to the level of normal children. There is, however, no reason to believe that ordinary differences in social environment (apart from heredity), differences such as those obtaining among unselected children attending approximately the same general type of school in a civilized community, upset to any great extent the validity of the scale" (18 : 116). Disagreement among psychologists concerning the relative influence of nature and nurture on intelligence has led to many experiments designed to give a more definite answer to the question.

Despite many elaborate experiments and much heated controversy on these questions, no great lessening of the differences in emphasis between the "environmentalists" and the "hereditarians" has resulted. In 1940 the National Society for the Study of Education published a yearbook (12) in two volumes on the influence of nature and nurture on intelligence. The interested reader is referred to these volumes for the most comprehensive treatment of the subject available. The issue is attacked from all points of view by the leading proponents of "hereditarianism" and "environmentalism" but without any appreciable reduction of the differences between them.

How constant is the I.Q.? This question is somewhat related to, but largely distinct from, the nature-nurture issue. If differences in intelligence quotients were due solely to differences in hereditary factors, an individual's I.Q. would not change significantly from one year to the next, because obviously his hereditary factors, or genes, do not change after he is conceived. If differences in I.Q. are due in part to differences in environment, the I.Q. may still remain fairly constant for most people if their environments do not change greatly in ways relevant to the development of intelligence. So the constancy or inconstancy of the I.Q. cannot settle the nature-nurture controversy.

But apart from this, the question of I.Q. constancy is important because it tells much about the predictive value of an I.Q. measurement. When I.Q.'s are obtained on a test and retest basis over an interval of from one month to say ten years, there is a very significant tendency for persons to have the same relative standing. For the average child, subjected to no radical change in the intellectual quality of his environment, the difference between I.Q.'s on test and retest over several months or years will be approximately five I.Q. points. The degree of constancy may also be expressed as a correlation of approximately .80 to .95 between the first and second measurements of I.Q. over several months or years, when representative groups of children are tested.

Since differences of five points in I.Q. are usually not educationally or psychologically significant, this degree of *average* constancy is highly valuable for predictive and guidance purposes. It means not that environmental changes are irrelevant to I.Q. but rather that such changes are relatively rare. For *most* children, the environmental factors that affect intelligence do not change markedly from one year to the next. They stay in the same family, neighborhood, and school, and the stimulating or stultifying effects of these factors on their intellectual growth remain roughly constant.

This also means that *some* individual children *will* vary widely —twenty or even forty points—in I.Q. Since education and guidance are concerned with the individual case, the average constancy described above does not do away with the need for caution in interpreting single I.Q. measures. Most school and guidance workers insist on at least two such measures at different times whenever important decisions concerning an individual child are at stake.

What methods, if any, are known at present by which the course of mental growth can be modified? That is, can modern nursery schools or superior foster homes improve the mental abilities of children? Or will the mental environment be adversely affected? At the State University of Iowa, the conclusions from studies designed to answer these questions have been decidedly in the affirmative. These conclusions have been challenged, however, on statistical, logical, and administrative grounds. We cannot here be concerned with the details of these arguments. Let us rather turn to general conclusions of practical significance to the classroom teacher.

1. The concept of intelligence or mental ability is culturally determined. What is regarded as intelligence varies with time and place. In our culture, spoken and written vocabularies are important. In other cultures, motor ability and skill might perhaps be more useful in distinguishing the able and the less able. Similarly, as it is now measured, intelligence has come to mean, in large part, aptitude for success in school.

2. Neither extreme "environmentalism" nor extreme "hereditarianism" is as correct as the middle point of view. Intelligence tests are neither instruments for measuring pure "native capacity" nor merely improved school achievement tests; whatever they

measure is influenced to a marked degree by experience and training and this influence should not be ignored in interpreting intelligence test scores.

3. Concerning the organization of intelligence, there seems to be a valid basis for believing as follows: (a) General intellectual ability probably is a reality (in the sense of Spearman's g), embracing many ways of thinking but with emphasis on the more general, abstract, and complex ones. (b) Group factors or primary abilities may also be distinguished; rather than being fixed, however, they are probably forms of behavior acquired in response to organized sets of environmental social stimuli.

EDUCATIONAL-VOCATIONAL DIFFERENCES IN MENTAL ABILITY

There are significant differences in the intelligence of students in different high-school curricula. The National Survey of Secondary Education found that in general the highest intelligence is found in the academic curriculum; the next highest, in the commercial courses; and the lowest average intelligence in the industrial arts or vocational curricula (11). Whether or not these differences are due to an unfair loading of the tests with such tasks as favor the abilities and interests of a particular type of student is a matter of indifference, since these significant differences are meaningful for guidance purposes regardless of value judgments concerning them.

Furthermore, there are significant differences in the intelligence of students in different subjects. In foreign languages, high-school and junior-college students had average I.Q.'s of 105 in Spanish, 108 in Latin, 111 in French, and 112 in German. Similarly, the I.Q. is of value in predicting a high-school student's probable success in English, mathematics, science, and average academic achievements. It has least value in estimating success in art, music, and home economics.

Moreover, there seem to be fairly definite intelligence requirements for certain occupations. That is, very few persons with intelligence test scores below a certain minimum have been found who have achieved success in these occupations. Tables showing this relationship between intelligence and a great number of occupations are presented in Bingham's *Aptitudes and Aptitude Testing* (5 : 44–59) and Strang's *Behavior and Background of Students in Colleges and Secondary Schools* (17 : 122–128).

A more recent study shows the results obtained with the Army General Classification Test (15). While this test is not labeled an intelligence test, its content is in general like that of group intelligence tests. Moreover, the correlation between scores on the AGCT and intelligence tests is high.

SPECIAL MENTAL ABILITIES OF PUPILS

Two Ways of Classifying Special Abilities

Our discussion of theories of mental organization mentioned the theories that "break down" intelligence into primary abilities on the basis of *factor analyses* of performances on mental tests. Thurstone, for example, now believes that it is possible to describe each individual by at least seven indices which should replace the intelligence quotient, mental age, and other scores for overall general intelligence. Each individual should be described by a profile of mental ability instead of by a single index of intelligence. Such a profile, composed of the scores in the primary mental abilities, is more helpful in educational and vocational counseling than the single composite intelligence rating that has been in common use for many years (21).

Should we break down general mental ability in such terms as Thurstone proposes or in terms of the more traditional "special aptitudes"? This is a question of practical convenience. In using Thurstone's approach it would be necessary to determine the degree to which various occupations require each of the primary abilities, then the degree to which an individual possesses each of the primary abilities, and finally the individual's fitness for various occupations on the basis of the agreement between his profile and the occupational profiles.

The more traditional approach makes the breakdown first in terms of *fields of endeavor* such as music, art, engineering, and then constructs measuring instruments specifically for the prediction of success in each of these fields. That is, tests designed to aid in vocational guidance have been based on attempted breakdowns of mental abilities into various aptitudes—artistic, musical, verbal, mathematical, legal, nursing, engineering, teaching, clerical, mechanical, and the like.

APTITUDES VS. SPECIAL ABILITIES

What is meant by the term *aptitude* as distinguished from *special ability?* Warren's *Dictionary of Psychology* defines aptitude as a "condition or set of characteristics regarded as symptomatic of an individual's ability to acquire with training some (usually specified) knowledge, skill, or set of responses such as the ability to speak a language, to produce music, etc." More briefly, *aptitudes are present traits considered as predictors of future achievement.* In using the term *aptitudes* we do not imply specifically inherited aptitudes. A good achievement test in algebra is a predictor of future achievement in engineering (i.e., it measures one aspect of engineering aptitude) just as much as pitch discrimination is one aspect of musical ability. Yet achievement in algebra is to a great extent the result of training, whereas ability to discriminate pitch has been found to be relatively little subject to training.

"Present traits" of the individual include not only his abilities but also his interests, adjustments, character, habits, and indeed all his other aspects. Special abilities are present traits that determine the individual's maximum performance of a relatively specific kind of task under the best possible conditions of motivation. In evaluating aptitudes we usually concentrate on the one or more aspects, including special abilities, most valuable for predicting success in a given future activity.

Special abilities are similar to other aspects of individuals in that they are not all equally strong in the same person, and people differ from one another in any single aptitude. Furthermore, like general mental ability, special abilities may be considered relatively stable. It is often far more economical to fit an individual's field of endeavor, either educational or vocational, to his present set of special abilities than to attempt to change them.

ACHIEVEMENT VS. APTITUDE

This does not mean that in evaluating special abilities we must search for aspects of the pupil which have not been influenced by experience and training. Aspects that have been subjected to much training—in other words, the present *achievements* of pupils—should be evaluated insofar as these achievements may be considered predictive of future achievement. What this means is that not merely tests of special abilities that are labeled "aptitude" may rightfully be used for the measurement of aptitudes.

The real distinction between achievements and aptitudes inheres not in what is measured but rather in the purpose for which it is measured—whether the point of view is backward-looking, to evaluate past learning, or forward-looking, whether our concern is with the pupil's past or with his future at any particular moment in our thinking about him. We may consider a pupil's capacity to profit from further training as represented by the ratio of his present achievements to the amount of training he has received to date. Hence his aptitude or capacity may be evaluated whenever it is possible to evaluate present achievement.

TASKS AND OPPORTUNITIES AS DEFINERS OF SPECIAL ABILITIES

The tasks to be done and the opportunities, either in school or in the world of work, are vital to our concern with special abilities or aptitudes. An acquaintance with these various tasks and opportunities, with the abilities and training they demand, with the earnings and satisfactions they return, and with changes in the opportunities to enter these fields are second in importance only to acquaintance with the pupil himself. Concerning opportunities in school, the sources of information are well known to most teachers. Information concerning the world of work has been made available by many books and services, such as those of Baer and Roeber (2) and Shartle (13). The following are also useful:

1. Bingham, W. V., *Aptitudes and Aptitude Testing*, Part 2: "Orientation Within the World of Work." Contains valuable discussions of manual occupations, skilled trades, clerical occupations, and the professions such as engineering, law, medicine, dentistry, nursing, teaching, music and art.

2. *Dictionary of Occupational Titles*, U.S. Employment Service, Department of Labor, 1949 (for sale by the Superintendent of Documents, Washington). Part I: *Definitions of Titles* (1581 pages) includes job definitions prepared by the U.S. Employ-

ment Service for use in employment offices and vocational services; 22,028 separate jobs are defined and 17,995 alternate titles are mentioned. It incorporates a significant occupational classification and code, and the glossary lists alphabetically definitions of technical terms and the names of machines and equipment. Common commodities sold in retail and wholesale trade are listed. Industries and jobs in each trade are listed.

The reason for our concern with occupational information at this point is that the specific definition of special abilities and aptitudes must eventually refer itself to such information. Traditionally, special abilities have been the focus of attention in discussions of vocational guidance, but it is only in the light of evidence concerning many other kinds of characteristics of the pupil that such guidance can be valid.

REFERENCES

1. Anastasi, Anne, and Foley, J. P., Jr., *Differential Psychology*, New York: The Macmillan Company, rev. ed., 1949.
2. Baer, Max F., and Roeber, Edward C., *Occupational Information, Its Nature and Use*, Chicago: Science Research Associates, 1951.
3. Binet, Alfred, *Les Idées modernes sur les enfants* (1909), p. 118, as quoted in Peterson, J., *Early Conceptions and Tests of Intelligence*, Yonkers: World Book Company, 1935.
4. Binet, Alfred, and Simon, T., "Methodes nouvelles pour le diagnostic du niveau intellectual des anormaux," *L'Année psychologique*, 11:191–244 (1905).
5. Bingham, W. V., *Aptitudes and Aptitude Testing*, New York: Harper & Brothers, 1937.
6. Doppelt, J. E., *The Organization of Mental Abilities in the Age Range 13 to 17*, Contributions to Education No. 962, New York: Teachers College, Columbia University, 1950.
7. Eells, K., Davis, A., Havighurst, R. J., Herrick, V. E., and Tyler, R., *Intelligence and Cultural Differences: A Study of Cultural Learning and Problem-Solving*, Chicago: University of Chicago Press, 1951.
8. Galton, Francis, *Inquiries into Human Faculty and Its Development*, London: Macmillan and Company, Ltd., 1883.
9. Garrett, H. E., "A developmental theory of intelligence," *American Psychologist*, 1:372–378 (1946).

10. "Intelligence and Its Measurement" (Symposium), *Journal of Educational Psychology,* 12:123–147, 195–216, 211–275 (1921).
11. Kefauver, G. N., *et al., The Horizontal Organization of Secondary Education,* National Survey of Secondary Education, Monograph No. 2, 1932.
12. National Society for the Study of Education, "Intelligence: its nature and nurture; Part I, Comparative and critical exposition; Part II, Original studies and experiments," *Thirty-ninth Yearbook of the National Society for the Study of Education,* Bloomington: Public School Publishing Company, 1940.
13. Shartle, Carroll L., *Occupational Information, Its Development and Application,* New York: Prentice-Hall, Inc., 1946.
14. Spearman, Charles, and Jones, L. Wynn, *Human Ability,* New York: The Macmillan Company, 1950.
15. Stewart, Naomi, "AGCT scores of Army personnel grouped by occupations," *Occupations,* 26:5–41 (1947).
16. Stoddard, G. D., *The Meaning of Intelligence,* New York: The Macmillan Company, 1943.
17. Strang, Ruth, *Behavior and Background of Students in Colleges and Secondary Schools,* New York: Harper & Brothers, 1937.
18. Terman, L. M., *The Measurement of Intelligence,* Boston: Houghton Mifflin Company, 1916.
19. Thomson, G. H., "The nature and measurement of the intellect," *Teachers College Record,* 41:726–750 (1940).
20. Thorndike, E. L., *et al., The Measurement of Intelligence,* New York: Teachers College, Columbia University, 1927.
21. Thurstone, L. L., "A new concept of intelligence and a new method of measuring primary abilities," *Educational Record,* Supplement No. 10, pp. 133–134, 1936.
22. Thurstone, L. L., *Primary Mental Abilities,* Chicago: University of Chicago Press, 1938.
23. Thurstone, L. L., and Thurstone, Thelma G., *Factorial Studies of Intelligence,* Psychometric Monographs, No. 2, Chicago: University of Chicago Press, 1941.

CHAPTER IX

Measuring General Mental Ability

ABSTRACT

*Teachers and administrators are more directly concerned with se-
lecting than constructing intelligence tests. The prediction of success
in school is probably the most usual purpose of intelligence tests. In
addition to conforming to some conceptual definition of intelligence,
these tests are constructed to satisfy such criteria as equality of opportunity, increased success as age increases, correlation of parts with total
test score, and ease of administration. Group tests are more useful than
individual tests in the majority of situations; similarly, verbal tests are
needed more often than performance or nonlanguage tests. Among
the types of material often used in intelligence tests are common observation, vocabulary, information, disarranged sentences, verbal analogies, spatial analogies, and number series. General achievement tests
in reading, English, and mathematics measure functions highly similar
to those measured by so-called intelligence tests.*

Nowadays almost everyone knows that intelligence tests are used
to evaluate the mental abilities of pupils. It is also common knowledge that the necessary tests are distinctly technical instruments.
Their authors use highly refined statistical, psychological, and
sociological procedures. There is consequently little occasion or
need for the classroom teacher to construct his own evaluation devices for measuring mental ability. The major problem for teachers is choosing a test from among the many available and using
it wisely.

The present chapter will seek to provide a general understanding of intelligence tests. Such an understanding is, of course, essential to the wise use and interpretation of measurements of intelligence. So, instead of the teacher's being concerned with the first two of the major steps of evaluation (see Chapter III) as part of his own practice and procedure, he is here concerned with the purpose and content of intelligence measurements and the technique of constructing an intelligence test merely as part of the background for selecting a test and then carrying out the next three steps: administration, interpretation, and evaluation of the device.

PURPOSE OF INTELLIGENCE TESTS

Accordingly, this discussion must begin with a statement of the purpose of the evaluation of mental ability as the first problem confronted by anyone undertaking to construct an intelligence test. The discussion in Chapter VIII has already supplied most of the answer to this problem. We saw there, however, that the most meaningful definition of intelligence for practical purposes emerges when we perform operations or construct tests to measure it. Let us turn, therefore, to the intelligence test builders, to see what operations they performed in constructing their tests. What were their purposes? How did they build their tests to achieve these purposes?

The first successful intelligence tester, Alfred Binet, shortly before the turn of the century, was seeking a technique with which to separate the school children of Paris into those who were mentally fit and unfit to be taught in the regular public schools. After great effort in many different directions, such as head measurements, physiognomy, graphology, palmistry, and sensory discriminations, Binet finally achieved a somewhat successful approach in terms of "higher mental processes." The point here is that his criterion for his test's "empirical" relevance was ability to succeed in school work. The content of his measuring instruments was derived not from an a priori, armchair reasoning process, but by an almost random process of trial and error toward a practical goal. This criterion, "success in school," has pervaded many subsequent operational definitions of intelligence. Whatever may be the fate of such general definitions as were noted in Chapter VIII or of theories of the organization or determiners of intelligence, ability to succeed in school must always remain a major part of our conception of intelligence, at least in our present civilization. Ever since Binet, teachers' judgments of pupil intelligence and teachers' marks, all based on judgments of the pupil's success in dealing with school subjects, have been important criteria for measurements of intelligence.

The question may be raised, "If school success and teachers' judgments of intelligence are such important criteria of intelligence tests, why do we need special instruments?" The answer traditionally given is that teachers' unaided judgments are not sufficiently reliable, relevant, or in many practical situations administrable. Binet investigated the ways in which teachers judge the intelligence of their pupils, both by using a questionnaire and by asking three teachers to come to his laboratory to judge the intelligence of children whom they had never seen before. He found that teachers "do not have a very definite idea of what constitutes intelligence, . . . tend to confuse it variously with capacity for memorizing, facility in reading, ability to master arithmetic, . . . fail to appreciate the one-sidedness of the school's demands upon intelligence, . . . are too easily deceived by a spritely attitude, a sympathetic expression, a glance of the eye, or a chance 'bump' on the head, . . . show rather undue confidence in the accuracy of their judgments." His observations of the teachers' actual procedures indicated that each one attempted to construct on the spot a poorly thought-out, unstandardized, errorful little intelligence test which resulted in little agreement among their estimates. "The teachers employed very awkwardly a very excellent method" (17 : 28–35). The intelligence test method of evaluating mental ability thus emerges as merely a refinement, organization, and standardization in scientific form of the teacher's or layman's "common-sense" but error-ridden approach.

This question was reëxamined by Hubbard and Flesher (14). They asked 24 different teachers in Grades II–VIII in four schools to estimate the intelligence quotients of their 763 pupils in 34 different classes. The mean of the 34 correlations they obtained between the teachers' estimates and the test I.Q.'s came to .72, considerably higher than the median r of .57 they found in five studies reported in 1922–1924. They attribute the higher accuracy of present-day teachers to a better understanding of the factors influencing the intelligence quotient; they believe that "the teachers of today are . . . less likely to offer snap judgments based on a 'chance bump on the head' or other extraneous factors. . . ."

Since many teachers are much less accurate than this, there is no reason to question the value of intelligence tests as an aid to teachers in judging pupils' intelligence. Hubbard and Flesher suggest that teachers can acquire valuable information by estimating their pupils' I.Q's before looking at test I.Q.'s, then comparing the mean of their estimates with the pupils' mean I.Q. as measured by a test, and examining individual cases in which large errors of over- or under-estimation were made.

CRITERIA FOR CONTENT OF INTELLIGENCE TESTS

Let us now examine the criteria used by Binet and subsequent intelligence test builders in the selection and arrangement of their test content. Every builder must select his content according to some conception of intelligence, explicit or implicit. Binet's conception stressed such characteristics of thinking as its power to keep going along purposeful lines, to criticize itself, and to adapt itself to a specific goal. This conception took many varied forms in test content: tests of time orientation, several kinds of memory, language comprehension, knowledge about common objects, free association, number mastery, constructive imagination, and ability to compare concepts, to see contradictions, to bind fragments into a unitary whole, to comprehend abstract terms, and to meet novel situations (17 : 46).

In addition to its agreement with some conception of intelligence, test content is subjected to a second criterion—equal opportunity of human beings *within a given culture* to have experience with that content. In setting up this requirement, intelligence test builders have hoped to hold constant the facor of environment or learning so that the differences between individuals that emerge from the testing will be ascribable to innate hereditary factors. To a large extent this attempt is justifiable, especially insofar as it excludes test content that is explicitly taught in the schools. It would be folly to use shorthand writing ability to measure high-school students' intelligence, since learning opportunity or environmental influences vary so greatly from pupil to pupil with respect to such test content. On the other hand, test builders and users must realize that this requirement—equal opportunity to learn test content—is seldom fully met, as we have already seen in Chapters V and VIII. This unwarranted assumption, that intelligence tests cover only what everybody has had an equal opportunity to learn, is responsible for much confusion in the nature-nurture controversy and for much unwarranted fatalism and determinism in the interpretation of test results.

To rule out differences in the previous experiences or training of pupils, the attempt is made to use equally familiar (or unfamiliar) material. Equally familiar material may be illustrated by such tests as asking a child to point to his nose, to draw a picture of a man, or to complete a picture in which one of the shadows is missing. Equally unfamiliar material may be illustrated by tests in which the individual is required to learn and apply an artificial language composed of nonsense syllables, or by maze tests. Test material in which environmental factors probably play a major role may be illustrated by vocabulary tests, arithmetic computation tests, and any other test involving words or mathematical symbols. The latter kind of material, obviously influenced to a large extent by learning opportunities and by the types of activity in which the individual is constrained to engage by the culture in which he lives, constitutes a major proportion of the content of many intelligence tests. It also varies in amount, as we have seen, in different tests. This fact, while it may invalidate the tests as measures of "innate ability," does not necessarily detract from their usefulness in guidance. Regardless of the unknown extent to which differences in pupils' scores are determined by differences in genes or environment, the ability reflected in such scores must still be taken into account in making vocational plans or understanding school success or failure.

INTELLIGENCE TESTS VS. ACHIEVEMENT TESTS

High correlations are usually obtained between a test of general intelligence and a battery of general achievement tests. T. L. Kelley (15), among others, has shown that this is the case. He obtained correlation coefficients, corrected for the unreliability of the tests correlated, which enabled him to estimate the community of function between intelligence and achievement tests. He concluded that the community of function among different intelligence tests is about 95 percent; between intelligence tests and achievement batteries, about 90 percent; between intelligence tests and reading tests, about 92 percent; between intelligence tests and arithmetic tests, about 88 percent. Although these figures are based on grade-school pupils, similar results between achievement and intelligence test scores would probably be obtained at any other age level. Kelley derived from these data his point of view that the distinction between intelligence and achievement tests is largely spurious and due to the "jangle" fallacy—the belief that two separate words or expressions for the same thing necessarily carry a real distinction.

If intelligence and general achievement tests cover the same ground to such a large extent, why do we need intelligence tests? The answer must be given in terms of practical usability and convenience. General scholastic achievement cannot usually be measured in as brief a time and with as short a test as can intelligence. Achievement in a single subject is usually measured by a test that is as long as the average intelligence test; to obtain a measure of general achievement would require several such achievement tests. Similarly, for pupils with varying educational background—from different school systems, for example—it is difficult to select an achievement test that is not prejudicial to some of them.

Ruch and Segel (16 : 24) state that verbal group intelligence tests are of most value when (1) used with achievement tests for pupils whose school attendance has been irregular, (2) transfers from other schools must be given tentative class assignments without delay even though adequate cumulative records are not available, (3) financial and other facilities permit extensive testing programs including both educational and mental tests, and (4) mental tests provide diagnoses of differential mental abilities such as memory, attention span, symbolic thinking, and so forth.

Another possible advantage is claimed for the intelligence test over general achievement test batteries as a measure of scholastic aptitude. Its novelty and apparent unrelatedness to ordinary

school subject matter may create greater interest and better testing morale on the part of students who have antipathies toward
one or more school subjects. A child may show low achievement
because of neuroticism, boredom, or poor teaching. The intelligence test may be able to reveal abilities that have escaped the influence of such debilitating factors.

Kelley used his argument of the community between intelligence tests and achievement tests mainly to inveigh against the
accomplishment quotient (A.Q.), "educational age divided by
mental age." However, he did admit that individuals can differ in
intelligence and achievement and that intelligence tests can reveal
such differences. Especially if the achievement in which we are
interested is not general but special—for example, music, computation, spelling, handwriting, etc.—the difference between it and
intelligence may easily be real and one which is demonstrable by
means of an intelligence test and a measure of the special achievement in question.

ITEM VALIDATION

Let us return to the criteria used in selecting the content of
intelligence tests. Having chosen and constructed a collection of
test situations, Binet tried them out on normal children of different ages. Then he applied a technique of evaluating the test material in terms of its difficulty and validity to insure even more the
success of his new type of intelligence test content; he determined
the percentage of success in a given test situation for each age
group of children tested. If this percentage increased little or not
at all or decreased in going from younger to older children, the
test was declared invalid on the justifiable assumption that the
average intelligence of normal children (that is, the mental age)
increases with chronological age. If the percentage of success increased rapidly with age and, furthermore, increased *within* a
given age group in accordance with elsewhere-obtained judgments
of the intelligence of the children in that group, the test situation
was judged valid and retained for the final form of the test. The
age level at which 66 to 75 percent of the children passed a test
was used to define the difficulty of that test situation in terms of
its age level. This way of defining difficulty was useful, as we shall
see later, in interpreting the scores of pupils.

Similar in principle to the criterion of an increasing percentage of success with increasing chronological age is the use of the total test score as a criterion for the validity of each separate item of test content. Using the total test score as the best available measure of intelligence, the test builder requires that each component of the test, each test situation or question, shall discriminate between those who make high, medium, and low total scores on the test. If the pupils are divided according to their total score into high, middle, and low groups, the percentage of success with a given item should rise as we go from the low to the high group. This is merely another way of saying that the correlation between single test items and total scores should be high. In practice this is achieved by any one of a great number of available techniques of statistical *item analysis*.

While the material is being selected for its validity, attention is paid to such considerations as ease of scoring, appeal to the student, time requirements, material or apparatus needed, and equal difficulty for both sexes. Large quantities of seemingly acceptable test material are often rejected on one or more of these grounds. Provisional test forms are constructed and tried out on appropriate samples of pupils and the results are critically examined so that only the most satisfactory test materials will be retained.

Finally one or more final forms of the test are constructed and administered to large representative samples of pupils. The samples are selected so that proper numbers of pupils are drawn from all the groupings that can be made according to factors which may have an effect on the test results. The standardization of the Revised Stanford-Binet test of intelligence took into account geographic distribution, socioeconomic status, rural or urban residence, and nationality or descent of the pupils tested in each age range. At this point the selection and standardization of test content requires much highly skilled labor and statistical analysis.

TYPES OF INTELLIGENCE TESTS

Even more than other types of evaluation devices, intelligence tests are classifiable as *individual* or *group* according to whether they can be given to only one or to more than one person at a time. A prime example of an individual intelligence test is the Stanford Revision of the Binet-Simon Scale; the group test may be illustrated by such tests as the Terman-McNemar Test of Mental Ability, the Henmon-Nelson Test of Mental Ability, the American Council on Education Psychological Examination, and the Ohio State University Psychological Test. The chief disadvantage of individual testing is, of course, the large amount of time required and the consequent high cost. Furthermore, the skill needed for proper administration of an individual intelligence test is usually gained only in a one-semester course in psychology at the university level, preceded in most universities by two or more introductory courses in psychology.

The advantages usually cited in favor of *individual* intelligence testing are its greater validity, and its interpretability in clinical terms. The first—higher validity—is largely illusory, for most available group tests have reliabilities higher than .85 and correlations with such criteria as school marks or teachers' ratings ranging upward from .40. Neither of these figures is sufficiently if at all exceeded by individual intelligence tests to warrant selection of the latter on these grounds. The other advantage, interpretability in clinical terms, refers to the possibility of more carefully observing the pupil's behavior during the test. Such observation may permit judgments concerning emotional adjustment, motivation, working habits, physical aspects, special interests, and the like, in addition to general intelligence. The individual test affords an opportunity for better detection of invalidating factors like faulty understanding of directions, lack of interest, and emotional disturbance. These factors may seriously invalidate group tests when given to children below eight years of age, to mentally defective children, and to badly maladjusted children. Bingham (2 : 228) noted this advantage even with adults: ". . . Distraught persons who really required professional psychiatric service were less often identified as such by the counselors who talked with them intimately about their problems than by the examiners who administered the individual performance tests and so had a chance to observe them under exceptionally revealing circumstances."

The advantages of individual tests can be greatly enhanced by an aid like the excellent *Examiner's Check List for Use in Noting and Interpreting Behavior During the Test Period* (2 : 229–235). This list presents points of behavior to be noted during the preliminary instructions and the execution of the task, the subject's attitude toward his performance, and his conduct at the end of the test and after the testing. The list is detailed and comprehensive, and shows much psychological insight in its suggested interpretations for each item of behavior noted.

Whatever advantages the individual intelligence test may have for testing very young children and enabling clinical observation, it is impractical in most schools for the majority of pupils. Since most evaluation of mental abilities can be made satisfactorily by means of group tests, only group tests will be discussed here. The reader is referred to books specializing in individual testing (3, 9, 10, 18, 23).

Another distinction between intelligence tests is that between *nonlanguage* and *language tests*. The latter require that the pupil be able to use and understand a given language—like English or arithmetic—and comprise by far the majority of group intelligence tests. Nonlanguage tests enable the measurement of pupils who are unable to read or write English, such as preschool children, foreign-born children, children with speech defects, deaf children, and others whose use of language is limited.

Sometimes a further distinction is made between *performance* and *paper and pencil* (or *printed*) *tests*. The former require the subject to do something with concrete materials, such as form boards, blocks, or picture puzzles; the latter involve no concrete material to be manipulated other than reading and writing materials. Performance tests are usually (but not necessarily) individual tests, whereas paper and pencil tests are usually designed for group administration. Fig. 11 shows how these two distinctions may be combined to yield four classifications, which are illustrated.

AVAILABLE GROUP TESTS OF INTELLIGENCE

The reader may be asking, What test should I use? This section will introduce some of the currently available intelligence tests to guide him in answering this question.

If in looking for an intelligence test suited to his own needs the reader were to consult the standard reference works for lists and descriptions of such tests, he could easily become bewildered.

Hildreth's *Bibliographies,* Buros' *Yearbooks,* publishers' catalogues, *Psychological Abstracts,* the *Review of Educational Research,* and the like, mention and contain information about literally hundreds of intelligence tests. How can one pick and choose among all these?

	Language	Nonlanguage
Performance	*Object vocabulary:* Given a word, the child is required to pick the object out of a collection of objects. *Directions:* Given directions orally, the child is required to carry them out.	*Form boards:* Given a form board and an opportunity to watch the examiner insert some pieces properly, the child is asked to insert the remaining pieces. *Blocks:* The examiner builds a design with blocks, destroys it, and the child reproduces it.
Paper and pencil, or printed	*Multiple-choice vocabulary:* Given a word and five choices, the child is asked to choose the one that means the same as the given word. *Arithmetic computation:* A series of numbers is to be added, subtracted, etc., as per instructions.	*Paper form board:* Given a diagram, the child is required to pick the drawing that shows its component parts. *Hands:* Given drawings of a hand from many angles and in many positions, the child marks whether the hand shown is the right or left one.

FIG. 11. Descriptions of 4 Different Types of Illustrative Tests Obtained by Combining 2 Distinctions Based on Kind of Tests.

BASES FOR PRESENT CHOICE

For our purposes, we have been able to make distinctions that cut down considerably the number of candidates for attention. (1) As mentioned above, we shall be concerned only with *group* rather than individual intelligence tests. (2) We shall not consider Canadian, British, and other tests developed and standardized outside of the United States. This exclusion is justified on the ground that differences in culture must always make the content and norms of these tests suspect for use in American schools. Since tests are available that do not involve this kind of risk, and since the dangers of inappropriateness due to subcultural differences within American society are already substantial, there is seldom justification in practical school work for using tests developed outside this country. (3) We need be concerned only with tests designed for use in schools, as against those developed for use in business and industry. (4) The evidence concerning the validity, administrability, and interpretability of the test still further limits the tests we need consider. This evidence is found in the test itself, the manual for it, and especially the bibliography of research publications on the test. The test itself and the manual should of course be consulted by any prospective user. For many tests, however, the bibliography of research publications is so long and technical that it may not be feasible for the prospective test user to track down, read, evaluate, and assimilate the long list of publications before deciding whether or how to use a test. Such tests are generally superior in validity—the extent to which the meaning and predictiveness of the test's scores are known—to others on which little or no research has been done. Other things being equal, then, we have chosen the tests about which a large amount of material has been published. Much of this material has been summarized in Buros' *Mental Measurements Yearbooks*. The "frankly critical" reviews in these yearbooks provide excellent grounds for deciding what test should be used in a given school situation. Below are the tests we have selected for special attention:

American Council on Education Psychological Examinations for College Freshmen, and for High School Students[1]

California Tests of Mental Maturity and their adaptations (Pub. 6, see p. 613).

Davis-Eells Test of General Intelligence or Problem-Solving Ability (Pub. 28)

Henmon-Nelson Tests of Mental Ability[2]

Kuhlmann-Anderson and Kuhlmann-Finch Intelligence Tests (Pub. 11).

Ohio State University Psychological Test (Pub.17).

Otis Quick-Scoring Mental Ability Tests (Pub. 28).

Pintner General Ability Tests (Pub.28).

Terman-McNemar Test of Mental Ability (Pub. 28).

The chief purpose of all these tests is to yield information about the learner's intellectual fitness to attain the objectives of educa-

---

[1] Cooperative Test Division, Educational Testing Service, Princeton, N.J.
[2] Houghton Mifflin Co., 2 Park St., Boston 7, Mass,

tion in school and college. These tests attempt to achieve this purpose in various ways; they have corresponding advantages and disadvantages for different facets of it.

GROUPS DESIGNED FOR

For one thing, they are applicable to different kinds of groups. The California and Pintner series provide various forms which cover the whole range of level of ability from kindergarten to college. The Henmon-Nelson, Otis, Kuhlmann-Anderson, and Kuhlmann-Finch series cover the elementary grades through college. The Davis-Eells tests are designed for Grades I through VI. On the other hand, the Terman-McNemar and the ACE Psychological (High School) tests are suitable primarily for the high-school grades and perhaps the junior-high-school level. The OSU Psychological Test and the ACE Psychological Examination for College Freshmen are intended primarily for the orientation testing of students entering college.

TIME REQUIRED

These tests differ also in the time required for administration. The total time required is estimated by adding to the amount of working time allowed the student. The range for the tests described here runs from 25 minutes (20 minutes' working time) for the Otis Quick-Scoring Test for Grades 1.5–4 to an unlimited amount of working time (with 120 minutes estimated as generally sufficient) for the OSU Psychological Test. On the basis of the time they require, we can divide tests into two groups: those that can be given in a single class period of 40 or 50 minutes, and those that require more than such a period. In elementary schools the school day is often not divided into fixed periods as it is in high schools and colleges. But elementary-school children cannot tolerate very long testing periods in one sitting. The tests that require less than 50 minutes are the short forms of the California Tests of Mental Maturity at the preprimary level, the Kuhlmann-Finch and Kuhlmann-Anderson tests, the Henmon-Nelson tests at all three levels, the Otis Quick-Scoring tests at all three levels, the elementary level of the Pintner General Ability Tests, and the Terman-McNemar test. All the other tests listed above require more than 50 minutes of administration time.

Logical Relevance

On strictly psychological grounds, the most important characteristic of any of these tests is its logical relevance—the kinds of score yielded, the psychological processes elicited, the ways in which the items were chosen and scored. The present group of tests can be divided into two kinds: those that yield only a single score, and those that yield a total score and in addition two or more subscores for different kinds of test content. In the first group are the Davis-Eells, Henmon-Nelson, Kuhlmann-Anderson, Kuhlmann-Finch, Otis, and Terman-McNemar tests. The two American Council tests yield a quantitative and a linguistic score in addition to the total score made up of both of these. The California tests yield separate scores for total mental factors, nonlanguage factors, and language factors, and scores for spatial relationships, logical reasoning, numerical reasoning, and verbal concepts. (The correlations between the language and nonlanguage factors at all five levels of the California Short-Form Tests of Mental Maturity—preprimary, primary, elementary, intermediate, and advanced—are all about .55. This means that differences between language and nonlanguage factor scores must be fairly substantial before any significance is attached to them.) The OSU Psychological Test yields two scores, reading and total. The Pintner tests yield only one score for each form, but both nonlanguage and verbal series of the tests are available, and at the elementary level there are two scales, one requiring reading while the other does not.

More important than the names of the scores, in judging the logical relevance of the test, is the content of the items. Just what do the items require? As we inspect these tests we gain an impression of "uniformity in diversity." Although details of format and style may differ from one test to another, throughout these group intelligence tests there is strong emphasis on knowledge of word meanings, ability to use words in solving problems; somewhat less frequently there is emphasis on number skills, as in handling number series items; still less frequent but nonetheless much in evidence are items dealing with spatial relations.

Examples of Verbal Test Content. Thus, in the ACE Psychological Examination for High School Students we find "same-opposite" vocabulary items like the following:

1. Many   1. ill   2. few   3. down   4. sour.
2. Ancient   1. dry   2. long   3. happy   4. old.

The task of course is to select the one of the four words at the right that means the same as or the opposite of the word at the left. The same test contains completion items in which the pupil is asked to think of the word that fits a given definition and mark the letter it begins with. Examples:

1. A contest of speed.   b   f   m   p   r
2. A place or building for athletic exercises.   c   d   g   h   t

In the California Short-Form Test of Mental Maturity, intermediate level, for Grades VII–X, much the same kind of ability is tested under the title of "Verbal Concepts." Here the pupil is told to mark the number of the word that means the same or about the same as the first word:

Blossom   1. tree   2. vine   3. flower   4. garden
Strange   1. real   2. tell   3. certain   4. unknown
Predatory   1. soft   2. stationary   3. plundering   4. lasting
Chuff   1. peeve   2. churl   3. cliff   4. laugh

The Henmon-Nelson tests contain items like these:

Stagnant water is:
     1. motionless   2. fresh   3. rapid   4. clear   5. foaming
Energetic means about the same as:
     1. sorry   2. sleepy   3. forceful   4. happy   5. brave

In the Otis Quick-Scoring Mental Ability Tests the following occur:

Which one of the five answers below tells best what a sword is?
     1. To cut   2. A weapon   3. An officer   4. A tool   5. To fight
Which word means the opposite of humility?
     1. Joy   2. Pride   3. Drive   4. Funny   5. Recklessness

In the OSU Psychological Test these items look like this:

Subservient is the opposite of
     1. existing   2. reproachful   3. accepting   4. commanding   5. critical
Flirt is the same as
     1. maid   2. shrew   3. coquette   4. vixen   5. virago

Examples of Numerical Test Content. Another kind of item that often occurs in group intelligence tests is called "number series." A series of numbers is given which sets up a pattern or sequence to be inferred by the examinee. Using this pattern he must determine one or more additional numbers to be inserted either within the given sequence or as the next numbers. Following are some items of this kind taken from the tests we are discussing.

In the California Short-Form Test of Mental Maturity: Elementary Level, Grades 4–8:

Directions: In each row of numbers below, there is one that does not belong. Find the number that should be omitted from each row among the answer numbers on the right, and mark its letter.

5 10 15 20 22 25 30 a. 5 b. 10 c. 15 d. 20 e. 22

3 4 7 8 10 11 12 15 a. 7 b. 10 c. 11 d. 12 e. 15

The Henmon-Nelson Test of Mental Ability for College Students also has such items, again differing slightly in form from those of other tests:

79. 4, 8, ..., 96, 480. What number should appear in the blank? (1) 40, (2) 48, (3) 32, (4) 24, (5) 16.

The Otis Quick-Scoring Mental Ability Tests: Beta Test: Form B, for Grades 4–9, has another version of the same kind of item:

One number is wrong in the following series. 1 2 4 8 16 24 64 What should that number be? 1. 12 2. 6 3. 3 4. 48 5. 32

And still another version in the same test:

Which of these series contains a wrong number?
1. 3–6–9–12–15 2. 1–4–7–10–13 3. 2–5–8–11–14 4. 1–3–5–7–9
5. 2–4–6–8–11

Further examples from other group intelligence tests could be given to make the point that, despite differences in detail, the types of items they contain are largely the same. For lack of space we omit similar illustrations of the uniformity in diversity to be found in the kinds of "spatial" items used in these tests.

Perhaps the most radically different kind of content is that of the Davis-Eells test. To minimize memory or specific learning requirements, this test calls for no reading and no special word knowledge. The problems, presented orally by the teacher, refer to pictures in the test booklet. They are intended to require mental processes similar to those called for "in solving most problems in life and in the school curriculum." To make the content interesting, it is based on the actual life of children as observed and reported by interviewers and field workers.

Arrangement and Homogeneity of Content. One important difference in these tests is that some, like the OSU Psychological and the Terman-McNemar, contain only verbal items, whereas others contain numerical and spatial materials as well. In the Ohio test this verbal content, in addition to the same-opposite items already cited, takes the form of (1) a section of items on paragraph reading in which the examinee is given a paragraph to read and a series of multiple-choice questions to answer on each paragraph and (2) a section of word relationships, or verbal analogies items, such as:

boy boyish infant   1. childish   2. infant-like   3. infant
    4. infantile   5. infantil

In the Terman-McNemar test the seven verbal subtests are entitled Information, Synonyms, Logical Selection, Classification, Analogies, Opposites, and Best Answer.

In the Henmon-Nelson and Otis tests the verbal material is supplemented by spatial and numerical types of items, but the three basic types are mixed, occurring in "spiral" sequence, each succeeding round of the various types of items being more difficult.

In a third kind of arrangement, the different types of test content are put into separate subtests which may or may not be scored separately. Thus, in the ACE Psychological Examinations same-opposite, completion, and verbal analogies items in separate sections are scored together to yield an L, or linguistic ability, score; and three separately timed subtests on arithmetical reasoning, number series, and figure analogies are scored together to yield a Q, or quantitative ability, score. Similar arrangements of different kinds of test content into separate parts are found in the California and Pintner tests.

Speed enters into performance on these tests in differing degrees, and this fact of course indicates that the tests measure correspondingly different aspects of mental ability. As indicated above, the Ohio test has no time limit. The time limits on the other tests are more or less adequate to allow all the examinees to attempt all the questions. The American Council tests, at the other extreme, all call for a fairly high speed, so that relatively few examinees ever have time to finish all the subtests.

EMPIRICAL RELEVANCE

The empirical relevance of these tests has generally been estimated by correlating the scores on them with scores on other intelligence tests, with school or college grades, and with scores on achievement tests of various kinds. The literature on the empirical relevance (or, in the more traditional terminology, validity) of some of the tests is voluminous. *The Fourth Mental Measurements Yearbook* lists 276 references concerning the ACE Psychological Examination for College Freshmen; illustrative titles of these studies are "The predictive value of the Thurstone Psychological Examination," "The relation of general intelligence, motor adaptability and motor learning to success in dental technical courses." The *Yearbooks'* bibliographies for the other tests on our list, although less extensive, are similar in kind and substantial, except for the Davis-Eells and Kuhlmann-Finch tests, published in 1952.

It is impossible to present here any detailed account of the findings of the many empirical studies of these tests. In general, their correlations with other tests of intelligence, individual or group, are about .70 or .80, depending in part, of course, on the "range of talent." Their correlations with school grades typically range from .30 to .70, the median correlations for various tests being approximately .45. Since the OSU Psychological Test has been continually refined against college freshman grades as the criterion, it yields correlations with grade point averages of about .60—probably the highest of those attained with any single test.

When these group tests of intelligence are correlated with objectively scored achievement tests in various school subjects, the resulting coefficients depend largely on the relevance of what is measured by the test to the kind of knowledge and understanding tapped by the achievement test. With tests in English, social studies, general science, and mathematics, the present tests generally correlate about .50 to .70. As the authors of the Davis-Eells test point out, "Such correlations must always be interpreted with extreme caution, particularly in the case of those dealing with achievement tests. . . . There is a tremendously important difference between 'problem-solving ability' as defined for purposes of this test and 'scholastic aptitude' as usually considered. Problem-solving ability involves reasoning, organization of material, insight, etc. Scholastic aptitude, with the present school curriculum, tends to place a much greater premium on memory and on work habits" (**6,** p. 11).

Reliability

The reliability of these group intelligence tests is usually estimated in the sense of internal consistency. Typically, this has involved obtaining the correlation between scores on odd- and even-numbered items and correcting with the Spearman-Brown formula to estimate the reliability of the whole test. On occasion, these coefficients will be reported for groups of pupils from a range of school grades, and the coefficients will accordingly be very high— at any rate, higher than that which would apply to any single grade level. For most teachers, however, reliability for the single grade level is of chief interest. The coefficients of internal consistency of these tests are generally adequate for the purposes to which the tests are put. They range around .90, occasionally extending down to .80 or .70, or as high as .95.

For some of the tests, reliability is reported in terms of the standard error, or probable error, of measurement, which is not influenced by the range of grades or "talent" used in making the estimate of reliability. Such standard errors of measurement are not comparable for different tests, because they are expressed in the raw score of the test being used.

For some of the tests, reliability is also reported as the correlation between equivalent or alternate forms of the test. These correlations typically are somewhat lower than the coefficients of internal consistency, ranging around .80—again depending on the range of "talent" of the population sample. Data on the reliability of these tests in the sense of stability are not often reported.

Administrability

The tests differ considerably in ease of administration. The ACE tests require careful instructions and timing for each of four or six subtests. All the tests for primary and preprimary levels can be given only to relatively small groups—not more than about 30 pupils—at one time. These tests for children also require careful self-training on the part of the administrator, because the directions to the pupils are highly detailed and must be given exactly.

At the other extreme are the Henmon-Nelson, Ohio, and Otis tests, which are almost "self-administering." They require little more of the examiner than that he distribute the test booklets, read a brief set of instructions aloud while the pupils follow along silently, give the starting signal, call time at the end of a single interval, and collect the tests.

The directions to examiner and pupil, apart from their differences in amount of detail and complexity, are uniformly clear and workable for all these tests.

Scorability

These tests, except those for the preprimary and primary levels, are arranged for the use of separate answer sheets that can be scored either mechanically, by electrical scoring machines, or visually, by means of stencils with holes punched in them. The Ohio, California, and Henmon-Nelson tests have devices that make it possible to mark more than a single answer sheet at a time, so that the test can be scored by more than one person independently and several records of the student's performance can be obtained. For the Ohio test, a set of answer sheets is punched with a pin that makes holes in several answer sheets at a time. For the California tests, an arrangement called "Scoreze" calls for marking an answer sheet which has carbon on the reverse; this enables marks to be placed on a second sheet on which the scoring key is preprinted. This second sheet provides a record of the pupil's performance which can be hand-scored and retained by the teacher. The Henmon-Nelson tests are set up for the Clapp-Young Self-Marking System, which is similar to "Scoreze" except that the original answer sheet is not machine-scorable. In short, consider-

able ingenuity has been used on all these tests to enable them to be
scored as efficiently as possible.

NORMS

The norms of an intelligence test may be as important as the
content. For the present tests, the norms differ markedly in form
and in the size and representativeness of the norm groups.

When tests yield only a single score, it is often expressed as a
mental age or as an intelligence quotient. But the norms for the
American Council tests are stated solely in terms of percentile
ranks for various college freshmen groups or high-school grades. A
passage in the manual of the ACE tests clearly expresses the view-
point of the authors, L. L. and Thelma Gwinn Thurstone, on
intelligence quotients and mental ages:

Mental ages and intelligence quotients do not exist for these tests.
Perhaps a few words of explanation should be given here. The intelligence quotient is, by definition, the ratio of the mental age to the
chronological age. The mental age equivalent of a test performance is
the chronological age for which that test performance is the average.
It follows from this definition that mental ages and intelligence quotients are indeterminate for the upper half of the adult population.
If a person scores above the average for adults in a psychological examination, then there exists no age for which his score is the average.
College students can be assumed to score above the average for the
adult population of the country, and, consequently, they cannot be
assigned any mental ages or intelligence quotients. This is not a
debatable question. It is a question of very simple and straightforward
logic.

Intelligence quotients are sometimes assigned to the upper half of
the adult population by changing the definition of mental age. For
example, a mental age 15 or 18 does not mean the average test performance of people of that age. Such mental ages are arbitrary designations of what the test author may choose to call superior adult
performance (7 : 7).

The *percentile rank* norms for the American Council tests are
based on many thousands of college freshmen tested in hundreds
of colleges all over the United States; perhaps the only type of
college not well represented is the eastern "Ivy League," whose

entering freshmen are often tested by the College Entrance Examination Board. Since these norms are determined by the colleges
that decide to use the test and also choose to report their score
distributions to the authors of the test, an unknown amount and
kind of bias enter into these norms. Accordingly, many of the
colleges that use the test develop norms based on their own students. In any case, norms are available for several different types of
colleges: four-year, teachers, and junior colleges. Similarly, norms
are provided separately for Q, L, and total scores, and for men,
women, and the combined group. The norms for the high-school
version of the ACE test are presented for Grades IX through XII
and are based on a total sample of 19,500 cases.

The California Short-Form Tests of Mental Maturity provide
norms which make possible the determination of mental ages and
intelligence quotients. Grade placement and percentile norms for
various age groups are also provided. According to the manual,
the norms for this test are based on a stratified sample of over
125,000 cases distributed normally as to mental ability, and typical
in age-grade relationships. The medians and standard deviations of
the I.Q.'s for the successive grade levels change in accordance with
known facts about the increasing selectivity of American schools
as grade level increases. Percentile norms are provided for I.Q.'s
of the normal population and for the various secondary-school
grades, as well as for college freshmen, sophomores, and graduates.
Each of these sets of percentile norms is based on large samples
ranging in size from 1000 cases for the college sophomores to 100,-
000 for the normal population.

The norms for the Davis-Eells test are based on 19,000 pupils in
Grades I to VI in fifteen states, selected as representative of the
urban population of the United States. Rather than an I.Q., the
test yields an Index of Problem-Solving Ability (IPSA) adjusted to
have a mean of 100 and a standard deviation of 16 for each age
group, by half years, from 6 to 13 inclusive.

The Henmon-Nelson test norms consist of percentiles for each
of the college years based on scores made by approximately 5500
students in colleges and universities of various sizes in different
parts of the United States, none of which uses any means of ex-
cluding students who have graduated from high school except that

they are unable to carry their work successfully. The norms for the high-school test consists of percentile ranks for each of the grades from VII through XII, and mental age equivalents for each possible raw score. Percentile rank scores are recommended by the authors. These norms according to the authors have been checked by returns from the testing of about 300,000 pupils in widely distributed areas of the United States.

The norms for the Ohio State test are in the form of percentiles based on the performance of freshmen at Ohio State University and other colleges in the state of Ohio. Norms are also provided for each year of high school.

The Otis tests yield raw scores that can be converted into age norms. When the pupil's chronological age is subtracted from the age norm equivalent to his raw score on the test, and the difference is added algebraically to 100, a "Gamma I.Q." is obtained. The norms for "Alpha," the high-school and college form, are based on equating experiments involving about 3000 students which the manual does not describe as to age, grade level, geographical location, or other characteristics. The norms for the "Beta" test are based on some 20-odd thousand pupils in Grades IV through IX, who took various forms of this test and of earlier tests by Otis and others. The deviation score method is also used to obtain I.Q.'s with the "Beta" test.

The Pintner tests were standardized on thousands of pupils drawn from many widely scattered communities at different socioeconomic levels. The scores on this test are also converted into age norms which can in turn be used to obtain I.Q.'s by the deviation method, i.e., by subtracting from or adding to 100 the difference between the pupil's age norm for his chronological age and his actual raw score, or by using special tables prepared for this purpose when this simple addition or subtraction is inappropriate.

The Terman-McNemar test's norms

. . . were established through a cooperative national testing program . . . in which approximately 190,000 tests were distributed to 200 communities in 37 states and 307 parochial schools in the diocese of Philadelphia. . . . The norms are based on the results from 148 communities in 33 states where answers were recorded in the test booklet. . . . To facilitate calculations, only a ten percent random sample of the test booklets was called for in setting up the norms. To insure the randomness of such a sample, communities were not notified of the serial numbers to be returned until after the tests were administered and scored. Each community tested all of the pupils in at least three consecutive grades in order to obtain at least one approximately unselected age sample from it. About one-half of the communities tested more than three grades while one-fourth of them tested the whole grade range. . . . Distributions of raw scores for separate age groups were run off; these were the basic data for setting up the standard score scale and the norms.

The norms thus obtained are presented in the form of standard score equivalents. Further, a table is provided for computing deviation I.Q.'s by determining the differences between the standard score obtained and the average standard score for other individuals of the same age. For ages 13, 14, and 15, the I.Q. is found by adding to or subtracting from 100 the pupil's deviation of score from the norm; for ages 10–12, and for ages 16 and above, the table provides I.Q. equivalents. It is also possible to convert these I.Q.'s into percentile ranks.

Choosing an Intelligence Test

The teacher, administrator, or research worker who needs a group intelligence test should realize that the foregoing account has only glanced over the major characteristics of the tests selected for the present discussion. In any given instance, the selection of a particular test should be based on a complex judgment concerning its advantages and limitations in relation to the unique conditions and purposes for which it is to be used. The test user should immediately look for a test that is designed for the age or grade range with which he is concerned; that does not require more testing and administration time than he has at his disposal; that yields a single score, or two different kinds of ability scores, or even more scores, depending on the purposes he has in mind; that is simpler to administer or that requires more complex timing and scoring, depending on the kind of personnel he has to administer the tests and the amount of training he can give them; whose content, based on his own examination and that of other test interpreters, appears to be related to the kinds of ability he considers most relevant to his purposes; and whose norms will be meaningful to the persons who will make the interpretations about student abilities.

Having thought through the circumstances and purposes of his intelligence testing program, he should then look through the manuals and other materials obtainable from the publishers of one or more of the tests described above or of other tests that may come to his attention. He should go to Buros' *Mental Measurements Yearbooks* to read reviews of the tests he is considering. He may consult Buros for references on these tests and read some of the studies, particularly those that refer to the kind of situation in which he is working. He should weigh the evidence thus obtained concerning the validity, administrability, and interpretability of the test for his purposes.

This description of the procedure for choosing intelligence tests may sound more formidable than it actually is. Many of the necessary judgments can be made easily and rapidly. The special circumstances obtaining for any test user may immediately reduce the tests that are real candidates for his testing program to a very small number. The few surviving tests then receive more intensive and searching scrutiny. The final decision will give the test user the group intelligence test that will provide the most valid information concerning the intelligence of his pupils for the particular purposes and conditions with which he is concerned.

STANDARDIZED ACHIEVEMENT TESTS USEFUL FOR APPRAISING INTELLECTUAL COMPETENCE

Group intelligence tests may be considered to measure *achievement* of intellectual abilities and skills of a kind not explicitly taught in school. Different kinds of items in group intelligence tests vary as to how much they deal with the kinds of achievement aimed at in schools. Some types of items are very similar, in what they demand, to some types of abilities and skills with which instruction at various grade levels is concerned. For example, the ability to read and comprehend a paragraph of complex verbal material resembles fairly closely the objectives of the teaching of reading in the elementary and secondary schools. Vocabulary and arithmetic reasoning items also have much in common with what is taught in classrooms.

Other kinds of items, on the other hand, seem to depart quite radically from anything taught in the schools. The ability to unscramble disarranged sentences, to distinguish between pictures of right- and left-sided objects, to solve number series problems, to detect and apply the principle involved in the difference in two geometrical figures, and the like, is certainly not taught directly in most schools, although it has obviously been learned. Information items of the kind presented in Test 1 (information) of the Terman-McNemar test come very close to tapping a kind of achievement—knowledge of specific facts—that is an objective of much of the instruction in geography, history, and general science in our elementary and secondary schools.

It would probably be quite possible to obtain consistent judgments from teachers on the degree to which different kinds of intelligence test items elicit abilities directly taught in the schools. That is, there is probably a continuum at one extreme of which are items entirely unrelated to formally recognized educational objectives, and at the opposite extreme are items indistinguishable from those that might properly be found in a test of achievement of instructional objectives in reading, English, arithmetic, algebra, history, or general science. If this is true, it means that intelligence tests differ from achievement tests only in the point on such a continuum at which the average "taughtness" of the items falls. The items on achievement tests require abilities that have a relatively high degree of "taughtness," or similarity to what is directly and explicitly taught in schools. The items on intelligence tests would probably have a lesser degree of such similarity. Nonetheless, the difference between intelligence and achievement tests is only a matter of degree, not a qualitative difference involving some mysterious, biologically inherited, intrinsic essence.

Intelligence tests are thus achievement tests—tests of the achievement of knowledge, skills, and abilities that result from the informal, unarranged interaction of the individual with his culture. When it can be safely assumed that the influences of this interaction are equal in kind and amount for a given group of persons, the differences in their "achievement" of these abilities and skills come to be called differences in their "intelligence." When the differences in these "achievements" can readily be traced to differences in the kinds of formal influences to which individuals have been subjected—such influences as schools, courses, teachers, curricula, textbooks, and the like—the differences are generally considered differences in "achievement."

This type of significance of intelligence test results implies that much the same meaning can often be attached to the results of achievement tests. Accordingly, the present section of this chapter on the measurement of mental abilities presents a discussion of general achievement tests, i.e., achievement tests that may be considered to measure characteristics highly similar to those measured by the kinds of intelligence tests described in the preceding section.

Rather than focusing on an inevitably unsuccessful attempt to peel away from intellectual ability all possible effects of differences in environment and training, the builders of intelligence tests for use in educational programs have concentrated on measuring achievement of maximally generalizable outcomes of intellectual influences of American society. By the same token, the authors of tests of general achievement for American schools have, knowingly or not, produced instruments for measuring general intellectual ability.

In making up a battery of general achievement tests, the test makers have to begin with a general outline of the areas and kinds of achievements they intend to measure. Often this outline is determined by the subject-matter areas and breakdowns that are traditional in the grade levels for which the test is intended. Sometimes the test makers transcend traditional subject-matter lines and develop integrated areas of achievement somewhat different from any of the official courses of study or curricula governing school programs.

At the primary grade levels, the American School Achievement Tests[1] deal with word recognition, word meaning, paragraph meaning, arithmetical computation, arithmetic problems, language usage, and spelling. The California Achievement Tests[2] for the same levels yield scores for reading vocabulary, reading compre-

[1] Publisher No. 20, see p. 614. [2] Publisher No. 6.

hension, total reading, arithmetic reasoning, arithmetic fundamentals, total arithmetic, mechanics of English and grammar, spelling, and total language. The Coordinated Scales of Attainment[3] break up achievement in the first three grades as follows: picture-word association, word-picture association, vocabulary recognition, reading comprehension, arithmetic experience, number skills, problem reasoning, computation, and spelling. On the other hand, the Metropolitan Achievement Tests[4] categorize achievement in the primary grades as follows: word pictures, word recognition, word meaning, numbers, reading, arithmetic fundamentals, arithmetic problems, spelling, and language usage. It is apparent that these batteries have much in common as to the way they conceive of achievement in the primary grades.

At the elementary grade levels, Grades IV to VI, many of the tests are organized along lines similar to those for the primary levels. Some, however, introduce tests organized along lines of the subject matter customary for these grade levels. The Coordinated Scales of Attainment, for Grades IV through VIII, yield scores for punctuation, usage, capitalization, reading, history, geography, social science, literature, computation, problem reasoning, and spelling. The Iowa Every-Pupil Test of Basic Skills[5] contains tests on silent reading comprehension (reading comprehension and vocabulary), work-study skills (map reading, use of references, use of index, use of dictionary, and alphabetizing or graphing), basic language skills (punctuation, capitalization, usage, spelling, and sentence sense), and basic arithmetic skills (fundamental knowledge, fundamental operations, problems, and total). The Metropolitan Achievement Tests yield scores for reading, vocabulary, arithmetic fundamentals, arithmetic problems, and language usage, and beginning with Grade V also provide scores on literature, geography, history and civics, and science. The elementary level tests of the Stanford Achievement Tests[6] are organized in terms of paragraph meaning, word meaning, language usage, arithmetic reasoning, arithmetic computation, literature, social studies, elementary science, and spelling.

The foregoing analyses of elementary-school achievement indi-

3 Publisher No. 11.
4 Publisher No. 28.
5 Publisher No. 22.
6 Publisher No. 28.

cate that these general achievement batteries conform to some extent to the ways in which general intelligence has been analyzed and also to the traditional subject-matter classifications of school curricula.

The content of such batteries has generally been determined on the basis of courses of study, curriculum practices, the opinions of curriculum experts in the various subject fields, textbooks and other instructional materials. The test makers also consult studies of word frequency, of teaching and learning problems, and the like.

The types of items, format, and make-up of these general achievement batteries resemble those of group intelligence tests. Batteries that are intended to provide uniform coverage of a major part of the grade range resemble the intelligence test series that attempt the same task; the kinds of norms and types of items are arranged to insure maximum comparability from one grade level to the next, and from one subscore to the next.

Selecting an appropriate general achievement test battery for use in a particular school resembles in many important respects the task of selecting an intelligence test described in the preceding section. Due attention must be given to the time required, the grade level, the kinds of norms provided, and the adequacy and representativeness of the samples on which the norms are based. Reliability data concerning total and part scores should be considered. Seldom if ever are there data on the empirical relevance of achievement tests. This means that the relevance of the test to the curriculum, the educational objectives with which the particular school is concerned, must be judged on the basis of a detailed examination, item by item, of the content of the test, the form of the items, the educational "philosophy" underlying the categories and processes embodied in the test items, the research and curricular studies on which the selection of test content was based, and the like. The same sources of information that can be used for intelligence tests serve also for general achievement test batteries.

What are some of the faults that reviewers have found with achievement batteries? Inspection of such criticisms may alert the reader to similar inadequacies in any test he may consider for his own use. Following are quotations of adverse criticisms from the *Fourth Mental Measurements Yearbook:*

Unfortunately, rigid time limits for the various sub-tests result in mixing measures of speed with measures of other factors such as paragraph comprehension and arithmetic problem-solving ability (p. 2).

Most schools will find the spelling sub-tests unsatisfactory since they are tests of recognition of correct spelling rather than tests of ability to reproduce from memory the correct spelling of a word (p. 2).

Are the norms sufficiently representative so that almost any school could use them with reasonable confidence? That question cannot be answered from the information available in the test manuals (p. 2).

[These] can be criticized, as were their predecessors, for the excessive difficulty of much of the primary battery, for an undesirable use of a term "diagnostic" to describe the analytical procedures (for analyzing types of errors made by pupils), and for the vagueness of statement in the accessory materials about the standardization procedures (p. 3).

The use of diagonal fraction lines is a real, but minor, flaw. The printing of reading selections and questions about them on different pages that require turning is a more serious criticism (p. 5).

. . . This reviewer would like to question seriously the use of primary batteries of standardized achievement tests generally. . . . Administrators . . . may profitably ask whether any values they derived from the results justify imposing this strain on pupils and the implied standards on teachers of such young pupils (p. 5).

. . . While the test has apparently been carefully made, it is little more than a miscellaneous collection of items on information . . . (p. 14).

Explanations for teachers on administering and scoring the test and on deriving and interpreting the scales' scores are complete and helpful. Nevertheless, group meetings to clarify the coordinated plan which permeates the entire program should be arranged in schools using these scales. The master manuals are worthy of study, although it is unfortunate that they provide little information on procedures used in arriving at the scale scores and the norms (p. 17).

In some items, especially in the reading test, some wrong answers are too nearly correct. However, many of the wrong responses are not at all plausible. An item analysis would probably reveal that one wrong response could be eliminated from most of the items without loss of effectiveness (p. 18).

A serious imbalance seems to occur in the test on English: here 60 items are devoted to language usage, 60 to capitalization and punctuation, and 60 to spelling—leaving only 69 items to the other five parts of the test, of which only 15 are devoted to literature. Since all items are given equal weight in scoring, literature becomes, in terms of number of items, only 6% of the total English course as tested (p. 20).

The authors indicate that considerable time and attention was given to analysis of content of academic high school curricula and to construction of items that would adequately sample such content. However, they fail to report the text books and courses of study which were included in the analysis so that it is impossible to describe precisely the type of high school program for which the sample of items is valid (p. 43).

Included as an important part of most general achievement test batteries are tests on reading, reading readiness, English usage, and mathematics. These are perhaps the most important of the so-called "tool subjects." Tests for measuring achievement of these tool subjects can be excerpted from the various achievement test batteries. It may often be more convenient, however, to use special tests for these purposes.

REFERENCES

1. American Educational Research Association, *Review of Educational Research,* Washington: American Educational Research Association.
2. Bingham, W. V., *Aptitudes and Aptitude Testing,* New York: Harper & Brothers, 1937.
3. Bronner, A. F., Healy, W., Lowe, G. M., and Shimberg, M. E., *A Manual of Individual Mental Tests and Testing,* Boston: Little, Brown & Company, 1928.
4. Buros, O. K. (ed.), *Mental Measurements Yearbooks,* Highland Park, New Jersey: The Mental Measurements Yearbook, 1938, 1940, 1949, 1953.
5. Cronbach, L. J., *Essentials of Psychological Testing,* New York: Harper & Brothers, 1949.
6. Davis, A., and Eells, K., *Manual, Davis-Eells Test of General Intelligence or Problem-Solving Ability,* Yonkers: World Book Company, 1953.
7. Educational Testing Service, *American Council on Education Psychological Examination for College Freshmen, Manual of Instructions, 1948 Edition,* New York: Cooperative Test Division of Educational Testing Service, 1948.
8. Eells, K., Davis, A., Havighurst, R. J., Herrick, V. E., and Tyler, R.,

Intelligence and Cultural Differences: A Study of Cultural Learning and Problem Solving, Chicago: University of Chicago Press, 1951.

9. Freeman, F. N., *Mental Tests,* Boston: Houghton Mifflin Company, rev. ed., 1939.

10. Garrett, H. E., and Schneck, M. R., *Psychological Tests, Methods, and Results,* New York: Harper & Brothers, 1933, Part II, Chapters 1, 2.

11. Gray, W. S., "Reading," *Encyclopedia of Educational Research,* New York: The Macmillan Company, rev. ed., 1950.

12. Hildreth, G. H., *A Bibliography of Mental Tests and Rating Scales,* New York: The Psychological Corporation, 1939.

13. Hildreth, Gertrude, *A Bibliography of Mental Tests and Rating Scales—1945 Supplement,* New York: The Psychological Corporation, 1946.

14. Hubbard, R. E., and Flesher, W. R., "Intelligent teachers and intelligence tests—do they agree?" *Educational Research Bulletin,* 32:113–122, 139–140 (1953).

15. Kelley, T. L., *Interpretation of Educational Measurements,* Yonkers: World Book Company, 1927.

16. Ruch, G. M., and Segel, D., *Minimum Essentials of the Individual Inventory in Guidance,* U.S. Dept. of the Interior, Office of Education, Vocational Division Bulletin No. 202.

17. Terman, L. M., *The Measurement of Intelligence,* Boston: Houghton Mifflin Company, 1916.

18. Terman, L. M., and Merrill, M. A., *Measuring Intelligence,* Boston: Houghton Mifflin Company, 1937.

19. Thurstone, L. L., *Primary Mental Abilities,* Psychometric Monographs No. 1, Chicago: University of Chicago Press, 1938.

20. Toops, H. A., *The Evolution of the Ohio State University Psychological Test,* Ohio College Association Bulletin No. 113, 1939.

21. Triggs, Frances O., "Description of the purposes and functions of the Diagnostic Reading Tests," *Educational and Psychological Measurement,* 8:3–14 (1948).

22. Triggs, Frances O., "Diagnostic reading tests as aids to remedial instruction," *School and Society,* 66:42–45 (1947).

23. Wechsler, D., *Wechsler Intelligence Scale for Children; Manual,* New York: The Psychological Corporation, 1949.

CHAPTER X

Measuring Special Abilities

ABSTRACT

In this chapter we shall concern ourselves with methods of evaluating special abilities for the purposes of guidance. Factor analysis and differential prediction studies provide the theoretical bases for evaluation of this kind. Work in factor analysis has resulted in substantial agreement on a list of significant, relatively uncorrelated abilities. Activities and jobs in American society provide a more realistic if less rigorous basis for analyzing special abilities. Available tests of special abilities consist of integrated batteries for a variety of occupational fields and of single, more narrowly focused tests.

·~·~·~·

THEORETICAL BASES OF SPECIAL ABILITY EVALUATION

In Chapter VIII we called attention to the problem of the organization of mental abilities. Three types of theory—the "sand," "gravel," and "cobblestone"—were mentioned. Whichever of these is closest to the truth, the "gravel" theory—that is, the theory of group and specific factors—is the only one that implies the possibility of a program of vocational guidance based on psychological testing. This has been pointed out by Hull (8 : 201–205). The "sand" or specific factor theory "pressed to its logical limit . . . would hold that the factors determining success in all activities— *both aptitude behavior and test behavior*—can be found in no other activity whatever; i.e., that they must be absolutely unique. Thus a test activity could never contain any of the determiners found in an aptitude activity. There could never be a correlation between the two." Similarly, the "cobblestone" or general factor theory "would preclude the possibility of forecasting by means of ordinary tests *whether a person would be more effective in one aptitude than another.* It would be impossible to differentiate the aptitudes within an individual. On this theory, a vocational guidance based on psychological testing would be impossible." On the other hand, the "gravel" or group factor theory in its strict form, assuming no universal factor or determiner running through all possible intellectual activity and rejecting specific or unique factors, would enable a test to correlate with one aptitude while not correlating at all with another. "In other words, the existence of group factors would permit the possibility of *differentiating* the potential aptitudes of an individual by means of tests."

We see thus that the hope of developing aptitude tests to predict vocational success is based on the degree to which the group factor theory is borne out. That is, aptitude testing requires the measurement of differences in the amounts of certain aptitudes possessed by an individual. The existence of such tests provides a decisive indication of the existence of group factors. These tests have already been produced in considerable variety. Thus, Hull and Limp (8 : 42–43) produced test batteries for shorthand, typewriting, high-school English, and high-school algebra which enabled the differentiation of the four aptitudes *from each other.* Many other tests of special abilities have been constructed that succeed in predicting specific achievement rather than general achievement.

We must distinguish between special *abilities* and all other aspects of pupils that are predictive of vocational success. In one sense, every aspect treated in this book may be considered an aptitude insofar as it is related to vocational success. Especially is this true of the interests of pupils, for many studies have shown that pupils differ widely in the degree to which their interests, or emotionally toned preferences, likes, and dislikes, fit them for various vocations. The emotional and social adjustments of pupils, their "personalities," distinguish them from one another in fitness for various vocations. The pupil's socioeconomic environment and background, his family, and the community in which he lives may be considered determiners of his fitness or aptitude for one vocation as against others.

In this chapter, however, we are concerned not with all aspects predictive of success, but only with those that are abilities.

An ability may be an achievement or development of the individual in the same sense as we consider the pupil's mastery of school subject matter to be an achievement. The abilities with which we are here concerned, however, may be distinguished from school achievements in that they are *relatively* not subject to change in the future, and have usually reached, through previous maturation and experience, about as high a level as is possible for the given individual at the time he is tested. At the time at which they are considered to be predictive of vocational success, these special abilities are generally no longer readily acquired.

It is well known that not all individuals possess these special abilities in the same degree. We cannot successfully characterize an individual's abilities or potentialities for success in a great number of varied tasks with a single general ability score. As most tests are at present constructed, two individuals with the same general ability score may differ in the composition of that general ability; one, for example, may have a high verbal ability and low mathematical ability while the other has a high mathematical ability and low verbal ability. Consequently, in attempting to guide pupils among the various curricula and vocations, some breakdown of general ability into special abilities is required.

PRESENT STATUS OF FACTOR ANALYSIS

In Chapter VIII two methods of making this breakdown were mentioned: (1) statistically derived "primary mental abilities," and (2) culturally determined fields of endeavor. The former may be illustrated by the following factors which have been reported by various factor analysts (**19** : 30–33):

A *verbal* factor, involved primarily in the tests that depend on the meanings of words and the ideas associated with them.

A *space* factor, which appears in tasks requiring reactions to spatial relations, such as reading plans or blueprints or telling whether two drawings represent one or more sides of an asymmetrical figure.

A *number* factor, requiring such simple numerical operations as multiplication, addition, subtraction, and division, but not the more complex tasks involving numerical reasoning.

A *memory* factor, requiring paired associations or the recognition of recently learned material.

A *mental speed* factor.

A *perceptual* factor, or readiness to discover and identify perceptual details.

Deduction and induction factors, measured respectively by syllogistic reasoning tests and by tests requiring the subject to find the rule that binds a number of items together and from it to classify or predict other items.

None of these factors bear a direct and obvious relationship to any specific vocation, such as automobile mechanic or lawyer. Some of them should, however, be involved more in some vocations than in others. The spatial factor is probably involved to a high degree in the work of a draftsman, whereas lawyers and writers need more of the verbal factor. The general nature of the uses of factor analyses of primary mental abilities in vocational guidance may be indicated as follows:

1. Find the degree to which each ability is predictive of success in each occupation. This would be in the form of a correlation coefficient, from which a weighting of the ability could be derived.

2. Obtain the score in each ability of the individual being counseled.

3. Multiply the ability scores by the weights and add the products. The resulting sum would be a measure of the individual's predicted success in that occupation.

Vocational counseling would indeed be a mechanical yet highly accurate procedure if results of Step 1 in the above procedure were available. Such an advanced stage has obviously not yet been reached, for the necessary primary abilities have not yet been isolated. And although tests to measure the extent to which individuals possess these abilities are to a considerable extent available, the weights of each ability in each occupation have not been determined. Perhaps after considerable progress has been made on the basis of much additional research along these lines, vocational guidance will become a matter of easy routine. For the present it is necessary to predict vocational success on the basis not of a few test batteries appropriate to all vocations but of many test batteries designed specifically for small groups of occupations.

THE NATURE OF AMERICAN VOCATIONS

It would be impossible, however, to construct a test for predicting success in each of the 20-odd thousand distinct jobs which have been defined by the United States Employment Service. Such a vast battery of tests, even if one could be constructed, would be of little use for guidance purposes because the problem of which test to give to which pupil would be almost insurmountable. As we saw in Chapter VIII, information concerning the thousands of distinct jobs or occupations in which the millions of workers in this country are employed is available. *The Dictionary of Occupational Titles, Part I,* has already been mentioned. This *Dictionary* is based on data collected by trained job analysts who at first hand observed workers at work, their duties, the machines and tools used, the hiring requirements of employers, and the estimated abilities necessary to make an adjustment in each job.

The problem of simplifying and clarifying the consideration of so many separate occupations for vocational guidance purposes becomes immediately apparent once the tremendous variety of American economic activity is realized. It is necessary, as Shartle (15 : 45–51) points out, to group occupations into families based on different lines of relationship, if the meanings of these vast accumulations of job descriptions are to be grasped. The U.S. Employment Service classification, based on the similarity of work performed and materials used, is as follows:

Major Occupational Groups and Divisions

0—Professional and managerial occupations.
   0–0 through 0–3   Professional occupations.
   0–4 through 0–6   Semi-professional occupations.
   0–7 through 0–9   Managerial and official occupations.
1—Clerical and sales occupations.
   1–0 through 1–4   Clerical and kindred occupations.
   1–5 through 1–9   Sales and kindred occupations.
2—Service Occupations.

2–0	Domestic service occupations.
2–2 through 2–5	Personal service occupations.
2–6	Protective service occupations.
2–8 and 2–9	Building service workers and porters.

3—Agricultural, fishery, forestry, and kindred occupations.

3–0 through 3–4	Agricultural, horticultural, and kindred occupations.
3–8	Fishery occupations.
3–9	Forestry (except logging), and hunting and trapping occupations.

4 and 5—Skilled occupations.
6 and 7—Semi-skilled occupations.
8 and 9—Unskilled occupations.

In Part II of the *Dictionary of Occupational Titles, Titles and Codes,* each of the thousands of jobs defined in Part I is classified along with other jobs to which it is related. Part II provides lists of occupations grouped according to the work performed and the materials used; the definitions of these jobs are easily found in Part I of the *Dictionary.* Similarly, if the definition of a job title is first found in Part I, jobs related to it may be found by looking up its code number in Part II and noting the occupational titles adjacent to it there. The definitions in Part I are also classified by industry, all occupations peculiar to a given industry being listed together; occupations found in all industries are excluded.

Other occupational classifications have been worked out to serve in vocational guidance. Among those mentioned by Shartle (15 : 48) are occupational classifications based on:

1. The personal worker qualifications required for success
2. The aptitude needed to learn the job
3. Educational prerequisites necessary for entrance

Such classifications may eventually answer such questions as these (15 : 48): "What are the occupations that might be open to a person whose chief ability and interest is in dealing directly with people? What are the occupations, regardless of industry, that might be entered by a youth who has the aptitude and interest for operating electrical machines, or the youth who has unusual finger dexterity, or unusual eye-hand coordination? What are the eighth-grade jobs, the high school jobs, the college jobs?" If we knew the

U. S. DEPARTMENT OF LABOR
UNITED STATES EMPLOYMENT SERVICE
WORKER CHARACTERISTICS FORM

Job title ....   *Schedule No.* ....

Indicate the amount of each characteristic demanded of the worker in order to do the job satisfactorily by putting an **X** in column A, B, or C.

RATING SCALE GUIDE

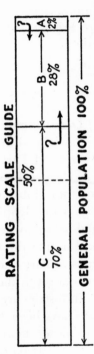

C 70%   ?   50%   B 28%   ?   A 2%

← GENERAL POPULATION 100% →

In checking these items, think of *persons in general* rather than workers in this job, department, or plant as a whole. *Consider each characteristic carefully before rating it. When in doubt between A or B amount, always rate the characteristic as B; when in doubt between B or C amount, always rate the characteristic as B. Thus the SIGNIFICANT characteristics of the job will not be submerged in the C column but will be focused more clearly in the B column.* If some characteristic is demanded which does not appear in this list, write it in and check as described above.

Amounts of Characteristics			Characteristics Required of Worker
C	B	A	
			1. Work rapidly for long periods.
			2. Strength of hands.
			3. Strength of arms.
			4. Strength of back.
			5. Strength of legs.

Amounts of Characteristics			Characteristics Required of Worker
C	B	A	
			26. Arithmetic computation.
			27. Intelligence.
			28. Adaptability.
			29. Ability to make decisions.
			30. Ability to plan.

6. Dexterity of fingers.
7. Dexterity of hands and arms.
8. Dexterity of foot and leg.
9. Eye-hand coordination.
10. Foot-hand-eye coordination.

11. Coordination of independent movements of both hands.
12. Estimate size of objects.
13. Estimate quantity of objects.
14. Perceive form of objects.
15. Estimate speed of moving objects.

16. Keenness of vision.
17. Keenness of hearing.
18. Sense of smell.
19. Sense of taste.
20. Touch discrimination.

21. "Muscular" discrimination.
22. Memory for details (things).
23. Memory for ideas (abstract).
24. Memory for oral directions.
25. Memory for written directions.

31. Initiative.
32. Understanding of mechanical devices.
33. Attention to many items.
34. Oral expression.
35. Skill in written expression.

36. Tact in dealing with people.
37. Memory of names and persons.
38. Personal appearance.
39. Concentration amidst distractions.
40. Emotional stability.

41. Work under hazardous conditions.
42. Estimate quality of objects.
43. Work under unpleasant physical conditions (qualify)_____
44. Color discrimination.
45. Ability to meet and deal with public.
46. Height.   Short   Medium   Tall
47. Weight.   Light   Medium   Heavy
48.
49.
50.

Definitions for added characteristics:

FIG. 12. Scale for Describing Jobs in Terms of Worker Characteristics.

14—8868

world of work and the pupil in this way, it would be possible to point out for him a family of similar jobs which best fit his traits. Knowing that a pupil has a high-school education, poor vision, an excellent sense of taste, high finger dexterity, poor memory for details, excellent memory for abstract ideas, low ability in arithmetical computation, a high degree of interest in mechanical devices, ability to estimate the size and form of objects, and many other similar traits and characteristics, we may eventually be able to provide him with a list of occupations which require his particular set of traits.

Preliminary results of this program of determining occupational relationships have been reported by Stead, Shartle, and associates (16 : 188–205). While their efforts are primarily directed toward the problems encountered in public employment services, vocational training and guidance workers and classroom teachers should also benefit from their approach. The worker characteristics form shown in Fig. 12 is filled out by trained job analysts for each job. The analyst indicates, by checking Column A, B, or C, "what amount of each characteristic is demanded of the worker in order to do the job satisfactorily."

This method of *estimating* rather than *measuring* worker characteristics required for success on a job is not too exact. It has the advantage, however, of being far speedier in yielding results for a large number of occupations.

The nature of this work in occupational classification has been summarized by Ward (16 : 206):

Eventually it may be possible to set up tables of occupations in which certain qualifications are of primary importance, such as personal appearance, ability to meet the public, strength, dexterities, coordinations, and amount of schooling. For the counselor, occupations may be identified in a code book by a family number for easy reference to the various groupings. . . .

Regardless of the method used in revealing occupational families and their relationships, it seems assured that counselors must be provided with such data if the occupational structure of industry is to be adequately understood.

This kind of information will have to be adapted to particular community situations and needs. Publications issued by the U.S.

Employment Service, such as the *Dictionary of Occupational Titles* and, eventually, sets of master pattern cards punched with the worker characteristics required for every kind of work in the country, will have to be supplemented by job information based on the particular community whose youth are to benefit from a particular vocational guidance program. The work of gathering local occupational information can probably be best done when organized as a coöperative community project involving schools, the public employment service, neighboring universities, and other agencies. Methods of developing local community programs for the promotion of occupational adjustment are described by Bell (1).

We have outlined some of the attempts to conceptualize the field of vocational guidance. On the side of the worker or pupil, an attempt has been made, by means of factorial analyses of tests of mental abilities, to isolate a relatively small number of primary traits on the basis of which predictions of vocational success can be made. On the side of the work to be done, the occupations or jobs, we have noted the attempts, particularly by the U.S. Employment Service, to develop a relatively small number of occupational groups in place of long lists of the thousands of currently indentifiable jobs.

SELECTION VS. GUIDANCE

The reader should realize that these attempts to reduce pupil and worker characteristics, on the one hand, and the vast number of different occupations, on the other, to a relatively small number of traits or occupational families find their justification in guidance more than in selection. Selection is concerned with a given job and the choice of workers for it. The job is already singled out and its characteristics and requirements are well defined; hence the task of constructing tests to predict success in it can proceed along the following well-established lines:

1. Develop a criterion of success in the activity or job for which workers are to be selected; for example, the production per hour of x units of quality q or better, with 5 percent spoilage allowed.

2. Analyze the job into the skills, activities, and other worker traits that are related to success in it.

3. Construct a test or set of test items to elicit the skills and activities determined in Step 2.

4. Apply these tests to a group of persons who will probably differ appreciably in success on the job and for whom criterion scores are available.

5. Determine the validity of the test in terms of the correlation between scores on the test and criterion scores.

If this procedure were to be used in guidance in the absence of any organization of occupations or workers' ability into relatively few groups, guidance would require (1) developing an aptitude test for each of the thousands of existing jobs, and (2) administering a large number of these tests to every individual who is to be guided into the occupation for which he is best suited. The impracticality of vocational guidance based on such a cumbersome and unwieldy procedure has motivated the isolation of primary characteristics and the organization of occupations into families.

GENERAL FUNCTIONS OF THE AVAILABLE DEVICES

Fortunately, the techniques and equipment already at hand can provide some valuable assistance in guidance work. A considerable number of special ability evaluation devices are available that enable the prediction of success in the different fields of work. Various techniques are available for narrowing down to a relatively small number the choice of tests to be given a particular individual. With them, broad areas of occupations can be eliminated as possibilities for a given person. The "narrowing-down" procedure uses all the information about a pupil in each of the various aspects with which this book is concerned. His scholastic achievement, physical aspects, general mental ability, social and emotional adjustment, and socioeconomic environment and background all provide a detailed and comprehensive picture of his make-up. From this picture it is possible to ascertain the jobs in which he is most likely to succeed. His attitudes and interests are of special importance in this respect. We shall be especially concerned with them in a later chapter. Here we merely note the possibilities of *vocational interest* evaluation for delimiting the field in which special ability tests should be given.

The role of the special ability test is thus supplementary; it serves to round out and complete the picture of the pupil's vocational strengths and weaknesses. Instead of a test for each vocational aptitude, only a few such tests are necessary in order to answer questions about a pupil not already answered by the other data concerning him. An illustration may clarify this point. Suppose that a pupil is undecided whether to enter an engineering college or to major in mathematics in a liberal arts college with a view to becoming an actuarial worker. His scholastic achievement indicates that he is equipped to do college work and is sufficiently strong in mathematics for either occupation. His physical status is adequate for either outdoor engineering work or indoor actuarial research. His general scholastic aptitude is of a high level and he rates equally high in both mathematical and verbal factors. His social and personal adjustment is of such a nature that he could manage men as an engineer or enjoy the solitary nature of actuarial research equally well. In the same way his attitudes and interests do not permit a discrimination between the two fields, and his socioeconomic environment and background, other than providing sufficient financial resources for either kind of training, do not afford any clue as to which would be the better vocational choice for him.

In such a hypothetical situation, probably also quite rare, a test of special ability might furnish the bit of evidence necessary to weight the balance in favor of one vocation as against the other. In this case, it might be found that the pupil's ability to handle spatial relations is far below that of most engineers. For the counselor would realize, along with Bingham (5 : 172), that "ability to perceive the sizes, shapes, and relations of objects in space and to think quickly and clearly about these relations is another distinct asset for a student of engineering. He must be able to see how the parts of a mechanism fit together, and to infer what happens to one part when another part moves. Many engineers, although not all, are facile visualizers. But all, whether excelling in their powers of visual imagination or not, must somehow learn to read diagrams and prepare blueprints, to make and read topographical maps and profiles, to translate two-dimensional sketches into three-dimensional models, and vice versa. Aptitudes for thinking about shapes, sizes, and spatial relations are particularly valuable in the study of drafting, descriptive geometry, and mechanics."

In this case, this difference between the pupil's ability to handle spatial relations and his otherwise high degree of potentialities for success in both engineering and actuarial work might be sufficient to enable his vocational guidance counselor to encourage him toward the latter and away from the former. The problem for this pupil would have been narrowed down by all the other data concerning him to the point where one special ability test, such as the Minnesota Spatial Relations Test, the Kent-Shakow Form Board, or the Minnesota Paper Form Board, might be sufficient to provide decisive evidence.

AVAILABLE SPECIAL ABILITY TESTS

What are the major fields for which special ability tests have been devised? What specific tests are available in each of these fields?

Two kinds of special ability tests can be identified in answer to these questions: (1) batteries of relatively uncorrelated tests intended to be valid for a variety of occupations and standardized on the same populations, and (2) single tests or batteries intended to be valid for a single type of occupation.

BATTERIES OF RELATIVELY UNCORRELATED TESTS

The first type, the relatively uncorrelated batteries, are groups of tests that have been developed by the same authors, put in a uniform format, standardized on the same groups of pupils or adults, and intended to maximize the validity of intraindividual as well as interindividual comparisons. If suitable for a particular kind of person and occupation, these batteries are much more useful than collections of tests developed and standardized by different authors.

Table 8 lists the scores yielded by five batteries of this kind. Here we shall describe one of these batteries that seems especially useful for guidance in secondary schools.

The Differential Aptitude Tests (DAT), intended for use in Grades VIII through XII, comprise the eight tests listed in Table

8; they are set up in seven booklets. The eight scores are designed explicitly for use in educational and vocational guidance. An exceedingly thorough test manual presents in great detail much in-

TABLE 8. Scores Yielded by Various Multi-Score Ability Test Batteries

Differential Aptitude Tests 18*	Guilford-Zimmerman Aptitude Survey 23*	SRA Primary Mental Abilities: Intermediate 22*	General Aptitude Test Battery (U.S.E.S.) 26*	Yale Educational Aptitude Test Battery 10*
Verbal Reasoning	Verbal Comprehension	Verbal Meaning	Intelligence	Verbal Comprehension
Numerical Ability	General Reasoning	Space	Verbal Aptitude	Artificial Language
Abstract Reasoning	Numerical Operations	Reasoning	Numerical Aptitude	Verbal Reasoning
Space Relations	Perceptual Speed	Number	Spatial Aptitude	Quantitative Reasoning
Mechanical Reasoning	Spatial Orientation	Word Fluency	Form Perception	Mathematical Aptitude
Clerical Speed and Accuracy	Spatial Visualization		Clerical Perception	Spatial Relations
Language Usage (Spelling and Sentences)	Mechanical Knowledge		Eye-Hand Coördination	Mechanical Ingenuity
			Motor Speed	
			Finger Dexterity	
			Manual Dexterity	

*Publisher Number (see pp. 613-614).

formation concerning the background and development of the battery. Indeed, the value of the tests derives at least as much from the manual and other aids as from the test content itself. Inspection of the manual should contribute much to an appreciation of the fact that mental tests consist not of the materials given the examinee but rather of these together with the data on relevance, reliability, and norms that adequate manuals should contain.

The DAT battery reflects a compromise between the factors resulting from factor analyses and the abilities considered important in guiding secondary-school youth in contemporary American society. Since the norms for the battery were obtained by giving all eight tests to the same groups of students, they can be used to describe the *intra*individual differences, i.e., strengths and weaknesses, already mentioned as essential to guidance. Furthermore, there are separate norms not only for each test but for each grade and sex. The large number of cases necessary to obtain such well-broken-down norms (about 47,000) were chosen from nearly 100 schools representing all regions of the United States and various social strata. The intercorrelations among the eight scores are given separately for different grades and both sexes. Correlations are also reported with other tests such as the ACE Psychological Examination, the Primary Mental Ability Tests, the General Aptitude Test Battery, and the Kuder Preference Record. The empirical relevance of the tests is further indicated by the consistently positive correlations of the various scores with grades in school courses to which they should logically be expected to be relevant. On the other hand, because many of the correlations are contrary to such expectation, the authors caution against uncritical predictions of achievement from test scores on the basis of merely the psychological "looks" of a test.

Since the tests are available separately, they can be used for testing single abilities in much the same way as the single-score special ability tests described later in this chapter. Even when not used as part of a battery, however, the tests have the advantage of norms based on good samples and linked to the norms of other tests.

Any battery of tests like the DAT implies the use of "profiles" as a basis for guidance. The student's eight percentile scores are plotted on a chart, as shown in Fig. 13 in the case study of Ellsworth Newcomb. The general height of the profile indicates the general ability level. The "jaggedness" of the profile, or the scatter of its various points around the average position of all eight, indicates how much the student differs "within" himself. The shape of the profile indicates the pattern of his abilities. These three characteristics of the profile may vary somewhat independently of one another. All three must, of course, be taken into account in counseling from profiles. To assist counselors in using such profiles, the authors of the battery have prepared a booklet (4) containing a series of illustrative cases, one of which follows.

Ellsworth Newcomb
Problem
Ellsworth wanted help in changing his career plans, since his low mathematics grades caused him to question his plans for engineering.

Tests
Differential Aptitude Tests. Grade 12.
An *Otis* test. Grade 12. IQ-120.
Ohio State University Psychological Examination. Grade 12. 69th percentile on college freshman norms.
Kuder Preference Record. Grade 12. Highest areas: Literary, Persuasive, Social Service; low areas: Mathematics, Science. (Actual scores not reported.)
Strong Vocational Interest Blank. Grade 12. A ratings: Social Science Teacher, Personnel Manager, Public Administrator, and three sales fields.

Report of Counseling in Grade 12
Ellsworth's engineering aspirations had arisen in part from advice given him by a local industrialist. His mathematics grades were A, D, C, and C, indicating difficulty with a subject crucial to engineering. His work experiences had been in selling; he had found this work pleasant and had done well at it. When Ellsworth and his parents reviewed the whole situation, Ellsworth decided to drop his plans for engineering and prepare for business administration. His low Clerical rating was observed but was not considered crucial to the decision. His high verbal ability and language skills, his successful work experience, and his personal qualities argued for this choice. He was later graduated in the second fifth of his class, and he is now in college.

Comments
Open-minded parents can be persuaded by facts—facts from achievement records, from work experiences, from job descriptions, from interest questionnaires, and from aptitude test results. In this case the data added up to a consistent pattern which suggested college-level

training but not in engineering. Whether he should study business administration or should complete a general liberal arts course with a social science or language major would be a matter of choice. If he had not wanted to go to college, on-the-job learning in industry or business (perhaps in selling) would have been consonant with his abilities and interests.

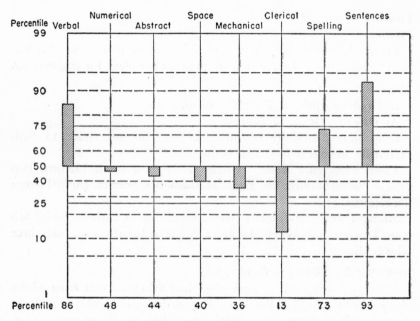

FIG. 13. DAT Profile of Ellsworth Newcomb.

One cannot help remarking that while well-meaning, successful persons in the community can be helpful to the school counselor, they sometimes may mislead young people because of their halo as advisers. Most counselors like to enlist the aid of local business and professional men, but the wise choice of such volunteers is not easy. The self-chosen vocational counselor can present embarrassing problems.

Ellsworth solved his problem neatly, partly because of the detailed information yielded by the *Differential Aptitude Tests*. Like the *DAT* Verbal and Language Usage scores, the *OSU* rating indicated college ability. Useful as such a single-score test can be, the *DAT* and interest test profiles were much more specific in providing a basis for choosing among possible college opportunities.

TESTS DESIGNED FOR SINGLE OCCUPATIONAL FIELDS

Tests of special abilities have been developed, and usually published, for the use of vocational guidance workers mainly in the following fields:

Mechanical ability
Motor ability
Clerical ability
Music ability
Art ability
Professional abilities, e.g., medicine, law, engineering, nursing, teaching

Mechanical Ability Tests. Mechanical ability tests may be classified as either (1) mechanical assembly tests, (2) spatial relations tests, or (3) tests of mechanical information. Typical of the first is the Minnesota Mechanical Assembly Test, a set of three boxes containing simple mechanical objects, such as a bicycle bell, a monkey wrench, and a metal pencil. The subject is required to assemble these within given time limits and his product is scored with partial credit. The test is valuable for predicting the success of junior-high-school boys in shop courses but is not very useful for older persons. It may be criticized on the ground of the possible large variation in scores resulting from crude and inadequate materials used in the simple mechanical objects.

Performance tests of spatial relations may be illustrated by the Minnesota Spatial Relations Test and the Kent-Shakow Form Boards. The Minnesota test consists of four boards with 58 odd-shaped cutouts which the pupil is instructed to put in their proper places in the board as rapidly as possible. The score, amount of time required, is intended to be an indicator of probable success in high-school shop courses and in such occupations as garage mechanic, manual training teacher, and ornamental iron worker.

The Kent-Shakow Form Boards contain five holes or recesses into which a graded series of eight sets of blocks must be fitted. The score, time required to fill the five recesses, is intended to be useful at all ages above six in determining fitness for mechanical occupations.

A paper and pencil test of spatial relations is the Minnesota

Paper Form Board, Revised, which consists of diagrams of disarranged parts of two-dimensional figures. The task is to select from five alternatives the diagram which indicates how the parts fit together. The score, number correct out of 64 items, may be interpreted in relation to the scores of engineering students, first-year vocational-school pupils, and elementary-school boys and girls of different grades and ages.

TABLE 9.   Mechanical Ability Tests

Name of Test	Grades Designed for	No. of Forms	Time (min.) Required to Give	Publisher No. (see list on pp. 613–614)
Minnesota Mechanical Assembly Test..................	7–10	I	60	25
Minnesota Spatial Relations Test......................	7–16	I	15–45	14
Kent-Shakow Form Board.....	1–17	I	20–40	15
Minnesota Paper Form Board, Revised..................	7–10	I	30	18
Detroit Mechanical Aptitudes Examination.............	7–16	I	40	20
O'Rourke Mechanical Aptitude Test......................	7–12	3	70	19
Stenquist Mechanical Aptitude Tests, I and II.............	5–12	I	95	28
Bennett Test of Mechanical Comprehension............	9–13 over	3	30	18
SRA Mechanical Aptitudes Test......................	9 over	2	40	22

Paper and pencil tests of mechanical information are illustrated by the Detroit Mechanical Aptitudes Examination; the O'Rourke Mechanical Aptitude Test: Junior Grade; the Stenquist Mechanical Aptitude Tests, I and II; the SRA Mechanical Aptitudes Test; and the Bennett Test of Mechanical Comprehension. The Detroit test consists of eight subtests: tool recognition, motor speed, size discrimination, arithmetic fundamentals, disarranged pictures, tool information, belt and pulleys, and classification. The O'Rourke Mechanical Aptitude Test proceeds on the assumption that the amount of mechanical information possessed by an individual reflects interest in and aptitude for mechanical activities. It presents pictorial and verbal material concerning the applicability of tools and mechanical processes in matching and multiple-choice form. The Stenquist Mechanical Aptitude Test requires the pairing of pictures of parts of common tools, contrivances, and machines. The Bennett Test of Mechanical Comprehension presents pictorial problems involving principles. The simple drawings call for a combination of information, ability to visualize spatial relations, and intuition of mechanical relationships, hydraulics, etc. The SRA Mechanical Aptitudes Test contains tests on tool use, space visualization, and shop arithmetic. The tool use test presents simple drawings of tools, for each of which the correct phrase concerning its use is to be selected from five choices.

The reader interested in further information on mechanical ability tests should consult the monograph by Bennett and Cruikshank (3), Jones and Seashore's review of the development of fine motor and mechanical abilities (9), and Buros' *Mental Measurements Yearbooks.*

Motor Ability Tests.   Important in many kinds of vocational and educational activity are the abilities required to move arms, hands, fingers, legs, etc., with certain degrees of accuracy, speed, coördination, and responsiveness to simple or complex stimuli. The Minnesota Rate of Manipulation Test is intended to measure rapidity of movement in working at simple tasks involving the hand and fingers. Part One, Placing, requires placing 60 cylindrical blocks in 60 regularly arranged holes in a board. The score is the total time required for four trials after one practice trial. Part Two, Turning, requires the subject to pick up each block from its hole, turn it over, and replace it with the other hand. After each

TABLE 10.   Motor Ability Tests

Name of Test	Grades Designed for	No. of Forms	Time (min.) Required to Give	Publisher No. (see list on pp. 613–614)
Minnesota Rate of Manipulation Test......................	10–adults	I	15–20	16
O'Connor Finger Dexterity Test..	10–adults	I	10–20	25
O'Connor Tweezer Dexterity Test.	10–adults	I	10–20	25
I.E.R. Assembly Tests for Girls, Abridged..................	7–12	I	20–40	25
Purdue Pegboard.............	9–16, adults	I	10	22

row of fifteen blocks, the direction and hand functions are reversed. Scoring is the same as for Placing. This test is considered useful in predicting success as a packer, wrapper, cartoner, or similar routine manipulative worker.

The O'Connor Finger Dexterity Test requires picking up three pins at a time from a tray and inserting them in small holes in a metal plate. The score is the time taken to fill the 100 holes in the plate. The test is useful in relation to occupations involving rapid handling of small objects, such as assembling clocks and radio fixtures or operating keyboard office machines. The O'Connor Tweezer Dexterity Test uses the reverse side of the metal plate; here the holes are large enough for only one pin at a time. The pins are picked up from the tray one at a time with tweezers and inserted in the holes as rapidly as possible. The score, time required for the 100 holes to be filled, is related to success in occupations requiring hand steadiness and eye-hand coördination, such as laboratory work, surgery, drafting, and watch repairing.

The I.E.R. Assembly Test for Girls: Abridged Form presents seven tasks, such as sewing a piece of tape on a strip of muslin and paper cutting and trimming. The tasks are selected for their interest to girls. The scoring of each task is a product of evaluation with partial credit. The test is intended to predict success at assembling jobs in terms of ability to work with the hands.

The monograph by Bennett and Cruikshank (3) goes into greater detail on the methods and results obtained in measuring manual dexterity.

One of their general findings applies particularly to guidance rather than selection uses of motor ability tests: "Vocational guidance (not selection) on the basis of motor skill alone is quite deplorable, except in the case of individuals who have gross incapacitating motor disabilities which may prove a deciding factor in vocational selection" (3 : 5).

Clerical Ability Tests. Obviously, many of the abilities (such as general intelligence and knowledge of grammar and spelling) required in clerical work are not distinctively "clerical" abilities. Four kinds of abilities were identified by Bingham (5) as underlying success in clerical work: (1) perceptual, as in observing words and numbers quickly and accurately; (2) intellectual, as in understanding and reasoning; (3) knowledge, as of spelling and punctuation or of technical information in some learned field; (4) motor, as in operating a typewriter or adding machine. One "clerical" job differs from another in how much and in what way it calls for these types of ability.

Some of the available clerical tests are concerned with just one of these kinds of ability, while others deal with several. The Minnesota Clerical Test consists of two parts, number comparison and name comparison. Numbers or names are presented in pairs separated by a line on which a check is to be marked if the members of the pair are exactly the same.

Examples: 147 √ 147, 3896   3897, 6487361   6489361;
             James   Jimes;   John L. Crawford √ John L. Crawford;
             C. Merriman Lloyd, Inc.   C. Merriam Lloyd, Inc.

The score, number correctly marked or left blank minus the number incorrect, is considered to be related to success in occupations requiring attention to clerical detail, such as bookkeeping, work as a bank teller, office machine operating, and stenography.

The DAT Clerical Speed and Accuracy Test, a part of the Differential Aptitude Tests, also presents letter and number combinations for measuring the perceptual speed and accuracy component of clerical ability.

The General Clerical Test represents a more comprehensive approach to clerical ability testing. It yields scores for clerical speed and accuracy, numerical ability, and verbal facility.

The Bennett Stenographic Aptitude Test, consisting of (1) writing and transcribing symbols and (2) identifying and respelling incorrectly spelled words, is intended to aid in predicting success in shorthand and typewriting training.

The Turse Shorthand Aptitude Test, also designed to predict success in stenographic training, has seven parts: (1) stroking, or making four alternating vertical and slanting strokes in a series of square boxes; (2) spelling, i.e., indicating which if any of three words is spelled correctly; (3) phonetic association, or spelling correctly words that are printed as they are pronounced, as "hoom" for "whom;" (4) symbol transcription, in which fourteen arbitrary shorthand-type symbols with letter values are to be used in transcribing six sentences; (5) word discrimination, or choosing words to complete thirty sentences meaningfully; (6) dictation, or writing in longhand four rapidly dictated sentences, each in ten seconds; and (7) word sense, or writing in full a word presented only in part or omitted from a paragraph. It is clear that these subtests cover most of the types of clerical abilities noted by Bingham.

TABLE 11. Clerical Ability Tests

Name of Test	Grades Designed for	No. of Forms	Time (min.) Required to Give	Publisher No. (see list on pp. 613–614)
Minnesota Clerical Test..........	7 up	1	15	18
DAT Clerical Speed and Accuracy Test......................	9 up	2	8	18
General Clerical Test............	9 up	1	50	18
Bennett Stenographic Aptitude Test	9–6	1	25	18
Turse Shorthand Aptitude Test....	8–10	1	50	28

A *Summary of Clerical Tests* prepared by Bennett and Cruikshank (2) provides more detailed discussion of the rationale and devices in this field than is possible here.

Music Ability Tests. The Seashore Measures of Musical Talent, Revised Edition, consist of two series of three double-faced phonograph records measuring sense of pitch, sense of intensity, sense of time, tonal memory, sense of rhythm, and sense of timbre. These subtests, based on a psychological analysis of musical talent, are played to the subjects, who record their answers on special blanks. For example, the first test, sense of pitch, presents a number of paired sounds and requires the subject to indicate whether the second sound is higher or lower in pitch than the first. The measures may be used to help predict success in music as an avocation or as a career. Series A, covering a wide range of difficulty, is used for unselected groups. Series B is intended for sharp discrimination among musically superior individuals.

The Drake Musical Memory Test consists of 24 original two-bar melodies to be played on a piano by the examiner or an assistant. Following each of the standard melodies, two to seven variations differing from the standard in key, time, or notes are presented.

The score, total number of errors in classifying the variations correctly, is said to correlate with music teachers' estimates of "innate musical capacity."

The Kwalwasser-Dykema Tests resemble the Seashore tests in using a set of phonograph records. Ten elements of musical ability are approached on the five double-faced records: tonal memory

TABLE 12. Music Ability Tests

Name of Test	Grades Designed for	No. of Forms	Time (min.) Required to Give	Publisher No. (see list on pp. 613–614)
Seashore Measures of Musical Talent.....................	5–16 and adults	2	60–80	21
Drake Musical Memory Test......	Ages 8 and over	2	25	20
Kwalwasser-Dykema Tests.......	5–16 and adults	1	60–80	18

(recognition), quality discrimination, intensity discrimination, tonal memory (completion), time discrimination, rhythm discrimination, pitch discrimination, melodic taste, pitch imagery, and rhythm imagery.

For further discussions of musical aptitude testing, the reader may consult the *Encyclopedia of Educational Research,* Buros' *Mental Measurements Yearbooks,* and the *Review of Educational Research.*

The following abstract of a research by Lundin (12) is quoted to illustrate briefly the rationale and procedure of musical aptitude testing and, indeed, of aptitude test research in general:

PROBLEM: In lieu of present existing inadequate measures of musical ability, the present investigation had as its aim, first, to develop a set of tests which would measure directly and objectively some musical behaviors not previously considered, and secondly to relate these measures to intelligence and other sensory acuities as measured by Seashore and Drake.

POPULATION: For preliminary item analysis 60 unselected freshmen and 15 musicians were used. For final testing 196 unselected freshmen and 167 musicians.

PROCEDURE: After preliminary item analysis on the basis of internal consistency and differences between the groups, tests were rerecorded on phonograph records using a Hammond organ and piano as media for sound.

RESULTS: The five tests selected were measures of (a) interval discrimination, (b) melodic transposition, (c) mode discrimination, (d) melodic sequences and (e) rhythmic sequences. The tests were validated on the musician group using professors' ratings in (a) melodic dictation, (b) harmonic dictation, (c) written harmonization, (d) general ability in theory, (e) performance, and (f) sum of ratings. Reliability coefficients were computed for groups separately for each test and total scores. Tests were correlated with years training, liking toward classical music, Seashore tests of pitch, rhythm and tonal memory, Drake test of tonal memory, and intelligence test scores (California Mental Maturity).

CONCLUSIONS: Validity coefficients are high. (*Total scores* and melodic and harmonic dictation .70, general ability .65, performance .51, total ratings .69.) Reliability coefficients range from .60 to .89. There is a low positive relation between *total scores* and training and liking toward classical music. Correlations with Seashore tests are low but positive. When the Seashore and Drake tests are validated against our criteria, validity coefficients for any one criterion used are almost without exception lower than ours. When correlated with intelligence as measured by the California test, our tests show close to a zero relationship for both groups.

Art Ability Tests. The Meier Art Tests: I. Art Judgment requires the selection of the more artistic picture in each of 100 black and white pairs. One of each pair is a reproduction of an artistic work of recognized merit; the other has been altered in some way so as to lower its merit, make it less pleasing, less artistic, less satisfying. The score, number of correct choices, may be interpreted with respect to norms for various grade levels from the seventh grade through senior high school. It furnishes a measure of one constituent of artistic talent, the "capacity for perceiving quality in aesthetic situations relatively apart from formal training."

The Horn Art Aptitude Inventory is a performance rather than a judgment test. In the first part the subject makes outline drawings of objects such as a house, box, and tree, and then of geometric forms such as six triangles, a square placed in another square, and a rectangle broken up with two lines. In the second part the subject uses lines printed in rectangles as bases for compositions drawn in the rectangles. The subject's products are scored by comparing them with examples of excellent, average, and poor work.

TABLE 13. Art Ability Tests

Name of Test	Grades Designed for	No. of Forms	Time (min.) Required to Give	Publisher No. (see list on pp. 613–614)
Meier Art Tests: I. Art Judgment..	7–12	1	45–60	4
Horn Art Aptitude Inventory.....	12–16	1	50	16
Knauber Art Ability Test........	7–16 and	1	180	2
Lewerenz Test in Fundamental	adults			
Abilities of Visual Art.........	3–12	1	105	6

The Knauber Art Ability Test requires drawing a design from memory, drawing figures within space limitations from memory, arranging a specified composition within a given space, creating and completing designs from supplied elements, spotting errors in drawn composition, and finally drawing a composition "using your own symbol for labor." The scoring is semisubjective, but high reliability coefficients are reported by the author. The test may be used to indicate progress in art classes and creative ability rather than aesthetic judgment.

The Lewerenz Test in Fundamental Abilities of Visual Art consists of nine tests: recognition of proportions, originality of line drawing, observation of light and shade, knowledge of subject-matter vocabulary, visual memory of proportion, analysis of problems in cylindrical perspective, analysis of problems in parallel perspective, analysis of problems in angular perspective, recognition of color. Both judgment or taste and creative ability seem to be tapped by this group of tests.

Professional Aptitude Tests. In 1940 Kandel (**10**) summarized the attempts and results obtained in the fields of medicine, law, and engineering. Nine years later, Stuit and others (**17**) brought together and analyzed the results of research on the prediction of success in training for engineering, law, medicine, dentistry, music, agriculture, education, and nursing. Their volume has tables summarizing the correlations with professional-school grades (usually first-year or first-semester grades) of students' previous school records, scholastic aptitude tests, special ability tests, and interest inventories. Although the present chapter is concerned only with special ability tests, it is pertinent to illustrate their conclusions with their table of recommendations for medicine (see Table 14). Similar tables of recommendations are provided for each of the other professional areas they consider.

In recent years professional aptitude testing has come more and more under the sponsorship of professional organizations that coöperate with technically competent testing agencies. The Educational Testing Service (7) has been foremost among the latter; it has developed testing programs for the selection of candidates for admission to colleges of medicine, law, and engineering; actuarial work; the U.S. Military, Naval, and Coast Guard Academies; the foreign service of the U.S. Department of State, and the like. Other workers have set up professional aptitude, or predictive, testing programs for the governing societies in dentistry (13) and pharmacy (14).

As aptitude testing for the professions has come under central sponsorship, it has become more oriented toward selection as against guidance. For the individual student concerned with choosing the path that will lead him into the right occupation for his particular characteristics, the kinds of tests that are readily available for use in guidance offices are still important. Consequently the recommendations by Stuit and others (17), and their approach in formulating these recommendations, are valuable to teachers and counselors concerned with vocational guidance.

GENERAL REFERENCES ON SPECIAL ABILITY EVALUATION DEVICES

In addition to the *Mental Measurements Yearbooks,* several other sources can provide valuable assistance in the selection, administration, and interpretation of devices for the evaluation of special abilities. Among these are the following:

Bingham, W. V., *Aptitudes and Aptitude Testing,* New York: Harper & Brothers, 1937.

Paterson, D. G., Schneidler, G. G., and Williamson, E. G., *Student Guidance Techniques,* New York: McGraw-Hill Book Company, Inc., 1938.

TABLE 14. Essential Qualifications, and Recommended Predictive Tests and Standards, for Success in Training for Medicine[1]

Essential Qualifications	Recommended Tests and Standards	
	High-School Graduates	College Students
Superior aptitude for college and medical-school work	Graduation in top quarter of high school * American Council on Education Psychological Examination for College Freshmen (Thurstone & Thurstone)	Undergraduate standing in upper third of class with minimum average of B * Miller Analogies Test[a] * Scholastic Aptitude Test for Medical Schools, Form 1 (Moss, Hunter, & Hubbard), (available in Veterans Administration guidance centers)
High achievement in the natural sciences	Average of B in high-school science courses * Cooperative General Achievement Tests, Revised Series	Average of B in college courses in biology, chemistry, and physics Cooperative College Biology Test ACS Cooperative General Chemistry Test for College Students Cooperative Physics Test for College Students Graduate Record Examination
Interests typical of successful physicians	* Vocational Interest Blank for Men, Form M (Strong), (score of B-plus or A on Physician key) Vocational Interest Blank for Women, Form W (Strong), (score of B-plus or A on Physician key) Kuder Preference Record (high Scientific and Social Service scores)	* Vocational Interest Blank for Men, Form M (Strong), (score of B-plus or A on Physician key) Vocational Interest Blank for Women, Form W (Strong), (score of B-plus or A on Physician key) Kuder Preference Record (high Scientific and Social Service scores)
Well-integrated personality	* Observation of counselee's behavior during interviewing and testing * Case history * An Inventory of Factors STDCR (Guilford) The Adjustment Inventory, Adult Form (Bell) California Test of Personality, Form A: Adult (Thorpe, Clark, & Tiegs)	* Observation of counselee's behavior during interviewing and testing * Case history * An Inventory of Factors STDCR (Guilford) The Adjustment Inventory, Adult Form (Bell) California Test of Personality, Form A: Adult (Thorpe, Clark, & Tiegs)

* Starred tests will probably constitute a good battery; the others are suitable alternatives.
a The Miller Analogies Test is available only through testing centers of the Psychological Corporation.

[1] Quoted by permission from D. B. Stuit *et al., Predicting Success in Professional Schools,* American Council on Education, 1949, p. 79.

Super, D. E., *Appraising Vocational Fitness,* New York: Harper & Brothers, 1949.

In *Psychological Abstracts* the subject index of each annual volume cites research and other publications on specific occupations and tests.

The *Review of Educational Research* has issues every three years on "educational and psychological testing" and "pupil personnel, guidance and counseling," which critically review the development of and research on special ability tests.

REFERENCES

1. Bell, H. M., *Matching Youth and Jobs,* Washington: American Council on Education, 1940.
2. Bennett, G. K., and Cruikshank, R., *A Summary of Clerical Tests,* New York: Psychological Corporation, 1948.
3. Bennett, G. K., and Cruikshank, R., *A Summary of Manual and Mechanical Ability Tests,* New York: Psychological Corporation, 1942.
4. Bennett, G. K., Seashore, H. G., and Wesman, A. G., *Counseling from Profiles, a Casebook for the Differential Aptitude Tests,* New York: Psychological Corporation, 1951.
5. Bingham, W. V., *Aptitudes and Aptitude Testing,* New York: Harper & Brothers, 1937.
6. Cattell, R. B., *Factor Analysis, an Introduction and Manual for the Psychologist and Social Scientist,* New York: Harper & Brothers, 1952.
7. Educational Testing Service, *Educational Testing Programs,* Princeton: Educational Testing Service, Undated.
8. Hull, C. L., *Aptitude Testing,* Yonkers: World Book Company, 1928.
9. Jones, H. E., and Seashore, R. H., "The development of fine motor and mechanical abilities," *Forty-third Yearbook of the National Society for the Study of Education,* Chicago: University of Chicago Press, 1944, Part I.
10. Kandel, I. L., *Professional Aptitude Tests in Medicine, Law, and Engineering,* New York: Bureau of Publications, Teachers College, Columbia University, 1940.
11. Kelley, T. L., "Talents and tasks, their conjunction in a democracy for wholesome living and national defense," *Harvard Education*

Papers, No. 1, Cambridge: Graduate School of Education, Harvard University, 1940.

12. Lundin, R. W., "Development and validation of a set of musical ability tests," *American Psychologist,* 2:350 (1947).

13. Peterson, S. A., "Aptitude testing program of the American Dental Association," *Colleges and Universities,* 23:212–216 (1948).

14. Remmers, H. H., and Gage, N. L., "The predictive testing program of the Pharmaceutical Survey," *American Journal of Pharmaceutical Education,* 11:54–62 (1947).

15. Shartle, C. L., "Guidance and occupational information," *Studies in Higher Education XL,* Proceedings of the Sixth Annual Guidance Conference held at Purdue University, November 29 and 30, 1940.

16. Stead, W. H., Shartle, C. L., *et al., Occupational Counseling Techniques: Their Development and Application,* New York: American Book Company, 1940.

17. Stuit, D. B., *et al., Predicting Success in Professional Schools,* Washington: American Council on Education, 1949.

18. Thurstone, L. L., *The Vectors of Mind,* Chicago: University of Chicago Press, 1935.

19. Wolfle, D., *Factor Analysis to 1940,* Psychometric Monographs No. 3, Chicago: University of Chicago Press, 1940.

PART THREE

Adjustment

CHAPTER XI

Emotional and Social Adjustment

ABSTRACT

Adjustment can be viewed as adjustment of the individual to himself and to others. It refers to continuous, fundamental, pervasive characteristics of behavior. Definitions of good adjustment, or mental health, cannot be restricted to the notion of passive conformity. Awareness of the basic socially derived needs of the individual helps in understanding the adjustment process. Manifestations of adjustment and maladjustment take many forms, often disguised. Many teachers have misinterpreted these symptoms. Adequate understanding of symptoms requires an appreciation of how adjustment mechanisms work. Personality develops in a cultural context that determines the ends served by these mechanisms.

•◦◦•

The two major impressions usually obtained by teachers and psychologists when they consider the field of emotional and social adjustment are that it is both immensely important and immensely confused. The importance of feeling well, of not being continually stirred up, and of getting along well with people is second only to the importance of living. And the number of possible points of view, of ways in which emotional and social adjustment may be analyzed, seems to be limited only by the number of individuals who attempt such analyses. Our consideration of these aspects of pupils will be guided and, we hope, given significance by our purpose—to meet the teacher's practical needs for evaluation data for guidance purposes. With this purpose in mind, let us consider the nature of adjustment.

THE NATURE OF ADJUSTMENT

Adjustment may be defined very generally as the process whereby a living organism varies its activities in response to changed conditions in its environment. An organism's needs can be fulfilled only by behavior that is effectively adapted to its opportunities. When external circumstances change, the organism must modify its behavior and discover new ways of satisfying its wants. The three fundamental ways in which the adjustment process can take place are new forms of response, a change in the environment, and the modification of the organic needs themselves. Conceived thus generally, adjustment may be identified with living itself. Thus, according to Shaffer, "As long as an animal continues to modify its responses it continues to live. If it fails to adjust in some degree, its existence is imperiled. When an animal ceases entirely to adjust, it is dead" (24).

The common understanding of the term "adjustment," however, includes only the more fundamental, continuous, and pervasive levels of activity and not such narrow functions as the eye's reaction to light, the finger's reaction to pain, and the "mind's" reaction to such a problem as $2 + 2 = ?$. That is, adjustment as it is generally understood means the satisfaction of certain drives, needs, basic motives, urges, desires, or tendencies which involve the whole organism.

Adjustment in this general sense can be thought of in two ways as it relates to the concept of mental health: (1) as mastery, i.e., making a deliberate choice from those actually available and modifying the environment in accordance with a need, and (2) as passive acceptance of social conditions (10). Much of the discussion of the concept of adjustment implicitly or explicitly contains the notion of strict conformity to the social norms of the culture. This meaning of adjustment and its use as an objective in psychotherapy have been vigorously criticized by Lindner, among others, in his book *Prescription for Rebellion* (16). As a cultural value it is characteristic of authoritarian, monolithic dictatorships. "The 'nerve of failure,' " says Riesman (22), "is the courage to face aloneness and the possibility of defeat in one's work without being morally destroyed. It is, in a larger sense, simply the nerve to be oneself when that self is not approved by the dominant ethics of a society."

Jahoda (10) proposes a threefold criterion of mental health: (1) positive adjustment to the environment (mastery); (2) unity of personality, i.e., freedom from conflicts of one's urges, one's reason, and one's conscience (in psychoanalytic terms, the id, the ego, and the superego); and (3) correct perception of reality. She points out, however, the lack of precision of these criteria. If two persons perceive reality differently, whose perception, if either, is correct? Why under unity of personality would we not accept a catatonic patient in a mental hospital as qualifying? At what point is manipulation or change of the environment to be rejected not because the individual is not mentally healthy but because the mastery technique has antisocial results?

Nevertheless, the teacher has no better criteria than these, and here, as often, he must make value judgments as best he can. One out of every twelve persons in this country spends some time as a patient in a mental hospital. In our overcrowded hospitals mental patients require about as many beds as all other patients together. These facts are grim indices of the size and importance of the problem of how, when frustrated, the drives, needs, basic motives, urges, desires or tendencies previously mentioned have led to socially if not always personally undesirable consequences (12 : 8–23).

IMPORTANT MOTIVES

Many lists of "urges" have been made. Among them have been self-preservation, race preservation, inquisitiveness, combativeness, fear, gregariousness, sociability, maternal love, sex, constructiveness, sympathy, rivalry, secretiveness, feeding, curiosity, self-assertion, questioning, imitation, jealousy, repulsion, submissiveness, shyness, modesty, playing, walking, friendliness, coöperation, and so on. It is impossible on the basis of scientific validity to choose the essential few from among these various lists. The inadequacy of words to symbolize dispositions and personality constellations, or determining tendencies, is well indicated by the abundance of such words.

However, no matter how vague and inadequate the words or symbols may be, it *is* possible to categorize the fundamental needs of human beings in American society into a brief but meaningful list. For our present purpose, which is to provide a basis for under-standing the emotional and social adjustment of pupils, we shall not be concerned with the so-called "unlearned" organic drives or goals such as air getting, temperature regulation, hunger, thirst, rest and sleep, elimination, and so on. Rather, we are concerned with the forms these drives take when they have been molded by interaction with the social-cultural milieu in which they must be satisfied. Here, it should be clear, we are going beyond the bounds of experimental information and must be guided chiefly by the requirements of clarity, simplicity, and meaningfulness. There-fore, let us now list the needs, desires, motives, urges, intentions, purposes (or whatever else is the most meaningful name for these aspects of pupils) in terms useful to classroom teachers.

The more important motives of pupils at all levels of education, as these motives are related to an understanding of the emotional and social adjustment of pupils in our culture, may be formulated as follows:

The desire for social approval: Favorable attention, sympathy, companionship, conformity to the mores, customs, and fashions of one social group are all basic needs of pupils. Social approval is one of the most powerful forces by which personality and be-havior are determined.

The desire for mastery: The urges to excel, to succeed, to over-come obstructions, to defeat a rival, to achieve a goal, to solve a problem, to dominate a situation are all manifestations of this type of motive. Success and mastery along some line of endeavor are essential to the emotional well-being of everyone.

The desire for new experience: Exploratory patterns, curiosity, in-ventiveness, concern with the fresh, the strange, and the un-familiar, all seem to be a basic need of human beings. A fixed routine in time or space can be followed for only a relatively small segment of one's lifetime before this urge toward novelty becomes irrepressible.

The desire for security: The feeling of being wanted, of being as-sured that one's presence and contribution are welcome, the need for stable affection from family and personal relationships, all constitute another important category of human motivation. The origin of this desire, in the physiological needs and the love responses of the infant, is strongly related to but not identical with the derivation of the need for social approval.

The desire for individuality: The need to assume adult responsibility, to take up obligations and become independent of the family's material and emotional support, to attain adult individuality or self-integration, is a motive derived largely from the needs of society. The continuously recurring truth that today's children must soon run the world has caused this desire for independence and responsibility to become an integral part of human make-up.

Essential to the proper understanding of these five categories of motivation is an appreciation of their interaction and interdependence. In all but the most elementary situations an individual's behavior is determined by combinations of motives; frequently all the strong motives of the individual are determiners of a single action. Our categories also make no claim to be definitive or complete. Like all such lists this one is merely a convenient descriptive device.

THE ADJUSTMENT PROCESS

Now, how is this discussion of motivation related to the classroom teacher's understanding of what aspects of emotional and social adjustment of pupils should be evaluated? The answer to this question comes out of an analysis of the process of adjustment. Such an analysis should show how motivation and adjustment are related so that they may be better understood.

The adjustment process may be analyzed into four principal steps:

1. The operation of a motive.
2. The presence of some obstacle to the immediate satisfaction of the motive. Such obstacles or thwarting factors may be divided into three general classes: *environmental obstacles,* such as walls around a prison, or an oversolicitous mother, or the mores and customs of society, or the activities of other persons; *personal defects,*[1] such as lameness, ugliness, mental defects, social defects

[1] Environmental and personal obstacles interact with one another. Thus the size of an environmental obstacle which will successfully thwart a motive is inversely proportional to the degree of personal defect of an individual in the area in which that obstacle operates.

such as lack of position or education, emotional instability; *conflict between antagonistic motives,* which, unlike physical forces, do not cancel each other but rather result in increased tension, vacillation, and nonspecific activity.

3. Responses, often trial-and-error reactions, using either motor or symbolic processes and guided in varying degree by past experience. At this stage emotional and social maladjustments usually arise. If the responses are not immediately successful in bringing about a satisfaction of the desire, an emotional response may arise leading to a persistent nonadjustive reaction, that is, excessive persistence in an unadaptive mode of activity. Failure to adjust continues, with thwarting and lack of satisfaction of the desire which in turn produces another attempt to overcome the obstacles, another thwarting, and another heightening of the emotional response—a vicious circle.

4. Solution, satisfaction, adjustment of the problem, desire, or motive. This is the goal of the adjustment process, the point at which it should result in personal happiness and social utility.

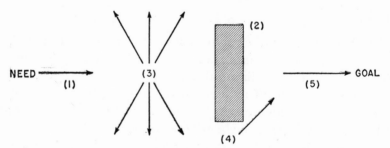

The organism (1) upon encountering an obstacle or difficulty (2) shows excess and varied activity (3) until one of the variant ways of reacting (4) resolves the difficulty and results in attainment of the goal.

FIG. 14. Schematic Representation of a Problem Situation and the Process of Adjustment. (After Dashiell, 5.)

This conception, shown schematically in Fig. 14, should serve to orient classroom teachers in their function of evaluating these aspects of pupils. The "mental hygiene" point of view, which substitutes understanding for censure and opens the way to objective evaluation and guidance, derives from this kind of analysis: maladjustment and undesirable behavior are "caused" by the interaction of the person with his environment. Moralistic, hostile reactions to people who exhibit maladjustment problems are incompatible with such an analysis.

THE MANIFESTATIONS OF MALADJUSTMENT

Let us now examine the manifestations of emotional and social adjustment. In what ways do children behave when they are in the third stage of the adjustment process mentioned above, when they are being satisfied or thwarted? What are the specific indications of poor mental health most frequently displayed by children in school? The preceding paragraphs have dealt in general with the causes of these indications. Now we are concerned with the indications themselves; in Chapter XII we shall deal with *how* emotional and social adjustment may be observed and traced more exactly.

The first reaction of many teachers to any attempt to describe emotional and social adjustment or maladjustment may be that this is something like "carrying coals to Newcastle." Who, they may ask, would know any better than the classroom teacher what is meant by adjustment and maladjustment? Unfortunately, the fact is that teachers often either ignore or admire (and therefore encourage) some of the forms of behavior that reflect poor mental health in their pupils. This has been shown by several studies of teachers' attitudes toward pupil behavior (1, 30, 31).

Teachers may regard as most serious children's behavior problems which attack the teacher's moral sensitivities, personal integrity, authority, or immediate teaching purposes. In contrast, the quiet, compliant, submissive, obedient child whose behavior is agreeable to teachers and who respects their authority is not considered a maladjusted child. Yet it happens that the amount of trouble a child gives a teacher is not a valid measure of his mental health. It is the consensus of clinical psychologists that the withdrawing modes of behavior are more serious and dangerous than the aggressive types because they are more likely to escape detection and more frequently lead to serious mental disorder. This last statement is based on evidence from studies concerning the earlier childhood characteristics of persons who later became mentally ill. The results obtained by Bowman (4) confirmed in general the findings reported by other observers (14) and justified the conclusion that persons who later developed functional mental illnesses exhibit distinctive personality traits long before there is any evidence of a definite mental disease. Friedlander (8) and Demerath (6) have reported essentially confirmatory findings. The most striking characteristics of the early histories of pupils who later became mentally ill, as distinguished from those who did not later become mentally ill, may be briefly summarized as follows: extreme seclusiveness, reticence, quietness, seriousness, conscientiousness, obedience, unusual achievement, frequent high standing in school work, dependence on adults, close emotional attachment to parents or teachers, relative inflexibility in adjusting to any change in the established routine, extreme sensitivity which increases with age. Perhaps most striking, these children were *not* "behavior problems" in the usual sense of that term but rather were usually "model" children.

We have not yet come to grips with the problem of what the teacher should evaluate in this area. What are the symptoms with which a teacher should be concerned in evaluating a pupil's emotional and social adjustment? Myers (19) has provided a useful classification of the specific types of mentally unhealthy pupils most frequently encountered in school:

1. The "unsociable" child
2. The "model" child
3. The "defensive" child
4. The "nervous" child
5. The "emotional" child

The "unsociable" child is always wandering off by himself, prefers to play alone, shows lack of interest in joining other children in their activities, is bookish, and usually likes nothing better than to stay in and do little chores for the teacher. Such a child is developing a habit of social withdrawal which does not provide a good foundation for later mental health. He may come to feel that he can have more fun when he is off by himself than when there are others around to interfere with his wishes, when he is keeping to himself, close-mouthed, uncommunicative, and secretive. Inattention or, more accurately, attending to *his own* ideas, hopes, fantasies, or daydreams, rather than to what the teacher or the rest of his social environment holds before him, is a simple way of accomplishing this end. Such daydreaming may be of the free type or it may be systematic, persistently following a central theme. Similarly, shyness or self-consciousness indicates not modesty but rather an undue preoccupation with oneself and a potentially dangerous lack of self-confidence.

The "model" child displays characteristics commonly regarded as virtues but carries them to such an extreme that they become symptomatic of poor mental health. Such virtues as neatness, conscientiousness, courtesy, honesty, ambition, caution, and thrift become excessive and are undesirable when they constitute a means of evading difficulties. The child who carries any of them to excess is often one who, having inadequacies in more important things, such as a real lack of any other of these virtues, finds that he can obtain the approval he craves by simply being a paragon in some other respect.

The "defensive" child rationalizes, that is, gives elaborate and logical-sounding reasons to explain an act which was really performed for purely emotional reasons. When carried to excess, this useful method of self-justification and fact-dodging, and its allied mechanisms, alibis and bragging, become harmful and symptomatic of mental ill health.

The "nervous" child is timid, fearful, anxious, shy, awkward, socially ill at ease, according to one understanding of this vague and misused term. Or this term may mean irritability, tenseness, and overactivity. It is not an explanation and does not refer to anything wrong with the nervous system. The "nervous" child does feel insecure and uncertain, and does believe he is different. Tics, such as grimacing, twitching, jerking, biting the nails, pulling the lips, shrugging, nodding, blinking, twisting, picking, scratching, and so on, are manifestations of the condition. These mannerisms are distinctly of less importance. More important is the neurotic device of exaggerating minor pains and illnesses in order to secure sympathy and attention.

The "emotional" child has unstable, uncontrolled habits of emotional expression. Inability or unwillingness to repress emotion is incompatible with group living. But mere repression is not enough, since emotion, whether repressed or not, arouses widespread organic disturbances of the vegetative functions, the digestive activities, gastric secretions, circulation, blood chemistry, and so on, with important effects on physical and mental health. Not merely emotional control but less occurrence of emotion itself is desirable. Among other things, this means that teachers should be extremely sparing in their use of fear as an incentive. Less emotionalizing will help lessen the fear of the child who has developed so many fears that he is almost always afraid, has no confidence in himself or others, and shows great anxiety about trying anything new or strange. He has disturbances of digestion, night-terrors, inability to go to sleep, restlessness, lack of appetite, food fussiness, and a general appearance of malnutrition.

The aspects of emotional and social adjustment with which teachers should be concerned may be given more specificity by the list of behavior problems in children presented in Table 15. This table, from Wickman's study, lists the fifty behavior problems most frequently reported by teachers, ranked according to the seriousness attached to them by consensus of thirty clinical psychologists.

Wickman's study, made in 1928, pointed up the differences between teachers and clinicians in their evaluations of the relative importance of children's behavior problems. It has been described as a "classic investigation" (7 : 164) and as "one of the most illuminating and interesting studies in the field" (15 : 76). We computed a rank order correlation of .85 between the ranking of these behavior problems by clinicians in Wickman's study and that by 42 other child psychologists on 23 of these behavior problems, as reported by Thompson (27) some twelve years later. This shows considerable consistency in the attitudes of clinical psychologists over a period of years in which there was a growing scientific interest in problems of mental hygiene and hence a possibility of new and different interpretations.

It is likely that Wickman somewhat "stacked the cards" by the different instructions he gave teachers and clinicians, thus artificially increasing the differences between them. Experimental results by Stewart (25) and replication and extension of Wickman's study by Stouffer (26) provide evidence on this point. It appears that the instructions given teachers influenced their ranking and that teachers and clinicians given the same instructions agree more

TABLE 15. Ratings by Mental Hygienists on the Relative Seriousness of Behavior Problems in Children (Ratings of 30 Clinicians) (30:127)

Type of Problem	Average Score	Rated Seriousness of Problem — Rating Scale
		Of Only Slight Importance (4.5) · Of Considerable Importance (12.5) · Of Extremely Great Importance (20.5)
Unsocialness	17.3	
Suspiciousness	16.4	
Unhappy, depressed	16.2	
Resentfulness	14.1	
Fearfulness	14.0	
Cruelty, bullying	13.5	
Easily discouraged	13.4	
Suggestible	13.3	
Overcritical of others	13.2	
Sensitiveness	13.1	
Domineering	13.0	
Sullenness	12.6	
Stealing	12.5	
Shyness	12.5	
Physical coward	12.0	
Selfishness	11.8	
Temper tantrums	11.7	
Dreaminess	11.3	
Nervousness	11.3	
Stubbornness	10.9	
Unreliableness	10.4	
Truancy	10.3	
Untruthfulness	10.3	
Cheating	10.3	
Heterosexual activity	9.9	
Lack of interest in work	9.6	
Enuresis (bed-wetting)	9.2	
Obscene notes, talk	8.8	
Tattling	8.8	
Attracting attention	8.5	
Quarrelsomeness	8.3	
Impudence, rudeness	7.6	
Imaginative lying	7.5	
Inattention	7.3	
Slovenly in appearance	7.2	
Laziness	7.2	
Impertinence, defiance	7.1	
Carelessness in work	7.1	
Thoughtlessness	6.8	
Restlessness	6.4	
Masturbation	6.4	
Disobedience	6.4	
Tardiness	5.6	
Inquisitiveness	5.3	
Destroying school materials	5.1	
Disorderliness in class	3.4	
Profanity	2.9	
Interrupting	2.8	
Smoking	2.3	
Whispering	0.8	

closely than when given Wickman's instructions. It is also probable that, during about three decades, teachers have changed significantly for the better in their insight. On this latter point, Mitchell (18), Schrupp and Gjerde (23), and Ullman (28) likewise found that mental hygienists and teachers have moved closer together in their judgments of the seriousness of behavior problems in children (circa 1950) than they were at the time of Wickman's study. Nonetheless, many individual teachers could be found whose attitudes depart quite radically from those of clinicians.

DEVELOPMENT OF ADJUSTMENT PATTERNS

In Chapter XII we shall be concerned with systematic, formal measurement and evaluation procedures. Here let us state with all possible emphasis that day-by-day, insightful, informal observations are the teacher's major guide, aided by the results of more formal approaches. What kinds of behaviors should the teacher be aware of and how do they come about? Let us first outline briefly an answer to the latter half of this question.

DEVELOPMENT OF PERSONALITY

Theories of "human nature" are at least as old as recorded history. "The striving of the human heart is evil from youth on and is desperately wicked," proclaimed the Old Testament prophet. This is not so different in content from the statement of a Harvard anthropologist that "man is still a super-ape, savage, predatory, acquisitive, primarily interested in himself and secondly in his immediate social groups (9)". The Darwinian theory of evolution has sometimes been interpreted as implying a relentless struggle for survival—"Nature red in tooth and claw." On the other hand, the thesis that coöperation, not competition, is the law of life and survival is ably presented by another anthropologist, Ashley-Montagu (3).

Sociologists, social psychologists, and particularly cultural anthropologists have in recent decades provided impressive evidence that man is a product of culture in ways as least as important as the ways in which he is a biological product. They have shown, too, that cultures differ enormously in the kinds of personality patterns they produce. Researchers in abnormal psychology, psychiatry, and child development have discovered a great deal about how the main personality dimensions of human beings develop. From the contributions of all these social sciences, let us sketch how our culture, interacting with man's biological make-up, shapes the personality.

From what the child development experts have discovered, it appears that perhaps the most important step in producing a mentally healthy child is to select for him parents who are emotionally mature and grown up, who love each other and their children, and so provide the proper atmosphere of emotional warmth and security. Even at best, however, each of us soon begins to experience, along with the joy of living, numerous hurts and frustrations in the new environment in which the parents and other members of the family are the most important ingredients.

When the individual is hurt, frightened, or frustrated, he has only two fundamental ways of responding. He can either "fight" or "run away." If he thinks himself cornered with no chance to run away, then he has no choice but to "fight," i.e., to try to change his environment. To a considerable degree his capacity to fight— and all that it implies in aggression, hostility, hatred—has been the instrument of his survival. Thus the individual accumulates a sizable reservoir of aggressions. When tensions are deeply aroused, the most direct means of handling them is by aggressive action. The person feels he must *do* something to relieve the pressure. Action is the primary requirement. The rationality of the action is a secondary and dispensable ingredient.

That this means of easing tension in a sense works was demonstrated by Grinker and Spiegel in their study of Air Force personnel in the North African campaign (2 : 54–55). Men in combat— men with guns in their hands who could take aggressive action— were significantly less subject to "nervous breakdowns" as a result of enemy attack than were noncombatants—ground crews, medical corpsmen, and others who could not strike back.

But the individual soon learns that direct expression of hostile feelings in the family and in other social situations is not acceptable, and he learns other ways of responding. He learns to try to control many of his aggressive impulses. As society becomes more and more complex, however, new aggressive impulses arise from new frustrations resulting from the group process itself. The very process of living together brings one person's wishes into conflict with those of others. These frustrations and irritations lead to hostile impulses which, if allowed direct expression, would probably lead to the disintegration of the group.[2]

In controlling aggressive impulses we do not destroy them. We either repress them, i.e., force them below the surface of our awareness, or mask them in various disguises. When we use any of these disguises adequately, hostile impulses can no longer be identified as aggression, at least by ourselves. But much as we might wish that the repression, or the disguise, had completely eliminated these unacceptable hostile feelings, it is abundantly established that a great deal of aggression remains in all of us beneath the disguise.

Repression is the simplest and, for most of us under ordinary circumstances a reasonably adequate solution. But we differ widely in the capacity to repress. In some individuals a backlog of too much feeling produces illness, physical or mental.

CULTURAL FACTORS IN PERSONALITY DEVELOPMENT

Society through its institutions molds the value systems, the systems of attitudes, by which its members regulate their behavior. Western industrial society with its administrative hierarchy relates people to each other through dominance-submission, superior-subordinate arrangements. No longer ago than the turn of the century most Americans were small, independent producers. At mid-century four out of five worked for a boss. It is a reasonable assumption that the frustrations inherent in the industrial system will mean that a large proportion of these people will be on not exactly friendly terms with the boss; more likely, they will "hate his guts."

Thus the ideal of democratic equality derived from a society of independent producers becomes more difficult to attain in a so-

[2] The frustration-aggression hypothesis originally proposed by Freud about 1920 and greatly elaborated by Dollard and others (*Frustration and Aggression,* Yale University Press, 1939) has been criticized on theoretical grounds in that many adjustment mechanisms related to frustration are nonaggressive. Withdrawal behavior is often observed as the result of frustration. In rebuttal it is pointed out that these responses are *learned* and that the primary response may very well always be aggression.

ciety characterized by giant industrial organizations in which the
individual may exist only as an anonymous, insignificant cog.
"The 'authoritarian personality' may be caused by certain child
rearing patterns; its growth, however, has also been fostered by
the mass character of industrial civilization" (**29** : 6).

Obviously the family is the primary socializing influence for the
individual. His interaction with it and with the expanding environment is fundamentally important in determining the kinds
of personality characteristics he will develop.

All theories of personality development agree on the importance
of early experience. Particularly appropriate for our purposes is
the formulation of a concept of "basic personality" by Linton
(**13**). For him, basic personality is a configuration based on the
postulates that "early experiences have lasting effects upon personality; similar experiences tend to produce similar personality
configurations; child rearing is culturally patterned and within
one society similar in all families though not identical; *child rearing differs from one culture to the next.*"

There is substantial evidence of genuine differences in child-
rearing practices between American middle-class and working-
class families (**20**). Whether these two groups can be thought of as
distinct "cultures" is still a matter of dispute. That differences
among high-school pupils with respect to personality characteristics are also related to socioeconomic status is evident from Purdue Opinion Panel poll results (**21**). Evidence has also been found
of significant differences in the attitudes of mothers of schizophrenics and mothers of nonschizophrenics toward child behavior
(**17**). The mothers of schizophrenics as a group were characterized
as being mainly restrictive; they believed in allowing a child no
freedom of choice, and in prescribing and carefully channeling his
behavior.

If the frustration-aggession hypothesis has any validity, child-
rearing practices may well be related to the social roles of the
parents. To quote a psychiatrist (**2** : 54–55):

The husband who is controlled at work, in politics, in leisure activities, even himself may feel that the one way in which he can assert his
masculinity is to control his wife, and any tendencies toward in-
equality of the sexes which already exist in that particular society may

become exaggerated unless the state counteracts this by making specific effort to elevate the status of women. Children, too, may become substitute foci of hostility—miniature scapegoats—on whom the father may feel it is safe to displace his anger and over whom he can exert authority to compensate for the feelings he has (but can not express) of being controlled from above. In such a situation a boy, as he identifies with his father, may get a head start toward his father's authoritarian pattern—he may become a miniature authoritarian, both controlling those weaker than he is and controlled by the stronger; hostile and insecure, with admiration only for power and only contempt for weakness.

The more desirable personality patterns implicit in a democratic way of life are of course equally the product of early learning in the social environment.

Adjustment Mechanisms

In this process of becoming "human," the individual develops various adjustment mechanisms. We shall review a few of the more important. Since entire books have been written on them, our discussion is necessarily only suggestive.

Adjustment mechanisms are ways of responding that help the individual either to protect himself from threats and discomforts or to improve his self-concept. They are activated as overt behavior when the individual does something about tension. They may also, however, involve only the mental and emotional aspects of behavior, with no observable activity, as when he builds "castles in Spain."

Rationalization is a mechanism which the individual uses to give plausible and socially acceptable reasons for his behavior rather than the "real" reasons which are often too painful to acknowledge. "The woman thou gavest me did tempt me and I did eat thereof" is one of the oldest recorded rationalizations. The failing freshman who, when interviewed by one of the authors, asserted that he could easily get all A's but said that he proposed to get a "well-rounded" education, was rationalizing.

Projection consists of attributing to an agency other than oneself one's own behavior, thoughts, or feelings, or responsibility for them, thus relieving oneself of guilt or anxiety. "The woman thou gavest me" etc., is also a specimen of this adjustment mechanism. "If everybody in the class didn't cheat, I certainly wouldn't cheat" is an example. Like rationalization, projection leads one to deceive oneself. It also is generally an unconscious process. It is to be noted that all projection is rationalization, but not all rationalization is projection.

In a somewhat but not wholly different context, the concept has been appropriated to the development of *projective techniques* designed to assay personality structure and dynamics by indirect means. This will be discussed in Chapter XII.

Repression is defined in Warren's *Dictionary of Psychology* as "the mental process by which perceptions and ideas which would be painful to consciousness are forced into the unconscious system while still remaining dynamic." Evidence for the operation of this process is found in studies that demonstrate a significantly readier recall of pleasant experiences than of unpleasant experiences and in psychiatric case studies showing that anger and hatred toward parents and suffering at their hands are buried in the unconscious, i.e., excluded from normal recall. Thus the individual may have feelings of guilt or hostility, although the experiences which originally cause these feelings are not subject to voluntary recall.

Suppression as distinguished from repression is the conscious activity of dismissing from consciousness or inhibiting the recall of unpleasant experiences, thoughts, and desires. Inhibiting the idea of "socking" the traffic officer who is about to give one a ticket, giving a soft answer when one would like to be loudly aggressive because of a perceived insult, turning one's thoughts away deliberately from a hated rival are examples of suppression.

Both suppressed and repressed feelings remain dynamic forces but serve the economy of living by conserving energy. Without them we would engage in fruitless and unadaptive dwelling on defeat or guilt-laden memories, or we might be so worried about the future as to be seriously disabled for living in the present.

Compensation is a mechanism by which an individual covers up or disguises an undesirable trait by calling a different one into play and exaggerating its manifestation. In a world dominated by adults, children use this mechanism frequently to relieve the disappointments, frustrations, and anxieties they develop. What to adults seems irrational behavior in children may be more usefully and constructively seen as compensatory behavior than as "innate wickedness" or "virtue." This mechanism is back of much youthful delinquency such as stealing, vandalism, fighting, and defiance of authority. Similarly, the unathletic boy may compensate by becoming an honor student.

Substitution is a kind of subspecies of compensation. It is a mechanism which reduces the tension produced by inability to achieve a desired goal by substituting another goal. Thus the jilted suitor throws himself into his work with redoubled energy.

If the original behavior or desire is heavily loaded with guilt feeling, *reaction formation* may occur. This is a complete reversal of the original behavior. The roué contributes heavily to a home for wayward girls; the parent who rejects his child shows inordinate concern for the child's welfare by extravagant demonstrations of affection; the ruthless "self-made" sharp practitioner in business becomes a philanthropist.

Fantasy or daydreaming is a mechanism by which desires are represented in imagination as already fulfilled. The youngster who "can't keep his minds on his studies" but instead stares vacantly out of the window is fleeing from the uninteresting and meaningless study assignment to a pleasurable "building of castles in Spain." In its extreme form this mechanism results in schizophrenia, in which the individual is completely cut off from reality and lives only in his imagination. Much commercial entertainment—movies, television programs, romantic literature—caters to less extreme forms of daydreaming.

Regression is a mechanism by means of which the individual returns to a mode of behavior possibly appropriate at an earlier stage of development. To say that an individual is "acting childish" is a popular way of describing the mechanism.

> Rock me to sleep, Mother, rock me to sleep,
> Mother come back from the echoless shore,
> Make me a child again just as of yore,

expresses quite precisely in poetic form the longing to be freed of the responsibilities and burdens of adult life. The young wife who runs home to mother and the high-school senior who has temper tantrums are other illustrations of people who use this mechanism. Mature adults at national conventions frequently exhibit a variety of regressive behavior.

Identification is "an unconscious mental process which expresses itself in the form of an emotional tie with other persons or situations in which the subject behaves as if he were the person (or thing) with whom or which he has this tie" (Warren's *Dictionary of Psychology*). The six-year-old who wears a cowboy outfit and behaves in accordance with his notion of the hypothetical cowboy is identifying with the cowboy. Children almost always identify with the parent of the same sex and sometimes with their teacher. Such identification accounts for much of the learning of attitudes that takes place throughout life.

Empathy as defined by Warren does not differ greatly from identification. It is "a mental state in which one identifies or feels himself in the same state of mind as another person or group." In informal language, it is the process of putting "oneself in the other fellow's shoes."

Sublimation is the unconscious process of redirecting one's energies into socially acceptable and socially useful rules and modes of behavior. The little boy's sadistic pleasure in mistreating a small animal may be sublimated into his becoming a professional surgeon. The unmarried woman teacher becomes the mother substitute for the whole roomful of children. The relatively young widow who has no children and disclaims all interest in men focuses her entire life on her work as a music teacher and spends her leisure time composing music.

This sketch describes some of the more important adjustment mechanisms. The concepts are not too precisely defined; clear distinctions among the mechanisms are not always possible. Nonetheless, the teacher will find such concepts useful in understanding pupil behavior more adequately than he could without them.[3]

[3] The interested student can become more familiar with the dynamics of human behavior by reading such books as the following: L. Kaplan and D. Baron, *Mental Hygiene and Life*, New York: Harper & Brothers, 1952; P. M. Symonds, *The Dynamics of Human Adjustments*, New York: Appleton-Century-Crofts, 1951; and L. E. Travis and Dorothy W. Baruch, *Personal Problems of Everyday Life*, New York: Appleton-Century-Crofts, 1941.

REFERENCES

1. Ackerson, Luton, "On evaluating the relative importance or seriousness of various behavior problems in children," *Journal of Juvenile Research,* 20:114–123 (1936).
2. Aldrich, C. K., "World Tensions and the Individual," in *The Garrison State—Its Human Problems,* Minneapolis: Social Science Research Center of the Graduate School, University of Minnesota, 1953.
3. Ashley-Montagu, M. F., *On Being Human,* New York: Abelard-Schuman, 1950.
4. Bowman, K. S., "Study of the pre-psychotic personality in certain psychoses," *American Journal of Orthopsychiatry,* 4:473–498 (1934).
5. Dashiell, J. F., *Fundamentals of General Psychology,* Boston: Houghton Mifflin Company, 1936.
6. Demerath, N. J., "Adolescent status demands and the student experiences of twenty schizophrenics," *American Sociological Review,* 8:513–518 (1943).
7. Fenton, N., *Mental Hygiene in School Practices,* Stanford University: Stanford University Press, 1948.
8. Friedlander, D., "Personality development of twenty-seven children who later became psychotic," *Journal of Abnormal and Social Psychology,* 40:330–355 (1945).
9. Hooton, E. A., quoted in the Chicago *Sun-Times,* April 11, 1953.
10. Jahoda, Marie, "Toward a social psychology of mental health," *Symposium on the Healthy Personality,* New York: Josiah Macy, Jr., Foundation, 1950, 221–298.
11. Jung, C. G., *Psychological Types,* New York: Harcourt, Brace & Company, Inc., 1923.
12. Kaplan, L., and Baron, D., *Mental Hygiene and Life,* New York: Harper & Brothers, 1952.
13. Kardiner, A., *Psychological Frontiers of Society,* New York: Columbia University Press, 1945.
14. Kasanin, J. N., and Veo, L., "A study of the school adjustment of children who later in life became psychotics," *American Journal of Orthopsychiatry,* 2:406–409 (1931).
15. Lee, J. M., and Lee, D. M., *The Child and His Curriculum,* New York: Appleton-Century-Crofts, 1940.
16. Lindner, R., *Prescription for Rebellion,* New York: Rinehart & Company, 1952.

17. Mark, J. C., "The attitudes of mothers of male schizophrenics toward child behavior," *Journal of Abnormal and Social Psychology,* 48:185–189 (1953).
18. Mitchell, J. C., "A study of teachers' and of hygienists' ratings of certain behavior problems of children," *Journal of Educational Research,* 39:292–307 (1949).
19. Myers, C. R., *Toward Mental Health in School,* Toronto: University of Toronto Press, 1939.
20. Orlansky, H., "Infant Care and Personality," *Psychological Bulletin,* 46:1 (1949).
21. Remmers, H. H., and Kirk, R. B., "Scalability and Validity of the Socio-Economic Status Scale of the Purdue Opinion Panel," *Journal of Applied Psychology,* 37:384–386 (1953).
22. Riesman, D., "A Philosophy for Minority Living," *Commentary,* 6:5 (1948).
23. Schrupp, M. H., and Gjerde, C. M., "Teacher Growth in Attitudes Toward Behavior Problems of Children," *Journal of Educational Psychology,* 44:203–214 (1953).
24. Shaffer, L., *Psychology of Adjustment,* Boston: Houghton Mifflin Company, 1936.
25. Stewart, Naomi, "Teachers' Concepts of Behavior Problems," *Growing Points in Educational Research, Official Report,* Washington: American Educational Research Association, 1949, pp. 302–310.
26. Stouffer, G. E. W., Jr., "Behavior Problems of Children as Viewed by Teachers and Mental Hygienists, A Study of Present Attitudes as Compared with Those Reported by E. K. Wickman," *Mental Hygiene,* 36:271–285 (1952).
27. Thompson, C., "The Attitudes of Various Groups Toward Behavior Problems of Children," *Journal of Abnormal and Social Psychology,* 35:120–125 (1940).
28. Ullman, C. A., *Identification of Maladjusted School Children,* Public Health Monograph No. 7, Washington: Government Printing Office, 1952.
29. Weisskopf, W. A., "Industrial Institutions and Personality Structure," *Journal of Social Issues,* 7:1–6 (1951).
30. Wickman, E. K., *Children's Behavior and Teacher's Attitude,* New York: Commonwealth Fund, 1928.
31. Yourman, J., "Children Identified by Their Teachers as Problems," *Journal of Educational Sociology,* 5:334–343 (1932).

CHAPTER XII

Evaluating Emotional and Social Adjustment

ABSTRACT

A first step in evaluating adjustment is screening relatively large numbers of individuals to identify those who need to be more deeply understood. Self-report inventories are useful for this screening. An account of the development of such an inventory suggests that the validity of this approach, properly defined, can contribute to the school guidance program. Evidence about a pupil from other pupils (e.g., sociometric data) and from the observations of teachers can lead to improved understanding of the individual pupil by teachers and counselors. Sociometry is useful in estimating the degree to which a pupil is being accepted by his peers. A teacher's informal observations depend for their validity on the teacher's own mental health, psychological concepts, and insight. Anecdotal records can aid in applying these observations but are primarily feasible for teacher training; extensive, formalized programs for collecting such records are rarely workable. Rating devices in various forms can be used to record and communicate impressions of personality. The general purposes and methods of projective techniques, as used by clinical psychologists, need to be understood by school personnel; the value of relatively spontaneous, unstructured responses of pupils can be gained by teachers by means of informal sentence completion tests.

◆～◆～◆～◆•

What can teachers do to evaluate the emotional and social adjustment of their pupils? The answer depends in part on whether the purpose is (1) to *screen,* out of a large number, the pupils whose maladjustments are serious enough to require special attention or (2) to *understand* the adjustment patterns of individual pupils as a basis for improving teaching and learning processes. In this chapter we shall deal with both purposes. The techniques to be considered do not fall sharply into these two categories. Yet some are definitely more appropriate for the first, whereas others make better sense for the second.

LARGE-SCALE SCREENING TECHNIQUES

Suppose a school superintendent, principal, board of education, or group of teachers have decided to do something about the maladjusted children in their schools. They all know a few individual pupils who are "odd" or have "got into trouble" with school or community authorities. These individuals almost select themselves for special attention. But the suspicion is well warranted that there are other pupils, less conspicuous in the everyday course of school affairs, who are at least as much, if not more, in need of special attention aimed at improving their emotional and social adjustment.

Some kind of relatively large-scale survey or screening program is called for. The occasion for the program—the realization of its desirability—may have arisen as a result of the teachers' discussion. Or the experience of past years may have led to the development of such surveys of pupil adjustment as a routine procedure. Whether the idea is relatively old or new, school personnel may eventually confront the problem of technique in conducting such a survey. The first section of this chapter is concerned with procedures of this kind.

Large-scale programs for identifying maladjusted pupils must be feasible administratively. This means that they must not require large amounts of time, money, and professional skill. The techniques that clinical psychologists and psychiatrists use for the diagnosis of an individual child or adult do not apply in this situation. Schools cannot have each pupil subjected to a time-consuming battery of diagnostic techniques, such as long clinical interviews or the projective techniques that must be applied individually by skilled professionals and interpreted with much subtlety and insight.

The sources of evidence that can be used for relatively large-scale surveys of pupil adjustment are (1) the pupil, (2) the pupil's peers, and (3) the teacher. By referring to the pupil as a source of evidence concerning his adjustment, we mean that his own opinions and descriptions of himself apply. In *some* ways, no one knows better than the pupil what his problems are, how he feels about himself, and how he gets along with other people. We can in a sense "talk" with him and "hear" his answers—in the survey situation—by the kind of one-way, standardized, printed "interview" known as the questionnaire or inventory.

The second source of evidence, the student's peers, refers to the attitudes, opinions, evaluations, and reactions to the pupil of those with whom he studies, works, and plays in school. Some aspects of his adjustment depend by definition on how his fellow pupils feel about him. When we ask pupils questions about their likes, dislikes, and preferences among their fellow pupils, we are using them as sources of evidence concerning pupil adjustment.

The teacher can serve as a source of evidence in the direct sense, because he has a direct opportunity to observe the pupil in and out of the classroom. Here we refer not to the formal observations that teachers make by means of tests and other devices, but to the informal, unarranged, everyday evidence that comes to teachers and results in perceptions of how pupils behave—i.e., feel, think, perceive, and act—in a variety of situations.

INVENTORIES: TECHNIQUES THAT USE THE PUPIL AS A SOURCE OF EVIDENCE CONCERNING HIS ADJUSTMENT

The techniques used to obtain evidence concerning his adjustment from the pupil himself are generally called inventories, surveys, schedules, or questionnaires. The term "test" is often avoided in referring to these devices because they do not call upon the pupil to perform at his best or maximum level; rather, they depend upon his willingness and ability to describe what is typical or generally true of himself.

We shall describe the inventory technique by giving an account of the SRA Youth Inventory (11). This inventory consists of 298 statements of problems in eight areas. In the hand-scored form the pupil is instructed as follows: "Read each statement in the questionnaire carefully. If it expresses something that has been a problem to you, make a mark in the answer box corresponding to that statement. If the statement does not express one of your difficulties, or does not apply to you, do not make any mark on the answer sheet, but go on to the next statement." Each of the following statements is taken from one of the eight areas:

Area	Illustrative Item
My School	1. I have difficulty keeping my mind on my studies.
Looking Ahead	35. What shall I do after high school?
About Myself	81. I feel "low" much of the time.
Getting Along with Others	115. I want people to like me better.
My Home and Family	156. I can't get along with my brothers and sisters.
Boy Meets Girl	208. I seldom have dates.
Health	251. I worry about my health.
Things in General	265. I am concerned with what life is all about.

The 298 statements were derived from anonymous essays by hundreds of students concerning the things that bother them most. The findings of the American Youth Commission and the New York State Regent's Inquiry, which has also studied problems of youth, were considered. After review and editing by educators and psychologists, the 298 items finally selected were put into the above eight groups.

The preliminary form was given to about 15,000 high-school students in Grades IX–XII in approximately 100 schools in all regions of the United States. In about half the schools the questionnaire was answered anonymously; in the other schools the students were asked to sign the ballot card on which they marked their answers before answering the questions. Subsamples from these two groups of schools, similar in school grade, sex, and religious preference, showed that slightly more often the "anonymous" students indicated that a given item expressed a problem that bothered them. The differences on most questions amounted to only two or three percentage points, the median being 1.7 percent difference. For group analysis purposes, it may therefore be inferred that signing or not signing the questionnaire makes little practical difference. But for any individual pupil the difference might be educationally or psychologically significant.

The answers of 2500 students were then selected for detailed analysis of the problem percentages. These 2500 were stratified according to sex, school grade, religion, urban or rural residence, and economic level. That is, separate percentages were computed for each of the groups resulting when the total group was broken down on each of these bases. To insure that the eight categories into which the 298 items had been classified were internally consistent and had psychological meaning, a coefficient of correlation (biserial) was computed between the score of each item (scored 0 or 1) and the total score in each of the eight areas. If an item correlated most highly with the total score of the area in which it had originally been placed, it was considered to have been correctly classified originally. If it correlated more highly with the total score in some other category, and would make sense in the latter category, it was reassigned. Reassignment was made for 27 items. The outcome of this procedure was that the eight categories could thus be considered fairly homogeneous both "logically" and "empirically." (See the Manual for refinements of procedure omitted here.)

An additional step was to ask seven professional workers in the fields of guidance, clinical psychology, and education to classify each of the items as to (1) whether "the statement simply indicates the recognition of a problem and a desire to do something about it," or (2) "whether it is more likely to indicate some more basic difficulty within the individual personality. Remember that you are to think of these items in relation to their significance to adolescents." On 101 items, at least six of the seven experts agreed that the item denoted a basic difficulty. The total score on these 101 items may be considered a measure of the student's social-emotional adjustment.

The reliability of the scores for each of the eight problem areas was estimated in the sense of internal consistency by means of the Kuder-Richardson formulas. These coefficients ranged from .75 to .94. All except one were above .84; that for the Health area was .75.

What is the relevance of the SRA Youth Inventory? If the purpose of the Inventory is to obtain an indication of what a student *thinks* are his problems, the items checked indicate his problems and the Inventory must be considered to have a very high degree of logical relevance in this sense. "As long as the student thinks that certain things bother him, it makes little difference whether the problems are real or whether he is unconsciously exaggerating their importance" (Manual). To estimate the empirical relevance of the Inventory scores requires some kind of external criterion. One such criterion might be the ratings of good or poor adjustment to the school situation obtained from the school personnel. The following evidence on the empirical validity of the basic difficulty score is reported in the Manual.

One such study, by Ullmann (15), is of special significance. In addition to providing some important data about the contribution of the *Youth Inventory* to the identification of maladjusted pupils, Ullmann's study indicates that the Basic Difficulty scale makes a unique contribution to the screening process by calling attention to the unrecognized adjustment problems of girls who are judged well adjusted by their teachers and fellow classmates.

The study was carried out in one county in Maryland. Nearly half of all white ninth-grade pupils in the county were included in the sample. There were 404 boys and 406 girls, coming from the classrooms of 23 different teachers. Three types of screening instruments were used:

Teacher ratings: An adjustment rating on a three-point scale was obtained for each pupil. Teachers also completed a specially developed forced-choice rating on each student. This required that they check the one item from 18 groups of items which best described the student. All items described student behavior that could be observed in the classroom.

Self-ratings: The *SRA Youth Inventory* (Basic Difficulty score) and the *California Test of Personality* (Self-Adjustment and Social Adjustment scores) were used to obtain the student's description of his own adjustment.

Sociometric ratings: Students identified three classmates who they felt were characterized by each of these traits: dependability, reliability, friendliness, honesty, and desire to be alone.

In analyzing the results of these measures Dr. Ullmann found two different pictures of adjustment. Teacher ratings identified four boys to one girl as severely maladjusted. Actual frequencies at each adjustment level were:

	Boys	Girls	Total
Well adjusted	251	313	564
Moderately maladjusted	102	80	182
Severely maladjusted	51	13	64

At the other extreme, the Basic Difficulty score of the *Youth Inventory* identified a few more girls than boys as severely maladjusted. The other measures, Forced Choice ratings, Sociometric ratings, and *California Personality Test,* fell in between these two extremes. Table 16 shows the proportion of boys to girls in the lowest 10 percent (maladjusted) on all measures except teacher ratings.

TABLE 16.   Number and Proportion of Boys and Girls with Scores in the Lowest Tenth on Five Measures of Adjustment (15)

Measure	Total Number	Number		Proportion	
		Boys	Girls	Boys	Girls
Forced Choice Rating	82	57	25	.141	.062
California-Self	82	46	36	.114	.089
California-Social	83	60	23	.149	.057
Y.I.—Basic Difficulty	86	34	52	.084	.128
Sociometric	81	59	22	.146	.054

On the whole, observer ratings correlated with each other. Self-descriptive tests correlated with each other but did not correlate highly with observer ratings. These intercorrelations are given in Table 17.

TABLE 17.   Intercorrelations of Six Measures of Adjustment of 404 Boys and 406 Girls (15)

Adjustment Measure	1	2	3	4	5	6
1. Teacher Ratings on 3-point Scale		.77	.56	.30	.33	.22
2. Forced Choice Ratings			.56	.28	.29	.15
3. Sociometric Ratings				.28	.28	.16
4. California-Self					.73	.61
5. California-Social						.47
6. Basic Difficulty Score						

It is evident from Table 17 that the two self-descriptive inventories correlate fairly well with each other. Most of the difference between the *Youth Inventory* Basic Difficulty score and the California scores may be accounted for in terms of the greater sensitivity of the *Youth Inventory* to the problems of girls.

According to Ullmann, the Basic Difficulty score makes a unique contribution to the screening of maladjusted students by drawing attention to the adjustment problems of girls who are considered well adjusted by their teachers and classmates. The score probably picks up maladjusted girls, as well as boys, whose overt behavior does not reveal their lower adjustment level.

In an experimental study sponsored by the Educational Records Bureau, Jacobs (7) also used teacher ratings as a criterion. From a school group of 164, twenty-three students were identified as "problems" by the principal and teachers. A comparison of the average area scores of the problem group and the total group showed no general trend toward greater incidence of problems among students considered as "problems." This finding is not surprising in the light of Ullmann's report on the discrepancy between self-rating and ratings based on overt behavior.

What happens when school counselors, instead of teachers, do the rating? Drucker and Remmers (4) sought to determine whether or not the *Youth Inventory* could rank teen-agers on the basis of good adjustment as recognized by trained personnel. They administered the *Inventory* to 392 seventh- and eighth-grade pupils attending an urban school in northern Indiana. Before the scores were known, eight regular school counselors were asked to designate, from among the students they knew well, the 20 percent who were *best adjusted* and the 20 percent who were *least well adjusted*. On the basis of the counselor ratings, the students were divided into two groups—136 pupils considered best adjusted and 120 considered relatively less well adjusted. Twenty-six students were not included in the analysis because of serious disagreements among the raters. The remaining 110 students were not well known to counselors.

The ability of the *Inventory* to differentiate between the two adjustment groups was studied in terms of the eight area scores and the Basic Difficulty score. Results, shown in Table 18, indicate that differences between the high and low adjustment groups were significant at the 1 percent level for several areas. Looking Ahead, which deals with vocational and educational future, and Things in General, which indicates a concern with problems of religion, philosophy, and world affairs, did not show significant differences between the two groups. The most significant differences occur in the Basic Difficulty scale and in the areas concerned with school and personal adjustment.

TABLE 18. Mean Scores and Standard Deviations of Well and Poorly Adjusted 7th and 8th Graders and of a National Sample of 7th and 8th Graders for the *SRA Youth Inventory*

Scale	Poorly Adjusted (N = 120) Mean	Sigma	Well Adjusted (N = 136) Mean	Sigma	Student's t	National Sample (N = 1000) Mean	Sigma
Basic Difficulty	19.1	16.2	10.6	10.7	5.01[a]	16.7	13.8
1. My School	7.7	5.2	4.4	4.2	5.61[a]	6.8	4.7
2. Looking Ahead	9.4	7.4	9.2	7.5	.01	10.6	7.8
3. About Myself	10.6	8.4	5.9	5.7	5.26[a]	9.1	7.2
4. Getting Along with Others	9.2	8.8	6.2	6.4	3.16[a]	9.4	8.0
5. My Home and Family	6.5	9.3	2.5	4.9	4.38[a]	5.4	7.2
6. Boy Meets Girl	4.9	6.4	3.1	4.2	2.63[a]	5.9	6.1
7. Health	3.4	4.1	2.2	2.5	2.71[a]	3.9	3.7
8. Things in General	4.5	6.7	3.2	4.8	1.73	5.7	6.6
Total	56.1	46.1	36.7	31.6	3.93	56.7	—

[a] Difference between means significant at or beyond 1% level.

It is noteworthy that the differences reported are not for extreme groups—such as the upper and lower 10 or 20 percent of a total group. Rather, they are based on a rough division of approximately 90 percent of the student population for which ratings were obtained. Such a division tends to make it less likely that significant differences will be found since there is bound to be considerable overlap between the well-adjusted and the less well-adjusted group. Despite such overlap, however, there was good agreement between counselor judgments and *Inventory* scores with regard to pupil adjustment.

Further evidence on the meaning of the eight category scores can be obtained from the intercorrelation among the eight categories. These are all positive, ranging from .20 between Areas 1 (My School) and 8 (Things in General), to .67 between Areas 3 (About Myself) and 4 (Getting Along with Others). If these scores were entirely determined by response sets of the kind described in Chapter V, the intercorrelations between the total scores of the eight problem areas would be of the same magnitude, about .88, as the reliability coefficients of these scores. The fact that they are not nearly so high indicates that the scores are largely due not to response sets but rather to more discriminative processes on the part of the student. The fact that all the intercorrelations are positive is not unreasonable since pupils with problems in one area may be expected to have problems in other areas as well.

Three kinds of norms are provided for the Inventory: (1) percentile rank norms for boys and girls in each of the eight areas of the Inventory; (2) the percentage of each of various subgroups checking each item on the Inventory, the subgroups being based on sex, grade, region of the United States, rural or urban residence, religion, and socioeconomic status; and (3) the percentile rank norms for each of the eight areas for each of sixteen subgroups obtained when sex, rural and urban residence, and grade are used to break down the total group.

The value of the Inventory for surveying problems and adjustments among groups of students follows from the approaches used in constructing and administering it. It tends to provide a relatively nonthreatening means of communication between the student and his teachers and counselors. The mere task of administering the Inventory establishes a social atmosphere in which consideration of emotional and social adjustment problems becomes acceptable. Students sense this atmosphere, realizing that other students may also have problems. They also realize that the school as an institution is willing to be concerned with students other than as learners of intellectual content. The specific information that his scores yield to the student can lay the basis for more constructive activity toward the solution of problems than he may have undertaken previously.

For all concerned—students, teachers, and administrators—the Inventory and its results are to be considered primarily a beginning step. What the student does about his problems from that point on, how the teacher adjusts his own activities and behavior to promote the adjustment of his students, how the administrator reëxamines his curriculum with the aid of Inventory results are all matters that require additional consideration, essentially outside the scope of this book. The Manual provides suggestions as to possible next steps for students, teachers, counselors, and administrators for realizing the potential values of the Inventory.

PROBLEMS IN APPRAISING ADJUSTMENT WITH SELF-INVENTORIES

The foregoing account should make clear the general procedure followed in the construction of inventories. Inventories have been widely criticized on various grounds. Their validity and usefulness depend, of course, on the purposes for which they are used. Many of the objections to them have been aimed against their use in situations for which they were not designed and for which they are not suitable.

1. One of the major problems with inventories is obtaining frank responses. Since adjustment is by definition an emotional and social matter, it is something that people are generally unable to consider in purely rational terms and without being influenced by their desire for social acceptance. Frankness of response will largely depend on the rapport established between the pupil and those whom he expects to examine his responses. The greater the degree of his trust in and acceptance of his teachers, the more he will try to give truthful answers to adjustment inventories.

In developing the SRA Youth Inventory, the authors, as already mentioned, had half of their large sample sign their answer sheets,

the other half being allowed to remain anonymous. In this situation, a nation-wide opinion poll, the differences between the percentages of signers and nonsigners who checked given items as
problems for themselves was in no instance greater than 6 percent.
So it is easy to overestimate the effect that lack of anonymity will
have on frankness of response. When the pupil is convinced that
the inventory is aimed at improving his own adjustment, at yielding benefits for himself, frankness may not be a substantial problem. But in other situations, such as employee selection, it is not
reasonable to expect that applicants will be frank when they can
readily see that their responses may damage their chances of getting hired.

2. A second problem is that, even if pupils want to be frank,
they may lack sufficient insight into themselves to be able to give
objectively true responses. This becomes important when the objective truth of a given response must be assumed. For example,
pupils may simply not know the truth about themselves concerning such questions as "Do you frequently have spells of the blues?"
and "Does your ambition need occasional stimulation through
contact with successful people?" People are prone to use the kinds
of adjustment mechanisms described in Chapter XI in answering
questions like these. When objective truth need not be counted
on, however, this difficulty is less relevant. It may not be the truth
of an answer that determines whether a pupil is adjusted, but
rather the way he feels about the question. As in the SRA Youth Inventory, it may be educationally and psychologically significant
that a pupil *thinks* he has a problem even if, on objective grounds,
he does not. So again the validity and usefulness of the inventory
approach depend on the use to be made of the results, the kinds
of interpretations to be given to them. When an outside criterion
of adjustment, such as counselors' ratings, is used, this difficulty
becomes unimportant to the degree that inventory results are
found to have empirical relevance to such criteria.

3. A third problem, not unique to this source of evidence concerning adjustment, is determining dimensions of adjustment.
The problem here is analogous to that involved in determining
the primary mental abilities through factor analysis. In the SRA
Youth Inventory, the dimensions of adjustment were determined

on logical grounds, on the basis of judgments and categorizations of professional workers in education, psychology, and sociology. Whether such logically determined dimensions are empirically valid was determined to some extent on the basis of the item analysis approach described above. For example, when Flanagan factor analyzed the Bernreuter Personality Inventory (6), he found that only two independent and internally consistent dimensions emerged—self-confidence and sociability—as against .the four (neuroticism, self-sufficiency, introversion, and dominance) that Bernreuter had attempted to build into his Inventory. A more recent attempt to apply factor analysis in determining dimensions of adjustment or "personality" was made by Guilford and Zimmerman. The Guilford-Zimmerman Temperament Survey (see Table 20) yields scores for ten "traits": general activity, restraint, ascendance, sociability, emotional stability, objectivity, friendliness, thoughtfulness, personal relations, and masculinity. The thirty items in each of these traits are internally quite consistent, so that the questions *within* a given trait correlate fairly highly with one another; the scores on one trait do not correlate highly with those on others, however, so that the ten traits may be considered fairly independent.

4. A fourth problem in appraising adjustment through self-inventories is a by-product of the trait approach which such inventories assume when they are used to obtain total scores based on responses to a large number of items. A trait is a form of behavior that is consistent for a given person over a wide variety of situations. A "careful" person is one who habitually looks up the spelling of a word in a dictionary when he is in doubt, looks up and down a street before crossing, checks his addition of a column of numbers, etc. When a person exhibits many such kinds of behavior in different situations, he is said to be "careful." But this also assumes that a given kind of behavior, when classified with other behaviors, has the same significance for the person doing the behaving as for the classifier.

It may be that behavior should be "sliced" differently for different persons. Some persons *will* be consistent according to some dimension such as "carefulness." But for others, carefulness may not be a relevant dimension at all; they simply are not consistent with themselves from one situation to another in the amount of "carefulness" they show. Instead of carefulness, one person's relevant trait might be "desire to impress others with his carefulness and other desirable traits when he knows they are watching." For another person, it might be "lack of confidence in his own intellectual ability but audacity in situations requiring motor skill and coördination." Hence the traits that are defined either logically or empirically, as by item analysis and factor analysis, will generally apply to many people, perhaps even a large majority, but *not* necessarily to every member of a group. When a trait classification is applied to individuals who are not organized as the trait scheme requires, the description becomes irrelevant. It is as if someone applied criteria emphasizing the strength and washability of furniture, which are relevant for tables and chairs used in restaurants, to a set of artistically designed antiques, for which they are irrelevant. Similarly, "self-confidence" and "sociability" might not be relevant dimensions for describing the personality of a physicist who shows great self-confidence and sociability at a meeting of the American Physical Society but not at a luncheon of the Rotary Club. Perhaps the relevant dimension for this physicist would be "need for social situation allowing intellectual conversation."

This difficulty of individualizing interpretation has been a factor in the increased popularity among clinicians of "projective" techniques, to be discussed below. One advantage claimed for such approaches, like the Rorschach inkblot tests, is that they call for attaching different significance to a given kind of response depending on the other responses it is found with. In other words, the various responses are considered as a pattern, in interaction with one another, in arriving at the description of the individual.

5. A final problem in using self-inventories in the measurement of adjustment is developing acceptable external criteria against which to validate these instruments. This difficulty is not, of course, unique to self-inventories. Since such inventories are seldom "disguised" and can therefore readily be "faked" by anyone motivated to do so, it follows that they should not be expected to yield valid results against external criteria of adjustment when they are administered under conditions that operate against frank

and insightful responses. Furthermore, on logical grounds alone, these inventories should not be expected to yield results that correlate perfectly, even when corrected for the unreliability of the measures, with appraisals of adjustment by other persons. An individual's report of his own adjustment cannot be expected to have the same content and significance as the adjustment perceived in him by someone else, however complete and extensive the other person's opportunity to observe has been. It is reasonable, however, to expect self-descriptions to be of some use in appraising adjustment when they are collected under conditions that make for a reasonable degree of frankness and insightfulness. If, as is done with such devices as the SRA Youth Inventory and the Mooney Problem Checklist, the purpose is defined as obtaining a record of problems that individuals say they have, and if this record is to be used merely as a springboard for counseling, to be supplemented by interviews and other procedures when necessary, the self-report approach must be considered to have substantial validity or usefulness.

VALIDITY OF INVENTORIES

When self-inventories have been validated against external criteria of adjustment, such as ratings by psychiatrists and clinical psychologists, or against "success" in school as defined by grades, their statistical and empirically defined "relevance" has seldom been found to be extremely high. Coefficients tend to range in various studies from nearly zero to .70. Table 19, based on Ellis' article, shows the results obtained in many studies of personality inventories. The external criteria, such as teacher's ratings and psychologists' diagnoses, cannot themselves be considered perfectly valid.

Such results of empirical studies have led some workers to reject self-inventories categorically. Ellis (5) came to the following conclusion from his review of many studies: "There is at best one chance in two that these tests will validly discriminate between *groups* of adjusted and maladjusted individuals, and there is very little indication that they can be safely used to diagnose individual cases, or to give valid estimations of personality traits of *specific* respondents. The older, more conventional, and more widely used

TABLE 19. Validity Data on Personality Inventories (Derived from Ellis, **5**)

r's Corresponding to Categories	Group Administration						Individual Administration	Totals
	Types of Criteria							
	Behavior Problem Diagnosis	Diagnosis of Delinquency	Psychiatric or Psychological Diagnosis	Rating Diagnosis	Test Inter-correlations	Over-rating[a]	Various Types of Criteria	
.70 to 1.00	2	15	36	12	9	6	10	90
.40 to .69	1	6	9	10	18	—	3	47
0 to .39	6	13	30	22	28	36	2	137
Totals	9	34	75	44	55	42	15	274

[a] Overrating refers to "whether or not respondents answer self-descriptive questionnaires with a high degree of accuracy and truthfulness." o to .39 here means "negative or mainly negative," which means that significant inaccuracy or untruthfulness was observed. The tabulation was made here, for simplicity, in accordance with Ellis' definitions of his meanings for coefficients of correlation as "negative" or "mainly negative" when r = o to .39.

forms of these tests seem to be, for practical diagnostic purposes, hardly worth the paper on which they are printed" (5 : 425).

It should be kept in mind that Ellis defines validity as follows: "A test of neuroticism, to be truly valid, must do what it is supposed to do: that is, clinically differentiate neurotics from non-neurotics" (5 : 390).

But his strictures will not apply to such tests when this is not what they are "supposed to do." If, for example, a test is "supposed" to give pupils in a school system an opportunity, under relatively nonthreatening conditions, to tell school personnel that they think they have certain problems and to compare themselves with other pupils of the same age, grade, and cultural background as to the kinds and numbers of problems they say they have, personality inventories and problem checklists such as the Youth Inventory can be considered valid.

In short, as in all educational and psychological measurement, validity is specific to a given kind of purpose. While personality inventories may not be valid for purposes for which they have frequently been used, they may have substantial validity when used not as indices of adjustment objectively defined, but as indices of self-reported adjustment.

ARE ADJUSTMENT INVENTORIES USEFUL?

A major question still remains: Are valid indices of self-reported adjustment useful in the work of the schools? Although it must always depend on the particular school situation, the answer to this question, at least as judged from the widespread use of such inventories by teachers and counselors in school situations, must be considered substantially affirmative.

Scathing criticisms of adjustment inventories continue to appear. For example, *The Fourth Mental Measurements Yearbook* (1) contains a review from which the following is an excerpt:

This is just another one of those toss-a-circle-around-the-symbol-for-your-problem inventories which holds no promise of contributing any more to our understanding of pupils' problems than the scores of others which represent the lowest form of the testmaker's art. In twenty-five minutes the student encircles numbers at the end of 180 problems to indicate whether they are big, medium, or small ones to him. The student is asked to give his honest and sincere opinions; this request should be warning enough that not much can be expected from the instrument. Many studies have shown that answers to this type of question can be faked consciously or unconsciously, and no check is provided in this inventory as to the sincerity and honesty of the students' opinions. The very fact that the student is asked to be honest and sincere may even suggest to those who had not thought about being insincere and dishonest that they could answer in that way. . . .

Since this reviewer sees *no* merit whatever in the procedure used in this inventory and such similar devices as the Mooney Problem Checklist and the SRA Youth Inventory, comparisons between them seem valueless. It is hoped that we will soon pass that naïve stage in educational and psychological thought in which we expect to get at important problems by a hurried mass approach. Perhaps these inventories will find their best use in bonfires celebrating our emergence from the ruts that the personality and adjustment testers . . . have carved out for us" (1 : 121–122).

In reply to invective of this kind, those responsible for constructive action under present-day conditions can only say, "What better alternatives are available for large-scale, feasible, useful screening of pupils as to emotional and social adjustment?" While the teachers, counselors, and administrators of our schools await an answer to this question, they have little choice but to continue to use adjustment inventories. Insistence on clinically sophisticated and profound techniques means that the schools will fail to do as adequate a job as is now possible. Although other techniques for appraising adjustment in the schools are available, none allows such a useful, large-scale program at so little cost.

KINDS OF ERRORS IN SCREENING

Any device for appraising adjustment, including adjustment inventories, can lead to two kinds of errors: (1) errors by which maladjusted individuals go undetected, i.e., "misses," and (2) errors by which individuals are identified as maladjusted by the inventory although, on the basis of other valid evidence, they are not maladjusted, i.e., "false positives." The latter kind of error is relatively easy to correct in the normal, everyday procedures of teaching and counseling in the schools. A pupil thus falsely identified as maladjusted may for some time receive special attention from his teachers and counselors, but the error of self-perception may soon become apparent as his normal adjustment manifests itself. Errors of the first kind, or "misses," are more serious. If the inventories alone were used, such errors would mean that pupils who need special attention from teachers, counselors, and perhaps clinical psychologists or psychiatrists would not be so identified.

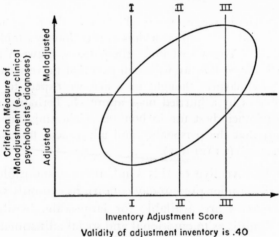

Validity of adjustment inventory is .40

For any given cutting score (I, II, or III) the cases in the upper-right quadrant are "hits," those in the lower-right quadrant are "false positives," those in the upper-left quadrant are "misses." Raising the cutting score increases the ratio of "hits" to "false positives" but also increases the number of "misses."

FIG. 15. Hypothetical Scatterplot of Inventory Scores Against a Criterion of Adjustment.

Even personality inventories with relatively low validity, such as .40—validity being defined as agreement with clinicians' ratings of adjustment—nonetheless by definition succeed to a greater than chance extent in correctly classifying individuals as to their adjustment. Whether the kinds and numbers of errors such inventories entail are to be tolerated depends on the kinds of human and financial cost that the school system can stand. To minimize the amount of undetected and unacted-upon maladjustment among children and youth means greatly increasing the financial outlay for skilled professional workers in mental health problems. In such a program the number of "misses" may be minimized. In less expensive programs, where resources are available only for the few children most in need, inventories can be used with relatively high "cutting" scores so that only the most serious cases are identified for special attention. This will also reduce the number of "false positives," as shown in Fig. 15.

In summary, we may say that the inventory approach to appraising emotional and social adjustment will do some good and will seldom do harm in the school program. The special attention that "false positives" may receive may be considered desirable in any case, as part of the program of individualized attention that modern education advocates. For the "hits," the pupils who are correctly identified as maladjusted by this relatively inexpensive procedure, the special attention thus directed to them may make an important difference in their emotional and social development. *Personality inventories certainly are not sufficient, and may perhaps not even be necessary to mental health programs in the school; nonetheless, in many schools and at the present status of psychological theory and technique they can be helpful.*

AVAILABLE ADJUSTMENT INVENTORIES

For lack of space we have described in detail only one adjustment inventory, the SRA Youth Inventory. Table 20, however, gives the names, grade levels designed for, and types of scores provided, for a representative list of the more widely used inventories designed for school situations. For each of these a sizable research literature has accumulated, and reviews are given in one or more of the *Mental Measurements Yearbooks*. Prospective users of inventories should make their choice according to the principles already discussed in the present volume.

SOCIOMETRY AND RELATED TECHNIQUES: METHODS THAT USE FELLOW PUPILS AS SOURCES OF EVIDENCE CONCERNING A PUPIL'S ADJUSTMENT

When we speak of social adjustment we refer to how an individual gets along with other people. For children in schools, this

TABLE 20. Adjustment and Personality Inventories

Name of Inventory	Grades Designed for	Kinds of Scores Provided	Publisher No. (see list on pp. 613–614)
Adjustment Inventory (Bell)	9–16, adults	Home, health, social and emotional adjustment. Also, for adult form, occupational adjustment	24
Cornell Index	13–16, adults	Psychosomatic and personality disorders	18
Guilford-Zimmerman Temperament Survey	9–16, adults	General activity, restraint, ascendance, sociability, emotional stability, objectivity, friendliness, thoughtfulness, personal relations, masculinity	23
Heston Personal Adjustment Inventory	9–16, adults	Analytical thinking, sociability, emotional stability, confidence, personal relations, home satisfaction	28
Life Adjustment Inventory (Wrightstone, Doll)	9–12	Adjustment to curriculum, reading and study skills, communication and listening skills, social skills and etiquette, boy-girl relationships, religion—moral ethics, functional citizenship, vocational orientation and preparation, physical and mental health, family living, orientation to science, consumer education, art appreciation and creativity, use of leisure time	1
Mental Health Analysis (Thorpe, Clark, Tiegs)	9–16, adults	Liabilities: behavioral immaturity, emotional instability, feelings of inadequacy, physical defects, nervous manifestations. Assets: close personal relationships, interpersonal skills, social participation, satisfying work and recreation, adequate outlook and goals	6
Minnesota Multiphasic Personality Inventory (Hathaway and McKinley)	Age 16 and over	Hypochondriasis, depression, hysteria, psychopathic deviate, masculinity and femininity, paranoia, psychasthenia, schizophrenia, hypomania. Control scores: question, lie, validity, K	18
Mooney Problem Checklist: 1950 Revision	7–9, 9–12, 13–16, adults. Also, ages 16–30 in Form for Rural Youth	Grades 7–9: Health and physical development, school, home and family, money—work—the future, boy and girl relations, relations to people in general, self-centered concerns. Other scores for other levels.	18

Name of Inventory	Grades Designed for	Kinds of Scores Provided	Publisher No. (see list on pp. 613–614)
Personality Inventory (Bernreuter)	9–16, adults	Neurotic tendency, self-sufficiency, introversion-extroversion, dominance-submission, confidence, sociability	24
Personality Survey (Symonds)	7–9	Age, intelligence, reading comprehension, pupil questionnaire, teacher rating, sociometric rating, absence, school marks, total adjustment	20
School Inventory (Bell)	9–12	Attitude toward school	24
SRA Youth Inventory (and Junior Inventory) (Remmers, Shimberg, Drucker, Bauernfeind)	4–8, 7–12	Grades 7–12: my school, looking ahead, about myself, getting along with others, my home and family, boy meets girl, health, things in general, basic difficulty	22
Thurstone Temperament Schedule	9–16, adults	Active, vigorous, impulsive, dominant, stable, sociable, reflective	22
Washburne Social-Adjustment Inventory	Age 12 and over	Truthfulness, happiness, alienation, sympathy, purpose, impulse-judgment, control, wishes, total	28

means largely how well a pupil gets along with his fellow pupils. In Chapter XI we discussed the desire for social approval as one of the basic needs that individuals develop in most societies, including our own. Whether an individual "deserves" social approval, whether in objective terms he should be approved by his peers, is beside the point. Regardless of how meritorious, how "good" in absolute terms he may be, what matters here is how others perceive him. In the preceding section of the present chapter we dealt primarily with how the individual sees himself. Now we are concerned with how others see him.

Whether a student is accepted by his fellows, whether they "want him around" for different kinds of activities, can of course be of tremendous importance to the student himself. His own perception of his standing among his peers is almost sure to make a great deal of difference to him. If his perception of it is correct, he will behave in ways that are appropriate; if it is incorrect, either it will be corrected by his fellows' reactions to him or he will con-

tinue to behave inappropriately and in one way or another alien-
ate himself from them. Apart from the accuracy of his own perception of his standing among his peers, his actual standing
is also important. It is less likely that an individual will develop
socially desirable habits of interacting with other persons if they
continually reject him. If the school is to be concerned with the
pupil's social development—which has important connections
with his intellectual development—it becomes necessary for school
personnel to identify the students who may need help in improving their social relationships.

The "Guess-Who" Method

The techniques used to study social adjustment in this sense are
all variations of the common-sense approach, "If you want to
know how other pupils feel about a given pupil, ask them." From
one point of view, the various methods are intragroup rating techniques. That is, the members of a small, closely knit group, such
as a classroom of pupils, are asked to react to one another. Of
these techniques, one of the more carefully designed is the "Guess-
Who" test of Hartshorne and May. Its use is adequately described by the directions:

Here are some little word-pictures of some children you may know.
Read each statement carefully and see if you can guess who it is about.
It might be about yourself. There may be more than one picture for
the same person. Several boys and girls may fit one picture. Read each
statement. Think over your classmates, and write after each statement
the names of any boys or girls who may fit it. If the picture does not
seem to fit anyone in your class, put down no name, but go on to the
next statement. Work carefully, and use your judgment.

1. Here is the class athlete. He (or she) can play baseball, basketball,
and tennis, can swim as well as any, and is a good sport.

....

2. This one is always picking on others and annoying them.

....

In scoring the "Guess-Who" test, many methods have been
tried, but adequate results have been obtained simply by totaling

the number of times a pupil's name appears, a positive value being given to "desirable" items and a negative value to "undesirable" ones. In practice it has been found that many pupils in the group are mentioned for a given item and that each pupil is mentioned for a fairly large number of items. Thus a rating is usually derived for many pupils over a fairly large number of items, and the results are quite reliable. Obviously, they provide evidence that the teacher can use in understanding a pupil's personality through the eyes of his fellow pupils. Results often surprise teachers; the pupil whom the teacher considered to be lonesome and ignored may turn out to be well liked and respected, while the one the teacher liked particularly because of his good manners and quick learning may be despised by his peers for his snobbishness.

A by-product of an intragroup rating scheme may be improved understanding of the sense of values of pupils—the things they consider important in persons. Such characteristics as neatness, courtesy, and quick obedience may prove, when "Guess-Who" rating results are inspected, to be negatively related to what pupils value in another, while positiveness, prankishness, or simply a high level of activity, hitherto scorned or ignored as virtues by teachers, may prove to be what attracts his classmates to a given pupil. The insight into pupils' values thus gained provides a basis for evaluating the social learning that inevitably goes on in school. Further, it can give the teacher some leads as to how to improve the standing of a pupil who is rejected by his peers. To make him more accepted, the teacher must either give him an opportunity to acquire the characteristics, traits, skills, and the like, that his fellow pupils value, or undertake to change the other pupils' values.

SOCIOMETRY

A general procedure that has been much used and studied since about 1934 is called *sociometry*. This technique was named and applied for many different purposes by Moreno (9). A "sociometric test" requires each member of a group, such as a classroom group, to choose one or more members for a given purpose. Jennings (8) offers the following as an illustration as to how a sociometric question may be worded:

We are going to need committees to work on such-and-such problems. Each of you knows with whom you enjoy working most. These may be the same persons with whom you work in other classes, or they may be different, so remember that we are talking about social studies. Put your name at the top of the page, and numbers 1, 2, and 3 on lines below. Opposite "1" put the name of a boy or girl with whom you would most like to work, after "2" your second choice, and after "3" your third. I will keep all of the choices in mind and arrange the committees so that everyone will be with one or more of the three people named. Remember, you may choose a boy or girl who is absent today if you want to. Write down the last name as well as the first name so that I will be sure to know whom you mean. As usual, we shall probably be working in these committees for about eight weeks, or until the Christmas holidays.

Chosen

	Boys					Girls					
Chooser Boys	Arnold	Ben	Charles	David	⋮	Alice	Betty	Cora	Doris	⋮	Number Chosen
Arnold		ABO	AOO								2
Ben	OOC		OOO	OBO		OBO					3
Charles	OBC										1
David	AOC		OBO								2
Girls											
Alice							ABC	OOC			2
Betty						ABC			OBO		2
Cora							OBC		OOC		2
Doris						AOO					1

	Arnold	Ben	Charles	David		Alice	Betty	Cora	Doris
Total A's	1	1	1	0		2	1	0	0
Total B's	1	0	1	1		2	2	0	1
Total C's	3	1	0	0		1	2	1	1
Combined	5	2	2	1		5	5	1	2
Number Choosing	3	1	2	1		3	2	1	2

FIG. 16. An Illustrative Sociometric Summary Sheet. (Adapted from Mary L. Northway, *A Primer of Sociometry*, Toronto: University of Toronto Press, 1952, p. 9.)

TALLY OF SOCIOMETRIC POSITIONS

No. of Boys ....; No. of Girls ....

Class/Grade ....
School ....
City ....
Date Given ....

Test Question: ....

How many choices were asked for? .... Total no. of choices made by all students? .... Maximum no. of choices possible (multiply size of group by number of choices allowed) ....

Enter in the spaces below the no. of pupils holding each position listed.

Frequency of Choice	Number of Pupils			
	Chosen	Chosen Mutually	Rejected[a]	Rejected Mutually[a]
Not at all	....	....	....	....
Once	....	....	....	....
Twice	....	....	....	....
Three Times	....	....	....	....
Four times	....	....	....	....
Five times	....	....	....	....
More than 5 times	....	....	....	....
Total no. of pupils[b]	....	....	....	....

Sample Breakdowns of Tally of Positions Along Group Factor Lines[c]

Frequency of Choice	No. of Choices Received		No. of Choices Received		No. of Choices Received	
	Boys	Girls	Negro	White	Live in Housing Project	Do Not Live in Housing Project
None	....	....	....	....	....	....
One	....	....	....	....	....	....
Two	....	....	....	....	....	....
Three	....	....	....	....	....	....
Four	....	....	....	....	....	....
Five	....	....	....	....	....	....
Total by category	....	....	....	....	....	....
Total no. of pupils	....	....	....	....	....	....

Further Questions

How many boys chose girls and were not reciprocated? ....

[Or how many white children chose Negro children and were not reciprocated?]

How many girls chose boys and were not reciprocated? ....

Number of mutual choices between boys and girls ....

Special Features

Note here any pattern which is of special interest to you, e.g., "Three of the unchosen pupils chose the same much-chosen pupil."

[a] Enter only if a rejection question was used.
[b] Totals of each column should equal the number of children in the group.
[c] Positions may be broken down into whatever categories for analysis will disclose whether particular group factors are operating to affect its structures.

Fig. 17. Tally of Sociometric Positions. In preparing his own forms, the teacher may substitute whatever categories are appropriate for breaking down the tally of positions and whatever further questions he may be particularly interested in. (Quoted by permission from Jennings, 8 : 20.)

It may be assumed that the pupils who are frequently chosen by other pupils for close association have a high degree of social acceptability to their fellow pupils. By requiring the pupils to choose their associates for other purposes, different dimensions of acceptability can be identified.

What advantages does this technique possess over the ordinary popularity contest or class election? Sociometric techniques have other uses than furnishing estimates of popularity. To achieve the additional purposes, it is necessary not merely to tally the number of choices each pupil receives from other pupils for a given purpose, but to construct a sociogram, beginning as Fig. 16.

A large summary sheet of squared paper is prepared on which the names of the group members are entered in alphabetical order along the side and across the top. If subgroups, such as boys, girls, fifth graders, and the like, are to be studied as such, the names should be alphabetized within each subgroup. The children's answer sheets are arranged in alphabetical order. On the basis of each answer sheet, entries are made on the summary sheet to indicate who chose whom for each of the sociometric questions. Thus, if Arnold chooses Ben on Question A, an "A" is entered on the row opposite Arnold in the column under Ben. If he chooses him on Question B, a "B" is entered. If he did not choose him on C, a zero is entered. The entries under Ben and opposite Arnold will then read "A," "B," "0." If Betty does not choose Arnold on any of the questions, the appropriate square has three zeros. The total entries in each column give the social acceptance score of the given pupils.

As this tally is filled in, the teacher may think of questions like the following: "How many mutual, or reciprocated, choices are there? Which individuals and what proportion of the class are very much in demand? What proportion is ignored? Do girls and boys choose each other? Are there any reciprocated choices across sex lines?" (8 : 19). The form shown in Fig. 17 is designed to facilitate the teacher's work in answering such questions.

Beyond this kind of tally, the social structure of the class as a whole can be presented by the type of sociogram illustrated in Fig. 18.

The positions near the center of the sociogram should be used

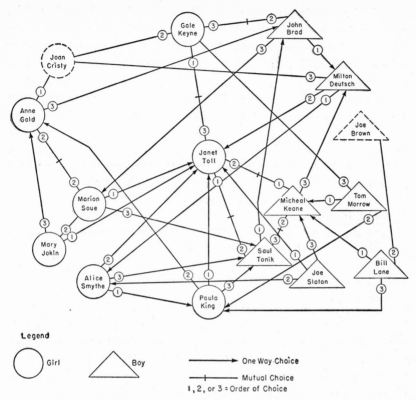

Legend

⬤ Girl   △ Boy   ———▶ One Way Choice

————┼———— Mutual Choice

1, 2, or 3 = Order of Choice

NOTE. For an absent boy or girl, use the respective symbol dashed, leaving any choice line open-ended (see Joe Brown above).

If rejections are obtained, the choice line may be made in dashes or in a different color.

Whenever a direct line from chooser to chosen cannot be drawn without going through the symbol for another individual, the line should be drawn with an elbow, as in the case of Bill Lane to Paula King.

FIG. 18. A Filled-In Sociogram, Presenting the Choice Patterns Graphically. Blank forms with empty circles and triangles may be mimeographed so that the teacher may fill in the names and draw in the choice lines after the test has been given. (Quoted by permission from Jennings, 8 : 22.)

for children who receive many choices; as distance from the center increases, the popularity or sociometric status of the child should decrease. It is often helpful, as is done in Fig. 18, to put the girls' symbols on one side and the boys' on the other side.

Many kinds of interpretation and analysis are possible once sociometric data have been collected. The interpretations can be enhanced by clinical insight, supplementary interview data, open questions and themes written by children, diaries, teachers' interviews with parents, and the like. The following from Jennings (8 : 23–24) illustrates merely the beginning of such an interpretation:

To a person looking at a sociogram for the first time, the whole thing may seem to be a meaningless jumble of circles, lines, and triangles. The first problem, then, is to trace the pattern and then gradually see its significance. After a little practice, sociograms can be read for major outlines of characteristic shape at a glance, and study is called for only in connection with details of the interaction of individual children. Once the picture is firmly in mind, or, indeed, while it is actually taking shape, all sorts of questions will suggest themselves for further study.

A good way to begin reading a sociogram is to concentrate on one person and follow all lines that lead from and to him. In the sample sociogram [Fig. 18], the circle marked "Mary Jokin" in the lower left corner has three arrows (unreciprocated choices) running from it to Janet Toll (first), Marian Soue (second), and Anne Gold (third). There are no arrows pointing at Mary. She has not received a single choice. Looking at Janet, we find her first choice is a boy, Saul Tonik, and it is reciprocated as Saul's second possibility; her second choice is another boy, Michael Keane, and is also reciprocated—she is first on Michael's list; her third choice is again reciprocated—by a girl this time, Gale Keyne, and represents another first choice. In addition, there are six arrows pointing at Janet, coming from two boys and four girls; moreover, four of these are first choices and the others second ones. Everyday life in the classroom must obviously be very different for Janet and Mary!

The various kinds of statistical analysis that have been devised for sociometric data have been summarized by Proctor and Loomis (10). Their discussion, although not difficult mathematically, indicates that the apparently simple and straightforward data collected with sociometric techniques can be treated statistically so as to answer a great variety of educational and psychological questions.

How sociometric data should be used for the improvement of social adjustments in children and youth is essentially beyond the scope of this book. Such data constitute only part of the information on which educational practice should be grounded. Jennings discusses this problem as follows:

The immediate thing to do about the findings of a sociometric test is to carry out the agreement made with the children when they were asked to indicate their choices. The class must be reseated as soon as possible, or the committees appointed, or the plans made for the party or the school trip, or whatever it was. . . . The principle for translating sociometric data into action is simple and the same for all purposes: each individual should be given the highest degree of satisfaction compatible with maximum happiness for everyone else and maximum stimulation for all. . . .

Most teachers notice an immediate effect on their students when they have carried out original agreements in this way. In most cases, this is a matter of eliminating those tensions that were due to blocked communication or feelings of not belonging. How this happens is illustrated by an anecdote in a primary school. Charles had been uncommunicative and apparently uninterested in his surroundings. On a sociometric test he was unchosen, and the child he had named first was Michael, the most asked-for boy in the class. When the new seating was announced, Charles found that he had been placed with his first choice. He smiled broadly, rushed up to Michael, and stretched out his hand to him saying, "I am happy to be by you, Michael." The other child rose to the occasion and said, "That's swell, I'll say!" as he proceeded to help Charles with his things. In this instance the two-way benefit of sociometric placement is to be noted. The overchosen boy had perhaps not known that Charles cared so much for him; he only knew, for his part, that he had neither chosen nor rejected Charles. In the new security given to Charles by Michael, the former's attitude toward schoolwork could be influenced by the specific desire to show Michael that he could do the work after all. An individual whose opinion he valued was now a reality in his interpersonal world. But the most significant result was that the opinion Charles held of himself took a more constructive turn (8 : 45–48).

Sociometry has often been used by groups of teachers engaged in improving their understanding of children in general. In the volume *Helping Teachers Understand Children,* two chapters are devoted to "studying the interaction of children in groups" (**13** :

275–363). Along with the description of uses and applications of sociometric data, these chapters present two cautions:

> [When newcomers to child study] undertook to give sociometric tests and to make diagrams, a great deal of confusion and anxiety resulted. The sociometric study of their classes, that challenged and interested the teachers with a year or more of experience in the program, proved to be too difficult to newcomers. . . . A sociogram is necessarily complex, being a visual representation of a constellation of attitudes toward each other that are expressed by the individual children making up the class. . . . No teacher should be asked to begin with a direct study of children's behavior by working at a problem of this level of complexity. We infer that teachers should have one or two years of experience in writing descriptive anecdotes and in organizing and interpreting the information provided by these anecdotes before they undertake to make and interpret sociograms.

> One further caution seems indicated. We question whether teachers should undertake sociometric tests in their classes unless they are also keeping anecdotal records about the children. . . . A sociogram is the most effective starting point and signboard for launching a study of social dynamics in school groups. It can direct observation, suggest hypotheses, and open teachers' eyes to unrecognized social realities. But it should be followed by the careful study of the child's society through time. Good descriptive anecdotal records . . . of the children's interactions are needed to confirm and to suggest alternatives to the interpretations initially made from the sociogram (13 : 362–363).

INFORMAL OBSERVATION: THE TEACHER AS A SOURCE OF INFORMATION ABOUT THE EMOTIONAL AND SOCIAL ADJUSTMENT OF STUDENTS

So far we have taken up the kinds of evidence that teachers can obtain from the pupil himself and from his fellow pupils. These kinds of information must of course be assimilated and interpreted before they can be used. But another type of evidence can be obtained by teachers without the intermediation of pupils or peers. This is what the teacher can observe for himself. As he interacts with learners in and out of the classroom there is much for him to see and hear. We refer particularly to what is called "expressive" behavior—the unique "style" of living that characterizes every one of us. A pupil's tone of voice, his rate of speaking, the kinds of words he chooses, his fluency, how much he talks in the presence of his fellows or of members of the opposite sex, whether he initiates conversations and topics of conversation, how often he agrees and disagrees with others, how often his opinion is ignored or sought by others, how often others agree or disagree with him, the amount of relaxed humor he displays as against grim seriousness, the degree to which he seems to be enjoying himself and works and plays constructively as against avoiding the task or activity expected of him—all these and myriad other cues present themselves continuously to teachers.

Obviously, no teacher can pay attention to all these items all the time. Nor can he be expected to "add" all these items of behavior together in any conscious and systematic way. The teacher must impose some organizing scheme on all this seeming chaos of behavior—indeed, he cannot keep himself from doing so. He will use stereotypes that are more or less correct, that is, norms and also expectations as to how the typical student will behave. These stereotypes are refined in various ways. He will have stereotypes concerning pupils of a given sex, a given age level, a given social class, a given body build, a given type of rural or urban residence, a given skin color or nationality, and the like. Much of what he observes in pupils will be immediately and unconsciously compared with these expectations. The comparison will result in more or less revision of the stereotype, depending both on how well the pupil fits the teacher's expectations and on how "flexible" the teacher is.

Ideally, the teacher comes to his pupils and his observations of their behavior with accurate knowledge, sound understanding, and appropriate expectations. As he observes and collects information about specific pupils and groups, his understanding of their characteristics is modified and comes closer to objective and social reality. The teacher who can understand pupils best is the one who is least rigidly bound by a small number of preconceptions concerning personality. The teacher who is himself insecure in his relationships with others, whose picture of himself is out of focus with the way he is perceived by others, will develop "blind spots" which will keep him from understanding his pupils. Needless to say, the teacher who has strong prejudices—hostile attitudes—toward members of any racial, religious, social, or nationality group cannot be expected to understand the emotional and social adjustment patterns of pupils who belong to those groups. He will misperceive the motives and desires of such pupils. His prejudices will prevent him from using the evidence that comes to his senses in a way that accords with social and psychological reality.

The foregoing does not mean that teachers should, or can, be free of stereotypes or even "prejudices"—in the sense of expectations and hypotheses. It is only incorrect and rigid stereotypes and prejudices that interfere with accurate understanding of pupils. "Correct" stereotypes as defined by social norms—such as those concerning the proper role for boys and girls in adolescent society —are indispensable to understanding adolescent boys and girls.

Thus the teacher's mental health, his emotional and social adjustment, affect the process of evaluating the emotional and social adjustment of pupils. In Chapter XVII we deal further with this aspect of the evaluation problem. The most important kind of work that the teacher does in evaluating emotional and social adjustment is the informal, everyday observation and interpretation that depend for validity on his own psychological security, social understanding, inner complexity, and wisdom. Training programs of the kinds described in *Helping Teachers Understand Children* (13) can contribute much to the teacher's equipment for this purpose.

ANECDOTAL RECORDS

Anecdotal records were mentioned earlier as supplementary materials for understanding sociometric data; this requires elaboration. Anecdotal records are brief reports of incidents in a pupil's life that are judged to be significant for his emotional and social adjustment. The choice of incidents to be recorded must be made in terms of some conception of the nature of adjustment and of what is significant, such as that outlined in Chapter XI. Anecdotes should include both an objective description of behavior and an interpretation of it. Traxler (14) has shown how a report that combines interpretation and recommendation can be broken down so as to be less confusing.

Combined report, interpretation, and recommendation. In a meeting of her club today, Alice showed her jealousy of the new president by firing questions at her whenever there was an opportunity. She tried to create difficulties by constant interruption throughout the period. The other students showed their resentment by calling for her to sit down. It is apparent that she is a natural trouble-maker, and I think her counselor should have her in for a serious talk.

Incident. In a meeting of her club today Alice fired questions at the new president at every opportunity. She interrupted many times during the period. On several occasions the other students called for her to sit down.

Interpretation. Alice seemed to be jealous of the new president and desirous of creating difficulty. The other students appeared to resent her action. The girl seemed to enjoy making trouble for others.

Recommendation. It would be advisable for the counselor to lead the girl tactfully into a discussion of her relations with the other students in an effort to bring about better adjustment.

The chief value of anecdotal records is to provide concrete, realistic information that goes beyond the use of ambiguous trait names or test scores such as "courteous," "considerate," "coöperative," and the like. A description of actual behavior tells more than any standard adjective or any phrase from an inventory or rating scale, about the living reality of a student's adjustment pattern.

Attempts have been made in schools and colleges to set up a system of anecdotal record keeping on a standard, routine basis. This means that the teacher should try to keep a record on all his pupils, making at least a few such records every day and attempting to cover all his pupils over a period of time. Administrative devices such as dictaphones, typist pools, filing systems, and summarizing techniques have been tried.

Despite these elaborate systems, anecdotal behavior records have tended to be discarded as a means of deriving information about the emotional and social adjustment of all the children in a school. If taken seriously, they make exorbitant demands on the time and energy of the teachers. Also, because of differences in points of view, teachers tend to select incidents for recording that are more or less irrelevant to each other. Observers, such as teachers, tend to overgeneralize on the basis of striking rather than typical incidents.

As a result of this experience, doubts have arisen as to the feasibility of keeping anecdotal records for all the children. On the other hand, practice in writing anecdotal records for one or two children may have important training values for the teacher.

It helps a teacher to see the actions of children in situational or social context instead of in terms of the teacher's educational intent. It helps break the habit of appraising all classroom behavior as either good or bad, to be commended or blamed, and builds up a habit of looking for the causes of behavior. In time, it supplies so much information about specific individuals that the teacher can see what a given situation really means to them and why they act as they do. In time it likewise permits teachers to see their theoretical concepts given flesh-and-blood reality in the conduct of living children. Moreover, when many teachers discuss their anecdote sequences with one another, the effect is to develop in each other a realistic appreciation of the range and variety of child behavior along with its many conditioning causes. These considerations confirm us in the belief that two or three years of observation and anecdote writing about one or two children is a very valuable professional activity for teachers (13 : 435).

COMMUNICATING IMPRESSIONS OF PERSONALITY TO OTHERS: RATING METHODS

When a pupil has been observed by his teacher in the classroom, in extracurricular activities, and elsewhere, the teacher is generally able to form impressions concerning the pupil in which he has some confidence. To communicate these impressions to other people, he can use one of many kinds of rating methods. Such methods make it possible to express in standard, brief, and quantitative form one person's description and evaluation of another.

The general ideas underlying rating methods for describing and evaluating adjustment are the same as those presented in Chapter VI for product and procedure evaluation. That is, we need (1) to analyze the pupil's adjustment or behavior patterns into various "traits" or other characteristics and (2) to provide a method of scoring each characteristic. Here we shall point out only the aspects of the procedure that are specific to adjustment evaluation.

The traits or modes of adjustment into which the pupil's emotional and social adjustments is analyzed are determined by some theory of adjustment and the purpose for which the ratings are made. The traits should be amenable to reliable evaluation. Research has indicated that judges agree better with one another—that is, are more reliable—in rating some traits than others. These studies suggest that traits that show up frequently are rated more reliably. The trait should be clearly defined and should have the same meaning for all the judges.

Various schemes have been developed for obtaining a rating on each trait; among them are descriptive, numerical, and graphic rating scales. These may also be combined in various ways. Descriptive rating scales provide lists of words or phrases, usually from three to seven, from which the rater selects the one most applicable to the person being rated. Numerical rating scales assign numbers for the various levels of each trait, from least to most; the numbers are proportional to the degree, or intensity, of the trait. Graphic rating scales have horizontal lines, defined at each end and perhaps at intermediate points, on which the rater checks the subject's standing with respect to each trait. Illustrations of these three types follow.

Descriptive Rating Scale

Directions: Place a check mark in the square before the phrase which represents your evaluation of the pupil.

Is this pupil honest? Can he be trusted to resist temptations to steal, lie, or cheat?

- ☐ Honest in all situations. Never dishonest.
- ☐ Usually honest. Rarely yields to temptation.
- ☐ Not dependably honest.
- ☐ Usually dishonest. Not to be trusted.
- ☐ Dishonest in all situations.

Numerical Rating Scale

Directions: Give the pupil a number from 0 to 10 to represent the degree to which he possesses the traits listed. 0 represents none of the trait, 5 an average amount, and 10 a maximum amount of the trait.

Is this pupil honest? Can he be trusted to resist temptations to steal, lie, or cheat?   ....

The graphic rating scale embodies the features of both of the others. In general, all three can be put in either the constant-alternative or the changing-alternative forms described in Chapter IV. When each trait is put in the constant-alternative form, the description of each level of the trait is the same for all traits and consequently must be in general terms. In the changing-alternative form, separate descriptions are provided for each level of each trait. The following illustrations of graphic scales show how alternatives for each trait may be either constant or changing:

Constant Alternatives

Is this
pupil honest?

| Extremely | Rather | Somewhat | Hardly | Not at all |

Is this
pupil neat?

| Extremely | Rather | Somewhat | Hardly | Not at all |

Changing Alternatives

Is this
pupil honest?

| Honest in all situations. | Usually honest. Rarely yields to temptation. | Not dependably honest. Yields to strong temptation. | Usually dishonest. Not to be trusted. | Dishonest in all situations. Pathologically deceitful. |

Is this
pupil neat?

| Always fastidious and immaculate. | Usually well groomed and orderly, with occasional lapses. | Clean and orderly about half the time. | Usually slovenly and unkempt but sometimes spruces up. | Invariably altogether unkempt and dirty. |

Suggestions for Constructing Graphic Rating Scales

In the development of graphic rating scales, the following suggestions for their construction have been made. It should be remembered, however, that these suggestions are for the most part based not on experimental findings but merely on common sense, which has frequently been refuted in the field of testing by experimental facts.

1. Alternation of Scale Directionality. Some writers on the subject suggest that the desirable end of the rating line should not always be on the same side of the page but should be randomly alternated. In this way, they believe, response set and halo effect (see below) may be somewhat reduced because the rater has to curb his tendency to check all the traits at the same end of the scale.

2. Explicit Trait Questions. Each trait should be introduced by a question phrased so as to describe the trait in objective, observable, tangible terms. For example, rather than merely labeling a trait "Emotional stability," it is better to follow this title with such questions as "How well poised is he emotionally? Is he touchy, sensitive to criticism, easily upset? Is he irritated or impatient when things go wrong? Or does he keep on an even keel?"

3. *Continuous Lines.* Either a great many or no segments should be marked off on the line. In this way the continuity of the trait is better emphasized and the rater can feel freer to place his check mark at any point along the line. In scoring the rating scale, a strip of paper marked off into as many divisions as is desirable can be placed along the line and the distance or number of divisions from the undesirable end of the line can be expressed numerically.

4. *Number and Position of Descriptive Phrases.* The descriptive adjectives or phrases, usually three or five in number, should be placed underneath the line with definite spaces between them.

5. *Order of Descriptive Phrases.* The extreme phrases should be put at the very end of the line, the neutral or average phrase at the middle of the line, and the intermediate ones in between.

6. *Diction of the Phrases.* The words used to describe each level should be fitted to the understanding of the persons who will make the ratings. Slang and colloquial expressions are sometimes advantageous.

7. *Phrasing of Extreme Levels.* The phrases at the ends of the line should not express levels of the trait so rare or extreme that raters will never check them.

8. *Phrasing of Intermediate Levels.* To induce raters to use a wider range of the line, the *meaning* of the intermediate levels should be closer to the average or neutral phrase than to the extreme phrases. This may help counteract the tendency for ratings to be concentrated around the middle of the line.

FORCED-CHOICE RATING TECHNIQUE

The technique known as forced-choice rating had its origin in the efforts made to overcome the markedly skewed distributions and low validities obtained with the usual rating scale. It was largely developed by the Personnel Research Section of the Adjutant General's Office (12). It markedly reduces the effects of halo and leniency by reducing the rater's knowledge of how he is rating an individual. A finished forced-choice scale consists of descriptive words or phrases usually presented in groups of two or four. The rater is required to select one word or phrase from each group as being *most* descriptive and one as being *least* descriptive of the subject. The items are assembled previously, and experimentally determined preference and discriminative indices are established for each one. The words and phrases are then assembled in such a way as to have about equal favorability but different empirical relevance. Thus the rater is forced to choose between phrases that appear equally valid for selection but differ in discrimination value as experimentally determined.

ERRORS IN RATING METHODS

Various errors may occur in obtaining an opinion about one person from another.

1. The person expressing an opinion may not know whereof he speaks. Unless he has had an opportunity to become acquainted with the subject and to observe him along lines pertinent to the question he is answering, he cannot give valid evidence.

2. Like the pupil who answers questions on a self-inventory, the rater must be both able and willing to give an "unbiased" judgment. The teacher's ability to have insight into a pupil's adjustment is, of course, less than in the case of the self-inventory, especially concerning the aspects of adjustment that are meant when we speak of the "inner" life of a person. But the teacher is more likely to be frank about a pupil than about himself. This advantage, however, may be lessened in the case of pupils with whom the teacher or other rater is *very* well acquainted through either long association or intimate friendship. When this relationship exists, ratings are often found to be too high, to show leniency and favoritism.

3. Inclusive of the second type is the "halo" effect in rating. This is the effect of the rater's overall impression of a pupil on his ratings of more specific aspects or qualities of that pupil. If a pupil is not thought well of in general, there is a tendency to rate him lower in at least some aspects than he would be were it not for the halo effect. The opposite tendency may appear when the pupil is considered to rank so high in general as to cast an emotional haze

over the opinion about him in specific aspects. A particular trait is subject to the halo effect when it is not easily or commonly observed or thought about, is not clearly defined, involves relationship to other people rather than being "self-contained," or is highly loaded with emotional or moral significance. To prevent the halo effect from distorting and invalidating ratings, the rater must constantly keep in mind the necessity of considering each trait separately, of not letting one rating be influenced by his other ratings of the pupil. For example, if a pupil is greatly admired and highly rated for his honesty, his popularity must still be considered separately and be neither raised nor lowered by the honesty rating.

Reliability can usually be improved by averaging the ratings of several raters. The reliability of the ratings obtained from equally well-trained and well-instructed raters will increase as the number of raters increases. But generally the increase is not worth the trouble after about ten ratings have been averaged, except in cases where larger numbers of raters are easily available and a high reliability is desired.

AVAILABLE RATING DEVICES

Table 21 provides information concerning commercially available rating devices that have been used in schools. Prospective users of these devices should base their choice on an inspection of the scale and on examination of information in the test manual, in Buros' *Yearbooks,* and in the literature as found in *Psychological Abstracts, Review of Educational Research, Education Index,* etc.

PROJECTIVE TECHNIQUES

Occasions arise when a teacher wishes he could get to know his pupils in ways unique to themselves. He wishes he could know "what is on the mind" of one of his pupils. The inventories discussed earlier in this chapter are "structured"; that is, they tend to fix the lines along which a pupil can respond and allow him to tell only the kinds of things that the authors of the inventory have built into it. For any individual pupil, such an inventory may miss ideas of particular significance simply because the unique ways in which that pupil sees himself and the world were not built into it. Furthermore, inventories depend on the willingness and ability of

TABLE 21.   Rating Devices

Name of Device	Grades Designed for	Traits Provided, and Other Characteristics	Publisher No. (see list on pp. 613–614)
Behavior Rating Schedule (Haggerty, Olson, Wickman)	Kdg.-12	15 behavior problems rated on frequency; 35 (intellectual, social, emotional, physical) traits rated on 5-point changing-alternative scales. Scoring based on empirical validation.	28
Winnetka Scale for Rating School Behavior and Attitudes (Van Alstyne)	Nursery school-6	13 classroom situations (e.g., "When there is a group project to be carried out") rated on 10-point scale according to five changing alternatives. Factor-analyzed. Norms.	13
American Council on Education Personality Rating Scale	9–13	5 traits (appearance and manner, industry, ability to control others, emotional control, distribution of time and energy). Descriptive and graphic forms. Space for illustrative instances. Intended especially for reporting to college entrance officers.	3
Vineland Social Maturity Scale (Doll)	Infancy through adulthood	117 items designed to indicate social age and quotient. Similar to individual intelligence test. 8 categories: self-help general, self-help eating, self-help dressing, self-direction, occupation, communication, locomotion, socialization.	11
Business Education Council Personality Rating Schedule	7–16, adults	29 traits in 8 groups: mental alertness, initiative, dependability, coöperativeness, judgment, personal impression, courtesy, health. Descriptions of levels worded as observable behavior.	12

the respondents to give valid answers. Sometimes the questions on such inventories arouse resistance, conscious or unconscious, that prevents valid responses from being made. This is particularly so when the pupil is interested in painting a favorable picture of himself, because of a lack of feeling of freedom and rapport.

By depending on what an individual is conscious of in himself, structured inventories also fail to get at the deeper, underlying structures of his personality which he is probably to a large extent unaware of himself. The mechanisms of adjustment, especially repression, discussed in Chapter XI, make it unlikely that any of us is conscious of enough about himself to be able to tell it in the straightforward fashion called for by most adjustment and personality inventories. Our unique "styles of life," ways of thinking, experiencing, and seeing ourselves in relation to the world are too deep within us to be called up at will and reported to someone else.

Projective techniques have been developed to surmount these limitations of structured approaches to personality. The general feature of projective techniques is that they present to the subject an ambiguous and unstructured stimulus which calls for a response, in the form of a perception, description, manipulation, and the like, that can be interpreted by the psychologist in terms meaningful for the personality of the subject.

THE RORSCHACH INKBLOT TEST

The classic and still most widely studied projective technique is the Rorschach. This test consists of a series of ten inkblots, mostly black and white but some with shades of gray and colors. Each of the inkblots is presented to the subject in turn and he is asked to describe it, to tell what he sees in it, to tell what it means to him. His responses are recorded in detail by the psychologist, who also asks questions to determine what parts of the inkblot are being used by the subject for the various parts of what he describes. As far as the subject can tell, there are no obviously right or wrong answers. A subject who wants to make a good impression has no cues to tell him how. The vagueness and the apparent meaninglessness of the task strip him of his defenses. He must tell the truth about himself even when he does not want to because there are no landmarks to tell him how or where he can hide. About all he can do in this situation is what the psychologist wants him to do— "behave naturally" and say what really comes to his mind.

From the complete record of the subject's responses, the psychologist makes various counts of different kinds. He counts the frequencies of various kinds of uses made of the inkblot—how often did the subject use the form of the inkblot, the color, the shading, the whole inkblot, parts of it? What kinds of things did he see in it, whole people or parts of people, animals or parts of animals, material objects? Were the things he reported similar to those usually reported by persons like himself, or were they unusual and bizarre? When he saw the color on some of the inkblots later in the series, did it "throw him for a loss" or was he able to respond at his normal rate?

Scoring and interpreting the Rorschach are complex and time-consuming affairs. Considerable study and supervised practice are required before the psychologist can acquire the necessary insight, subtlety, sophistication, and habits of complex thinking about personality. Moreover, before taking this training, he should have had considerable training in personality theory and dynamics. Laymen who lack a substantial background of psychological training cannot expect to learn to use this test validly.

These facts about the Rorschach indicate that it is not for use by most teachers or school guidance personnel. It is rather a tool for clinical psychologists and psychiatrists, or others who have had the intensive and specialized training it requires. Its main significance for teachers is for them to be aware of its existence and potentialities. For special studies of learners, in attempts to unravel particularly knotty adjustment problems, the teacher may increasingly expect to have school psychologists and other specialized personnel refer to the Rorschach and to the evidence obtained with it.

The concept of validity (relevance and reliability) cannot as yet be applied to the Rorschach in the same way as for the other types of tests discussed in this volume. The Rorschach does not yield a single total score or even a set of scores that has the same significance for all individuals. In interpreting the Rorschach, the psychologist continually relates one kind of response to others and changes the interpretation of each accordingly. The meaning of Rorschach responses depends on the total pattern of responses, on the uses to be made of the test results, and on other knowledge about the subject.

Much controversy still goes on concerning the Rorschach. Some psychologists are convinced that it produces almost perfectly valid information concerning an enormous range of facets of personality, but others are skeptical about its value for any purpose. Even those who use it and are convinced of its value differ as to the meaning of specific kinds of response and scores. No attempt to evaluate these controversies can be made here. School personnel should be aware that the test is probably more widely used by clinical psychologists than any other single test. Although more research has been published on it than on any other test (*The Fourth Mental Measurements Yearbook* cites 1219 references on the Rorschach) many of these studies, as Cronbach (2) has shown, have used inadequate or wrong statistical techniques.

THE THEMATIC APPERCEPTION TEST (TAT)

The TAT is probably the second most widely used projective test. It consists of twenty-odd ambiguous drawings that are shown to the subject one at a time. He is asked to make up a story about each picture, telling what has happened, what is happening, and what will happen. Some of the pictures are different for men and women and for boys and girls, although some are the same for everyone. Again, the stimulus (picture) is so unstructured as to allow for enormous variety in the kinds of responses. The subject's unique set of choices from these infinite possibilities is interpreted by the psychologist as revealing the subject's needs, frustrations, and attitudes—toward himself, others, and the world about him. The psychologist carefully records the stories as they are told; he may spend hours poring over them to extract their significance, hidden more or less to anyone except those trained for the task.

As with other projective techniques, the basic principle is that what the subject sees in the ambiguous stimulus tells more about himself than about the stimulus. The assumption is made that he identifies with someone in the picture and attributes to (projects upon) the pictured person his own needs, wishes, anxieties—in short, the things that are "on his mind" but repressed deep within his personality, out of conscious reach.

Several schemes for interpreting TAT stories have been developed. Among the more important of these are those of Murray (who with Morgan originated the technique), Tomkins, Stein, Henry, and Holt. Murray's scheme calls for analysis in terms of the needs and press (forces acting upon) of the individual. The analysis is made idea by idea or action by action, each component of the story being taken apart and allocated to a given kind of need or press. A count is then made to obtain the total number of the various kinds of need and press; the total interpretation is based on an all-over impressionistic synthesis of these materials.

As with the Rorschach, the TAT requires advanced training in clinical and abnormal psychology if it is to be used validly. Scoring and interpretation have been much less standardized for the TAT than for the Rorschach. Generally, the scheme used depends not only on the particular authority using the test but also on the situation and purposes of the test.

OTHER PROJECTIVE TESTS

Besides these two widely used projective techniques, dozens of others using different kinds of auditory and visual stimuli have been developed. Drawing, finger painting, doll play, phonograph records of nonsense syllables and musical phrases—indeed, almost any kind of material and task that allows the subject to give free rein to his imagination—have been used. Most of these have not been as well standardized and studied as the Rorschach and the TAT. The consensus among psychologists is that these techniques are promising, merit a great deal of research, can prove useful in the hands of properly qualified people, but are uniformly in need of validation—i.e., studies demonstrating their usefulness in diagnosing personality and adjustment, and in predicting behavior.

The incomplete sentences technique, or sentence completion test, has also been used as a projective approach to personality. Two such tests have gained some recognition: the Rotter Incomplete Sentences Blank, developed by Julian Rotter, and the Sentence Completion Test,[1] developed by Rohde and Hildreth. Both tests ask the subject to complete each sentence with what first comes into his mind. His completions are then analyzed for evidence of his wishes, desires, fears, and attitudes.

For the classroom teacher it is conceivable that rough-and-ready applications of the sentence completion approach can be made to yield information that has some of the advantages of projective methods. Any teacher who wants to get pupil reactions to the classroom situation and to himself in a relatively unstructured fashion can draw up his own set of incomplete sentences, administer them

[1] Publisher No. 18. See p. 614.

to his students, and apply his own psychological and educational insight to the interpretation of the responses. Teachers have long constructed their own rating scales for securing pupil ratings of themselves. When such scales are administered to his classes year after year, the teacher can develop his own set of norms for making the results more meaningful.

The same procedure, applied to the sentence completion technique, can produce similar information without depending on the teacher's ability to anticipate the aspects and dimensions of the classroom situation that are most meaningful to the pupils and hence to himself. The following incomplete sentences illustrate some that might be useful to a teacher:

1. My teacher ....
2. The kids in this class ....
3. The things we have to study ....
4. Homework ....
5. The books we read ....
6. The things about school that bother me ....
7. Boys ....
8. Girls ....
9. I don't understand ....
10. My parents think that school ....

No teacher without advanced psychological training can expect to interpret the responses with as much depth, insight, and complexity as is brought to the task by the clinical psychologists who have been foremost in the development of the projective techniques. Nevertheless, teachers can secure valuable information by home-made incomplete sentence techniques. They may learn things about their own behavior and characteristics as seen by pupils that can be useful in improving their teaching processes.

When used in the way sketched above, the incomplete sentence technique has the advantage of being unstructured but it is probably not so disguised as to prevent pupils from giving what they consider acceptable responses. To minimize the tendency to say only the "right" things, pupils should probably be allowed to remain anonymous. If excellent rapport is known to exist between the teacher and one or more pupils, they may be asked to sign their names on another occasion when alone with the teacher or counselor; the results can be used for improving his understanding of these particular pupils.

REFERENCES

1. Buros, O. K. (ed.), *The Fourth Mental Measurements Yearbook,* Highland Park, N.J.: Gryphon Press, 1953.
2. Cronbach, L. J., "Statistical methods applied to Rorschach scores," *Psychological Bulletin,* 46:393–429 (1949).
3. Cunningham, Ruth, *et al., Understanding the Group Behavior of Boys and Girls,* New York: Bureau of Publications, Teachers College, Columbia University, 1951.
4. Drucker, A. J., and Remmers, H. H., "A validation of the *SRA Youth Inventory," Journal of Applied Psychology,* 36:186–187 (1952).
5. Ellis, A., "The validity of personality questionnaires," *Psychological Bulletin,* 43:383–440 (1946).
6. Flanagan, J. C., *Factor Analysis in the Study of Personality,* Stanford University: Stanford University Press, 1935.
7. Jacobs, R., "A report on the experimental use of the *SRA Youth Inventory* in the fall testing program of the Educational Records Bureau," *Educational Records Bulletin No. 56,* New York: Educational Records Bureau, 1950.
8. Jennings, Helen H., *Sociometry in Group Relations,* Washington: American Council on Education, 1948.
9. Moreno, J. L., *Who Shall Survive? A New Approach to the Problem of Human Inter-Relations,* Washington: Nervous and Mental Disease Publishing Company, 1934.
10. Proctor, C. H., and Loomis, C. P., "Analysis of sociometric data," in Jahoda, Marie, Deutsch, M., and Cook, S. W. (eds.), *Research Methods in Social Relations, Part II: Selected Techniques,* New York: Dryden Press, 1952.
11. Remmers, H. H., and Shimberg, B., *The SRA Youth Inventory,* Chicago: Science Research Associates, 1949.
12. Staff of Personnel Section of the Adjutant General's Office, "The forced choice technique and rating scales," *American Psychologist,* 1:267 (1946).
13. Staff of the Division on Child Development and Teacher Personnel, American Council on Education, *Helping Teachers Understand Children,* Washington: American Council on Education, 1945.

14. Traxler, A. E., "The Nature and Use of Anecdotal Records," *Supplementary Bulletin D,* New York: Educational Records Bureau, 1939.

15. Ullmann, C. A., *Identification of Maladjusted School Children,* Public Health Monograph No. 7, Washington: Government Printing Office, 1952.

PART FOUR

Attitudes: Opinions, Interests, Appreciations, Etc.

CHAPTER XIII

The Nature of Attitudes

ABSTRACT

Attitudes can be analyzed in the same way as intelligence. The concept has many synonyms in both folk language and psychological terminology. Attitude structure, organization, and functioning are fundamentally important aspects of personality. The dimensions of attitudes are favorableness, intensity, salience, generality, degree of "publicness," and commonness in different individuals and groups. Determiners of attitudes are chiefly social and hence need to be understood for guidance purposes.

THE IMPORTANCE OF ATTITUDES

We noted in Chapter II that attitudes are an important part of many statements of instructional objectives. Educational philosophers, curriculum builders, administrators, and teachers are all becoming increasingly aware that educational procedures and curriculum content can and do change attitudes (19). And even where attitudes are not subject to the influence, conscious or unconscious, of the school but are shaped by out-of-school experiences, the school cannot escape the need for being concerned with these aspects of pupils. Counts (8 : 217) states the basic issue that confronts all mankind today: "The essence of any civilization is found in its values—in its preferences, its moral commitments, its aesthetic judgments, its deepest loyalties, its conception of the good life, its standards of excellence, its measures of success, its teachings regarding the things for which and by which men should live and, if need be, die. The issue at stake in the coming years is nothing less than the birth, the death, and the survival of values." This statement is put into our conceptual context if for *values* we read *attitudes*.

This point of view means that education cannot proceed as if human beings were intellectual machines activated by pure reason. From the standpoint of both society and the individual, the importance of attitudes needs only to be mentioned in order to be appreciated. (For the present let us define attitudes roughly as "feelings for or against something.") Socially, the system of morals which governs any given group or society can be truly said to be a matrix of attitude patterns that constitutes the "flywheel of society," to use the phrase of William James. To the extent that these attitude patterns function in the lives of individuals in society without creating undue stresses and strains, they constitute characteristics of a society that is stable with respect to its aims and purposes. Education must therefore be concerned with whether it is producing types of attitude patterns that are desirable as the integrating forces in society.

Does this imply a system of indoctrination rather than of education? These two words are charged with feeling. Educators have upheld the slogan that children must be taught *how* to think but not *what* to think. However, this slogan contains a fundamental psychological self-contradiction. Thinking does not occur in the abstract or in a vacuum but proceeds in terms of the individual's background of attitude patterns and experience. Hence, in the process of teaching *how* to think we shall inevitably and necessarily also to a considerable extent be teaching *what* to think.

From the standpoint of the individual, attitudes are important for mental hygiene. The individual's own evaluation of his conduct and desires in relation to the system of social values *as he understands them* constitutes the basis for social-emotional adjustment leading either to a happy, effective, socialized individual or, at the other extreme, to a complete disintegration of the personality. The individual's attitudes toward his associates, playmates, teachers, institutions, customs—all have a basic effect on his mental ease or dis-ease. His attitudes also affect what he perceives, what he remembers, and, in fact, what he thinks. "Our intellect," said G. Stanley Hall, "is a mere speck afloat on a sea of feeling."

The attitudinal make-up of the pupil is this sea of feeling. The integration of the intellectual-emotional life of pupils is as much a matter of attitude as is social integration, the problem of holding society together.

More specifically, attitudes are a vital concern of guidance, and consequently of educational evaluation, because they affect:

1. The pupil's fitness for various curricula. Unless a pupil has a favorable attitude toward a set of instructional objectives and sets them up as desirable goals for himself, the educative process will be relatively ineffective.
2. The pupil's fitness for various occupational goals. Bingham (5 : 82) has summarized the reason for concern with attitudes as related to occupational fitness in terms of answers to the questions whether (a) the individual will like the actual work of an occupation; (b) the individual will find himself among congenial associates, with interests similar to his own; (c) symptoms of the individual's future abilities may be uncovered; (d) alternative fields of occupation which may not yet have been seriously considered may be discovered.
3. The pupil's fitness for effective and desirable participation in a democratic social order. Attitudes toward social groups, institutions, practices, and policies, such as Negroes, freedom of speech, initiative and referendum, or a peaceful world, are all attitudes in which society and the schools have a real stake. Most important of all, perhaps, are the pupil's attitudes toward the acceptance of social responsibility. Any guidance concerned with the basic essentials of individual and social progress requires the evaluation of the pupil's respect for his future right to vote, his amenability to social change, and his sensitivity to social problems.

DEFINITION OF ATTITUDES

As we stated above, attitudes may be roughly defined as feelings for or against something. This definition serves to provide a framework on which may be hung a more rigorous definition.

The term "feeling" points to the difference between attitudes and detailed, rational, intellectual, cognitive mental operations. Attitudes are linked to the emotions; pleasant and unpleasant associations—fear, rage, love, and all the variations and complications in these emotions brought about by learning—play a part in attitudes.

The phrase "for or against" expresses the directionality of attitudes, the fact that they are characterized by approach or withdrawal, likes or dislikes, avoidant or adient tendencies, favorable or unfavorable reactions, loves or hates, as these are responses to specific or generalized stimuli.

The word "something" signifies that attitudes are not merely mental images or verbalized ideas, but rather take on meaning only when they are considered in relation to some object, situation, or stimulus.

A further characteristic of attitudes is that they have an effect on behavior which may be so great that the attitude enables the prediction of behavior, or which may be influenced in such a way by other forces, social and attitudinal, that the behavior will not follow the expressed attitude, as when a pupil who expressed opposition to cheating proceeds to cheat on an examination. A fifth characteristic of attitudes, to be treated later in more detail, is that they are learned.

In summary, an attitude may be defined as an emotionalized tendency, organized through experience, to react positively or negatively toward a psychological object.

ATTITUDES AND CERTAIN ALLIED CONCEPTS

Certain concepts allied to attitudes, some of them essentially synonyms or near-synonyms, may be considered here, since they are frequently used in popular discussion and technical literature. Such concepts are *interests, motives, values, appreciation, tastes, mores, morality, morale, ideals, social distance,* and *character.* Other similar concepts could be listed, but these will serve the purpose of the present discussion—to show that each of these concepts, from a dynamic, functional point of view, is constituted of attitudes.

Interests as observed are presumably the reflection of attractions and aversions in our behavior, of our feelings of pleasantness and unpleasantness, likes and dislikes. In action they are characterized by seeking-acceptance at one end of the scale and by avoidance-rejection at the other (10 : 15). A distinction may be made between attitudes and interests in that the latter merely indicate the degree to which the individual prefers to hold an object before his consciousness whether he reacts approvingly or disapprovingly toward that object, whereas attitudes indicate his reaction in terms of its direction, pleasantness or unpleasantness, agreement or disagreement. But since we do not prefer to hold an object before our consciousness unless we agree with it or find it pleasurable, the distinction is a very fine one, and attitudes and interests are for practical purposes identical. If this is the case, why do we use the term attitude instead of interest? The answer is that theoretical and experimental social psychology has produced a vast literature around this concept and has used the word "attitude" to denote it. However, in vocational psychology and guidance the term "interest" has been mainly used. Bingham (5 : 62) defined interest as a "tendency to become absorbed in an experience and to continue it." The similarity of this definition to that for attitudes is apparent. The use of a separate term for such a tendency serves only to complicate our thinking and to hinder the application of experimental and theoretical work in attitudes to the field of "interest." So we shall use the term attitude as inclusive of what vocational psychologists and guidance workers have called "interests."

Motives are related to attitudes in that the latter, with their directionality and feeling tone, constitute an important aspect of motives. A highly favorable attitude toward a particular teacher may motivate a pupil to emulate that teacher. Attitudes have been defined (18) as predispositions to motive arousal. Motives are in this sense more specific and temporary. When goals are reached, motives are satisfied, but the attitude, or tendency to have the motive, persists from one occasion to the next.

Values are the things of social life (mores, customs, ideals, institutions, taboos, etc.) that are objects of affective regard. These values may be positive—freedom, education, the family, law observance, justice, etc.—or negative—cruelty, crime, injustice, intolerance, ignorance, poverty, etc. The saint and the racketeer differ chiefly in their value systems. The concept of values is thus essentially a synonym for attitudes, usually referring to dominant and pervasive systems of attitudes.

Appreciation is used loosely in at least two widely different senses. In "I appreciate your point of view," the term obviously has the connotation of understanding or comprehending—a cognitive, intellective meaning. Appreciation of literature, music, graphic and plastic art—in short, aesthetic appreciation—on the other hand, connotes emotionalized, affective processes. It is in this latter sense that the term concerns us. Its kernel here is the acceptance-rejection notion, and this is readily subsumed under the concept of attitudes. *Taste* is practically synonymous with *appreciation*.

Mores, morality, and *morale* are conveniently treated together. Mores are defined by Sumner (22 : 59) as "the ways of doing things which are current in a society to satisfy human needs and desires, together with the faiths, notions, codes, and standards of well-living which inhere in those ways, having a genetic connection with them." The mores "are social ritual in which we all participate unconsciously" (22 : 62); they define "right" and "wrong" for a particular social group. Though usually having a rational origin, many of the mores become obsolescent through changing social conditions but tend nevertheless to continue as categorical imperatives, not to be questioned. They are subjectively highly emotionalized; violations of them are "wrong," "sinful," "obscene," "in bad taste," and, in general, not tolerated by the group. Their emotional loading brings them readily within the purview of the concept of attitudes, at least from the operational, measurement point of view.

The term *morality* in its popular meaning has come in this country to be restricted largely to sex morality but is properly used as referring to all social sanctions implemented by the mores. The moral act, then, is one that is in harmony with the mores either in doing what they demand or in refraining from doing what is contrary to them. The moral person is one who observes the mores. *Morale* refers to the *esprit de corps,* the emotional integration of a group. It is the integrating pattern of attitudes with reference to attitude objects judged to be of vital concern to the group. These attitude objects may be threats or goals the achievement of which is endangered by the absence of morale. We have the morale of an army or of the civilian population in war, the morale of the classroom, of an industrial organization, of a teaching staff.

Ideals are the conscious aspects of the mores (**6** : 472–473). Conscious striving toward "ways of doing things" most acceptably is the essence of ideals. They are the individual's conscious adjustment to the demands of society, the public, as conceived and understood by him. The public may be a "phantom" public and have no counterpart in reality. Consider, for example, the attempted control of a small boy's behavior by means of Santa Claus or the "bogy man." Robert Burns' lines,

> The fear of hell's a hangman's whip
> To haud the wretch in order,

describe a type of attitudinal social control familiar to all western cultures.

Social distance refers to the difference between the mores or the ideals of individuals and groups and implies tension or clashes inherent in different sets of mores and ideals. Social distance exists between management and labor, rich and poor, the younger generation and the older, one national or racial group and another. Strikes, lynchings, race riots, and even wars are the reflections in large part of the social distance between groups of human beings. Insofar as such distance persists we have failed to achieve the "brotherhood of man." The reduction of social distance between groups and the evaluation of the individual on his merits are part of the democratic ideal.

Character has ethical connotations sufficiently unambiguous to require little analysis here. The person of character is the moral person as defined in terms of attitudes. He behaves in accordance with individual ideals that are socially approved.

This sketchy exploration of the meanings of related terms may suffice to show the central nature of the concept of attitudes. Further elaboration of the concept in all its varied aspects is contained in Dewey's classic *Human Nature and Conduct* (**9**) and in the writings of the Allports (**2**, **3**).

DIMENSIONS OF ATTITUDES

It is often helpful to think of attitudes as having various dimensions. Having these in mind can lead teachers to more adequate ways of thinking about the attitudes of their pupils.

1. FAVORABLENESS

Favorableness is the dimension that is most often considered and measured. It is the degree to which one is for or against a given attitude object. When people speak of someone's attitude toward the United Nations, progressive education, or the core curriculum, they most likely have in mind the person's favorableness toward these things. Those who believe that capital punishment should be abolished are unfavorable toward this practice; those who believe it should be abolished except for a smaller number of crimes than it now applies to, are somewhat less unfavorable, and so on. Favorableness is the basic dimension of attitudes, as was indicated in our definition of attitude.

2. INTENSITY

Intensity is the strength of the feeling. Two people can have equally intense attitudes but be at opposite extremes on favorableness. The relationship between intensity and favorableness has often been found to be V- or U-shaped. That is, the more favorable or unfavorable the attitude, the more intense it is; people who are neutral have the least intense attitude. An example of this is seen in attitudes toward so-called "progressive" education. Those who are ardently in favor of or opposed to progressive education can be found on any large university campus, along with perhaps a still larger group who are neutral, indifferent, and have attitudes of little intensity on the matter.

3. SALIENCE

Salience is the readiness with which the attitude can be aroused, its "closeness to the surface" in a person's mind. Some people, when asked what they consider the most important problem facing humanity today, immediately think of preventing war; others, the "curse of drink"; still others, juvenile delinquency. Salience is best discovered by asking unstructured questions so that the respondent's attitudes appear freely. Among first-graders, attitudes toward age groups are highly salient; when they meet a new child they are immediately impressed with whether or not he is older than they are. Among adults, attitudes toward occupations are more salient;

when they meet a stranger they are more interested in what kind of work he does, and their attitudes toward occupations are more likely to determine their attitudes of respect for or interest in him.

4. GENERALITY, OR RANGE CONSISTENCY

Although discussed below, this aspect of attitudes also belongs in any consideration of dimensions of attitudes. The number and variety of attitude objects toward which a person has a single, internally consistent, overall attitude are a reflection of the generality of his attitude. Some people may be labeled "liberals" or "conservatives" because they have consistent attitudes toward a wide range of objects, such as racial and nationality groups, government planning, socialized medicine, world government, federal aid to education, religious denominations, labor unions, civil liberties, and the like. The fact that knowing whether a person is "liberal" or "conservative" makes possible fairly accurate predictions of his attitudes toward such a variety of topics indicates that, by and large, many attitudes tend to be highly generalized, with a wide range and substantial internal consistency.

5. PUBLIC VS. PRIVATE ATTITUDES

This is not a sharp twofold distinction, but a continuum. Public attitudes are those that people will talk about freely in almost any social situation; a simple example is attitude toward different kinds of weather. A less public attitude might be that toward the major political parties. Kinsey's elaborate interviewing techniques were required in part because some attitudes toward sex behavior are highly private in American society. The more a person thinks his attitudes are likely to be disapproved or punished, the more private he is likely to keep them. This is one reason why attitude questionnaires are sometimes administered anonymously.

6. COMMON VS. INDIVIDUAL ATTITUDES

When many people have attitudes of more or less favorableness, intensity, and the like toward a given attitude object, we speak of common attitudes. Individuals may, however, have attitudes toward things that no one else is aware of or cares about. A man's attitude toward one of his neckties, and a teacher's attitude toward a given pupil's reading habits are examples of attitudes that are more individual than, for example, the man's attitude toward the Republican party or the teacher's attitude toward his principal.

THE ORGANIZATION OF ATTITUDES

With attitudes as with mental abilities, questions concerning organization are concerned mainly with the degree of specificity or generality or the size of the organizational units to be observed in an individual's personality or behavior. That is, are attitudes organized into large structures or small ones, into "cobblestones" or "grains of sand"? For example, are we justified in calling a person "liberal" or "conservative" and, from this general label, inferring his attitude toward a large number of more specific attitude objects such as races, nationalities, internationalism, labor, income taxes, and so on?

In response to these questions about attitudinal organization some researches have drawn conclusions in favor of specificity and some in favor of generality. Perhaps the most influential of the researches supporting the doctrine of specificity have been Hartshorne and May's studies (12) of the traits and attitudes of honesty, service, and self-control. Broadly stated, their conclusions are that we are unjustified in considering these traits and their related attitudes as general characteristics of children. They are related to the specific situation in which a child is placed, and an individual behaves similarly in different situations only insofar as these situations are alike. For example, although the child who cheated in one classroom situation may cheat in another, the same child may be scrupulously honest in athletics, party games, etc. Stealing money was unrelated to stealing answers on examinations. Consequently these two researchers considered the traits and attitudes centering in the concept of honesty to be highly specific.

Other studies have come to very different conclusions concerning the organization and interrelationships of attitudes. For example, Cantril (7) examined the responses of a sample of college students to a series of terms, statements, personality sketches, and the Allport-Vernon Study of Personal Values. He found evidence for generality of some sort in mental life independent of specific content. Similarly, Herrick (13) used a group of mental tests, rating

devices, autobiographical sketches, and interviews and drew conclusions in favor of the existence of general attitudes on certain
social issues and matters of conduct in a college student group.

Further evidence in favor of some generalization of attitudes
in individuals is found in the significant correlations among various attitudes, such as those toward pacifism, communism, and the
church. Radicalism-conservatism has been found to be a general
attitude enabling prediction of more specific attitudes toward
races, national ideals, imperialism, militarism, international good
will, birth control, religion, etc. In the study cited above, Herrick
was able to show by factorial analysis that the data of Hartshorne
and May contain certain "group factors" or clusters of character
traits and attitudes, a finding in sharp disagreement with the
extreme specificity inferred by those authors.

A quite general authoritarian personality pattern, very different
from the democratic personality pattern, has been discovered
through extensive research (1).

In a series of studies Gough (11) comes to such conclusions as
the following:

. . . It appears that the more anti-semitic students are on the average less liberal in social outlook, less tolerant of other races and groups,
less internationally minded, more nationalistic, more cynical concerning the ideals of democracy, less impressed by the record of achievement in securing human rights and privileges in this country, less
tolerant and trusting of others in a general way, less magnanimous, less
respectful of others' integrity, less able to overlook and ignore minor
irritations and frustrations, less concerned with resolving and rectify-
ing problems once they do arise in interpersonal interaction, and are
less sociable. In respect to socio-economic status, the more prejudiced
students come from poorer homes, and tend to exhibit characteristic
fears, insecurities and doubts which are often associated with such
backgrounds. The prejudiced subjects are clearly less intelligent, and,
as would now be expected on the basis of previous data, show the attitudes and beliefs which the California group designated as "anti-
democratic."

In another paragraph he summarizes as follows:

If a brief review is attempted of the factors which seemed to characterize the more anti-semitic subjects in the several samples, it seems

that the following impressions emerged: (1) lower intellectual level; (2) disadvantaged economic background; (3) less sociability and participation in school activities; (4) inferior academic performance; (5) greater uneasiness and discomfort in social situations; (6) greater tendency to complain of personal dissatisfactions, problems, and annoyances; (7) narrowness of outlook in regard to national and international affairs; (8) debunking attitude toward questions of political-social ideals and goals; (9) antagonism toward many out groups, not just some particular out groups; (10) emphasis on nationalism, chauvinism, and conservatism; (11) feelings of victimization and exploitation.

All of these factors are similar to those observed in other studies and seem to justify the conclusion that there is a discoverable and identifiable network of attitudes and beliefs, into which the specified ethnic opinions are characteristically integrated.

The differences in the conclusions concerning generality and specificity may in part be due to differences in the ages of the groups studied. That is, generality of attitude organization may become greater as age increases; the integration and self-consistency of attitudes would thus be a function of the amount of time during which an individual has been under the influence of the socially organized sets of attitude patterns by which his own consistency was judged. Consequently, teachers should adjust their expectations of consistency in a pupil's attitudes to his age and maturity; high-school pupils will be less consistent than college students but more consistent, integrated, and predictable from situation to situation and from one attitude to another than elementary-school pupils.

Another factor determining the degree of generality is the narrowness of the attitude considered. The more narrowly we define an attitude, the more closely it is related to other similarly narrowly defined attitudes and the higher the degree of generality we will infer. If we consider attitudes toward the prohibition of wines and beer as one attitude, and attitudes toward the prohibition of whiskey and brandy as another distinct attitude, we shall find these two attitudes highly correlated and conclude that we have evidence of a general attitude toward the prohibition of alcoholic beverages. But this illustrates merely the procedure used in constructing instruments to measure attitudes, whereby a group of closely knit, internally consistent statements of attitudes are assembled so as to provide a statistically reliable test. If this is the case, what should be our criterion for distinguishing between unitary attitude entities and attitudes which should be considered merely as components or elements of attitudes? Where should we stop in our breakdown of attitudes? There is, of course, no absolute rule in this matter. Attitudes should be considered separate from other attitudes as our practical concern dictates.

If a teacher has reason to be concerned with a pupil's attitudes toward work in general, that may be considered an attitude. A more specific problem will lead the teacher to be concerned with attitudes toward a specific kind of work, such as homework or classroom tasks. A still more specific problem will lead him to be concerned with homework in a specific subject, such as algebra or history. These considerations may be summarized by a quotation from Newcomb (16 : 1029):

The needed caution is simply that *no* attitudes as measured are genuine entities in the sense that there is anything "absolute" about them. For practical purposes any set of verbal responses which is statistically reliable may be considered an entity and given an appropriate name. Any measured attitude, no matter how reliable, might conceivably be broken down into two or more different attitudes with slightly different labels. A single label implies nothing concerning singleness of attitudes. Indeed, the concept of singleness has meaning only in regard to the object of reference. If the attitude measured has reference to a custom, person, or institution commonly accepted as an isolable phenomenon and is reliably measured, it may be regarded as an entity.

In summary, the generality or specificity of attitudes may be considered to be a function of (1) the degree to which attitude objects or attitudes themselves are organized into sets of related clusters by the society in which an individual lives; (2) the degree to which an individual has absorbed the structure or organization of the society in which he lives, which in turn is the function of his age, maturity, and sensitivity to social forces; and (3) the narrowness with which an attitude is defined, the broader more-inclusive attitudes being more likely to be independent, self-contained, and "specific" than attitudes more narrowly conceived.

DEVELOPMENT OF ATTITUDES IN THE INDIVIDUAL

Why does a given individual have a certain attitude? Where shall we look for the causes or origins of a person's attitudes? Why do people differ in attitudes? Why are some liberal and some conservative, religious or atheistic, favorable or unfavorable toward a given teacher, a given subject, vocation, or any other attitude object?

Environmental modification of the human organism begins with conception. Apart from embryonic development, the changes wrought by environmental contact are manifested from birth on during the early years and even months of life. Here the individual acquires his first attitudes and exhibits his first learned behavior. In brief, he develops personality. Original drives are overlaid by social experiences organized into attitudinal systems.

The newborn child quickly acquires certain feeding habits. He comes to regard favorably those who contribute to the gratification of his needs, and unfavorably those who frustrate his activities. The baby's attitudes toward his parents carry over to others. As the child grows in his capacity to respond to those outside his family group, his social attitudes—e.g., coöperativeness, selfishness, dominance, conformity, and the like—become definite.

As the child acquires "human nature" which will equip him for life in a society of human beings, the area of his relevant experience expands. The attitudinal patterns become incorporated in his personality. Attitudes will be modified, through learning, in accordance with his own goals and drives. This means that he will acquire attitudes like those of his parents, his friends, and the other primary groups (permanent face-to-face groups) of which he is a member. As he grows older, secondary groups (not face-to-face, or temporarily face-to-face groups) with which he is associated will elicit certain attitudes. In general, the closer the relationship between an individual and others, the greater the potency of the relationship in the formation of attitudes.

The development of attitudes involves the integration of numerous specific responses of a similar type. Such attitudes determine the entire adjustment of the individual. If a child is frustrated by his classroom teacher and believes that the teacher is discriminating against him, he will tend to react negatively to the teacher's future criticisms. Accordingly, the term "attitude" is merely a convenient way of referring to the preparedness that exists within the organism for some future activity. It is to be emphasized that such preparedness is neither automatic nor routine, but has cognitive and conative aspects that differentiate attitudes from habits and reflexes as commonly regarded. Furthermore, attitudes toward inanimate forces, institutions, and values, although culturally determined, vary in intensity between individuals and within the same individual at different times.

The baby grows into childhood, youth, and adulthood with attitudes as an important aspect of his learned behavior. Attitudes are evolved from association with his family group, with children in his play and school group, and in general through social-psychological interaction. An adult's occupation and his responsibilities of citizenship and parenthood are important in attitude development. It is inconceivable that cultural stability, language, and dependability in human affairs could exist without attitudes. Yet the fact that attitudes do change accounts for social innovations, social conflict, and social changes (**20** : 3–4).

Another point of view as to the determiners of attitudes is provided by the classification of related variables by Newcomb (**16** : 912–1046). He deals with the relationships between attitude and (1) individual characteristics, (2) experimental variables, (3) life experiences, and (4) other attitudes.

1. Under the heading of individual characteristics are included sex, age, intelligence, and such nonintellectual characteristics as muscle coördination, suggestibility, persistence, susceptibility to majority influence, ability to break long-established habits, speed of reaction time, tendency to sacrifice accuracy to speed, ability to think in unusual terms, neurotic tendency, ascendance-submission, and other personality variables.

2. Under the heading of experimental modification Newcomb deals with investigations in which attitudes have been measured before and after the introduction of some experience presumed to modify them, these experiences being in turn classified into those occurring within the classroom and those occurring as extraschool experiences. The school experiences are chiefly those due to par-

ticular curricular materials, especially in the social sciences, and those due to specific teachers, usually either liberal or conservative with respect to broad issues. The extraschool experiences include motion pictures, radio and television programs, pamphlets, speeches, and other forms of "propaganda."

The characteristics of methods which appear to be most effective in the experimental modification of attitudes are summarized as follows: (a) They should be vivid, novel, emotionally charged, and realistic (as opposed to laboratory-like). (b) There should be neither strong opposing influences nor opportunity to become familiar with the complexities of or the objections to the point of view being advanced. (c) The methods should use individuals, groups, institutions, or symbols thereof, which have prestige value for those whose attitudes are to be affected.

3. Under the heading of life experiences as determiners of attitude are included the more "normal," everyday kind of experiences. Typical of these are such factors as educational level reached or amount of education received, college military training in the R.O.T.C., the experience of college fraternity life, familiarity and contact with races and nationalities, continued experiences of association with a particular family, allegiance to particular religious groups, racial or national background, socioeconomic status, residence in rural or urban environment or in different national or cultural areas.

The influences of these "natural" experiences are summarized as follows: (a) Few generalizations are justifiable concerning experiences which are more or less individual rather than being associated with a particular group or a particular locality. (b) Experiences regularly associated with family, race, or church groups enable better prediction of attitude. (c) Experiences shared by larger communities geographically defined enable practically no prediction of attitude, except for urban-rural differences in racial prejudice and superstitious belief and for sectional differences in this country with regard to Negroes and Orientals.

4. Under the heading of the interrelationship of attitudes, Newcomb deals with the question of generality and specificity which has already been discussed in this chapter.

Our discussion of the determiners of attitudes may be concluded with a reference to the two most broadly conceived classifications of such determiners: personality differences on the one hand, and conformity-enforcing agencies or social institutions on the other. The first of these will tend to produce variability within groups, and the second produces differences between groups. In considering a pupil's attitudes for the purpose of guiding him educationally, vocationally, or personally, the teacher should look to these two kinds of factors for an explanation of his attitudes. The teacher's understanding of the nature of attitudes, their organization, and their determiners will enable him to make better use of the concept of attitudes in evaluating the pupil. Let us now turn to the consideration of what attitudes the teacher should evaluate.

ATTITUDES SIGNIFICANT FOR GUIDANCE

As already stated, the most convenient way to denote an attitude is by its attitude object, that is, by the thing toward which the attitude is held. The reason for this is that all other properties of an attitude—its directionality, its feeling tone, its motivating power—are not sufficiently different from attitude to attitude to enable them to be used as definite labels for a particular attitude. Consequently, in choosing the attitudes that are most significant for guidance, we shall be concerned mainly with attitude objects.

Any attempt to classify or bring some sort of systematic order into the field of attitude objects, if it were to lay claim to any other than mere practical usefulness, if it were to make pretensions toward scientific validity or unique truthfulness, would have to be based on some metaphysical system whereby the contents of the universe were ordered. Obviously, no such attempt can be made here. Rather we need to select and arrange attitude objects solely for the purpose of clarifying and simplifying the evaluation of pupils for guidance purposes. Horne (14) attempted by the questionnaire and rating scale techniques to determine what a representative population regarded as socially significant attitude objects and to rank these objects in order of social significance. From his studies there emerged 233 attitude objects which were classified by two psychologists into eight categories:

1. Personality
2. Education
3. Economic activities
4. Family
5. Government
6. Social problems
7. Recreation and exercise
8. Religion

All the 233 attitude objects fitted into one of the categories, the two judges agreeing almost completely as to the classification of the objects. Another classification of attitudes is apparent in a paper by Nelson (17) which summarizes the experimental literature on social attitudes under four headings: attitude toward personal ideals, attitude toward political issues, racial attitudes, and religious attitudes.

The classification made by Horne will be used as a framework on which to formulate our presentation of attitude objects significant in guidance. We shall use his eight headings with illustrations drawn either from his study or from other sources.

Personality

Personality as an attitude object classification refers to such broad, all-embracing concepts as "personal values" and "level of aspiration." According to Spranger (21), an individual's personality is best understood through his values, his evaluative attitudes toward the common attributes of a number of classes of situations. Spranger distinguished six types of values: theoretical, economic, aesthetic, social, political, and religious. The theoretical man values truth. The economic man values wealth. The aesthetic man values beauty. The social man values people for their own sake. The political man values power. The religious man values a "mystical unity with the cosmos." The significance of Spranger's theory has been enhanced by the construction of a test (4) to measure the relative strength of these six values in an individual, so that at certain age levels (above about fifteen years) it is possible to acquire valuable data concerning a person's attitudes along these all-embracing lines.

The level of aspiration concerns the goal which an individual sets for himself in the achievement or solution of any task or problem. It is his attitude toward a statement of what he should achieve. Knowledge concerning the pupil's level of aspiration and its relationship to his abilities constitutes perhaps the most important basis for predicting an individual's achievement.

Attitudes as major personality factors guide and channel perception and learning. A gift of a side of beef will be perceived as rewarding by an orthodox Jew but as punishing by a Hindu. The reverse will be true of a gift of a ham. Staying after school to help the teacher tidy the classroom and clean the blackboard is rewarding to "teacher's pet" but punishing to the boy who would rather be out playing baseball.

Experimental results demonstrate the principle clearly. In an interesting experiment, Levine and Murphy (15) found that of two groups equal in learning ability as tested on neutral material, the group with strongly anti-Soviet attitudes learned more rapidly and remembered better a passage "excitedly anti-Communist" than one more "moderately pro-Communist." The other, pro-Communist, group learned more rapidly and remembered better the pro-Communist selection. Not a few experiments are reported in the psychological journals showing similar selective perception and learning related to attitudes, needs, and frames of reference.

Obviously, other attitudes that color personality have been distinguished and may prove valuable. Those we have pointed out should serve as illustrations and bases for further thinking on the question of such attitudes.

EDUCATION

School subjects, teachers, pupil-pupil and pupil-teacher relations, and teaching practices, such as homework, classroom drill, examinations, and study periods, are perhaps the most obvious attitude objects within the field of school work. Certain administrative aspects of the schools, such as the size of classes, the grading system, the system of records and reports, the length of the school day, vacations and holidays, pupil participation, are also objects toward which pupil attitudes may be significant for guidance.

ECONOMIC ACTIVITIES

In the economic area, attitudes toward specific vocations, either as measured directly or as inferred from the similarities between an individual's interests and the interests of those engaged in a particular occupation, are obviously of high importance for guidance.

FAMILY

Attitudes toward parents, brothers and sisters, the home and community environment, and toward the family as an institution may throw considerable light on questions arising in the field of personal guidance and, consequently, in all guidance.

GOVERNMENT AND SOCIAL PROBLEMS

General liberalism-conservatism has been the most explored aspect of this field. Social sensitivity, or awareness and feeling of responsibility for social problems, is a similarly inclusive aspect. Racial attitudes, international attitudes, attitudes toward government ownership, social insurance, civil liberties, conservation, immigration, and other specific social institutions and practices may become foci in the measurement both of the outcomes of social science instruction and of the pupil's fitness for his proper role in a democratic society.

RECREATION AND EXERCISE

What an individual likes to do for fun, his preferences and interests in the fields of recreation and exercise, has been considered important in the field of educational evaluation not only for its own sake but for the light these attitudes throw on vocational interests and personal and social adjustment. That is, questions concerning recreational interests have constituted a large part of tests and inventories in these other fields. Their use in this way, of course, does not preclude their more narrow function as indices of recreational organization which schools and communities should provide or consider in their plan to meet the needs of youth.

RELIGION

The complexity of this field of attitude objects, the wide variation between communities in the nature of their concern with religious attitudes, the traditional American separation between church and state agencies, all operate to render this area too difficult to be treated here. It is included merely for the sake of completeness. Teachers and school administrators will be able to distinguish the more meaningful objects within this attitude area in the light of their own particular community situations and needs.

REFERENCES

1. Adorno, T. W., *et al., The Authoritarian Personality,* New York: Harper & Brothers, 1950.

2. Allport, F. H., *Social Psychology*, Boston: Houghton Mifflin Company, 1924.
3. Allport, G. W., "Attitudes," in Murchison, Carl (ed.), *Handbook of Social Psychology*, Worcester: Clark University Press, 1935.
4. Allport, G. W., Vernon, P. E., and Lindzey, G., *A Study of Values*, Boston: Houghton Mifflin Company, 1952.
5. Bingham, W. V., *Aptitudes and Aptitude Testing*, New York: Harper & Brothers, 1937.
6. Briggs, T. H., *Secondary Education*, New York: The Macmillan Company, 1933.
7. Cantril, H., "General and specific attitudes," *Psychological Monographs*, Vol. 42, No. 192, 1932.
8. Counts, G. S., *Education and American Civilization*, New York: Bureau of Publications, Teachers College, Columbia University, 1952.
9. Dewey, John, *Human Nature and Conduct*, New York: Henry Holt & Company, Inc., 1922.
10. Fryer, Douglas, *The Measurement of Interests*, New York: Henry Holt & Company, Inc., 1931.
11. Gough, H. G., "Studies of social intolerance," *Journal of Social Psychology*, 33:237–246, 247–256, 257–262, 263–269 (1951).
12. Hartshorne, H., and May, M., *Studies in the Nature of Character*, New York: The Macmillan Company, 1928–1930, Vols. I–III.
13. Herrick, V. E., "The generality and specificity of attitudes," Ph.D. thesis, University of Wisconsin Library (unpublished); referred to in Young, Kimball, *Personality and Problems of Adjustment*, New York: Appleton-Century-Crofts, 1940, p. 288.
14. Horne, E. P., "Socially significant attitude objects," *Studies in Higher Education XXXI, Bulletin of Purdue University*, 37:117–126 (1936).
15. Levine, J. M., and Murphy, G., "The learning and forgetting of controversial material," *Journal of Abnormal and Social Psychology*, 38:507–517 (1943).
16. Murphy, G., Murphy, L. B., and Newcomb, T. M., *Experimental Social Psychology*, New York: Harper & Brothers, rev. ed., 1937.
17. Nelson, Erland, "Attitudes: III. Social attitudes," *Journal of General Psychology*, 21:417–436 (1939).
18. Newcomb, T. M., *Social Psychology*, New York: Dryden Press, 1950.
19. Remmers, H. H., "Attitudes as educational objectives," *University of Washington, College of Education Record*, 7:68–75 (1941).

20. Remmers, H. H., *Introduction to Opinion and Attitude Measurement,* New York: Harper & Brothers, 1954.
21. Spranger, E. *Types of Men* (transl. by P. J. W. Pigors), Halle: Niemeyer, 1928.
22. Sumner, W. G., *Folkways,* Boston: Ginn and Company, 1906.

CHAPTER XIV

Measuring Attitudes and Interests

ABSTRACT

Attitudes can be evaluated as educational outcomes or, when considered as interests, as related to vocational and educational choices. For the former purpose, the two main approaches are (1) single questions and (2) scales and questionnaires. Single questions need to be carefully worded; their validity can take a variety of forms. Scales can be made by Thurstone's equal-appearing intervals method or in the form of straightforward summated questionnaires. Guttman's scale analysis provides a way of estimating the degree to which adding weighted responses to a series of questions is justified by the uni-dimensionality, or homogeneity, of the attitudes measured. Although much disputed, the results of attitude measurement techniques can have significant meaning when properly interpreted. Disguised techniques furnish data that are free of some of the limitations of the older approaches. Published attitude scales have been less used than those designed for special situations and purposes.

As educational-vocational interests, attitudes are most often appraised by means of interest inventories, although observational procedures and information tests have also been used. The Study of Values, the Kuder Preference Record, and Strong's Vocational Interest Blanks have used different approaches and formats. These devices, and many not so well understood, have in one sense the same meaning: the systematic, quantitative recording of one's values, or likes and dislikes, for various goals and activities. Like most such inventories, these can be "faked"; accordingly, scores on them have straightforward significance only when individuals respond frankly.

In Chapter XIII we discussed the importance of attitudes in the integration both of individuals and of the societies in which they live. We offered a general definition of attitudes, indicated the relationships of attitudes to other allied concepts, and discussed problems of the organization and determiners of attitudes. The chapter concluded with a citation of attitudes considered possibly significant for educational guidance.

TWO FUNCTIONS OF ATTITUDE MEASUREMENT

First we point out a distinction between two functions of attitude measurement. (1) The attitudes of pupils may be evaluated as educational outcomes, as indications of the degree to which pupils have acquired certain attitudes set up as objectives of instruction. Attitudes may be and have been considered as objectives of instruction in all areas of the curriculum, including social studies, mathematics, natural science, art, and language studies. (2) Attitudes may be evaluated as part of the attempt to predict the adjustment of pupils to various school curricula and vocations, and to life outside of and after formal schooling.

This distinction between the two functions of attitude measurement arises from the difference in the degree to which the attitudes measured are set up as instructional objectives. Attitudes toward curricula and vocations are not established as goals; pupils may fully achieve instructional objectives and yet differ widely among themselves in their attitudes, preferences, or interests in various curricula and vocations. It may be considered desirable, for example, for all pupils to acquire certain attitudes toward democratic principles; but for all pupils to acquire certain attitudes toward the "technical" curriculum in high school as distinguished from the "academic" or the "commercial" curriculum is not set up as a goal of educational endeavor.

ATTITUDES AS EDUCATIONAL OUTCOMES

APPROACHES TO THE EVALUATION OF ATTITUDES

Techniques for measuring and evaluating attitudes range widely in objectivity, reliability, and possibility of standardization.

While attitudes may be inferred from overt behavior (effort expended for a cause, relative amounts of money spent for goods and services, and the like), most of the systematic work has concerned itself with indices of attitudes based on opinions expressed or endorsed. We shall therefore consider the various devices of this kind that have been developed.

THE SINGLE QUESTION

The crudest method of measuring attitudes is the ballot or single-response counting, as exemplified in various public opinion polls. These polling devices are in effect two-point "scales." For example, in measuring attitude toward capital punishment, the item in question might be "Capital punishment is necessary." The proportion of "agree" and "disagree" votes would then be taken as an index of the existing attitude for a given population.

RELEVANCE

What do answers obtained with questions like this mean? Several types of meaning, or relevance, can be distinguished. They are not essentially different from those described for educational measurement in general in Chapter V. The following illustrate the specific form they take in attitude measurement.

1. If we are interested only in knowing the present attitude of a group of students toward capital punishment, it can be argued that their anonymously recorded opinions are as relevant as they are reliable, since by definition we are interested only in these opinions with no implications for further student behavior. Relevance and reliability by definition becomes synonymous.

2. "Real-life voting" criteria are often available as bases for validating responses to single questions of this kind. The best known illustrations of such validation are doubtless the predictions of elections from preëlection polls.

3. Another type of criterion is the agreement of the answers with known social commitments. Clearly, membership in the Temperance League or the Prohibition party would validate answers to questions on the desirability of the sale and use of alcoholic beverages; membership in the Seventh-Day Adventist sect would validate questions about the desirability of observing Sunday.

4. Expert opinions frequently serve as criteria of relevance.

Questions designed to get at citizenship attitudes were used in surveys of a sample of college graduates by *Time* (19), and by Drucker and Remmers (8) with high-school and college students. These questions were validated by submitting them to political scientists, psychologists, sociologists, and educators; the questions that produced substantial agreement as to the best answer of three alternatives—"agree," "disagree," or "doubtful"—were used in the surveys.

5. Nonverbal, usually future, behavior is still another kind of criterion. Soldiers' responses to opinion survey questions made it possible to predict the proportion of veterans of World War II who would take advantage of the educational provisions of the G.I. Bill of Rights (8.0 percent predicted, 8.1 percent did). Consumer and market research also uses this type of criterion. Manufacturers validate surveys of consumer acceptance of their product against actual sales.

QUESTION WORDING

One of the greatest problems of opinion and attitude research involves wording a question to be presented to groups who may differ widely in cultural background, age, etc., so that it means the same to all concerned. At best it is possible only to minimize the errors arising from this source; they cannot be eliminated completely.

Since meanings are built up in the individual through experience, and since no two individuals have identical experience, it follows that in strictest logic no verbal symbol, no word, can have exactly the same meaning for any two individuals. "Meanings are in persons' minds, not in words," says Thorndike. "At least 99% of meanings depend upon the past experience and present attitude or 'set' of the hearer (or reader)" (42).

Cantril administered questions taken from national surveys by Gallup, Roper, and the National Opinion Research Center, to a sample of forty subjects and also interviewed them intensively. He demonstrated extensively the difficulties of question wording (4 : 3–4).

Terris (41) used 144 randomly selected questions from surveys made by the same agencies as those studied by Cantril and measured readability by applying special readability formulas (Flesch and Dale-Chall). Over 90 percent of the questions were too difficult for 12 percent of the population and about 70 percent were beyond the grade level comprehension of nearly half of our population. Such studies clearly indicate the need for close attention to vocabulary difficulty and for pretests of opinion and attitude questions.

McNemar (24) and Cantril (4) have both pointed out the importance of providing a frame of reference and standards of judgment for the respondent. Cantril finds that people with stable standards of judgment will be inclined to answer a given question the same way, regardless of the particular wording. No absolute frame of reference for all individuals is possible; but one question in a list of questions can through its context make clear the meaning of another question. In determining areas of ignorance the single-question polls seem to do a good job, and hence provide the teacher with a useful tool for discovering instructional needs of pupils.

Payne (27) has devoted an entire book to the problem of question wording. Much educational questionnaire research could profit from the guidance it provides.

RELIABILITY

For the single question, it is obvious that only the test-retest method of estimating reliability is feasible. In this method the time interval must be long enough to preclude the memory factor. Besides being indeterminate—how can one tell when the first answer has been forgotten—there is also the hazard of real changes in attitude having taken place. Stating questions in an alternate form is a possibility, but to make such questions comparable is very difficult.

Few investigations of the reliability of the single question have been made. Cantril (4) reported on the reliability of this question: "Do you think Roosevelt is doing a good job, only a fair job, or a bad job running the country?" For a group of 286 persons he reported an interview and reinterview agreement of 79 percent, which for the given situation approximates a correlation coefficient of .90. The same group gave 87 percent consistent answers to a question concerning whom they voted for in the last presidential election, and 86 percent on whether they owned a car. Such reliabilities for single questions compare favorably with those for the better psychological tests of all sorts. Unfortunately, it cannot be assumed that such reliability will always occur.

In a study of the consistency of responses to positively and negatively worded statements about armaments and war debts Hayes (20) found that the correlation coefficients varied from .60 to .70. For questions on government ownership, taxes on risk, tariff, unemployment relief, and veterans' relief, the coefficients ranged from .40 to the .60's. For five other current issues the agreement ranged from the .30's down to .10. These low coefficients, however, may reflect failure to construct comparable questions rather than low reliability.

We should note that although few reliability coefficients for single questions have been published, much research has been reported on correlates of responses to single opinion and attitude questions (usually, to be sure, in terms of differences of percentages rather than coefficients of correlation) from which at least a kind of "lower bound" of reliabilities may be inferred. Obviously, as a matter of statistical logic, zero reliability for a question would also produce zero correlation with any other variable. The literature is replete with reports of many significant correlations of answers to single questions with such variables as sex, age, socioeconomic status, membership in religious, fraternal, or political groups; from any of these correlations, the minimum reliability necessary to produce the observed correlation can be inferred.

ATTITUDE SCALES AND QUESTIONNAIRES

Attitude Scales

Thurstone's equal-appearing-intervals technique proceeds by the following steps (43): First a large number of statements expressing opinions concerning an attitude object are collected. All of them must express an attitude toward (a feeling for or against) a single object—the policy, practice, institution, group, or anything else—the attitude toward which is to be measured. Mere statements of fact concerning the attitude object are not suitable, nor are opinions which do not carry a connotation of favorableness or unfavorableness. The statements in this initial collection should range along the entire continuum from extreme favorableness through neutrality or indifference to extreme unfavorableness. They should be unambiguous, and they should not be "double-barreled" or express more than one complete thought, because a person may agree with one part of the statement and disagree with the other part.

After the initial group of statements has been collected and edited, they are given to a group of judges to be rated on a scale of nine or eleven points which represent equal steps from the most favorable extreme through neutrality to the most unfavorable extreme of attitude toward the particular object.

The scale value, i.e., the average (median) of the ratings along the favorable-unfavorable continuum, is then determined for each statement. Some of the statements, however, will be judged more uniformly than others. That is, the amount of scatter (quartile deviation) of the judgments will differ for the various statements. The ambiguity of a statement in expressing a given degree of favorableness or unfavorableness toward the attitude object can be measured by this spread. The ambiguous items are thus eliminated.

After the scale values of all the statements in the preliminary collection have been determined and only the unambiguous and relevant ones have been selected, the number of statements can be reduced so as to include in the final attitude scale only those which represent approximately equal steps along the entire continuum of favorableness-unfavorableness. The scale is administered by asking subjects to place a check mark after all the statements they endorse as an expression of their own sentiment, opinion, or attitude. The subject's score on the scale is the mean or the median scale value of the opinions he has endorsed.

Obviously the amount of labor required in constructing a scale to measure attitude toward any psychological object is so great that it would be impossible to build scales for all possible significant attitude objects. Remmers (31) attempted to overcome this difficulty to some extent by developing generalized or master attitude scales which can be used to measure attitude toward any one of a *class* of attitude objects, such as school subjects or vocations. The statements in the general attitude scale are not related specifically to any single attitude object; but if the name of the appropriate object is filled in at the head of the scale, they can be interpreted meaningfully for any representative of the class of objects for which the scale is intended. The scale values of Remmers' scales are determined by Thurstone's equal-appearing-intervals technique whereby large numbers of preliminary statements are rated on an eleven-point scale from complete unfavorableness through neutrality to complete favorableness.

The Remmers master scales are illustrated by the excerpt of the Kelley-Remmers Scale for Measuring Attitude Toward Any Institution shown in Fig. 19. Whereas in the Thurstone scales the statements are arranged in random order, in the Remmers scales they appear in order of decreasing favorableness. This arrangement has been found (31 : 16) to decrease greatly the time and labor required for scoring without affecting the accuracy of the measurement.

The validity of the master scales has in many instances (31) been determined in terms of their correlations with comparable specific scales in the Thurstone series. These correlations have in general been sufficiently high to warrant the conclusion that both types of scale measure essentially the same attitude. For instance, when the Kelley-Remmers Scale to Measure Attitude Toward Any Institution was used to measure attitudes toward communism, it yielded scores which correlated almost perfectly with those obtained by the Thurstone Scale for the Measurement of Attitude Toward Communism.

ATTITUDE QUESTIONNAIRES

Before the equal-appearing-intervals technique was applied to attitude scales the simple questionnaire was most widely used to measure attitudes. Attitude questionnaires are collections of statements or questions to which an individual responds *yes* or *no*. For some of the statements a *yes* response indicates attitude in a certain direction, whereas for others a *no* response indicates this direction. The statements are not scaled as to intensity or degree of favorableness-unfavorableness. Rather a measure of degree is obtained by

A SCALE FOR MEASURING ATTITUDE TOWARD ANY INSTITUTION

Ida B. Kelley   Edited by H. H. Remmers

Form A

Please fill in the blanks below. (You may leave the space for your name blank if you wish.)

Name_____

Male   Female (encircle one)   Date_____

Age_____   Class if in School_____

Directions:

Following is a list of statements about institutions. Place a plus sign (+) before each statement with which you agree with reference to the institution or institutions listed at the left of the statements. The person in charge will tell you the institution or institutions to write in at the head of the columns to the left of the statements. Your score will in no way affect your grade in any course.

Institution						
						1. Is perfect in every way.
						2. Is the most admirable of institutions.
						3. Is necessary to the very existence of civilization.
						4. Is the most beloved of institutions.
						5. Represents the best thought in modern life.
						6. Grew up in answer to a felt need and is serving that need perfectly.
						7. Exerts a strong influence for good government and right living.
						8. Has more pleasant things connected with it than any other institution.
						9. Is a strong influence for right living.
						10. Gives real help in meeting moral problems.
						11. Gives real help in meeting social problems.
						12. Is valuable in creating ideals.
						13. Is necessary to the very existence of society.
						14. Encourages social improvement.
						15. Serves society as a whole well.
						16. Aids the individual in wise use of leisure time.

FIG. 19. Excerpt from Remmers-Type Attitude Scale.

adding all the responses, *yes* or *no,* which indicate attitude in a given direction. The greater the number of statements of one type with which a person agrees, and the greater the number of statements of the opposite type with which he disagrees, the more favorable is his attitude.

Illustrative of such questionnaires is the Harper Social Study (18) developed in 1925 to measure the liberalism-conservatism of teachers and college students. As in most other attitude questionnaires, the responses which indicated a given attitude were determined by consultation with authorities on the various issues presented.

Wrightstone (46) has constructed a Scale of Beliefs which employs the questionnaire procedure. His questionnaire, a series of statements concerning racial, international, and national-political issues and attitudes toward national achievements and ideals, includes an equal number of expressions characteristic either of liberals or of conservatives. The statements were validated (1) by comparison with a list of beliefs represented in textbooks commonly used in American schools, (2) by a statistical study of the ability of each statement to discriminate between liberals and conservatives, (3) by the rankings social scientists gave to the statements in order of liberalism or conservatism, and (4) by determination of the degree to which the liberal statements agreed and the conservative statements disagreed with expressions of editorial opinions in liberal journals such as the *Nation* and the *New Republic.* The student marks either *yes* or *no* for each statement and his score for liberalism or conservatism is computed directly from the number of liberal or conservative statements with which he agrees.

SCALES AND QUESTIONNAIRES COMPARED

One distinction between questionnaires and scales is the refinement the latter possess as to the degree of favorableness represented by each statement, and consequently the method of scoring. Since scale statements are given values differing in magnitude as well as direction, the score is the average magnitude endorsed. A questionnaire score, on the other hand, is simply a summation of the responses in a given direction, each response being equally weighted for lack of scaling. A major difference between the questionnaire and the scale is the fact that questionnaires require norms for interpretation of the scores, whereas scales do not because they incorporate such norms by virtue of the procedure used in their construction.

The measures provided by questionnaires suffer from certain theoretical disadvantages. In the first place, each statement is equally weighted, although some of them probably indicate a far greater degree of what the whole scale measures than others. It is impossible to say, for example, that a score of 75 indicates as much greater liberalism than a score of 50 as a score of 50 indicates a greater liberalism than a score of 25. But this is a justifiable interpretation from scores on attitude scales constructed by the equal-appearing-intervals technique. In the second place, such questionnaires include a large variety of statements indicating attitudes toward a great many things on the assumption that since they all differentiate between liberals and conservatives, a general factor of liberalism or conservatism runs throughout the questionnaire. Thus it is difficult to interpret in specific terms what a score on such a questionnaire means because the attitude object is so generally and vaguely defined. With attitude scales constructed by Thurstone's technique, or with Remmers' master attitudes scales, the attitude is strictly and unambiguously delimited in terms of a single attitude object or class of objects. Thus, one of the statements in a questionnaire may deal with the Negro, another with the Chinese, another with Germans, and still another with Russians; all these attitudes are then grouped together as a class of ethnic attitudes without any evidence that such an overall grouping is justified for a given individual. With the equal-appearing-intervals approach, attitude toward each of these nationalities and races would be measured separately and no assumptions concerning their interrelationship would be made. A clearer, more understandable picture of a pupil's attitudinal make-up can probably thus be obtained.

On the other hand, whenever it is desired to assume such general overall attitudes as liberalism-conservatism, the questionnaire approach can furnish valuable results. This is especially true when such general attitudes constitute an objective of school instruction.

UNI-DIMENSIONAL QUESTIONNAIRES

One of the recurring problems in mental measurement is to insure that the set of responses that is given a single total score actually "hangs together" and can be treated as if it had a single meaning. This is the same as the problem of internal consistency discussed in Chapter V, where coefficients of internal consistency were presented. It is also, in a sense, the same as the problem of organizing mental abilities, or of expressing a year's educational achievement in a single score. In Chapter VIII we discussed the fact that a given measure of intelligence may represent different combinations of relatively independent kinds of mental ability, such as verbal and numerical. In the same way, a measure of attitude, denoted by a single score, may represent the adding together of two very different kinds of attitudinal responses unless the scale used for measuring the attitude can be considered "uni-dimensional."

Most of the methods for measuring attitude have provided some way of checking on the degree to which all the statements or items in the questionnaire are related to the same attitude. During World War II, however, Guttman (15) developed a procedure for scaling which tried to solve this problem. This had a better mathematical rationale than had hitherto been provided. In *Measurement and Prediction*, Volume 4 of the Studies in Social Psychology in World War II, Guttman (36) presented a full account of the theory and practice of this technique, called "scale analysis."

Perhaps the best way to show what Guttman means by a uni-dimensional scale is to consider a scale that is known to meet perfectly the requirements of uni-dimensionality. Suppose we wanted to measure people's heights, but that a standard unit of measurement, such as a foot rule or a yardstick, was not known and was not available to us. Lacking any predetermined unit of measurement, suppose we chose ten sticks, each of a different length, as a measuring instrument.

The operation of measuring would involve standing each stick up alongside each individual and recording whether he is taller or shorter than the stick. We would record a plus if he is taller and a minus if he is shorter. Our data for each individual would then consist of ten marks, each of which might be either plus or minus.

We might now determine how many individuals received a plus on each of our measuring sticks. We could then arrange the sticks in order from the one on which the greatest number of people re-

TABLE 22.   A Perfect "Scale"

	1		2		3		4		5		6		7		8		9		10		Scale Score
Stick number	+	−	+	−	+	−	+	−	+	−	+	−	+	−	+	−	+	−	+	−	
Arbitrary weights	1	0	1	0	1	0	1	0	1	0	1	0	1	0	1	0	1	0	1	0	
O	x		x		x		x		x		x		x		x		x		x		10
A	x		x		x		x		x		x		x		x		x			x	9
Z	x		x		x		x		x		x		x		x			x		x	8
X	x		x		x		x		x		x		x		x			x		x	8
S	x		x		x		x		x		x		x			x		x		x	7
W	x		x		x		x		x		x		x			x		x		x	7
E	x		x		x		x		x		x			x		x		x		x	6
D	x		x		x		x		x		x			x		x		x		x	6
C	x		x		x		x		x		x			x		x		x		x	6
V	x		x		x		x		x			x		x		x		x		x	5
F	x		x		x		x		x			x		x		x		x		x	5
R	x		x		x		x		x			x		x		x		x		x	5
T	x		x		x		x			x		x		x		x		x		x	4
G	x		x		x		x			x		x		x		x		x		x	4
B	x		x		x		x			x		x		x		x		x		x	4
N	x		x		x		x			x		x		x		x		x		x	4
H	x		x		x			x		x		x		x		x		x		x	3
Y	x		x		x			x		x		x		x		x		x		x	3
U	x		x		x			x		x		x		x		x		x		x	3
J	x		x			x		x		x		x		x		x		x		x	2
M	x		x			x		x		x		x		x		x		x		x	2
K	x		x			x		x		x		x		x		x		x		x	2
I	x			x		x		x		x		x		x		x		x		x	1
L		x		x		x		x		x		x		x		x		x		x	0
P		x		x		x		x		x		x		x		x		x		x	0
Freq.	23	2	22	3	19	6	16	9	12	13	9	16	6	19	4	21	2	23	1	24	

(The vertical label "INDIVIDUAL" appears along the left margin beside rows V through L.)

ceived a plus down to the one on which the smallest number received a plus.

We would now find that anyone who received a minus on Stick
1 would have received minuses on all the other sticks; an individual who received a plus on Stick 1 and a minus on Stick 2 would
have received minuses on all the subsequent sticks, and so on. The
individual who received a plus on Stick 10 would have received
pluses on all the other sticks. Each individual would thus fall into
one of 11 "patterns of response." These patterns could be arranged
in order from "tallest" to "shortest" and we would thus have a
scale for measuring height. It may be noted that since this instrument is uni-dimensional, it would be impossible for an individual
to receive a minus on Stick 1, a plus on Stick 2, and a minus on
Stick 3. In fact, there are 1013 possible "patterns of response"
which would *not* have occurred. Only the eleven patterns numbered 0 to 10 in the last column of Table 22 could occur.

A picture called a *scalogram* could be made of the 11 "patterns
of response" made by the people with our ten-stick measuring instrument; it would look like Table 22. Each row represents "responses" for one person, and each pair of columns represents the
distribution of marks for one stick, first the pluses, then the minuses. Ignore the "arbitrary weights" for the present.

The "quantitative scale variable" is indicated at the right. It
may be obtained merely by assigning rank-order numbers to each
successive different pattern of response, running from the pattern
characterizing the tallest. These can be any numbers, as long as the
rank order is preserved.

If instead of measuring height with sticks of varying length, we
are measuring attitude, the sticks will take the form of statements
pertinent to the attitude being measured. Suppose, for example,
that attitude toward a textbook is being measured. The items
might read as follows:

This textbook is one of the best I have ever used.
Agree Strongly   Agree   Don't Know   Disagree   Disagree Strongly
The tables and graphs in this textbook make things quite clear.
Agree Strongly   Agree   Don't Know   Disagree   Disagree Strongly
I found the summary at the end of each chapter useful.
Agree Strongly   Agree   Don't Know   Disagree   Disagree Strongly

Any student that can't learn efficiently from this textbook doesn't belong in this course.

Agree Strongly Agree Don't Know Disagree Disagree Strongly

The authors of this textbook have a lucid style.

Agree Strongly Agree Don't Know Disagree Disagree Strongly

This textbook seems to go into various topics in just about the kind of detail the topic deserves.

Agree Strongly Agree Don't Know Disagree Disagree Strongly

Suppose there were about a dozen such items expressing attitudes concerning the textbook. If these items were given the members of the class in which the textbook was used, we could score the responses of each student with a 4 if he chose the response most favorable to the book and a 0 if he chose the least favorable one. We would then add the numbers assigned each student's responses to get his total score. If we arrange the students in rank order from top to bottom of their total score as was done in Table 22, and if the items are arranged from those which elicit the most favorable response to those which elicit the fewest favorable responses, as was done at the top of Table 22, by using various inspectional and counting techniques we can determine the degree to which this particular set of items applied to this particular set of students constitutes a uni-dimensional scale.

If the responses followed the perfect kind of step pattern shown in Table 22, the scale would be considered perfectly uni-dimensional. In practice, of course, perfect scales seldom occur in attitude questionnaires. Rather, there will be some inconsistencies, or so-called "errors of reproducibility." These inconsistencies arise whenever a student who responded favorably on an item that is more "difficult" or calls forth fewer favorable responses fails to respond favorably on an "easier" item, i.e., one which, for all students, called forth more favorable responses.

Since the concept of uni-dimensionality can be applied to any kind of mental measurement, such as achievement in mathematics, an illustration from this field may make the concept clearer. Suppose we had five problems in mathematics: (1) addition of 1-digit numbers, (2) multiplication of mixed numbers, (3) solution of a quadratic equation, (4) one on trigonometry, and (5) one requiring integral calculus. If such a test were applied to a representative sample of the people in a large town, the items would probably be found to rank in difficulty in the above order. Further, the scores would probably range from zero, obtained by an illiterate or feeble-minded person, to 5, obtained by the city engineer. If a person obtained a score of only 1, we would be fairly certain that he passed the simple addition problem and failed all the rest. If he obtained a score of 2, we would be certain that he passed the simple addition and the multiplication of mixed numbers problems, and failed all the rest. If no one succeeded on an item that was more difficult than the easiest item he failed, the test would be considered perfectly uni-dimensional.

It is conceivable, however, that a person who obtained his training in another culture might know trigonometry but not elementary algebra (quadratic equations). Such a person might therefore fail Item 3 and pass the more difficult Item 4. This would constitute an inconsistency, or "error in reproducibility." It would indicate that the scale was *not* perfectly uni-dimensional for this group of persons.

In the same way, an attitude scale would be uni-dimensional if no such errors in reproducibility appeared. Guttman has stated that questionnaires which yield 90 percent accuracy of reproducibility may be considered uni-dimensional. There are various other requirements that the data must meet in addition to reproducibility, but this requirement is the most distinguishing characteristic of scale analysis procedures. Table 23 shows the kinds of errors in reproducibility that may occur in practice.

Guttman's "Cornell" technique for making a scale analysis of the responses to a set of attitude questionnaire items obtained from a given group of students is fairly simple.

1. Assign weights to the response alternatives for each question, using the successive integers beginning with 0. Assign a weight of 0 to the most unfavorable choice, 1 to the next most favorable, and so on.

2. Obtain a total score for each pupil by adding the weights of the response alternatives he has chosen.

3. Arrange the pupils' answer sheets or questionnaires in rank order of their total scores.

4. Prepare a table with one column for each choice of each item

TABLE 23. Hypothetical Patterns of Responses Illustrating Perfect Reproducibility (Item 1) and Various Types of Error in Reproducibility (Items 2–4)

Score	Item 1			Item 2			Item 3			Item 4		
	2	1	0	2	1	0	2	1	0	2	1	0
30	x			x			x			x		
30	x			x			x			x		
29	x			x				x		x		
27	x			x				x			x	
26		x		x				x			x	
26		x		x				x			x	
24		x		x					x		x	
23		x		x				x		x		
21		x			x				x		x	
21		x			x			x		x		
20			x		x				x		x	
18			x		x				x		x	
16			x	x					x		x	
14			x	x					x	x		
14			x		x				x		x	
12			x		x			x		x		
11			x			x			x		x	
11			x		x				x		x	
9			x		x			x			x	
8			x			x			x			x
6			x			x			x			x
3			x			x			x			x
Freq.	4	6	12	10	8	4	2	8	12	7	12	3

and one row for each pupil, like that for the measuring-stick illustration, Table 22. In that example, each item (stick) had only two response alternatives—pass or fail—but there should be as many columns for each item as there are response alternatives for it.

5. Indicate each individual's responses to every item by putting an x in the row for him and in the column for the response alternative he chose. These entries are made in descending order of total score, as shown in Table 22. The arrangement of people with the same total score is arbitrary.

6. Enter the total frequency of choice of each response alternative at the bottom of each column of the table. Inspect the table to see how well the pattern of the scalogram approximates a perfect pattern such as that shown in Table 22. This is done by establishing cutting points between the categories of each item. A cutting point is the point in the order of responses on the scalogram at which most of the responses in a higher category are above it and most of the responses in the next adjacent lower category are be-

low it. For instance, the cutting point for Item 1 in Table 22 is between Individual I and Individual L; that for Item 5 is between Individuals R and T, etc. A cutting point is established between each pair of adjacent categories in an item so that each item has one less cutting point than it has response alternatives. There will probably be some individuals with responses in the higher category who are below the cutting point in the rank order, and some individuals with responses in the lower category who are above the cutting point. These inconsistent responses are errors of reproducibility for any given placement of a cutting point. In deciding where to place each cutting point in an actual scalogram, we consider each possible location of the cutting point and count the errors of reproducibility there would be below it to the left and above it to the right for each possibility. We locate the cutting point where there are the smallest possible total number of errors of reproducibility around it. If there are several possible positions with the same minimum number of errors, the placement of the cutting point may be arbitrary, or it may be partially determined by some of the considerations to be mentioned below. After all the cutting points have been established, we can extend them, either mentally or with dotted lines as in Table 22, across the entire table, so that they break up the rank order of the people into several groups. The people falling between any two successive dotted lines are considered all of one kind and are given new rank-order designations, either with numbers or with letters of the alphabet.

7. Count up all the errors of reproducibility in the entire scalogram, subtract this from the total number of responses in it, and express the remainder as a proportion or percentage of the total number of responses. This proportion or percentage is the coefficient of reproducibility. For instance, in Table 22 there are 25 × 10, or 250, responses recorded and there are no errors of reproducibility, so we have a coefficient of reproducibility of 250/250; this equals 1.00 or 100 percent reproducibility.

8. If the coefficient of reproducibility is 90 percent or greater, the sample of items administered to the sample of individuals may be considered to be a uni-dimensional scale, according to Guttman, *provided the following additional criteria are met:*

a. Homogeneity of content—are the items relevant to the same area of attitude when judged subjectively and intuitively as to their meaning or content? The items must "make sense" as relevant to a definable "universe of content" that is defined educationally, psychologically, sociologically, or in some other conceptual terms.

b. Range of marginal frequencies—Does the highest percentage of persons (the modal response frequency) responding in a given way to each item have a fairly wide range? For two-choice items the range of modal frequencies should be from about 50 to 90 percent. For three-choice items it should be from about 33 to about 90 percent. This inspection is made to insure that a high coefficient of reproducibility is not obtained simply because all the items are responded to in the same way by very high percentages of the subjects. The error of reproducibility for a given item cannot be less than the modal response percentage for that item. If all the items had modal response percentages of 90 percent or greater, the 90 percent requirement for the coefficient of reproducibility could be met spuriously. Every response category in the scalogram should contain more nonerror responses than error or "misplaced" responses.

c. Random scatter of errors—Are the errors of reproducibility in any particular response category scattered rather than bunched together within a narrow range of the overall rank order of individuals?

9. If there are items with more than two response categories and the criteria for scalability are not met in the first trial, this means that the subjects did not interpret the various response alternatives for a given item in the same way. The appropriate procedure here is to combine into a single response category the adjacent response categories which the subjects seem to interpret in the same way, as indicated by the scalogram structure of responses. Examine the first trial scalogram for adjacent categories within an item in which responses seem to "intertwine" or scatter up or down the rank order of individuals more or less together. Combine such categories. Assign new arbitrary weights to these new categories for each item, obtain new total scores for each indi-

vidual on the basis of these new scoring weights, and repeat Steps
1–7.

The entire process of combining response categories, making a
scatter diagram, counting errors of reproducibility, etc., should
be repeated as often as necessary, until all the items have been reduced to dichotomies, or all the criteria for scalability are satisfied.
If a 90 percent coefficient of reproducibility cannot be obtained
even after all the items have been dichotomized, it must be concluded that the universe of content from which the sample of items
was drawn is nonscalable and not uni-dimensional. If all the
criteria are met except that of a 90 percent coefficient of reproducibility, the set of items may be considered a sample from a "quasi-
scalable" universe of content—one that has a single dominant
variable and many other small factors running through it. If either
a scale or a quasi-scale can be obtained, it is meaningful to speak
of persons as "higher" or "lower" in the area measured by the
scale.

The "Scale-Discrimination" Technique

One of the problems in using scale analysis is selecting the initial set of items to be tested for scalability. Edwards and Kilpatrick
(10, 11) have developed a technique for overcoming this difficulty.
Their "scale-discrimination technique" amounts to combining the
three methods discussed above: equal-appearing intervals, summated questionnaire, and scale analysis. The first part of the procedure consists of developing a set of items and assigning them
median or mean scale values on the basis of judges' ratings of the
items on an equal-appearing-interval favorable-unfavorable continuum. The ambiguous items, those that show the greatest scatter
of judges' ratings as to favorableness, are rejected. The remaining
items are administered as a summated questionnaire to a group
of subjects like those on whom the scale will eventually be used.
The discriminating power of each item is then ascertained by an
item analysis procedure such as that described in connection with
the SRA Youth Inventory (Chapter XII). The most discriminating
items at various points along the favorableness continuum are retained and are then subjected to a scale analysis, as described in
the preceding section.

VALIDITY OF SCALES AND QUESTIONNAIRES

Various technical issues in attitude scale construction and interpretation have been raised by such writers as McNemar (24, 25), Conrad (5), Crespi (6), and many others. The present discussion will not examine the details of these arguments; for a critical review of the technical literature on attitude scales the reader should consult Newcomb (26 : 889–912) or McNemar (24). The validity of the attitude measuring devices here discussed has been much disputed.

It is sometimes maintained that attitude measurements should serve as predictors of behavior and that any set of measures which does not correlate highly with nonverbal or "real-life" behavior toward the attitude object should be considered invalid. In general, there is a very low correlation between tests of knowledge and judgment of ethical matters and the actual performance of individuals in activities to which the knowledge or judgment might be considered related. Thus pupils might know the rules of honesty and be able to apply them in verbally expressed situations without necessarily being themselves honest in those situations. In the same way, various studies have shown that measures of attitudes may fail to predict what pupils will do in actual situations.

On the other hand, it is maintained that the failure of attitude scales to meet this kind of test does not mean that they are without value. For if the responses they elicit can be considered adequate measures of the verbal form which "feelings for or against something" may take, they are in themselves valuable regardless of their relationship to nonverbal or "real-life" behavior. An attitude is seldom the sole determiner of behavior even in the situations to which the attitude seems most closely related. Other attitudes and the situational context may work at cross purposes with the attitude which has been measured so that the resultant effect upon behavior is not what would be expected from knowledge of the single attitude.

Furthermore, the verbal expression of an attitude frequently is also the most fundamentally important expression of that attitude for the purposes of living. What indication of one's attitude toward the United Nations would be more adequate than what one says about the United Nations? Our most practical behavior toward such an agency or institution could hardly be other than verbal. Our attitudes toward candidates for political office are, of course, measured for the practical purposes of government by means of the crude two-point, yes-no, verbal attitude scales known as election ballots.

This amounts to saying that the important distinction is not one between verbal and nonverbal behavior, but rather between test, or laboratory, behavior and "real-life" behavior. If the real-life behavior is verbal behavior, as in voting or discussing a matter at a public meeting or chatting with one's neighbors, it is acceptable as a criterion for the validation of an attitude measurement. If a sample of verbal behavior is taken as a measure of an attitude, as with an attitude scale or questionnaire, and is found not to correlate with nonverbal behavior presumably relevant to the attitude, this does not necessarily mean that the verbal expression of attitude on the questionnaire was invalid. For example, measurements of attitude toward cheating on examinations were found not to correlate with actual cheating behavior unobtrusively observed by an experimenter. This means that the measurement of verbal attitude is invalid as a predictor of this particular kind of behavior (cheating) under particular social conditions, but not necessarily invalid for another purpose, such as predicting attitude toward cheating in other situations. The often-made distinction between "real" vs. "expressed" attitudes is misleading and confusing. Any attitude is "real" in relation to its social context.

One criterion of attitudes frequently used for the validation of attitude scales is membership in groups and organizations of known attitudinal make-up. Thus Thurstone and Chave's Scale for the Measurement of Attitude Toward the Church was able to differentiate clearly between divinity students and other college students, between active and inactive church members. Similarly, scales designed to measure attitudes toward the Negro have been found to yield very different average scores when filled out by northern and by southern university students. Attitude scales toward war and prohibition and liberalism and conservatism in political affairs and many other psychological objects have been validated in this fashion. Stouffer (35) used as a criterion for the validity of his prohibition attitude scale a set of thousand-word compositions written by students concerning their feelings and experiences from childhood on as related to prohibition and drinking liquor. Ratings of the composition by four judges who read each case history and scored it for attitude on a graphic rating scale correlated highly with scores on the attitude scale which Stouffer constructed by the Thurstone method. The attitude scale and the compositions were completely anonymous, being matched solely by means of code numbers. It is obvious, however, that both the scale and the compositions provided verbal responses. These might very well differ from the individuals' actual drinking behavior.

Another technique considered to provide a validation of attitude scales involves determining whether the scales reflect the changes in attitude to be expected when individuals are subjected to experiences, such as lectures or movies, that are designed to have a strong effect on attitudes in a given direction. Thus Peterson and Thurstone (30) administered a scale of attitudes toward the Chinese to a group of junior- and senior-high-school pupils both before and after they were shown a movie designed to shift attitudes toward the Chinese in a favorable direction. The pupils' attitudes toward the Chinese as reflected in their average scores on the scale became distinctly more favorable, as might be expected from the nature of the experience to which they were subjected; this may be considered evidence for the validity of the method of measuring attitudes.

Kelley (22) validated the master Scale for Measuring Attitude Toward Any Institution against the differences between scores for attitude toward Sunday observance obtained by Seventh-day Adventists, whose actual conduct and overt commitments led to the expectation of low (unfavorable) scores, and by groups of Methodists, Baptists, and United Brethren. Fig. 20 shows that the attitude scale discriminated almost perfectly between these two groups. The correlation with the specific Thurstone Scale for Attitude Toward Sunday Observance was .83, which indicates the similarity of results obtained with master and specific scales.

Striking validation of a master scale, the Remmers-Thomas Scale for Measuring Attitudes Toward Any Proposed Social Action, was obtained by Peters and Peters (28) in their study of the

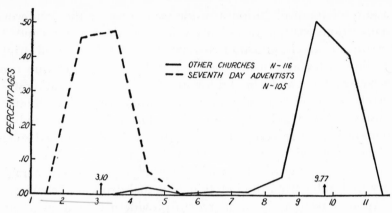

FIG. 20. Attitude Toward Sunday Observance.

effect of pupil self-government on attitudes toward law enforcement. Two groups of pupils, one of which participated in a thoroughgoing scheme of pupil government of school while the other had no self-government, were asked to indicate on the master scale their attitudes toward the judge's decisions in ten actual cases of law violation. The cases were selected to exemplify the desires to gain wealth, to save the life of a member of the family, to gain or keep friends, to improve the family's living conditions, and violation through ignorance of the law—all of these being considered instances of the principal reasons for children's disobedience of law. The attitudes of the pupils who were experiencing self-government were significantly more favorable toward law enforcement than those of pupils without self-government.

The persistence of attitude changes effected by instructional activities has been studied by means of master attitude scales. Hall (16) found that the attitudes of pupils toward social insurance, capital punishment, labor unions, and Negroes could be changed by means of articles read to them by the teacher. The changes were in the directions expected and tended to persist over a period of at least six months with little change after an initial regression. Similar results were obtained by Williamson and Remmers (45) with the attitudes of rural and urban pupils toward such conservation issues as allowing the government to tell the farmer how to farm, allowing each farmer to farm as he pleases, clean farming, taxing all the people to plant new forests, and draining swamps. Typical results are shown in Fig. 21. The pupils' attitudes toward clean farming became less favorable as a result of the instructional

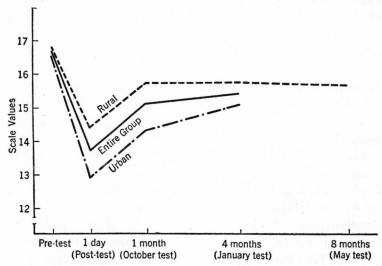

FIG. 21. The Persistence of Attitude Changes.

materials designed to have this effect, and the effects lasted for at least four months for the urban and eight months for the rural pupils.

DISGUISING ATTITUDE QUESTIONNAIRES

Attitude scales and questionnaires face the same difficulty as do the self-inventories used for evaluating adjustment. That is, individuals may not be willing to be frank and honest about their attitudes. This difficulty may be overcome either (1) by establishing a high degree of rapport or (2) by disguising the attitude scale so that the subject does not realize that he has anything to conceal. The necessity for rapport becomes evident whenever there are socially defined "right" and "wrong" attitudes toward a particular attitude object in a particular situation. Pupils living in an open-shop cotton-mill town that was completely owned and operated by antiunion mill operators would be wary of expressing attitudes explicitly favorable to trade unions unless their responses could be made anonymously or they had complete trust that their teacher would keep their answers strictly confidential.

One way of disguising the attitude scale depends on a distinction between "stereotypes" and the clusters of opinions and behaviors underlying such "stereotypes." An attitude toward a stereotype such as "fascism" is the individual's conscious response to statements containing that word. Stagner (34) constructed an instrument to measure fascist attitudes in which the term does not appear but in which such components of fascism can be expressed as opposition to labor unions, to various national and racial groups, to democratic procedures, and to freedom of expression for radical groups. He found that people who were distinctly opposed to the stereotype "fascism" might still be favorable to many of the policies and practices that fascism directly implies. Thus the disguised attitude scale was able to reveal attitudes which an attitude scale employing stereotypes would have concealed.

Another promising indirect attitude-measurement technique is the error-choice (2, 44, 17) or the direction-of-perception technique (1). Hammond (17) suggested that attitudes can be indirectly measured by the bias shown in answering a mixture of factual and nonfactual questions concerning a given topic or issue. Insofar as the respondent is unaware of the true interest of the questions, they provide a structured projective technique that, like other projective techniques, minimizes attitude test set. Examples of nonfactual items from Hammond's Information Test follow (17).

Financial reports show that out of every dollar (1) 16¢, (2) 3¢, is profit.
Man-days lost because of strikes from January to June, 1946, were (1) 34.5 million, (2) 98.6 million.
Most unions have initiation fees (1) over, (2) under, $35.
There (1) is, (2) is not, freedom of religion in Russia.

Weschler (44) constructed an error-choice inventory under the guise of an information test on labor-management relations designed to elicit constant errors due to known bias. Its administration to university students yielded results as hypothesized. Income, political preference, and labor affiliation were related to inventory scores, but age and sex were not.

In a subsequent study Weschler (44) administered a revised form of the Labor Relations Information Test to a group of advanced university students and a sample of management people, labor union officials and members, and labor mediators. He points out that, although a good attitude-measurement technique, error choice, when applied to labor-management problems, would have to be constantly revised to take cognizance of the latest developments in labor relations. He includes suggestions for avoiding methodological mistakes in further error-choice measurement.

Sample questions from Weschler's Labor Relations Information Inventory follow.

Factual Information Items.
  In 1948, the majority of strikes were caused by issues over (a) collective bargaining terms of existing agreements, (b) union recognition.
Nonfactual "Error-Choice" Items.
  During April of 1948, the coal and meat strikes increased the number of work days lost through voluntary stoppage to (a) 10 million work days, (b) 6 million work days.
    Correct answer: 8 million work days.
  During the strike wave of April, 1948, the percent of estimated working time lost was (a) 1.1% (b) 2.2%.
    Correct answer: 1.6%.
  The 1948 increases in the price of steel were: (a) proportional to the union's wage gains, (b) comparatively greater than the union's wage gains.
    Correct answer: Not accessible.

An interesting classification of indirect approaches to the measurement of attitudes has been devised by Campbell (2):
  1. Nondisguised-structured: the classic direct attitude tests of Thurstone, Wrightstone, *et al.*
  2. Nondisguised-nonstructured: the free-response interview and questionnaire approaches, the biographical and essay studies.
  3. Disguised-nonstructured: the typical "projective" techniques.
  4. Disguised-structured: tests which approximate the objective testing of attitudes.
Further, Campbell suggests that any number of methods of

measuring attitudes indirectly may be developed by means of the following general procedure:

First, take *a plausible task:*
    a. which your respondents will all strive to do well,
    b. which is sufficiently difficult or ambiguous to allow individual differences in response, and
    c. which can be loaded with content relative to the attitude which you seek to measure.

Next, test the responses of individuals for persistent selectivity in performance, for correlated or non-random errors.

Measurements conforming to this developmental approach should be useful in the analysis of attitudes. The generality of Campbell's procedure may suggest to the reader the wide range of possible attitude-measurement techniques.

AVAILABLE ATTITUDE EVALUATION DEVICES

Apart from the devices already discussed, various commercially available attitude scales and questionnaires may be mentioned for their possible value in the evaluation of attitudes judged to be significant outcomes of the educational process.

What Would You Do? is a questionnaire developed by Eckert and Wilson for use in the Regents' Inquiry into the Character and Cost of Public Education in the State of New York. It is intended as a measure of the allegiance of pupils to the fundamental principles of American democracy—free speech, freedom of the press, free assembly, and the obligation to participate, even at some personal sacrifice, in group action for the common good. The questionnaire is in two separate booklets, each presenting 15 situations with three alternatives. The pupil is to indicate his acceptance of, neutrality toward, or rejection of each of the 45 alternatives in a booklet.

The situations in one booklet deal with school problems in which pupils are relatively free from faculty interference and control. A typical item is the following:

One of the freshman pupils has never been vaccinated and refuses to be so now. He says that he alone should decide, for he will be the one to suffer if he ever gets smallpox.

(a) I feel strongly that each pupil should be free to do as he pleases in this matter .... + ? —
(b) I think that it is the duty of the school doctor to point out the dangers if he is not vaccinated, but that nothing further should be done .... + ? —
(c) I believe that every student should be vaccinated whether he wishes to be or not .... + ? —

The situations in the other booklet deal similarly with community affairs and adult problems. The item comparable to that just quoted is the following:

One of the men in the steel mill is told by the company doctor to have typhoid inoculations. He refuses to do so, saying that he would rather run the risk of getting sick, and that it will be his own affair if he gets typhoid later.
(a) I feel strongly that each man should be free to do as he pleases .... + ? —
(b) I think it is the duty of the company doctor to point out the dangers if he is not inoculated but that nothing further should be done .... + ? —
(c) I believe that the company should compel him to do so under threat of discharge .... + ? —

The two booklets are administered at different testing periods without time limits; usually fifteen to twenty minutes suffices for each booklet. Each response is scored according to weights ranging from 0 to 4 on the basis of the degree to which the responses were found to discriminate between pupils with high and low total scores. Norms are provided for Grades VII through XII based on New York State schools. The reliability of the total score on both booklets combined is about .80 for a single grade range as determined by the split-half method.

The Regents' Inquiry found greater differences between schools than between grades in any single school. This indicates that schools and their communities may perhaps be characterized by a general liberal attitude which pervades all school grades and distinguishes one school from others.

Other devices for attitude evaluation which may prove useful in various school situations are Lentz's C-R Opinionaire, designed to measure general conservatism or radicalism with respect to human affairs; Lewerenz and Steinmetz's Orientation Test, designed to elicit opinions concerning a large number of superstitions and delusions; and the Illinois Opinion Inventories, designed to survey students' and parents' opinions concerning their schools.

TABLE 24. Attitude Scales and Questionnaires

Name of Test	Grades Designed for	Time (min.) Required to Give	Publisher No. (see list on pp. 613–614)
Master Attitude Scales............	7–16, adults	5	9
What Would You Do?.............	7–12	40	8
C-R Opinionaire..................	9–16, adults	20	7
Orientation Test.................	9–16, adults	60	6
Illinois Opinion Inventories.........	6–8, 9–12, adults	30–50	28

Publication of standardized devices for measuring opinions and attitudes, in the sense of this section, has not flourished, probably because of their relatively temporary relevance. Instead, many teachers and school systems have developed their own devices shaped to their particular objectives. Since 1940 a national service, the Purdue Opinion Panel, has made available to high schools a periodic attitude survey on important issues. The participating schools are furnished with a report on the responses of their own students and a detailed analysis of the responses of a nationally representative sample of high-school youth. This analysis breaks down the responses according to sex, grade, religious preference, political preference, region, socioeconomic status, and mother's educational level. The areas of attitude surveyed range from personal to national and international problems. Beyond this service to schools, the Panel has accumulated the most extensive and thoroughly analyzed storehouse of data on the attitudes of adolescents in the United States.

ATTITUDES AS EDUCATIONAL-VOCATIONAL INTERESTS

APPROACHES TO THE EVALUATION OF INTERESTS

To ascertain a pupil's interests, several approaches can be used.
1. The pupil might be asked to write an account of the activi-

ties, vocational and avocational, in which he finds the greatest pleasure and those from which he derives the least enjoyment.

2. Direct observation of the student, both by his fellow students and by his teachers and parents, could be employed. These observations could be accumulated in the form of anecdotal records previously described. The amount of time the individual spends in various activities, the degree of pleasure or displeasure he shows in them, the breadth or narrowness of his interests in them might all be inferred from these observations. The observations could range over such activities as school subjects, recreation, jobs, or hobbies.

3. Experimental situations might be set up in which the individual is required to participate in various activities which could serve as samples of those in which his interests are being evaluated. Conclusions concerning interests could then be drawn from his behavior in the experimental situation. Thus pupils might be required to canvass a neighborhood for advertisements for the class yearbook. Their enthusiasm and success in such an activity might serve as the basis for statements concerning each one's interest in commercial work involving dealing with people.

Typical school activities may similarly serve as experimental tryout situations. The interest of pupils in such school subjects as mathematics, history, bookkeeping, chemistry, physics, or English composition may be meaningfully interpreted for interest in various occupations.

Ability in school subjects is by no means an adequate indicator of interest in them or in the occupations related to them. Symonds (40 : 244–245) in summarizing the evidence on the relationship between ability and interests concluded that the relationship between abilities and interests is distinct but not close and that for junior-high-school pupils it is low enough so that one can usefully supplement the other for the purposes of guidance. The disparity between abilities and interests has also been found at the high-school and college levels. For example, Garretson (14 : 72) reported only a slight relationship between the degree of preference for and ability in a curriculum as measured by objective tests of curricular aptitude. Whereas he concluded that his preference questionnaire was valid for the determination of curricular "inclination," he did not consider it useful for predicting the degree of success that would be achieved by the pupil in the curriculum for which he shows the greatest preference.

The low correlation between (1) measured interests and (2) abilities or achievements as measured by tests or school grades has often been found. In the typical study of this kind the scores of a number of students on, say, "scientific" interests are correlated with their scores or grades in scientific subjects. There is, however, a different approach that may change the picture; this is to correlate interests and abilities *within* the person. If we take a student's profile of scores on an interest inventory and correlate this with his profile on a battery of achievement or ability tests, we may find that his higher or stronger interests do tend to coincide with his higher or stronger areas of achievement or ability.

Apart from all the approaches to interest evaluation mentioned above, there are a number of paper and pencil testing devices for the quantitative determination of a pupil's vocational and curricular interests. These tests are for the most part of two kinds: direct approaches to the individual's likes and dislikes, and indirect approaches which assume some relationship between interest and a measure of information or ability in a given field.

Which of these two types of interests should be measured depends on various considerations. Various kinds of errors may accompany an individual's report of his interest. (1) An individual may not tell the truth about his feelings or inner experiences. A boy may be unwilling to be frank about his liking for a given occupation because he considers its socioeconomic status too low. The boy who glories in working with automobile engines as a "grease monkey" but whose parents have taught him to disrespect working with his hands may commit a prevarication error in reporting his interest. (2) An individual may report interest on the basis of *false* information concerning the activity. The boy may report an interest in engineering simply because he considers it to be outdoor masculine work but he has no appreciation of its mathematical nature. (3) A third error results from reporting one's interest on the basis of information which is *inadequate* in range and extent. The boy who reports an aversion to selling on the basis of a childhood failure in selling magazines may be unjustifiably generalizing for all selling occupations from an insufficient sample of that kind of work.

Despite these sources of error, measures of interest have been found on the whole to have a satisfactory degree of validity in correlating with happiness and success in various kinds of activity.

The assumption underlying the use of information tests in measuring interest has been well expressed by Flanagan (12). Defining interest in an activity as "the extent to which an individual selects these activities in preference to others in a free choice situation," Flanagan measured interest in terms of the relative strength of an individual's information on contemporary affairs in six fields: political events, social and economic events, science and medicine, literature, fine arts, and amusements.

Information tests sample the person's knowledge concerning a sample of facts in a given field. If he has been interested in that field, he will presumably have tended to select reading and sources of information about it in preference to other fields of interest. Consequently he should have more information because of his wider and more attentive reading and activity in that field. A further assumption is that facts and events in a preferred field will be better *remembered* as well as more sought out and attended to by individuals interested in that particular field. But Fryer, in surveying the correlations of these tests of interests with other estimates of interest and with measures of ability and achievement, concludes (13 : 290) that "there is no valid evidence that something different to ability is measured by information tests. What is thought to be an evidence of interest in these measures of information may be but a measure of the extent to which these tests are measures of the same abilities. The safest conclusion . . . is that information tests measure information. But the theory persists that in achievement, as evidenced in the acquisition of information, there is present an effect of interests as well as of abilities."

Let us now turn to illustrations of standardized interest evaluation devices. We shall discuss the methods by which the specific devices were constructed and the scores they provide.

The Allport-Vernon-Lindzey Study of Values, Revised Edition,[1]

[1] Published by Houghton Mifflin Company.

is designed to yield measures of the six evaluative attitudes
which, according to Spranger, are the most revealing aspects of
personality. These values, described in Chapter XIII, are measured by the test through responses to 30 two-alternative items and
15 four-alternative items. The two-alternative items are illustrated
by the following:

1. The main objects of scientific research should be the | (a) | (b) |
   discovery of pure truth rather than its practical applications.
   (a) Yes; (b) No ....

If the pupil agrees with alternative (a) and disagrees with (b), he
writes 3 under (a) and 0 under (b); if he has a slight preference
for (a) over (b), he writes 2 under (a) and 1 under (b). Agreement
with (b) or slight preference for (b) is similarly indicated. Illustrative of the four-alternative items is the following:

1. Do you think that a good government should aim chiefly at—
   ....   a. more aid for the poor, sick and old
   ....   b. the development of manufacturing and trade
   ....   c. introducing more ethical principles into its policies and
                  diplomacy
   ....   d. establishing a position of prestige and respect among
                  nations.

The pupil writes 1, 2, 3, or 4 before each alternative to indicate
the order of his preference for them.

Extensive research with the Study of Values reviewed by Duffy
(9) has in the main corroborated the findings and expectations of
its authors with respect to norms, retest constancy, and differences
between the sexes in evaluative attitudes. The scores have been
shown to be significantly related to academic achievement and to
various educational and occupational groupings. The six scores
yielded by the test may thus prove valuable for acquiring self-understanding and providing a basis for educational and vocational
guidance.

Several shortcomings of the test have, however, been revealed.
Studies have shown, by means of correlation coefficients and factor
analysis, that the political and economic values may be considered
nearly synonymous and that the aesthetic value is nearly the op-

posite of the same aspect of people. Thus Lurie (23) combined these three values into one which he called "Philistinism" on the basis of his factor analysis of an original battery of tests of the six values.

Some writers have considered the scoring system of the Study of Values a further disadvantage. This is because scores for each value are obtainable not in absolute amounts but merely as the relative strengths of the values within each person. Thus a person who has a high real value for all six categories may obtain scores for some of the six that are lower than those made by another person who has lower real values for those categories. A high score in one value is obtainable only at the expense of scores in other values; every individual is given a total of 180 points which he distributes among the six values. This feature may be desirable if the object is to study not "how much" evaluative attitude an individual has but rather how he chooses to distribute his preferences when given equal quantities of preference to express.

The Kuder Preference Record[2] requires the pupil to choose which of three described activities he would ordinarily prefer most and which least. Illustrative triads are:

Browse in a library.
Watch a rehearsal of a large orchestra.
Visit an aquarium.

Sell vegetables.
Be an organist.
Raise vegetables.

Build bird houses.
Write articles about birds.
Draw sketches of birds.

From pupils' choices among hundreds of such items, scores are obtained to indicate interests in (1) scientific, (2) computational, (3) musical, (4) artistic, (5) literary, (6) social service, (7) persuasive, (8) clerical, (9) mechanical, and (10) outdoor activities. The procedure for scoring the responses is simple and can be done by the student; it involves counting the number of punctured circles on the reverse side of specially prepared answer sheets. The ten

[2] Published by Science Research Associates.

scores have been related to specific occupations. Suggestions are given in the test manual for interpreting the scores for vocational guidance. The procedure for further research in this direction is set forth. Validity is indicated by the average profiles of groups of students who have chosen various occupations. In each of these profiles the high and low scores indicate to a striking degree that different occupational groups are differentiated by the Kuder Preference Record.

Evidence is provided in the manual that the scores do not correlate substantially with those on Thurstone's Primary Mental Abilities Test. However, the scientific, computational, and literary scales seem to correlate positively with average college grades, and the persuasive, artistic, and social service scores tend to correlate negatively.

Another very extensively used device for the evaluation of interests is Strong's Vocational Interest Blank,[3] which is available in forms for men and for women. Strong's thorough volume (39) provides detailed information on the theory, development, and research data related to this device. The blank consists of approximately 400 items dealing with (1) likes and dislikes for occupations, (2) likes and dislikes for school subjects, (3) likes and dislikes for amusements, (4) likes and dislikes for activities, (5) likes and dislikes for peculiarities of people, (6) order of preference of activities, (7) order of importance of factors affecting one's work, (8) order of preference of men one would most and least like to have been, (9) positions one would most and least prefer to hold in a club or society, (10) comparison of interests between two items, (11) self-rating of present abilities and characteristics. The likes and dislikes are indicated by circling one of the three letters, L I D, to indicate like, indifference, and dislike. The orders of preference are indicated by checking in one of three columns. The blank is scored by means of 50 separate scoring keys which provide scores indicative of masculinity-femininity, maturity of interest, occupational level, and interest in 41 specific occupations and six occupational groups.

These scoring keys were made by giving the test to large samples of men who had been successfully engaged in their occupation

[3] Published by Stanford University Press.

for at least three years prior to taking the test. Each of the 400 items is given a weight for each occupation which is derived from the difference between the proportion of men in the given occupation who marked the item in a certain way and the proportion of "men in general" who marked the item in that way. At least 250 men less than 60 years of age were included in each of the occupational criterion groups. The greater the difference between the proportion of men in the occupational group who like, dislike, or are indifferent to each item and the proportion of "men in general," the larger the weighting given to that response as an indicator of interest in that occupation. The weights range from plus 4 through 0 to minus 4.

In scoring the blanks, the scoring process must be repeated separately for each occupation for which a score is desired. Thus if measures of interests in 30 occupations are desired, the blank must be scored 30 times. Obviously, scoring is a laborious procedure and constitutes perhaps the major drawback of the blank. In his manual, Strong discusses three methods of scoring: hand-scoring, scoring with the Hollerith machine, and with the International Test Scoring Machine. Engineers Northwest[4] provide a special answer sheet and a scoring service for answers recorded on their answer sheet, on IBM answer sheets, or on the test booklet. Several attempts (38, 33, 29) have been made to simplify the scoring.

Contrary to the finding of Strong, and of Rock and Wesman, Peterson and Dunlap have found (29) that by using a range of item weights from plus 1 through 0 to minus 1 instead of plus 4 through 0 to minus 4, scores could be obtained which correlated on the average about .96 with those obtained by using the more variable weights. When the scores from these reduced weights were used to predict the scores which would be obtained by using Strong's more variable weights, the predicted scores agreed almost perfectly with those obtained by Strong's scoring method. Serious changes in the scores occurred only about 3 percent of the time and could be easily checked by rescoring whenever necessary. Strong (39 : 626–633) has objected that this results in loss of differentiation. To quote him on the crucial point (p. 633): "If the present cost were one

[4] 100 Metropolitan Life Building, Minneapolis 1, Minnesota.

hundred dollars, some decreased accuracy might be justified for the sake of cutting the cost in half. But when the present cost is a dollar, one wonders about saving fifty cents at the expense of inaccurate counseling of some people. Is it worth the chance of error?"

The reliability of the scores for the various occupations is on the average about .88 for college seniors by the split-half technique. When 285 college seniors were retested after a period of five years, the retest correlation on 21 occupational scales averaged .75. The validity of the blank as it differentiates men successfully engaged in one occupation from men successfully engaged in other occupations has also been found to be quite high. For example, only 15 percent of 933 non-engineers rate A in engineering interests, in contrast with 75 percent of engineers who rate A. The blank also differentiates well between men of high and low incomes in the same occupation. Thus, 67 percent of insurance agents with ratings of A were found to be successful on this basis in contrast to only 6 percent of those with ratings of C. The permanence of interest scores over twenty-two years has been reported by Strong (37). The median correlation for 228 individuals tested while in college and again twenty-two years later was .75.

The retest reliability of the scores of high-school students has, in general, been found to be somewhat lower than that obtained with college students. This decrease is not so great as to make the scale entirely without value for the evaluation of high-school students' interests. Canning, Taylor, and Carter (3) concluded that the blank indicates certain facts about the interests of high-school boys with considerable reliability. "Thus, if the high school boy receives a 'C' rating on the first test, there is an 83 per cent chance that he will receive the same rating and only a 1 per cent chance that he will receive an 'A' rating two years later. And if he receives an 'A' rating on the first test, there is an 88 per cent chance that he will receive a rating of 'B' or higher two years later."

A score for measuring maturity of interests, or the extent to which an individual has attained a stable, long-lasting set of interests, has been developed by Strong. An occupational-level key is also available for showing whether a student can probably find a satisfactory occupation among those that make relatively few demands on the worker or whether he prefers for his adjustment one of the more professionalized and exacting occupations at the upper socioeconomic level.

Satisfactory interpretation of the blank and counseling of students on the basis of information obtained with this device are possible only for those who have a good understanding of its technique, are acquainted with the extensive research literature, and are familiar with the accumulated experience of people who have used it in counseling. On the basis of his extensive experience, Darley (7) has prepared a manual in which he stresses the importance of "pattern analysis" rather than specific occupational keys and discusses such problems as the interpretation to be given to scores in which no significant interest pattern, or no A ratings, appear.

That interpretation of interest ratings obtained with the Strong blank should not be straightforward in the narrow sense is indicated by correlation coefficients obtained by Johnson (21) between various scores and first-year grade-point averages for freshman engineering students. The score for engineering interests correlated .23 with grades; but equally high coefficients were obtained for the certified public accountant, mathematician, and psychologist interest scores; the correlation coefficient of the score for chemist was .33, the highest coefficient obtained. Thus in counseling students concerning their chances for success in the college engineering curriculum, as much help is available from several other scoring keys as from the score for engineering interests.

The Strong Vocational Interest Blank is usually valuable as a stimulater of thought about vocations, of self-scrutiny, and of attention to interests as a factor in vocational choice. In making a vocational choice, information about a student's abilities is, of course, at least as important as his interests. Even when there is much reason to suspect the meaningfulness for a given individual of the scores he obtained, the educational advantages of using a vocational interest blank in guidance are still considerable.

OTHER INTEREST MEASURING DEVICES

We have discussed three instruments in some detail because they are widely used and are best supported with evidence on their validity. Dozens of other interest inventories, varying in usefulness and demonstrated validity, have been published. Even when based on much careful work prior to publication, they have not had nearly as much postpublication research as the three we have discussed. For example, the *Fourth Mental Measurements Yearbook* lists 273 references on Strong's Vocational Interest Blank for Men.

Buros' *Mental Measurements Yearbooks* contain reviews of many of these less familiar inventories. Among them are the Cleeton Vocational Interest Inventory, the Lee-Thorpe Occupational Interest Inventory, the Michigan Vocabulary Profile Test, the Dunlap Academic Preference Blank, and the Gregory Academic Interest Inventory. Many other inventories are merely cited by Buros.

GENERAL SIGNIFICANCE OF INTEREST INVENTORIES

Interest inventories have been criticized as being subject to "faking," in that the student can make his scores come out much as he wants them to. This criticism has been supported by considerable experimental evidence. This does not mean that such inventories are not valid for guidance. An interest inventory is essentially a means whereby the student can communicate with himself and his counselor. It is better than unorganized introspection and conversation because it is systematically organized and makes possible comparisons with other persons of known occupational status. The student is free to tell himself anything he wants to. But if he is motivated to learn his own interests accurately, he can do so more efficiently and thoroughly with an interest inventory than without one.

REFERENCES

1. Bernberg, R. E., "The direction of perception technique of attitude measurement," *International Journal of Opinion and Attitude Research,* 5:397–406 (1951).
2. Campbell, D. T., "The indirect assessment of social attitudes," *Psychological Bulletin,* 47:15–38 (1950).
3. Canning, L., Taylor, Kathryn, V. F., and Carter, Harold D., "Permanence of vocational interests of high school boys," *Journal of Educational Psychology,* 32:481–494 (1941).

4. Cantril, Hadley, and associates, *Gauging Public Opinion*, Princeton: Princeton University Press, 1944.

5. Conrad, H. S., "Some principles of attitude measurement: a reply to 'opinion-attitude methodology,'" *Psychological Bulletin*, 43:570–589 (1946).

6. Crespi, L. P., "'Opinion-attitude methodology' and the polls—a rejoinder," *Psychological Bulletin*, 43:562–567 (1946).

7. Darley, J., *Clinical Aspects and Interpretation of the Strong Vocational Interest Blank*, New York: The Psychological Corporation, 1941.

8. Drucker, A. J., and Remmers, H. H., "Citizenship attitudes of graduated seniors at Purdue University, U.S. college graduates, and high school pupils," *Journal of Educational Psychology*, 42:231–235 (1951).

9. Duffy, Elizabeth, "A critical review of investigations employing the Allport-Vernon 'Study of Values' and other tests of evaluative attitude," *Psychological Bulletin*, 37:597–612 (1940).

10. Edwards, A. L., and Kilpatrick, F. P., "A technique for the construction of attitude scales," *Journal of Applied Psychology*, 32:374–383 (1948).

11. Edwards, A. L., and Kilpatrick, F. P., "Scale analysis and the measurement of social attitudes," *Psychometrika*, 13:99–114 (1948).

12. Flanagan, J. C., *Measuring Interests*, Advisory Service Bulletin No. 4, New York: Co-operative Test Service, May, 1940.

13. Fryer, D., *The Measurement of Interests*, New York: Henry Holt & Company, Inc., 1931.

14. Garretson, O. K., *Relationships Between Expressed Preferences and Curricular Abilities of Ninth-Grade Boys*, New York: Bureau of Publications, Teachers College, Columbia University, Contributions to Education No. 396, 1930.

15. Guttman, L., "A basis for scaling qualitative data," *American Sociological Review*, 9:139–150 (1944).

16. Hall, W., "The effect of defined social stimulus material upon the stability of attitudes toward labor unions, capital punishment, social insurance and Negroes," *Studies in Attitudes III, Studies in Higher Education XXXIV, Bulletin of Purdue University*, 1938, pp. 7–19.

17. Hammond, K. R., "Measuring attitudes by error-choice: an indirect method," *Journal of Abnormal and Social Psychology*, 43:38–48 (1948).

18. Harper, M. H., *Social Beliefs and Attitudes of American Edu-*

cators, New York: Bureau of Publications, Teachers College, Columbia University, Contributions to Education No. 294, 1927.

19. Havemann, E., and West, Patricia S., *They Went to College,* New York: Harcourt, Brace and Company, 1952.

20. Hayes, S. P., Jr., "The interrelations of political attitudes: II. Consistency in voters' attitudes; III. General factors in political attitudes; IV. Political attitudes and party regularity," *Journal of Social Psychology,* 10:359–378, 379–398, 503–552 (1939).

21. Johnson, A. P., "The prediction of scholastic achievement for freshmen engineering students at Purdue University," *Studies in Higher Education XLIV, Bulletin of Purdue University,* 1942.

22. Kelley, Ida B., "The construction and validation of a scale to measure attitude toward any institution," *Studies in Attitudes, Studies in Higher Education XXVI, Bulletin of Purdue University,* 35:18–36 (1934).

23. Lurie, W. A., "A study of Spranger's value-types by the method of factor analysis," *Journal of Social Psychology,* 8:17–37 (1937).

24. McNemar, Quinn, "Opinion-attitude methodology," *Psychological Bulletin,* 43:289–374 (1946).

25. McNemar, Quinn, "Response to Crespi's rejoinder and Conrad's reply in appraisal of opinion-attitude methodology," *Psychological Bulletin,* 44:171–176 (1947).

26. Newcomb, T. M., "Social attitudes and their measurement," in Murphy, G., Murphy, Lois B., and Newcomb, T. M., *Experimental Social Psychology,* New York: Harper & Brothers, rev. ed., 1937.

27. Payne, S. L., *The Art of Asking Questions,* Princeton: Princeton University Press, 1951.

28. Peters, Fridiana and Peters, M. Rosanna, "Children's attitude toward law as influenced by pupil self-government," *Studies in Attitudes, Series II, Studies in Higher Education XXXI, Bulletin of Purdue University,* 1936, pp. 15–26.

29. Peterson, Bertha M., and Dunlap, J. W., "A simplified method for scoring the Strong Vocational Interest Blank," *Journal of Consulting Psychology,* 5:269–274 (1941).

30. Peterson, Ruth C., and Thurstone, L. L., *Motion Pictures and the Social Attitudes of Children,* New York: The Macmillan Company, 1933.

31. Remmers, H. H., "Generalized attitude scales—studies in social-psychological measurements," *Studies in Attitudes—A Contribution to Social Psychological Research Methods, Studies in Higher Education XXVI, Bulletin of Purdue University,* 1934, pp. 7–17.

32. Remmers, H. H., and Kirk, R. B., "Scalability and validity of the socioeconomic status scale of the Purdue Opinion Panel," *Journal of Applied Psychology*, 37:384–386 (1953).

33. Rock, R. T., and Wesman, A., "The comparative efficiency of various methods of weighting interest test items," *Psychological Bulletin*, 36:569 (1939).

34. Stagner, R., "Fascist attitudes: Their determining conditions," *Journal of Social Psychology*, 7:438–454 (1936).

35. Stouffer, S. A., "Experimental comparison of a statistical and a case history technique of attitude research," *Publications of the American Sociological Society*, 25:154–156 (1931).

36. Stouffer, S. A., *et al.*, *Measurement and Prediction*, Princeton: Princeton University Press, 1949.

37. Strong, E. K., Jr., "Permanence of interest scores over 22 years," *Journal of Applied Psychology*, 35:89–91 (1951).

38. Strong, E. K., Jr., "Procedure for scoring an interest test," *Psychological Clinic*, 19:63–72 (1930).

39. Strong, E. K., Jr., *Vocational Interests of Men and Women*, Stanford University: Stanford University Press, 1943.

40. Symonds, P. M., *Diagnosing Personality and Conduct*, New York: Appleton-Century-Crofts, 1931.

41. Terris, Fay, "Are poll questions too difficult?" *Public Opinion Quarterly*, 13:314–319 (1949).

42. Thorndike, E. L., "Psychology of semantics," *American Journal of Psychology*, 59:613–632 (1946).

43. Thurstone, L. L., and Chave, E. J., *The Measurement of Attitudes*, Chicago: University of Chicago Press, 1929.

44. Weschler, I. R., "An investigation of attitudes toward labor and management by means of the error-choice method," *Journal of Social Psychology*, 32:51–62, 63–69 (1950).

45. Williamson, A. C., and Remmers, H. H., "Persistence of attitudes concerning conservation issues," *Journal of Experimental Education*, 8:354–361 (1940).

46. Wrightstone, J. W., *Wrightstone Scale of Civic Beliefs*, Yonkers: World Book Company, 1938.

PART FIVE

Environment and Background

CHAPTER XV

Environment and Background

ABSTRACT

Environment and background are distinct from other aspects of pupils in being determiners rather than dimensions. The teacher needs to understand the relationships between various factors in the environment and background and the various aspects of pupils considered in other chapters. The home, the community, and the school are categories of the environment. In the home, parent-to-parent, parent-to-child, and child-to-child relationships all have important effects on pupils' emotional and social adjustment and attitudes. Social class, role, and status as concepts and in relation to techniques of measurement have basic significance in adjustment. Economic conditions, social customs, movies, other recreational activities, and the mass media of communication significantly affect attitudes and emotional adjustment. Teachers, teaching practices, curricula, and other constituents of the school similarly have their impact on the pupil.

◆◆◆

Thus far in our discussion of aspects of pupils which should be evaluated, we have been concerned only with results, effects, outcomes, or the present status of the pupil. When the evaluation of each of these aspects is carried on over a period of time, it becomes possible to conceive of yesterday's "present status" as a background, cause, or determiner of today's "present status." Or as the poet long ago phrased it, "The child is father of the man." For example, our evaluation of the pupil's freshman achievement in mathematics makes possible prediction and understanding of his senior achievement in mathematics; in this case, freshman

427

achievement is background of senior achievement. But when we have evaluated achievement, mental abilities, adjustments, and attitudes, we still have the whole constellation of pupil aspects denoted by the phrase "environment and background."

This chapter will develop what is meant by environment and background, organize this field into categories, and discuss the significance of these categories as determiners of the other aspects of pupils.

GENERAL SIGNIFICANCE OF ENVIRONMENT AND BACKGROUND

In using data concerning a pupil's environment and background, it is important to realize that none of these data taken alone permits hard-and-fast prediction of a student's standing in other aspects. This is so because overlapping occurs in any aspect of pupils when they are grouped according to a single item of environment or background. For example, although there is a significant correlation between father's occupation and pupil's intelligence, the overlapping among occupational groups makes it impossible to improve very appreciably over a sheer guess the prediction of an individual student's intelligence or achievement from his father's occupation. So it is with other items of background and environment. Furthermore, significant relationships do not always have the same significance for guidance. Some relationships are direct; others may merely reflect mutual dependence on a common third factor. For instance, is the relationship between a pupil's achievement in school and his father's occupation a direct one, or is it due to some underlying factor on which occupation of the father is itself dependent? These considerations point to the need for caution in drawing inferences from any single fact about a pupil's background or environment.

We shall think of environment and background as consisting of the *home*, the *community*, and the *school*. The interdependence of these three divisions is self-evident, since knowledge concerning any one of them almost always enables us to form fairly safe conclusions about some aspects of the others. That is, knowledge that the father of a *family* heads a great corporation enables a safe prediction about the general nature of the *community* in which his children live and of the *school* which they attend. Before we turn to each of these divisions, an excellent summary statement of what has been happening in our culture and to the family as part of the culture merits quotation (**20 : 434**):

Numerous and rapid changes in the general culture have had profound effects upon the family and, in turn, upon its educational functions. Separate employment, including that of women, in industrial and commercial institutions; urban residence with congested living quarters and the impact of heterogeneous cultures; commercial dining and recreational establishments; disappearance of neighborhood standards and controls; increasing use of paper and substitution of abstractions and symbols for reality; increased mobility through revolutionary changes in transportation and communication; and increasing emphasis upon money as an end and as the chief criterion of value are some of the changes which have affected the family. Concurrently, within the family members tend more to work, dine, and play separately or by age and sex groupings rather than as families; spatial, psychological, and social mobility are increased; the social and economic status of women is less conditioned by the family; economic and social competition produces strains; persons of divergent cultures marry more frequently; and family tensions and disorganization are indicated by higher divorce rates. Relationships are increasingly complex and impersonal. The adult generation is confused by the relatively rapid changes which have occurred in the material culture while the nonmaterial institutions are slow or lagging in their adjustments. The adult and immature generations are more isolated than formerly.

Our discussion of the nature of social and emotional adjustment in Chapter XI as it relates to environmental-cultural factors is obviously in point here.

HOME BACKGROUND AND ENVIRONMENT

The pupil's home and family may be considered from three points of view:

1. Parent-to-parent relationships
2. Parent-to-child relationships
3. Child-to-child relationships

These categories are neat and tidy only in a logical sense and on paper. In psychological actuality these interrelationships are inextricably interwoven. The family is a small microcosm in which the child undergoes his first and probably most important social-izing experience. The family in turn through its various members interacts with the society, the culture in which it has its being.

One principle in considering parental behavior is that the same behavior may have widely different implications according to its context. That is, the same parental act has different significance for different children depending on how they perceive it. A highly disturbing experience for a child who sees himself as weak and helpless may be a positively constructive and developmental ex-perience for the child who perceives himself as strong and compe-tent.

Moreover, once the child comes to see adults as sources of strength, warmth, approval, and protection, he is much more likely to remember and accept confirming experience and not to notice conflicting experience. On the other hand, a child who perceives adults as threatening, hostile, and punitive will tend to find a great deal of evidence to support his view and will tend to ignore contrary experience (43).

Along the same lines, Sorokin (41) found that college students who believe people in general to be essentially "good" reported significantly more pleasant relationships with their parents than did those who believe people to be essentially "bad." In other words, those who accepted the possibility of peaceful, altruistic, coöperative relations with others had pleasant relationships, while those who thought that social relations were essentially a matter of the "law of the jungle" had unpleasant relations with their parents.

Similarly, Sperling (42) found that disturbed behavior of the parents might be reflected in similar disturbed behavior of the child, or the child might act out repressed problems of the parents.

The effects of children's frustrations in the home have been re-ported in a number of studies. Hollenberg and Sperry (22) experi-mentally confirmed the hypothesis that highly frustrated children would be aggressive in doll play. Children subjected to excessive control at home showed significantly greater frequency of aggres-sion than those not so restrained. Similar results were reported by Sears (39).

The effects on children of separation from a parent have also been considered. Bach (2) studied the father fantasies of 20 father-separated children from six to ten years of age and those of 20 control father-home children by means of a standardized doll play technique. The father-separated children produced an idealistic and feminine fantasy picture of the father when compared to the control children, who elaborated the father-aggressive tendency. Boys showed more of these aggressive fantasies than girls. Sears and others (40) analyzed the aggressive behavior of 126 children and found that boys from father-absent homes are less likely to have fantasy aggressions than boys from father-present homes.

These studies of father-separated families carried out during World War II lead to the general question of the effects of crises, especially wartime crises, on families. Boulding (5) concluded that any event, however cataclysmic, does not necessarily produce a family crisis. Rather, three factors are involved: (1) hardship of the event, (2) the family's resources to meet the event, and (3) the family's definition of what constitutes a crisis.

Since men and women tend to project authority patterns they experienced as children into their own marriage and family relations (24), it is not surprising that Ellis (17) found a significant correlation between early family experience of girls and their later love behavior histories. Similarly, Wolford (51) found that non-dating seniors in high school had less wholesome relationships with their parents and less wholesome feelings of self-regard than those who dated. This is consistent with Abrahamsen's report (1) that the sex impulses of sex offenders developed irregularly because of early destructive influences in childhood and adolescence, especially in relationships with parents, brothers, and sisters.

CHILDREN'S OPINIONS ABOUT THE FAMILY

Children's opinions about family relationships reflect and influence their social development. Williams (49) concluded from a study of some 1500 high-school students in Michigan and Georgia, made by means of questionnaires, discussion groups, and 100 interviews, that parents and youth need education regarding attitudes toward dating, mutual understanding, sharing responsibilities, and work and play. About half his subjects were not finding the companionship or partnership they thought they needed, and about one-fourth of them, who probably needed to, did not talk problems over with their parents. In a nation-wide sample of some 3000 high-school pupils, another study (36) found that from 10 to 20 percent of these young people indicated a lack of mutual confidence between themselves and their parents. Some friction points were parental supervision, allowances, use of the family car, and bickering among brothers and sisters.

In a national survey aimed specifically at teen-agers' perceptions of parent-child relationships (33, 34) students were asked not only how they felt about various issues but also how they thought mothers and fathers would feel about them. Following is an illustrative item:

When high school students are out for an evening, should their parents know just where they are?

Your answer:
.... Always
.... Often
.... Only sometimes

How would *mothers* answer this?
.... Always
.... Often
.... Only sometimes

How would *fathers* answer this?
.... Always
.... Often
.... Only sometimes

The following few highlights illustrate the way the home environment is seen by many students in American high schools:

59% feel parents should seldom decide upon their child's future occupation.

31% indicate that what happens on dates should never be discussed with parents.

31% think parents often talk too much about what their children ought to do.

24% feel that parents hardly ever understand the problems of modern youth.

47% believe parents often worry too much about the possibility of teen-agers "going bad."

44% think fathers would say that parents are too easy in the way they handle their children.

62% believe mothers think that parents usually trust their children as much as they can.

59% would never justify whipping or slapping as punishment.

39% say young people should seldom be punished by being made to stay at home.

61% indicate that young people should usually be allowed to drive the family car on dates if they have a driver's license.

81% say that petting or "necking" is at least sometimes all right when out on dates.

44% approve of "going steady" as a usual occurrence.

43% believe it is usually a parent's duty to prevent young people from choosing the wrong kind of friends.

53% think parents should always know where their children are when they are out for an evening.

74% say that parents allow their children enough spending money.

60% feel parents should always try to protect young people from making the mistakes they themselves made in their youth.

48% believe that parents usually set a good example for young people to follow.

90% think the family should at least sometimes get together and talk over each other's problems.

Hackett (19) analyzed the results of this survey and extended the study by obtaining answers from some 1200 parents in a midwestern urban community, and also their estimates of how their children would answer. On almost no question on the poll did these young people feel that their parents would be in complete agreement with them. The parents were somewhat better able to predict how their children would answer than the children were able to predict their parents' answers.

DELINQUENCY AND THE HOME

Delinquency has long been viewed as a symptom of inadequacies in the home environment. A monumental study by the Gluecks (18) deserves mention because it reveals the complexities of the personal and environmental factors that operate in producing delinquency. They carefully matched 500 delinquent boys with 500 nondelinquent boys on age, general intelligence, national (ethnico-racial) origin, and residence in underprivileged neighborhoods. By means of projective tests, psychiatric interviews, and sociological case studies, including interviews in the home and records from various social institutions, the Gluecks compared the two groups and arrived at important conclusions summarized as follows:

The delinquents as a group are distinguishable from the non-delinquents: (1) physically, in being essentially mesomorphic in constitution (solid, closely knit, muscular); (2) temperamentally, in being restlessly energetic, impulsive, extroverted, aggressive, destructive (often sadistic)—traits which may be related more or less to the erratic growth pattern and its physiologic correlates or consequences; (3) in attitude, by being hostile, defiant, resentful, suspicious, stubborn, socially assertive, adventurous, unconventional, non-submissive to authority; (4) psychologically, in tending to direct and concrete, rather than symbolic, intellectual expression, and in being less methodical in their approach to problems; (5) socio-culturally, in having been reared to a far greater extent than the control group in homes of little understanding, affection, stability, or moral fibre by parents usually unfit to be effective guides and protectors or, according to psychoanalytic theory, desirable sources for emulation and the construction of a consistent, well-balanced, and socially normal superego during the early stages of character development. While in individual cases the stresses contributed by any one of the above pressure-areas of dissocial-behavior tendency may adequately account for persistence in delinquency, in general the high probability of delinquency is dependent upon the interplay of the conditions and forces from all these areas.

In the exciting, stimulating, but little-controlled and culturally inconsistent environment of the underprivileged area, such boys readily give expression to their untamed impulses and their self-centered desires by means of various forms of delinquent behavior. Their tendencies toward uninhibited energy-expression are deeply anchored in soma and psyche and in the malformations of character during the first few years of life (18 : 281–282).

PARENT-CHILD RELATIONSHIPS

From the standpoint of parent-to-parent relationships, families may be classified on an accord-discord scale—accord homes being integrated and coöperative and discord homes being the opposite. The connection between parent-to-parent relationships and personality development has been implicitly recognized by all students of the subject. When the two parents deeply love each other in the fullest sense of that relationship, and the atmosphere is democratic and permissive, the children are much more likely to be mentally healthy than if the opposite prevails.

That parental behavior affects the personality development of the children in various ways has been shown by a number of studies. Only a few will be briefly cited here by way of example. Baldwin (3) found that lack of democracy in the home produced a quiet, well-behaved, nonresistant, socially unaggressive child restricted in curiosity, originality, and fancifulness. Freedom and permissiveness, on the other hand, permit the child to become active, outgoing, and spontaneous. In a study of parental behavior McKeown (29) found that encouraging behavior was quite common among parents of normal children but very rare among parents of schizoid or behavior problem children.

Cass (10) found that children with special personality problems are likely to have mothers who have little awareness of their child's needs but impose a high degree of control on him. Rabban (31) found that working-class children adopt the appropriate sex roles earlier than middle-class children. Thus it seems that some of the problems of middle-class children may arise from the fact that clear-cut role models are not offered to them.

The White House Conference on Child Health and Protection (48 : 299–300) stated its conclusion concerning the significance of the home for the child's personality development as follows: "Of paramount influence are the subtle, intangible relations of family life such as affection, confiding in parents, trust and loyalty of child to parents . . . and control by other means than punishment. In importance for child development they seem to outweigh by far the role of the external aspects of the home, upon which emphasis has in the past been placed, such as economic status of the family, number of rooms to a person, and formal education of the children."

In this connection it is of interest to know the attitudes of high-school students toward child behavior and management, for in a relatively short time they will be marrying and having children. Evidence from the Purdue Opinion Panel clearly shows that our culture in this area provides differential sex roles and that girls, even at the ninth-grade level, are significantly better "child psychologists" than boys. Moreover, the differences between boys and girls increase with increase in grade level (33, 34). If this differential continues after marriage (What does father read and what does mother read?) it may well be a factor in family friction. Mother will want to treat the children as the child psychologists advise, but father will want to treat them as he was treated—as he learned child management at home. A few sample items from this poll will illustrate the differences between boys and girls.

		Percent Agreeing with Experts	
	Experts	Boys	Girls
Elimination of emotional tension in the home corrects much misbehavior in children.	Agree	61	71
Early home life appears to be the single most powerful factor in shaping an individual's personality patterns.	Agree	73	82
The mother who talks and gurgles to her child (not baby talk) will develop a child with finer speech which will be developed more quickly than the mother who is relatively silent.	Agree	50	65
A child's ability to get along with others may be improved by his attending nursery school.	Agree	54	73
It is natural for children to be curious about sex.	Agree	79	89
If a child is alone too much, he fails to learn how to get along with people.	Agree	77	90
A child's stuttering may be due to emotional tension in the home.	Agree	53	65
Racial prejudices in children are usually the result of the attitudes of the parents and other adults.	Agree	70	81
Praise is more effective than blame in dealing with children.	Agree	63	76
A child's hands should not be held down while he is being fed.	Agree	61	72

	Experts	Percent Agreeing with Experts	
		Boys	Girls
Parents may have attitudes which cause intense rivalry among brothers and sisters, which in turn profoundly affects the individual child's outlook on life.	Agree	68	82
One of the first steps in treating thumb sucking and nail biting is to make the child comfortable and free from criticism.	Agree	40	57
A child may be seriously maladjusted and still be considered a model child by his parents.	Agree	73	82
A child should be included in the family planning for charity and gifts.	Agree	76	90
The child should help make plans and be allowed to help prepare for the new baby.	Agree	57	81
Putting a child to bed as punishment may be an effective way of getting him to dislike sleeping.	Agree	55	69

Of the total 90 items in the poll, on only four were boys more frequently in agreement with the child experts than the girls were.

Concerning affection between parents and child it is convenient to conceive of a scale ranging from overprotection to rejection. Overprotection arises when the parents secure excessive emotional satisfaction from satisfying the demands of the child without imposing any restrictions or limitations on these satisfactions. It is an excessive performance by the parent of his function of protecting the child. It may result in stunting the child's progress toward self-reliance and independence, both by withholding opportunity for practice and by fostering an overattachment of the child to the parent. Rejection is the opposite of overprotection in that it means denial of affection and care to the child. Thus the child is cast upon his own inadequate resources for emotional and social security and affection. Either or both parents may reject him, with consequences both for the parents' relationships with each other and for the other parent's relationship with the child, as when rejection by one parent results in overprotection by the other. Such rejection in the form of criticism, punishment, or lack of affection, or disguised in the form of overprotection, has been found to have definite effects on child personality. Symonds (45) concluded that the rejected child is likely to show aggressive traits and to be antagonistic toward others. Similarly, Burgum (9) and Witmer and her colleagues (50) found rejected children to be in need of clinical treatment. For a book-length treatment of the problem, the reader is referred to Symonds' survey of the entire field of parent-child relationships (46).

CHILD-TO-CHILD RELATIONSHIPS

Child-to-child relationships are usually considered in terms of the relationship between birth order, or ordinal position in the family, and other aspects of the child. For example, what are the effects on a child's intelligence, personality, health, and adjustment, of being the only child in a family, or the last-born of twelve children, or a boy with five sisters, or other such situations? Perhaps the most complete classification of ordinal positions has been made by Krout (26), who was able to distinguish twenty-six ordinal positions, thirteen for each sex. To groups of subjects representing each of these twenty-six positions, Krout administered a schedule from which he determined (1) by which parent a child was most favored or disciplined, (2) which parent dominated the family, (3) to which siblings the subject was most attached, submissive, or dominant, and (4) the attitudes of dominance, submissiveness, and attachment of each subject toward males and females outside his family. While the results are too elaborate to be presented here, it is sufficient for our present purpose to state that significant relationships were found between ordinal position and behavior patterns within the family.

The personality characteristics of the only child, in either kindergarten or university, have only infrequently been found to differ in any practically important degree from those of children who have siblings. Remmers (32) found that "only" children were significantly more frequent among distinguished (honor) students than were students who had brothers or sisters. But despite the smallness of the relationships and the consequent impossibility of forecasting with certainty from knowledge of ordinal position in the family, this factor still remains a suggestive and potentially enlightening source of understanding concerning the guidance problems of any particular pupil.

A more fruitful point of view considers child-to-child relationships and their effects on such aspects of pupils as attitudes and social relationships. Hero worship or shame for a brother or sister, jealousy, the older child acting as a parent substitute for one or more of the younger children may explain much about the personality of a particular pupil. In the latter case, imitation, suggestion, and identification would exist as frequently in the relation between younger and older children as they would in the relation of child to parent.

SOCIAL CLASS MEMBERSHIP

In this country the concept of social class is repugnant and alien. The Declaration of Independence with its ringing statement, "All men are created equal," and the strong democratic tradition derived from a pioneering society conquering a new continent constituted a sharp break with the concepts of the Old World. The values derived from this tradition survive today.

From this country's very beginning as an independent nation, however, there has been a history of class distinction and class conflict. That the framers of the Constitution were well aware of their economic and class interests was Beard's conclusion (4). Industrialization brought many signs of an increasing consciousness of class, sharpened especially by the economic depression of the 1930's. A number of studies in recent decades by sociologists, cultural anthropologists, and social psychologists have reflected this growing awareness of class (21, 28, 47, 23, 12).

MEANING OF "SOCIAL CLASS"

What do we mean when we speak of "social class"? Social scientists are by no means in agreement on any one definition but they would probably all endorse the raw statement that social classes are categories of people—any particular category being alike in a number of ways—and can be generally ranked as "higher" or "lower" according to some criterion or characteristic. Disagreement begins when we ask what that criterion is. This disagreement results not from differences in the social scientists' actual knowledge, but from their different interpretations of these facts, or their different technical approaches to the study of social class. The major approaches can be roughly classified as objective and subjective. Defining social class by objective characteristics concerns such measures as *income, occupation, education, type of dwelling,* etc. Subjective characteristics are *attitudes, choice of friends, feeling of belonging to a social class,* etc.

As already noted, earlier investigators have shown that social classes differ in a number of respects. People with similar social backgrounds appear to be alike in many ways—more so than people with widely varying backgrounds. Children of less favored parents do not get as much or as good an education as children from more favored families; neither do they obtain as well-paid jobs. Many clubs and associations that are perfectly democratic in their aims often "screen" their members according to their social class background. People tend to marry and seek friends among persons "of their own kind." Such screening practices not only reflect discriminatory attitudes on the part of the "uppers," they indicate genuine differences in what the various classes "want" and "like." In an intensive study of children in Grades I-VIII in a small industrial city, Stendler (44) discovered clear evidence of class structure and class dynamics: increasing awareness of class symbols with increase in grade level, different degrees of consciousness of class symbols among the three class groupings she found, differences in attitude toward different social classes. Out-of-school activities differed in important ways for the different class groups—upper-middle-class children joined more organizations, took more paid lessons, and worked after school less often. A significant difference existed between in-school and out-of-school choice of friends, in-school choices being more democratic and working-class children being most frequently named as those with whom the chooser would least like to associate.

In judging their own social class position these grade children were less accurate than in judging that of their schoolmates. The highest two grades showed considerable accuracy in rating other children's social class position when accuracy was measured as similarity to adult ratings. In these grades also the choices of future occupation tended to indicate "some appreciation of what they realize their lives can be."

That social class membership has significant impact on personality is reflected in the results of one of the Purdue Opinion Panel Polls (37). Both an objective and a subjective criterion of social class membership was used in this study. (1) The pupils checked each of twelve alternative occupational descriptions as to whether it was more, equally, or less desirable than the occupations of the father or main provider and also (2) they indicated in which social class (upper, middle, working, or lower) they thought they belonged. The study was designed to test the existence and relationship to social class status of three main attitudinal patterns— the *deferred gratification pattern* (postponing immediate pleasures for greater future pleasures, involving control and restriction of behavior), *level of aspiration,* and social-political *ideology* (individualistic or class oriented). Illustrations of these follow:

Deferred gratification: "If you won a big prize, say two thousand dollars, what would you do?

.... spend most of it right away on things I and my family want.
.... save most of it for education or for business."

Level of aspiration: Pupils were asked to indicate on a list of occupations those they considered "not good enough" for their own lifework.

Ideology: "If I ever go into politics, I would like to become known as a strong backer of

.... American union ideas.
.... American business ideas."

Typically, the "middle-class" pattern of opinion placed more emphasis on deferred gratification, on the higher levels of aspiration, and includes greater assimilation of the ideas and goals of "American businessmen," with a corresponding rejection of union or labor ideals.

Evidence for the reality of social classes and their effects on attitude and individual behavior is clear. Ninety-four percent of the high-school students believed that social classes exist in America, and 37 percent of the same pupils said that differences among the classes are large. Furthermore, choice of friends, educational and vocational goals, and attitudes toward violence and aggression and toward a number of school activities were all related to social class position.

We do not, however, wish to overemphasize these trends. Although the differences are "real" enough, i.e., statistically reliable, the differences in actual numbers are generally not large and the groups overlap considerably. Table 25 shows the relationship

TABLE 25.   Social Class Self-Identification of 2500 High-School Students, Grades 9 to 12, Related to Father's Occupational Grouping

Father's occupation	Upper Class	Middle Class	Working Class	Total[a]
A. Professional and managerial....	12	68	19	99
B. Middle-level job dealing with people......................	6	69	24	99
C. Middle-level job working with tools........................	4	59	35	98
D. Unskilled labor...............	3	47	48	98

[a] Totals are not an even 100 because a few students failed to answer.

between father's occupational grouping and the social class self-identification of the student. The classes are obviously not rigid divisions in our society. But they are social realities and their existence is frequently a barrier to "equal opportunity" to develop one's potentialities fully, a goal of our democratic society. Equally important, social class differences in opportunity mean that fulfilling our society's manpower requirements for economic, military, political, and cultural competence is retarded.

IMPLICATIONS FOR TEACHING

Implications for the teacher are fairly clear. Pupils of different social background and environment, with different training in the home, have widely differing attitudes toward the school situation. These attitudes frequently influence pupils' dropping out of school and their "problem" behavior. Since teachers tend to judge pupils by their own middle-class standards, serious lack of understanding between teachers and pupils can arise. Recognizing some of these factors as determiners of a pupil's attitudes and behavior, the teacher can more easily understand his behavior and view him in a helpful if not more sympathetic manner. If education is to accomplish its goals, the educator needs to be aware of the factors that shape the pupil's personality, for these factors affect the receptivity of a pupil for the educational "stuff" to which he is exposed. How many thousands of pupils dropped out of school last year because of lack of "interest"? Not for lack of ability, not for lack of financial means, but for lack of favorable attitudes?

Differences in neighborhood environment and home values—not merely objectively measured "mental abilities"—determine the achievement of the individual pupil. Knowledge of such factors enables the educator to direct attention to problems connected with pupils whose backgrounds vary. We can find out how the interests of less favored pupils differ from those of pupils with a favorable background, and we can appeal to those interests.

There is a final reason for the value of such knowledge as we have been discussing here. Rational persons in our society value democracy and seek to eliminate threats of totalitarian rule. Communism and fascism thrive on "class struggle"—the greater the inequalities of opportunity the greater the totalitarian threat. Reducing these inequalities through democratic processes strengthens resistance to such movements. One Purdue Opinion Panel asked whether "everyone willing to work hard is able to get ahead in America." One out of every four students in the sample said no. Therein lies a challenge to education.

STATUS AND ROLE

Two concepts of great importance in education have evolved in modern social science—*status* and *role*. Shakespeare anticipated their formulation some three hundred years ago:

> All the world's a stage,
> And all the men and women merely players.
> They have their exits and their entrances;
> And one man in his time plays many parts.

The children in each classroom constitute a small society with many lines of association and social interaction. The kinds of lines of association and interaction create what has been called an "atmosphere" for the group. In this atmosphere the children learn not only assigned lessons but ways of responding to each other and to the teacher. Through these interactions and others outside the classroom, each child also develops a self-concept.

As Linton has pointed out (27 : 263–272), even the simplest primary society, such as a primitive village, has a relatively complex status structure; the individuals who compose the society are classified and organized in several ways simultaneously. Among these status systems, for example, are the sex system, the prestige system, the family system, association groups, friendship units, work groups, clubs, and usually secret societies. Status, then, is "the place in a particular system which a certain individual occupies at a particular time."

The concept of role designates the "sum total of the culture patterns associated with a particular status and includes the attitudes, values, and behaviors ascribed by the society to any and all persons occupying this status. A role, then, represents the behavior of the individual appropriate to his status, what he must do to validate his status."

This rather abstract formulation can be clarified by fictional examples. Ben Harmon III is the son of the local banker in a midwestern city, the oldest of three children in the family, and a senior in high school. On a mental test which he took as a freshman, he scored an I.Q. of 120. He is taking the college preparatory course and plans to major in business administration in college. He has already visited the state university campus and his father's fraternity there, but he is undecided whether to attend it or try to enter Princeton University.

Among his association groups are the younger set at the country club, the Athletic Boosters, the Episcopal Church, and the football team. His various leadership roles include being an older brother to his younger sister and brother, president of the Athletic Boosters, and editor of the school paper; he also served as president of the mock legislative session organized by the Social Science Department of the high school.

In his sex roles, he took dancing lessons at the age of eight, is very much on a "man-to-man" basis with his father, and is gentle and patient with his ailing mother, who "enjoys" poor health. He dates the daughter of the owner of a grocery chain.

His friendship roles are related to the younger country-club set already mentioned, and to the group of young people from the part of town called Crestview, a number of whom have adjoining summer homes in Minnesota. Each school morning, four or five of his neighborhood friends ride with him in the convertible his father gave him for Christmas.

Contrasting statuses and roles are those of Tony, whose grand-parents came in the steerage from Ruritania. Tony is the son of a laborer and the oldest of eight children. He too is a senior in high school and also achieved an I.Q. of 120. He is taking the voca-tional course and works part time in a garage. Ambitious, he often wishes that he could attend college and be a part of the prestige system that this implies. He has been awarded a scholarship but will be unable to use it because part of his earnings are needed to help support his family. By saving a little of them, he hopes to complete work at the local technical institute.

Tony's association groups are those related to the Catholic Church, which he attends regularly, and to the street-corner gang that congregates at the local drugstore on week-end nights. He is also a member of the high-school glee club, in which he frequently sings tenor solos.

In his family and sex roles, he is on good terms with his father, and is his mother's pride, with his excellent high-school record and his prestige as a member of the glee club. He occasionally takes Maureen Sullivan, a steelworker's daughter, to a movie, but this creates some conflict because of the expense. He will need his money if he is to attend the technical institute next year.

Obviously the statuses and roles of Ben and Tony differ de-cidedly, and hence their own expectations. While we have con-cerned ourselves with them as seniors in high school, their statuses and roles began to differentiate very early in their school careers, and they acquired correspondingly different systems of attitudes, values, and other personality characteristics.

That various kinds of personal, self-perceived problems related to role behavior differ significantly as between pupils from families of lower and higher social class is clear from the following tabulation of responses from the SRA Youth Inventory (35):

Problem	Percentage Having the Problem in Each Social Class	
	Lower	Higher
What shall I do after high school?	51	37
Should I go to college?	36	26
I wish I could afford college	24	9
How do I select a vocation that doesn't require college?	16	6
What jobs are open to high-school graduates?	45	25
How do I go about finding a job?	37	30
I feel that I'm not as smart as I should be	36	27
I get stage fright when I speak before a group	55	45
I wish I could carry on a pleasant conversation	36	28
I want to learn to dance	35	25
There aren't enough places for wholesome recreation where I live	46	34
I can't find a part-time job to earn spending money	30	20

Qualitatively the following more predominantly *upper*-group problems look very different. While the preceding items may be generally classified as ego-centered, that characterization does not apply to the following:

Problem	Percentage Having the Problem in Each Social Class	
	Lower	Higher
I have a desire to be important to society and my own group	14	27
How can I help to make the world a better place to live in?	27	39
What can I do to help improve our government?	13	20
What can I do about the injustice all around us?	13	23
I am worried about the next war (1949)	29	37
Is there something I can do about racial prejudice?	21	39
I wonder about the afterlife	20	29

THE COMMUNITY ENVIRONMENT
AND BACKGROUND

The community part of the pupil's total environment and background includes the parts of the environment that are neither of the family nor of the school. The community environment and background includes such social factors as economic depression or prosperity, war, customs and traditions, leisure-time activities (such as reading, playing, and camping), motion pictures, radio, and television. Economic conditions can influence pupils both directly through their effect on attitudes and opportunities and indirectly through their effect on the home and school. War or its anticipation, prolonged depression and unemployment may produce severe personality disorganization. During the depression of the 1930's, Rundquist and Sletto (38) gave tests to several thousand high-school students, college students, people on relief, and other adults. Comparison of the employed and unemployed revealed wide differences in attitudes toward the economic order and in general adjustment. Edmiston and Swaim (16) found that delinquency rates and length of school term were inversely related. However, economic status was not controlled in their study; probably these variables are correlated because both of them depend on economic conditions.

Thus economic conditions affect pupils directly if they are about to enter the world of work, and indirectly through the adjustment engendered in their parents by the economic situation. War and unemployment produce crowded living conditions and inadequate places to play and study, and these in turn increase the difficulty of making adjustments at home and in school. From a study of children's attitudes as influenced by economic deprivation, Meltzer (30) concluded that economic insecurity is associated with emotional insecurity, but that above certain low limits economic security does not imply emotional security since children from the middle class manifested better adjustment than children from the upper economic levels. In the early 1930's the effects of the depression on the social attitudes of high-school and college youth produced what has been termed "the revolt on the campus." Buck (8) has shown how the depression lessened the disapproval of debt and "socialistic" plans on the part of 2000 university students. Breemes, Remmers, and Morgan (6) similarly reported that a decided increase in the liberalism of groups of college sophomores between 1931 and 1934 had not been lost by comparable groups of students measured in 1937 and 1939. There had thus been a shift in student opinion at the beginning of the depression which had remained stable through the next six years of the nation's economic and political development.

Social customs, traditions, or mores, as was stated in Chapter XIII, constitute a conservative, change-resistant force in the community. The attitudes of the community at large toward social institutions and personal values exert a profound influence on the individual pupil. That these mores frequently lag behind changing actualities is evident from the social history of the depression of the 1930's. Middletown, the typical American small city, had undergone profound social and economic changes, but the thinking of its citizens had remained substantially the same (28).

In Chapter XIII we intimated that differences between urban and rural areas, between North and South and other geographical divisions can profoundly affect pupil attitudes. For example, Davis (14) was able to compare the influence of such disparate mores as those obtaining in Soviet Russia and in our own country. In 1927 Davis found that Soviet school children actually respected the occupational title "ditch-digger" far more than "banker." Here is a striking case of the importance of community customs for individual attitudes.

The effect of leisure-time activities on adjustment, their constructiveness or destructiveness, may similarly be significant. A pupil's hobbies, the voluntary activities he finds to be inherently interesting, and the role he takes in these leisure-time activities when they involve other individuals may reveal the developmental level of his personality. A pupil may fail to grow from one developmental level of play into the next. The child who engages only in individual activities and fails to join groups, as in becoming a member of a "gang," may be showing symptoms of serious maladjustment. The individual who fails to observe the customary sex differences in play activities or to take a normal interest in the opposite sex at a certain period in his development similarly deserves the teacher's concern. Of obvious importance to the pupil's total adjustment would be his membership in a delinquent gang from which he acquired attitudes and habits rendering him incapable of assuming a constructive role in society.

The role of movies, radio, and television in molding attitudes of adults and children has been demonstrated by several researches (see Chapter XIII). Bruel (7) reported on motion pictures which provide experiences conducive to the development of neuroses and found that these experiences are not limited to early childhood. The significance of the radio may similarly be judged from the study by DeBoer (15). He found that about one-third of the children he studied lay in bed thinking over what they had heard on the radio, and that 30 percent had recently dreamed about some radio program, three-fourths of these dreams being of the nightmare type. Coffin (11) found that in two matched groups of 137 families each, the 137 television-owning families had 24 percent less out-of-home activities than in the nonowning families. He also found that the influence of television was stronger among middle-class families than among families of higher economic status.

In a Purdue Opinion Panel poll (37), 40 percent of the students who had television in their homes reported that watching television interfered with their school work. About a third (32 percent) felt that the "crime and improper behavior" shown in TV programs are at least somewhat harmful, but nearly half (44 percent) of those who had no access to television believed this. Here reading about such programs led to more unfavorable opinions than did actually seeing the programs.

There is also an interesting relationship between this belief and socioeconomic status in the group of nonviewers. Of the low-status group, 42 percent believed that some programs are harmful; 47 percent of the middle group believed this; but 55 percent of the high group had this attitude. Possibly we have here a concealed relationship between the reading of newspapers and periodicals on the one hand and the attitudes expressed on the other.

For all types of television program preferences—plays, sports, mysteries, family comedy, quiz shows, variety shows, and western movies—there is a negative relationship between socioeconomic status and the proportions of those in the three income groups who watch television very often. The greatest range is for mysteries —63 percent for the low status group, 55 percent for the middle, and 49 percent for the high.

There is one exception to this negative relationship—opera. Opera is preferred by 8 percent of the low group, 10 percent of the middle group, and 13 percent of the high group.

The potency of these media as forces for maladjustment means that they can be equally potent as forces of constructive education. In any case, educators in the traditional sense must take account of, evaluate, and use the influences of these new "educators" —the mass-communication media of the twentieth century.

THE SCHOOL ENVIRONMENT AND BACKGROUND

This part of the pupil's environment can be evaluated only if teachers and school administrators are willing to evaluate themselves and their own work (see Chapters XVI and XVII). The mental hygiene of teachers and administrators, the teaching practices resulting from it and from their professional training and equipment, the curricular organization of the school, its administrational organization, the school's physical facilities, its provisions for individual differences, its marking system, guidance system, and all other aspects of its functioning can and should have a vital effect upon the pupil. Here it is our purpose only to round out the discussion of pupil background and environment by drawing attention to the role of the school conceived as part of a pupil's environment.

REFERENCES

1. Abrahamsen, G., "Study of 102 sex offenders at Sing Sing," *Federal Probation,* 14:26–32 (1950).
2. Bach, G. R., "Father-fantasies and father-typing in father-separated children," *Child Development,* 17:63–80 (1946).
3. Baldwin, A. L., "Socialization and the parent-child relationships," *Child Development,* 19:127–136 (1938).
4. Beard, Charles A., *An Economic Interpretation of the Constitution of the United States,* New York: Macmillan Company, 1913.
5. Boulding, Elsie, "Family adjustments to war separation and reunion," *Annals of Political and Social Science,* 272:59–67 (1950).
6. Breemes, E. L., Remmers, H. H., and Morgan, C. L., "Changes in liberalism-conservatism of college students since the depression," *Journal of Social Psychology,* 14:99–107 (1941).
7. Bruel, O., "A moving picture as a psychopathogenic factor: a paper on primary psychotraumatic neurosis," *Character and Personality,* 7:68–76 (1938).
8. Buck, W., "A measurement of changes in attitudes and interests of

university students over a ten-year period," *Journal of Abnormal and Social Psychology*, 31:12–19 (1936).

9. Burgum, Mildred, "Constructive values associated with rejection," *American Journal of Orthopsychiatry*, 10:312–326 (1940).

10. Cass, Loretta K., "An investigation of parent-child relationships in terms of awareness, identification, projection and control," *American Journal of Orthopsychiatry*, 22:305–313 (1952).

11. Coffin, T. E., "Television effects on leisure time activities," *Journal of Applied Psychology*, 32:550–558 (1948).

12. Davis, A., and Dollard, J., *Children of Bondage*, Washington: American Council on Education, 1940.

13. Davis, A., Gardner, B., and Gardner, Mary R., *Deep South*, Chicago: University of Chicago Press, 1941.

14. Davis, Jerome, "Testing the social attitudes of children in the government schools of Russia," *American Journal of Sociology*, 32:459–471 (1927).

15. DeBoer, J. J., "Radio and children's emotions," *School and Society*, 59:369–373 (1939).

16. Edmiston, R. W., and Swaim, E. H., "Juvenile delinquency and provisions for education," *School and Society*, 55:195 (1942).

17. Ellis, A., "Some significant correlates of love and family attitudes and behavior," *Journal of Social Psychology*, 30:3–16 (1949).

18. Glueck, S., and Glueck, Eleanor, *Unraveling Juvenile Delinquency*, New York: The Commonwealth Fund, 1950.

19. Hackett, C. G., "An opinion polling technique in a study of parent-child relationships," *Studies in Higher Education No. LXXV*, Lafayette: Purdue University, Division of Educational Reference, February, 1951.

20. Hayes, W. F., "The family and education," in Monroe, W. S. (ed.), *Encyclopedia of Educational Research*, New York: The Macmillan Company, 1950.

21. Holcombe, A. N., *The Middle Classes in American Politics*, Cambridge: Harvard University Press, 1940.

22. Hollenberg, Eleanor, and Sperry, Margaret, "Some antecedents of aggression and effects of frustration in doll play," *Personality*, 1:32–43 (1950).

23. Hollingshead, A. B., *Elmtown's Youth*, New York: John Wiley & Sons, Inc., 1949.

24. Ingersoll, Hazel L., "A study of the transmission of authority patterns in the family," *Genetic Psychology Monographs*, 38:225–302 (1948).

25. June, A. W., *Life, Liberty, and Property,* Philadelphia: J. B. Lippincott Company, 1941.

26. Krout, M. H., "Typical behavior patterns in twenty-six ordinal positions," *Pedagogical Seminary and Journal of Genetic Psychology,* 55:3–30 (1939).

27. Linton, R., "Social Roles," in Swanson, G., Newcomb, T. M., and Hartley, E. (eds.), *Readings in Social Psychology,"* New York: Henry Holt & Company, Inc., rev. ed., 1952.

28. Lynd, R. S. and Helen M., *Middletown in Transition,* New York: Harcourt, Brace & Company, Inc., 1937.

29. McKeown, J. E., "Behavior of parents of schizophrenic, neurotic and normal children," *American Journal of Sociology,* 56:175–179 (1950).

30. Meltzer, H., "Economic security and children's attitudes toward parents," *American Journal of Orthopsychiatry,* 6:590–608 (1936).

31. Rabban, M., "Sex-role identification in young children in two diverse social groups," *Genetic Psychology Monographs,* 42:81–158 (1950).

32. Remmers, H. H., "Distinguished students—what they are and why," *Studies in Higher Education XV, Bulletin of Purdue University,* 31 (1930).

33. Remmers, H. H., and Drucker, A. J., "How high school youth believe children should be brought up," *Purdue Opinion Panel Report No. 24,* 9 (1949).

34. Remmers, H. H., and Drucker, A. J., "Teen-agers' attitudes toward problems of child management," *Journal of Educational Psychology,* 42:105–113 (1951).

35. Remmers, H. H., and Shimberg, B., *The SRA Youth Inventory, Manual,* Chicago: Science Research Associates, rev. ed., 1953.

36. Remmers, H. H., Drucker, A. J., and Hackett, C. G., "Youth looks at the parent problem," *Purdue Opinion Panel Report No. 23,* 9 (1949).

37. Remmers, H. H., Horton, R. E., and Mainer, R. E., "Attitudes of high school students toward certain aspects of television," *Purdue Opinion Panel Report No. 36,* 12 (1953).

38. Rundquist, E. A., and Sletto, R. F., *Personality in the Depression,* Minneapolis: University of Minnesota Press, 1936.

39. Sears, R. R., "Symposium on genetic psychology. III. Effects of frustration and anxiety on fantasy aggression," *American Journal of Orthopsychiatry,* 21:498–505 (1951).

40. Sears, R. R., Pintler, Margaret, and Sears, Pauline S., "Effects of

father-separation on pre-school children's doll play," *Child Development,* 17:219–243 (1946).

41. Sorokin, P. A., "Affiliative and hostile tendencies of college students," *Explorations in Altruistic Love and Behavior,* Boston: Beacon Press, 1950.

42. Sperling, Melitta, "Children's interpretation and reaction to the unconscious of their mothers," *International Journal of Psychoanalysis,* 31:36–41, 1950.

43. Stagner, R., "Homeostasis as a unifying concept in personality theory," *Psychological Review,* 58:5–17 (1951).

44. Stendler, Celia B., *Children of Brasstown,* University of Illinois Bulletin No. 59, April, 1949.

45. Symonds, P. M., "A study of parental acceptance and rejection," *American Journal of Orthopsychiatry,* 8:679–688 (1938).

46. Symonds, P. M., *The Psychology of Parent-child Relationships,* New York: Appleton-Century-Crofts, 1939.

47. Warner, W. L., and Lunt, P. S., *The Social Life of a Modern Community,* New Haven: Yale University Press, 1941.

48. White House Conference on Child Health and Protection, *The Young Child in the Home,* New York: Appleton-Century-Crofts, 1936.

49. Williams, M. J., "Personal and familial problems of high school youth and their bearing upon family education needs," *Social Forces,* 27:279–285 (1949).

50. Witmer, Helen L., *et al.,* "The outcome of treatment of children rejected by their mothers," *Smith College Studies in Social Work,* 8:187–234 (1938).

51. Wolford, Opal P., "How early background affects dating behavior," *Journal of Home Economics,* 40:505–506 (1948).

CHAPTER XVI

Measuring Environment and Background

ABSTRACT

Personal relationships within the home can be evaluated through various informal channels such as interviews with parents, pupils, and neighbors. Observational and questionnaire techniques may also be used. Rapport is crucial to the validity of these evaluations. Socio-economic status can be evaluated by means of scales designed especially for this purpose; some can be filled out by students, but others require careful observation and interviewing. Thorndike's Ten-Item City Yard-stick provides a usable technique for determining the general goodness of life in a city. Average scores of representative pupils on socioeconomic status inventories and various social indices are also useful for acquiring insight into the nature of the community environment and background.

~·~·~·

In Chapter XV the environment and background of pupils was viewed as the home, the community, and the school. We considered the home in terms of parent-to-parent, parent-to-child, and child-to-child relationships. Social class membership, social role and status provide overall concepts for understanding significant dimensions of the environment. The present chapter will consider techniques for measuring and evaluating these aspects of the pupil's environment and background.

PARENT-TO-PARENT RELATIONSHIPS

The parent-to-parent relationships in the pupil's home environment have an importance in his adjustment and guidance that is

454

easily appreciated. In most situations, however, the evaluation of these relationships is difficult for the classroom teacher. This difficulty arises from the traditional aura of privacy that surrounds relationships between parents. How they feel toward each other, the sources of the major satisfactions and discontents in their life with each other, are usually considered to be strictly a "family matter" and none of the teacher's "business." A pupil may be maladjusted in school and be obviously suffering because of insufficient parental stability and emotional security, but it is nonetheless hazardous for a teacher to take direct steps toward investigating the relationships between his parents. Such efforts may easily be misunderstood as "prying" and may lead to serious conflict between teacher and parents and even between the school and the community as a whole.

Situations may arise in which it becomes almost imperative that some knowledge of interparental relationships be gained to determine whether certain aspects of a pupil's adjustment can be traced to some phase of the relationship between his parents. The teacher who lives in a community and is associated with the pupils' parents in matters of community concern will frequently be able to observe and evaluate these relationships through all the informal channels by which people ordinarily come to know one another. A friendly and receptive teacher who combines an interest in parents with a sense of professional responsibility can sometimes gain the parents' confidence to such an extent that informal interviews with them will yield relevant information.

When it is desirable to make a direct attempt to acquire insight into interparental relationships, a higher degree of parent-teacher rapport than usually exists must first be established. The procedure for establishing this will vary from parent to parent, but its general nature has been indicated by Baruch (2). In studying the "coexistence" of reported tensions in interparental relationships with behavior adjustment in young children, she employed interviews similar to those used by psychiatrists. As a result of frequent continuous contacts, parents felt at ease with the interviewer and were willing to relate intimate details concerning their lives. They observed her close relationship with their children and her interest in them. In the interviews parents were encouraged to express not only intellectualized facts but also their feelings and emotions. An attempt was made to encourage them to gain insight into their own emotions on the ground that these greatly affected their children and that no emotion could be a justifiable cause of guilt feelings.

The participation of parents in such interviews is best gained by explaining their purpose and their thoroughly confidential nature. The interviewer must make it clear that no confidences will ever be revealed to anyone. Furthermore, interviews should not adhere rigidly to any fixed schedule or outline. Within wide limits of relevance, parents should be encouraged to talk along any lines they choose in the freest and most natural manner possible.

In encouraging interviewees to reveal material that might be highly embarrassing or a source of feelings of shame and unworthiness, Baruch used the technique of reassurance on the basis of the commonness of similar facts in the lives of most people. The widespread occurrence of masturbation at various ages, of antagonism to parents and siblings, of childhood stealing, or of adolescent sex experimentation may all need to be pointed out to interviewees to keep them at ease and to maintain and improve rapport during the interview.

Myers (10) tried to evaluate interparental relationships through a questionnaire which can be filled out by high-school pupils. He prepared a set of questions one of whose six sections dealt with relations between parents. The other sections dealt with home membership, supervision, discipline, parent-child relations, and relations between children. The reliability of the complete questionnaire was .913 for the group of high-school students used in the study. When the questionnaire was filled out by guidance workers in the school and by social case workers in the community in the light of their knowledge of the pupil's family background, there was complete agreement between the pupils' answers and the raters' markings in 85 percent of the items.

PARENT-CHILD RELATIONSHIPS

Many studies of the influence of various parent-child relationships on children's adjustments have been made. Symonds (17) has classified these relationships along two dimensions: dominance-submission and acceptance-rejection. A parent's fluctuation between acceptance and rejection is called ambivalence; fluctuation between dominance and submission is called inconsistency.

Fitz-Simons (7) has prepared a guide for estimating parent attitudes to be used in evaluating case studies of parent-child relationships. After an elaborate case study has been made on the basis of many interviews with parents and observations of actual parental behavior and home situations, the guide can be applied so as to provide a quantitative index of the degree to which a parental attitude toward a child is negative or positive. Whenever the majority of the items recorded in the body of the scale fall on the positive side but certain Key-points in the scale indicate that the parent's attitude is essentially negative, that attitude may be considered overprotection or concealed rejection. In interviewing parents and pupils, during visits to the pupil's home, and in talks with the pupil at school, the teacher can use the concepts provided by Fitz-Simons as central points around which to arrange an evaluation of the parents' relationship to the child.

The child's attitude toward his parents may similarly be determined through interviews. As usual, rapport must be established in the friendliest, most mutually respectful terms possible if the interview is to have maximum success. Simpson (14) used a direct approach among others, asking the child, "Whom do you like best at home?" Meltzer (9) has used what he terms the Single Free Association Interview. He met each child individually and engaged in a preliminary conversation to further rapport. The child was then instructed about the procedure as a game that would be fun and take only a little time. Thus the experimenter would say a key word and the child would "shoot out," without holding back, the first ten ideas or words that came to his mind in connection with the given word, regardless of whether they were silly or embarrassing. After some preliminary trials with innocuous words the pupils were given the word "mother" and then "father."

By this technique Meltzer hoped to secure the fundamental underlying attitude of the child toward his parents with a minimum of disguises and socially acceptable pretenses. As typical of the results obtained with his method, Meltzer presents the following:

Fourteen-year-old Italian girl from low economic level school—I.Q. 95. Father thirty-five years old; mother forty-four. Parents are Catholic and go to church regularly. Girl associates with family friends. Attended a settlement house and quit because considered children there too rough. Fairly popular in classroom. Cries easily if disappointed. Is leader in athletic activities in school.

Reaction to Mother: Nice—gentle—kind—kind to animals—nice to people—polite—she's not very good-looking—she likes comedians and she likes Russian music—she likes Polish music too,—she's not so nice sometimes (sometimes she has to scold you)—she doesn't like to go to shows—she doesn't care for nice clothes—likes to go riding (auto)—she likes to read stories.

Reaction to Father: Rather good-looking—unselfish—likes to hunt and fish—likes to work—likes animals—likes dogs—he likes always to be out in the open air—he owns a clubhouse—he has picnics almost every Sunday—he likes to tinker with guns—he likes to give things—he likes to have good times—when he gets to scolding he scolds for rather a long time but that's not so often.

From such reactions to the words "mother" and "father," teachers can acquire insight into a pupil's attitudes toward his parents, the degree of his dependence on them, the parents' characteristic role in his world, and similar determiners of his feelings of emotional security and personal worth.

Classroom teachers do not usually have the training in clinical psychology necessary for the best application of Meltzer's technique. It may prove serviceable when used with children with whom a high degree of rapport has been established. The interpretation of the results obtained will be necessarily qualitative rather than quantitative but may be sufficient when the teacher's main purpose is to discover whether a pupil's attitudes toward his parents are at the root of some difficulty in adjustment.

Stott (15) constructed a questionnaire to measure for a group of rural pupils in Nebraska what he calls the "Family-Life Variable" or the pattern of confidence, affection, and companionability in the pupil's home life. Typical items in his questionnaire are given below. The positive aspect of the Family-Life Variable is manifested by adolescents who tend to say:

1. They rarely assume the attitude expressed by "What my folks don't know won't hurt them."

2. They try out what their parents advise.
3. They deserve the punishment they get.
4. Every member of the family has "his say" in what the family does as a group.
5. Their parents listen to their side when they disagree with the parents.
6. Their parents sometimes admit that they are wrong.
7. They like to do extra little things to please the other members of the family.
8. They would enjoy being shut in with the family on a rainy day.

The negative aspect of the variable is represented by pupils who admit:

1. They think "Oh, what's the use" after trying to explain their conduct to their parents.
2. They "talk back" to mother.
3. They get scolded for every little thing.
4. Father resents it when they disagree with him.
5. Other young folks seem to have more fun with their families than they.
6. Their parents do things that make them appear foolish.
7. Father nags and scolds.
8. They have more fun away from home.

Scores obtained by two children in the same family on a questionnaire of 64 such items correlated with each other to only a very low degree. This indicates that family life may be a different matter for each of the children in a family, rather than a general, objective home environment. That is, the responses of students to such questions reveal their own personal adjustment to their parents and their family situations relative to themselves rather than absolute and for the family as a whole. One of the children in a family may be well adjusted and derive emotional satisfaction from his relationships with his parents, while another child in the same family may see his family in a different light and be maladjusted in it. Thus it appears that within the same general family situation there may be very different *affective* environments for different children in the family.

All the foregoing has referred to a variety of attempts to make sense out of the relationships between parents and children. Inevitably, however, the suspicion remains that important aspects of these relationships have been neglected. For this reason we turn to one of the most comprehensive attempts to describe parent-child relationships in all the complexity that everyone, from his experience in growing up in a family, knows these relationships to have. This attempt was made at the Samuel S. Fels Research Institute by Champneys, whose 30 items for such rating are reproduced here (1).

1. Home atmosphere
- 1.1 Adjustment of home: The general internal adjustment of the family, its stability, satisfaction and happiness.
- 1.2 Activeness of the home: The activity level of the home, its quickness and alertness.
- 1.5 Discord in the home: A general atmosphere of conflict, discord, recrimination in the home.
- 1.6a Sociability of the family: The degree to which the energies of the family are directed outward from the home toward society. Degree of participation in community affairs.
- 1.7 Coordination of household: The smoothness with which the routines of the house are carried on. The effectiveness of the schedule.
- 1.91 Child-centeredness of the home: The degree to which the organization of the household is built around the child's needs and welfare.

2. Contact of child and mother
- 2.11 Duration of contact with mother: Hours per day of contact.
- 2.12 Intensity of contact with mother: The reactivity of the parent in contacts.

3. The control and influence of parent on child
- 3.11 Restrictiveness of regulations: The restrictiveness and severity of the standards to which the child is expected to conform.
- 3.12 Readiness of enforcement: The vigilance with which the parent enforces regulations; his follow up; his watchfulness for infraction of rules.
- 3.13 Severity of penalties: Rated in terms of their impressiveness for the particular child, not in terms of objective standards.
- 3.14 Justification of disciplinary policy as presented to child: The parent's tendency to explain reasons for requirements and penalties. The logic of the policy from the child's point of view.

3.15 Democracy of regulation and enforcement policy: The extent to which the child shares in the formulation of regulations.

3.16 Clarity of policy of regulations and enforcement: The clearness with which the standards of child conduct are manifested to the child.

3.17 Effectiveness of policy: The degree to which the child's behavior meets the standards set by the parent. In the eyes of parent, how well behaved is the child.

3.18 Disciplinary friction: The amount of overt parent-child conflict over questions of policy.

3.21 Quantity of suggestion: The parent's tendency to make suggestions, requests, commands, hints and other directive attempts.

3.22 Coerciveness of suggestion: The extent to which the parent's suggestions are dictatorial and coercive.

3.3 Accelerational attempt: The parent's deliberate efforts to increase by special training the child's maturation rate.

4. *Babying and protectiveness*

4.1 General babying: The parent's tendency to help child over difficulties even when the child is perfectly capable.

4.2 General protectiveness: The parent's tendency to keep the child sheltered from threats and hazards of all sorts.

5. *Criticism and evaluation of the child*

5.1 Readiness of criticism: The parent's tendency to express and evaluate attitude toward the child's behavior regardless of whether it is an approving or disapproving one.

5.2 Direction of criticism: The extent to which the criticism is approving or disapproving. A high rating indicates approval.

6. *Readiness of explanation*

61. Readiness of explanation: The parent's tendency to satisfy the child's intellectual curiosity. His response to "why?" and "how?"

7. *Emotional relationships between parent and child*

7.1 Solicitousness for child's welfare: Tendency to be overconcerned and anxious for the child's well-being.

7.2 Acceptance of the child: Acceptance of the child as an intimate and inseparable partner, sharing in all areas of parent's life.

8. *Miscellaneous*

8.1 Understanding: The extent of the parent's insight into the child's wishes, needs, point of view, level of development, etc.

8.2 Emotionality: The emotionality of the parent in his behavior toward the child.

8.3   Affectionateness: The parent's expression of affection to the child.

8.4   Rapport: The closeness of the psychological relationship between parent and child.

As the reader inspects this list of 30 dimensions of parent behavior, he may feel that they are not all distinct, that some of them generally tend to go along with others. When these 30 variables were used by a highly trained observer in describing 125 families on the basis of careful observations and interviews, this was indeed found to be the case. This observer's ratings were intercorrelated and then subjected to what was termed a "syndrome analysis." This consisted of putting together the variables that tended to be highly intercorrelated and also made psychological sense when viewed as aspects of a common tendency. The following three syndromes emerged from this analysis:

Democracy in the home:

3.14 Justification of policy
3.15 Democracy of policy
3.22 Non-coerciveness of suggestions
6.1   Readiness of explanation
5.2   Direction of criticism (approval)
3.16 Clarity of policy
8.1   Understanding of the child
3.11 Nonrestrictiveness of regulations

Acceptance of the child:

7.2   Acceptance of the child
8.4   Rapport with the child
8.3   Affectionateness toward child
5.2   Direction of criticism (approval)
3.17 Effectiveness of policy
1.91 Child-centeredness of the home
3.18 Nondisciplinary friction

Indulgence:

4.2   General protectiveness
4.1   General babying
1.91 Child-centeredness of the home
7.2   Acceptance of the child

7.1 Solicitousness for child's welfare

2.11 Duration of contact with mother

2.12 Intensity of contact with mother

If each of these syndromes were considered to exist at three levels, high, middle, and low, we could immediately specify 27 different patterns of parent behavior. Actually, most of the families fell into seven groups.

Since not all 27 varieties of families were found, this meant that the syndromes were themselves not completely independent. This was also found to be true of the seven common factors isolated by Roff (13). These seven factors were "concern for the child," "democratic guidance," "permissiveness," "parent-child harmony," "sociability-adjustment of parents," "activeness of home," and "non-readiness of suggestion."

But these seven factors were themselves correlated. Consequently, in a search for underlying factors of a broad character, Lorr and Jenkins (8) performed a "second-order" factor analysis of the intercorrelations among the seven factors isolated by Roff. Their three factors may be represented by the following three questions:

1. How far does this home sustain and encourage dependence and how far does it deny satisfaction to dependence?

2. How far do its methods of child training reflect democratic practices and values, or to what extent are they authoritarian and undemocratic?

3. To what extent is there a strict orderliness in the home and to what extent is the home lax and unorganized?

These successive analyses of the dimensions of parental behavior can be used in various ways. The most abstract set, the three proposed by Lorr and Jenkins, are at once the most inclusive and, by the same token, the least concrete. Roff's seven dimensions provide more detail, and the original set developed by Champneys, with all their overlapping, make possible the most specific ways of describing parent-child relationships.

Data concerning parent-child relationships must usually be evaluated informally by means of conversations with pupils and their parents and observations of the behavior of parents and children in such areas as have been indicated by the above illustrative items. Aggressive problem behavior of pupils may thus sometimes be traced to rejection by one or both parents. Excessively submissive or withdrawing behavior may similarly be traced to over-accepting or submissive parental attitudes toward the pupils. Inconsistent parental attitudes in either dominance-submissiveness or acceptance-rejection (ambivalence) also usually result in some form of child maladjustment.

CHILD-TO-CHILD RELATIONSHIPS

Child-to-child relationships within the family frequently operate in conjunction with parent-child relationships to produce the particular pattern of adjustment or maladjustment exhibited by a pupil in school. Frequently some insight into the parents' relationships to the other children in the family and of the latter to each other is necessary to make a given pupil's mode of adjustment more understandable. The relationships of the parents to the other children in the family can be evaluated by the techniques discussed above.

In general, it is not sufficient to ascertain merely that a pupil is an only or an intermediate or a youngest child. The factor of "only-ness," or position in order of birth, has been found to have a less predictable effect on the personality of the individual than the more directly psychological relationships between children. In this connection it is worth noting that all first-born children are "only" children until a second child is born. Such relationships between children as hero worship, shame, jealousy, and parent-child substitution may prove to be fruitful hypotheses or "things to look for" in investigating the relationship between children in the same family.

Whenever it is possible to observe two children of the same family together, it may be possible to classify the relationship between them and to draw inferences from this relationship regarding the adjustment of a pupil. Frequently, however, such inferences may be obtained merely from conversations with a pupil about brothers and sisters and from known facts concerning his educational achievement, physical status, mental abilities, emotional and social adjustment, and the attitudes of his brothers and sisters. If a pupil has a sibling who is markedly superior or inferior in one or more of these aspects, these facts may be inserted into the total picture of his personality when it is interpreted as a basis for guidance. The pupil whose brother has preceded him in school and been a star athlete and the valedictorian of his high-school class may, for example, easily set goals for himself that are too high in the light of his own abilities. Feelings of inferiority and discouragement may result from such a relationship. A pupil's adjustment to the opposite sex may similarly be related to the presence or absence of siblings of the opposite sex in his own family. The boy who is surpassed by his younger brother in gaining academic honors or other forms of social approval; the girl with very masculine brothers who becomes a tomboy; the boy who expresses like or dislike of a vocation or curriculum because of his older brother's favorable or unfavorable experience with it—these relationships and many others between children in the same family frequently provide the major clue to understanding adjustment problems in providing guidance for an individual pupil. The literature of psychology gives no hard and fast rules for interpreting such family relationships. Rather the teacher must use all his ingenuity, powers of observation, and ability to establish rapport in ascertaining the facts of these relationships and interpreting their unique meaning for the adjustment of the individual pupil.

SOCIOECONOMIC STATUS

SINGLE INDICES

The socioeconomic status of a pupil's family may be evaluated on the basis of a single index or, more adequately, through the investigation of a larger number of carefully selected indices. In small communities or in rural schools, the socioeconomic status may be so homogeneous and easily identifiable from the teacher's general knowledge of the community that any formal investigation is unnecessary. When this is not the case, a teacher can ascertain it only by an explicit attempt to secure relevant information. The most frequently used single index of socioeconomic status is father's occupation. Various ways of classifying occupations have been used for this purpose. Occupational classifications according to socioeconomic status deal not with the types of abilities required, but with the social prestige, income, or general "goodness of living" which usually follows in the wake of a given paternal occupation. Beckman (3) has presented a classification of occupations according to the intelligence, skill, and education or training required as well as the socioeconomic prestige given to them. For each of the following five grades Beckman listed representative occupations of which we shall present only the first three:

I. Unskilled manual occupations
   Farm laborers
   Lumbermen, raftsmen, and woodchoppers
   Laborers (construction, manufacturing, road, warehouse, etc.)
II. Semi-skilled occupations
   Fishermen and oystermen
   Mine operators
   Filers, grinders, buffers
IIIA. Skilled manual occupations
   Farm owners and tenants
   Apprentices to building and other skilled trades
   Bakers
IIIB. Skilled white-collar occupations
   Freight and express agents
   Mail clerks and carriers
   Radio, telegraph, and telephone operators
IVA. Subprofessional occupations
   Opticians
   Undertakers
   Actors and showmen
IVB. Business occupations
   Owners and proprietors of garages, truck, and cab companies
   Conductors (steam railroad)
   Postmasters
IVC. Minor supervisory occupations
   Farm managers and foremen ·
   Mine foremen and overseers
   Manufacturing foremen and overseers
VA. Professional occupations (linguistic)
   Authors, editors, and reporters
   Clergymen
   College presidents and professors

VB. Professional occupations (scientific)
    Architects
    Artists, sculptors, and teachers of art
    Chemists, assayers, and metallurgists
VC. Managerial and executive occupations
    Owners and managers of log and timber camps
    Mine operators, managers, and officials
    Manufacturing managers and officials, and manufacturers

It is evident that this ranking is by no means perfectly correlated with financial income. The cultural, aesthetic, and social prestige of the occupation is the major criterion. The income of many skilled workmen is greater than that of some professional workers such as clergymen or teachers, but the social status of these latter occupations is usually considered superior. The advantages enjoyed by pupils whose fathers rank high in this classification usually enable them to attain superior average status in educational achievement and adjustment.

Income as an index of socioeconomic status must, of course, take into account the size of the family and the age and sex of its members. Sydenstricker (16) included these factors in his "Ammain" scale. Each member of the family is assigned a number of units based on sex and age, and the sum of the units for all the members of the family is obtained. The monthly family income is then divided by this total to obtain the index of socioeconomic status.

Other single indices of socioeconomic status are such possessions as a telephone, an automobile, a vacuum cleaner, or a bathtub. The inadequacy of these single indices of the home environment for the understanding of an individual pupil's background is self-evident; homes that are distinguished from one another by one of these factors almost inevitably overlap to a large degree in their possession of other desirable environmental factors. For example, homes with a telephone differ widely from one another in parental occupation, family income, cultural advancement, and aesthetic sensitivity. Some of them may rank below homes without telephones in these various aspects of the home environment. This overlapping holds true for other single indices; families with the same paternal occupation or family income index may differ widely from one another in other aspects of the home environment.

Multiple Indices

To overcome the lack of precision and inadequate coverage of the total scope of factors affecting a family's socioeconomic status, various methods employing multiple measures of environment have been devised.

The Kerr-Remmers American Home Scale[1] contains 50 items answerable by any pupil in the sixth grade or above. The items are classified into cultural, aesthetic, economic, and miscellaneous sections. This classification was made by a type of factor analysis so as to obtain meaningful clusters of items while reducing the intercorrelations of the clusters to a minimum; minimizing the intercorrelations serves to make the scores on the four parts as independent as possible and to increase the diagnostic value of the scale. By using statistical analysis in conjunction with subjective opinion concerning the significance of each item, it was possible to insure that the *actual* interrelationships of the items, as well as their surface meaning, would influence the grouping.

The correlation with American Home Scale scores of 60 pairs of siblings was .84. Reliability by the split-half method was found to be .89, and by the Kuder-Richardson formula .91. The following illustrate the types of items on the Kerr-Remmers scale:

House and Home: Answer these questions by checking "yes" or "no" in the space below.
Does your family have:
A. a vacuum cleaner?   Yes .... No ....
B. an electric or gas refrigerator?   Yes .... No ....
C. a bathtub or a shower with running water?   Yes .... No ....
D. a telephone?   Yes .... No ....
E. an automobile?   Yes .... No ....
F. Have you had paid lessons in dancing, dramatics, expression, elocution, art, or music outside of school?   Yes .... No ....

The foregoing items also constitute the brief scale for measuring socioeconomic status used by the Purdue Opinion Panel. Remmers and Kirk (12) have furnished evidence concerning the scalability (uni-dimensionality) and validity of this brief scale.

[1] Published by Psychometric Affiliates, Box 1625, Chicago 90, Illinois.

For the rapid and efficient evaluation of the socioeconomic status of large numbers of pupils in the upper elementary and secondary-school grades, the American Home Scale provides a highly practicable technique. The scale has been standardized only on urban homes. The value of the particular items in any instrument that measures socioeconomic status may vary from time to time as social customs and technological facilities change. Fireplaces in the home may eventually become signs of cultural retardation rather than cultural advantage. The value of such items as "Central heating system?" and "Does your family leave the city every year for a vacation?" may vary widely in different geographic sections of the country. Such considerations, however, reduce the meaningfulness of the scores obtained to only a slight degree. Within ordinary limits of time and geography the scale provides evaluations of real significance.

The Index of Status Characteristics developed by Warner and others (19) requires that an interviewer obtain the necessary information on four characteristics of the person whose status is being measured: occupation, source of income, house type, and dwelling area. The information concerning each one of these is rated on a 7-point scale; this rating is then multiplied by a weight of 4 for occupation, 3 for source of income, 3 for house type, and 2 for dwelling area. The sum of these weighted ratings is interpreted by processes described in detail in Warner, et al. (19). In general, these authors have found that in any fair-sized urban community six levels of social class can be identified: upper-upper, lower-upper, upper-middle, lower-middle, upper-lower, and lower-lower.

A comparison of the rationale, content, technique, and results of the American Home Scale and the Index of Status Characteristics has been made by Finch and Hoehn (6). Apart from the fact that the American Home Scale can be administered by untrained persons during the normal routine of the classroom, whereas the ISC requires individual administration, it is of interest that the results of the two measures were found to be highly but definitely imperfectly correlated when applied to a sample of 197 school children aged 12 and 13 in a midwestern city. The correlation between the two scales was .71. If the reliabilities of the two instruments are assumed to be roughly what was reported by their authors in earlier studies, this would mean that even when corrected for imperfect reliability, the correlation between the two scales would be less than 1.00. An additional conclusion by Finch and Hoehn is as follows: "The quality of *ISC* results depends upon painstaking application by skilled observers. The *AHS* uses a questionnaire form that can be conveniently administered and scored by persons with relatively little technical training. This questionnaire form introduces a special limitation because it includes obvious status-bearing items. On signed questionnaires such as these, there is a strong tendency for respondents to give false answers to questions characterized by a high level of ego-involvement" (6 : 66).

THE COMMUNITY

Thorndike (18) has provided a list of items to evaluate the "general goodness of life for good people" in American cities. A reading of his engrossing and enlightening little book, *Your City,* is necessary for a more complete and critical understanding of his technique; here, however, it is only possible to describe his general approach for measuring the general goodness of one's own city. Thorndike demonstrates that American cities differ from one another widely in such factors as retention of boys and girls in school, number of domestic installations of gas per 100 inhabitants in 1930, number of telephones per 100 inhabitants in 1930, number of radios per 100 inhabitants in 1930, infant death rate for 1926–1934, death rate from typhoid fever for six years near 1930, and many other items that may be considered related to health, creature comforts, education, recreation, social decency, literacy, and similar factors. The full meaning of "general goodness" of living in a community may, of course, be obtained only from the specific items which enter into Thorndike's measurements.

Thorndike measured 310 cities with an index consisting of 37 items carefully selected from an original group of 297. Selecting the 200 cities remaining after the exclusion of (1) residential suburbs and other cities adjoining much larger cities, (2) the cities of the old South, and (3) the giant cities, he found that "the goodness of life in a city is explainable only in part (about one-fourth) by wealth and income. . . . The goodness of life in a city has deeper roots than its present wealth and income" (18 : 62).

On the other hand, the personal qualities of the residents, such as the number of persons per 1000 inhabitants graduating from public high schools, or the percentage of literacy in the total population, or the per capita number of deaths from syphilis (reversed), explained about 43 percent of the goodness of life in a city. That is, "cities are made better than others in this country primarily and chiefly by getting able and good people as residents. . . . The second important cause of welfare is income" (18 : 67).

Of Thorndike's 37 items, many cannot be obtained conveniently. In order to enable ordinary citizens to secure a fairly accurate measure of the general goodness of their own city, Thorndike has provided the Ten-item City Yard-stick. These ten items can be obtained for "almost any city in a few hours, and . . . will tell fairly well how the city stands in its general goodness."

The Ten-item City Yard-stick can provide teachers with a better idea than is otherwise obtainable of the kind of community in which they are teaching and in which their pupils live. Other notions of the general goodness of a community can be obtained by averaging the scores of large numbers of pupils on scales of socioeconomic status. Its general nature is thus described in terms of averages of the units, components, or individual families of which it is composed. The community within a community represented by an individual school or classroom may be described by the average socioeconomic status of the homes from which its pupils come.

The technique of estimating the "goodness of living" of a city by averaging the scores of its pupils on a scale of socioeconomic status was applied by Remmers and Kerr (11). They measured 16,455 eighth-grade pupils in 42 different cities by means of the American Home Scale. The correlations between average American Home Scale scores and Thorndike's G (goodness) index was .34; with Thorndike's P (personal factors) and I (income indices) the correlations were substantially zero. Since the two measuring devices correlate only slightly, the relative effect of what they measure on the adjustment of children remains an open question.

⟮In becoming acquainted with the community, the neighborhood, or the broad segment of environment in which pupils live, the teacher may use all the informal approaches that are available to any socially sensitive citizen. Talking with one's neighbors, with the parents of pupils, with "the man on the street," will provide valuable insights into the political, economic, and social structures of the community. The political corruption or decency of a town or city, the real centers of political power—whether these are in the hands of a local manufacturer, the Chamber of Commerce, or any other nongovernmental group—can thus be ascertained. The local economic structure, the dominant industry, the rising and declining branches of economic enterprise, the population trends and shifts, the transportation facilities can all be readily studied and evaluated by a teacher who is an alert member of the community. The local newspaper may be a valuable index to the attitudinal make-up of the community, its liberalism or conservatism. Its attitudes toward school policies and curricula should be closely followed by the teacher who is concerned with the whole pupil. Only by living in and with the community can he understand the major sources of pupil and parent attitudes. The religious composition of the community, whether it be Catholic, Protestant, Jewish, or any other faith, must similarly be understood by the teacher as part of the total picture of the environment and background.⟯

THE STATE AND NATION

The home, the school, and the community are all part of a larger political and social unit, the state. It is well known that the forty-eight states differ markedly in the social, economic, and political dimensions that affect the development of their children⟯ A striking illustration of this fact was found by Davenport and Remmers (4). They used an index of the educational product of a state's school system: the average score, obtained by candidates for the A-12 V-12 college training program, on selection examinations given during World War II. These mean scores were correlated with a variety of variables concerning the states, with the results shown in Table 26.

These substantial relationships probably have no simple mean-

TABLE 26. Correlation Between State Mean on A-12 V-12 Test
and Certain Data on State School Systems
(All r's corrected for broad groupings)

State mean and average teacher's salary................	.63 ± .06
State mean and average total per-pupil cost.............	.77 ± .04
State mean and average current per-pupil cost...........	.80 ± .03

ing. A complex of factors is involved; the degree of industrialization, urbanization, and cosmopolitanism characterizing the state enters into the determination of its students' achievement on examinations. This means that improvement of this achievement could not be brought about overnight merely by increasing the salaries of teachers or the per pupil expenditures for schools. Such findings indicate that school personnel can better understand the achievement of their students in the light of the total culture of the state in which they work.

In another study the same authors (5) carried out a factor analysis of 13 variables concerning the forty-eight states, including each state's average score on the qualifying examination. They found four factors: a state economic factor, a rural-urban factor, a North-South factor, and a fourth unnamed factor.

The multiple correlation of four variables—automobile registrations per thousand, number killed in World War I per thousand, residents in *Who's Who* per hundred thousand, and telephones per thousand—with the average state scores was .962. The authors conclude: "These data are all state data; they do not apply to individuals. Without much facetiousness, however, we interpret these results to mean that the possibilities of reaching a high educational achievement are much greater if one comes from a high income state which is highly urban, which is not in the South, and which has such advantages as library service available to most of its population, has a high proportion of foreign-born citizens, a large number of residents in *Who's Who*, and many telephones."

In evaluating the community in which his pupils live, the teacher should not disregard the total society, the world of which all communities and nations are a part. War and peace, economic prosperity and depression, political stability and chaos all have their effects on pupils and must be comprehended in the total picture of the pupil's environment and background. The repercussions of world events on one's own community should be observed and interpreted in relation to pupil adjustment. Especially in communities of heterogeneous national origin or racial composition should the effects of international relations be evident.

Population movements within the nation, like those dealt with in Steinbeck's *The Grapes of Wrath* and Leighton's *The Governing of Men,* may introduce further conflicts within a community. Migrants and their cultures may require special understanding by a teacher both for their own worth and for their effect upon and relationships with the more permanent members of the community.

Class-consciousness within a community needs to be appreciated and evaluated if the social adjustment of pupils is to be fully evaluated. To what extent is there a feeling of difference, a social distance, between rich and poor? How homogeneous is the socioeconomic status of a group of pupils in a given school? And to what extent does class-consciousness facilitate or hamper the social interaction and adjustment of any pupil or group of pupils?

REFERENCES

1. Baldwin, A. L., Kalhorn, Joan, and Breese, Fay Huffman, "Patterns of parent behavior," *Psychological Monographs,* Vol. 58, No. 3 (Whole No. 268) (1945).
2. Baruch, Dorothy W., "A study of reported tension in interparental relationships as co-existent with behavior adjustment in young children," *Journal of Experimental Education,* 6:187–204 (1937).
3. Beckman, R. O., "A new scale for gauging occupational rank," *Personnel Journal,* 13:225–233 (1934).
4. Davenport, K. S., and Remmers, H. H., "Educational achievement as compared with money spent on schools," *School and Society,* 61:333–335 (1945).
5. Davenport, K. S., and Remmers, H. H., "Factors in state characteristics related to average A-12 V-12 test scores," *Journal of Educational Psychology,* 41:110–115 (1950).
6. Finch, F. H., and Hoehn, A. J., "Measuring socio-economic or cultural status: a comparison of methods," *Journal of Social Psychology,* 33:51–67 (1951).
7. Fitz-Simons, Marion J., *Some Parent-Child Relationships as Shown*

in Clinical Case Studies, New York: Bureau of Publications, Teachers College, Columbia University, Contributions to Education No. 643, 1935.

8. Lorr, M., and Jenkins, R. L., "Three factors in parent behavior," *Journal of Consulting Psychology,* 17:306–308 (1953).

9. Meltzer, H., "Sex differences in parental preference patterns," *Character and Personality,* 10:114–128 (1941).

10. Myers, T. R., *Intrafamily Relationships and Pupil Adjustment,* New York: Bureau of Publications, Teachers College, Columbia University, Contributions to Education No. 651, 1935.

11. Remmers, H. H., and Kerr, W. A., "Home environment in American cities," *American Journal of Sociology,* 51:233–237 (1945).

12. Remmers, H. H., and Kirk, R. B., "Scalability and validity of the socio-economic status items of the *Purdue Opinion Panel,*" *Journal of Applied Psychology,* 37:384–386 (1953).

13. Roff, M., "A factorial study of the Fels Parent Behavior Scale," *Child Development,* 20:29–44 (1949).

14. Simpson, M., *Parent Preferences of Young Children,* New York: Bureau of Publications, Teachers College, Columbia University, Contributions to Education No. 652, 1935.

15. Stott, L. H., "Parent-adolescent adjustment, its measurement and significance," *Character and Personality,* 10:140–150 (1941).

16. Sydenstricker, E., and King, W. I., "The measurement of the relative economic status of families," *Quarterly Publications of the American Statistical Association,* 17:842–857 (1921).

17. Symonds, P. M., *The Psychology of Parent-Child Relationships,* New York: Appleton-Century-Crofts, 1939.

18. Thorndike, E. L., *Your City,* New York: Harcourt, Brace & Company, Inc., 1938.

19. Warner, W. L., Meeker, Marchia, and Eells, K., *Social Class in America, a Manual of Procedure for the Measurement of Social Status,* Chicago: Science Research Associates, 1949.

CHAPTER XVII

Evaluating School Personnel

ABSTRACT

The teacher's importance as a factor affecting the intellectual and emotional development of pupils is so great that no thoroughgoing evaluation of the pupil's environment can be made without evaluating the pupil's teacher. Teachers can be evaluated either on the basis of the changes they bring about in pupils or on those aspects of themselves that are presumably related to their effectiveness in bringing about desirable changes in pupils. The first basis, while of unquestionable validity, is beset with so many difficulties as to be impracticable in most situations. The second should be applied in terms of both cognitive and noncognitive attitudinal aspects. Various tests of mental ability and intellectual-cultural attainment are available for evaluating cognitive aspects. Teachers' attitudes and opinions concerning child psychology and pupils' emotional and social adjustment may be evaluated by means of various inventories. Other aspects of the teacher's effect on pupils may be ascertained by pupil ratings of teachers. The procedure for obtaining these ratings is practicable and the results are valid when properly interpreted. Counselors and administrators can be evaluated by devices parallel to those used for teachers—inventories and rating scales.

.~.~.~.

THE TEACHER

"Common sense," psychology, and psychiatry agree that the teacher is the most important factor in the school situation with respect to pupil adjustment. This is true whether we conceive of

476

the teacher's functions in the narrow sense of teaching only sub-ject matter or in the broader sense of the school's concern with the pupil's whole personality—physically, intellectually, emotionally, and socially. The pupil's learning is conditioned not only by "how much the teacher knows" (subject matter) but also to a considera-ble extent by the personality traits of the teacher and the psy-chological relationships between teacher and pupil.

Since the teacher plays so important a role in the various aspects of pupils with which this volume is concerned, any thoroughgoing evaluation of the pupil's environment must include evaluation of the teacher.

The importance of the teacher to the pupils' learning and ad-justment derives from his position as one of the major channels for the transmission of the facts, knowledge, skills, attitudes, and ideas of our culture. It is his function to change pupils in the direc-tion of greater saturation with the desirable elements of the cul-ture in which they live. This role endows teachers with an author-ity that increases their power to mold pupil personality. Pupils spend more of their waking hours with teachers than with any other adult, including parents. They are probably more imitative of their teachers, more susceptible to their influences for good or evil, than is true of any other adult other than their parents. Conse-quently, if a teacher is to understand a pupil, he must understand himself.

TEACHER SELF-EVALUATION

How can teachers be evaluated? Our answers to this question will be made primarily from the point of view of the teacher eval-uating himself rather than being evaluated by school superintend-ents, principals, or supervisors. This point of view means that this evaluation becomes essentially a democratic process of self-supervi-sion based on the assumption that the teacher is eager for self-im-provement, rather than that supervision from above is necessary to motivate him toward improving his work in guiding pupil devel-opment. Most of the techniques described below can be applied either by administrators and supervisors or by teachers themselves. These techniques have been more frequently used by research workers and administrators than by teachers. But the major emphasis in the discussion is the potentiality of these techniques for self-evaluation.

APPROACHES TO TEACHER EVALUATION

The approaches to teacher evaluation may be of two kinds (24, 28). One evaluates the merit of teachers on the basis of the changes they produce in pupils. This approach is simply a reflection of the primary aim of all educational endeavor, namely, to effect desirable changes in pupils. The merit of any other instrumentality of education, be it a textbook, a school building, a principal, a curriculum, or a teaching method, may similarly be evaluated in terms of its effectiveness in producing these changes. The other approach evaluates any aspects of teachers that may be considered *related* to their effectiveness in producing desirable changes in pupils. Among the aspects which have been considered thus related are all those discussed in terms of pupils in this book. The teacher's own scholastic achievement, general and special mental abilities, emotional and social adjustment, attitudes and interests, socioeconomic environment and background, and physical aspects may all be evaluated when it is desired to estimate his effectiveness in producing desirable changes in pupils.

TEACHER EVALUATION BASED ON PUPIL CHANGES

General Nature. Let us first consider in more detail the nature of the "pupil-changes" approach to the evaluation of teachers. This approach involves first of all some definition of the types of changes teachers should effect. These changes may be defined in terms of any of the various aspects of pupils thus far discussed. Needless to say, the aspect that is most often considered a criterion of teaching success is the pupils' achievement of instructional objectives as these were presented in Chapter II. Typical of these objectives are ability to solve arithmetic problems, ability to read rapidly and with comprehension, and understanding of a particular topic in American history. When instructional objectives are formulated so as to include particular attitudes toward activities, institutions, or other attitude objects, the teacher's success may be evaluated through desirable changes in pupils' attitudes. It has been shown (19, 20) that teachers who differ in liberalism have significantly different effects on their pupils' liberalism and information concerning contemporary affairs.

Among other aspects of pupils thus considered are various traits of character and personality, themselves essentially attitude configurations, which may not be explicitly included in formal lists of instructional objectives but are nevertheless considered desirable products of any teacher's influence on his pupils. Obviously, such aspects as pupils' physical traits, general mental ability, and socioeconomic background are not usually expected to change appreciably under the teacher's influence and consequently are seldom used as criteria for the evaluation of teachers. Physical health and the pupil's home environment may, however, be improved as the result of instruction in applied dietetics, home economics, and similar fields. The school or teacher could then reasonably be evaluated on the basis of the changes in diet, health, or aesthetics of the home at which instruction is aimed. Such an evaluation program has been outlined by Clark (7) in an attempt to determine whether the schools can improve the diet of a community.

In any case, whatever aspect of pupils is selected as the one in which certain changes are desired, the general scheme for teacher evaluation is to secure a measure of the status of the pupils *before* and *after* they come under the teacher's influence. The difference between these two scores is taken as the measure of the change in pupils during the time they have been under his influence. Arithmetic achievement, for example, can be measured with a standard arithmetic achievement test before and after the pupils have been taught by a given teacher. If the scores on the test greatly increase, it may be inferred that the teacher is capable and efficient in teaching arithmetic, whereas if only a small increase or a decrease has occurred the opposite conclusion is drawn. But certain cautions are necessary if these conclusions are to be valid.

ADVANTAGES AND DIFFICULTIES

The major advantage of this approach to the evaluation of teaching success is its unquestionable validity, for there can be no argument against the thesis that the teacher who produces desirable changes in his pupils in the most aspects and to the greatest degree is the best teacher. If this approach were readily available to school administrators and individual teachers, the problem of teacher evaluation might be considered solved.

In practice, however, this approach is so difficult that it is usually used only in experimental research as a criterion for more practical procedures and devices for teacher evaluation. The difficulties should be discussed both for the light they throw upon the nature of this approach and for the insight thus afforded into the problems of educational research. The use of the criterion of pupil changes raises the problems of defining what changes are desirable and of measuring such changes. These problems refer immediately to the what and the how of educational measurement and pupil evaluation.

A second set of difficulties in evaluating through pupil changes involves the problem of insuring that any differences or changes observed are due solely to the influence of the teacher and not to other influences. A group of pupils may achieve instructional objectives to a greater or lesser degree, dependent on any of the following factors other than the teacher's influence:

1. General mental ability of the pupils
2. Special mental abilities of pupils related to particular types of achievement
3. Past educational experiences, or the amount and quality of the instruction received in earlier grades. It is difficult to hold this factor constant solely by equating scores on an achievement test given before a specific teacher's influence becomes active.
4. Pupil motivation
5. The pupil's socioeconomic background and environment, especially the cultural level of the home and community in which he lives
6. The instructional materials, such as textbooks, manuals, workbooks, maps, visual materials, laboratory equipment, and notebooks which the teacher can use
7. The amount and quality of the supervisory assistance and leadership provided to the teacher
8. The teaching load and extracurricular duties of the teacher
9. The general attitude toward work that characterizes the school as a whole or particular segments of the community

10. The quality of instruction in areas of the curriculum other than the one for which a given teacher is responsible or in which he is being evaluated. This is important because the influence of all of a pupil's teachers and of instruction in all areas of the curriculum often has an effect on the pupil's achievement of any specific set of instructional objectives

11. The pupils' achievement of objectives other than those evaluated by the test or other device. The real worth of a teacher's influence may be reflected not so much in his pupils' information and knowledge, which are most easily evaluated by available tests, as in their attitudes and emotional and social adjustments

Because of the difficulty of taking into account all of these and other factors in pupil achievement, the approach to teacher evaluation through desirable changes in pupils cannot readily be used either by school administrators or by teachers themselves for self-evaluation. Elaborate experiments (10) have been carried out in the attempt to evaluate teacher effectiveness through pupil changes, but the results have been largely disappointing. The accomplishment quotient (A.Q.) has often been used as a means of holding pupils' mental ability constant while evaluating a teacher's effectiveness in increasing his pupils' achievement on such standard tests as the Stanford Achievement Test. Since accomplishment quotients are practically worthless for either individual or group measurement, it is not surprising that the results have not been found significantly correlated with estimates of teaching efficiency obtained elsewhere. The approach to teacher evaluation through standardized achievement tests of pupils has not yet reached a stage of development where it can be used with any confidence.

This does not mean that "before and after" evaluations of pupils have no value. Their validity in measuring pupil growth must be distinguished from their much lower practical value as indices of teacher merit. Such evaluations can reveal very effectively the kinds and amounts of changes that have been produced in pupils over a period of time by *all* the change-producing agencies that affect them. The problem of tracing the individual causes of these changes and isolating the effect of the teacher from all other effects is far more difficult and cannot be solved by the routine use of "before and after" tests.

EVALUATING ASPECTS OF TEACHERS RELATED TO EFFECTIVENESS

Because of the difficulty of evaluating teachers through changes in pupils measured by standardized tests, a more frequent approach has been to evaluate the aspects of teachers judged to be related to desirable changes in pupils. These aspects may be classified into two groups: (1) the teacher's mental ability and scholastic success, and (2) his attitudes and interests, emotional and social adjustment, and background and environment, as these are related to the development of pupils' emotional and social adjustment and attitudes.

Cognitive Aspects of Teachers

The criteria used to evaluate a teacher's mental ability and intellectual attainments in general culture, specific knowledge of teaching methods, and subject matter include the following:

1. Grades in teacher training courses
2. Amount and quality of scholarly publications
3. Membership and participation in professional societies
4. Out-of-school contacts—services to the community and state
5. Standardized objective tests of mental ability and achievement

The methods of applying each of these criteria are so straightforward that they need be discussed here only briefly. The teacher in training or the teacher on the job usually realizes the implications concerning himself of the grades he has received in teacher training courses, of his activity or lack of it in producing scholarly publications, and of his contacts outside the school. The teacher who receives A or B grades throughout his educational career and especially in the courses in the teacher training curricula will usually, other factors being equal, be considered superior. School administrators almost always give consideration to the scholastic record of any candidate for a teaching position. In self-evaluation, the teacher needs no instructions in interpreting his own record in these respects. The last of these criteria, however, may profitably be discussed at greater length.

The mental ability of teachers may be evaluated with many of the tests of general mental ability that are used with college freshmen and adults; they were discussed in greater detail in Chapter IX. Among them are the Ohio State University Psychological Test and the American Council on Education Psychological Examination. The intellectual attainments of teachers can be determined by means of standardized achievement tests similar to those used in evaluating the achievement of secondary-school and college students. At present the most adequate battery of tests for this purpose is probably the National Teacher Examinations of the Educational Testing Service.

The National Teacher Examinations are widely used as an aid to school systems in the selection of teachers for certification, employment, or promotion. . . . The examinations are designed to measure the professional knowledge, mental ability, general cultural background, and special preparation of candidates for teaching positions.

Each February the NTE are administered to candidates in a nation-wide administration at ETS-supervised examination centers. After scoring the tests, ETS forwards a confidential report of the results to each applicant and to school systems or colleges as directed by the candidate.

The NTE consist of two groups of tests, the Common Examinations and the Optional Examinations. The Common Examinations include tests of professional qualifications considered desirable for teachers in general. The Optional Examinations comprise individual tests of methods and subject matter specific to elementary education and to various high school teaching fields. Both groups of tests are intended to measure those abilities and skills which can be assessed by written examinations. Scores on the tests are usually employed in conjunction with other measures of teaching promise.[1]

The Common Examinations include the following tests:
1. Professional Information
2. General Culture
   a. History, Literature, and Fine Arts
   b. Science and Mathematics

[1] Application blanks and other information may be obtained from National Teacher Examinations, % Educational Testing Service, P.O. Box 592, Princeton, New Jersey.

3. English Expression

4. Nonverbal Reasoning

Optional Examinations are available in the following fields:

1. Education in the Elementary School

2. Kindergarten-Primary Education

3. Biological Sciences

4. English Language and Literature

5. Industrial Arts Education

6. Mathematics

7. Physical Sciences

8. Social Studies

The National Committee on Teacher Examinations has emphasized that the extremely important noncognitive factors in teaching success are neglected by the examinations it provides. However valuable may be the information concerning teachers that is provided by the examinations—and their value is admittedly great—the fact remains that they do not approach such aspects as attitudes, emotional and social adjustment, and environment and background.

Probably the best idea of the nature of the National Teacher Examinations can be obtained from an inspection of typical items in certain of the fields tested. Some of the items, quoted by Flanagan in 1941 (13), were as follows:[2]

Professional Information, Part I, Education and Social Policy

45. Substantial modifications in the high school curriculum have been necessary since the [First] World War to allow for

   1 expansion of the college preparatory curriculum. (14%, 5%)

   2 the presence in high school of many persons with slight aptitude for book learning. (61%, 88%)

   3 studies on a more difficult level, necessitated by better preparation in the grades. (3%, 3%)

   4 emphasis on cultural rather than vocational subjects because of decreased employment opportunities. (5%, 2%)

   5 consolidation of rural high schools. (10%, 2%)

   omitted (7%, 0%); *not reached* (0%, 0%)

---

[2] After each answer the percentage of all candidates selecting that particular choice is given; the second figure is the percentage of the individuals with scores in the highest 10 percent who chose that answer. The correct answers are printed in bold-face type.

Professional Information, Part II, Child Development and Educational Psychology

19. If a child is *continually* a difficult behavior problem, the teacher might best
    1 **refer his case to a competent authority for investigation.** (71%, 90%)
    2 discuss the problem with other teachers. (9%, 5%)
    3 isolate him from the rest of the class. (2%, 0%)
    4 have him transferred to another class. (2%, 0%)
    5 devise a more effective form of discipline. (16%, 5%)
    omitted (1%, 0%); *not reached* (0%, 0%)

Professional Information, Part III, Guidance and Individual and Group Analysis

18. A boy applying for entrance to a highly selective school attained a percentile score equivalent to the 67th percentile of the previous year's entering class in that school. The school counselor is justified in concluding that the boy
    1 probably should not be admitted to the school. (8%, 8%)
    2 if admitted, would probably fail in his work. (2%, 0%)
    3 if admitted, would have to work harder than the average entering student in order to avoid failure. (30%, 17%)
    4 **if admitted, would probably do slightly better than average work.** (36%, 70%)
    5 if admitted, should be about 67th best in the entering class of one thousand. (10%, 2%)
    omitted (14%, 3%); *not reached* (0%, 0%)

Professional Information, Part IV, Secondary School Methods

38. To be successful, the "no-failure" policy adopted in some schools requires
    1 **the individualization of programs of study.** (60%, 80%)
    2 decreasing attention to the superior students. (4%, 3%)
    3 the abandonment of school grades. (20%, 12%)
    4 emphasis on vocational education. (4%, 2%)
    5 elimination of pupils who cannot do satisfactory work. (4%, 2%)
    omitted (8%, 1%); *not reached* (0%, 0%)

KNOWLEDGE OF CHILD PSYCHOLOGY

The National Teacher Examination on Professional Information approaches to some extent the teacher's understanding of pupils, of educational policies and procedures in dealing with the problems of individual pupils. Another instrument that provides an evaluation of the teacher's professional equipment in child and adolescent psychology is the Kelley-Perkins How I Teach inventory (16).[3] Its purpose is "to measure what teachers know about the wants, needs, problems, developmental status, and incipient personality disturbances of children and adolescents" (16 : 17). Based on material in books concerned with child and adolescent psychology, case histories of problem children, descriptions of teachers most liked and disliked, and observations made during visits to classrooms, these items were classified into three groups: teaching practices, opinions, and factual results of experimental study. Scoring was based on the judgments of ten recognized authorities.

Items which the judges disagreed on or considered ambiguous or irrelevant, or on which there was too close agreement between them and a preliminary sample of 84 grade and high-school teachers, were eliminated. Thus the items were endowed with what might be called "logical relevance."

Furthermore, items which elicited markedly different average responses from grade and high-school teachers were eliminated or revised, so that the inventory could be used with both groups. A further evidence of validity was the significance of the difference obtained between teachers who were rated "plus" by their principals and those who were rated "minus." "Plus" teachers were those whom the school administrators considered to understand children best, whom they would choose as teachers for their own children; "minus" teachers were those whom the administrators considered to understand children least and to whom they would hesitate to send their own children. Another evidence of validity was the significance of the differences obtained between teachers in school systems known to emphasize the "progressive," mental hygiene point of view, and those in more traditional schools.

Some of the items on practices and opinions are as follows:

Directions: Check each of the following actions or practices in terms of what your own practice is (or would be) in dealing with this prob-

[3] Published by Educational Test Bureau, 720 Washington Ave. S.E., Minneapolis, Minnesota.

lem or situation. For instance, if you judge the practice to be "decidedly good" write the number 5 after the practice.

Use this scale: 1—decidedly harmful; 2—probably harmful; 3—doubtful value; 4—probably good; 5—decidedly good.

1. Requiring an additional assignment from a pupil who misbehaves in class. ....
2. Commending the high school pupil for not being interested in having dates. ....
3. Threatening to punish the pupil who tells lies. ....
4. Expecting a pupil to be able to give adequate reasons for his undesirable behavior. ....
5. Telling the child who masturbates that it leads to ruined health. ....

The meaning of such items is discussed by Kelley and Perkins as follows:

These items which discriminate so decidedly between the teachers in the upper and lower tenths of the total group suggest several implications for the training of teachers. In general, the teachers in the lower group did not understand certain principles of child and adolescent development. These teachers do not realize that all behavior is an attempt to meet some need; they do not realize the nature of individual differences; they do not understand how to motivate children; they do not consider the effect of failure; they do not realize the importance of heterosexual adjustment; and they are unaware of the laws of learning and present knowledge relative to formal discipline.

According to many of these items, the action of this lower group would often result in making the child more insecure, in fostering hatred, rivalry, and jealousy, and in increasing conflict and tension. The answers to many of the statements suggest the teachers' own needs for achievement, dominance, and even self-punishment. Training in the principles of mental hygiene must emphasize the necessity of seeking the real causes of behavior rather than punishing the symptoms of maladjustment (16 : 53).

The Minnesota Teacher Attitude Inventory is designed "to measure those attitudes of a teacher which predict how well he will get along with pupils in interpersonal relationships, and indirectly how well satisfied he will be with teaching as a vocation" (8 : 3). It was built by drawing up hundreds of items dealing with attitudes considered relevant to teacher-pupil relationships. These items were given to two groups of 100 teachers each, selected by their principals as, on the one hand, the one or two teachers who were liked very much by their pupils and who had excellent working relations with pupils, and as, on the other hand, the one or two teachers at the opposite extreme—highly disliked by the pupils. The percentage of teachers in each of these two extreme groups who chose each of the response alternatives for each item was computed; items for which the percentages of teachers in the two groups differed significantly were retained and assigned weights according to the amount of the difference and its psychological meaningfulness. These items were then readministered to a new sample of teachers for whom three kinds of criterion data were available—ratings by their pupils on items that would reveal the degree to which the pupils liked their teacher, ratings by their principal as to disciplinary ability and similar matters, and ratings by a specialist in the area of teaching effectiveness. Scores on the Inventory were found to correlate significantly with each of these three criteria. In several studies the correlations all ranged around .45, with multiple correlations against all three criteria of about .60. The general conclusion from several studies of this Inventory is that it provides a measure of teacher attitudes that are known to be relevant to the effectiveness of the teachers' relationships with their pupils.

Teacher-pupil relations are, of course, not merely a function of the attitudes of teachers; the values and other characteristics of pupils are also involved. This has been indicated by Della Piana and Gage (9), who found that the correlation between teachers' scores on the Minnesota Teacher Attitude Inventory and ratings by pupils was a function of the values of pupils. The pupils in 97 fourth-, fifth-, and sixth-grade classrooms of a midwestern city were measured on a values inventory which asked them to "choose things about teachers" they would rather have in their teacher. Each item required them to choose between a description of a teacher designed to reflect "cognitive merit" and one designed to reflect "affective merit." For example, when the pupils were asked whether they would rather have a teacher who "explains things clearly" or one who "treats us fairly," the first choice would indicate a cognitive value, and the second would indicate an affective value. The classrooms were found to differ significantly among themselves in the average strength of the cognitive as against the affective values of the pupils in them. When the 20 classrooms with the strongest cognitive values were selected, the correlation between the MTAI scores of the teachers and the mean rating of their pupils proved to be only .06. When the 20 classrooms with the weakest cognitive values (and, by the same token, the strongest affective values) were selected, the correlation between teachers' MTAI scores and mean ratings by their pupils was .56. The difference between these two correlation coefficients is statistically significant. It indicates that the validity of the MTAI against pupils' ratings is a function of what pupils want in their teachers. If pupils want a teacher who is fair, nice, sympathetic, understanding, etc., the teacher's attitudes on the MTAI relevant to these matters will correlate substantially with pupils' ratings of the teacher. This will not be the case when pupils are more concerned with the degree to which the teacher explains things clearly, teaches "lots of things," and the like.

The ultimate validation of any such inventory will, of course, be in terms of changes in pupil adjustment. Two groups of teachers might be chosen, one with high scores and the other with low scores on the inventory. The pupils of these two groups of teachers could then be evaluated as to their emotional and social adjustment when they first came under the influence of the teachers and again after they had been under this influence for a semester or a year. If the pupils of the first group of teachers either improved or did not change in emotional and social adjustment, while the pupils of the second group of teachers deteriorated, this would be clear evidence that scores on such an inventory are indications of the probable effects of teachers on pupil adjustment. Needless to say, the initial status of the pupils' adjustment and all other factors affecting it while they were under the influence of the two groups of teachers would have to be controlled.

ATTITUDES TOWARD THE ROLE OF THE SCHOOLS

It is frequently desirable to ascertain the degree to which teachers are aware of and in agreement with "progressive" ideas con-

cerning the role of schools in modern society. An instrument entitled What Should Our Schools Do?[4] has been made available for
this purpose. A series of 100 statements is presented to which the
teacher or citizen indicates his attitude by underlining *agree* or
disagree. The statements cover the following seven broad categories of school policy:

1. Willingness to accept change in the local educational program and
   research or experimentation in various aspects of the local school
   situation. (21 items)
2. Readiness to accept an intellectually tolerant point of view, one of
   freedom from personal bias or prejudice. (17 items)
3. Approval of the general idea of extending the scope of educational
   services in the areas not now generally accepted within the common
   school or public school system. (13 items)
4. Desire to broaden the curriculum or to take the school out of the
   classroom and into the community life, and vice versa. (9 items)
5. Willingness to reject the theory of formal discipline or to accept the
   proposal of breaking down the *solid subjects*. (22 items)
6. Acceptance of the policy of individualizing the educational resources of the school or acceptance of the primary policy of education of *personalities* as against desiring to have mass instruction.
   (21 items)
7. Acceptance of possible related consequences involved in a program
   of liberalizing the educational program. (8 items)

The "progressivism" not only of teachers but also of others in
the community—counselors, school administrators, school board
members and parents—may be evaluated. In this way the community environment of the school and its pupils may be revealed in
relation to its favorableness for the school's concern with all important aspects of pupils.

That a somewhat general factor of "educational enlightenment"
may exist is indicated by the coefficient of correlation of .64 obtained[5] between the scores of 170 college students of education on
the How I Teach Inventory and the What Should Our Schools Do
questionnaire. Students who were enlightened concerning pupil

[4] Published by the Bureau of Publications, Teachers College, Columbia University,
New York.

[5] In an unpublished study reported to the authors by the late Professor Kenneth
Davenport.

behavior and adjustment problems also tended to have more "progressive" attitudes toward the role of the schools.

The Illinois Opinion Inventories are intended to appraise the attitudes of parents, teachers, and pupils toward the role of the school and also toward the degree to which the schools are achieving the objectives that these kinds of persons would set up for schools (14). These instruments are intended not to "measure" opinion against any norms, but rather to provide a means for intracommunity expressions of satisfaction and dissatisfaction with the schools. The results of such opinion surveys are generally to be used as springboards for discussions by interested persons in the community of ways in which the schools can be improved.

The SRA Educators Opinion Inventory[6] is designed to obtain in detail the opinions and judgments of educators about the strong and weak points of the school or school system in which they operate (30). It consists of 148 items, the first 130 of which call for "agree—?—disagree" responses to such items as:

I think my work load is about right for me.

The superintendents and their assistants tend to ignore our suggestions and complaints.

The citizens in this community are generally glad to give time and energy in order to help the school program.

This school system is doing a better-than-average job in preparing pupils for life.

A special section of 12 items concerning policies, procedures, and programs require responses of "satisfactory—?—unsatisfactory," as does also a final section of 9 questions on physical facilities and working conditions, such as lighting, ventilation, noise, and the like.

RATINGS OF TEACHERS BY SCHOOL ADMINISTRATORS

A second method of evaluating aspects of teachers presumably related to teaching success is to have school administrators, superintendents, principals, or supervisors rate teachers by means of any one of the many available teacher rating scales. These scales are

[6] Published by Science Research Associates, 57 West Grand Avenue, Chicago 10, Illinois.

usually not fitted for self-evaluation, as is evident from the decrease in the validity coefficient from .55 to .20 obtained by Barr (1) with the Torgerson Teacher Rating Scale when it was administered by a school administrator and then by the teacher herself. The criterion of validity in Barr's study was formed from a composite of two measures of pupil's gains on the Stanford Achievement Test, a composite of seven rating scales applied by school administrators, and a composite of nine tests commonly associated with teaching success. Whether this criterion is itself valid depends of course on the validity of the achievement tests, rating scales, and teacher trait tests of which it is composed.

Since one of the major purposes of the present chapter is to provide teachers with methods for *self-evaluation,* rating scales designed for use by school administrators are not highly relevant and may be dismissed with a few brief general comments. The validity of these scales depends first of all on the traits they list as significant for any consideration of teaching merit. Second, it depends on the rater's skill, knowledge, and familiarity with these aspects of teachers.

In one sense, of course, the administrator's ratings are highly important with respect to what happens to teachers as a result of the ratings, for it is clear that such ratings, when made "for keeps," affect the promotions, salary increases, and dismissals of teachers. In this sense they are the most valid ratings that are made. Their validity in relation to changes in pupils, however, is generally unknown.

RATINGS OF TEACHERS BY PUPILS

Pupils have the most opportunity to observe a teacher in action. Consequently, teachers can be evaluated on the basis of their pupils' ratings on various aspects of teaching merit. Numerous rating scales for this purpose have been designed. Probably the most widely used is the Purdue Rating Scale for Instruction, a graphic rating scale covering 10 aspects of teachers and 15 other aspects of the classroom situation. The scale is shown in Fig. 22, pp. 494–495.

The unique value of pupils' ratings stems from the directness of their approach to certain highly important factors in the learning situation—attitudes or the emotionally toned feelings, opinions, and reactions. As one of the present authors points out elsewhere (21): "All psychologists . . . agree upon the importance of the affective or feeling components of learning . . . Children's attitudes are of primary importance in the effective acquisition of knowledge, skill, interests, attitudes, ideals, etc., with which the school purports to concern itself."

Furthermore, the indirect objectives of instruction, or concomitant learnings such as attitudes toward subjects, attitudes toward the ideas represented by a teacher, and the pupil's attitudes toward himself as well as toward the more immediate, direct instructional objectives are similarly affected by his reaction to his teacher's personality and methods. Just as achievement tests in the usual sense are used to evaluate one group of effects of the teacher on pupils, so pupils' ratings of teachers may be used to evaluate another, equally important group of effects.

ARGUMENTS FOR AND AGAINST PUPIL RATINGS OF TEACHERS

Before we describe the available devices for pupil ratings and the typical results obtained with them, we should consider some of the arguments against and in favor of this procedure. Arguments against it include the following:

1. Pupils are incompetent to judge the merit of either the process or the results of teaching, incapable of distinguishing between bad and good teaching, and prone to judge what the teacher does rather than what he gets the pupil to do. This argument may be answered on the grounds that even if, as is doubtful, it states the truth, it is important to ascertain pupils' attitudes toward their teachers because they exist and exert a powerful influence on the effectiveness of instruction. The adage, "You can lead a horse to water but you can't make him drink," applies here.

2. Attaching importance to pupil ratings commits the democratic fallacy of implying that that teaching is best which pleases the majority of pupils, and that teaching should be adjusted to achieve this end. This argument may be answered on the grounds that the best educational process *is* in essence democratic, and the use of pupil opinion makes possible a wholesome kind of coöperative effort to improve the learning situation.

3. Pupils are inclined to make snap judgments that are conse-

Note to Instructors: In order to keep conditions as nearly uniform as possible, it is imperative that no instructions be given to the students. The rating scale should be passed out without comment at the beginning of the period.

Note to Students: Following is a list of qualities that, taken together, tend to make any instructor the sort of instructor that he is. Of course, no one is ideal in all of these qualities, but some approach this ideal to a much greater extent than do others. In order to obtain information which may lead to the improvement of instruction, you are asked to rate your instructor on the indicated qualities by darkening one of the spaces on the line at the point which most nearly describes him with reference to the quality you are considering. For example, under Interest in Subject if you think your instructor is not as enthusiastic about his subject as he should be, but is usually more than mildly interested darken the space indicated thus: Fill the chosen space solidly with the special electrographic pencil; leave no stray marks.

Interest in Subject...........

Always appears full of his subject. | Seems mildly interested. | Subject seems irksome to him.

Name of Instructor.......... Course.......... Date..........

This rating is to be entirely impersonal. Do not sign your name or make any other mark on the paper which could serve to identify the rater.

1. Interest in Subject..........
Always appears full of his subject. | Seems mildly interested. | Subject seems irksome to him.

2. Sympathetic Attitude toward Students..
Always courteous and considerate. | Tries to be considerate but finds it difficult at times. | Entirely unsympathetic and inconsiderate.

3. Fairness in Grading..........
Absolutely fair and impartial to all. | Shows occasional favoritism. | Constantly shows partiality.

4. Liberal and Progressive Attitude..........
Welcomes differences in viewpoint. | Biased on some things but usually tolerant. | Entirely intolerant, allows no contradiction.

5. Presentation of Subject Matter..........
Clear, definite and forceful. | Sometimes mechanical and monotonous. | Indefinite, involved, and monotonous.

6. Sense of Proportion and Humor..........
Always keeps proper balance; not over-critical or over-sensitive | Fairly well balanced. | Over-serious; no sense of relative values.

7. Self-reliance and Confidence..........
Always sure of himself, meets difficulties with poise. | Fairly self-confident; occasionally disconcerted | Hesitant, timid, uncertain.

8. Personal Peculiarities..........
Wholly free from annoying mannerisms. | Moderately free from objectionable peculiarities. | Constantly exhibits irritating mannerisms.

9. Personal Appearance..........
Always well groomed, clothes neat and clean. | Usually somewhat untidy; gives little attention to appearance. | Slovenly; clothes untidy and ill-kept.

10. Stimulating Intellectual Curiosity..........
Inspires students to independent effort; creates desire for investigation. | Occasionally inspiring; creates mild interest. | Destroys interest in subject; makes work repulsive.

Note to Students: Following is a list of factors which are important to many courses but over which the instructor often has little control. You are asked to rate the course on each of the factors by darkening one of the spaces at the right of each statement. Use the special electrographic pencil. Leave no stray marks.

If the course is extremely poor with respect to the factor darken space 1, thus:

If the course is below average with respect to the factor darken space 2, thus:

If the course is average with respect to the factor darken space 3, thus:

If the course is above average with respect to the factor darken space 4, thus:

If the course is excellent with respect to the factor darken space 5, thus:

For example: If you feel that the course is not contributing very much to the attainment of your ultimate goal; but on the other hand, is not a complete waste of time you would probably respond to item number 20 by darkening space 2, thus:

20. How the course is fulfilling your needs (consider your ultimate as well as your immediate goals)

11. Suitability of the method or methods by which subject matter of the course is presented (recitation, lecture, laboratory, etc.)

12. Suitability of the size of the class (consider the subject matter and type of class—lecture, lab, etc.).

13. The degree to which the objectives of the course were clarified and discussed

14. The agreement between the announced objectives of the course and what was actually taught

15. Suitability of the reference materials available for the course.

16. Suitability of the laboratory facilities available for the course.

17. Suitability of the assigned textbook.

18. The use made of tests as aids to learning

19. Amount of freedom allowed students in the selection of the materials to be studied (considering the subject matter)

20. How the course is fulfilling your needs (consider your ultimate as well as your immediate goals).

21. Range of ability in the class (are there too many extremely dull or extremely bright students?).

22. Suitability of the amount and type of assigned outside work.

23. The weight given to tests in determining the final grade for the course.

24. Coordination of the tests with the major objectives of the course.

25. Frequency of tests.

26. The overall rating of the Instructor.

Fig. 22. The Purdue Rating Scale for Instruction, by H. H. Remmers and D. N. Elliott.

quently unreliable. But the available statistical evidence indicates that the average ratings of teachers by a group of pupils about equal in number to those in the average classroom have a reliability as great as or greater than that of most standardized achievement tests.

4. Pupils' judgments of teachers may be affected and distorted by such irrelevant factors as grades, amount of work required by the teacher, the pupil's interest in the subject, the difficulty of the subject, the preëstablished reputation of the teacher, the general attitude toward school, and a lack of seriousness in making the ratings. It can be answered that correlational studies have shown little relationship between most of these factors and ratings of teachers; in particular, pupils' grades, attitudes toward subjects, amount of work required by teachers, and general attitude toward school have been found to correlate to only a low degree, or not at all, with their ratings of teachers. It is more difficult to ascertain the effect of preëstablished reputation, but insofar as such an effect exists and influences present ratings, it also constitutes desirable evidence concerning a teacher. The lack of seriousness in making ratings would tend to lower the reliability of the ratings; however, since ratings have been found to be reliable, it follows that pupils have in most investigations taken a serious attitude toward this assignment. In any case, it is possible to eliminate this factor by taking effective steps to establish rapport with pupils when the assignment is explained to them.

Although differences between the sexes, or between pupils in the upper and lower half of their class in school marks, are significant only infrequently in ratings of a given teacher, they do occur. If the pupils in such classifications are asked to mark their sheets with symbols such as X or F, separate tabulations can be made of the ratings by boys and by girls or other groups.

5. Pupil ratings tend to disrupt the morale of the teaching staff by arousing hostility, self-consciousness, discouragement, disrespect between colleagues, and attempts to cater to adverse pupil opinion through activities irrelevant to good teaching. Whenever such a danger seems to be present, teachers should be permitted to keep their ratings strictly confidential rather than being required to submit them to their administrative officers. This situation did not

seem to be present in most of the published reports dealing with the problem.

6. Pupil rating tends to have a disruptive effect on the morale of pupils; they may come to feel that they are the judges of the worth of teachers, curricula, and school activity. No evidence of this has been found in any of the rating schemes whose results have been published. Bowman (4) states, on the basis of several years of experience with having student teachers rated by their pupils, that pupil morale is improved by the opportunity.

Arguments in favor of pupil rating other than those mentioned in refuting negative arguments are as follows: (1) The inevitably powerful effect of pupils' opinions of teachers, in the form of gossip, on pupils, teachers, and administrators makes it advisable to recognize the influence, bring it into the open, and capitalize fully on its value. In a very real sense no teacher has a choice as to whether he wants to be rated. The only real choice open to him is whether he wants to know what the ratings are and thus profit by them. Hence (2) a collection of pupil ratings enables a teacher to exercise a sort of self-supervision based on objective evidence obtained from those in the best position to observe him. (3) Obtaining pupils' ratings of teachers is an eminently practical procedure; it costs little, requires only a few minutes, and fits easily into the regular routine of any classroom.

DEVICES FOR SECURING PUPIL RATINGS OF TEACHERS

The Diagnostic Teacher-Rating Scale (31) is designed for elementary-school children in Grades IV to VIII. The scale is divided into two parts—a survey instrument by means of which a rather generalized picture of pupils' attitudes can be obtained, and a diagnostic instrument with two comparable forms which provide detailed and specific information regarding the strengths and weaknesses of teachers. In both scales, seven different aspects of the teacher's work are considered:

1. Liking for teacher
2. Ability to explain
3. Kindness, friendliness, and understanding
4. Fairness in grading
5. Discipline (keeping order with the children)

6. Amount of work required

7. Liking for lessons

On the general scale the aspects of teachers are put as questions and the pupils are instructed to rate them on a five-point scale. The diagnostic scale provides for each general aspect seven statements selected from several hundred such statements evaluated and scaled by Thurstone's method for the construction of attitude scales (see Chapter XIV). Thus, the diagnostic scale consists of seven shorter scales with approximately equal scale distances between the diagnostic statements.

The reliability of this scale has been found by Tschechtelin, Hipskind, and Remmers (32), using the split-test procedure, to range from .86 for "Amount of Work Required" to .96 for "Liking for the Teacher."

The validity of such a measuring instrument may be considered from four different points of view.

1. Since the scale is designed to measure the attitudes of pupils, it is sufficient to say that to the extent that reliable measures are obtained they are also valid since we are concerned not with the characteristics teachers actually possess in the sight of some omniscient judge, but with the characteristics they possess in the eyes of the children they teach. In the words of T. L. Kelley (17 : 9), "If competent judges appraise Individual A as being as much better than Individual B as Individual B is better than Individual C, then it is so, as there is no higher authority to appeal to."

2. The logic underlying its construction is another argument for the validity of the scale. Insofar as verbalized opinions are measures of attitudes and the scale measures verbalized opinions, it must also measure attitudes.

3. Evidence for the validity of the short scale may be inferred from the degree to which it differentiates between the teachers whom the pupils selected as the best teacher and the poorest teacher they had ever known. A complete twofold division with no overlapping was found between the two distributions of scores.

4. Another argument for validity rests on the lowness of the intercorrelations among the seven aspects of teachers measured by the diagnostic scale and the highness of the correlations obtained between the general and the diagnostic scales. The lowness of the

intercorrelation coefficients indicates that each of the attitudes measured is relatively independent of all the others.

In the Bryan-Yntema Rating Scale for the Evaluation of Student Reactions (6), designed for use at the secondary-school level, the pupil records his opinion of the teacher in answering the following:

1. What is your opinion concerning the sympathy shown by this teacher?
2. What is your opinion concerning this teacher's ability to maintain discipline?
3. What is your opinion concerning his (or her) fairness in marking?
4. What is your opinion concerning the ability of this teacher to explain things clearly?
5. What is your opinion of the ability this teacher has to make the classes lively and interesting?
6. What is your opinion concerning the ability of this teacher to plan classroom work and keep students busy in class?
7. What is your opinion concerning the extent to which this teacher speaks in a lively manner with a clear and distinct voice?
8. What is your opinion concerning the pride this teacher takes in his personal appearance?
9. What is your opinion concerning the value that this subject has for you?
10. What is your opinion concerning the general (all-round) teaching ability of this teacher?
11. On what question from 1 to 8 (omitting the last two) did you give the lowest rating? Please state in a sentence or two why you gave a low rating on this question. (Your writing will not be recognized if you print your words or use a backhand slope.)
12. Please name one or two things you especially like about this teacher. (Print or use backhand slope when answering.)
13. Is this teacher in the habit of doing something, not mentioned above, that you do not like? If so, what is it?

According to the authors of the scale, the regular classroom teacher can in most instances obtain just as frank and honest ratings when he conducts the class during the rating as when he calls in another teacher to obtain them.

In scoring the rating scales, the teacher assigns values of 1 to "excellent" ratings, 2 to "good," 3 to "average," 4 to "below average," and 5 to "poor."

The average ratings for the ten aspects of teachers evaluated by the scale should be interpreted in the light of the pupils' responses to Questions 11, 12, and 13.

The reliability coefficients of the ratings obtained from 30 pupils range between .83 and .92. With larger groups of pupils these coefficients would, of course, be increased.

The Purdue Rating Scale for Instruction, described earlier, has been widely used in both high schools and colleges. The median reliability of ratings for 205 college instructors obtained with this scale was .90. Ratings of characteristics of the course had a median reliability of .82. Each of these reliability coefficients was obtained by selecting the ratings of 20 students for each instructor, dividing these into two random halves of 10 rating scales each, computing the mean for each set of 10 ratings on each trait, correlating the two sets of means, and correcting by the Spearman-Brown formula.

The most extensive study of students' ratings of teachers was that made in Indiana, in which 26,014 students rated 460 college teachers in ten different institutions (22). The ratings were studied as to their relationship to the students' sex, year in school, veteran or nonveteran status, and scholastic standing in the class. Of these, only one was found to be related—whether or not the student was a graduate student. The ratings by graduate students were higher than those made by undergraduates.

The ratings were also studied as to their relationship with the teachers' sex, teaching experience, highest academic degree held, and academic rank. Of these factors, only the last was related to the student ratings. Teachers with the lowest academic rank received somewhat lower ratings; beyond this rank, however, ratings were not systematically related to rank except for three traits which appear to be either amenable to teacher training or important for continued teaching. These three traits were "presentation of subject matter," "self-reliance and confidence," and "stimulating intellectual curiosity."

Elliott (12) later studied relationships among four criteria of teacher effectiveness in a required general chemistry course for engineering freshmen. The four criteria were (1) students' ratings of instructors, (2) teacher's knowledge of correct teaching practices involving mental hygiene principles, (3) teacher's knowledge of the subject matter taught, and (4) students' achievement after ability had been statistically equalized for all instructors. The teachers whose students achieved relatively more on objective measures of knowledge and understanding of the work after the influence of differences in the students' ability had been statistically controlled, received relatively higher ratings from their students. In short, the student ratings reflected not merely their liking for or dislike of their instructor, but the amount they learned under him, objectively measured.

USE OF PUPILS' RATINGS TO IMPROVE TEACHING

Ward, Remmers, and Schmalzried (33) studied the extent to which teachers change their teaching behavior when they are apprised of pupils' attitudes, as obtained with the Purdue Rating Scale for Instructors, and when a training program to improve weak spots is undertaken. Forty student practice teachers in a high school were rated by their pupils about one month after they began teaching and again at the end of the semester. Between the two ratings the supervisor conferred with each student-teacher concerning the general standing and specific strengths and weaknesses revealed by the first rating. Each student-teacher knew that the ratings would be repeated at the end of the semester.

The effect of the first ratings and conference was revealed by the differences between the two ratings. Only one of the forty student-teachers failed to gain in average rating on the ten traits. The average gain in all traits for the entire forty was highly significant. The greater gains were made in ratings for "self-reliance and confidence" and "sense of proportion and humor." The diagnostic and remedial value of the ratings was reflected both in the relatively greater gains in the two traits in which student-teachers are probably most deficient, and in the general gains.

THE COUNSELOR

IMPORTANCE OF THE COUNSELOR

That the role of school counselor is growing in importance is attested by the fact that at mid-century fifteen states issued certificates to public-school counselors and two additional states granted teaching certificates which recognized majors or minors in guidance work (34). College and university catalogues list a great variety of courses designed to train people as professional counselors. A large and growing number of private individuals and organizations provide counseling services on a fee basis.

A counselor may be defined as a professionally trained individual who in face-to-face verbal relationships consciously attempts to assist another person or persons to modify attitudes or other behavior concerned with educational, emotional, and vocational issues (25, 29). This definition obviously characterizes the counselor as a teacher, albeit with specialized professional functions and training.

APPROACHES TO EVALUATION

Viewing the counselor as a teacher, as one who attempts to produce desirable changes in the person counseled, makes it obvious that the rationale of evaluating the counselor will in general be the same as that of evaluating the teacher. The twofold approach described earlier in this chapter applies here: (1) evaluation of the changes actually produced by the counselor, and (2) evaluation of aspects of the counselor believed to be related to his competence in this function. The reader is therefore referred to that discussion for consideration of the advantages and limitations of each of these approaches.

In spite of the rapidly growing importance of counseling, the institutionalization of counseling and the counselor, and the expanding legal recognition of counseling as a profession, the evaluation of counselors and counseling is still largely in the "talking stage"—programmatic and, at best, exploratory. Training programs and certification requirements are obviously based on value judgments about aspects that are considered to be related to competence in counseling. Equally obviously, the validation of these value judgments and assumptions requires the use of the more ultimate criterion of changes produced in those counseled.

A test developed by Benz and Remmers (2, 3) is designed in two equivalent forms to indicate acquaintance with counseling techniques, the counselor's philosophy of counseling, and his awareness of some of the basic principles of human behavior. The examinee answers items in the test by indicating whether he agrees, disagrees, or is uncertain. The 100 items in the two forms of the test are exemplified by the following three:

Counselors should be removed, as far as possible, from any disciplinary activities.
A good counselor will solve extremely difficult problems for a student.
If a student makes contradictory statements, the counselor should hasten to point out the inconsistency.

Preliminary percentile norms based on 346 high-school teachers are provided. Reliability was found to be .834 for the combined scores on both forms of the test. Its validity at present is clearly chiefly that of logical relevance, although fourteen veterans' counselors obtained significantly higher scores than did various groups of teachers, and counselors with higher test scores were more critical of counseling services in the university than were persons with lower test scores (11). At present the chief function of the test is probably serving as a basis for discussion. It has not been sufficiently validated to be used in the selection and placement of counselors.

Counseling programs, it is quite generally agreed by those competent to judge, are very much in need of evaluation with respect to their effectiveness. We shall give space here only to a brief citation of one of the better attempts at evaluating a guidance program in terms of changes produced in the people counseled. Rothney and Roens (26) worked with 825 subjects for various lengths of time, but made their evaluation of continuous counseling with only 129 subjects who were counseled for the five years they attended Grades VIII to XII in a typical high school. The investigators compared the high-school and posthigh-school performances of the counseled subjects with a control group who had been matched with the experimental group on eight variables. The results were summarized by Rothney and Danielson (25 : 133) as follows:

(a) Significant differences between the experimental and control groups of students in terms of academic achievement while in high school; (b) more employment among noncollege guided groups; (c) more definiteness concerning vocational plans and means of attaining them; (d) better adjustment on the job or in post-high-school training; (e) greater awareness of educational problems; and (f) better information on how to meet problems and where to seek advice. They concluded that counseling of youth can contribute significantly to the accomplishment of the objectives of the secondary school.

THE ADMINISTRATOR

If the school is a significant part of the pupil's environment, we need to be concerned with the individuals who shape that environment in ways important to the pupil—the principal of the school and the superintendent of the school system. Although in many school systems the "supervisor," as distinct from the principal and the superintendent, is an important determiner of the school environment, we shall deal explicitly only with the two officials just mentioned. In smaller school systems especially, the principal and supervisor are often the same person. Many decisions are made by principals and superintendents, in their roles as educational leaders, that determine the opportunities of teachers and pupils to achieve educational objectives.

Superintendents and School Boards

Much of the foregoing discussion in this chapter applies to principals and superintendents. In much of their work they too are "teachers." Hence their knowledge of educational practices and procedures—and particularly their "philosophy" concerning the proper functions of the public school—will affect the type of curriculum provided by the schools. In working with the board of education, the superintendent, as its professional leader, must bring to the laymen elected by the community the significant information and points of view that will be involved in a myriad of decisions. How should money be spent? On gymnasium equipment or new uniforms for the varsity teams? On typewriters or pianos? On shop equipment or a higher salary for a Latin teacher? In short, in his interaction with the school board the superintendent is constantly involved in decisions concerning "values." His own values will not always prevail; indeed they will be shaped by those of the community and the board members with whom he works. But to a large extent he must act as the "teacher" of the school board. When research has demonstrated that a given technique or procedure facilitates the achievement of important educational objectives, his role is often that of persuading, or "selling," the school board that the expenditures required for it are justified.

SUPERINTENDENT AND SUBORDINATES

The superintendent and the principal also have significant relationships with their "subordinates," namely, the teachers and non-professional staff of the school. Here the important dimensions of the relationship are analogous to those between the teacher and the pupils. Here, as in all social relationships, the mutual "role expectations" of the participants may make a difference. What the teachers have learned to expect from the holder of a given position such as the superintendency or principalship necessarily affects their own behavior. When they have learned that all decisions should be made by their principal, they will come to him for "the word" on whether reading assignments should be uniform for all the pupils in a given classroom, on whether Johnny should be kept after school, and on whether the pupils should be seated in straight rows or in a circle. Such teachers will resist their principal's efforts to have them assume professional responsibilities. Teachers learn their own "role" largely from the way in which the principal and the superintendent act theirs.

The opposite kind of learning probably occurs less often; that is, administrators less often "learn" from their teachers how they should behave because the administrators have predominant "power" to distribute rewards and punishments to teachers. Hence it is largely the administrators who shape the ways in which the school system is governed—democratically or autocratically, by group decisions or administrative fiat. If preparing children for democratic living is accepted as a function of the schools, it becomes necessary that the school itself provide opportunities for teachers and pupils to experience the problems and opportunities of democratic school government.

How can administrators determine the extent to which they are meeting the role expectations of their subordinates? Good rapport with teachers makes possible the type of conversation and informal impressions that will provide administrators with more or less accurate information on this score. But a vicious circle can evolve here. Poor rapport—impaired communication between administrators and teachers—can keep the administrator ignorant of the existence and reasons for low morale on the part of the teaching staff. The worse the rapport and the lower the morale, the poorer his opportunity to learn about the condition and take appropriate steps to remedy it.

RATINGS BY SUBORDINATES

One way to break the "vicious circle" and gain more systematic information concerning the attitudes of teachers that are so important to the proper functioning of administrators is to use anonymously filled-out devices such as rating scales and opinion questionnaires. Properly designed and administered, these devices can yield information on the general state of morale among teachers and on specific healthy and diseased areas of administrator-teacher relationships.

The Purdue Rating Scale for Administrators and Executives (15, 23) has been designed for this purpose. It consists of 36 items to be filled out by subordinates to indicate their personal appraisal of the administrator. The items are grouped in the following ten categories:

1. Intellectual balance
2. Emotional balance
3. Administrative leadership
4. Administrative planning
5. Use of funds
6. Capacity for work
7. Accomplishment
8. Relations with subordinates
9. Public relations
10. Social responsibility

By summarizing the ratings of his subordinates, computing the mean of his ratings on each item, and plotting this mean on a profile chart, the administrator can obtain a picture of his relative strengths and weaknesses as compared with those of other administrators whose mean ratings were used in preparing the percentile norms. For example, the administrator who gets a mean score of

3.3 on the item "Welds staff into a unit with clearly recognized goal" would have a percentile rank of about 12 with respect to other school administrators who have been rated by their teachers. The mean rating of 3.3 on this item is intermediate between the phrases "(4) very well," and "(3) quite well." On an absolute basis, the administrator might consider this a satisfactory rating, but interpretation in terms of percentile norms would certainly modify this idea. Similarly, Item 5, "Is concerned with his own personal problems," would yield a percentile rank of 50 if the mean of ratings by subordinates is 3.7, intermediate between "(3) sometimes," and "(4) seldom."

In a staff evaluation project carried out in Indiana colleges and universities (22), 54 administrators in nine institutions were rated by their subordinates with the Purdue Rating Scale for Administrators and Executives. The average number of raters per administrator was 15. A summary quotation from this study gives the more salient results:

An investigation of the reliability of the items indicated that all of them were acceptably free of chance fluctuations. The 36 coefficients of reliability for 20 raters were all above .700, and 15 of the 36 coefficients were above .900. The combined, or "average," reliability of all the items was .89.

Because of the technique used in determining reliability, it was possible on sound logical grounds to consider reliability and validity of the items as synonymous. Validity of the scale as a unit was checked against an internal measure of staff morale as a criterion, and a coefficient of .812 was obtained.

The halo effect was demonstrated to be at least less than of major importance.

A factor analysis of the 36 items was performed, and the three factors which emerged were named: fairness to subordinates, administrative achievement, and democratic orientation. There was evidence that a majority of the items were measuring other characteristics than those included in the three factors.

A study was made of the relationships between personal data of the administrators and the ratings they received. It was concluded that none of the following factors have a dependable relationship with total scale ratings: age; salary; years in present position; years connected with the institution; years of administrative experience; years of teaching experience; percentage of contractual time spent in administration, teaching, research, or extension; and professional activities—including memberships in professional societies, attendance at their meetings, papers read to them, and number of professional publications. It was also found that the type of administrative position held —whether as dean, department head, president, or other—made no significant difference.

Another study was made of the relationships between characteristics of groups of raters and ratings they gave their superiors. The age, rank, and years of college teaching of the subordinates showed a slight positive relationship. The proportion of their time they spent in administration was also positively related. Characteristics of no significance were: salary, formal degrees, years under present administrator, sex, and professional activities.

Another study that used the same rating scale obtained data from a national sample of 88 administrators at the elementary and public-school level, rated by 1153 teachers. For this self-selected sample the reliability was only .67—appreciably lower than that obtained in the previous study of college and university administrators, and probably a function of the more restricted range of ratings (18).

REFERENCES

1. Barr, A. S., *et al.,* "The validity of certain instruments employed in the measurement of teaching ability," in Lancelot, W. H., *et al., The Measurement of Teaching Efficiency,* New York: The Macmillan Company, 1935.
2. Benz, S. C., "An investigation of the attributes and techniques of high school counselors," *Purdue University Studies in Higher Education No. LXIV,* Lafayette: Purdue University, Division of Educational Reference, October, 1948.
3. Benz, S. C., and Remmers, H. H., *How I Counsel,* Personnel Evaluation Research and Service, Division of Educational Reference, Purdue University, 1950.
4. Bowman, E. C., "Pupil ratings of student-teachers," *Educational Administration and Supervision,* 20:141–147 (1934).
5. Bryan, R. C., "Pupil rating of secondary school teachers," *School Review,* 44:357–368 (1938).
6. Bryan, R. C., and Yntema, O., *A Manual on the Evaluation of*

Student Reactions in Secondary Schools, Kalamazoo: Western State Teachers College, 1939.

7. Clark, H. F., "An effort to extend the measurement of the results of schooling into the social and economic fields," American Educational Research Association, *An Appraisal of Technics of Evaluation: Symposium,* February 26, 1940, pp. 20–24.

8. Cook, W. W., Leeds, C. H., and Callis, R., *The Minnesota Teacher Attitude Inventory,* New York: The Psychological Corporation, 1951.

9. Della Piana, G. M., and Gage, N. L., "Pupils' values and the validity of the Minnesota Teacher Attitude Inventory," *Journal of Educational Psychology,* 46 (1955).

10. Domas, S. J., and Tiedeman, D. V., "Teacher competence: an annotated bibliography," *Journal of Experimental Education,* 19:101–218 (1950).

11. Drucker, A. J., and Remmers, H. H., "The validity of university counselor self-ratings," *Journal of Educational Psychology,* 40:168–173 (1949).

12. Elliott, D. N., "Characteristics and relationships of various criteria of college and university teaching," *Purdue University Studies in Higher Education No. LXX,* Lafayette: Purdue University, Division of Educational Reference, 1950.

13. Flanagan, J. C., "An analysis of the results from the first annual edition of the National Teacher Examinations," *Journal of Experimental Education,* 9:237–250 (1941).

14. Hand, H. C., *What People Think About Their Schools: Values and Methods of Public-Opinion Polling as Applied to School Systems,* Yonkers: World Book Company, 1948.

15. Hobson, R. L., "Some psychological dimensions of academic administrators," *Further Studies in Attitudes, Series XVIII, Purdue University Studies in Higher Education No. LXXIII,* 1950.

16. Kelley, Ida B., and Perkins, Keith J., "An investigation of teachers' knowledge of and attitudes toward child and adolescent behavior in everyday school situations," *Studies in Higher Education XLII, Bulletin of Purdue University,* 1941.

17. Kelley, T. L., *The Influence of Nurture upon Individual Differences,* New York: The Macmillan Company, 1926.

18. Kirk, R. B., "Guidance for the school administrator," *Sixteenth Annual Guidance Conference, Purdue University Studies in Higher Education No. LXXIX,* 1951.

19. Kroll, A., "The teacher's influence upon the social attitudes of

boys in the twelfth grade," *Journal of Educational Psychology,* 25:274–280 (1934).

20. Mason, H. M., "Effects of high school social studies teachers' attitudes upon attitudes of their pupils," *Studies in Higher Education XLIV, Bulletin of Purdue University,* 1942.

21. Remmers, H. H., "The college professor as the student sees him," *Studies in Higher Education XI, Bulletin of Purdue University,* 1929.

22. Remmers, H. H., and Elliott, D. N., "The Indiana college and university staff evaluation program," *School and Society,* 70:168–171 (1949).

23. Remmers, H. H., and Hobson, R. L., *The Purdue Rating Scale for Administrators and Executives,* Lafayette: Purdue University, Division of Educational Reference, 1950.

24. "Report of the Committee on the Criteria of Teacher Effectiveness," *Review of Educational Research,* 22:138–263 (1952).

25. Rothney, J. W. M., and Danielson, P. J., "Counseling," *Review of Educational Research,* 21:132–139 (1951).

26. Rothney, J. W. M., and Roens, B. A., *Guidance of American Youth,* Cambridge: Harvard University Press, 1950.

27. Ryans, D. G., "The investigation of teacher characteristics," *Educational Record,* 34:371–396 (1953).

28. "Second report of the Committee on Criteria of Teacher Effectiveness," *Journal of Educational Research,* 46:641–658 (1953).

29. Snyder, W. U., "The present status of psychotherapeutic counseling," *Psychological Bulletin,* 44:297–386 (1947).

30. Spencer, L. M., Gehlmann, F., and Maris, Edith F., *In Your Opinion: What Los Angeles Educators Think of Their School System,* Los Angeles City Board of Education, 1953.

31. Tschechtelin, Sister M. Amatora, and Remmers, H. H., *Diagnostic Teacher-rating Scale,* Lafayette: Division of Educational Reference, Purdue University, 1940.

32. Tschechtelin, Sister M. Amatora, Hipskind, Sister M. John Frances, and Remmers, H. H., "Measuring the attitudes of elementary-school children toward their teachers," *Journal of Educational Psychology,* 31:195–203 (1940).

33. Ward, W. D., Remmers, H. H., and Schmalzried, N. T., "The training of teacher-personality by means of student-ratings," *School and Society,* 53:189–193 (1941).

34. Woellner, R. C., "Training and certification of school counselors," *School Review,* 58:6–9 (1950).

PART SIX

Physical Aspects of Pupils

CHAPTER XVIII

Physical Aspects of Pupils

ABSTRACT

Teachers should be concerned with the physical aspects of pupils because of the relationships of physical aspects to school attendance and performance, vocational choice, and emotional and social adjustment. We describe briefly the major physical aspects with which teachers should be concerned. The teacher should accept the medical profession's encouragement in evaluating students' physical aspects. Teachers have been found to have little knowledge of their pupils' physical defects. But they can readily be trained to fulfill their functions of cooperating with school nurses, being alert to pupils' physical needs, referring pupils to physicians, keeping histories of pupils, and making routine inspections and measurements. Evaluation of physical aspects is recognized as a function of teachers in the school laws of most states. This recognition has frequently been supported by the medical profession, teacher training centers, and authorities on pupil health.

·~·~·~·

Since the material of this and the following chapter represents a departure from what has traditionally been included in books on educational tests and measurements, we present some of the reasoning which led to its inclusion and a discussion of how this work of the teacher should fit in with that of other health agencies.

REASONS FOR TEACHERS' CONCERN WITH PUPILS' PHYSICAL ASPECTS

Why should classroom teachers be concerned with the evaluation of the physical aspects of their pupils? Justification for this concern has traditionally been given in terms of the supposed connection between mind and body. Mental activity has been recognized as inseparable from physical activity. Consequently it has been assumed that the quality and quantity of mental work depend as certainly on the condition of the bodily machine as do the quality and quantity of work produced by any less complex man-made machine. Scientific research, however, has greatly modified our notions about this relationship. Although this research has been going on since the beginning of the century, it is not yet widely known or appreciated. The research findings which contradict common notions concerning the relationship between mind and body were summarized by Paterson (9 : 269–270) at the end of his exhaustive survey of the data, as follows: ". . . Prevalent notions regarding the intimacy of the relationship between physical traits and intellect have been greatly exaggerated. Search in the realm of gross anatomy for a physical correlate of intellect has yielded uniformly negative results. . . . Such structural characteristics as height and weight, . . . head size and shape, . . . skeletal development measured by precise X-ray photography, . . . dentition, . . . physiological development measured in terms of pubescence, . . . complicated morphological indices of body build, . . . deleterious physical conditions, . . . glandular therapy, . . . disease processes [except when they] directly attack the central nervous system, especially the higher centers . . ." have all been found to be relatively unrelated to mental development and temperament.

Although "body" and "mind" are not related in the ways discussed above, there is still ample justification for the teacher's concern with pupils' physical aspects. Good health is obviously something to be desired and achieved for its own sake. Also physical condition is directly related to the working efficiency of pupils. Poor health causes absence from school and from work; it can decrease the amount of energy available for the learning process, for participation in social relationships, for the maintenance of emotional stability, and for other forms of pupil development.

Similarly, the physical aspects of pupils are directly related to their vocational fitness. Since different occupations require different physical capacities of those who work in them, realistic guidance must take physical capacities of pupils into account. Numerous instances of physical qualifications for occupations come to mind. The almost perfect physical equipment required for admission to the United States Military and Naval Academies; the perfect vision required of airplane pilots; the durable vision required of lawyers, accountants, draftsmen; the physical and nervous stamina required of medical students and physicians; the pleasant, presentable physiognomy and general appearance required of those engaged in occupations involving direct face-to-face contacts with other people, such as selling; the strength and endurance required of many industrial workers—all these are instances of physical requirements for occupations toward which many high-school students have aspirations.

Teachers can introduce a distinctly realistic note into their occupational counseling by calling attention to the physical requirements for occupations and relating the pupils' own physical status to them.

Educational guidance, also, should take into account the physical aspects of pupils. Obviously a student's physical capacity determines his ability to acquire the education necessary for any occupational goal. The amount of school work and other activity in which a pupil should be encouraged to engage may be determined by his physical status. A list of the kinds of adjustments that may be made to health needs has been made by Brown (2 : 40):

1. Shortening of academic program
2. Curtailment of outside activity
3. Withholding approval of athletics or permitting participation in accordance with individual needs
4. Use of a convalescence room for students needing rest and relaxation
5. Lengthening the noon hour
6. Mid-morning lunch of milk and orange juice recommended
7. Correction of physical defects by outside medical aid
8. Systematic health inspection and coöperation with health agencies
9. Classroom adjustment for the physically handicapped. Allotment of front seats for the hard-of-hearing pupils and provision of special lighting for defective vision

    10. Provision of corrective physical exercises for students who lack some muscular control, exhibit nervous movements and are slightly crippled

Concern with the health and physical characteristics of pupils has led national organizations of the educational profession to publish reports and yearbooks (1, 14) on these matters. These volumes provide more extended treatments of the problems, methods, devices, and policies considered in this and the following chapter.

OVERVIEW OF PHYSICAL ASPECTS OF PUPILS

What do we mean by the physical aspects of pupils? These aspects have been listed in convenient form in a monograph by Rogers (11). His list, with notes concerning the frequency of occurrence of certain physical defects, follows.

GROWTH

Normal development in height and weight is a fundamental indicator of normal health. The satisfactoriness of such development can, of course, be judged only roughly. Pupils must not be expected to conform exactly to the standards set in height-weight-age tables because differences of race and heredity make pupils differ in these respects. A short stocky boy may be perfectly healthy and normal as to growth but in terms of the height-weight-age table be "too short" for his weight and age; and conversely for a tall slender boy or girl. The Physical Growth Record for Boys and Girls has been developed for plotting growth in height and weight according to the child's physical type: thin, medium, or stocky. Moreover, growth is not always regular; but if a pupil moves sharply out of the channel of growth appropriate for his physique, medical attention is required to make sure nothing is wrong.

CARRIAGE

The customary position of the head and shoulders and the general position in which the child places his body when standing or sitting may be interpreted by the teacher as an indication of the state of general health. When not due to inheritance or to some bony deformity, bad posture is to be taken as a sign of fatigue or general weakness resulting from wrong feeding or some other condition of poor hygiene.

Skin and Hair

Uncleanliness of the skin and hair is important for guidance evaluation both for aesthetic reasons, in that it may affect the social adjustment of pupils, and for reasons of practical efficiency. Its importance in the latter respect may be judged from the following quotation: "The worst problem in health counseling (in secondary schools) is that of skin disease, particularly scabies, which causes more continued absences than any other disease" (6 : 88). Apart from the cleanliness of the skin and hair and the presence of such skin diseases as ringworm, impetigo, and scabies, the teacher should note the general appearance and color of the pupil's skin. Cold or purplish appearance of the arms, hands, and lips suggests that something may be wrong with the organs of circulation, that the pupil is not properly fed, or that he is insufficiently clothed.

Eyes

Even today, perhaps, there are teachers who forget the importance of the pupil's eyes. There is no excuse for a teacher's being ignorant of whether a pupil is handicapped by defective eyesight. Failure in school work, social maladjustment, and emotional instability can often be traced to visual defects. Nearsightedness, farsightedness, astigmatism, squint-eyes, and cross-eyes are the major types of visual defect for which teachers should be on the alert.

The size of the problem of student vision is indicated by the finding that approximately 33 percent of the students entering the University of Minnesota in the fall of 1936–37 were found to have visual errors of sufficient severity that they should have worn glasses (13 : 516). Data for elementary and secondary schools indicate a similar frequency of visual defects (10 : 6).

Ears

Hearing is only slightly less important than vision. A considerable number of students have impaired hearing, and more are thus handicapped than we usually suppose. Boynton's data, cited above, show that 5.4 percent of her university students had impaired hearing in both ears of such grade that it probably was some handicap. Slowness, dullness, or mistakes in a child's schoolroom responses should make one suspect poor hearing; a special test seems almost indispensable. Subnormal hearing may be detected with either an audiometer, a watch, or the voice test. Actual ear disease is indicated by the presence in the ear of a light yellow discharge that is readily seen on looking into the ear.

Nose

Except when afflicted with a cold or hay fever, every pupil ought to be able to breathe freely through his nose. Defective breathing was found in 6 percent of the children in New York state, in 13 percent of rural Indiana boys (Porter County Survey), and in 4 percent of Detroit children (10 : 15). Although the condition tends to improve eventually, and is practically nonexistent among adults, while it exists it is often a menace to health and to the integrity of hearing.

Teeth

Although the decay of the first teeth is not a normal condition (though it is so common as to seem so), already at six or seven years of age uncared-for children usually have several decayed teeth each, mostly of this first set. The second set of teeth, however, begins to appear at this time and should be preserved if possible. The first of these "permanent" teeth appear just back of the molars of the first set and often begin to decay within a few months. Tooth defects, the most frequent kind of defect in school children, occur in about 80 to 90 percent of them. Yet the dental profession claims that practically all of the permanent set can be saved. By early detection and treatment, probably 90 percent of the caries can be easily controlled. (4).

Throat

The condition of the tongue, the soft palate, the uvula, and the tonsils is extremely important and not difficult for teachers to evaluate. Boynton found that about 22 percent of University of Minnesota students had tonsils that were enlarged or gave evidence of being infected. The figure for the University of California is similar, 30 percent. "The examiners of nearly 600,000 school children in New York State in 1923–24 reported 16 per cent as having diseased or hypertrophied tonsils" (10 : 13).

BREATH

Rogers quotes a distinguished physiologist as saying that "bad breath has caused more misery than all the bad laws ever enacted" (11 : 16). The teacher who finds that a pupil has bad breath from day to day should do what he can to see that the cause, whether in the mouth, nose, or alimentary organs, is found and removed.

NECK

The teacher should be concerned mainly with whether the pupil has a wry neck, in which the head is drawn toward one side and the face turns toward another; or whether he has enlarged lymph glands, visible as lumps on the side of the neck at the edge of the bandlike muscles that descend obliquely on either side from just behind the ear to the upper margin of the breastbone and the collarbone. Goiter is another condition for which teachers should be on the alert.

CHEST

Here the teacher should note the existence of serious deformities, ability to breathe deeply, expansion of the chest equally on both sides, normal speed in ordinary breathing, or the presence of a chronic cough. Breathing abnormally quickly on slight exertion and a purplish color of lips or hands both may indicate a badly working heart and hence should be referred to a physician.

BACK

A stoop, an angular projection of the back ("gibbus" or "hunchback"), unequal height of shoulders, and unequally protruding shoulder blades are the main features which teachers should note here. In the Cleveland schools in one year 0.5 of 1 percent of the pupils in the first grade showed this condition.

LEGS

A limp or an evident deformity should be noticed, as well as any shortening of one leg.

FEET

Deformities of any kind, such as flat feet and calluses, and the shape, size, and condition of the shoes and stockings should be noted.

CLOTHING

Neatness, cleanliness, suitability to temperature, and proper use of overshoes should be noticed by the classroom teacher.[1]

COMMUNICABLE DISEASES

Teachers can easily learn to recognize the general signs of sickness in pupils and the general signs and symptoms of such common school-age diseases as the following: measles, scarlet fever, diphtheria, tonsillitis, smallpox, chickenpox, mumps, German measles, and whooping cough. The periods of communicability and the incubation periods, or the time required after exposure for the disease to develop, are also valuable facts for teachers.

RELATIONSHIP OF TEACHER TO OTHER HEALTH AGENCIES

What should be the relationship of the classroom teacher to other social agencies that are concerned with pupils' physical health, particularly the medical and nursing professions?

The amount of trained medical help available to classroom teachers varies from zero in one-room country schoolhouses, through a single trained nurse for an entire township school system, through one or more nurses and physicians for an entire school system, through a resident physician for a single school, to the elaborate, hospital-like student health services in our large state universities. What the classroom teacher will evaluate concerning the physical aspects of his pupils must vary in each of these situations. Consequently it is impossible to give a fixed set of rules for all of them. The medical profession does not think teachers are "meddling" when they evaluate the physical aspects of their pu-

---

[1] This list includes only the physical aspects for whose evaluation teachers are readily qualified. A more extensive treatment, intended for physical educators and school nurses is given in G. G. Deaver, *Fundamentals of Physical Examination,* Philadelphia: W. B. Saunders Company, 1939.

pils. On the contrary, as is seen in the following quotation from Rogers (11 : 1), it is highly favorable to this sort of evaluation:

The committee on legislation of the White House Conference on Child Health and Protection urged the training of teachers for the detection of signs of communicable disease and of gross physical defects. One of the forty-eight physicians of this group remarked that the ability of the teacher in this field "is the keystone of medical inspection." There can be no substitute for such service, for the appearance of communicable disease in a schoolroom does not await the coming of a physician or nurse, and no one is in such a position of vantage for observing any lapse of the child from a condition which seems, for him, normal.

Rogers also draws the following conclusion from his discussion of physical-mental relations:

The thoroughgoing training school for teachers will include as a fundamental in its curriculum the close observation of physical traits of the instruments (i.e., pupils) with which they are to work. The material to be studied is always at hand in the pupils of the training school, and such a course of physical examination may well supplement the didactic work in physiology and hygiene which it will serve to bring home to the student in a practical way. Nor does it require a long and laborious schooling to prepare the teacher in such physical appraisement. If nice distinctions were to be made in physical examination or decisions as to the treatments of diseases or defects, such would be the case, but these are not in the domain of the teacher but are left to the physician or dentist.

Teachers in service can be trained for this work by the school physician, who does not need to go searching for illustrations of physical defects.

While her powers of observation will be sharpened more rapidly by good training, the teacher, with the help of such directions as are offered herewith, can do effective work.

A rich source of ideas concerning the teachers' knowledge of the health deficiencies of their pupils and concerning their participation in the health program is the monograph by Franzen which reports on the School Health Study of the American Child Health Association (5). Concerning teacher recognition of the health needs of their pupils, Franzen concludes (5 : 19):

1. Teachers have knowledge of only a very small proportion of the cases that are in definite need of professional attention. [See Table 27.]

2. There is definite evidence that the teacher is able to perform a very useful function in initiation and reference.

3. The teacher alone can combine selection, education and continuity of attention. She is best situated to refer cases for examination, use the material for habit structure, and maintain a continuing interest in the encouragement of corrections.

TABLE 27. Recognition by Teacher of Health Needs
(After 5 : 19)

Defect as Defined	No. Children Examined	Percentage of Children Truly Having Defect as Defined		Percentage of Children with True Defect Who Were Reported by the Teacher (Efficiency Quotient)		Percentage of Children Who Were Reported by the Teacher as Having Defect and Show the Defect by Measurement (Accuracy Quotient)	
		Girls	Boys	Girls	Boys	Girls	Boys
Vision............	7366	16	12	14	16	61	59
Teeth............	2510	14	14	11	14	55	64
Growth and development.....	2338	18	17	16	12	43	45
Hearing[a].........	4559	3		19		32	

[a] Not reported separately by boys and girls because 3 percent of the group makes the numbers inadequate for such a division.

4. The great need at present is for instruction and supervision of the teacher by coordinated action of health education supervisor, nurse and medical examiner.

To this last conclusion we would add "teacher training institutions."

In the School Health Study, of which Franzen's monograph is the final report, there were four major phases: (1) construction of health tests and their application to 70 groups of school children, (2) removal of extraneous influences and allowance for economic status, (3) selection of distinctive aspects of procedure which are correlated with school health tests, and (4) grouping of selected items and interpretation so as to yield the elements of school health procedures which bring school health results. In the generalizations of this fourth phase we find valuable indications of the relationships which a teacher's health work should have to the work of other school health agencies. The first of these principles, characteristic of school health programs that actually produce results, is *sympathetic coöperation between nurse and teacher* (5 : 58). This includes items giving evidence of:

Discussion and agreement between nurse and teacher about health procedure and policy.

Discussion and agreement between teacher and oral hygienist about health procedure and policy.

Active records which involve a mutual recognition of the health needs of children by teacher and nurse.

Classroom information included in nurse's home visit preparation.

Teacher initiative relative to the health of her pupils and reference to the nurse.

Presence and participation of teacher in physical examination and of nurse in classroom inspections.

The only aspect of nurse-teacher rapport that had a satisfactory frequency of favorable occurrence is initiative by the teacher and reference to the nurse. The other five Franzen judged to be in great need of improvement, at least in the presumably typical schools which participated in the School Health Study.

The second generalization concerning the nature of the effective school health program deals with *physical examination by a trained medical doctor*. When all the items of such an examination are separated into those which do and do not have a measurable school health effect, we find that those which do have such an effect are the ones that are characteristic of an *extended* examination. No two-minute line-ups contain these desirable items—desirable because they have a proved relation to school health results as measured.

Thus the thorough, effective physical examination includes such items as individual hearing tests, palpation of cervical glands, accurate measurements of distances in hearing, and a dental examination by a dentist rather than a physician which makes a distinction between temporary and permanent teeth. These items occurred in less than half of the survey units included in the School Health Study.

To increase the possibilities for more frequent examinations by physicians Franzen recommends that the relation between teachers and physicians be changed so as to develop more fully the teacher's potentialities for referring cases to physicians. Teachers can be trained so as to increase the validity of their suspicions concerning pupils' teeth, vision, hearing, nutritional status, and skin conditions. Thus aided by teachers' referrals, physicians and nurses will be able to give adequate attention to the pupils who are referred rather than having to spend much time in necessarily superficial inspections.

In order to enable physicians to make fewer but more intensive physical examinations of pupils, it is recommended that teachers keep histories based on an intimate knowledge of individual children extending over a long range of time.

The medical examination should be a subsequent reference service. That is, measurement and "history" can better be supplied by others, such as teacher or nurse, thus permitting the physician to concentrate on his appropriate function, diagnosis.

Franzen's third generalization concerns *teachers' knowledge, opinions, and beliefs.* Not technical knowledge but methods of teaching, manner of approach, knowledge of children, opinion of relative value of health practices, progressive attitudes toward methods of teaching, and acquaintance with authoritative health books and journals stand forth as characteristics of teachers that discriminate best between programs that do and do not increase school health. It is along the lines of this third generalization that the teacher can most independently go about making his contribution to school health. No nurse or physician is necessary for a teacher to attain the enlightenment which Franzen found so highly related to the physical and mental health of pupils.

LEGAL CONSIDERATIONS IN THE EVALUATION OF PHYSICAL ASPECTS

Political and social recognition of the importance of pupil health has led to the inclusion in school laws of references to the evaluation of pupils' physical status. The following paragraphs from the school laws of the state of Indiana **(8)** may serve as an illustration of a permissive law:

225. *Medical inspection of children*
 1. That all school trustees and township trustees are herewith permitted and recommended to institute medical inspection of school children at any time, the said trustees may require teachers to annually test the sight and hearing of all school children under their charge, the said test and uses thereof to be made according to the rules hereinafter authorized.
226. *Medical inspection defined*
 2. The term, medical inspection, as used in this Act, shall be held to mean the testing of the sight and hearing of school children and the inspection of said children by school physicians for disease, disability, decayed teeth, or other defects, which may reduce efficiency or tend to prevent their receiving the full benefit of school work.

These laws were written in 1911. Even then recognition was given to the role of the teacher in evaluating the physical aspects of pupils. The medical profession has frequently been instrumental in bringing about the passage of such laws. Hoag and Terman (7 : 64) report that in 1906 when the legislature of Massachusetts was considering a mandatory provision by which vision and hearing were to be tested by teachers, sittings were held during which a mass of evidence as to the feasibility of the plan was offered by some of the best-known (medical) specialists of the state.

The following quotation from Burks and Burks (3 : 156–157) is also illustrative of the essential lack of novelty in what has been said here concerning the teacher's role in evaluating pupils' physical status. In 1913 they wrote: "Minnesota is even training her teachers to make general physical examinations, the claim being that trained teachers can recognize 90 per cent of the defects of children. . . . Swarthmore College, recognizing the direct responsibility of teachers toward the health of children, has actually added a course of medical inspection to its teacher's preparatory course. School children are brought to the college every week and the students under the supervision of the physical director are taught the methods of inspection and examination."

REFERENCES

1. American Association of School Administrators, "Health in Schools," *Twentieth Yearbook*, Washington, rev. ed., 1951.

2. Brown, Marion, *Leadership Among High School Students*, Teachers College Contributions to Education No. 559, New York: Teachers College, Bureau of Publications, Columbia University, 1933.

3. Burks, F. W. and J. D., *Health and the School*, New York: D. Appleton and Company, 1913.

4. Cross, H. D., "Possibilities in dental hygiene," *American Journal of Public Health*, 16:234–236 (1926).

5. Franzen, Raymond, *An Evaluation of School Health Procedures*, New York: American Child Health Association, 1933.

6. Hess, Frederick, "Health counseling service at Louisville," *Proceedings of the Conference on Guidance and Student Personnel Work*, Evanston: Northwestern University, 1936.

7. Hoag, E. V., and Terman, L. M., *Health Work in the Schools*, Boston: Houghton Mifflin Company, 1914.

8. McMurray, Floyd I., *School Laws of the State of Indiana*, Department of Public Instruction, Indianapolis, Indiana, 1939. (The laws were prepared under his direction.)

9. Paterson, D. G., *Physique and Intellect*, New York: Appleton-Century-Crofts, 1930.

10. Rogers, J. F., *Physical Defects of School Children*, Department of the Interior, Office of Education, School Health Studies No. 15, Washington: Government Printing Office, 1925.

11. Rogers, J. F., *What Every Teacher Should Know About the Physical Condition of Her Pupils*, Department of the Interior, Office of Education Pamphlet 68, Washington: Government Printing Office, 1936.

12. Wheatley, G. M., Koplik, L. H., *et al.*, *What Teachers See*, New York: Metropolitan Life Insurance Co., 1951.

13. Williamson, E. G., *How to Counsel Students*, New York: McGraw-Hill Book Company, Inc., 1939.

14. Wilson, C. C. (ed.), *School Health Services; A Report of the Joint Committee on Health Problems in Education of the National Education Association and the American Medical Association with the Cooperation of Contributors and Consultants*, Washington: National Education Association, 1953.

CHAPTER XIX

Evaluating Physical Aspects of Pupils

In this chapter we present the techniques whereby teachers can evaluate the physical aspects of their pupils. The role of the teacher in providing this evaluation and health service must always be as a supplement to other health agencies the school may provide, such as school nurses and physicians. Teachers cannot be expected to possess, except in very slight degree, the technical information required for detailed diagnoses of physical defects and diseases. They must serve merely in the capacity of enlightened laymen. They should be willing to accept the encouragement of the medical profession that they can do effective work in detecting physical disorders incompatible with normal growth, development, and educational progress, or dangerous to other members of society. If every pupil could be examined by a physician every day of the school year, it would be unnecessary for the teacher to be concerned with this type of evaluation. Since this is manifestly impossible even in the largest city school systems, the teacher must be the best possible substitute in providing such service. It has been demonstrated in many schools that only a short time is required for teachers to become sufficiently acquainted with the signs and symptoms of physical disorders to be able to evaluate their pupils in this way and call attention to conditions that need examination by a physician.

We now take up the techniques and considerations involved in evaluating each of the physical aspects of pupils discussed in Chapter XVIII.

VARIOUS PHYSICAL ASPECTS AND MEANS OF EVALUATION

Growth

Determining the pupil's weight and height are the two most important procedures involved in evaluating his growth. The chief value in weighing and measuring pupils is in the educational experience for them, not as an index of pupil health. Height-weight-age tables can easily be misinterpreted. Equally healthy children of the same age may vary considerably in height or weight, or in both together. Differences in diet, race, nationality, and constitutional body type are not taken into account by such tables. Even more refined measurements of the size and weight of the body, based on elaborate anthropometric procedures, do not provide a safe way of determining a pupil's physical fitness.

Jenss and Souther (3) correlated four indices of body build (the Baldwin-Wood Weight-Height-Age Tables, the ACH Index of Nutritional Status, the Nutritional Status Indices, and the Pryor Width-Weight Tables) against clinical judgments by a physician. The subjects of their study were 713 seven-year-old children of both sexes. None of the four indices proved to be an efficient method of identifying children who, according to the physician's criteria of nutritional status, need of medical and dental care, etc., are likely to be physically unfit. "The indices are neither selective nor sensitive, as they fail to identify a considerable number of boys and girls whom a given criterion selects as likely to be in need of medical care or nutritional advice and assistance, and, in addition, they often identify children who were not selected by the criterion" (3 : 94). The interest of pupils in their own growth is, however, well satisfied by means of periodic measurements with a scale.

Measures of height and weight become most meaningful when plotted over a period of years. One device that has been developed for this purpose is the Physical Growth Record for Boys and Girls.[1] These forms show height and weight zones for normal boys and girls of ages four to eighteen. The height zones show the range for each age that should be considered short, moderately short, aver-

[1] Available from the National Education Association, 1201 Sixteenth St., N. W., Washington, D.C., or from the Order Department of the American Medical Association, 535 N. Dearborn Street, Chicago 10, Illinois.

age, moderately tall, and tall. The weight zones similarly indicate the range from light to heavy. The charts include directions for measuring height and weight, plotting the record, and interpreting the child's growth.

The terms "underweight" and "malnourished" should not be considered synonymous. The former relates to a height-weight-age table, and the latter to the pupil's own most healthy condition. Nevertheless, the measurement of height and weight with reference to tables can be valuable in revealing whether a pupil has gained satisfactorily from year to year and in interesting him in his progress. The most valid guide in evaluating growth, however, must always remain the personal experience, training, and insight of the observer. Teachers seldom differ greatly among themselves in their opinion concerning the healthy or unhealthy *appearance* of a pupil. It is this appearance, rather than size, to which we must attend when we speak of nutrition. Underheight and underweight are, of course, important and should be kept in mind, but more important are the pupil's appearance of vigor or lethargy, alertness or dullness, the clearness of his eyes, the glow or pallor of his skin, and the lack or overabundance of layers of fatty tissues beneath the skin.

POSTURE OR CARRIAGE

The posture or carriage of a pupil is easily evaluated by comparing his way of holding his body, of carrying himself—standing, walking, or sitting—with the standards of good posture. These standards are illustrated in Fig. 23.

It is essential in evaluating posture to create a situation such that the pupils will not self-consciously assume a pose rather than their usual posture. Thus, misleading results are usually obtained if pupils are lined up in groups for the examination of posture or shadow graphs.

One way to bring out typical posture is that used by Kephart and Floyd (5). To determine whether children had head tilt—a tendency to tilt the head noticeably to one side when standing erect and looking at an object twenty feet in front—they ostensibly tested the pupil's vision with an eye chart. As the child reached the point where it became difficult for him to recognize the letters on

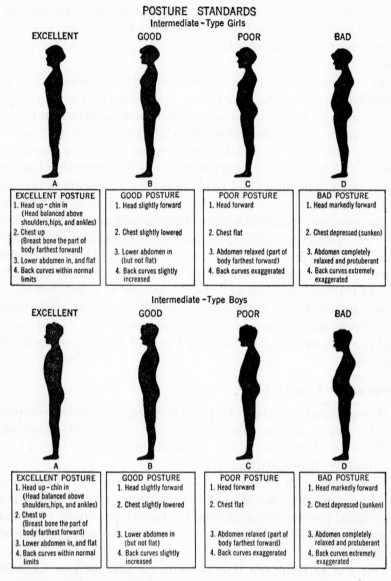

POSTURE STANDARDS

Intermediate – Type Girls

EXCELLENT	GOOD	POOR	BAD
A	**B**	**C**	**D**

EXCELLENT POSTURE	GOOD POSTURE	POOR POSTURE	BAD POSTURE
1. Head up - chin in (Head balanced above shoulders, hips, and ankles)	1. Head slightly forward	1. Head forward	1. Head markedly forward
2. Chest up (Breast bone the part of body farthest forward)	2. Chest slightly lowered	2. Chest flat	2. Chest depressed (sunken)
3. Lower abdomen in, and flat	3. Lower abdomen in (but not flat)	3. Abdomen relaxed (part of body farthest forward)	3. Abdomen completely relaxed and protuberant
4. Back curves within normal limits	4. Back curves slightly increased	4. Back curves exaggerated	4. Back curves extremely exaggerated

Intermediate – Type Boys

EXCELLENT	GOOD	POOR	BAD
A	**B**	**C**	**D**

EXCELLENT POSTURE	GOOD POSTURE	POOR POSTURE	BAD POSTURE
1. Head up - chin in (Head balanced above shoulders, hips, and ankles)	1. Head slightly forward	1. Head forward	1. Head markedly forward
2. Chest up (Breast bone the part of body farthest forward)	2. Chest slightly lowered	2. Chest flat	2. Chest depressed (sunken)
3. Lower abdomen in, and flat	3. Lower abdomen in (but not flat)	3. Abdomen relaxed (part of body farthest forward)	3. Abdomen completely relaxed and protuberant
4. Back curves within normal limits	4. Back curves slightly increased	4. Back curves exaggerated	4. Back curves extremely exaggerated

FIG. 23. Posture Standards for Girls and Boys. (After 3 : 10–11.)

the chart, a camera in front of him was snapped and a full-length front-view photograph of him was obtained. Judgments made by different judges of the photographs as to the presence or absence of head tilt were found to agree closely. There was also a high degree of constancy as to whether a given child showed head tilt from one day to another.

Very poor posture can be corrected and is worth correcting. Klein and Thomas (7) found that training pupils according to the exercises in *Posture Exercises, a Handbook for Schools and for Teachers of Physical Education* (6) strikingly reduced the prevalence of poor posture in school children. Furthermore, this improvement was associated with improvement in health, efficiency, and school work as revealed in attendance, deportment, and scholarship.

Skin and Hair

General cleanliness can usually be evaluated by simple observation. It can be fostered by emphasizing it in the classroom, drawing the pupils' attention to its desirability, and discussing with them the harmful aesthetic, social, and physical effects of uncleanliness. In general, uncleanliness facilitates infection by parasites and the spread of contagious diseases.

Among the various skin diseases for which teachers should be on the alert are ringworm, impetigo, scabies, acne, and eczema. Ringworm shows itself by a slightly raised, reddish scaly spot which enlarges, the center clearing and the edges advancing as a superficial scaling in the form of a circular or oval "ring." It may occur on any part of the body, on the face, neck, or arms, and also on the scalp or between the toes. Treatment is usually effective for ringworm on the body, but very difficult when on the head or feet.

Impetigo appears as a crust of fingernail size, irregular in shape and honey-yellow in color, usually on the face or hands and often behind the ears. New spots can result from the material being carried from one lesion to other parts of the skin. Since the disease is highly contagious, the pupil should be kept out of school.

Scabies is evidenced by red points and lines on the skin that indicate the punctures and pathways of the itch mite that causes it. The itch mite is an insect which bores into the skin and causes an intense itching; scratching is the most obvious symptom. The mites themselves are too small to be seen easily. Because they are easily transmitted, especially within families, and can easily cause secondary infection, cases of scabies should be excluded from school. Reinfection readily occurs unless the underlying colonies of the itch mite in clothes or bedding or other persons are eliminated. For this, the whole family must be treated and its clothes and linen sterilized by heat.

Acne is most frequent during adolescence, being characterized by pimples or "furuncles" on the skin of the face. The discharge from one pimple produces new lesions when spread to other portions of the skin; hence the disease easily becomes chronic, leaving unsightly scars. The mental hygiene aspect of acne is especially important because its unsightliness is apt to make adolescents feel miserable. Teachers should be on the lookout for incipient cases, caution pupils against fingering the lesions, and advise prompt medical attention. Soap and water are an excellent preventive, and the frequency with which the condition clears up when boys begin to shave suggests that cleanliness can also assist in the cure. Attention to diet, especially the limitation of sweets, cocoa, and chocolate, also helps in many cases.

Eczema takes the form of patches of roughness that crack, scale, and at times exude moisture. Frequently chronic, it is often due to allergy, the sensitivity of the individual either to certain foods or to something in the clothes or environment that comes in direct contact with the skin. It is not contagious, but its discomfort and unsightliness should lead pupils to seek prompt medical attention.

Apart from these skin infections, the teacher should be on the alert for contagious diseases which manifest themselves by the appearance of the skin, such as measles, German measles, scarlet fever, chickenpox, and smallpox. In general, they are characterized by a rash of red spots whose size and distribution on the body vary according to the disease. The scarlet fever rash is like a generalized blush; whole portions of the body appear red. The German measles rash is composed of separate little red spots, closely set and merging together in places, but presenting the isolated lesions somewhere on the body. The measles rash has larger spots than German measles, and they tend to form blotches of smaller or larger size. In these three diseases the rash spreads from the neck downward over the chest, abdomen, and extremities; the scarlet fever rash generally avoids the face, but the other two do not.

Chickenpox differs greatly from these three diseases, for typically it occurs as tiny water blisters known as vesicles that rupture easily and are surrounded by a narrow zone of redness. Instead of spreading downward in the wavelike fashion of the other diseases, chickenpox lesions come out in groups in the spaces between the older lesions. In this disease, several stages of lesions are present at one time, and they are more abundant on the body than on the face or limbs. Smallpox differs from chickenpox in that the vesicles are all at the same stage, first little red bumps that gradually change into lesions with pus. It is further differentiated from chickenpox in that it affects the arms, hands, legs, feet, and face more than the trunk.

The pupils' hair should be watched mainly for the presence of lice and of nits, or the eggs of the lice. Any prolonged itching and scratching of the scalp should lead the teacher to suspect these conditions. The live lice are too small to be found easily, but the nits are easily seen as oval gray bodies clinging to the hair, especially behind the ears and on the back of the head. Like scabies, the condition is easily transmitted, especially within families, and generally the entire family must be treated at a time. Like scabies, head lice are more common in pupils from lower economic strata but are not confined to them. Lice should be eradicated as a sign of uncleanliness and a cause of discomfort and infections of other kinds. Live nits can be killed by applying appropriate medication to the scalp; they are removed by softening with vinegar and combing. The condition is simple to treat in boys—merely cutting the hair short.

EYES

Several methods can readily be used by teachers in evaluating pupils' eyesight. Among these are the Snellen Chart,[2] a check list

[2] For very young pupils who have not yet learned the alphabet, special Snellen Charts with only E's pointing up, down, or to either side are available. Snellen Charts may be obtained from the American Medical Association, 535 N. Dearborn Street, Chicago 10, Illinois, and from the National Society for the Prevention of Blindness, 50 West 50th Street, New York City.

of observable behaviors, the Eames Eye Test, and the Betts Tele-binocular. The Snellen Chart should be kept out of sight and in a clean place to prevent the pupils from becoming familiar with the letters and to keep it in good condition. When in use, it should be placed so that the pupil can stand at a distance of exactly 20 feet from it; it should be in a good light (about 10 foot-candles) that is evenly distributed, and the general illumination in the room should not be less than one-fifth of the chart illumination (not less than 2 foot-candles). The light should not shine into the pupil's eyes but should come from the side. The height of the chart should be such that the child's eye will be level with the 20-foot line. The 20-foot distance from the chart should be marked off, and also the 15-, 10-, and 5-foot distances; these shorter distances are used only for teaching small children to use the chart and for those who cannot see the 20-foot line at 20 feet. The pupil should cover one eye with a cover card; both eyes should remain open during the test. If the pupil wears glasses, he should be tested first with them and then without. Squinting and straining should not be permitted.

A standardized routine should be followed to avoid confusion: test the right eye first, then the left eye, and then both together. Beginning at the top of the chart with the larger letters, the pupil should read all the letters he can. If he reads all of them, including those for the distance at which he is placed, he is not nearsighted, but he may be farsighted or moderately astigmatic, or have muscular strain when using both eyes. If he reads smaller letters than are expected of the normal eye (as in reading the 15-foot line at 20 feet) his vision is keener than that of the average person. Inability to read the line expected of the normal eye, but only the 30- or 40-foot line at 20 feet may indicate nearsightedness, astigmatism, defects in the refractive media of the eye, corneal scars, or even fairly high degrees of farsightedness.

The visual acuity for each eye should be recorded as a fraction whose numerator is the pupil's distance from the chart and whose denominator is the distance at which normal eyes can read the line. For example, 20/20 means normal visual acuity, i.e., the pupil can read at 20 feet the letters that normal eyes can read at 20 feet; 20/200 means such defectiveness that the pupil can read at only 20 feet what normal eyes can read at 200 feet; 20/15 means being able to read at 20 feet what the normal eye can read at only 15 feet. These fractions should not be considered as percentages of normal vision.

Measurements with the Snellen Chart should be correlated with observations of pupils' visual behavior in the classroom. The following list of observable behaviors that are symptomatic of disturbances of vision has been suggested:

Attempts to brush away blurs.
Blinks more than usual when reading.
Holds the book far away from face when reading.
Holds face close to the page when reading.
Holds the body tense when looking at distant objects.
Is inattentive during reading lessons.
Is inattentive during wall-chart, map, or blackboard lessons.
Is inattentive during class discussion of field trips or visits to museums.
Is irritable over work.
Reads only brief periods without stopping.
Reads when he should be at play.
Rubs eyes frequently.
Screws up face when reading.
Screws up face when looking at distant objects.
Shuts or covers one eye when reading.
Thrusts head forward to see distant objects.
Tilts head to one side when reading.
Has poor alignment in penmanship.
Has reversal tendencies in reading.
Tends to look cross-eyed when reading.
When reading, tends to make frequent changes in distance at which he
  holds his book.
When reading, tends to lose the place on the page.
Confusion in reading and spelling: o's and a's, e's and c's; n's and m's;
  h's, n's, and r's; s's and t's.
Apparently guesses from a quick recognition of parts of the word in
  easy reading material.

The Eames Eye Test[3] consists of seven parts, each of which is aimed at the detection of eye defects needing professional care. (1) The visual acuity test is the conventional Snellen-type test. (2) The lens test is similar to the visual acuity test except that the

[3] Obtainable from the World Book Company, Yonkers, New York.

pupil attempts to read the letters while looking through a lens designed to detect farsightedness. (3) The astigmatic chart test is the conventional radiating-line test for astigmatism. (4) The coördination test requires the pupil to look at a card depicting a chicken and a box through a hand stereoscope. (5) The fusion test uses a card on which moon and stars appear, to detect defects of binocular vision. Tests (6) and (7) are for fusion of type and eye dominance, aspects of pupil vision that may be of interest to school psychologists and remedial teachers.

The Eames test represents a valuable compromise between the overly simple Snellen Chart and the more elaborate Betts Telebinocular described below. Its relatively low cost and ease of administration and interpretation increase its value for classroom vision testing by teachers in order to discover eye troubles that need professional attention without regard to specific diagnosis. Evidence that the Eames Eye Test has a high degree of reliability and validity, in terms of agreement with retests and with an oculist's examination, has been presented by Eames (1).

The Betts Telebinocular is an instrument for testing (1) the ability to fuse images created in the two eyes and (2) the ability to perceive depth. It consists of a pair of binocular lenses mounted on a stand and equipped with a staff or stand to which is attached a movable slide holder. The slides, placed at various positions along the stand, are viewed through the binoculars. From the pupil's report of what he sees in the various slides, the examiner can determine visual acuity, muscular balance, ability to fuse images, astigmatism, and the like. Some technical knowledge is required for the correct use and interpretation of the Telebinocular; this can be acquired only by working with the instrument itself. If the school system can afford to make the instrument available to teachers, they can easily learn to use it and will find it a valuable supplement in evaluating vision.[4]

Although only a small percentage of boys are color-blind, and a still smaller percentage of girls, pupils should be examined for color blindness because of its implications for educational and vocational guidance. Obviously, the color-blind boy should be

[4] Information concerning the Telebinocular is available from the Keystone View Company, Meadville, Pa.

discouraged from aspiring to any occupation, such as railroad engineering, where color blindness is a severe handicap. The Holmgren test for color blindness makes use of a standard test of various colored yarns which the pupil is required to group according to color. The Ishihara test for color blindness requires the pupil to read numbers formed by various colored dots on a background of colored dots. The special materials required for either of these tests can be obtained from any scientific supply company.

EARS

A pupil's hearing can be tested most accurately by the audiometer, an instrument developed by the Bell Telephone Laboratories and the Western Electric Company.[5] Several different types are available, only some of which are adapted to testing hearing in school. The 4A audiometer, consisting of a phonograph and a telephone apparatus whose headset is clamped to the ear, enables the testing, one ear at a time, of any number of children up to forty at the same time. The testing room must, of course, be very quiet. The pupil is required to write on a special form the numbers dictated to him by the phonograph through the earphone. The completed forms, when compared with a key or standard, enable an estimate of the amount of hearing loss. For some children as many as four tests may be necessary to secure reliable results; children who cannot write must be tested in some other manner.

The 5A audiometer, for individual testing, has a similar earphone but requires the pupil to push a button that lights a light when he no longer hears a buzz or hum whose intensity the examiner regulates by turning a dial. The amount of hearing loss is read directly from the dial on the instrument. Advantages of the 5A are its simplicity, the short time (15–30 seconds) required for the test, and the possibility of testing kindergarten children as readily as college students. Marked hearing defects for higher-pitched notes, however, are not always detected with the 5A.

When an audiometer is not available, cruder but valuable examinations can be made with the whispered speech test or the

[5] Information concerning audiometer equipment can be obtained from the Council on Physical Medicine and Rehabilitation, American Medical Association, 535 N. Dearborn Street, Chicago 10, Illinois.

watch-tick test. In the speech test, the examiner first roughly stand-
ardizes the intensity of the whisper that can just barely be heard at
20 feet by several people whose hearing is known to be normal.
One ear is tested at a time, the other ear being closed by the pupil's holding the palm of his hand over it. His eyes should be
closed, or his back should be turned toward the examiner. The
room should be as quiet as possible. The pupil is asked to repeat
whispered words or numbers. If he fails at 20 feet, the examiner
moves up a foot at a time and repeats the whispering until the pupil succeeds in hearing him. The results of the test are expressed as
in the Snellen Chart eye test: if the pupil can hear the standardized whispered voice, he has 20/20 hearing; if he can hear only at
15 feet, he has 15/20 hearing, and so forth.

The watch-tick test is still more convenient, because it provides
a more constant stimulus and requires little space. Here again the
room should be very quiet. A watch of medium size and quietness
should be used. If possible, a stopwatch should be used, for this enables the examiner to interrupt the ticking sound to check the validity of the pupil's responses. The standard distance, that at which
persons of known normal hearing can hear the watch tick in a
quiet room, is first determined. In actual testing, the examiner
should stand behind the pupil and cut off his side vision with a
card held at the side of his head. The watch should be held at about
the level of the pupil's head. The watch is held at arm's length
from the pupil's ear, then gradually brought closer until the pupil
signifies that he hears the tick; the distance of the watch from the
ear at this point is measured. Hearing acuity is again expressed in
the form of a fraction, pupil's distance over standard distance. If
this fraction is less than one-half, the pupil should be referred to a
physician.

Observation of pupils' listening habits often reveals to the alert
teacher those who are having trouble in hearing. Some of the signs
of deafness are (2 : 21):

    Listlessness and inattention
    Frequent mistakes or failure in carrying out instructions
    Failure to respond when questioned
    Turning one ear toward the speaker
    Defects in speech

Peculiar qualities of the voice

Falling below par in subjects that are taught orally

Avoiding people

Discharging ears (frequently detected by odor)

Earaches

Noises in head (children sometimes complain of a buzzing or
   ringing sound)

By looking into the pupil's ears, the teacher can see whether discharges of light yellow material are present. If they are impacted and hardened or overly abundant, the pupil should be referred to a physician.

NOSE

Defects of the nose most frequently show up in the form of habitual mouth breathing. The pupil's mouth usually sags open, he has a vacant expression on his face, pinched nostrils, dull eyes, drooping eyelids, and round shoulders. The clearness of each nasal passage is easily tested by pressing on one side of the nose and having the pupil try to breathe through the other with the mouth shut. Habitual mouth breathing due to obstructed breathing passages can easily cause many other physical maladjustments. It should therefore always receive medical attention.

Whether a pupil has hay fever of any kind is an important item in some cases of vocational guidance. Hay fever should be suspected in children who seem to catch "colds" regularly in the late spring, summer, or early autumn. Sneezing, nasal discharges, and red, inflamed, or discharging eyes are all symptoms of colds and hay fever.

TEETH AND MOUTH

In the absence of a dentist, the teacher can make a first approximation toward examining the pupils' teeth. Since whatever defects are discovered will have to be referred to a dentist for correction and rediscovered by him, the chief value of the teacher's examination of teeth does not lie in the detection of dental defects. The educational value of such examinations and the advice that should accompany them are the major outcome of the teacher's work.

In examining the teeth the teacher should first observe the pupil with jaws closed and lips drawn apart, so that the efficiency of the bite can be seen. If a large number of teeth do not meet each other in the normal bite, chewing may be seriously affected. The teeth should next be examined with the mouth wide open and the head thrown back. It is possible for even the untrained to note inflamed or ulcerated gums, decayed teeth, and general oral uncleanliness. Furthermore, the teacher should be alert to note irregularities of the jaws or teeth which mar facial appearance and speech. Any defects should be brought to the attention of the pupil's parents and referred to a dentist for correction. The pupil's breath should also be noted during the dental examination as well as during daily contacts with him.

THROAT

The throat should be inspected with the pupil facing a good light, usually without the use of a tongue depressor; the pupil should open his mouth wide, extend his tongue, and utter a prolonged "ah!" If a tongue depressor is necessary, care should be taken that it is disposed of immediately after use to prevent its being handled or used again. If possible, the tonsils should also be inspected. The size of the tonsils, whether large or small, is not of itself significant. Symptoms for which teachers should be on the alert are a fiery red throat, with or without yellow spots on the tonsils, and also the presence of a small or large grayish patch on the tonsils or adjacent soft palate. Any of these conditions should be brought to the attention of a physician. The health history of the pupil is of special significance here, frequent attacks of tonsillitis or rheumatism, huskiness of the voice, or hacking little coughs all being cause for concern.

NECK

Enlarged lymph glands are the most frequent defect or disease in the region of the neck. They are detected by touch as lumps occurring in a slanting line from behind the angle of the jaw toward the junction of the breast and collarbones. Enlarged glands may indicate infection in the nose, mouth, or throat; decaying teeth, or possibly chronic infections, including tuberculosis. The pupil with enlarged lymph glands should receive immediate and thorough medical care.

Goiter, or abnormal enlargement of the thyroid gland on either side of the windpipe at the base of the neck, is another relatively frequent disturbance in the neck region. In some localities where there is a deficiency of iodine in the drinking water or food, simple goiters are common. Since the seriousness of a goiter can be determined only by a physician, all children with enlarged thyroid glands should be referred to a physician.

CHEST

Serious deformities of the chest are usually visible through the clothing. A projecting breastbone—known as pigeon breast—or flaring lower ribs may thus be noticeable. The ability to breathe deeply, equal expansion of the chest on both sides, normal speed in ordinary breathing, and the presence of a chronic cough should all be the subject of the teacher's observation. Similarly, such symptoms of a badly working heart as abnormally fast breathing on slight exertion, as when walking up stairs or playing games, and a purplish color of the lips (cyanosis) can also be observed by the alert classroom teacher and referred to a physician.

BACK

Such abnormalities as a stoop or an angular projection of the back or other structural defects of the skeleton can be observed by teachers. Serious lateral curvatures can be detected by looking at the pupil from behind when he stands with feet together and both knees straight and noting whether one shoulder or hip is higher than the other or whether one shoulder blade stands out more than the other.

LEGS AND FEET

Bowlegs, knock-knees, limping, legs of unequal length, and stiff joints should all be looked for; examination for flat feet can be made by having the pupils remove their shoes. The gait may indicate defects of the legs; a shuffling gait may indicate flat feet. The fit of stockings and shoes, whether too large or too small, should also be observed. Clubfoot, while relatively rare, is of sufficient importance in the pupil's adjustment to be given special attention in his cumulative record.

CLOTHING

Besides the shoes and stockings, the clothing should be evaluated for neatness, cleanliness, and suitability to weather; it should be called to the attention of parents whenever found lacking in any of these respects. Teachers should also see that pupils do not wear overshoes indoors.

SPEECH DEFECTS AND ABNORMAL NERVOUS CONDITIONS

Lisping, stuttering, involuntary twitchings, nervous tics, and similar phenomena can readily be observed by teachers. All such conditions should be brought to the attention of school psychologists, mental hygienists, or speech pathologists, because special attention can frequently remedy these handicaps to pupil adjustment.

USE OF THE CLINICAL THERMOMETER

Whenever a school is not staffed with a nurse or physican, the teacher should know how to use and interpret a clinical thermometer. It is probably safe to say that whenever a pupil has a temperature more than half a degree above or below 98.6° Fahrenheit, he should receive attention from a physician.

A *summary* of important points for observation has been drawn up by Rogers (8). This summary, with a small number of additions, may be used as a check list in the teacher's observation of pupils' physical aspects.

General:
General impression of physique (age, race, and heredity taken into consideration)
Vigor or weakness
Alertness or listlessness
Good or bad color
Cleanliness or uncleanliness
Face and lips:
Cleanliness

Pallor
Cyanosis or pallor of lips
Flush of fever
Ringworm, impetigo, or other disease
Hair and scalp:
Cleanliness and neatness
Signs of vermin or disease
Eyes and vision:
Frequent errors in reading

words or numbers

Complaints of headache, pain, blurred vision

Holding book too close

Evidence of difficulty in seeing at a distance

Congested eyes

Red or crusted lids

Test with Snellen letters

Color-blindness tests

Ears and hearing:

Dullness and slow response

Presence of discharge from ear

Special test with watch, voice, or audiometer

Nose:

Inability to breathe freely with mouth closed

Throat:

Signs of inflammation

Diseased tonsils

Obstructing tonsils

History of frequent sore throat

History of rheumatism

Teeth:

Decayed permanent teeth

Need of adjustment

Diseased gums

Uncleanliness

Neck:

Enlarged lymphatic glands

Enlarged thyroid glands

Wry neck

Chest:

Deformity

Rapid breathing, especially after slight exertion

Small expansion

Unequal expansion

Cough

Back:

Round shoulders

Stoop

Projection backward of spine

Unequal height of shoulders

Unequal height of hips

Projection of one shoulder blade

Arms:

Signs of scabies or ringworm

Coldness or bluish appearance

Legs:

A limp

Unequal length or other deformity

Feet:

Deformities

Shoes and stockings—shape, size, and condition

Clothing:

Neatness

Cleanliness

Suitability

Nervous disorders:

Speech defects

Involuntary movements

EDUCATIONAL GUIDANCE BASED ON THE EVALUATION OF PHYSICAL ASPECTS

In general, evaluation of the pupils' physical aspects should be followed by the referral of cases needing attention to physicians and parents. Teachers must frequently stimulate parents to see that their children receive needed medical care. And after a physician has diagnosed and treated a physical defect, the teacher must see that the treatment is carried out insofar as he can control environmental conditions and pupil behavior in and outside the school.

ORGANIZING THE EVALUATION OF PHYSICAL ASPECTS

The daily inspection or morning health review should become a classroom habit for both teachers and pupils. During the first few minutes after school opens in the morning, the teacher should see whether each pupil seems up to his usual healthy condition. Any pupil who deviates markedly from what is normal should be noted and given special attention, or "inattention," during class work. Anyone who shows signs of an acute or communicable disease should immediately be isolated until a decision is reached about his remaining in school for the day.

A more systematic and complete physical examination should be made periodically during the school year, say at the beginning, middle, and end. The findings for each pupil should be entered in a permanent cumulative record. Record forms for this purpose have been devised by the American Medical Association.

COMMUNICABLE DISEASES

Most of the common communicable diseases are readily transmitted soon after they set in; hence the teacher can perform a valuable service in preventing their spread by detecting pupils with acute illnesses as soon as possible. Once he has become familiar with the normal appearance of his pupils, it is not difficult to recognize deviations from the normal that indicate the onset of sickness. Some of the *general signs* of disease are: listlessness, weakness, drowsiness, flushed face, undue pallor, headache, sneezing, running nose, red and watering eyes, coughing, vomiting, or sore throat; an eruption on the face, neck, or arms also indicates disease. Teachers will find useful for reference purposes a list of the early symptoms of some of the common diseases that attack school children. The appearance of these symptoms in any pupil should be sufficient to have that pupil sent or taken home. The symptoms of the common diseases for which the teacher should be on the alert are as follows:

Measles. Cold in the head, with sneezing, running nose, red and watering eyes, cough, fever. The eruption does not appear until the third day.

Scarlet Fever. Vomiting, sore throat, fever; a fine scarlet rash appears within 24 hours on the neck, chest, arms, and, to some extent, the face.

Diphtheria. General signs of illness. There may be vomiting or a chill or only great prostration. The throat may be red and there may be a patch of gray membrane. The child may complain of sore throat. Fever is present, though it is usually not high.

A watery nasal discharge that irritates the upper lips should make one suspect nasal diphtheria during an epidemic.

Tonsillitis. The throat is sore; there may be a chill or chilly sensations and usually high fever. There is great prostration. The throat is much inflamed, and yellowish spots may be present on the tonsils.

Smallpox. Chill, fever, backache, headache, nausea, and vomiting are usually present. The eruption appears on the second or third day. The symptoms may be very mild and the disease may be difficult to distinguish from chickenpox.

Chickenpox. An eruption of discrete, red, raised spots appears usually first on the forehead. There may be fever, but other symptoms are slight.

Mumps. There is swelling of the parotid gland, in front of and below the ear, on one or both sides; this region is painful, especially when swallowing; and there are general signs of illness.

German measles. The symptoms are similar to those of measles but are mild. In about 50 percent of the cases there is no fever, the first sign of the disease being the eruption which appears first on the face and consists of discrete spots of a deep pink color.

In case of an epidemic of any disease, the teacher should, of course, become familiar with the symptoms of that disease.

REFERENCES

1. Eames, T. H., "The reliability and validity of the Eames Eye Test," *Journal of Educational Research,* 33:524–527 (1940).

2. Indiana State Board of Health, *Aids to the Teacher and Pupil in Health Promotion*, Indianapolis, 1941.

3. Jenss, Rachel M., and Souther, Susan P., *Methods of Assessing the Physical Fitness of Children*, Washington: U.S. Department of Labor, Children's Bureau Publication No. 263, 1940.

4. Joint Committee on Health Problems in Education of the National Education Association and the American Medical Association, *Conserving the Sight of School Children*, New York: National Society for the Prevention of Blindness, Publication 6, 1935.

5. Kephart, N. C., and Floyd, W., "Classroom environment and pupil welfare," *Journal of Educational Psychology*, 45:52–59 (1954).

6. Klein, A., and Thomas, L. C., *Posture Exercises, a Handbook for Schools and for Teachers of Physical Education*, Washington: U.S. Department of Labor, Children's Bureau Publication No. 165, 1926.

7. Klein, A., and Thomas, L. C., *Posture and Physical Fitness*, Washington: U.S. Department of Labor, Children's Bureau Publication No. 205, 1931.

8. Rogers, J. F., *What Every Teacher Should Know About the Physical Condition of Her Pupils*, U.S. Department of the Interior, Office of Education Pamphlet 68, Washington: Government Printing Office, 1936.

PART SEVEN

Administering and Interpreting the Evaluation Program

CHAPTER XX

Administering the Evaluation Program

ABSTRACT

This chapter concerns the procedures for administering evaluation devices. The topics to be discussed are (1) rapport between teacher and pupils, (2) the frequency with which various types of evaluation devices should be administered, (3) a general overall schedule for evaluations throughout a pupil's school career, (4) the environmental conditions under which evaluations should be made, (5) the importance of and procedures for strict adherence to standardized conditions of administration, (6) open-book examinations, and (7) student participation in evaluation.

•~•~•~•

RAPPORT

IMPORTANCE OF RAPPORT

Rapport is a relationship between pupil and teacher such that the pupil has confidence in and is willing to coöperate with the teacher. Rapport is necessary, in varying degrees, for the administration of all kinds of evaluation devices. Its absence will mean "nervousness" and inefficiency on the part of the pupil. He will not be able to do full justice to his own achievement. He may become so tense as to look for absurd subtleties in the directions for the test; his ability to recall or recognize things which he knows well may become "blocked."

In evaluating physical aspects of pupils, physicians have found that inadequate rapport results in increased pulse rate and blood pressure; pupils may attempt to deceive teachers concerning their posture, their health habits, or their general state of physical well-being. General and special mental ability may not be expressed validly if examiners do not establish rapport before giving the test. Its importance in administering a self-inventory, a vocational interest questionnaire, or an attitude scale has already been emphasized in the chapters dealing with these devices. Rapport is needed throughout the evaluation program.

SECURING RAPPORT

How can rapport be established and maintained? No specific rules can be given. Procedures vary with pupils, situations, and teachers. For the pupil who is too highly motivated, so eager to perform well on a test that he becomes tense and inefficient, the testing situation should be deëmphasized and put in its proper perspective. The lackadaisical pupil who does not take the testing situation seriously and will not put forth his best efforts should be given some indication of the importance of doing well. The discouraged pupil who has little hope of doing creditably on a test should be given encouragement in as subtle and friendly a way as possible; perhaps, to increase his confidence, he should be given a goal lower than that which the teacher knows he can achieve. The over-confident pupil whose conceit leads him to exert less than his full energies may need self-comparison with higher standards to show him that he has not exhausted the possibilities of achievement.

The pupil who is fearful or ashamed of the truth about himself may need to be reassured that the information will be considered confidential. The value of self-understanding as a basis for more adequate adjustment may need to be pointed out. The teacher should adopt a completely noncritical, "nonmoral" attitude when attempting to evaluate a pupil's emotional and social adjustment. In some cases, however, pupils who are ashamed of certain facts about themselves should be reassured; for example, they can be told how frequently the same facts are true about other pupils.

In general, moderate encouragement and praise should be given to pupils when evaluating their status in intellectual or cognitive matters, and receptiveness and sympathetic understanding should keynote the teacher's role in evaluating physical aspects, emotional and social adjustments, attitudes and interests, and environment and background. In evaluating the former the teacher should be a skilled "stimulator"; in the latter he should be a skilled "respondent," neither praising nor blaming but simply understanding. The pupil should not be given the impression that in a certain respect he is good or bad, sinful or virtuous, desirable or undesirable. In this way his hesitancy to talk about what is "on his mind" may be overcome and the basis laid for guidance in accordance with valid evidence.

The teacher's "personality" will determine the specific expression in any given situation of each of these general policies and procedures for establishing rapport. Sincerity and honesty blended with "a light touch" and seriousness are necessary in all relationships with pupils. The words used in giving encouragement and praise must always be natural and friendly, yet dignified. The teacher should be sensitive to the pupils' reactions to his approach and be flexible so that he can modify it in accordance with these reactions. In establishing and maintaining rapport there is no substitute for the teacher's adaptability and "social intelligence."

When announcing that tests or examinations are to be given, the teacher should attempt to prevent them from assuming undue importance and becoming crises. Teachers and pupils should take examinations "in their stride" rather than permit them to become a major focus of the educative process. Continuous, regular study habits should be emphasized as preferable to "cramming" in preparing for examinations. As far as possible the teacher should explain that the purpose of evaluation is to enable both himself and the pupils to find out how well they are achieving educational objectives so that he can give them better help.

When a test is given to fairly large groups, the examiner should make some preliminary remarks that will place it in its proper perspective. Its purpose, the uses to which the results will be put, the value to the pupils of the information it provides, should all be explained. Standardized group tests are usually accompanied by preliminary instructions, to be read by the examiner, concerning the importance or unimportance of speed, how the pupil should handle items that are too difficult for him, the desirability of guessing or not guessing on responses about which he is not certain, and similar points designed to establish the mental set most conducive to valid results. When such instructions are not provided, as for teacher-made tests, they should be prepared in advance.

SCHEDULING VARIOUS TYPES OF EVALUATION

ACHIEVEMENT OF INSTRUCTIONAL OBJECTIVES

The *frequency* with which the various aspects of pupils should be evaluated depends on both the nature of the aspects and the facilities available to the teacher. There have been many investigations of the effect of different frequencies on the achievement of pupils. Some of these investigations have indicated that more frequent tests result in increased learning, but others failed to show this.

Similarly, the beneficial effects of more frequent testing may be greater for pupils of lower than higher mental ability. The superiority of the more frequently tested pupils as evidenced at the end of a semester may disappear when the two groups of pupils, experimental and control, are retested at a later date, say from six to twelve weeks after the final examination. The best practice for classroom teachers is probably determined by the organization of the subject matter in a given course of study. The teacher may also be guided by obtaining an expression of the pupils' attitudes toward frequency of testing; he may well be surprised to learn that pupils prefer more frequent tests, if they are not "counted" on grades, as better incentives to regular study habits and as aids in avoiding the necessity of "cramming."

Pretests may be used to discover the achievement of instructional objectives which pupils already possess as a result of previous school and out-of-school experiences. The results of these tests can be used to plan the relative emphases in instruction and, perhaps, to show when certain parts of the course may be omitted. When well constructed, pretests also may serve as stimulators of interest in the materials to be studied. Such a test may indicate to pupils the kind of achievement they may expect to acquire from the instruction they will receive; if the test has been interestingly written, they may learn for themselves the areas in which they are strong and weak and distribute their learning efforts accordingly.

GENERAL MENTAL ABILITY

The general mental ability of pupils should be evaluated less frequently than every semester but more often than once in the school career. In general, two considerations determine the grades in which intelligence tests should be given. First, the imperfect although high degree of constancy of intelligence level as indicated by general mental ability tests makes it desirable that the scores or ratings of pupils on these tests be "refreshed" at intervals during their school career in order to reveal any fluctuations which may result either from real changes in their rate of intellectual growth or from errors of measurement due to imperfections in the tests. Second, the need for mental ability and other measurements is greater at some stages in a pupil's school career than at others.

It is probably sufficient to give a group test of mental ability to every pupil in the school every third or fourth year. Probably the best time for this testing is when the pupils begin a new kind of experience or must make a choice among various curricula. Thus, entrance in the first grade is a desirable time because of the lack of preliminary data on a pupil that will help a teacher become acquainted with him in the shortest possible time. The beginning of elementary schooling at the fourth- or fifth-grade level should also be accompanied by a measurement of intelligence and other relevant characteristics since it is known that the predictive value of test scores decreases appreciably over a period of two or three years.

On entering junior high school in the seventh grade the pupil may have to choose among various subjects. Another testing at this point should provide fresh data with which to guide his choice. Entering high school in the ninth grade, where a choice is usually made among such curricula as academic, commercial, and technical, is another point at which a mental test is desirable. Similarly, the last year of secondary education, before the pupil goes to work or enters college, provides an advantageous time for mental ability tests or their equivalent in a battery of achievement tests as a basis for vocational guidance.

In a given school year the test should be given early enough to permit the score to be used for guidance purposes during the rest of the year. If decisions concerning curricula have to be made at the beginning of the year before tests can be given, scored, and made available to counselors and students, the tests should be given at the end of the preceding semester.

Special Abilities

Tests of special abilities should be given whenever information is necessary for counseling the pupil, as when choices of curricula and vocations are to be made, or failures or successes in school work require investigation and explanation. These tests, with the exception of art and music aptitude tests, will probably be given mainly in the latter years of high school. A test of mechanical aptitude at the beginning of high school may help to throw light on the desirability of a technical curriculum for a given pupil.

Emotional and Social Adjustment

The emotional and social adjustment of pupils should be evaluated informally and continuously, on every possible occasion, every day of their school career. It is probably desirable for all pupils to fill out an inventory at intervals. The same applies to sociometric procedures and other techniques in which the teacher and fellow pupils are used as sources of data for guidance of a given pupil.

Attitudes and Interests

Considered as aspects of personality, attitudes and interests merit the same kind of evaluation as was described in the preceding paragraph. Insofar as they are assigned a role in educational outcomes they may be evaluated with the same frequency as the achievement of other instructional objectives. Thus they may be measured before and after certain educational experiences, at the beginning and end of a school year. When considered mainly as factors affecting pupils' choices among curricula and vocations, attitudes and interests are usually evaluated at the beginning of high school and toward the end of high school or in college by means of interest blanks. Every pupil should fill out these blanks rather than only those who express a need for educational or vocational guidance.

ENVIRONMENT AND BACKGROUND

The environment and background of pupils, like their emotional and social adjustment, require continuous evaluation. When a pupil changes teachers, the results of this evaluation should be passed on to the next teacher in the form of a cumulative record for each pupil.

PHYSICAL ASPECTS

Evaluations of the physical aspects of pupils also vary in frequency and extensiveness. The teacher should of course observe his pupils every day and seek to discover any who are ill and in need of medical care. In the lower grades this may be a formal, organized classroom inspection of cleanliness, clothing, and general health. In the upper grades, a more casual and informal approach, although lacking the motivational force of formal inspection, is probably adequate.

In no case should pupils be permitted to complete their school careers without being thoroughly examined by a physician. However cursory this examination may be under the most limited circumstances, it is probably better than none at all. The frequency of periodic health examinations by physicians prescribed by the American Medical Association (2 : 7) is as follows:

From two to five years of age, semiannually

From five to fifteen years of age, every two to three years

From fifteen to thirty-five years of age, every two years

These frequencies are minimal, of course; they should be increased whenever a teacher or nurse notices abnormal changes in the appearance or behavior of a pupil.

According to one manual (1 : 49–50), "The average child could well be examined twice during the high-school years—at entrance and before graduation. The last examination may be combined with that required for a work certificate.

"The present trend is to de-emphasize the annual periodic school health examination. In many cases, the time consumed by the annual repetition of the examination used all possible time available of medical, dental, nursing, and teaching staff. Annually, defects of vision, hearing, teeth, tonsils, nutrition, and personality were rediscovered, recorded, and filed away. Lack of personnel has led to hasty, perfunctory, and inexpert examinations so that no effort could be made to sort out even those cases needing immediate medical care."

The organization and planning of the total evaluation program of a given school system, school, or classroom can best be carried out coöperatively by the supervisor, principal, and teachers. This planning and organization, by whatever course it proceeds, should result in (1) a schedule of testing and evaluation for each semester, including dates, places, and devices for each test; and (2) a program for training and instructing teachers regarding each of the tests to be used and the procedure for administering it.

OPEN-BOOK EXAMINATIONS

To promote examinations that require "thinking" rather than mere recall of textbook information, examinations have been suggested which permit the use of textbooks and notes. These open-book examinations may test the worth of a course, encourage sound preparation on the part of the pupil, present a more natural situation, and necessitate comprehensive thought questions (12).

These examinations need not be in the form of essay questions; short-answer questions of the types described in Chapter IV can readily be put in such a form as to require ability "to see situations in the whole," to "use facts in solving problems," to "draw inferences from known to unknown situations," and in general to achieve broader, more permanent objectives of instruction than mere memorization of the facts and procedures stated in textbooks and lecture notes.

Questions for open-book examinations must be constructed so that the pupil cannot answer them by simply turning to the proper page in a textbook. They must be arranged so that he is required to use his understanding of the large sections or basic principles in the book, to draw together under a single heading the scattered definite cases of a fundamental generalization, or to cite specific instances of a major trend.

It is possible to construct similar examinations in all subjects insofar as the teaching of these subjects stresses something more than the memorization of facts and procedures from textbooks, lectures, or other sources. In constructing open-book examinations teachers will be forced to stress mental processes other than memory. A similar shift in emphasis will occur in pupils' study habits and methods of preparation for examinations. Such evidence as is available indicates that open-book examinations appeal to pupils as more "natural" and representative of the type of use they will make of their achievement in out-of-school life.

In real life, problem solving goes on with the available resources at hand. Consumers, voters, professional people such as lawyers, engineers, and physicians, use "open-book" methods to solve their problems. The Stalnakers (13) have reported their experience with these examinations in the humanities at the University of Chicago. By splitting the final examination into a three-hour morning open-book session and a three-hour afternoon closed-book session they were able to compare the relative standing of the students on the two types of examinations. In general, they found that the relative standing did not change and that both types of examinations gave results similarly related to the scores on an intelligence test. This means that the open-book gave neither more nor less advantage to the more intelligent student than did the closed-book examination. Whatever merit open-book examinations may have will be shown in the types of questions they necessitate and by the kind of study habits they stimulate in students.

STUDENT PARTICIPATION IN EVALUATION

Should teachers and school administrators monopolize decisions concerning content and procedures in evaluation? Or should students participate in making such decisions? Modern psychology and democratic social values agree that important educational objectives can be achieved by having students participate. Many individual teachers and school systems have increasingly been placing responsibility on students for determining the time, content, and techniques for evaluating their achievement. Nor is this restricted to any particular level of education; it is being done from the first grade to the university level (11).

An example of such participation at the first-grade level is given in the following (6 : 28–29):

In one school, the first grade children attempted to evaluate their own level of development with respect to points that *they* as a group felt to be important. Since they thought that their parents would be interested, they reported to them, too. The teacher worked with each child to help him get a reasonably correct concept of his performance level before the group finished the project. Here is the report as they developed it.

Dear Father and Mother,
This is my report to you. All the children helped decide the things to report on.

1. I am a quiet worker. ....
2. I am a good listener. ....
3. I remember my jobs. ....
4. I finish my work. ....
5. I let other people have turns. ....
6. I keep my hands at home. ....
7. I work to make the First Grade a nice place. ....
8. I am a good helper. ....
9. I try to be a nice person in the rest room. ....
10. I walk in the halls (not run). ....
11. I try to be kind. ....
12. I am a good neighbor in groups. ....
13. I cross streets safely. ....
14. I am fair when I play. ....
15. If I stay for lunch, I try to be a good helper. ....

Signed

....
....

An illustration at the college level is provided by a course taught by one of the present authors with this textbook. After considerable discussion of the objectives to be achieved in the course, the students decided that one desirable activity for themselves would be to specify these objectives in detail, design appropriate test exercises to evaluate their achievement, administer the tests, score and interpret them, and finally report the results to the class.

The first four weeks of the course were spent in a fairly rapid reading of the textbook, after which the 33 students in the course divided themselves into 11 committees of three each. Each of these committees was responsible for one periodical test, so that each student in the course took 10 tests at weekly intervals. This procedure proved to be highly motivating. Indeed, the instructor's chief function often became that of umpire when the wording of a particular item was hotly challenged by one or another of the students who had missed it. Moreover, a healthy group rivalry developed in the matter not only of item wording but also of completeness of reporting the results, including estimating the reliability of the test, reporting the number of times each item was missed, and making recommendations for turning the test results into the grade equivalents used by the university.

Obviously, this general procedure can be applied in any subject-matter area, with innumerable modifications, and at all levels. The instructor tends to become a resource person rather than the sole purveyor of wisdom as to what is important in the course. In the example just cited, some of the committees asked the instructor to review their questions before they were administered; others did not. Here again the amount of control exercised by the teacher may vary considerably.

STEPS IN ADMINISTERING TESTS TO PUPILS

Administering a test or a battery of tests involves the following steps. We state them as they would apply to a comprehensive, large-scale testing program for an entire school or school system. For smaller testing programs, as when one teacher gives his own students a test, many of these steps will be unnecessary or be modified in obvious ways.

1. *Responsibility.* If the examination is to be administered to more than one classroom, as when a test of mental ability is given in one day to all the pupils in a school, the responsibility for planning and executing the details of the testing program should be given to a single member of the school staff who will make thorough preparation for every detail and supervise each of the following steps.

2. *Securing tests.* If the tests to be used are standardized, externally made, and commercially available, they should be ordered well in advance of the date on which they are to be given. Most publishing companies require about ten days between receipt of an order and delivery of the tests. If the test is locally constructed or teacher-made and is to be given in printed form, the manuscript should be in the hands of the mimeographer or printer at least a week before the test is to be

used. After the mimeograph stencils have been cut or the test is in page proof, it should be proofread meticulously, one person reading from the manuscript and another checking the stencil or proof. All capitalizations and punctuation, spacings and indentations should be closely inspected for correctness and for the probable legibility of the printed copy.

3. *Schedule.* If the whole school is to be tested at once or if several tests are to be given over a period of time, a schedule of hours and rooms in which specific tests will be given should be mimeographed and distributed to every teacher concerned in the testing program.

4. *Distractions.* Distractions during tests should, of course, be avoided as much as possible. A sign should be put on the door of the room warning visitors to keep out because testing is going on. Noises from the street or from other classrooms should be reduced if possible to the point where they no longer distract. Pupils should be informed if they are to disregard school bells and continue working past the regular school period.

The importance of distractions can be overestimated. Charges are often made by students or parents that testing conditions were unfair because of distractions. Yet Super, Braasch, and Shay (14), in a carefully controlled experiment, found that *average* scores on clerical ability and intelligence tests were unaffected by a trumpeter's playing a musical scale in the next room, a person's bursting into the room and loudly whispering a question to the examiner, a student's loudly breaking a pencil and exclaiming, a loud argument between two persons outside the door, a trumpet solo by a novice, and the examiner's ringing the timer too soon and saying "Go on with the test." All these distractions were introduced under seemingly natural conditions and were noticed by the students, who were unaware of the purpose of the experiment. Nonetheless, the scores of *individual* students *may* be affected.

5. *Distribution of tests to examiners.* If more than one classroom is being tested at a time, the tests should not be distributed before the day of the examination. Packages for each classroom should be made up with the proper number of tests, answer

sheets, special pencils, or other materials well in advance of the day set for the testing.

6. *Examiner training.* Each person, examiner or teacher, who will administer the test should be provided with a test manual and a sample copy of the test several days in advance and urged to study the details of its administration closely, preferably by taking the test himself. In this way, by the time the test is to be given he should be thoroughly familiar with the oral and written directions for it, the ways in which responses should be indicated, and the time limit for each part.

7. *Adherence to directions.* Strict adherence to the test manual in the matter of answering pupils' questions after a test has begun or assisting pupils with test items, unfamiliar words, or misunderstood directions is absolutely necessary with standardized tests if the scores are to be interpreted in the light of the norms provided. If the directions in the manual are violated, it may be impossible to tell whether the norms still apply.

8. *Proctors.* One proctor for every fifty pupils in excess of fifty should assist the examiner in handing out and collecting test materials and making sure that the pupils are following instructions.

9. *Examiner's check list.* Before giving the test, each teacher or examiner should have a written check list of his duties covering in proper order such procedures as (a) seating pupils, (b) announcing the nature and method of the test, (c) distributing writing materials, (d) distributing answer sheets, (e) distributing test booklets, (f) giving instructions for filling in names and other personal data, (g) reading aloud the general directions for the whole test, (h) the time limit for each subtest, (i) collecting the test booklets, answer sheets, and writing materials, and (j) packaging and forwarding the collected materials.

10. *Timing.* If the examination is given with certain time limits, they should be observed carefully by means of a watch or clock with a second hand or, if available, a stop watch. All timepieces should be checked for accuracy. If possible, one of the proctors should check the time throughout the test with his own timepiece. In timing tests the examiner should *write down* the

exact hour, minute, and second at which the signal to start is given. The time at which the signal to stop is to be given should be computed and also written down.

11. *Supervision*. While the pupils are working on the test, examiners and proctors should move about the room unobtrusively to make sure that everyone is recording his answers in the proper way and is working on the right part of the test. Watching a pupil over his shoulder or moving quickly about the room should be avoided because it may distract pupils from their work.

12. *Ending the test*. The examiner should make sure that all the pupils stop work immediately when the time is up. The answer sheets, or test booklets if answers are recorded in them, should be collected, and then writing materials.

13. *Notations*. After the tests have been collected, any necessary notations of a given pupil's abnormalities in testing should be made, such as the need to leave the room or marked conditions of anxiety, or such disruptions of the entire group as a fire drill. They can then be taken into account in interpreting the scores. In the case of standardized tests the examiner should be especially careful to note any discrepancies between the conditions, directions, or time limits under which the test was administered and those stipulated in the test manual.

SCORING EVALUATION DEVICES

Despite the objectivity of short-answer test scoring, certain procedures and precautions are indispensable if this step in evaluation is to be carried out with a maximum of accuracy and efficiency. The necessity for extreme care in planning and executing the scoring of evaluation devices has been indicated by several studies (5, 7, 9), which have found that scoring errors occur with appalling frequency. Both "constant" errors due to failure to understand scoring directions with resultant scores which were consistently too high or too low, and "variable" errors due to carelessness in marking, adding, computing, or transcribing scores were found with sufficient frequency to warrant (1) the careful training and instruction of scorers and (2) the practice of rescoring at least a sample of any group of test booklets.

Order of Scoring

If one person is to score all the tests, a given page (or in the case of essay tests each question) in all the booklets should be scored first, then the next page, and so on, rather than scoring all of one booklet before going on to the next. If so many booklets must be scored that several scores are necessary, each person should specialize on a given page or group of pages of the booklet but should score only one page in all the booklets at a time.

Rescoring

If a large number of booklets are to be scored and sufficient clerical help is available, it is always worth while to rescore them so as to eliminate the errors that almost inevitably occur in a clerical task like this. If complete rescoring is not feasible, every fifth or tenth booklet should be rescored to obtain a rough idea of the frequency and magnitude of scoring errors. The rescoring of a sample sometimes uncovers such inaccuracy as to make it desirable for the remainder of the test booklets to be rescored and thus checked.

Scoring Devices

Before scoring can begin, it is necessary to have scoring keys or stencils. Standardized tests are provided with scoring keys, stencils, or other devices which enable rapid and accurate scoring. These keys are of the following four major types:

1. Strip keys are used with tests in which the answer spaces are *aligned* along one side of the page in the test booklet. They contain the correct responses in a vertical column on a narrow strip of paper and are used in scoring by placing them adjacent to the column of responses in the test booklet.

2. Window stencils are used when the answer spaces are *scattered* over the page of the booklet rather than being in a single column. These stencils are usually made of heavy paper or plastic in which circular or oblong holes are punched. When the stencil is placed over the page of the test booklet the answer spaces are visible through the holes. The number of pupil responses which agree with the correct answers on the stencil can be counted, yielding

the pupil's score for that page of the test. Frequently, the stencil has heavy black lines connecting the holes so as to guide the scorer's eye movements.

3. A third frequently used scoring device is the International Test Scoring Machine shown in Fig. 24. For tests to be scored by this machine the pupils' responses must be recorded with a special soft pencil whose marks on paper will conduct electricity, and the answer sheet must be specially cut and printed. The answer sheet is scored by inserting it in the test scoring machine, pressing a lever so as to bring the sheet against contact units inside the machine, and reading the score registered by a needle on a meter. The machine is set to distinguish between right and wrong answers by means of a window stencil prepared and inserted in it beforehand. Many different varieties of scoring formulas, part scores, and weighted scores can be obtained by setting various switches on the machine. International Test Scoring Machines are now available at many testing centers and university bureaus. For large-scale testing programs such machines often provide the most accurate and least troublesome means of scoring objective tests.

4. Another set of scoring devices are test or answer sheets whose reverse side has been prepared in such a way that correct answers will fall within circles or squares printed on that side. The Clapp-Young Self-Marking Tests (4) have answer sheets attached to each page of the tests. Answers to the multiple-choice items are indicated by placing an X in the appropriate one of a row of small squares. The X is duplicated by means of a thin coat of carbon on the reverse side of the answer sheet onto another sheet which contains only the squares for the correct answers. If the pupil writes his X in the correct square, it will be transferred by the carbon into the square on the second sheet. The teacher can then score the tests simply by counting the number of duplicated X's which fall in the small squares on the second sheet. Toops has devised a method of answering and scoring by which the pupil punches holes with a stylus in appropriate squares on an answer pad; his answers are scored by counting the number of holes or "pyramids" which appear within squares on the reverse side of the answer sheet. This method is also used in one form of the Kuder Preference Record.

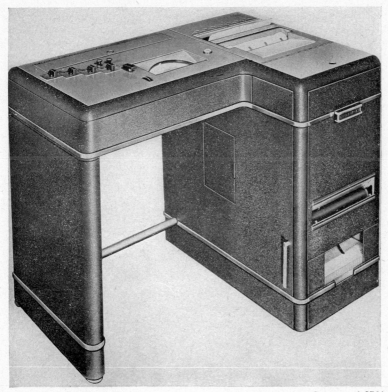

FIG. 24. The International Test Scoring Machine.

5. Some exciting new developments in test scoring and processing making use of recent developments in electronics are reported in the *Proceedings of the 1953 Invitational Conference on Testing Problems*.[1] The reader interested in these new developments will be especially interested in the papers by E. J. Hankes, "New developments in test scoring machines" (pp. 157–159) and E. F. Lindquist, "The Iowa electronic test processing equipment" (pp. 160–168). If the machines described in these two papers as having been designed and in process of construction live up to their advance billing, they will make the IBM scoring machine a museum piece. The DUS (Digital Universal Scorer) as described by Hankes will eliminate the need for special pencils, permit schools to make their own answer sheets, will automatically convert raw scores to standard and percentile scores, will print the scores, raw or converted, is portable ("under 50 pounds cased"), and will be purchasable for $385 to $650, depending upon the accessory items desired.

Lindquist describes a much more elaborate machine that is to remain the property of the State University of Iowa in its Measurements Research Center. The cost of this equipment, if its manufacture had been turned over to an electronic engineering firm, Lindquist estimates, would have been about half a million dollars. The basic rate of the equipment is 6000 answer sheets per hour, and its impact on psychological and educational research promises to be very great. It is designed to score, transform scores to derived scores, cross-foot, cumulate and compute means of scores, squares of scores and cross products, print complete reports, tabulate frequency distributions, and make item counts—all during a single run of the answer sheets through the machine. It will, according to Lindquist, do the work of a staff of sixty working for five weeks in only twelve hours of continuous machine operation.

MARKING RESPONSES

If a strip key or window stencil has been selected and prepared, as is the case with most teacher-made tests, rules should be set up concerning which kind of responses, correct or incorrect, should be marked and in what way. If only correct responses are to be considered in the scoring formula, it is usually most economical of

[1] Educational Testing Service, Princeton: 1953.

effort to mark only wrong answers and omissions so that the score can be obtained by subtracting the number of marks from the total number of items. If a scoring formula involving both right and wrong answers and omissions is being used, all three kinds of responses should be marked, each in a different way, such as a dash (—) for correct responses, an x for incorrect responses, and a zero for omissions. A colored pencil should usually be used in making all marks. Neatness and uniformity of size and spacing in marking responses will increase the accuracy of scoring.

SUMMING MARKS

The next step is to count the number of marks of each kind and record on each page or at the end of each subtest the totals of rights, wrongs, and omissions. This is a major source of error if not done carefully.

APPLYING THE SCORING FORMULA

The totals of correct responses, incorrect responses, and omissions must then be substituted in the scoring formula being used. See Chapter IV for frequently used formulas.

TRANSCRIBING SCORES

Scores for each page or subtest must usually be transcribed to the front page of the test. This also is frequently a source of error.

CONVERTING SCORES

The transcribed raw scores often have to be converted into some form of derived score, such as percentile, *T*-score, or scaled score. This is usually done by referring to a table that gives the derived score to which each raw score is equivalent. Derived scores will be discussed in Chapter XXI, but it is pertinent here to say that this last step in scoring also requires great care if accuracy is to be achieved.

REFERENCES

1. American Association of School Administrators, "Health in School," *Twentieth Yearbook,* Washington, 1942.

2. American Medical Association, *Periodic Health Examination,* Chicago: American Medical Association.

3. Anderson, C. J., "Is the exemption system worthwhile?" *School and Society,* Vol. 3 (1916).

4. Clapp, F. L., and Young, R. V., *The Clapp-Young Self-Marking Tests,* Boston: Houghton Mifflin Company.

5. Dearborn, W. F., and Smith, C. W., "The result of re-scoring 530 Dearborn tests," *Journal of Educational Psychology,* 20:177–183 (1929).

6. Harris, F. E., *Three Persistent Educational Problems: Grading, Promoting and Reporting to Parents,* Lexington: Bulletin of the Bureau of School Service, College of Education, University of Kentucky, Vol. 24, 1953.

7. Herbst, R. L., "How accurately do teachers score achievement tests?" *Journal of Educational Research,* 22:405–408 (1930).

8. Kemmel, H., "Exemption from examinations and grades," *School and Society,* 8:112–114 (1918).

9. Pintner, R., "Accuracy in scoring group intelligence tests," *Journal of Educational Psychology,* 17:470–475 (1926).

10. Remmers, H. H., "Exemption from college semester examinations as a condition of learning," *Studies in Higher Education XXIII, Bulletin of Purdue University,* November, 1933.

11. Simpson, R. H., *Improving Teaching-Learning Processes,* New York: Longmans, Green & Co., Inc., 1953.

12. Stalnaker, J. M., and Ruth C., "Open-book examinations," *Journal of Higher Education,* 5:117–120 (1934).

13. Stalnaker, J. M., and Ruth C., "Open-book examinations: results," *Journal of Higher Education,* 6:214–216 (1935).

14. Super, D. E., Braasch, W. F., and Shay, J. B., "The effect of distractions on test results," *Journal of Educational Psychology,* 38:373–377 (1947).

CHAPTER XXI

Interpreting Test Scores: A Little Statistics

ABSTRACT

Since single raw scores are relatively meaningless, test scores must be related to one another when interpreted. Ranking and frequency distributions furnish a beginning in this direction. Frequency polygons, histograms, and ogives increase the interpretability of frequency distributions. Arithmetic means and medians furnish measures of central tendency or points most representative of frequency distributions. The range, quartile deviation, and standard deviation measure the spread or scatter of the scores around the measure of central tendency. The normal curve and its area relationships aid in the interpretation of statistical measures.

Test scores can be made comparable by means of various derived scores such as z-scores, T-scores, and percentiles. The closeness and direction of relationships between paired variables can be ascertained by means of rank-difference or product-moment coefficients of correlation and by scatter diagrams. To estimate the degree to which the statistical measures obtained are subject to the fluctuations of random sampling requires computation of standard errors and levels of confidence as a means of testing null hypotheses. Derived scores may take the form of age, grade, or percentile norms, standard scores, or quotients. Norms in any form become meaningful only insofar as the sample of pupils used for deriving them is fully specified and described. Norms are most useful when comparable from one aspect of pupils to another. Achieving comparability requires either an anchor test or the use of the same pupils in establishing the norms of all tests that are to be made comparable.

~·~·~·~

After the teacher has constructed or selected an evaluation device and has administered and scored it, the result is a *raw score* for each pupil. In this chapter we discuss the procedures necessary for the next step in the evaluation process, namely, the interpretation of raw scores.

Apart from providing the techniques necessary for interpreting raw scores, we shall also furnish the basic statistical equipment for understanding the literature of experimental education, which consists largely of statistical interpretations of controlled observations.

We shall also describe methods for computing the coefficients of correlation needed to estimate reliability and empirical relevance, as these were discussed in Chapter V. For teachers who select rather than construct evaluation devices, this chapter should provide an understanding of the techniques by which the commercially available devices have been constructed and evaluated and should thus improve the teacher's own judgment in test selection.

This chapter, although the last in the book, may be studied earlier. Knowledge of these elementary statistical methods is assumed in many of the preceding chapters. In some institutions a first course in statistics is prerequisite to the course for which this book is intended; others do not have this requirement. The point at which this chapter should be read depends on the student's needs.

THE MEANINGLESSNESS OF A SINGLE RAW SCORE

Suppose a teacher has given a test of reading ability. Let us suppose further that one pupil obtained a raw score of 104 on it.

What is the meaning of this score of 104? Taken by itself, a single raw score has little meaning. If the teacher knows the number of items in the test or the total possible score, the raw score can be used to determine the percentage of correct responses given by the pupil. Even this, however, is not meaningful as an indication of the pupil's status because the difficulty of tests cannot be determined on the basis of a single pupil's responses. For example, a twelfth-grade pupil may receive the total possible raw score on a test; yet unless the teacher has some basis for comparison, such as the performance of other twelfth-grade pupils on this test or a standard of achievement based on social utility, it is conceivable that this pupil's performance is no better than that of, say, the average seventh-grade pupil. The same situation prevails whether a pupil receives zero or an intermediate score on a test. Some basis for comparison is always necessary for the interpretation of a single raw score.

THE RELATIVE NATURE OF TEST SCORE INTERPRETATION

The comparisons necessary if raw scores are to be given meaning may be made either against absolute standards or against norms based on other pupils. Absolute standards enable the teacher to consider a pupil qualified regardless of the relationship between his performance and that of other persons. Thus if it is considered desirable and satisfactory for a pupil to be able to write his own name legibly, a test item that requires this and is answered correctly by the pupil can easily be interpreted. Similarly, if a job requires the ability to lift one-hundred-pound weights at a given rate of speed, the individual's success at this can be readily interpreted regardless of the performance of other people. Standards define the minimum degrees of excellence society can accept in the performance of given tasks. Whenever absolute standards are available, even a single test score can readily be interpreted simply by comparing it with the standard. These interpretations are valuable even in such simple forms as those that denote a pupil's performance as "successful" or "failing."

The absence of absolute standards for achievement of instructional objectives, general and special mental abilities, attitudes and interests, and other highly important aspects of pupils makes norms widely used in the interpretation of raw scores. It is impossible to set up definite levels or kinds of performance in these aspects of pupils without *relating* the performance of pupils one to another. The spelling ability of a pupil of a given chronological age or school grade or level of mental ability cannot be interpreted meaningfully as successful or failing by an absolute standard. We can only know the degree to which this ability is creditable by relating it to the spelling ability of other pupils. This is so because we can never have for such aspects of pupils any external yardstick independent of other pupils which will enable us to say that a pupil spells well or poorly, regardless of his status in comparison with other pupils. The impossibility of defining levels of performance on any given test without relating the scores to those of other pupils results in the necessity for techniques for making the indicated comparisons between pupils, or norms. Statistical methods provide the techniques necessary for interpreting the raw scores of individual pupils.

Sims makes the point that, with available standards, some interpretation of a single score is possible on the basis of the teacher's previous knowledge of the pupil, and without norms. Examples are: "The student whose factual learning is entirely acceptable to the teacher but whose attitudes toward the same problems are not; the student whose emotional blocking prevents him from using his ability to reason sensibly on problems relating to labor unions; the student whose motivations are all in the direction of pleasing the teacher" (8).

Ranking: A First Step in Test Score Interpretation

If instead of a single score the teacher has the scores of two pupils, the first step in interpretation can be taken by noting which of the two scores is higher. It is then probable (but not certain!) that the pupil with the higher raw score has more of the achievement, ability, or other aspect which the test is supposed to measure. As the number of raw scores increases, the range of interpretability also becomes greater because the teacher has more of a basis for interpreting each single score. A simple ranking, or arrangement of scores in order of magnitude, enables him to interpret each raw score as an indicator of test performance. The relative nature of the interpretation of test scores is evident from this procedure—for the impossibility of stating whether a given score is successful or failing we substitute the possibility of determining which score is best, better, worse, and worst.

Grouping and Frequency Distributions

A fairly large number of test scores, say thirty or more, can usually be interpreted more readily when put into groups. The re-

TABLE 28. Scores for 100 University Sophomore Students on Forms A and B
of the Purdue Reading Test

Student	Form A	Form B	Student	Form A	Form B
1	62	65	51	74	72
2	115	106	52	71	74
3	117	98	53	88	96
4	120	125	54	64	67
5	84	73	55	83	81
6	87	78	56	119	112
7	80	82	57	115	108
8	110	90	58	97	76
9	93	95	59	114	120
10	100	96	60	129	123
11	89	91	61	68	71
12	101	97	62	94	101
13	103	100	63	75	83
14	63	71	64	122	121
15	104	94	65	80	77
16	74	74	66	87	88
17	76	81	67	107	111
18	115	125	68	88	87
19	104	103	69	108	106
20	71	74	70	113	118
21	68	66	71	129	133
22	95	85	72	61	80
23	104	92	73	93	96
24	86	78	74	66	65
25	105	98	75	89	91
26	113	113	76	109	79
27	82	74	77	108	82
28	104	102	78	92	96
29	114	94	79	97	95
30	85	99	80	88	82
31	•78	75	81	64	42
32	107	100	82	105	98
33	79	81	83	111	89
34	104	54	84	108	99
35	93	94	85	126	125
36	70	83	86	113	94
37	45	51	87	108	101
38	107	106	88	95	72
39	74	66	89	116	114
40	118	114	90	121	111
41	71	91	91	95	96
42	90	80	92	84	76
43	90	89	93	98	86
44	100	84	94	123	116
45	114	119	95	107	115
46	92	102	96	68	56
47	106	107	97	85	92
48	117	128	98	48	69
49	62	69	99	101	89
50	105	98	100	128	107

sult of this grouping is a *frequency distribution.* The nature of grouping and frequency distributions is probably best clarified through the procedures involved. Table 28 gives the raw scores obtained by 100 university sophomores on Forms A and B of the Purdue Reading Test. Each form of the test is, of course, a test in itself. In the table, numbers are substituted for the students' names.

As these scores stand, their interpretation would obviously be difficult if not impossible without a table of norms or other interpretative aids provided by the test authors. If the test were teacher-made, the teacher would have to supply his own norms or aids. Ranking the scores is the first step in interpretation. However, grouping the scores in a frequency distribution results in a form of ranking and a condensation of the data into a smaller, more comprehensible number of categories. The steps for grouping the Form A scores into a frequency distribution are as follows:

1. Determine the *range* of the scores. The range is 1 plus the difference between the highest and the lowest score. Look through the list of scores and find the highest and lowest. Subtract the lowest from the highest. The highest score for Form A is 129; the lowest is 45. The range is 1 plus the difference between 129 and 45, or 85.
2. Determine the size of the *class interval* to be used. A class interval is one of the groups in which scores are tabulated. The number of class intervals should usually be between 10 and 20. The class interval is preferably chosen so that its mid-point is an integral multiple of the size of the class interval. By dividing the range by 10 and then by 20 we can get some idea of the size of class interval to use. Dividing 85 by 10 gives 8.5; by 20 it gives 4.5. The size of the class interval should therefore be between 8.5 and 4.5. If we use intervals of odd numbers of units, the computation in obtaining subsequent statistical measures is easier; hence the size of the class interval should be an odd number between 4.2 and 8.4. We choose a class interval of 7.
3. List the class intervals in a column beginning with the highest.

At this point we need to discuss the limits of a single raw score. Any single score, say 75, represents a distance stretching all the way from somewhere above 74 to somewhere below 76. At what point between 74 and 75, and between 75 and 76, shall we set the *limits* of 75? If we had 10,000 pupils all of whom achieved a score of 75 we could be sure that in achievement on this particular test they were not really *exactly* alike. A few had ability such that they just barely made the response that gave them a score of 75 and a few had ability such that they just barely failed to make the response that would have given them a score of 76. The remainder were somewhere between these two extremes. The distribution of these 10,000 pupils all of whom scored 75 would appear as in Fig. 25 if they had been measured with a finer scale on the same abilities.

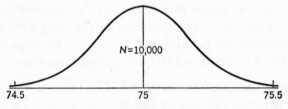

FIG. 25. Theoretical Distribution of Test Scores
Given a Value of 75.

We may say, then, that 75 represents a mid-point whose limits are 74.5 and 75.5; or 75 is the most representative score for all pupils with scores of 74.5 or more, and 75.5 or less. Thus, in setting down the column of class intervals, we might write for the upper *real* limit of each interval a number that is half a unit greater than the highest score in that interval, and for the lower *real* limit, a number that is half a unit less than the lowest score falling therein. Inspection of Table 29 shows that for Form A the limits of the highest interval are 129.5–136.5. This consideration applies to the computation of various statistical measures described below. In accordance with common practice we have written the *integral* limits rather than the *real* limits in Table 29.

Table 29 shows the columns of class intervals for Form A and Form B scores. The highest class interval for Form A is 130–136, the next is 123–129, and so on down to 39–45. Since the ranges of the scores for both forms were nearly the same, the same column of class intervals is used for both.

TABLE 29.   The Scores in Table 28 Grouped into a Frequency Table, Illustrating the Computation of the Arithmetic Mean and the Median

	Form A				Form B			
	(tally)	f	d	fd	(tally)	f	d	fd
130–136					/	1	6	6
123–129	ℋ/	5	5	25	ℋ/	5	5	25
116–122	ℋ/ ///	8	4	32	ℋ/	5	4	20
109–115	ℋ/ ℋ/ //	12	3	36	ℋ/ //	7	3	21
102–108	ℋ/ ℋ/ ℋ/ ///	18	2	36	ℋ/ ////	9	2	18
95–101	ℋ/ ℋ/	10	1	10	ℋ/ ℋ/ ℋ/ ////	19	1	19
88–94	ℋ/ ℋ/ ///	13	0		ℋ/ ℋ/ ////	14	0	
81–87	ℋ/ ////	9	−1	− 9	ℋ/ ℋ/ //	12	−1	−12
74–80	ℋ/ ////	9	−2	−18	ℋ/ ℋ/ ///	13	−2	−26
67–73	ℋ/ //	7	−3	−21	ℋ/ ///	8	−3	−24
60–66	ℋ/ //	7	−4	−28	////	4	−4	−16
53–59			−5		/	1	−5	− 5
46–52	/	1	−6	− 6	/	1	−6	− 6
39–45	/	1	−7	− 7	/	1	−7	− 7
		$N = 100$		50		$N = 100$		13

$$M = \text{Assumed mean} + \frac{\Sigma fd}{N}\,(i)$$

$$= 91 + \frac{50}{100}\,(7) = 94.50 \qquad\qquad 91 + \frac{13}{100}\,(7) = 91.91$$

$$\text{Median} = \frac{N}{2} \text{ measure}$$

Adding frequencies from below,

$1 + 1 + 7 + 7 + 9 + 9 + 13 = 47$; this takes us to 94.5, the real lower limit of the interval containing the median; 3 more to get $\frac{N}{2}$;

$1 + 1 + 1 + 4 + 8 + 13 + 12 = 40$; this takes us to 87.5, the real lower limit of the interval containing the median; 10 more to get $\frac{N}{2}$;

$$\therefore 94.5 + \frac{50 - 47}{10}\,(7) = 96.60\text{, the median.}$$

$$\therefore 87.5 + \frac{50 - 40}{14}\,(7) = 92.50\text{, the median.}$$

4. Tabulate each raw score by making a mark after the appropriate interval for each raw score which falls within it. For every fifth score in an interval make a diagonal mark connecting the preceding four. After all the 100 scores have been tabulated, total the number of marks in each interval and write it in the column labeled f, for *frequency*. The frequency in each class interval is thus the number of scores that fall within it. The sum of the frequencies in all class intervals is obviously the same as the total number of pupils whose test scores are being interpreted. Write this total frequency, or N, at the bottom of the frequency column.

GRAPHIC REPRESENTATIONS OF FREQUENCY DISTRIBUTIONS

Often a frequency distribution of test scores can be better comprehended when shown graphically. For this purpose three major types of graphs are used: the *frequency polygon*, the *histogram*, and the *ogive*. In the frequency polygon and histogram, the horizontal axis represents the scale of magnitude of scores, and the vertical axis represents the frequency or number of cases of scores at each of the points along the scale of magnitude. The horizontal axis is pointed off in the same class intervals as those used in the frequency distribution, beginning at the left with the lowest class interval and proceeding to the right with as many intervals as are necessary to include the complete range. The vertical axis is similarly pointed off, beginning with zero at the bottom and proceeding upward to the largest frequency. A frequency polygon and a histogram differ in that in the polygon the frequency in each class interval is indicated by a *point* above the center of the class interval. These points are then connected by *straight lines,* as is shown in Fig. 26. In the histogram, on the other hand, the frequency in

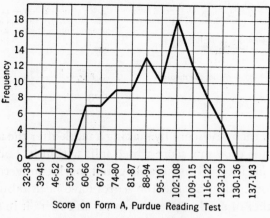

FIG. 26. Frequency Polygon.

each class interval is indicated by a *rectangle* whose base is equal to the width of the class interval and whose altitude shows the frequency within that class interval. This procedure is indicated in Fig. 27.

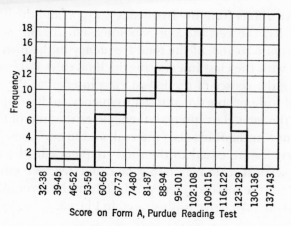

FIG. 27. Histogram.

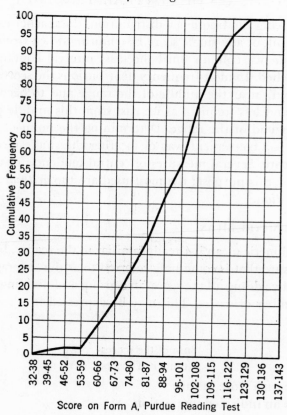

Score on Form A, Purdue Reading Test

FIG. 28. Ogive or Cumulative Frequency Curve.

The ogive differs from the frequency polygon and the histogram mainly in that the vertical axis is pointed off in *cumulative* percentages, from 0 to 100, of the total frequency in the distribution. Beginning with the class interval in which no cases fall, we place a point above the center of the lowest class interval at the point on the vertical scale proportional to its frequency, add to this the frequency in the next class interval, then add to the sum of these two the frequency in the third class interval, and so on. These cumulative frequencies are equal to the total frequency in the distribution. The vertical scale may either be converted into cumulative percentages of the total frequency or be left in the form of cumulative frequencies. An ogive is illustrated in Fig. 28.

MEASURES OF CENTRAL TENDENCY

After making the frequency distribution, the teacher can determine the rank of any single score by counting down from the top of the frequency column until the class interval containing the score it reached. In most frequency distributions the scores tend to be "bunched" near the middle of the range and to become relatively less and less frequent as we pass from this middle point toward either end of the range. Determining the point of "central tendency" is a convenient way of locating the single most representative score. Several measures of central tendency, or averages, are used for this purpose; the most used are the *arithmetic mean* and the *median*.

THE ARITHMETIC MEAN

The arithmetic mean is already familiar to the reader, because it is the measure that is commonly referred to as the "average." It is computed by adding all the scores in a group and dividing the sum by the number of scores. This may be expressed in a formula as follows:

$$M = \frac{\text{Sum of the scores}}{\text{Number of scores}} = \frac{\Sigma X}{N}$$

where X = each score in turn
Σ = an indicated summation
N = number of scores

In a frequency distribution, the computation of the arithmetic mean is facilitated by a short method that is expressed in the following working formula:

$$M = \text{Assumed mean} + \frac{\Sigma fd}{N}i$$

where $f =$ the frequency in each class interval

$\quad d =$ deviation, in class intervals, of each class interval from the assumed mean

$\quad i =$ size of the class interval (in Table 29 this is 7)

The steps in applying this short formula are as follows:

1. Select an assumed mean at the mid-point of some class interval. To save labor, it should be about where the calculated mean is likely to come. In the illustrative problem shown in Table 29 this is 91. This class interval is thought of as extending from 87.5 to 94.5 in accordance with our previous discussion of the real limits of scores.

2. Set the assumed mean equal to zero and call the class intervals (mid-points) one-step deviations from the guessed mean. Above the assumed mean the deviations are plus; below, they are minus. This step involves the assumption that the mid-point is most representative of all the measures in the interval. In Table 29 this column of deviations is labeled d.

3. Multiply the frequencies by the deviations so as to obtain the next column of figures, labeled fd in the table.

4. Obtain the algebraic sum of the fd's. In Table 29, Form A, the algebraic sum of the fd's is 50.

5. Divide the sum of the fd's by N. In Table 29, Form A, this quotient equals .5.

6. Multiply this quotient by the size of the class interval. In Table 29, Form A, this product is 3.50.

7. Add this product to the assumed mean. In the illustrative problem, this is $91 + 3.50 = 94.50$. It is obvious that if the assumed mean is chosen so as to make Σfd negative, the product will be negative and will be subtracted (algebraically added). That the arithmetic mean obtained by the short method will be the same regardless of the assumed mean will be seen if the reader carries out these steps using another assumed mean such as 98.

The Median

The median is defined as the point in a frequency distribution on either side of which lie 50 percent of the cases. It is, then, the $\frac{N}{2}$th measure. Computing this average requires somewhat less labor than does the arithmetic mean. It is better as a measure of central tendency if it is desired not to weight the scores in proportion to their deviation from the average. If the scores are not grouped in a frequency distribution, the median is obtained by arranging them in order of magnitude, or ranking them, and counting down from the highest score until the $\frac{N}{2}$th measure is reached. If there is an even number of scores, there will be no single middle score but rather two; the median is the arithmetic mean of the two. Suppose we have the following eighteen raw scores arranged in order of magnitude:

| 33 | 32 | 32 | 30 | 29 | 28 | 27 | 26 | 26 |
| 24 | 22 | 21 | 20 | 20 | 18 | 17 | 16 | 16 |

Since there are eighteen scores, $\frac{N}{2}$ is equal to 9. Counting down to the ninth score from both ends of the distribution shows that 26 and 24 are the two middle scores. The arithmetic mean of these two is 25, or $(26 + 24) \div 2$. The procedure for computing the median of grouped scores is as follows:

1. Compute $\frac{N}{2}$, or the total number of scores divided by 2.

2. Begin at the lower end of the distribution and cumulate the frequencies up to the class interval containing the median. In Table 29, Form A, this gives 47.

3. Divide the number of measures required to fill out $\frac{N}{2}$ by the frequency of the interval containing the median and multiply the result by the value of the class interval. In Table 29, Form A, this is $\frac{3}{10} \times 7 = 2.10$. This step involves the assumption that the measures in a class interval are equally distributed throughout the interval.

4. Add this amount to the lower real limit of the class interval which contains the median. In Table 29, Form A, this equals $94.5 + 2.10 = 96.60$. The median obtained by this method will be the same regardless of from which end of the frequency distribution the $\frac{N}{2}$ count is made. This can be shown by adding the frequencies from the top of the distribution downward. This also provides a ready check on the correctness of the computation made by starting from the low end. To illustrate, in Table 29, Form A, $5 + 8 + 12 + 18 = 43$; seven more scores are required to fill out $\frac{N}{2}$. The median therefore equals 101.5 (that is, the upper limit of the class interval, 95–101) $minus$ $\frac{7}{10} \times 7 =$ 96.60

Measures of central tendency, whether means or medians, are useful in several ways. (1) They provide a point in a frequency distribution by which the teacher can tell whether the scores of given pupils are above or below the average performance of the class or whatever other group is involved. (2) Comparisons between groups can be made whenever two or more groups have taken the same test. Given the average scores of two classes, one of which took the test a year later than the other, the teacher can compare the average of the first class with that of the second.

The choice of the mean or the median depends on whether it is desired to include or exclude the influence of the extreme or highly atypical scores which sometimes occur. If some pupils obtain perfect or zero scores on a test, they are not fairly measured, for the test is too easy or too difficult to reveal their true performance. By using the median the teacher can exclude the influence of these atypical scores on the typical score of the group.

If we wished to compare communities as to average family income, the arithmetic mean would tell how they compared when extremely wealthy and poor families are taken into account. This would be useful for comparing community wealth for school tax purposes. The median would not be influenced by the extremes of wealth and poverty; it would yield better comparisons of the typical standards of living in the communities. In other situations, the mean is often more desirable, especially since it lends itself better to mathematical treatment in the computation of further statistical measures to be described below.

MEASURES OF VARIABILITY

Another feature of the frequency distribution, the variability of the scores, needs to be described. Two frequency distributions may have the same central tendency and yet be quite dissimilar in variability, as shown in the following illustration:

Class Interval	Class I f	Class II f
120–129	1	—
110–119	2	—
100–109	4	—
90–99	7	—
80–89	10	15
70–79	12	18
60–69	15	21
50–59	12	18
40–49	10	15
30–39	7	—
20–29	4	—
10–19	2	—
0–9	1	—

The mean or the median of the distributions for both Class I and Class II is 65; yet it is evident that the scores in Class I are far more scattered around the mean or the median than are those in Class II. The pupils in Class I differ among themselves far more widely than those in Class II. Obviously it is desirable to compute an index of variability rather than to rely merely on the impression gained from inspection of a frequency distribution.

THE RANGE

One measure of variability is the range, or 1 plus the difference between the highest and lowest scores. In the illustration above, the range for Class I is 1 plus (125 − 5), or 121, and that for Class II is 1 plus (85 − 45), or 41. The range, however, is unsatisfactory as a measure of variability because of its complete dependence on the extreme scores in a distribution. One atypical pupil in Class II could have greatly increased the range if his score had fallen in the highest or lowest class interval, but the scatter of the majority of the pupils would not have been changed. Because of this, the range is not a dependable measure of variability.

THE QUARTILE DEVIATION

Another measure of variability is the quartile deviation, or semi-interquartile range. It is defined by the following equation:

$$Q = \frac{\text{upper quartile} - \text{lower quartile}}{2} = \frac{Q_u - Q_1}{2}$$

The upper quartile is the point in a frequency distribution *above* which lie 25 percent of the cases. The lower quartile is the point in the distribution *below* which lie 25 percent of the cases. In Table 30 we find for Form A that the upper quartile, Q_u, equals 108.5, and the lower quartile, Q_1, equals 80.5; therefore the quartile deviation, Q, equals $\frac{108.5 - 80.5}{2}$, or 14.0. For Form B, Q_u equals

TABLE 30. Illustrating the Computation of the Standard Deviation (σ), Probable Error ($P.E.$), and Quartile Deviation (Q)

	Form A				Form B			
	f	d	fd	fd²	f	d	fd	fd²
130–136					1	6	6	36
123–129 卌	5	5	25	125	5	5	25	125
116–122 卌 ///	8	4	32	128	5	4	20	80
109–115 卌 卌 //	12	3	36	108	7	3	21	63
102–108 卌 卌 卌 ///	18	2	36	72	9	2	18	36
95–101 卌 卌	10	1	10	10	19	1	19	19
88–94 卌 卌 ///	13	0			14	0		
81–87 卌 ////	9	−1	−9	9	12	−1	−12	12
74–80 卌 ////	9	−2	−18	36	13	−2	−26	52
67–73 卌 //	7	−3	−21	63	8	−3	−24	72
60–66 卌 //	7	−4	−28	112	4	−4	−16	64
53–59		−5			1	−5	− 5	25
46–52 /	1	−6	− 6	36	1	−6	− 6	36
39–45 /	1	−7	− 7	49	1	−7	− 7	49
	N = 100		50	748	N = 100		13	669

$$\sigma = 7\sqrt{\frac{748}{100} - \left(\frac{50}{100}\right)^2}$$

$$= 18.82$$
$$P.E. = .6745\sigma = 12.69$$
$$Q = \frac{108.5 - 80.5}{2} = 14.00$$

$$\sigma = 7\sqrt{\frac{669}{100} - \left(\frac{13}{100}\right)^2}$$

$$= 18.08$$
$$P.E. = .6745\sigma = 12.18$$
$$Q = \frac{103.06 - 78.88}{2} = 12.09$$

103.06, and Q_1 equals 78.88; therefore Q equals $\dfrac{103.06 - 78.88}{2}$, or 12.09. The quartile deviation is probably the best measure of variability for the kind of purpose for which the median is the best measure of central tendency, that is, in situations where we wish to discount extremely high and low scores.

THE STANDARD DEVIATION

The standard deviation, the most commonly used measure of variability, is the square root of the mean of the squared deviations of the scores from the arithmetic mean. This definition is better comprehended in terms of the following fundamental formula:

$$\text{Standard deviation} = \text{sigma} = \sigma = \sqrt{\frac{\Sigma d^2}{N}}$$

$$d = X - M = \text{deviation of each score from the arithmetic mean}$$

A shorter method is again available. The working formula for the short method is:

$$\sigma = i \sqrt{\frac{\Sigma f d^2}{N} - \left(\frac{\Sigma f d}{N}\right)^2}$$

The notation here is the same as for the formula for M. The computation of the standard deviation (sigma) is shown in Table 30 for the data on Forms A and B of the Purdue Reading Test. The steps in computing it follow:

1. Make a frequency distribution of the test scores.
2. Assume a mean at the mid-point of some class interval, preferably near the middle of the distribution, and lay off deviations, in steps of one, above and below this mid-point. Note, however, that it is not necessary to compute the mean.
3. Obtain the fd's by multiplying each frequency by the deviation of the mid-point of the class interval from the assumed mean.
4. Obtain the fd^2's by multiplying each fd once again by the corresponding d (since $fd^2 = fd \times d$).
5. Add the fd's, divide by N, and square the result.
6. Sum the fd^2's and divide by N.
7. Subtract the $\left(\dfrac{\Sigma f d}{N}\right)^2$ obtained in Step 5 from the result obtained in Step 6.

8. Obtain the square root of the difference obtained in Step 7.
9. Multiply the obtained square root by the class interval. This product is the standard deviation of the distribution of scores.

THE NORMAL CURVE

INTERPRETING THE STANDARD DEVIATION

To interpret a standard deviation, the reader should have an introduction to the ideal, theoretical, mathematically defined frequency distribution known as the normal curve of error, the normal probability curve, or normal distribution. The normal curve is a mathematical ideal in the sense that it is a product of pure reason rather than of experimental results. Its importance in statistics is due to the fact that it has been found to coincide closely with the actual distribution of certain types of data to be described below. Wherever a given phenomenon is the result of a large number of factors none of which has a disproportionately great influence, and all of which act independently of one another, the shape of the distribution of the frequencies or magnitudes of the phenomenon will tend to approach the normal curve.

An example of such a phenomenon is the frequency with which varying numbers of heads will be obtained if ten coins are tossed simultaneously many times. The range of the frequency distribution of the number of heads is from 0 to 10 and the theoretical mean is 5. The actual mean obtained from a large number of throws will be very close to 5. The frequencies with which different numbers of heads will be obtained will decrease as we proceed from 5 upward to 10 or from 5 downward to 0. The distribution will be bell-shaped, as shown in Fig. 29.

Human traits may or may not be distributed in a form similar to the normal curve. The form of the frequency distribution of a human trait depends not only on the trait but also on the way it is measured and on the sample of persons included in the frequency distribution. Thus human skin or eye color is not distributed normally because people fall into fairly distinct groups according to these traits. Human height is a more continuous trait, people being less distinctly grouped according to height.

Similarly, one test of mental ability of a given group of pupils may yield scores that fall into a bell-shaped distribution. But an

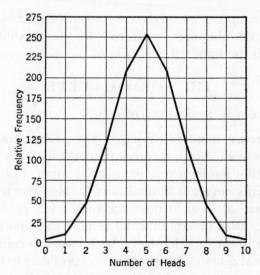

FIG. 29. Theoretical Frequency Distribution of Number of Heads Obtained in Tossing 10 Coins.

easier test may yield scores that pile up toward the high end of the range of scores, or in a *negatively skewed* distribution, as shown in Fig. 30. A too difficult test may yield scores that fall into a *positively skewed* distribution.

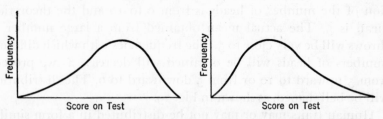

FIG. 30. Negatively Skewed (Left) and Positively Skewed Distributions of Test Scores.

The group included in a distribution of human heights might include half Japanese and half Scandinavians. The resulting frequency curve might have two peaks, i.e., be *bimodal,* with one peak at the average Scandinavian height and the other at the average Japanese height, as in Fig. 31. So it is evident that human traits are not necessarily distributed according to any fixed law, such as the normal curve. Hence the normal curve is not useful in the sense of relevance to the aspects or traits of pupils with which this volume is concerned.

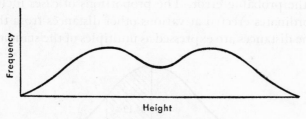

FIG. 31. Bimodal Distribution.

But for another class of data the normal curve *is* descriptive of the form of distributions. This class includes the various statistical measures discussed in this chapter, such as arithmetic means, medians, proportions, standard deviations, semi-interquartile ranges, and differences between means, standard deviations, proportions, etc. As shown below, if we know that a given set of measures is distributed normally and if we know the standard deviation of the set of measures, we can infer the frequency with which measures of various magnitudes will occur.

AREA RELATIONSHIPS

One property of the normal curve that is used in the interpretation of frequency distributions is the following: The *area* under the curve included between a vertical line (or ordinate) erected at the arithmetic mean of the curve and a vertical line (ordinate) erected at a given distance from the arithmetic mean, where the distance is expressed as a multiple of the standard deviation, is always the same proportion of the total area under the curve. The area included between the ordinates at the mean and one standard deviation from the mean will always include 34.13 percent of the total area under the normal curve. This is shown in Fig. 32.

If the difference between the mean ordinate and another ordinate is equal to .6745 standard deviation, the area between the two ordinates will equal 25 percent of the total area under the normal curve. This distance, .6745 standard deviation, is known as the *probable error;* it is evident that 50 percent of the total area under a normal curve will be included between ordinates erected on both sides of the mean ordinate at a distance of one probable error from it. In a normal distribution, the quartile deviation equals the probable error. The proportions of cases included between ordinates erected at various other distances from the mean, when the distances are expressed as multiples of the standard devia-

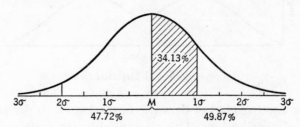

FIG. 32. Relationship Between Sigma Distances of Ordinates from Mean and Area Included Between Ordinates.

tion, are shown in Table 31. The reader should practice using this table by verifying the figures for various values given in this chapter.

Since the area included under any part of a curve is analogous to the number of cases in that area, the various proportions of the area may be interpreted directly as proportions of the total number of cases in a frequency distribution. The importance of the standard deviation follows from this equivalence of area to number of cases.

So, between plus and minus one standard deviation from the mean will be included approximately two-thirds (68.26 percent) of the total number of cases; within plus and minus one probable error from the mean will be included approximately 50 percent of the cases. Within plus and minus two standard deviations from the mean will be included roughly 95 percent of the cases, and between plus and minus three standard deviations from the mean will be included practically all, or 99.74 percent, of the cases. These interpretations of the standard deviation are valid, of course, only to the degree that the frequency distribution obtained approximates the normal curve.

TABLE 31. Percentage of Total Area Under the Normal Curve Between Mean Ordinate and Ordinate at Any Given Sigma Distance from the Mean

$\frac{x}{\sigma}$	.00	.01	.02	.03	.04	.05	.06	.07	.08	.09
0.0	00.00	00.40	00.80	01.20	01.60	01.99	02.39	02.79	03.19	03.59
0.1	03.98	04.38	04.78	05.17	05.57	05.96	06.36	06.75	07.14	07.53
0.2	07.93	08.32	08.71	09.10	09.48	09.87	10.26	10.64	11.03	11.41
0.3	11.79	12.17	12.55	12.93	13.31	13.68	14.06	14.43	14.80	15.17
0.4	15.54	15.91	16.28	16.64	17.00	17.36	17.72	18.08	18.44	18.79
0.5	19.15	19.50	19.85	20.19	20.54	20.88	21.23	21.57	21.90	22.24
0.6	22.57	22.91	23.24	23.57	23.89	24.22	24.54	24.86	25.17	25.49
0.7	25.80	26.11	26.42	26.73	27.04	27.34	27.64	27.94	28.23	28.52
0.8	28.81	29.10	29.39	29.67	29.95	30.23	30.51	30.78	31.06	31.33
0.9	31.59	31.86	32.12	32.38	32.64	32.90	33.15	33.40	33.65	33.89
1.0	34.13	34.38	34.61	34.85	35.08	35.31	35.54	35.77	35.99	36.21
1.1	36.43	36.65	36.86	37.08	37.29	37.49	37.70	37.90	38.10	38.30
1.2	38.49	38.69	38.88	39.07	39.25	39.44	39.62	39.80	39.97	40.15
1.3	40.32	40.49	40.66	40.82	40.99	41.15	41.31	41.47	41.62	41.77
1.4	41.92	42.07	42.22	42.36	42.51	42.65	42.79	42.92	43.06	43.19
1.5	43.32	43.45	43.57	43.70	43.83	43.94	44.06	44.18	44.29	44.41
1.6	44.52	44.63	44.74	44.84	44.95	45.05	45.15	45.25	45.35	45.45
1.7	45.54	45.64	45.73	45.82	45.91	45.99	46.08	46.16	46.25	46.33
1.8	46.41	46.49	46.56	46.64	46.71	46.78	46.86	46.93	46.99	47.06
1.9	47.13	47.19	47.26	47.32	47.38	47.44	47.50	47.56	47.61	47.67
2.0	47.72	47.78	47.83	47.88	47.93	47.98	48.03	48.08	48.12	48.17
2.1	48.21	48.26	48.30	48.34	48.38	48.42	48.46	48.50	48.54	48.57
2.2	48.61	48.64	48.68	48.71	48.75	48.78	48.81	48.84	48.87	48.90
2.3	48.93	48.96	48.98	49.01	49.04	49.06	49.09	49.11	49.13	49.16
2.4	49.18	49.20	49.22	49.25	49.27	49.29	49.31	49.32	49.34	49.36
2.5	49.38	49.40	49.41	49.43	49.45	49.46	49.48	49.49	49.51	49.52
2.6	49.53	49.55	49.56	49.57	49.59	49.60	49.61	49.62	49.63	49.64
2.7	49.65	49.66	49.67	49.68	49.69	49.70	49.71	49.72	49.73	49.74
2.8	49.74	49.75	49.76	49.77	49.77	49.78	49.79	49.79	49.80	49.81
2.9	49.81	49.82	49.82	49.83	49.84	49.84	49.85	49.85	49.86	49.86
3.0	49.87									
3.5	49.98									
4.0	49.997									
5.0	49.99997									

MAKING TEST SCORES COMPARABLE

We have considered the meaninglessness of a single raw score. This applies not only to the interpretation of raw scores on a single test or the interpretation of a pupil's standing on a single test, but also to the interpretation of the relative standing of a single pupil on two or more tests. That is, raw scores from different tests are not directly comparable. Suppose that Ray Brown, a ninth-grade pupil, made the following scores at the end of the semester:

Algebra 52
Problems of Democracy 116
Mechanics of Written English 163
Attitude Toward High School 8.4

These raw scores tell us nothing. They are not on a common scale. We need to know his *relative* standing, that is, his standing in comparison with a defined group, such as all ninth-grade pupils in his school or in the county, state, or nation. We cannot tell from the raw scores alone whether Ray Brown was better in algebra than in Problems of Democracy, and so on. To compare his standing in the four different evaluations, we need to take into account the degree to which he was above or below average. If on one of the tests, say algebra, the pupils' scores did not differ much from one another, their standard deviation would be small. To achieve a relatively high standing in the algebra test, Ray would not need to exceed the average of his class by as many raw score units as would be necessary if the standard deviation were large. Obviously, then, both central tendency and variability must be taken into account in finding the relative standing of any pupil within a group. Of the many methods for making scores on different tests comparable in central tendency and variability, we shall discuss *standard scores,* T-*scores,* and *percentile scores.*

STANDARD SCORES

A standard score, or z-score, is defined as the deviation of a score from the arithmetic mean in standard deviation units. The formula for z-scores is:

$$z = \frac{X - M}{\sigma}$$

z = standard score M = arithmetic mean of raw scores
X = raw score σ = standard deviation of raw scores

All raw scores below the arithmetic mean will thus be converted into negative z-scores. The arithmetic mean will equal the z-score of zero. A score one standard deviation above or below the arithmetic mean will equal a z- score of +1 or −1 respectively. In z-scores, the standard deviation becomes the unit distance of a frequency distribution. The usefulness of these scores may be illustrated by comparing Ray Brown's relative standing on each of the four evaluation devices. By obtaining the required additional information, the arithmetic mean and the standard deviation of each test, and substituting in the formula, we obtain z-scores.

	X (score)	M	X − M	σ	z
Algebra.....................	52	47.92	+4.08	10.00	+0.41
Problems of Democracy.......	116	120.26	−4.26	21.02	−0.20
Mechanics of Written English..	163	163.00	0.00	23.19	0.00
Attitude Toward High School..	8.4	7.20	+1.20	2.40	+0.50
Combined z-score (arithmetic mean)					.18

It is now clear that Ray is well above average in algebra and in Attitude Toward High School, slightly below average in Problems of Democracy, and exactly average in Mechanics of Written English. Every pupil's relative standing can be found in the same manner.

T-SCORES

T-scores serve the same purpose as z-scores and are based on the same principle; they have the advantage, however, of being always positive and expressed in larger units, thus removing the necessity of dealing with negative numbers and decimal fractions. These advantages are obtained by converting the mean of the distribution to 50 and the standard deviation to 10 by means of the following formula:

$$T\text{-score} = 50 + \frac{10\,(X - M)}{\sigma} = 50 + 10z$$

A T-score of 60 means a score one standard deviation above the mean; a T-score of 70 lies two standard deviations above the mean, and so on. T-scores of 40, 30, and 20 similarly indicate scores at one, two, and three standard deviations *below* the mean respectively. The changes from z-scores to T-scores are illustrated on page 592, based on Ray Brown's z-scores given above.

Any distribution of raw scores can be similarly transformed to any arbitrarily chosen mean and standard deviation. For example,

	z-score	T-score
Algebra.........................	+0.41	54
Problems of Democracy............	−0.20	48
Mechanics of Written English......	0.00	50
Attitude Toward High School.......	+0.50	55

in some testing programs the mean is transformed to 500 and the standard deviation to 100 for all tests.

PERCENTILES

A third method of making test scores comparable is through the computation of *percentile rank;* this indicates the percentage of all the scores in a frequency distribution that are exceeded by a given raw score. If a raw score is equivalent to a percentile of 50, it exceeds 50 percent of the scores in a group. A raw score equivalent to a 99th percentile exceeds 99 percent of all the scores in a group; a raw score equivalent to the 1st percentile exceeds only 1 percent of the scores in a group. The 50th percentile is thus equal to the median; the 75th percentile equals the upper quartile, Q_u, and the 25th percentile equals the lower quartile, Q_l. Percentile equivalents for each raw score are computed by arranging the raw scores in order of decreasing magnitude and finding for each the number of scores lying below it. Each of these numbers is then divided by the total number of scores, and the quotient is multiplied by 100. When the scores are grouped into a frequency distribution and all within a given class interval are assumed to have the same value, we determine for each class interval the total frequency of the scores in the intervals below it.

For such purposes it is frequently desirable to make a *cumulative frequency distribution*. This is done by adding the frequencies, beginning with the class interval at the bottom. This procedure is illustrated in the following, based on the figures used in Table 29, Form A of the Purdue Reading Test. The ogive for this cumulative frequency distribution is shown in Fig. 28.

If it is justifiable to assume that the frequency distribution obtained closely approximates a normal curve, z-scores, T-scores, and percentile ranks can all be converted one into another. A z-score of 1, meaning a raw score falling at one standard deviation above the mean, is then known to be equivalent to the 84th percentile, as is also a *T*-score of 60.

	Frequency *f*	Cumulative Frequency
130–136	—	
123–129	5	100
116–122	8	95
109–115	12	87
102–108	18	75
95–101	10	57
88–94	13	47
81–87	9	34
74–80	9	25
67–73	7	16
60–66	7	9
53–59	—	2
46–52	1	2
39–45	1	1
	100	

MEASURES OF RELATIONSHIP—CORRELATION

Scattered throughout this book are references to relationships between various aspects of pupils, between various methods of evaluating these aspects, between successive applications of the same evaluation device, and others. These relationships have been variously named according to the kind of measurements involved. The relationship between two applications of the same device obtained either by splitting the device into equivalent halves, by retesting with the same device, or by applying two equivalent forms of the same device, has been considered under the heading of *reliability*. Relationships between measurements obtained with an evaluation device and some criterion or external standard of the same aspect of pupils or the degree to which scores obtained on the test agree with elsewhere-obtained ideas of the degree of that aspect in a pupil, have been considered under the heading of *relevance*. Relationships between various aspects of pupils, such as general mental ability and scholastic achievement, socioeconomic environment and emotional adjustment, have been considered in the discussions of the aspects of pupils which should be evaluated.

The classroom teacher may often want to know the relationships between measured aspects of pupils. Such relationships inform him about the nature of the pupils, their learning processes, and reactions to teaching procedures. They help in understanding the evaluation devices in terms of reliability, relevance, and overlapping functions. In the present section we shall consider techniques by which the teacher can determine such relationships. An understanding of these techniques will prove useful not only in working with data locally obtained but also in reading the literature of experimental education and the manuals for the externally made, standardized evaluation devices.

The Closeness and Direction of Relationships

Relationships vary in closeness and in direction. The *closeness* of a relationship is the degree to which one variable changes as the other changes. For example, as the length of one of its sides increases, the area of a square also increases according to a completely fixed, close relationship. Or as temperature increases, the height of the mercury in a thermometer also increases, following the temperature very closely. On the other hand, the body weight and general mental ability of a group of people are not closely related; that is, intelligence does not increase as body weight increases. An intermediate degree is illustrated by the relationship usually found between a pupil's scores on mathematical and verbal ability tests; while some pupils excel in both tests and others do poorly, there are many pupils who differ greatly in their standing on the two.

The *direction* of a relationship refers to whether one variable increases as the other variable increases. In a positive relationship, a high degree of one variable is accompanied by a high degree of the other. If the temperature is high, the column of mercury will be high; or if a pupil's score on one test of mental ability is high, it will be high on another test of mental ability. In a negative relationship, low scores on one variable are accompanied by high scores on another variable. The relationship between pupils' scores on a test of mental ability and the number of their failures in school subjects is negative. With some variables the direction of relationship may differ at different stages or levels of one of the variables. Such combinations of both positive and negative relationships are called *curvilinear*. Physical strength increases with chronological age up to a certain level and then decreases as persons approach old age. The length of a shadow decreases as the day grows older during the first half and increases during the later half of the day.

TABLE 32.   The Computation of r from an Assumed Mean of Zero

Student	Score on Form A(X)	Score on Form B(Y)	X^2	Y^2	XY
1	62	65	3,844	4,225	4,030
2	115	106	13,225	11,236	12,190
3	117	98	13,689	9,604	11,466
4	120	125	14,400	15,625	15,000
5	84	73	7,056	5,329	6,132
6	87	78	7,569	6,084	6,786
7	80	82	6,400	6,724	6,560
8	110	90	12,100	8,100	9,900
9	93	95	8,649	9,025	8,835
10	100	96	10,000	9,216	9,600
11	89	91	7,921	8,281	8,099
12	101	97	10,201	9,409	9,797
13	103	100	10,609	10,000	10,300
14	63	71	3,969	5,041	4,473
15	104	94	10,816	8,836	9,776
16	74	74	5,476	5,476	5,476
17	76	81	5,776	6,561	6,156
18	115	125	13,225	15,625	14,375
19	104	103	10,816	10,609	10,712
20	71	74	5,041	5,476	5,254
21	68	66	4,624	4,356	4,488
22	95	85	9,025	7,225	8,075
23	104	92	10,816	8,464	9,568
24	86	78	7,396	6,084	6,708
25	105	98	11,025	9,604	10,290
Σ	2,326	2,237	223,668	206,215	214,046
$\dfrac{\Sigma}{N}$	93.04	89.48			

$$r = \frac{\Sigma XY - NM_x M_y}{\sqrt{\Sigma X^2 - NM_x^2}\sqrt{\Sigma Y^2 - NM_y^2}}$$

$$r = \frac{214,046 - 25(93.04)(89.48)}{\sqrt{223,668 - 25(8658.44)}\sqrt{206,215 - 25(8006.67)}}$$

$$r = \frac{5915.5200}{6623.5968} = .893$$

Data Required for Determining Relationships

How can the closeness and direction of the relationship be found? The first requirement is that the variables themselves be obtained and paired. Usually the pairing is done on the basis of individual persons, as when each pupil in a group is measured by two tests. The net result should be three columns of data, the first denoting the pupil, the second denoting his score on one of the variables, and the third denoting his score on the other variable. The list of scores on Form A and Form B of the Purdue Reading Test in Table 32 shows a list of paired scores for 25 students.

Rank Correlation

Several methods may be used to ascertain the closeness and direction of the relationship between the two series of measures. If the data are in the form of ranks rather than raw scores or derived scores, the *Spearman rank-difference coefficient of correlation* (rho) should be used. The formula for this coefficient is

$$\text{rho} = 1 - \frac{6 \, \Sigma D^2}{N(N^2 - 1)}$$

where D = difference between a pair of ranks
N = number of pairs of ranks

We illustrate the use of this formula by applying it to the ranks of ten pupils on two different tests. These data and the necessary computations are shown below.

Pupil	Rank on Test I	Rank on Test II	D	D^2
A	6	5	1	1
B	9	4	5	25
C	4	1	3	9
D	5	3	2	4
E	3	8	5	25
F	8	6	2	4
G	10	10	0	0
H	2	9	7	49
I	7	7	0	0
J	1	2	1	1
				118

$$\text{rho} = 1 - \frac{6 \, \Sigma D^2}{N(N^2 - 1)}$$

$$= 1 - \frac{6(118)}{10(99)}$$

$$= 1 - \frac{708}{990} = 1 - .715$$

$$\text{rho} = .285$$

Coefficients of correlation approach +1.0 to the degree that the relationship between the variables is close and positive, −1.0 to the
degree that the relationship is close and negative, and .00 to the
degree that there is an absence of any relationship between the two
variables. The rank-difference method can, of course, be applied to
scores if they are first ranked, but when the number of cases exceeds say 30, the ranking becomes time-consuming. For this and
other reasons the rank-difference coefficient is seldom used for large
numbers of cases.

SCATTER DIAGRAMS

If the paired variables are in the form of scores instead of ranks,
the direction of the relationship between the variables is most conveniently found by plotting each pair of scores on a two-way table.
A scatter diagram for the paired scores in Table 32 is shown in
Fig. 33. The vertical axis is pointed off in regular steps for as many
class intervals as are used in the frequency distribution of one of
the variables, and the horizontal axis is similarly pointed off for
the other.

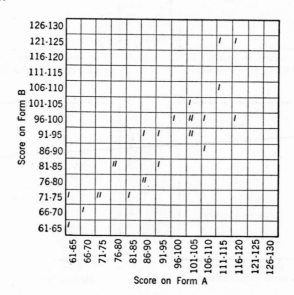

FIG. 33. Scatter Diagram of 25 Paired Scores
on Forms A and B of the Purdue Reading
Test.

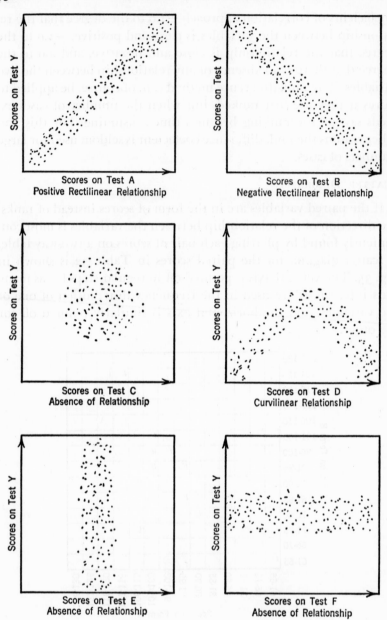

FIG. 34. Types and Degrees of Relationship Between Two Tests.

Each pair of scores is then plotted by entering the vertical axis at the proper point for the size of the score of one of the variables and then moving across horizontally until the proper point for the score on the other variable is reached; at this intersection a mark is made for this pair of scores. The process is repeated until all the pairs have been plotted.

Most two-way tables are arranged so that the horizontal axis indicates increasing scores to the right, and the vertical axis from bottom to top. For a positive relationship the scores tend to fall in a diagonal band from the lower left to the upper right corner of the table. For a negative relationship they fall in a diagonal from the upper left to the lower right corner. Absence of relationship is indicated to the degree that the tabulated pairs of scores tend to fall on neither of these diagonals but rather along a horizontal or vertical line or in a circle. These various relationships are shown in Fig. 34.

Sometimes the pairs of scores tend to fall in a curved line; teachers should be on the lookout for such *curvilinear relationships*. Special statistical methods are necessary for finding the degree of such relationships.

PEARSON PRODUCT-MOMENT COEFFICIENT OF CORRELATION

A scatter diagram is a visual aid in discovering whether using the formula for the Pearson product-moment correlation coefficient is justified. If inspection reveals no marked tendency toward curvilinearity, the formula applies. This coefficient (r) is defined by the following formula, which shows it to be the arithmetic mean of the products of the paired z-scores:

$$r = \frac{\Sigma z_1 z_2}{N}$$

where r = Pearson product-moment coefficient of correlation
z_1 and z_2 = paired z-scores on each of the variables
N = number of pairs of scores

Using this formula, however, is quite laborious. Many more convenient formulas yield the same results. Algebraically it can be shown that the coefficient defined by the above formula can also be obtained by means of the following formula which is much easier to apply:

$$r = \frac{\Sigma XY - NM_xM_y}{\sqrt{\Sigma X^2 - NM_x^2}\ \sqrt{\Sigma Y^2 - NM_y^2}}$$

where X and Y = raw scores on each variable

M_x and M_y = arithmetic means of the two distributions

The application of this formula is illustrated for the 25 pairs of measures in Table 32. The reader should follow through the computations in this table for an understanding of the procedure.

STATISTICAL SIGNIFICANCE OF MEASURES OBTAINED

Suppose a teacher has given a test to two groups of pupils, computed the arithmetic means of the distributions of the scores, and obtained the difference between the two arithmetic means. Only rarely will the two averages be the same; the average performance of one group will almost surely be higher than that of the other. Is the difference obtained due to chance fluctuations or does it reflect a real difference in the populations of pupils of whom the two groups are samples?

This question arises because the measures obtained with measuring instruments are often based on parts or samples of the total group of people or phenomena about which it is desired to generalize. A given group of pupils is only a small part of the total population of pupils of whom we should like to be able to say that an obtained difference holds true. Similarly, a single administration of an evaluation device is only a small sample of all possible administrations.

Whenever we seek to generalize about a whole on the basis of our knowledge of a part of it, we are involved in *sampling error*. This is illustrated by a bucketful of spherical balls, a given proportion of which are white and the remainder black. Let us say there are 1000 balls in a bucket, half of them white and half black. If an experimenter were to blindfold himself and pick out one of the balls, the chances would be 50–50 that the one selected would be black and, similarly, 50–50 that it would be white. If this ball were put back in the bucket, the balls thoroughly mixed up, and another selection made, the same chances for drawing a black or a white ball would prevail. If this were done an infinite number of times, the number of white balls chosen would equal the number of black ones chosen. But in only, say, 100 choices the proportion of black balls chosen will frequently differ from exactly one-half.

If we take a great many groups of 100 random choices from the bucketful of balls, the arithmetic means of the number of black ones per 100 choices will differ from one another and can be placed in a frequency distribution. The arithmetic mean of this distribution of number of black balls per 100 chosen will approach 50 as the number of groups of 100 choices is increased.

The distribution of numbers of black balls per 100 choices will also have a standard deviation, which is computed by a special formula and is called the *standard error* of the proportion. If we knew at the beginning the proportion of black and white balls in the bucket, we could calculate in advance the standard deviation of the distribution of the proportion of black balls, and by using our knowledge of the area relationship under the normal curve we could predict the frequencies with which various proportions of black balls would be obtained in the long run. This is so because most statistical measures are known to fall into a normal distribution when large numbers of them are calculated on the basis of samples containing, say, 30 or more members drawn at random.

Let us look at the analogy between this illustration and the conditions under which teachers or experimenters interpret statistical measures and the differences between them. If one wishes to generalize about all of a particular group of pupils, say all pupils taught with a certain textbook or all pupils of a given age or sex, on the basis of the limited numbers of pupils available for evaluation or experimentation, the entire group is comparable to the entire bucketful of black and white balls, and the sample of pupils is comparable to the 100 balls chosen at random in each group of selections.

Similarly, if a teacher wishes to generalize, on the basis of a single administration of the test, about the scores obtained by a group of pupils every time it is administered, or to draw conclusions concerning a pupil's "true" score on a test on the basis of a single form of the test, the true score is comparable to the known proportions of black and white balls in the bucket, and the single form of the test is comparable to a single group of 100 selections of balls. If another sample of pupils belonging to the class about which one wishes to generalize were chosen, it would not be expected that the same values of the statistical measures, such as means, would be obtained.

If many other similar samples of pupils from the same class were used, the statistical measures would differ from one another and could be placed in a frequency distribution which would itself have an arithmetic mean and a standard deviation. If it were possible to test a single group of pupils a great number of times without introducing practice and other effects, the scores of a single pupil would be expected to fluctuate around his theoretical "true" score. These scores could also be placed in a frequency distribution whose mean and standard deviation could be computed, the mean closely approaching the pupil's "true" score on the given test and the standard deviation being called *the standard error of measurement* or the *standard error of the score*.

Such standard errors (1) of measurement, (2) of means, (3) of standard deviations, and (4) of differences between means or standard deviations are all standard deviations of distributions of scores, means, standard deviations, and differences, obtained from great numbers of random samples drawn from the same population. The usefulness of these standard errors depends on the fact that scores and statistical measures based on a sufficiently large number of random samples are known to fall into a normal distribution. Then by using the area relationships under the normal curve we can estimate the frequency with which various scores, arithmetic means, standard deviations, or differences between means or standard deviations will occur if we continue to draw samples beyond the single one upon which our knowledge is usually based.

Given the mean and standard deviation of a normal distribution of statistical measures, we can estimate the probability that a given statistical measure will deviate from the mean by a certain amount. The probability that the statistical measures obtained could *not* have arisen by chance may then be considered the *level of confidence* with which we may accept it as true of the whole population.

Suppose we hypothesize that there is no real difference between the intelligence of boys and girls. Such hypotheses, that the true difference between two statistical measures based on complete populations is zero, are called *null hypotheses*. Yet we usually obtain a difference greater or less than zero. If the null hypothesis is borne out, this difference will be within the fluctuations of random sampling. If the null hypothesis is disproved, the difference based on random samples drawn from the population will be a real difference greater or less than zero in the population.

How can we test the null hypothesis? We can do this if we have (1) the obtained difference between the statistical measures based on random samples of the population, and (2) the *standard error* of the difference between the statistical measures. The standard error, S.E., of the obtained difference is computed with special formulas whose derivation is beyond the present discussion. The formulas for the standard errors of various statistical measures are as follows:

(1) $$\text{S.E.}_M = \frac{\sigma_{\text{(sample)}}}{\sqrt{N-1}}.$$

(2) $$\text{S.E.}_{Mdn} = \frac{5}{4} \cdot \frac{\sigma_{\text{(sample)}}}{\sqrt{N-1}} = \frac{5}{4}\text{S.E.}_M.$$

(3) $$\text{S.E.}_\sigma = \frac{\sigma_{\text{(sample)}}}{\sqrt{2(N-1)}};$$

(4) $$\text{S.E.}_Q = \frac{.787\,\sigma_{\text{(sample)}}}{\sqrt{N-1}} = .787\,\text{S.E.}_M.$$

(5) $$\text{S.E.}_{(M_1 - M_2)} = \sqrt{(\text{S.E.}_{M_1})^2 + (\text{S.E.}_{M_2})^2 - 2r_{12}(\text{S.E.}_{M_1})(\text{S.E.}_{M_2})}.$$

(6) $$\text{S.E.}_{(\sigma_1 - \sigma_2)} = \sqrt{(\text{S.E.}_{\sigma_1})^2 + (\text{S.E.}_{\sigma_2})^2 - 2r_{12}(\text{S.E.}_{\sigma_1})(\text{S.E.}_{\sigma_2})}.$$

(7) $$\text{S.E.}_r = \frac{1 - r^2}{\sqrt{N-1}}.$$

To test the null hypothesis with respect to an obtained statistical measure, we find the number of standard errors above or below zero at which the measure would fall in a normal distribution. This is done by forming a fraction, or *critical ratio*, whose numerator is the obtained difference and whose denominator is the standard error of the difference. Then by using the table of areas under the normal curve included between the mean and ordinates erected at various standard deviation distances along the range above and below zero, we find the probability that the obtained difference could have occurred in a population of differences whose mean is zero. If the difference is shown to fall at a point so many standard errors from the mean of zero that only five out of 100 or one out of 100 such measures could have occurred through fluctuations in random sampling, the measure obtained is said to be significant at the 5 percent or 1 percent *level of confidence,* respectively. Following are the computations for two illustrative cases.

Illustrative Problem I: Range within which the obtained mean may be expected to deviate from the true mean.

Mean of a Class on an Attitude Scale

$M = 8.67$ $\qquad\qquad$ $\sigma = 2.4$ $\qquad\qquad$ $N = 37$

$$\text{S.E.}_M = \frac{\sigma}{\sqrt{N-1}} = \frac{2.4}{\sqrt{36}} = \frac{2.4}{6} = .4$$

Therefore the chances are 68 out of 100 that the obtained mean deviates from the true mean .4 score point.

The chances are about perfect (99 + out of 100) that the obtained mean does not deviate from the true mean by more than three $S.E._M$'s, or by more than 1.2 score points.

Illustrative Problem II: Significance of a difference between means

Scores on an Arithmetic Test

Class A	*Class B*
$N = 37$	$N = 50$
$M = 75$	$M = 82$
$\sigma = 6$	$\sigma = 14$

$$\text{S.E.}_{MA} = \frac{\sigma}{\sqrt{N-1}} = \frac{6}{\sqrt{36}} = 1 \qquad\qquad \text{S.E.}_{MB} = \frac{14}{\sqrt{49}} = 2$$

Difference between means $= M_B - M_A = 7$

$$\text{S.E.}_{(M_B-M_A)} = \sqrt{(\text{S.E.}_{MA})^2 + (\text{S.E.}_{MB})^2} = \sqrt{(1)^2 + (2)^2} = \sqrt{5} = 2.236$$

$$\text{Critical ratio} = \frac{M_B - M_A}{\text{S.E.}_{(M_B-M_A)}} = \frac{7}{2.236} = 3.13$$

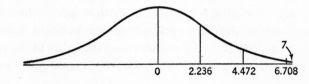

0 $\qquad$ 2.236 $\qquad$ 4.472 $\qquad$ 6.708

Interpretation: A critical ratio of 3.13 will occur less than once in one hundred times (see Table 31) in a distribution of differences between means when the true difference between means is zero. Hence the obtained difference probably belongs not in this distribution but rather in a distribution of differences whose mean is greater than zero. The null hypothesis can thus be rejected at better than the 1 percent level of confidence.

DERIVED SCORES

The major function of the statistical techniques thus far described is the interpretation of scores obtained by pupils on educational and psychological tests. Of these techniques the measures of central tendency and of variability are most important in setting up norms. A *derived score* is a raw score expressed in terms of norms. Norms are the levels of performance on a test attained by defined groups of pupils. They are to be distinguished from standards in that they describe *what is* rather than *what should be*.

Among the various types of norms are (1) age norms, (2) grade norms, (3) percentile ranks, (4) standard scores, and (5) quotients. We shall briefly describe each of these, and its various advantages and disadvantages.

Age Norms

Age norms are obtained by giving a test to representative groups of pupils at various age levels and computing measures of central tendency of the distribution of the scores obtained in each age group. It can then be said that a given raw score indicates a level of performance typical of a certain chronological age. For mental ability tests the raw score is interpreted as a *mental age*, for reading tests as a *reading age*, and so on. If the average score of all ten-year-old pupils on a test is 46, any pupil who scores 46 on that test will receive a derived score of ten years on it, regardless of his chronological age. By assuming that there is a regular increase in test score from one age level to the next, some authors of standard tests provide norms for intermediate age levels, say ten years and three months. The test score obtained by adding one-fourth of the difference between the eleventh- and tenth-year raw scores to the latter would be a raw score equivalent to ten years and three months.

Age norms have the advantage of being readily understandable, especially for interpreting measures which are highly correlated with age, such as mental ability, reading ability, and various skills taught in the elementary grades. Their utility is limited, however, for other aspects of pupils, especially those related to the instructional objectives of secondary schools and other higher educational levels. Very high or very low scores are difficult to interpret with age norms because the latter usually do not go beyond fairly intermediate raw score levels. In this case it is necessary to "extrapolate," which generally involves dubious assumptions.

A third disadvantage of age norms is their dependence on administrative policies concerning age at school entrance, retardation and acceleration, and other factors determining the selection of the pupils upon whom the norms are based. If the sample used to establish norms for the ten-year level is composed of pupils who have made regular progress through school, the norms will be different from those based on ten-year-olds whose progress has been retarded. Unless the proportions of retarded, normal, and accelerated pupils of a given chronological age are well defined, the age norms based on them will lack real meaning.

Grade Norms

Grade norms characterize a pupil's raw score as equivalent to that achieved by typical pupils at a given grade level. These norms are obtained by giving a test to representative groups of pupils at various grade levels and computing measures of central tendency for the pupils in each grade. The average score of the group in a given grade can then be used in interpreting raw scores as equivalent to the test performance of that level. As for age norms, the validity of grade norms depends greatly on the selection of the schools and pupils used in deriving them. Large numbers of schools in widely scattered areas whose promotion and retardation policies are representative must be used if grade norms are to be valid for interpreting scores on tests given throughout the nation.

Norms for intermediate grade levels, say for the fifth month of the fifth grade, are usually obtained by a interpolation similar to that for age norms.

Grade norms in elementary schools depend on the relative emphases given to various subjects at different grade levels. If a sub-ject is emphasized in one grade and neglected in another, the rate at which increases in raw scores on a test in that subject may be ex-pected in successive grade levels may be considerably affected. This is especially true for the applicability of norms established in other school systems.

Furthermore, grade norms are particularly liable to the danger of becoming standards to be attained by all pupils; the violence thus committed to the principle of individual differences among pupils has been emphasized in this volume. A further disadvantage of grade norms is their inapplicability to extreme scores obtained by pupils in the lowest and the highest grade for which norms are provided. Raw scores beyond these limits can usually be inter-preted only vaguely.

In the secondary school, grade norms are usually supplanted by *semesters-of-study norms,* a given raw score being interpreted as the average for pupils who have studied a subject for a certain number of semesters.

Percentile Ranks

Percentile rank norms have the advantage of easy interpretabil-ity. They depend just as completely, however, on the description of the group of pupils used in obtaining them as do age and grade norms; the group must be fully described in all aspects related to performance on the test. It is usually necessary to specify the meas-ures of central tendency and variability of the distribution of chronological age, mental age, grade placement, semesters of study, and socioeconomic status of the groups used in deriving norms for standardized achievement tests. Rural or urban residence, sex, and education of parents are also frequently related to aspects of pupils and thus logically require differential norms.

Percentile ranks suffer from the unique disadvantage that they inevitably result in unequal units along the scale of performance on a test. Such units are undesirable for two reasons. First, a false impression is given the unwary concerning the differences in per-formance between scores, say, at the 50th and 55th percentile levels and at the 90th and 95th levels. The latter, for all bell-shaped dis-tributions of raw scores, is always a larger actual difference than the former, even though the differences in percentile rank are equal. Second, percentile ranks are not arithmetically manipulatable for computing means and standards deviations. The percentile rank of two averaged raw scores is not equal to the average of their separate percentile scores. Another disadvantage is the variation in reliability of different ranks. Despite these disadvantages, percentile ranks are so readily understood that they are used as norms for many standard tests.

STANDARD SCORES

Standard scores are based on the principle of the z-score and T-score already discussed. They avoid the disadvantage of the unequal units of percentile norms. Standard score norms transform the distribution of raw scores into a distribution with a specified central tendency and variability.

Although not so readily understood by most test users, standard scores have the advantages (1) of providing equal units along all parts of the scale of performance on a test and (2) of being based on the most reliable statistical measures obtainable from a frequency distribution, namely, the arithmetic mean and standard deviation. There is still the necessity of specifying the nature of the group of pupils on whom the norms are based. Hence standard scores are liable to the danger already discussed in connection with age, grade, and percentile norms. When standard scores are interpreted in terms of percentile ranks, they always involve the assumption that the raw scores are distributed according to the normal curve.

QUOTIENT NORMS

Quotients are frequently used in connection with age norms to obtain a measure of the relative status of a pupil's performance. The best known of the quotients, the *intelligence quotient* or I.Q., is obtained by dividing the pupil's mental age by his chronological age and multiplying by 100. That is, $\text{I.Q.} = 100 \times \dfrac{\text{MA}}{\text{CA}}$. Since for the typical child mental age equals chronological age, intelligence quotients over 100 indicate mental ability superior to that of the average child and those below 100 indicate inferior mental ability. The intelligence quotients obtained with group tests of mental ability have been in many cases equated to those obtained with the Stanford-Binet individual intelligence test.

In general, the aim has been to arrange the norms so that the intelligence quotient remains constant for a given pupil as he grows older. This goal has been only partially realized because of the fact that the standard deviation of the distribution of mental ages increases in general for groups of pupils of increasing chronological age. This results in increasing I.Q.'s for pupils with I.Q.'s greater than 100 and in decreasing I.Q.'s for pupils with I.Q.'s less than 100.

Furthermore, the inapplicability of the mental age concept for chronological age levels above about fifteen years makes intelligence quotients have doubtful meaning for older pupils and adults. Mental age does not increase with chronological age throughout an individual's lifetime; the curve of mental growth levels out somewhere during early adulthood for most persons. Consequently, since mental age cannot keep pace with chronological age, the I.Q. should decrease as a person grows older unless some limit is placed on chronological age. For the Stanford-Binet intelligence test, and consequently for most group intelligence tests, chronological age is held constant after an individual reaches the age of about 16.

The *educational quotient,* E.Q., can be found whenever an educational age or subject-matter age is known. The educational quotient then equals educational age divided by chronological age and multiplied by 100. Its advantages and limitations are those of the intelligence quotient, especially as far as the limitations of age norms discussed above are concerned.

The *accomplishment quotient,* A.Q., represents an attempt to obtain a measure of whether a pupil is achieving instructional objectives to the limits of his mental ability. It is equal to educational age divided by mental age and multiplied by 100. If the tests used to determine educational age and mental age were not administered at the same time, the educational quotient and intelligence quotient may be substituted; the accomplishment quotient then equals $\dfrac{EQ}{IQ} \times 100$.

The initial promise of the accomplishment quotient has not

been realized for several reasons. (1) Not only must it inevitably be based on imperfectly reliable tests, but it accentuates the unreliability of the tests on which it is based. (2) The age norms for the two tests used in determining the A.Q. are seldom derived from the same group of pupils and hence the norms are seldom strictly comparable. (See the discussion of comparable norms below.)

Educational malpractice, we fear, is fairly common in that the A.Q. concept is applied to the results of one achievement test or a battery of a few such tests. Since the correlation between a mental ability test and a single achievement test is far from perfect (typically between 0.4 and 0.6), the so-called "regression effect" insures that pupils above the average on the mental test will on the average be relatively lower (nearer the average) on the achievement test. Conversely, pupils below average in mental ability will on the average have relatively higher achievement scores than mental test scores. Hence brighter-than-average pupils will typically have A.Q.'s of less than 100, and below-average students will typically have A.Q.'s of more than 100.

The teacher who is unaware of the fallacy of the A.Q. often puts pressure on the brighter students to achieve "up to their capacity," perhaps often with unfortunate consequences on pupil emotional response and usually without success. Only when the achievement of the above-average pupil in mental ability is significantly *below* the average of the group with which he is being compared can the teacher conclude with any confidence that the pupil "is not achieving up to his capacity."

For a more detailed and extensive discussion of this problem the reader may consult Goodenough (3 : 334–336) and Conrad (1 : 798–799).

Finally, it is now well known that a battery of achievement tests and a measure of I.Q. are so closely correlated (about .9) as to make it extremely dubious whether the two types of tests are not merely measures of each other.

Precautions in Test Interpretation

1. Perhaps most important of all, preference should be given to tests whose norms have been made comparable to those of other tests. Such tests have all been standardized on one group of pupils

or else their norms have been equated to one another through an anchor test. Information relevant to this consideration is usually contained in the manuals or literature of the tests that offer this great advantage in interpretability.

2. Test users should not accept test norms at face value; they should attempt to secure and evaluate all available data concerning the sample of pupils used in deriving them.

3. When selecting standardized tests of a given aspect of pupils, preference should be given to the tests which have been standardized with large samples of pupils carefully selected for their representativeness and which give evidence of having been submitted to careful statistical analyses designed to yield reliable and meaningful norms.

4. Many local factors should be taken into account when interpreting the standing of pupils according to norms derived on a nation-wide basis. Among these factors are (a) the legal age of school entrance, (b) the average age of actual school entrance, (c) promotion and retardation policies, (d) the rate and selectivity of elimination from school, (e) the grade placement, time allowances, and general nature of the curricula, (f) the efficiency of the teaching personnel, (g) the composition of local pupils in mental ability and other aspects related to the one being evaluated, (h) the relative emphasis in the local school situation on academic, social and vocational development, and similar factors. The meaning of the derived scores for a given group of pupils may then be interpreted in the light of these factors.

In many practical situations it is necessary to use norms whose applicability to local conditions is questionable or unknown. To the extent that this is so, the data obtained with them cannot be interpreted meaningfully for the individual pupils with whom guidance is concerned. A way out of this difficulty may be found, however, if *local norms* are computed. These should be derived as percentiles or standard scores.

REFERENCES

Many works are available which cover more extensively, with fuller illustrations and explanations, the use of statistical methods in educational measurement and evaluation. Among them are:

1. Conrad, H. S., "Norms," in *Encyclopedia of Educational Research,* New York: Macmillan Company, 1950.
2. Garrett, H. E., *Statistics in Psychology and Education,* New York: Longmans, Green, & Company, 2nd ed., 1947.
3. Goodenough, Florence L., *Mental Testing,* New York: Rinehart & Company, Inc., 1949.
4. Guilford, J. P., *Fundamental Statistics in Psychology and Education,* New York: McGraw-Hill Book Company, Inc., 2nd ed., 1950.
5. Johnson, Palmer O., and Jackson, Robert W., *Introduction to Statistical Methods,* New York: Prentice-Hall, Inc., 1953.
6. Lindquist, E. F., *A First Course in Statistics,* Boston: Houghton Mifflin Company, rev. ed., 1942.
7. Peters, C. C., and Van Voorhis, W. R., *Statistical Procedures and Their Mathematical Bases,* New York: McGraw-Hill Book Company, Inc., 1940.
8. Sims, V. M., "Questioning some assumptions underlying current achievement testing," *Educational and Psychological Measurement,* 8:565–573 (1948).
9. Walker, Helen M., *Elementary Statistical Methods,* New York: Henry Holt and Company, Inc., 1943.

APPENDIX

Publishers

1. Acorn Publishing Company
   Rockville Centre, New York
2. Alma Jordan Knauber
   3331 Arrow Avenue
   Cincinnati, Ohio
3. American Council on Education
   744 Jackson Place
   Washington, D. C.
4. Bureau of Educational Research & Service
   State University of Iowa
   Iowa City, Iowa
5. Bureau of Publications
   Teachers College
   Columbia University
   New York City
6. California Test Bureau
   5916 Hollywood Boulevard
   Los Angeles, California
7. Character Research Institute
   Washington University
   St. Louis, Missouri
8. Committee on Publications
   Harvard Graduate School of Education
   Cambridge, Mass.
9. Division of Educational Reference
   Purdue University
   West Lafayette, Indiana
10. Educational Records Bureau
    437 West 59th Street
    New York, New York
11. Educational Test Bureau
    720 Washington Avenue, S. E.
    Minneapolis, Minnesota
12. Harvard University Press
    Cambridge, Mass.
13. Horace Mann School Educational Press
    Winnetka, Illinois
14. Marietta Apparatus Co.
    Marietta, Ohio
15. Nilsson, G. A.
    16 Maverick Road
    Worcester, Mass.
16. Office of Educational Research
    Rochester Institute of Technology
    Rochester, New York
17. Ohio State University Press
    Columbus, Ohio

18. Psychological Corporation
    522 Fifth Avenue
    New York, New York
19. Psychological Institute
    3506 Patterson Street, N. W.
    Washington, D. C.
20. Public School Publishing Co.
    509–513 North East Street
    Bloomington, Illinois
21. RCA Manufacturing Company
    Camden, New Jersey
22. Science Research Associates
    1700 Prairie Avenue
    Chicago, Illinois
23. Sheridan Supply Company

P.O. Box 837
Beverly Hills, California
24. Stanford University Press
    Stanford University, California
25. C. H. Stoelting Co.
    424 North Homan Avenue
    Chicago, Illinois
26. United States Govt. Printing Off.
    Washington, D.C.
27. Vocational Guidance Centre
    371 Bloor Street W.
    Toronto 5, Canada
28. World Book Company
    Yonkers, New York

Index

The italicized page numbers after names denote references at the ends of chapters. The subheadings are alphabetized according to the first noun in the subheading; i.e., initial prepositions, etc., are to be disregarded.

Set in Linotype Baskerville
Format by Katharine Sitterly
Manufactured by Kingsport Press, Inc.
Published by HARPER & BROTHERS, *New York*